SECOND EDITION

# Human Behavior in the Social Environment

*The Developing Person in a Holistic Context*

Vimala Pillari

*Kansas Newman College*

Brooks/Cole Publishing Company

I(T)P® *An International Thomson Publishing Company*

Pacific Grove • Albany Belmont • Bonn • Boston • Cincinnati • Detroit • Johannesburg
London • Madrid • Melbourne • Mexico City • New York • Paris • Singapore
Tokyo • Toronto • Washington

Sponsoring Editor: *Lisa Gebo*
Marketing Team: *Jean Thompson,*
 *Romy Taormina, Deanne Brown*
Editorial Assistant: *Shelley Bouhaja*
Production Editor: *Timothy Wardell*
Production: *Greg Hubit Bookworks*
Manuscript Editor: *Molly Roth*

Permissions Editor: *May Clark*
Interior Design: *John Edeen*
Cover Design: *Roy Neuhaus*
Typesetting: *Fog Press*
Printing and Binding: *Malloy Lithographing*

*For more information, contact:*

BROOKS/COLE PUBLISHING COMPANY
511 Forest Lodge Road
Pacific Grove, CA 93950
USA

International Thomson Editores
Seneca 53
Col. Polanco
11560 México, D.F., México

International Thomson Publishing Europe
Berkshire House 168-173
High Holborn
London WC1V 7AA
England

International Thomson Publishing GmbH
Königswinterer Strasse 418
53227 Bonn
Germany

Thomas Nelson Australia
102 Dodds Street
South Melbourne, 3205
Victoria, Australia

International Thomson Publishing Asia
221 Henderson Road
#05-10 Henderson Building
Singapore 0315

Nelson Canada
1120 Birchmount Road
Scarborough, Ontario
Canada M1K 5G4

International Thomson Publishing Japan
Hirakawacho Kyowa Building, 3F
2-2-1 Hirakawacho
Chiyoda-ku, Tokyo 102
Japan

Printed in the United States of America

10 9 8 7 6 5 4 3 2 1

**Library of Congress Cataloging-in-Publication Data**
Pillari, Vimala.
 Human behavior in the social environment : the developing person
in a holistic context / Vimala Pillari. — 2nd ed.
  p.  cm.
 Includes bibliographical references and index.
 ISBN 0-534-35028-3
 1. Social psychology.  2. Life cycle, Human.  3. Human behavior.
4. Developmental psychology.  5. Social ecology.  6. Social service.
I. Title.
HM251, P537  1998
302—dc21
                    97-26560
                     CIP

Dedicated to my son
Kapil

*May all your dreams come true*

# Contents

# 3

## Infancy   73

# 4

## The Preschool Years   107

# 5

## Middle Childhood   141

# 6

## *Adolescence*   179

# 7

## *Early Adulthood*   223

# 8

## *Middle Adulthood*   265

## 9

### *The Older Years*   *305*

# Preface

Why do people behave the way they do?

I am rushing through the streets of New York City to the library. It's cold and there is a tremendous amount of old snow clinging grudgingly to the sidewalks. An old woman, bent with age, is trying hard to step off the curb and cross the street. I, like the rest of the passersby, notice the old woman but rush past her in a hurry. As I do, something in me protests: My family background and upbringing come to mind and stop me. I walk back to the old woman and help her across the street. She looks up, and her large, warm, grey eyes startle me as she smiles and says, "I like it here, people always help me." I am amazed at her inner strength and her belief in people. Her personality shines through—as I walk away, she waves and says, "Have a good day."

Seventeen-year-old Chris, an extremely well-behaved student, suddenly loses his temper with his classmate, beats him badly, and is suspended from school.

John and Wendy, who apparently have been "happily married," obtain a divorce after their youngest child leaves home.

This book is for students who want to understand human behavior in the social environment. It is especially prepared for graduate and undergraduate students in social-work programs and fulfills the requirements of the Council on Social Work Education. The Council recommends that the course on human behavior in the social environment encompass the psychological, sociocultural, and biological aspects of development, so that students can understand these dimensions of social work as well as offer constructive interventions.

## Organization of the Book

There are two ways of writing and teaching a course on human behavior in the social environment: the topical approach and the chronological approach. In the topical approach, only one aspect of development is traced through the lifespan. For instance, moral development is traced from childhood through old age. I have chosen to use the chronological approach, which looks at the functioning of all aspects of development in various stages of life from conception to old age. I also chose the chronological approach in accordance with the desires of my students, who found it to be more meaningful and easier to relate to than the topical approach.

The multifaceted aspects of development are presented in the nine chapters of this text: The Study of Development and Behavior; Conception, Pregnancy, and Childbirth; Infancy; Preschool Years; Middle Childhood; Adolescence; Early Adulthood; Middle Adulthood; and The Older Years. Each chapter discusses various theories of development, along with the biological, social, and psychological factors that influence development. Case studies, highlighting racial, ethnic, class, or gender factors, are presented from a social worker's perspective to illustrate points or explain concepts.

Every chapter deals with the implications of practice, so that students of social work can understand the roles they can play in helping people during various stages of their lives.

## Notes on the Second Edition

The second edition of *Human Behavior in the Social Environment* has therefore been an exciting journey in terms of updating the book in new and varied ways. I now present multicultural factors with examples, new citations, and current knowledge regarding fast-developing topics such as diverse lifestyles, pregnancy, AIDS, and women's issues. I have also modified and expanded discussions concerning the implications of such issues for social work; in this way, students can view human behavior in terms of "how to" help people facing such issues at different points in their life-span development.

At a more general level, I have provided (1) more attention to how cultural, social, and economic factors affect the development of people at various life stages, (2) a stronger focus on the intricate interplay among biological, psychological, and environmental factors in shaping development, and (3) more illustrations to show that developmental outcomes depend on the "goodness-of-fit" between individuals and their socializing environments.

This edition still provides a framework for students to view the person-situation configuration over the course of the life span. I present the life-cycle stages of an individual in the context of his or her family, community, and culture. I also take into consideration the challenges and stressors of everyday life and life tasks. Attention is given to the social, economic, and cultural factors that affect the well-being of individuals, as well as to the variations in development and functioning that arise from cultural diversity.

I aim at presenting a book that students can easily comprehend and that faculty can use as a source book. As in the first edition, case examples help make difficult concepts more down-to-earth for students. My goal, in short, has been to provide a book that speaks directly to its readers and encourages them to participate actively in an ongoing discussion.

All the chapters in this edition were "pretested" by my own students, who pointed out what was not clear to them and offered suggestions. So, with the valuable help of my student-critics, I have attempted to make this edition more substantive, challenging, and accessible than the first.

## Supplementary Aids

To help make the book practical and comprehensive, I have developed an instructor's manual that contains chapter outlines, summaries, key terms, and suggestions for class lectures, discussions, role-play, and effective media materials. The manual will present exercises in each chapter from a social worker's perspective. The workbook can be an important tool for professors who wish to incorporate into their own teaching some of the ideas, suggestions, and exercises from each chapter.

An updated test bank is available to all instructors who adopt the book. The test file for each chapter consists of a variety of multiple-choice items (with answers) and essay questions (both conceptual and applied). Many new conceptual questions have been added in this edition.

An exciting addition to the first book is a second book, *Human Behavior and the Social Environment: Families, Groups, Organizations and Communities* (with Dr. Moses Newsome). We felt that we needed to write a second book that highlights the growth of individuals in other varied aspects of human behavior: different types of families, in various group settings, in macroorganizations, and in multiple communities. Having taught for several years, I felt that presenting the life-span development in one book and other connected systems in another book would offer students and faculty the flexibility of using either one or both books, such as using one of them as a text and the other as a reference. This second book is also accompanied by an instructor's manual and a test bank; I urge instructors to take a close look at the manual, which can help them a great deal in their teaching efforts.

## Acknowledgments

First and foremost I would like to thank Dr. Isaac Alcabes for his constructive criticisms and his moral support throughout the writing of this book. I wish to thank my students for their enthusiastic support and interest, especially those who read and commented on the chapters of the book and helped make it a book *for* students: Laura Woodruff, Gloria Jensen, Neeta Mehta, Klynn David Donaldson, Janine Bateman Hansen, Ralph Laub, Todd Powers, Birdie Rasmussen, and William Sawyer.

I would like to thank the following reviewers for their valuable suggestions: Janice Adams, Indiana Wesleyan University; Leola Furman, University of North Dakota; Gloria Jensen; Munira Merchant, Valparaiso University; William Roberts; and Mary Swigonski, Rutgers University—Newark Campus.

I also wish to thank Moses Newsome, Jr., Norfolk State University, Dennis Laray Welker for his patient and caring support from Media Services, Brigham Young University, and Arnold Barnes at Indiana University.

At the Brooks/Cole family, my special thanks to Claire Verduin, to Lisa Gebo for her support and masterful guidance, to Timothy Wardell, to Greg Hubit, and to Molly Roth for her intense dedication and support in working with me closely on the book.

Last but not least, my special thanks to Steve and Kapil for their support and encouragement.

*Vimala Pillari*

# 1

# The Study of Development and Behavior

## INTRODUCTION

Human behavior is fascinating as well as perplexing. People's behavior can make us laugh, cry, be angry or be reasonable. We learn to distinguish that John has a "nice" sense of humor and Tom's humor is "dry." Why do people behave in different ways? What influences one person to become a preacher and another a murderer? What kind of a person are you? Why are you different from your parents' best friends' children? Answers to such questions can be found through the study of human behavior and the environment in the life-span perspective.

Through such study, we find that our upbringing plays a role in who we are. We also see that we are never totally separate from others, that our lives are intermingled. Each one of us, however, weaves a unique tapestry, best achieved when we respect and accept differences and learn from them. Diversity and differences are rich, positive, and mutual sources of knowledge, growth, and change for all concerned. Further, the assumptions we make of ourselves are influenced by our individual and collective histories; the way we view ourselves, the world, and its people affects the way we behave in our daily lives.

As social workers, we help others make decisions, solve problems, and grow as individuals and members of society. Exploring the dynamics of human behavior in relationship to environments can help us achieve these goals. Further, by understanding how people develop from conception to old age, we gain insights about our clients and ourselves; this knowledge increases our ability to help clients deal with problem situations. In short, understanding people equips us to help both individuals and society fulfill their potential.

This book presents human development and behavior within the social environment from a life-span developmental perspective. In this view, development occurs at all points of a person's life cycle, from conception to death. Traditional views of human development have emphasized maturation and growth during infancy, childhood, and adolescence; stability during adulthood; and degeneration and decline during old age. This book rejects the traditional notion that children flower in childhood, stop abruptly at the end of adolescence, remain static in early adulthood, and begin at midlife a steady withering. Instead it reflects the conviction that growth and change take place in all age levels at different points in a person's life. The life-span view of human development attempts to describe, explain, and optimize intraindividual changes in behavior. It also attempts to describe and explain changes in the way a person interacts with the environment throughout life.

To understand the life-span developmental perspective, we should be aware of certain terms. In his classic book, *A Theory of Data*, Coombs (1964) distinguishes behavior, raw data, and data. *Behavior* is described as everything that is potentially observable about a person or event. *Raw data* are bits of information the investigator selects and constructs as empirical facts for further analysis. *Data* refers to the body of facts that have already undergone interpretation according to the investigator's chosen method. Coombs reveals two dimensions of scientific activity: (1) the discovery, selection, and construction of raw data out of the total pool of behavior and (2) the mapping of raw data; that is, those procedures used for empirical verification and falsification.

Theorists constantly use data to support their points of view. In this book, I draw on the theories that support the life-span perspective, that help us investigate, enrich and understand human development and behavior in the social environment. A life-span perspective provides a framework for identifying common, critical issues that individuals encounter in their everyday lives.

## THE STUDY OF DEVELOPMENT AND BEHAVIOR

Before we proceed, the term *development* has to be explained. There is some consensus that development refers to change—but not all changes are developmental. An accident in a house can bring about changes in people's lives; these are nondevelopmental changes, defined as random, unorganized, and unsystematic. Nondevelopmental changes could also be called *nonnormative life events,* such as the death of a young parent or the birth of a child with congenital defects. Nonnormative changes also include happy events such as unforeseen opportunities in a foreign country or a sudden financial inheritance. When such unexpected events occur, they would cause more stress than a developmental event would, because the person was not prepared for it and may need special help in adapting. Human beings have tremendous potential to create their own positive nonnormative events and actively participate in their own development.

On the other hand, developmental changes are systematic, organized changes in a culture, a society, a community, a group, a family, or an individual. In an individual, systematic changes take place at different stages such as childhood and old age. Further, developmental changes in individuals are multidirectional.

Heinz Werner (1957), a major theorist, described development as a process characterized by increasing differentiation and hierarchical integration. *Differentiation* implies that human organisms change during development from simple, general forms to more complex, specific forms. The first few weeks following conception, cells are undifferentiated; that is, they do not perform any specialized function. After a few weeks, however, they become differentiated into skeletal cells, digestive cells, circulatory cells, and so on. This process also applies to behavioral and psychological functioning. In the first year of life, for example, the gross reflective motor actions of the newborn change into more complex, specialized, and voluntary patterns of behavior. In the same way, notions of what is acceptable and unacceptable become clearer as a person develops and becomes integrated.

*Hierarchical integration* refers to the way differentiated parts and functions of the individual become increasingly coordinated into organized systems during development. When a child begins to walk, his or her individual motor responses become integrated into a complex, coordinated motor system that results in walking. Hierarchical integration implies that as development proceeds, the more primitive and psychological systems of an individual become subordinated to more sophisticated systems. Though the developmentally less-advanced behaviors remain with the individual, they are overshadowed and controlled by such systems (Brodzinsky, Gormly, & Ambron, 1986). When 15-year-old Johnny is pestered by his 8-year-old sister, he can understand and overlook it as her way of getting attention. However, if he were tired after a tough day at school or trying to prepare for an exam, he might get angry with her and stomp out of the room. Like many of us, Johnny has the capacity to control his immature cognitive, emotional, and behavioral responses, and in most cases he does. Occasionally, however, the usual mechanisms fail or are put aside. At these times, developmentally less-advanced behaviors emerge.

The processes of differentiation and hierarchical integration characterize the way people generally change over the course of a life span. A *stage of development* is a period of life distinguished by a specific underlying structure expressed by certain behaviors. Some characteristics distinguish and differentiate each stage from the stages that precede and succeed it. Stage theories propose that development generally moves in one direction, with each stage incorporating the gains made in earlier stages (Levin, 1986; P. H. Miller, 1993). However, changes in adulthood occur in different directions. Some developments continue to increase, as in expansion of vocabulary for older people, but others decrease, as in reaction time or the ability to do physical work. As they grow older, some people develop new abilities. For instance, Winston Churchill started to paint in his older years, a previously unexplored area. Creativity is a part of life, and some people continue to develop it throughout their lifetimes.

## DETERMINANTS
## OF DEVELOPMENT

Every one of us is unique. Our thoughts, feelings, attitudes, and behavior are like no one else's. What makes us the way we are? Why do we follow a specific developmental path uniquely our own? Our differences proceed from two major factors: heredity and environment. *Heredity* refers to the genes parents pass on to their children at the time of conception. *Environment* refers to the wide array of circumstances an individual experiences from the time of conception to death.

Historically, controversy has marked the debate on how important heredity and environment are in a person's development. By contrast, some recent research constructs a relatively systematic theoretical and operational model, based on a bioecological perspective, of genetic-environmental interaction in human development (Plomin 1990). In this view, hereditary and environment both play greater or lesser roles in various aspects of development. Some behaviors, such as walking, can best be explained in terms of a genetic blueprint that guides maturation. Other behaviors, such as what sorts of games we play, are best explained in terms of how individuals and society influence us. Thus, the critical question concerning development is not which factor—heredity or environment—is responsible for our behaviors but how these two factors interact so as to propel us along our unique developmental roads (Brodzinsky et al., 1986).

Experiences that we face could be biological—such as exposure to disease, drugs, or inadequate nutrition—or social—such as the interactions one has within the family, among peers, in school, through the media, and within our specific community and culture. All these factors intertwined with heredity influence the way we grow, feel, act, and behave. Social development is an important aspect of life, and we shall focus on its influences in the next few pages.

## SOCIAL DEVELOPMENT
## AND BEHAVIOR

*Social development* is the process by which individuals adopt behaviors that are customary and acceptable to the standards of their reference group. Every group has expectations of its members according to their status, class, gender, and life stage. Children learn social roles under various circumstances. Within each of these roles, the group expects children as well as adults to learn those behaviors the group accepts as relevant. Next, they must develop appropriate attitudes toward their reference group, which permits interaction in social settings and creates opportunities necessary for social self-image, self-esteem, and reinforcement. Finally, individuals learn to participate in social interactions and become sociable; however, their degree of sociability varies according to their upbringing and lifestyle as well as personality. Though few people conform to all the expectations of their group, gaining social approval in important matters requires most people to reconcile their needs with group expectations. Thus, a well-socialized individual will eventually become skilled at knowing how far ahead of the group one can be and yet be perceived as a leader or a fashion setter rather than a deviant.

The term *social* is used for a person who has fully learned these processes. A gregarious person is a sociable, outgoing person who has learned various social aspects of his or her life and has also received much reinforcement. An unsocial person is someone who has not learned the social processes well and is likely to spend time alone. An antisocial person is aware of the reference group's expectations and has developed an antagonistic attitude toward the group. A nonsocial person has not experienced the processes of socialization.

Many traits developed by children as part of the socialization process remain stable throughout life. Culture, social norms, and expectations of the social group all affect people's growth.

According to the cultural context view, an individual's culture is an ongoing and important determinant of his or her development (Steuer, 1994). For example, Kojima (1986) evaluated 58 documents about child rearing in the Japanese culture during the Edo period (1600–1867 C.E.). The Edo culture prompted some child-care ideas and practices that differed from those encountered in Euro-American culture. The Edo culture was rigidly divided into well-defined unequal social classes. Learning young that maintaining harmonious relationships among people of differing ranks was extremely important, children were taught to be scrupulously polite to people who outranked them as well as very considerate to servants and others below them on the social scale.

In any culture, people often need to adjust their coping styles as they reach old age. This may occur because stereotypes of age-appropriate behavior have been imposed on the elderly by themselves and younger people. On the other hand, roles can ease the transition to old age. In traditional conservative India, when the head of the family, say a 72-year-old man enters a room in his home, his children would stand up as a mark of respect to him.

## Roles

As they surveyed the literature written between 1900 and 1950, Neiman and Hughes (1951) at first found the term *role* to be a hopeless mass of different types of definitions, usages and implications. Their analysis, however, reveals the evolution and categorization of roles:

1. Roles are a basic factor in socialization. Personality organizes the roles that a person plays in group life and can be defined as the sum of all such roles.
2. Roles are culturally determined patterns of behavior. Although culture sets the limits of role variation, a given culture may allow alternative roles.
3. A role is a culturally defined social norm that dictates reciprocal action.
4. *Role* is a synonym for *behavior*. For example, an individual's role as a middle-aged person implies a set of behaviors associated with being that age.
5. Roles are also defined by participation in a specific group. *Role* refers to a person's assumption of or assignment to a part in a specific situation. For example, the president of the United States is respected as the head of the country, regardless of his educational qualifications or family background, as long as his term as president lasts.

In examining such problems as socialization and interdependence among individuals, role theorists have revealed much about the organization and characteristics of social positions and processes of conformity and sanctioning. They have also examined specialization, as well as the performance and division of labor.

As we grow up, we all learn roles in terms of their relevancy for us. We also take on multiple roles, which often produce conflicting demands for time and attention. At the same time, though, such roles provide structure for our daily behavior and enhance our feelings of well-being (Thoits, 1986).

Another problem related to roles is role ambiguity. One can describe it as having neither a place nor formal recognition in the social system. Role ambiguity occurs in many social situations. For instance, a foster parent may feel that she is the parent of a child she has taken care of from the time the child was 6 months old. However, if the natural parent reappears when the child is 6, society may decide the foster parent can no longer act as the child's parent. A young teenager who has been sexually abused by her father will be confused about her role because she does not know whether she is a child, a daughter, a responsible parent, or her father's lover—even though these roles were forced on her (Strean, 1979).

Learning roles is an important aspect of every individual's development. Children learn about social roles early in life; young children are not allowed to assume a variety of roles that are appropriate to older children and adults. As young children grow, they become socialized by acquiring verbal skills and through role-playing. Children with good verbal skills tend to feel comfortable in role enactment. Children learn not only their own roles but also to ascribe roles to their peers, often simplistic ones such as "crybaby" or "bully." The following case vividly presents the effects of upbringing or social roles.

Seven-year-old Mala is an only child from a wealthy, well-known family in India. She has been taught to be respectful to older children and address them as "brother" or "sister." Mala's parents visit North America with their daughter and decide to send her to a private school in New York. Arrangements are made for Mala to stay temporarily with some American friends. When Mala meets the older children and adolescents of the host family, she addresses them as "sister" or "brother". Because the American children do not understand her socialization or her culture, they burst out in laughter when she addresses them this way. Limited by their own cultural upbringing, they call Mala "weird." After permanent living arrangements are made, Mala progressively stops addressing others as siblings as she begins to fit into a new culture.

In almost all cultures, role learning is an important aspect of an individual's development. Within the family, too, children learn to differentiate between the role of father and mother and tend to follow their gender roles. Similarly, they learn rules related to ethnicity and social class. Roles learned in the home are modified as children receive formal education. There are at least five types of identity that children begin to follow as they grow up (Gordon, 1976):

1. Sexual identity, which is consistently reinforced and is the most pervasive type
2. Ethnic identity, which influences personal values, association patterns, and often the choice of a marriage partner
3. Occupational identity, which relates to the adult's role in the workplace as well as at home

4. Membership identity, which is seen as the link between the formal and informal organizational life of the community
5. Political identity, which describes a person's membership in a political party as a leader, loser, or peacemaker

## Transmission of Norms

Throughout the life span, socialization also means the transmission of *norms,* which are rules of behavior, the appropriate ways of acting in a group that its members have accepted as legitimate. Group norms regulate the performance of the group as an organized unit (Napier & Gershenfeld, 1993).

Although some people speak of a "generation gap," research suggests that cultural as well as behavioral norms continue to be transmitted from one generation to another. Sociologists describe three elements of the transmission mechanisms that maintain intergenerational solidarity: (1) association or objective interaction between generations, (2) affect or the degree of sentiment among family members, and (3) consensus or agreement on values and opinions (Bengston, 1976).

Many cultures have similar ways of discouraging the open expression of feelings. In U.S. culture, openness and honesty are seen as the best policies, but the truth is that most people in this culture find it considerably difficult to assert themselves or confront others, particularly in facilitative rather than destructive ways. When we look at norms from other cultures, though, we find even less openness than in U.S. society. In Asian culture, for example, free participation and exchange of opinions contradict the mores of humility and modesty (Ho, 1987). In Hawaiian culture, "it is totally unacceptable to resolve conflicts openly and through confrontation" (Young, 1980, p. 14). In Ireland, communication patterns differ from the American ideal as McGoldrick indicates:

The Irish often fear being pinned down and may use their language and manner to avoid it. The affinity of the Irish for verbal innuendo, ambiguity, and metaphor have led the English to coin the phrase, "talking Irish" to describe the Irish style of both communicating and not communicating at the same time (1982, p. 315).

The norms developed in one community or group are carried on for generations. Thus, norms with intergenerational similarities continue even though there may be some apparent ideological differences in the younger generations based on their peer interactions. For instance, Samuel, a teenager, adores hard rock music and "hangs out" with teenagers who enjoy "talking trash," smoking cigarettes, and listening to heavy metal music. In the confines of his bedroom, however, Samuel confesses that when he grows up he would like to be like his father—be successful in business, get married, and have two children.

In spite of continuity of norms, change is as much an aspect of the human life span as constancy. On the assumption that change is predictable, developmental theorists continue with their research in order to understand life better. As people develop, they learn norms and values or modify them in ways that are acceptable to their social groups. Guisinger & Blatt (1994) indicate that Western psychologists give greater importance to self-development than to interpersonal relatedness, stressing the development of autonomy, independence, and identity as central factors in the mature personality. In contrast, women, many ethnic groups, and non-Western societies have generally placed a greater emphasis on relatedness. They argue that individualistic biases are outdated and propose a view based on interpersonal relationships, whereby an increasingly mature sense of self develops through such relationships as well as the influence of family and societal norms. For example, a 27-year-old mother of four who is a full-time homemaker has chosen caretaking as her main role. A single 27-year-old woman who has just graduated from law school defines herself as a wage earner and a lawyer.

## More to Learn About Change

Human beings experience all kinds of changes besides evolving norms. Change is basically physical, psychological, and social. When we look at physical factors, we begin to see why each person, and thus his or her behavior, is unique. What gives the body and its organs stability in the face of chemical and structural turnover? For instance, a scar from a childhood accident can stay with a person throughout life. The mature human brain contains about a trillion neurons, each of which connects to roughly 3000 cells (Tanner, 1990); clearly, the brain is enormously complex. Cells found in the brain and different parts of the human system carry out different kinds of functions. Each time cells divide, chromosomes transmit their information to every new cell. As the cells of certain systems accumulate experience, we can each recognize the uniqueness of our own history. There is memory in the immunological system as well; when we recover from an infectious disease, the system may impart immunity if we encounter that disease in the future. Knowledge about the laws of change in the human organism over its life span is by no means a finished business. Much information remains to be discovered at the psychological as well as biological level; further, an appreciation of the mechanisms and limits of change would, I believe, lead to a more enlightened society.

## SCIENCE AND THEORIES OF HUMAN BEHAVIOR

### Tools of Science

Human behavior has always been a fascinating puzzle waiting to be solved. By using the tools of modern psychology, we increase our ability to solve this puzzle.

The first tool for collecting data and theories is *scientific psychology*. Psychologists have been studying human behavior in the laboratory and in real-life settings for a long time, giving us many helpful facts about people. Many theories of behavior have stood the test of time. Often, we can fruitfully draw on these theoretical viewpoints to help us understand human behavior.

A second tool that we use is the *scientific method,* which gives us an extremely powerful way of collecting data and evaluating it to help us understand and solve human problems. We shall discuss data collection later in the chapter.

Scientific pursuits of human behavior are related to the sociopsychological context of cultural and scientific developments. Instead of presenting a unity of thought, science embodies multiple viewpoints.

Science can be described as a social enterprise; it is not private and cannot be understood exclusively in terms of criteria internal to the scientific method. Therefore, we need to understand scientific pursuits in terms of the sociopsychological context of cultural and scientific developments. According to Weimer (1979), scientists encounter not different data but different arguments in the constructive rhetoric and rational criticism of their colleagues. To deliver this rhetoric fruitfully, scientists must rely on shared *structures of proof,* either explicit or tacit, that they adopt or create in order to develop their own theories (Weimer, 1979). These structures of proof are applications of the scientific method.

## Social Science Theories

One can describe a *theory* as a set of interrelated statements about a phenomenon. Theories are attempts to answer questions, such as the following: What is human nature? Are human beings driven by passions, or are we rational and goal oriented? How can we as social work practitioners develop knowledge? Can we accumulate it through insight in small sequential steps, or are we motivated by reward, punishment, curiosity, and inner pain? What is a con-

science, and how can it be developed? Can we look at developmental psychology for answers to these basic questions? The answers vary by each theory of human development and the set of assumptions about behavior on which each theory is based. Theories allow social scientists to formulate significant questions as well as organize their data meaningfully within a larger framework. Without theories, we would be overwhelmed by unusable data.

All of us have our own theories about the issues that will be discussed in this book. Often we find ourselves leaning toward one kind of explanation rather than another. For instance, one can view juvenile delinquency as a problem that young, irresponsible people create for themselves or that results from a poor environment; that is, delinquent young people could be viewed either as deviants and perpetrators or as victims suffering from a lack of nurturing and training in their families. Similarly, some parents may feel that 5-year-old children can make their own decisions about what to study at school, while other parents may not. We find that we have broad assumptions about the degree to which individuals are responsible for their behavior and the degree to which we can rely on human rationality to direct human actions.

In some settings, social work practitioners are free to follow the theories of human behavior they personally espouse; in others, they may have to adopt the theories accepted by an agency. Because different theories may be suited to different aspects of behavior, practitioners need to be familiar with many approaches.

The general orientations regarding human behavior and development tend to fall into two categories. First, the *mechanistic* view sees human interactions as complex phenomena one can understand in terms of elementary parts, like a machine. That is, the whole is viewed as the sum of its parts the way physicists and chemists try to see the nature of things by studying atoms and molecules.

In contrast to this view, the *organismic* view sees people as active organisms, who cannot be reduced to parts and still be understood completely. When combined, the constituent parts possess characteristics that they lack when viewed in isolation; that is, the whole person must be studied.

The contrast between the mechanistic and the organismic views reveals that human behavior can be studied from any conceptual framework. The type of perspective used dictates the questions that will be asked as well as the manner of interpreting data. Therefore, in making use of research, one must take the researcher's perspective into account.

## VIEWS OF HUMAN BEHAVIOR

Many views of human behavior have been debated and used. To understand a few basic perspectives, let us look at the following case.

> Erika is 16 years old. She learned to speak English when she was 7 as she entered the United States from Russia. People quickly discovered that she was quite talented and had a high IQ. She was in medical school by 13 and was successfully competing with older students; she revealed an ability to learn that amazed her professors and her friends. Even so, she still followed teenage fads and was not quite ready for serious sexual relationships.

How can we analyze and understand Erika? Here, I present three different ways of understanding her: biological, intrapsychic, and social/behavioral.

### The Biological Viewpoint

Some theorists emphasize the importance of biological factors that determine who you are and what you can do. They believe that everything a person thinks and feels is controlled by electrical and chemical activity in the brain and the rest of the body. Thus, to these theorists the body controls the mind and not the other way around.

From the biological perspective, Erika can be defined primarily in terms of her brain: Her high

level of comprehension is attributed to psychological and behavioral factors that are a natural consequence of a highly developed brain and nervous system. However, other people with highly developed brains and intelligence do not turn out like Erika. The mere flow of electricity through the nervous system does not explain Erika's development sufficiently for most people.

### The Intrapsychic Viewpoint

Most theorists believe that everything that goes right or wrong in someone's psyche or behavior cannot be explained in simple biological terms. Many behavioral theorists would probably adopt an *intrapsychic viewpoint* to understand Erika. The scientists try to understand what goes on inside the individual's mind, rather than just look at how a person's brain functions.

Intrapsychic theorists are primarily interested in mental processes. Scientists study these processes in many ways.

1. They observe what people actually do and say in a variety of settings.
2. They give standardized tests to people and then compare their responses with those of others.
3. They pay special attention to the statements that people make about their inner thoughts and feelings.

Intrapsychic theorists explain these objectively measured behaviors in terms of mental processes such as perceptions, motives, values, attitudes, memories, and personality traits. The intrapsychic view maintains that the mind dominates most of the body activities, whereas the biological view shows that the body has complete control over the mind. As you may see by now, each viewpoint by itself does not offer a complete explanation of human behavior.

### The Social/Behavioral Viewpoint

Erika has both a body and a mind. But she is also a social being. Erika's thoughts and behaviors are influenced by her family and others. Especially bright children often show quite different behavior patterns, depending on the type of family and home they grew up in.

Many people ignore the importance of the environment in shaping human thoughts and actions. From the social/behavioral perspective, there is little about Erika's performance and emotions that cannot be explained in terms of what she learned from her social environment.

## The Holistic Approach

Which of the three viewpoints—biological, intrapsychic, and social/behavioral—gives you the greatest understanding of Erika? Truly, it is the combination of all three approaches taken together. Like the rest of us, Erika is quite complex, with a biological, a psychological, and a social side to her that have received a great deal of nurturing for her to be talented, focused, and well-integrated as a person. Thus in the holistic approach, we look at these three aspects of a person.

There is no one theory that all practitioners universally accept; each theory has its dedicated adherents and its impassioned critics. Whereas some practitioners align themselves with a single body of thought, the most thoughtful students of human behavior will find that each theory contributes something to their understanding, with no theory ultimately sufficient in itself. When practitioners employ theories to understand human development and behavior, they increase their ability to devise successful interventions. Throughout this book we shall discuss and evaluate ego and cognitive theories of human development, emphasizing the influence of social environments and examining these theories from a life-span perspective. Many of these theories combine intrapsychic and social perspectives and thus present a holistic view. Though I do not present a thorough analysis of every theory in all its aspects, I shall cover the strengths and weaknesses of each theory as developmental life events are discussed. Various types of assess-

ment and help offered to people are based on these theories of behavior.

## THE EGO AND ITS FUNCTIONS

To comprehend the transactions between the ego and the environment and their significance for a person's growth and understanding, one must first understand the ego and its functions.

In tracing the development of Freud's thinking about the *ego*, Heinz Hartmann (1964) points out that Freud defined it as an organism with constant *cathexis*—the concentration of psychic energy on a particular person, thing, idea, or aspect of life—and assigned to it such functions as defense, reality testing, perception, memory, attention, and judgment. Hartmann sees the ego as synonymous with the conscious mind and defines it as a sense organ for perception, for thought processes, and thus for the reception of external and internal stimuli.

Hartmann is regarded as the father of ego psychology. His work is a direct outcome of the introduction of Freud's revised concept of the ego. This theory opened up questions about the development of the ego and its functions.

When Hartmann presented his first paper on ego psychology in Vienna in 1937, it was a turning point in modern psychoanalytic theory. This paper is considered to be a natural sequel to Freud's previous formulations of the structural hypothesis and his contributions to psychoanalytic thought, and it continues to modify our ideas about people and their functioning. Concepts that originated with Hartmann—the undifferentiated phase, the conflict-free sphere, conflict-free ego development, and primary and secondary autonomy—give evidence of the tremendous impact of his theories.

Hartmann defines the *conflict-free ego sphere* as the ensemble of functions that at any given time exert their effects outside the region of mental conflicts. He indicates that people are born with a preadaptation to an average expectable environment and are equipped with an innate apparatus for establishing relationships with their environments. Thus Hartmann views the individual as having biologically endowed potentialities and an ever-developing ability to respond to the environment. According to Hartmann, the organism can not only adapt to the environment but also change it in a creative process of mutual adaptation. This task of the ego is more or less related to understanding reality.

The ego performs several functions: perceptive, cognitive, adaptive and protective, object-relationship, and executive and integrative. The ego's *perceptive* functions include perception of self (based on self-awareness, self-image, and body image), perception of others in relation to self, and reality testing. *Cognitive* functions include remembering and the ability to associate, to differentiate, and to select behaviors on the basis of anticipated outcomes and logical thinking. They also include communicating verbal and nonverbal information.

*Adaptive and protective* functions of the ego involve using defensive mechanisms in order to satisfy needs as well as to handle related feelings. Such defense mechanisms reduce anxiety or protect the ego from it. They are essential for maintaining balance: Usually people are called well adapted if their productivity, ability to enjoy life, and mental equilibrium are undisturbed. What does it mean to say that a person has adapted meaningfully? What makes a person succeed or fail in a given situation? A person's degree of adaptivity is defined in terms of how well he or she responds to various environmental situations—that is, expected, typical situations or unexpected, atypical ones (Hartmann, 1964).

The *object-relationship* functions of the ego deal with affect, capacity for intimacy, nurturance, and the capacity for extended social relationships. The executive and integrative functions of the ego include the following:

1. Planning and establishing priorities in relation to goals, interests, and motives
2. Decision making—that is, making choices that involve considering both negative and positive consequences

3. Social functioning—that is, goal-directed behavior and delay of gratification, which are means of carrying out social roles and responsibilities
4. Problem solving and the capacity to learn, to relearn, and to integrate new learning
5. The ability to reach a compromise between what one wants and what one can realistically get or achieve
6. Maintaining a sense of balance and wholeness while modifying one's behavior through making changes in oneself or through transactions with the environment.

To function effectively, all people need to adapt themselves to their life situations, dealing with such life phases as infancy, childhood, adolescence, adulthood, marriage, employment, old age, retirement, and death and bereavement. At times, they need to deal with unusual life situations such as war and other crises.

## EGO THEORISTS

### Erik Erikson

Erik Erikson, a psychoanalyst, has extended the Freudian notion of the ego and explored the influence of the environment on individual development. Erikson (1980) sees the development of a person as eight different stages of life, each having a characteristic concern:

| | |
|---|---|
| Infancy | Basic trust versus basic mistrust |
| Early childhood | Autonomy versus doubt and shame |
| Play age | Initiative versus guilt |
| School age | Industry versus inferiority |
| Adolescence | Identity versus role confusion |
| Young adulthood | Intimacy versus isolation |
| Middle age | Generativity versus stagnation |
| Old age | Ego integrity versus despair |

Erikson specifies that the successful resolution of a turning point or crisis at every stage leads to meaningful development. A *crisis* or a *critical period* is that time when a given event would make the greatest impact on a person. Psychoanalysis emphasizes such periods. For example, Freud believed that the experiences a child undergoes before age 5 seriously affect his or her development. Erikson believes that in every stage of life there is a critical period for emotional as well as social development.

According to Erikson, an individual undergoes major conflict at each stage. The ultimate personality of the individual depends on whether these conflicts have been successfully resolved. This theory also emphasizes the influence of social and cultural factors on personality development.

One advantage of Erikson's theory is that it covers the entire life span. However, a major drawback of the theory is its lack of emphasis on women's development. Erikson has been accused of having an antifemale bias for failing to take into consideration the social and cultural factors that influence gender-specific attitudes and behaviors. Other general widely spread criticism includes the fact that one cannot easily assess some of his concepts objectively and use them as the basis of follow-up research.

## Robert White

Another theorist who moved away from Freudian thinking and developed his own school of thought is Robert White. Whereas traditional psychoanalytic theory says that all motivations of the ego are derived from motives that serve the id, White (1960) maintains that the ego assigns motives to the ego proper. According to White, the ego begins to comprehend reality even when a child is very young. For instance, a child who wishes to break a vase may hesitate because of the consequences. Many times, a child may give in to impulses because he or she does not know what else to do; however, as the ego increases in strength and as rational thought

intervenes, the child spends more time deliberating before taking action. The ego learns to avoid failure or punishment by identifying situations associated with it.

In addition to the concept of the ego, White stresses the notion of competence. *Competence* is the ability to interact with the environment in ways that promote self-maintenance and personal growth. White describes competence as a major driving force in life. All people strive to govern their circumstances. Children learn to care for themselves by learning simple skills, later extending the competence to school work and small chores. Still later in life, people receive job training. In all these cases, people must also acquire certain social skills. Successful living truly depends on a person's competence. White's theory is exciting because it emphasizes people's ability to grow and change, based on their drive for competence.

White maintains that the careful study of children's exploratory play, even at age 1, reveals the characteristics of directiveness, selectivity, and persistence. Selective manipulation and exploration are aspects of competence, and one general motive lies behind them. White calls this motive *effectance* because its most characteristic feature is the production of effects on the environment. For a baby, those effects could consist of any changes in sensory input that follow activity or exertion. Before long, however, the child is able to intend particular changes and to be content with only these. The baby cries and is fed. Producing such changes causes what White calls the feeling of efficacy (White, 1960).

White presents his ideas of development in the classification originated by Freud:

- The oral stage
- The anal stage
- The phallic stage
- The latency stage
- Adolescence

These stages will be discussed in appropriate chapters.

## Jean Piaget

Jean Piaget was an important advocate of the organismic theory. A great deal of the information we have about children comes from this great Swiss psychologist.

*The organismic perspective* As you know, the organismic perspective focuses on the person as a whole, not the sum of his or her parts. Further, this perspective sees people as active organisms who, through their own actions, can bring about their own development. Organismic theory emphasizes the process. Individuals are viewed as dynamic, in a constant state of activity. Unlike the psychoanalysts, organismic theorists do not focus on unconscious motivations. Rather, they emphasize a view of the child as someone who actively constructs his or her own world.

Organismic theory concerns itself with qualitative changes (the nature of what changed) rather than quantitative ones (the leaps from one stage of development to another). Organismic theorists often describe development as a sequence of qualitatively different, discontinuous stages, so that later behaviors cannot be predicted from earlier ones. They do not attach importance, as other theorists do, to the fact that external reinforcements shape a child's responses.

*The world of the child* Piaget explored the various aspects of children's thoughts in terms of stages, each of which represents a qualitative change in type of thought or behavior. According to his stage theory, all individuals have to go through the same stages in the same order, even though the actual timing varies from one person to another, making any age demarcation only approximate. Thus each stage builds on the one that went before and lays the foundation for the next stage. Every stage has many facets.

According to Piaget, the child's cognitive world develops through a *scheme*—a personal representation of the world—that becomes increasingly complex and more abstract. Thus cognitive development takes place in a two-step process, whereby one's ideas are expanded to include this new knowledge.

### DEVELOPMENTAL STAGES*
### ACCORDING TO PIAGET (1970)

| | |
|---|---|
| Infancy | Sensorimotor—the knowledge that external objects exist |
| 2 to 7 years | Preoperational—mentally representing absent objects and using symbols to represent objects |
| 7–11 years | Concrete operational—reversibility of actions; thoughts limited to concrete objects |
| 11 through adulthood* | Formal operational (beginning to develop for some)—seeing all possible combinations of elements of a problem to find a solution, real or imaginary |

*Ages are the author's approximation.

The two-step process of cognitive development arises from the action of the organism on the environment and from the subsequent action of the environment on the organism. We shall discuss these stages further in upcoming chapters.

Recognized as the world's authority on how children think, Piaget has developed a meaningful theory of how children grow intellectually. He has established a unique way of evaluating the development of logical thinking. Further, Piaget has inspired more research than any other theorist of the past few decades, while also stimulating many practical innovations in education.

Piaget has not escaped the critics, however. Some charge that he primarily discusses only the "average" child's abilities and he does not consider such influences on performance as education and culture. He says very little about emotional and personality development, except as it relates to a person's cognitive development. One of the chief criticisms has concerned the study of subjects. Many of Piaget's ideas about cognitive growth emerged from his highly personal observations of his own three children and from his idiosyncratic way of interviewing children.

## Lawrence Kohlberg

Profoundly influenced by Piaget, Lawrence Kohlberg focuses on the moral development of individuals in his moral stage theory. He believes people go from premoral to moral development.

Quite comprehensive, Kohlberg's theory presents a clear sequential pattern. He builds on Piaget's theory that moral development is related to cognitive development. By finding the reasons for people's choices, Kohlberg has uncovered a great deal about the thinking that underlies moral judgment. He has also inspired much research as well as many classroom programs on morality. These are the levels and stages in the revised version of Kohlberg's theory of moral reasoning (adapted from Kohlberg, 1976):

LEVEL 1: PRECONVENTIONAL
    Stage 1: Heteronomous morality
    Stage 2: Individualism, instrumental
           purpose, and exchange

LEVEL 2: CONVENTIONAL
    Stage 3: Mutual interpersonal
           expectations, interpersonal
           conformity and relationships
    Stage 4: Social systems and
           conscience

LEVEL 3: POSTCONVENTIONAL OR
           PRINCIPLED
    Stage 5: Social contract or utility and
           individual rights.

Over the course of these five stages, a person's social perspective increases in scope, including more people and institutions; it also moves from physicalistic reasoning (preoccupation with bodily matters) to relatively abstract reasoning about values, rights, and implicit contracts (Colby, 1978, Kohlberg, 1976, 1978).

Kohlberg's theory has been criticized on two counts. First, it concerns itself only with moral thinking, as opposed to behavior, thereby ignoring the fact that a person's moral thinking and behavior may contradict each other. Second, his view of morality is narrow in that it focuses on a sense of justice, omitting other aspects of morality, such as compassion and integrity.

## Carol Gilligan

Carol Gilligan's insightful theory of women's development and the differences between men and women will be discussed in later chapters. However, her theory about how women's moral development relates to that of men will help us place Kohlberg's perspective in a realistic context.

Gilligan (1982) believes that psychology has consistently and systematically misunderstood women—that is, misunderstood their motives, their moral commitments, the course of their psychological growth, and their sense of what is important in life. Several developmental theorists have based their theories on the observation of men's lives. Gilligan attempts to correct misconceptions about women and refocus psychology's view to include the female life cycle. Rooted in both research and common sense, her thinking contributes to a more meaningful understanding of human experience. When life-cycle theorists use her theory and begin to observe the lives of women as they have those of men, their vision encompasses the experiences of both genders and their theories become correspondingly more fertile.

Further, to understand both men and women and offer them constructive help, we must understand their respective emotions, sense of self, and development. Both male and female practitioners would increase their effectiveness by examining the differences and similarities between men's and women's development.

Gender-role differences exist in various cultures throughout the world. The extent of these differences is so great that researchers refer to a broad "gender asymmetry" (Mukhopadhyay & Higgins, 1988). Often, cross-cultural studies of gender differences discuss "male dominance" or "female subordination" because gender-role differences almost always favor men.

Many studies have examined the role of *biological differences* in gender asymmetry. "These studies have assumed that a 'universal fact' like asymmetry, must have a 'universal cause,' so they have looked for 'universal determinants' such as biological causes for aggressiveness, strength and reproductive function" (McConnell & Philipchalk, 1992).

Although biological differences do establish some gender asymmetry, cultures often magnify such differences. For instance, men and women may be taught that "men's work" requires more strength than women's work, even when the difference may be slight. Biological differences can be crucial in defining roles in one culture and almost insignificant in another. For instance, in many cultures women do not hunt, presumably because they are restricted by their strength or reproductive functions. However, women in the Agta culture of the Philippines hunt regularly, even when they are pregnant. These women take hunting trips of the same distance and duration as the men and also kill more or less the same number of animals (Estioko-Griffin, 1985; Goodman, Griffin, Estioko-Griffin, & Grove, 1985).

Because cultures are so diverse, researchers rely less and less on "universal causes" to explain gender asymmetry; instead, they recognize that the causes for gender-role differences are many and complex. These causes may vary from person to person and from culture to culture (Mukhopadhyay & Higgins, 1988).

Many psychologists have productively researched women's development: J. B. Miller, N. Chodorow, D. Dinnerstein, M. Greenspan, and others. We sahll discuss their thinking throughout the book.

## THE ENVIRONMENT

No study of human behavior is complete without a consideration of environments. The idea of an environment, particularly in reference to human behavior, is complex; it is difficult to distinguish between inner and outer environments. Leaving aside philosophical as well as scientific issues, any conceptualization of the environment should take into account its physical, social, and cultural aspects. The physical environment comprises the built world as well as the natural world. The social environment comprises a network of human relations at various levels of organization. Both the physical and the social environments are affected by the cultural values, norms, knowledge, and beliefs that pattern social interaction and determine how we use and react to the physical environment (Germain, 1979). Also, many of the effects of the physical environment on people's behavior depend on *where* people are and *what* they do. In short, the structure of behavior is based on people's abilities and motivations, the process of development is based on person-environment transactions and "goodness-of-fit," and the goals of behavior are based on task learning and social competence.

### Emphasizing the Objective

Whereas the study of physical environments—that is, geography—provides descriptive answers to questions such as "Where do certain activities take place?" those working in psychology and social work often ask complementary questions about *why* certain activities take place in certain locations and *what* psychological consequences they cause. In answering such questions, reference to psychological processes such as perceptions, cognition, the formation of preferences, and decision making become important.

Traditionally, both geography and psychology have emphasized the objective rather than the subjective environment. For instance, in psychology this emphasis reached its peak during the heyday of behaviorism (Skinner, 1974). Observable behavior was seen as the result of antecedent environmental factors (stimuli) and individual or organismic factors (needs). Though this conceptualization has been replaced by one that sees individuals as processing available information and acting on it, we should never forget that the objective environment does affect the individual.

A valuable contribution from geography is its emphasis on objective environmental constraints (Desbarats, 1983; Eagle, 1988; Lenntorp, 1978). Similarly, scarce, nonrenewable resources act as constraints and induce stress in people. Such factors have direct and indirect psychological impacts on individuals, whether or not they are aware of them (Mitchell, 1984). An environment and the people in it are constantly interacting. For instance, if someone drops a match in the forest and it starts a fire, that fire will in turn affect people, who will in turn try to put out the fire, run, and so forth.

## The Importance of the Environment

As life advances and experiences increase, both internal and external phases of behavior and growth change consistently. Human beings follow universal laws of growth and development. For instance, people everywhere go through the same stages of development, in the same order, thereby growing older in similar ways. Although the physical aspects of maturation unfold naturally and predictably, they vary according to the rate and extent of development, which in turn depend on environmental influences. For instance, a child seriously malnourished on account of poor environmental conditions might develop an ineffective intellectual system. The social environment includes families, friends, workplaces, organizations, and governments. Social institutions that include educational, religious, recreational, and social welfare are also part of the social environment.

The environment began to play a major role in the profession in the 1940s, when Roger Barker began to emphasize naturalistic observation in his research (see Barker & Schoggen, 1973; Barker & Wright, 1955). He wanted to start from the beginning, detailing observations of

children's behaviors in their everyday life. His emphasis on naturally occurring behavior in natural settings is called *ecological psychology*.

L. S. Vygotsky's work, influenced by attempts to understand development in its social context, ended abruptly with his untimely death in 1934. His works have been published in the United States since 1978. This Russian psychologist suggests that culture determines how the mind of a child will develop. He views development as a dynamic process of adaptation and readaptation of the child to his or her social world.

Vygotsky (1930/1978) discusses the role of culture by pointing out the historical changes that impinge differentially on the development of succeeding generations of children. For instance, as societies develop, their use of tools and language often tends to become more elaborate. Vygotsky believes that children at later historical times tend to create more elaborate cognitive structures to keep up with their culture's advancing technology and language.

One U.S. psychologist influenced by this thinking, Urie Bronfenbrenner, is best known for his work in ecological psychology (Bronfenbrenner, 1990). Bronfenbrenner defines *development* as the individual's growing ability to understand and influence his or her ecological environment. He characterizes the environment as "a set of nested structures, each inside the next, like a set of Russian dolls" (Bronfenbrenner, 1979, p. 3).

## Layers of the Human Environment

There are several layers that make up a human environment, as Bronfenbrenner suggests. First, *microsystems* are individual organisms who form the layer closest to the developing child and represent settings and social relationships he or she experiences regularly, such as family members who live at home, friends, schoolmates, and neighbors. The child and these microsystems influence each other. For example, a child who cries a great deal may have an effect on parents, who may become anxious or irritable.

*Mezzosystems,* the next layer, comprise the relationships between and among microsystems. They can be a small group, such as a family or work group. At times, it is difficult to differentiate clearly between a microsystem (a person) and a mezzosystem (a small group). Again, a mezzosystem emphasizes the relationship between two or more microsystems. For example, a child whose parents know the teacher and help the child in school work may have a very different educational experience than children whose parents know little about their school and do not help with homework. In another example, say a family moves into a new neighborhood. In this new small neighborhood, a group of young people actively participate in outdoor swimming. Under their influence, all young members of the new family begin to learn to swim.

Third, *exosystems* are one layer removed from the child. Though he or she does not actively interact with exosystems, they may influence the child indirectly. If the Board on Higher Education cut funding for certain programs, this would affect the school system, the faculty, and the student body. Although students may not have direct contact with the policy makers, this exosystem would affect the students' progress and satisfaction with the educational system.

*Macrosystems* form the outer layer of the ecological environment. They include organizations and settings that affect the beliefs, ideologies, and accepted behavior practices of a person's general culture. Macrosystemic influences become obvious when we see how relationships and institutions are restructured from one culture to the next. For example, most classrooms in France appear to be similar to one another, unlike those in the United States (Bronfenbrenner, 1979).

For another example of a macrosystem, let us look at the code of conduct for the male stereotype. As Eagley indicates, men have to act "tough," hide their emotions, earn a good income, get the right kind of job, compete intensely, and win at any cost (1987). When growing up in such a culture, boys and men must face tremendous stress, because no one can win *all* the time.

## Ethnic Groups

While we are discussing the social environments, a word on ethnic groups will be helpful, because the United States is a multicultural country. Many scholars have made culture the central element of their definition of an ethnic group— that is, "a human group that shares certain cultural characteristics such as language or religion" (Yinger, 1985, p. 159). Many (Jaret, 1995) define an ethnic group as a set of people who share a unique culture or subculture that gives them a distinctive, perhaps an "exotic" way of life. When social scientists think about a group of people belonging to a cultural group, they often have in mind a variety of behavior patterns and institutional forms such as the following:

1. A common language, dialect, or nonverbal communication style that is distinctive and customary
2. A particular kinship system, patterns of family statuses and roles, or style of family interaction
3. Special foods and dietary customs
4. Distinctive religious beliefs and rituals
5. Styles of dressing or grooming that give them a unique appearance
6. A time frame or calendar with holidays or celebrations that represents a unique temporal cycle
7. Distinctive musical or artistic forms of expression

Many social scientists view any group that is distinctive on several of these items to be an ethnic group and think of ethnicity as the cultural traits and ethos that characterize the group.

As social workers, however, we should not accept all cultural definitions of ethnicity, for they present some real problems. For example, some ethnic groups may have many members who do not really live according to the authentic standards and norms of their culture; thus, it is only a half-truth to call the group culturally distinctive. Particularly in the United States, there is an unconscious and conscious blending of cultures and people, making it difficult to define "the authentic nature" of an ethnic group in this country. Many people attempt to portray ethnic cultures in a rather rigid or even stereotyped manner, based on the past—such as immigrants from the "old country" or Indians from the "Wild West." Thus, a frequent complaint by some Native-American Indians is that their ethnic identity is questioned if they do not look or act according to an outdated image of what a "real" Indian is supposed to be.

In reality, all ethnic cultures are dynamic, adaptive, and ever changing; ethnic groups in the United States have evolved and become culturally and organizationally very diverse (Jaret, 1995). However, different types of environmental influences have a tremendous effect on different peoples. In all cultures, people have different roles to play which in turn interact with the environment, which then affects people. Given their importance, environmental influences on human development will be discussed throughout this book.

## SOCIAL RESEARCH

The study of human behavior is complex. A great deal of information is gathered from a diverse array of sources, as well as from different disciplines, and the information is interpreted. As we have seen, any study of people's behavior benefits greatly from a commitment to the scientific method, a particular approach to examining phenomena. To understand human behavior in a scientific manner is to develop knowledge based not on speculation but on facts obtained through systematic observation and research and to formulate conclusions based on this data. This approach distinguishes science from philosophy. To understand human behavior, researchers must examine, question, interview, and observe

people methodically. They cannot rely just on what they believe or wish to believe about human behavior. The procedures by which researchers make observations and collect and examine data are called *research methods.*

The purpose of research is to study phenomena by examining relationships among variables. One might say that the goal of research, in human behavior or any other field, is to reduce the degree of error in stating relationships among variables. Research methods consist of a set of rules and procedures that help researchers make valid inferences about phenomena.

Before we discuss research methods, I wish to make a few comments. Often, students complain that they do not want to study methodology because it is not usually easy to read and assimilate. Although this may be true to some extent, I believe that your ultimate understanding of human development and behavior will be more enlightened, realistic, and rewarding if you take some time to study these methods. Further, you will create a solid basis for evaluating the different studies you will read. Understanding research methods, or the logic of scientific investigation, could even inspire you to pursue your own research interests. Let us, then, look at several issues in data collection.

### Different Methods of Describing and Measuring Behavior

Can we predict how people will behave at various points in their development? Yes, to some degree, on the basis of two kinds of study. People can either be observed as they go about their daily lives or be studied under planned conditions. The three principal techniques used to study people are naturalistic, clinical, and experimental.

*Naturalistic studies*    Naturalistic studies depend on observation. Researchers observe people in their natural setting, making no effort to alter their subjects' behavior. Such studies provide the practitioner with *normative information*—information that reflects average behaviors at given times. This data may be based on average groups of people or could be derived from individual case studies.

Naturalistic studies commonly take the form of case studies. A *case study* is used to obtain an extensive description of a single individual. This could contain information about the observed behavior of a child, parent, or group of people. Anything that an investigator thinks is important and that would add to our knowledge base could be studied.

Case studies have been used extensively. Baby biographical studies usually consist of observing babies from the time they were born. Typically, the researcher studies one baby. For example, Charles Darwin in 1877 published notes about his son and advocated the long-term study of babies and children as a way to understand our species (Dennis, 1936). Freud used this method as the basis for his influential theory of personality development. Piaget (1952) based his highly original theories on his meticulous day-to-day observations of his own three children. Helping professionals who need a rounded picture of their clients' lives often use this method, which would also be useful if a newly identified developmental or behavioral phenomenon needed to be explored and described in detail (Marcell & Thomas, 1993; Mendelson, 1992).

Though biographies can offer useful information about normative development, as a research tool they do have some shortcomings. Many such studies record information but do not explain behavior. Usually studies of babies are done by parents, who may suffer from observer bias: The recorder emphasizes certain aspects of behavior over others. Parents, for example, tend to downplay their own child's negative behavior. Moreover, isolated biographies tell about a particular child, but such information cannot be applied to all children in general (Papalia & Olds, 1992).

The value of a case study is determined by the care an investigator uses in describing procedures and separating inferences from facts (Wells, 1987). But even when a case study meets the highest standards, further study is needed to determine how far the findings can be generalized.

Apart from individual cases, naturalistic studies could involve observing vast numbers of people and recording information about their development at various ages to derive average ages of appearance of various skills and behaviors and formulate other growth measures (Papalia & Olds, 1992).

While using naturalistic observational techniques, we need to maintain a record of a person's ongoing behavior. As you can imagine, recording a person's behavior can present many challenges. These challenges include (1) specifying which of all the behaviors that occur will be recorded, (2) determining how the recording will be done, and (3) making recordings accurately and consistently.

Once we have decided on the level of specificity we desire, we can collect data in different ways. For example, to study aggressiveness in a child, we might do the following. First, we would make a brief description of everything the child does. Then we would divide the observation period into time intervals and check whether aggressiveness occurs or does not occur at each interval. We could also create a description of each aggressive episode that occurs and ignore all other overt behaviors. The purpose of our study would guide us on which approach to use.

Another data-collection technique is *time sampling,* whereby researchers record the occurrence of a certain type of behavior, such as aggression, babbling, or crying, during a given time period. One researcher used this technique to study the ways infants and their parents interact with each other. The researcher went into the homes of forty 15-month-old babies and observed the lives of those children 2 hours a day for 2 days. He watched the parents and children interact without giving them any instructions. Throughout each 2-hour session, he observed and recorded during alternating 15-second periods, using a checklist he had drawn, up to

15 parent behaviors and 8 infant behaviors (Belsky, 1979). The conclusion he reached was that fathers and mothers are more alike than different in the ways they treat their babies. Parents showed a slight preference for paying attention to a child of the same sex as themselves. Parents interacted more with their babies when they were alone, and babies were more sociable, than when both parents were present.

*Clinical studies*    Clinical studies follow one of two methods: clinical or interview. The *clinical method* was developed by Piaget, who combined careful observation with individualized questioning. A procedure for tailoring the test situation to the individual being questioned offers researchers a flexible way of assessing thought. This open-ended, individualized method differs from standardized testing, which makes the testing situation as similar as possible for all respondents. With the clinical method, a researcher can probe the meaning underlying what a subject says. However, this method can lead to bias. Its flexibility requires an interviewer to ask questions as well as draw inferences, both of which could be biased. The only way to assess this method is to compare the results of a large number of researchers who have varying points of view on the subject (Papalia & Olds, 1992).

Researchers use the *interview method* to understand one or more aspects of people's lives, such as effects of family myths on family members' behavior toward each other (Pillari, 1986). Interviews are either structured or unstructured. In *structured interviews,* all subjects are asked to answer the questions in the same order. In *unstructured interviews,* the investigator is free to ask any type of question that the conversation with the interviewee might suggest. Structured interviews tightly control the information elicited from subjects, whereas unstructured ones allow for a more natural flow of conversation and greater latitude regarding question topics. Investigators could also use interview approaches that lie between these two extremes.

The type of interviewing used in a particular study should be determined by the purpose of research, not by a personal preference for one type of interview over another. Structured interviews are usually used to collect comparable data from all subjects. Unstructured interviews are likely to be more useful when an investigator is doing probing, exploratory research.

One drawback of this type of research is that it depends on information taken mainly from the interviewee's memory, which is often faulty. Some interviewees may have forgotten certain events, and others may distort their replies to make them more acceptable to the interviewers or to themselves.

Because questionnaires are essentially structured interviews on paper, they can elicit comparable information from all subjects but can also fall prey to the frailties of human memory. The questionnaire is used when data must be gathered from large numbers of subjects in a limited time. A written instrument, though, automatically eliminates the illiterate and young children who cannot read.

*Experimental studies*    There are three principal types of experiments: those conducted in the laboratory, those conducted in the field (a setting that is part of the subject's everyday life), and those that make use of naturally occurring experiences, such as hospitalization, which we call *natural experiments.*

In laboratory experiments, subjects are brought into the laboratory and their reactions to certain controlled conditions are recorded. Their behavior may be contrasted with the same individuals' behavior under different conditions or with the behavior of other individuals who are subjected to the same or different laboratory conditions. In the first case, parents and children might be brought into the laboratory together in order to measure the strength of parent-child attachment. Researchers compare what happens when a parent leaves the child and what happens when a stranger leaves the child. In the second case, an experiment might be constructed in which some children see a person behaving aggressively while other children do not, and then both groups are measured to determine the degree to which they act aggressively.

In field experiments, researchers introduce a change into a familiar setting, such as the subject's school, home, or workplace. A field experiment might offer an enrichment program to some young children in a day-care center but not to others in the center and measure the effects on some variable.

Natural experiments, on the other hand, do not manipulate behavior but instead compare two groups of subjects whose exposure or nonexposure to a certain life experience represents the variable the researcher is studying. Natural experiments might measure the effects of certain calamities, which for ethical reasons cannot be replicated. Examples include hospitalization, malnutrition, teenage pregnancy, and divorce.

## Methods of Data Collection

Most of the data cited in this book pertain to an individual's development and behavior in the social environment. The designs commonly used for developmental research are longitudinal, cross-sectional, and time-lag studies. Sequential strategies combine some features of the first two.

*Longitudinal design* In a *longitudinal* study, the same group of people is studied more than once to ascertain similarities and differences in behavior and development. Without longitudinal observations of the same people, researchers could not learn which behaviors a person tends to exhibit throughout the life span. Just a few longitudinal studies of human behavior have been done, because they are expensive and time consuming (Livson & Peskin, 1980).

One advantage of longitudinal studies is that they provide a good picture of development within individuals, not just an overview of differences among age groups. Moreover, by following the development of a specific behavior over an extended time, researchers can answer ques-

tions about its developmental stability. Often they can determine what earlier conditions or experiences influenced the development of the behavior in question (Schaie & Herzog, 1983).

Longitudinal studies also present problems. Samples tend to be small because few people are willing to participate in this type of study. Some people drop out. Some people's awareness of or familiarity with tests influence their behavior, thus biasing the study.

As more researchers became interested in studying adulthood and aging, several investigators undertook longitudinal studies of intelligence. The researchers measured IQ scores of the same people at different periods in their lives. The results surprised many, for they showed that IQ scores do not decline with age (Woodruff, 1985). According to Cattell, there are two types of intelligence. *Fluid intelligence,* or the ability to take information and deal with it quickly, declines with biological capacity; *crystallized intelligence,* or accumulated knowledge and experience, increases with age. The result shows an overall IQ that remains stable throughout most of a person's adult life (Cattell, 1971; Horn & Donaldson, 1980).

*Cross-sectional design.* In *cross-sectional* studies, different groups of people are studied at one time, and observations can be completed relatively quickly. A study of how social relationships develop might use this method. Instead of observing one group of people every year for 20 years, the researcher would observe groups of individuals in, say, various age groups. To compare the levels of moral reasoning of 25- and 50-year-olds, a social worker might interview subjects in each age category within a relatively short period, perhaps a week or two. If the former demonstrated higher levels of moral reasoning than the latter, the researcher might conclude that young adults are morally more sensitive than older adults. The researcher might further hypothesize that adults lose their ability to draw moral conclusions as they age.

Quick and relatively inexpensive, cross-sectional studies give the researcher a good overview of the developmental phenomenon under investigation. Yet this type of research also has limitations. It is difficult to control fully and adequately all the variables that affect behavior differently. One may not be certain whether differences among the various age groups are due to difference in age or due to other factors. The researcher thus has to match the individuals on many important variables other than age (for example, race, parents' education, background, income level, or type of housing) to rule these out as possible causes of difference. However, full comparability is hard to achieve.

One might expect cross-sectional studies to yield results that are comparable to those obtained from studying the same group of people over time and just as efficient. However, the results of cross-sectional and longitudinal studies are rarely consistent.

*Sequential strategies*    To nullify the weaknesses of longitudinal and cross-sectional designs, researchers have worked at combining these two approaches. *Sequential designs* include the *short-term longitudinal method* and the *cross-sectional short-term longitudinal method.* Sometimes developmentalists combine cross-sectional and longitudinal approaches to learn about life-span development (Schaie, 1965, 1986). The sequential approach begins with a cross-sectional study of individuals of different ages. A chosen number of months or years after the initial assessment, the same individuals are tested again; this is described as the longitudinal aspect of the design. At this later time, a new group of subjects is assessed at each age level. The new groups at each level are added at a later point in order to control for changes that might have taken place in the original group of subjects: Some subjects may have dropped out of the study, or retesting might have improved their performance. Normally the sequential approach is complex, expensive, and time-consuming, but it provides information one cannot obtain from cross-sectional or longitudinal approaches alone. Regarding life-span development, researchers have employed sequential techniques to understand intellectual functioning.

*Time lag design*    In contrast to these designs, time-lag studies do not allow the researcher to see the differences in behavior associated with particular times in people's history. For instance, if researchers want to discern the characteristics associated with a particular age group—say, 20—at different times of measurement, the researcher might compile data from 1970, 1980, and 1990. The time-lag design is not used in research as frequently as longitudinal or cross-sectional designs.

## Issues in Data Collection

In planning a questionnaire for data collection, a social work researcher has to consider some important questions: Do the subjects being surveyed represent the total population? Are the respondents' answers on questionnaires consistent from one testing to another? Does the questionnaire accurately reflect reality? These three questions arise from concepts of sampling, reliability, and validity.

*Sampling*    *Sampling* refers to the method of choosing sample subjects for study. Researchers frequently employ the principles of random selecting to insure that every member of the population being studied has the same chance of being chosen for the study. A *random sample* is an unbiased sample of the population that may represent the entire group.

For example, children in a randomly selected sample will possess a wide range of skills proportionate to that of the population of young children as a whole. If researchers manipulate a variable, such as social praise, to note its effects on problem solving in the random group, they can then assume that its effect would be similar if measured in the larger population of children. Thus, using random-sampling principles allows researchers to generalize their results beyond a relatively small number of subjects.

*Reliability*   *Reliability* is the degree of consistency with which a test or scale measures something. If a measure produces approximately the same results each time it is used, the measuring instrument is reliable. Reliability also refers to the amount of agreement among individuals observing the same kind of behavior. An important question to bear in mind is whether observer 1 and observer 2 are measuring the same thing. Both measurement instruments and data-collection procedures must be reliable if the data gathered in a study are to be accurate.

*Validity*   *Validity* refers to the degree to which a test or scale measures what it is supposed to measure. *Internal validity* pertains to how well a relationship between two variables has been identified or interpreted. A study's internal validity could be affected by alternative interpretations such as the presence of a third variable.

For example, to permit repairs in a residential home for physically disabled people, the residents are sent to their relatives' homes. When the repairs have been completed and the residents return, they appear to be happy. There is a correlation between improvements in their housing and a dramatic increase in their morale, but could a third variable account for their happiness? Yes, for their visit with relatives could have had a positive effect on them. Further, there is no way to determine which of the plausible explanations is accurate (Lerner & Hultsch, 1983).

*External validity* concerns how much we can generalize findings. If the observations made in a subset of a population are statistically predictive of that population—that is, they accurately describe the larger population—then they are externally valid. Also, external validity requires internal validity.

Like internal validity, there are many potential threats to external validity. For one, it involves more than generalization across a sample to a population. That is, external validity applies to inferences made from a sample of observations to a population of potential observations; every observation represents a unique combination of person, place, measurement, treatment, and historical time variable (Lerner & Hultsch, 1983), which can work against generalizability.

## Ethical Issues in Research

The methods of research, manipulation of variables, and other aspects of study and experimentation imply interactions between investigators and participants. According to the ethical principles set by the American Psychological Association in 1992, researchers are obligated to maintain humane, morally acceptable treatment of all living beings (American Psychological Association [APA], 1992). The guide for researchers, entitled *Ethical Principles in the Conduct of Research with Human Participants* (1992), presents the following:

1. Individuals cannot be involved in research without their knowledge or consent.
2. The participants should be informed of the nature of the research study.
3. Participants should not be misinformed about the true nature of research.
4. The researcher should not coerce individuals to participate in research.
5. The researcher should not fail to honor promises or commitments to participants.
6. The participants should not be exposed to undue physical or mental stress.
7. The researcher should not cause physical or psychological harm to participants.
8. The researcher cannot invade the participant's privacy without the participant's permission.
9. The researcher has to maintain confidentiality of information received and should not withhold benefits for participation in control groups.

Ethical problems arise not because researchers are bad or do not care but rather because of the kinds of variables involved and the nature of people themselves. One must weigh the cost of research against its benefits. For example, it would be difficult to study a significant event such as the death of a spouse without exposing subjects to mental stress. Before agreement to participate, however, bereaved subjects should be informed of the nature of the mental stress that they may have to deal with while discussing the topic. Severe stress is never justified. The knowledge derived from research is valuable, but sometimes its cost in human terms would be too great; the end does not always justify the means.

## THE LIFE-SPAN DEVELOPMENTAL PERSPECTIVE

As you know, this book uses the life-span perspective as a framework for studying human behavior in the social environment. However, I do not mean to suggest the superiority of this approach over others. It merely gives us a way to examine some of the issues and puzzles of human behavior. By looking at the development of a person from birth to death, we begin to understand how each period of development and behavior has its own challenges and frustrations and how it relates to other periods of development as well as human behavior in general.

The infant and the preschooler learn how to control their behavior and develop a sense of relation to the world of family and play. The school child adjusts to a new environment (school) and a new adult (teacher) while learning to read, write, and develop friendships with peers. The adolescent comes to grips with himself or herself in terms of the world of school work, career, and social development. The young adult further clarifies vocational direction and lifestyle and may begin intimate social or family relationships. The middle-aged adult consolidates self-growth and development by generating activities that support and strengthen career, social, and family

associations. Finally, the aging adult faces the prospect that life will be over and that death is inevitable.

In the life-span perspective, each part of a person's life is influenced by earlier ones, and each in turn affects those that follow. Each is just a part of the whole. Development is seen as involving multiple patterns of change for different behaviors and different people at various points in time.

As researchers probe the changes that a human being undergoes "from womb to tomb," they describe and explain various age-related behavioral changes (Papalia & Olds, 1986, 1992). The life-span approach portrays the developing individual as embedded in a complex matrix of social and contextual influences that interact over time. From this matrix evolve dynamic interactions among variables that help structure human behavior and development.

The life-span view allows us to interpret these interactions in helpful ways. Manturzewska (1990), for example, studied the life-span development of 165 Polish professional musicians. These musicians were predominantly male, came from families with a musical tradition, had parents who were either intelligentsia or craftsmen, and were born in small or large towns. The researcher found a developmental pattern. The majority started their musical instruction between 5 and 6 years of age, had a mean of 16 years of systematic study, were guided by a master musician, achieved their greatest artistic accomplishment between 25 and 45 years of age, and retired after age 70.

As the life-span view suggests, many incidental and formal causes influence behaviors as well as behavioral changes. Thus, to look for a single determinant of behavior is highly illusory, even futile. We can categorize a particular determinant as necessary and/or sufficient, but we must then view it in relation to its context—the determinants in which it is embedded and factors that affect those determinants, such as historical changes (Labouvie, 1982). Thus, the task in using the life-span perspective is not only to identify a particular determinant as necessary and sufficient but also to specify the contexts in which a determinant or set of determinants is (1) sufficient and necessary (2) necessary but not sufficient (3) sufficient and not necessary, or (4) neither necessary nor sufficient in reference to occurrence or form of behavioral changes that are being studied (Labouvie, 1982).

Finally, one strength of the life-span view is its multidisciplinary approach to understanding and working with human beings. The life-span perspective incorporates knowledge from several academic disciplines that study human development and behavior. The information presented in this book is taken from psychology, social work, sociology, history, biology, anthropology, medicine, and law.

Now let us look at the components of the life-span perspective.

## Issues

A life-span perspective or orientation presents human behavior in terms of long-term sequences and patterns of change, which one can view in the context of either interindividual changes (in relationships among individuals) or intraindividual changes (changes within an individual). A focus on the latter emphasizes specificity and is person centered. In contrast, a focus on the former emphasizes generality and is group centered.

Life-span developmentalists usually focus on three tasks: description, explanation, and optimization (Baltes, 1973). First, all changes that characterize development must be described. Second, they must be explained; one must show how antecedent or current events make behavior take the form that it does over time. Third, once development has been described and explained, it should be optimized; one should attempt to prevent unhealthy development and foster change as helpfully as possible. For instance, during adolescence and young adulthood, men as well as women choose roles—those socially defined forms of behavior that will influence

their adult lives. The study of life development shows that men and women do not commonly enter roles of equal status in areas such as vocation. Men usually enter higher-status vocations than do women. Studying this disparity, life-span developmentalists would describe childhood role-related behaviors and their relation to adult role-related behaviors. They would explain it in terms of the psychology, development, and mental outlook of women as they differ from those of men. To do this, developmentalists would likely draw ideas from such theorists as Carol Gilligan and Jean Baker Miller. Finally, the life-span developmentalists would attempt to promote higher-status role choices in women and thus enhance or optimize their development. They would also explain why recent or current events in the lives of older people reflect how they behaved in adolescence and young adulthood and thus show how such behavior shapes the rest of a person's adult life.

The life-span developmental approach and its relevant issues emerge especially when we study the long-term sequences of change in historical contexts. One cannot create life-span developmental theories without considering issues such as how we choose explanatory paradigms, how we construct and explain them, how we select and construct concepts, and how we describe change itself. Each of these issues is multifaceted, and discussions elsewhere have focused on some facets more than others. Illuminating as many facets as possible, though, helps to refine the objectives of the life-span developmental approach and to document its usefulness.

## Some Organizing Principles

*Chronological age* A dimension in which behavior changes are recorded, *chronological age* is a useful tool for describing change patterns that are homogenous enough to exhibit a high correlation between age and behavior change (Baltes & Willis, 1977). If there are large between-person differences in these patterns, then the use of a chronological dimension is likely to be unproductive.

*Cohort*    One can define *cohort* as a group of individuals experiencing some event in common, such as year of birth—someone born in 1956 would belong to the 1956 cohort. The specific range of time involved is arbitrary. For example, Nesselroade, Schaie, and Baltes (1972) analyzed measures of dimensions of intelligence obtained from members of eight birth cohorts taken at two points in time (1956 and 1963). They found that 59-year-olds measured in 1963 (1904 cohort) scored higher than 59-year-olds measured in 1956 (1897 cohort). Further, they reported that cohort differences reflect not only biological but also environmental influences.

Such environmental influences are also referred to as *normative history-graded influences*. These include, for example, the worldwide economic depression of the 1930s, the political turmoil of the 1960s and 1970s caused by the Vietnam War, the major famines in Africa in the 1980s and the prominent effects of AIDS, and homelessness and the gang cultures in the 1990s. They include cultural factors as well, such as the changing role of women and the impact of the computer.

*Life transitions*    *Life transitions* refer to normative life events such as marriage, the birth of children, and retirement. Although not all people experience these events, they are sufficiently normative to serve as a potentially useful organizing variable.

Throughout the entire life-span, the developmental tasks that individuals face are innumerable. One cannot list or study every aspect of growth one person encounters in a lifetime. Even so, general categories of tasks allow us to catalog the common developmental tasks within a culture.

Different cultures make different demands on their members; all people face developmental tasks peculiar to their time and place. Nonetheless, one can find patterns of development that even

diverse cultures share. For example, in most cultures today, the developmental tasks of each generation differ from those of its predecessors. Each individual moves from a state of helpless dependence as an infant through varying degrees of independence as an adolescent to a mature level of interdependence with others as an adult. This mature level is the product of the environmental conditions and the body-mind factors that contribute to a person's holistic growth and development, which continue throughout adulthood.

## The Life Span: An Overview

As we have seen, the life-span perspective views human behavior in terms of developmental tasks that characterize various stages of growth. Thus, although the life span is a continuum, we can see it in definable segments: gestation and birth, infancy, the preschool years, later childhood, adolescence, young adulthood, middle adulthood, and old age. The remaining chapters of this book correspond to these stages.

Pregnancy (Chapter 2) begins with conception and continues while the fetus develops in the mother's uterus. Pregnancy usually arouses new feelings in the parents and confers new roles and responsibilities; it also involves plans for the expectant mother. The months of anticipation culminate in the baby's birth, uniting the new baby, mother, and father in a new family.

The birth of the child appears to be an important transition for the parents. About 120 couples were studied during various stages of new parenthood: when the woman was in midpregnancy, when the baby was 6 weeks old, and when the baby was 8 months old. Some of the negative experiences that they reported were fatigue, loss of sleep, extra work, and demands on the mother's time. Husband-wife relationships were strained, and the emotional costs of parenthood included an overwhelming sense of responsibility, uncertainty about parental competence, anxiety, frustration, and depression as well as resentment at the restriction of adult activities, finances, and careers. On the other hand, these parents mentioned that the child's upbringing brought them a sense of fulfillment and a new meaning in life, strengthening the cohesiveness of their marriage (Miller & Solie, 1980).

The tasks of infancy (Chapter 3) represent the beginnings of independence. By the end of infancy, average children have usually acquired some autonomy and are feeding themselves with solid food. They have usually begun to walk. All such tasks represent many hours of practice, accomplished through play as well as work. At this point in an infant's life, his or her parents are solely responsible for the child's well-being. Children need early stimulation, and parents need resources and support to develop parenting skills (Duvall & Miller, 1985).

Children begin preschool development (Chapter 4) between the ages of 2½ and 6. Preschool children tend to develop according to predictable principles of human development. They attain more autonomy and notable advances in initiative and imagination. During the preschool period, most children become toilet trained, and they are greatly impressed with a sense of their own bodies. They get around easily and communicate freely with words as well as symbols. They like to know how to do things such as working with blocks, playing with utensils, and riding a bicycle.

Most preschoolers' development occurs through exposure to social interactions and to a physical environment that lets them make experiments in competence. A preschool that encourages children to test their skills is of immeasurable value to the child; most middle-class homes cannot furnish enough educational toys and activities to provide the same enrichment. There are also nursery schools geared to underprivileged children—to stimulate their perception of the world around them, their development of a sense of meaningful transaction with their immediate environment, and their enthusiasm for learning. These children have the opportunity to make new discoveries, to think, and to reason, and as they grow older they can concentrate on an activity for longer and longer periods.

Middle childhood (Chapter 5) is represented as a period of stable physical growth from age 6 to 12. During this fascinating period, elementary school children proceed through a wide range of normal physical, mental, and social development. They enter school as little children and emerge seven years later in various stages of puberty. Growth in height is steady until 9 to 12 years of age. Weight increases slowly, and there is a more mature distribution of fat in most children of this age than in younger children. Appetite varies from poor to ravenous, and digestion is usually good. The school years are vigorous, healthy, and meaningful for most children. Some say that in this age group children are in a latency period and are easy to deal with; however, theorists do observe and describe various dimensions in different ways.

During this period, parents or chief caretakers still provide overall care of the children, who lead a less hectic life and grow at a slower rate than they did as infants or preschoolers. They are generally satisfied with their relationships with their parents and are involved to a considerable degree in family activities.

Adolescence (Chapter 6) is the period of physical, cognitive, and emotional change from childhood to adulthood. Adolescence is difficult to define. A person in adolescence is not just reaching reproductive maturity but is also making changes that are biological, social, cultural, and historical.

The developmental tasks of adolescents were originally discerned from intensive longitudinal studies. It was found that young people often have to identify their own developmental tasks; their ethnic, racial, and social-class identities influence the priorities they set and the way they accomplish them. Lower and lower-middle-class teenagers, not content with past patterns, strive for upward mobility and set tasks for themselves accordingly. Similarly, some middle-, upper-middle-, and upper-class young people, unwilling to live up to the traditions of their families, may rebel and become downwardly mobile by adopting the behaviors and goals of lower-class people.

Of teenagers who drop out of school, about 15% to 20% are from impoverished homes. Usually children with poor grades have the highest dropout rates. Most of the jobs available at this level of educational attainment are routine, menial, and temporary; they tend to be part time and to provide lower wages and fewer benefits than jobs held by older workers. Also, jobs within their sector are unusually unstable and may be supervised by rigid, supposedly autocratic employers, many of whom, particularly in the fast-food industry, are not much older than the novice worker.

Older adolescents from lower-income families, especially those from minority backgrounds, often make compromises in their career plans (Lauver & Jones, 1991). Such youth aspire to less prestigious occupations than middle-class youth and begin to doubt their ability to attain high-status jobs, as many of them do not feel encouraged.

Before the end of their teen years, many have become delinquent. Some underprivileged adolescents tend to give their primary loyalty to their peers; often, professionals and researchers focus on the importance of peer relationships at this stage. However, adolescents' interactions with their parents are also extremely important. As young people emancipate themselves from their parents, they tend to become quite critical of them, to the point of disrespect and defiance. At the same time, adolescents feel that parents undervalue and do not respect them. Studies show that parents as well as high school students exaggerate the power that adolescents have in the family, but they agree on the degree of closeness to one another (Jessop, 1981).

The adolescent's main developmental task is to forge a coherent sense of self, to verify an identity that can span the discontinuity of puberty as well as make possible an adult capacity for love and work. Chapter 6 will emphasize ego and gender-sexual identity because this is the period when young people start to develop an identity with which they are comfortable, moving toward a lifestyle in which ego identity overlaps with gender/sexual identity. Some young people make a commitment to a specific lifestyle at this time, whereas others wait until they reach their early twenties or so.

For the first two decades of life, the young person lives within a system of expectations based on age and grades. In young adulthood (Chapter 7), the person emerges from this system into a future of his or her own making. People's success as an adult depends on how they make plans and choices for their future. Face-to-face with an adult world, the young person is eager to learn as well as perform. Further, formal or theoretical education offers little guidance in making life's most crucial decisions.

Young adulthood is in some ways the most individualistic part of a person's life. Elder (1985), a leader in understanding young adulthood, discusses two central themes in the life of a young adult—trajectory and transition. A *trajectory* is the path of one's life experiences in a specific domain, particularly in terms of work and family life. The family trajectory includes marriage, parenthood, grandparenthood, and widowhood. A *transition* is the beginning or end of an event or role relationship. In the work trajectory, for example, a transition could be getting one's first new job, being laid off, or going back to school. Further, transitions create a lifelong trajectory. In this period, young people grow with a sense of purpose, or directionality. This feeling motivates young people toward achievement. For many, the self-imposed command is "I will make it, now."

People in middle adulthood (Chapter 8) have been called the "sandwich" generation because they face developing new ways of responding to both grown children and aging parents. People ages 40 to 65 differ from younger people in that older people have to learn to accept limitations, make compromises with reality, and move on. Parents in their mid-fifties and mid-sixties may enter the postparental years, and retirement takes them into the final stage of the family life cycle. Through these middle years, the husband and wife form a nuclear family and maintain their husband-wife interaction as a central interpersonal relationship; a single parent develops strong social networks. At this time, each occupies a variety of positions in the family: spouse, parent, grandparent, mother- or father-in-law, and child of aging parents. Adults in their middle years form the bridging generation between younger and older members of the family, who periodically look to them for strength and support.

The departure of children from their parents' homes establishes their independence and is the turning point in the life of the family; new patterns must be established and former habits abandoned as inappropriate. The period when children leave home has been called the "launching stage" (Mattessich & Hill, 1987). For families with few children this period may last only a few years, but in large families it may last for 10 to 15 years. Further, alternative patterns clearly exist now in U.S. families. About 30% of children in their twenties return home, so that many parents have one or more of these adult children living at home (Aquilino, 1990). By the time adult children marry, they are almost always ready to leave the parental home. When children leave home, their parents may become closer, whereas others may end their marriage in divorce. Parents also review and evaluate their performance as parents when they see the kinds of lives their children have established for themselves. Erikson & Kivnick (1986) found that many parents continue to build their identities on the accomplishments of their children. Parents also find new targets for the energy and commitment they had previously directed toward the care of their children.

Other issues arise in this age period. The older parent who stayed home and took care of the children may find it hard to let go of them, especially if he or she clings to the children and refuses to let them go. Parents can encourage their children to become autonomous by seeking other outlets for the need to provide nurturance or by throwing themselves into a career or community service. Parents who accept their children as adults and respect their independence are better able to accept the children's autonomous lifestyles and continue their own lives.

In short, the tasks of middle adulthood are to face the completed responsibility of taking care of a child and to deal with the changing patterns and ways of living in middle age. Physical changes may affect health and cognitive processes. Both parents and children have to make intergenerational adjustments, and divorce or widowhood may occur. Sometimes career adjustments create a new work environment that becomes important and consuming.

Aging adults (Chapter 9) represent the last part of life-span development. Most people in the United States are living longer than their predecessors. Life expectancy has increased dramatically since the turn of the 20th century; for both men and women, life expectancy is 73 years of age and rapidly increasing (Butler, 1981). The number and percentage of older people in the nation will double by the end of the 21st century. Death rates for people over 65 years of age, particularly women, have fallen considerably over the past 40 years; the over-65 population grew twice as fast as the nation's total population between 1960 and 1990. Millions of people born in the baby-boom years of the 1950s will be in their seventies by the year 2020 and will account for an exceptionally large percentage of the population (U.S. Bureau of the Census, 1983). A discussion of aging in the United States must also acknowledge the changing gender composition of the population of older ages. In 1991, 55% of people 65–69 years old, 57% of those 70–75 years old, and 72% of those over 85 years old and over were women. Though this trend is seen all over the world, the difference is more accentuated in developing countries (U.S. Bureau of the Census, 1992). The imbalance is more noticeable today than it was 50 yeas ago, when there were as many women as men in the over-65 category (U.S. Bureau of the Census, 1983). Also, as old age becomes commonplace in the United States, families will have to come to terms with their aging family members.

Aging parents have to face certain developmental tasks. By that time, most children have become established adults with concerns for the well-being of their aging parents, and many of them participate in the plans being laid by and for the aging couple. If an aging couple lives for a long time, their developmental tasks are intertwined as they face the rest of their lives together. Both must adjust to the common task of developing a lifestyle that is meaningful to each of them.

Widowhood or divorce may end the marriage, but most older couples continue together as long as they live, carrying out the final stage of the family life cycle through their joint developmental tasks. These involve adjusting to retirement income, making satisfactory living arrangements, and adjusting to changes in both their bodies and their minds. Maintaining their marital relationships, maintaining contact with their own families, keeping active and involved, and finding meaning in life are all important for older people. Another important aspect of aging is reminiscing, which is not a sign of senile adjustment but the basis for reviewing their lives. Reminiscing makes it easier for older people to adjust to difficult situations and contributes to a perspective in which life makes sense.

Later in life, many vigorous or demanding activities are no longer possible. Religious faith and practices can also present challenges. Many older people who are religiously inclined may stop going to church because of failing health, reduced income, or feelings of being unappreciated or being pushed out of church by younger generations. Older people do not merely want to live longer—they want to live more fulfilled lives. They also have to deal with the concept of death and dying. Older people who have accepted the idea of death are better able than others to communicate with their families about their fears and sometimes their desire to die. Old

age is part of human development and evolution. Older people who are kind and caring did not become that way overnight, and neither did those who are quarrelsome and angry. Temperament in old age results greatly from what they have done in their lives over the years. Integrity of personality is really a conservation of one's lifestyle—that is, the consolidation, protection, and retention of the ego integrity one has accrued over a lifetime, despite loss and the divestment of usual roles and functions.

In each stage of human development, diversity and multiculturalism can greatly influence human behavior. Awareness of differences helps us as social workers assist clients when they face problems. Given the stress, poor environmental supports, lack of experience, or even poor habits people face, they may think that they have no alternatives, no way to help themselves. In spite of the running thread of U.S. culture, different cultures provide different support systems to their families. As such, we shall consider these differences as we explore human behavior throughout the book.

## CHAPTER SUMMARY

- People are affected by developmental and nondevelopmental events. The latter include the death of a young parent or the birth of a child with congenital defects, as well as any other unexpected events.
- In development, people accomplish necessary tasks of growth, integrating them at each stage. Because each stage builds on the previous ones, development is hierarchical and moves in one direction. Development includes social factors, such as playing different roles as well as acquiring and passing on social norms.
- Science offers many tools that can help us understand human behavior. This includes developing a theory, which always involves a particular point of view.

- There are different ways of looking at people, such as the biological, intrapsychic, and social/behavioral viewpoints. These viewpoints taken together approach a holistic perspective.
- The ego is also an important factor contributing to this perspective. Erikson, White, Piaget, Kohlberg, and Gilligan offer theories that help us understand how the ego affects social behavior.
- Studying the environment is essential to understanding human behavior. Human environments include microsystems, mezzosystems, exosystems, and macrosystems. Ethnic differences deserve special attention as environmental influences on development.
- An overview of research methods helps us understand studies that describe and measure behaviors. There are three research methods available for studying people: naturalistic studies, which often take the form of case studies; clinical studies, which include the clinical and the interview methods; and experimental studies, which include laboratory, field, and natural experiments.
- The designs commonly used for human-development studies are longitudinal, cross-sectional, sequential, and time-lag designs. In a longitudinal design, each person is studied more than once. In a cross-sectional study, different groups of people are studied at one time, and observations can be completed relatively quickly. Sequential strategies involve testing subjects more than once to determine the differences that show over time for different groups of people. The time-lag design allows the researcher to see the differences in behavior that are associated with particular ages at various times in people's history.
- Issues in data collection include sampling, reliability, and validity. Random sampling is a way of insuring that every member of a given population has the same chance of being selected for a study. Reliability describes the degree of consistency with which a test or scale measures something. Validity is the degree to which a test or scale measures what it is supposed to measure.
- Social research presents many ethical issues; the APA offers helpful ethical guidelines for researchers.
- The life-span perspective offers a helpful way to understand human behavior. One can assess the determinants of behavior as necessary and/or sufficient regarding changes in a particular behavior.
- Interindividual changes occur between people; intraindividual ones take place within the individual.
- Life-span developmentalists have three tasks: description, explanation, and optimization.
- Three organizing principles help us apply the life-span perspective: chronological age, cohort, and life transitions.
- The stages in the human life span are pregnancy and the birth of a child, infancy, preschool years, middle childhood, adolescence, young adulthood, middle adulthood, and old age. Each stage is characterized by developmental tasks that confront each individual.

## SUGGESTED READINGS

Gonzalez, I., Miren, A., & Valera, J. B. 1990. There is nothing so practical as a good theory: Social psychology and social development issues in the Philippine context. *Philippine Journal of Psychology, 23,* 1–18.

Hartson, H. R., & Smith, E. C. 1991. Rapid prototyping in human-computer interface development. *Interacting with Computers, 3*(1), 51–91.

Jacklin, C. N. 1990. Female and male: Issues of gender. *Annual Progress in Child Psychiatry and Child Development,* pp. 111–126.

Lipsitt, L. P. 1992. Discussion: The Bayley Scales of Infant Development: Issues of prediction and outcome revisited. *Advances in Infancy Research, 7,* 229–245.

Parham, T., & Austin, N. L. 1994. Career development and African Americans: A contextual reappraisal using the nigrescence construct [Special Issue: Racial identity and vocational behavior]. *Journal of Vocational Behavior, 44*(2), 139–154.

Prosser, G. 1992. Psychological issues when others mediate your life. *Educational and Child Psychology, 9*(1), 17–26.

## SUGGESTED VIDEOTAPES

Chariot Productions (Producer). (1994). *Language of life: Understanding the genetic code* (27 minutes). Available from United Learning, 6633 W. Howard St., Niles, IL 60714-0718; 800-424-0362; Email: bistern@interaccess.com; Website: www.unitedlearning.com

Concept Media, Inc. (Producer). (1991). *Cognitive development: First 2 ½ years* (25 minutes). Available from Concept Media, Inc., P.O. Box 19542, Irvine, CA 92623-9542; 800-233-7078; Email: info@conceptmedia.com; Website: www.conceptmedia.com [Piaget]

Concept Media, Inc. (Producer). (1992). *Cognitive development: First 2 ½ to 6 years* (28 minutes). Available from Concept Media, Inc., P.O. Box 19542, Irvine, CA 92623-9542; 800-233-7078; Email: info@conceptmedia.com; Website: www.conceptmedia.com [Piaget]

Concept Media, Inc. (Producer). (1992). *Psychosocial development* (23 minutes). Available from Concept Media, Inc., P.O. Box 19542, Irvine, CA 92623-9542; 800-233-7078; Email: info@conceptmedia.com; Website: www.conceptmedia.com

Jeulin (Producer). (1995). *Genetics I: Fundamentals of DNA* (13 minutes). Available from HRM Video, 175 Thompkins Ave., Pleasantville, NY 10570; 800-431-2050; Website: www.hrmvideo.com

Jeulin (Producer). (1995). *Genetics II: Breaking the genetic code* (18 minutes). Available from HRM Video, 175 Thompkins Ave., Pleasantville, NY 10570; 800-431-2050; Website: www.hrmvideo.com

## REFERENCES

American Psychological Association. (1982). *Ethical principles in the conduct of research with human participants*. Washington DC: Author.

American Psychological Association. (1992). Ethical principles of psychologists and code of conduct. *American Psychologist 47,* 1597–1611.

Aquilino, W. S. (1990). Likelihood of parent-child coresidence, *Journal of Marriage and the Family, 52,* 405–419.

Baltes, P. B. (1973). Prototypical paradigms and questions in lifespan research on development and aging. *Gerontologist, 13.*

Baltes, P. B., & Willis, S. L. (1977). Toward psychological theories of aging and development. In J. E. Birren & K. W. Schaie (Eds.), *Handbook of psychology of aging*. Belmont, CA: Wadsworth.

Barker, R. G., & Schoggen, P. (1973). *Qualities of community life: Methods of measuring environment and behavior: Applied to an American and English town*. San Francisco: Jossey-Bass.

Barker, R. G., & Wright, H. F. (1955). *The Midwest and its children*. New York: Harper & Row.

Belsky, T. (1979). Mother-father-infant interaction: A naturalistic observational study. *Developmental Psychology, 15,* 601–607.

Bengston, V. L. (1976). The "generation gap" of aging family members. In E. Olander & A. Haddad (Eds.), *Time, self and roles in old age*. New York: Behavioral Publications.

Brodzinsky, D. M., Gormly, A. V., & Ambron, S. R. (1986). *Lifespan human development*. New York: Holt, Rinehart & Winston.

Bronfenbrenner, U. (1979). *The ecology of human development*. Cambridge, MA: Harvard University Press.

Bronfenbrenner, U. (1990). Who cares for children? *Research and clinical center for child development 12,* 27–40.

Butler, R. N. (1981, August 24). Interview: Latest on extending the human lifespan. *U.S. News and World Report.*

Cattell, R. B. (1971). *Abilities: Their structure, growth, and action*. Boston: Houghton Mifflin.

Colby, A. (1978). Evolution of a moral-developmental theory. *New Directions in Child Development, 2,* 89–104.

Coombs, C. H. (1964). *A theory of data*. New York: Wiley.

Dennis, W. (1936). The bibliography of baby biographies. *Child Development, 7,* 71–73.

Desbarats, J. (1983). Spatial choice and constraints on behavior. *Annals of the Association of American Geographers, 73,* 340–357.

Duvall, E. M., & Miller, B. C. (1985). *Marriage and family development*. New York: Harper & Row.

Eagle, T. C. (1988). Context effects in consumer spatial behavior. In R. G. Golledge & H. J. P. Timmermans (Eds.) *Behavioral modeling in geography and planning* (pp. 299–324). London: Croom Helm.

Eagley, A. H. (1987). *Sex differences in social behavior: A social-role interpretation*. Hillsdale, NJ: Erlbaum.

Elder, G. H. (1985). *Life course dynamics: Trajectories and transitions 1968–1980*. Ithaca. NY: Cornell University Press.

Erikson, E. H. (1990). *Identity and the life cycle*. New York: Norton.

Erikson, E. H., & Kivnick, H. Q. (1986). *Vital involvement in old age*. New York: Norton.

Estioko-Griffin, A. (1985). Women as hunters: The case of an Eastern Cagayan Agta group. In P. B. Griffin & A. A. Estioko-Griffin (Eds.), *The Agta of Northeastern Luzon: Recent studies*. Cebu City, Philippines: San Carlos Publishing.

Germain, C. B. (1979). *People and environments*. New York: Columbia University Press.

Gilligan, C. (1982). *In a different voice*. Boston: Harvard University Press.

Goodman, M. J., Griffin, P. B., Estioko-Griffin, A. A., & Grove, J. S. (1985). The compatibility of hunting and mothering among the Agta hunter-gatherers of the Philippines. *Sex Roles 12,* 1199–1209.

Gordon, C. (1976). Development of evaluated role identities. *Annual Review of Sociology, 2.* 112–115.

Guisinger, S., & Blatt, S. Individuality and relatedness: Evolution of a fundamental dialect. *American Psychologist, 49*(2), 104–111.

Hartmann, H. (1964). *Essays on ego psychology*. New York: International Universities Press.

Ho, M. K. (1987). *Family therapy with ethnic minorities*. Newbury Park, CA: Sage.

Horn, J. I., and Donaldson, G. (1980). Cognitive development in adulthood. In O. G. Brim, Jr., and J. Kagan (Eds.). *Constancy and change in human development*. Cambridge, MA. Harvard University Press.

Horn, J. I. & Donaldson, G. (1980). Cognitive development in adulthood. In O. G. Brim, Jr., & J. Kagan (Eds.), *Constancy and change in human development*. Cambridge, MA: Harvard University Press.

Jaret, C. (1995). *Contemporary racial and ethnic relations*. New York: Harper Collins.

Jessop, D. J. (1981). Family relations as viewed by parents and adolescents: A specification. *Journal of Marriage and the Family, 43,* 95–106.

Kohlberg, L. (1976). Moral stages and moralization: The cognitive-developmental approach. In T. Luck-ona (Ed.), *Moral development and behavior,* New York: Holt, Rinehart & Winston.

Kohlberg, L. (1978). Revisions in the theory and practice of moral development. *New Directions for Child Development, 2.*

Kojima, H. (1986). Japanese concepts of child development from mid 17th to mid 19th century. *International Journal of Behavioral Development, 9,* 315–329.

Labouvie, E. W. (1982). Issues in lifespan development. In B. B. Wolman, G. Stricker, S. J. Ellman, & P. Keith-Spigel (Eds.), *Handbook of developmental psychology*. New Jersey: Prentice-Hall.

Lauver, P. J., & Jones, R. M. (1991). Factors associated with perceived career options in American Indian, White, and Hispanic rural high school students. *Journal of Counseling Psychology, 38,* 159–166.

Lenntorp, B. (1978). A time-geographic similarities model of individual activity programmes. In T. Carlstein, D. Parkes, & N. Thrift (Eds.), *Human activity and time geography* (pp. 162–180). London: Arnold.

Lerner, R. M., & Hultsch, D. F. (1983). *Human development*. New York: McGraw-Hill, 1983.

Levin, I., (1986). *Stage and structure: Reopening the debate*. Norward, NJ: Ablex.

Livson, N., & Peskin, H. (1980). Perspectives on adolescence from longitudinal research. In J. Adelson (Ed.), *Handbook of adolescent psychology*. New York: Wiley.

Manturzewska, M. (1990). A biological study of the lifespan development of professional musicians. *Psychology of Music, 18*(2), 112–139.

Marcell, M. M., & Thomas, C. S. (1993, March). Behavioral profile of an adolescent with a chromosome 4 deletion. In M. M. Marcell (Chair), *Unusual and prototypical cases as guidelines for developmental research*. Symposium conducted at the biennial meetings of the society for research in child development, pp. 15–32, New Orleans, LA.

Mattessich, P., & Hill, R. (1987). Life cycle and family development. In M. B. Sussman & S. K. Steinmetz (Eds.), *Handbook of marriage and family* (pp. 437–469). New York: Plenum.

McConnell, J. V., & Philipchalk, R. P. (1992). *Understanding human behavior* (7th ed.). New York: Harcourt Brace Jovanovich.

McGoldrick, J. (1982). Irish families. In M. McGoldrick, J. K. Pearce, & J. Giordano (Eds.), *Ethnicity and family therapy*. New York: Guilford Press.

Mendelson, M. J. (1992, Fall). Let's teach case methods to developmental students. *Social Research on Child Development Newsletter,* pp. 9–13.

Miller, B. C., & Sollie, D. L. (1980). Normal stresses during transition to parenthood. *Family Relations, 29,* 459–465.

Miller, P. H. (1993). *Theories of developmental psychology* (3rd ed.). New York: Freeman.

Mitchell, J. (1984). Harvard perception studies: Convergent concerns and divergent approaches during the past decade. In T. F. Saarinen, D. Seamon, & J. L. Sell (Eds.), *Environmental perception and behavior* (research paper #209, pp. 33–59). Chicago: University of Chicago Department of Geography.

Mukhopadhyay, C. C., & Higgins, P. J. (1988). Anthropological studies of women's status revisited: 1977–1987. *Annual Review of Anthropology 17,* 461–495.

Napier, R. W., & Gershenfeld, M. K. (1993). *Groups: Theory and experience* (5th ed.). Boston: Houghton Mifflin.

Neiman, L. J., & Hughes, J. W. (1951, December). The problem of the concept of role: A resurvey of the literature. *Social Forces,* pp. 141–149.

Nesselroade, J. R., Schaie, K. W., & Baltes, P. B. (1972). Ontogenetic and generational components of structured and quantitative change in adult behavior. *Journal of Gerontology, 27,* 222–228.

Papalia, D. E., & Olds, S. W. (1986). *Human development* (3rd ed.). New York: McGraw-Hill.

Papalia, D. E., & Olds, S. W. (1992). *Human development* (4th ed.). New York: McGraw-Hill.

Piaget, J. (1952). *The child's conception of number.* London: Routledge & Kegan Paul.

Piaget, J. (1970). Piaget's theory. In P. H. Mussen (Ed.), *Carmichael's manual of child psychology* (Vol. 1). New York: Wiley.

Pillari, V. (1986). *Pathways to family myths.* New York: Brunner/Mazel.

Plomin, R. (1990). *Nature and nurture: An introduction to human biological genetics.* Pacific Grove, CA: Brooks/Cole.

Schaie, K. W. (1965). A general model for the study of developmental problems. *Psychological Bulletin, 64,* 92–107

Schaie, K. W. (1986). Beyond calendar definition of age, time and cohort: The general developmental model revisited. *Developmental Review, 6,* 252–277.

Schaie, K. W., & Herzog, C. (1983). A fourteen-year cohort sequential analysis of adult intellectual development. *Developmental Psychology, 19,* 531–543.

Skinner, B. F. (1974). *About behaviorism.* New York: Knopf.

Steuer, F. B. (1994). *The psychological development of children.* Pacific Grove, CA: Brooks/Cole.

Strean, H. S. (1979). Role theory. In F. J. Turner (Ed.), *Social Work Treatment.* New York: Free Press.

Tanner, J. M. (1990). *Fetus into man: Physical growth from conception to maturity.* Cambridge, MA: Harvard University Press.

Thoits, P. A. (1986). Multiple identities. Examining gender and marital status differences in distress. *American Sociological Review, 51,* 259–272.

Turner-Hansen, A., & Holaday, B. (1995). Daily life experiences for the chronically ill: A lifespan perspective. *Family and Community Health, 17*(4), 1–11.

U.S. Bureau of the Census. (1983). *Population of the United States, 1970–2050.* Current Population Reports, Series P-25, Nos. 917 and 922. Washington DC: U.S. Government Printing Office.

U.S. Bureau of the Census. (1992). *Statistical abstract of the United States.* Washington DC: U.S. Government Printing Office.

Vygotsky, L. S. (1978). *Mind in society: The development of higher mental processes.* (M. Cole, V. John-Steiner, S. Scribner, & E. Souberman Senes (Eds.) Cambridge, MA: Harvard University Press. (Original work published in 1930, 1933, 1935).

Weimer, W. B. (1979). *Notes on the methodology of scientific research.* Hillsdale, NJ: Erlbaum.

Wells, K. (1987). Scientific issues in the conduct of case studies. *Journal of Child Psychology and Psychiatry, 28,* 783–790.

Werner, H. (1957). The concept of development from a comparative and organismic point of view. In D. Harris (Ed.), *The concept of development: An issue in the study of human behavior.* Minneapolis: University of Minnesota Press.

White, R. W. (1960). Competence and the psychosexual stages of development. In R. Jones Marshall (Ed.), *Nebraska Symposium on Motivation: Vol. 8.* (pp. 97–141). Lincoln: University of Nebraska Press.

Woodruff, D. S. (1985). Arousal: Sleep and aging. In J. E. Birren & K. W. Schaie (Eds.), *Handbook of the psychology of aging.* New York: Van Nostrand Reinhold.

Yinger, J. M. (1985). Assimilation in the United States: The Mexican Americans. In W. Conner (Ed.), *Mexican Americans in comparative perspective.* Washington DC: Urban Institute Press.

Young, S. (1980). The Hawaiians. In J. McDermott, W. Tsing, & T. Maretzki (Eds.), *People of culture of Hawaii.* Hawaii: University Press of Hawaii.

# 2

# Conception, Pregnancy, and Childbirth

# INTRODUCTION

Nita is going through her second divorce and discovers to her dismay that she's pregnant with her second child. She is apprehensive and nervous—as her "contested" divorce drags on in court. It is a painful and lonely time for Nita. Often, she does not feel like eating although she has reached her sixth month of pregnancy. By the seventh month she is concerned and forces herself to "eat for two." How will this crisis of divorce and its aftermath affect the unborn child?

As its title suggests, this chapter will deal with a developmental period that comprises three distinct phases. After a look at the psychosocial context of pregnancy, I shall present the biological and developmental aspects of how a human being is created and delivered. This information can help social workers give clients an accurate image of this stage of life; it will also help workers understand what such clients are going through.

Though this part of the chapter will touch on many contextual concerns, the sections that follow take a closer look at specific circumstances that social workers may find helpful, such as the mechanisms of inheritance. Next, we shall look at two significant issues—infant death and abortion—that deserve special attention. The chapter concludes by offering an idea of how social workers can apply the information in this chapter to their own practice.

# THE PSYCHOSOCIAL CONTEXT OF PREGNANCY

Each person functions within a uniquely conceived reality in which the present is defined in terms of the past and the future, and the past is constantly redefined in terms of the present. Time moves on for everyone. That which was the future becomes the present and rolls away to join the endless ocean of the past. Time never stops, ever, for anyone! Individuals rely on past experiences to make sense of the world around them and select behaviors that are appropriate to their interpretations of the day-to-day events of their lives (Darling, 1983).

The human capacity for adjustment is almost infinite. When prepared for a particular situation, such as pregnancy, people often adjust relatively smoothly to it. Even if not prepared for a pregnancy, expectant parents usually learn to accept it in time. The parental role begins with the decision to have children. For infants, the process of growth begins at the moment of fertilization. The mother's social role begins as soon as the pregnancy is confirmed by tests.

One's behavior is the direct result of one's definition of a given situation. The meaning of "having a baby" varies for prospective parents, depending on whether the pregnancy is wanted or unwanted, whether the parent is single or has a partner, and so forth.

Pregnancy and childbirth are often viewed with awe and amazement. As one woman put it, "You just eat right after you know you are pregnant and then comes this miniature human being carrying your and your significant other's heredity in his or her genes. It is a miracle!" Many factors come together to create this miracle. Like any other developmental period of a person's life, pregnancy has both personal and social aspects. Pregnancy and childbearing entail stress and continual coping and adapting. From the conception to the adulthood of the child, and sometimes beyond, the parent/parents have to deal constantly with an enormous variety of situations, expected and not. Pregnancy itself is affected by both parents' genetic endowments; the woman's age and general health; the intrauterine environment; complications such as toxemia, anoxia, Rh incompatibility, drugs, alcohol, reduction of hormones, and stress; and the prevailing family environment.

Pregnancy, particularly the first, can create problems for prospective parents, single or married. However, those with support systems and/or stable marriages tend not to suffer great stress (Doering, Entwistle, & Quinlan, 1982).

Experienced parents as well as women in their first pregnancies feel concern over the health of the unborn child (Darling, 1983). A childless couple who have experienced one or more miscarriages or stillbirths have to cope with a tremendous amount of stress. As one first-time mother says, "I had two miscarriages before I became pregnant with Ricky. . . . I thought maybe I had bad genes or something. . . . It was in the back of my mind through the whole pregnancy" (Darling, 1983).

Pregnant women are surrounded by a psychosocial environment that affects their pregnancy. Their views of pregnancy are colored by opinions received from friends, relatives and neighbors. Women in the midst of marital conflicts who have inadequate support systems and women who have problems with their own personal identity are more likely to experience emotional stress than others (Fleming, Ruble, Flett, & Shaul, 1988). Strong emotional reactions such as prolonged anxiety or depression may influence fetal development as the maternal hormones are secreted and cross the placenta barrier. However, evidence on this is mixed (Sameroff, 1983; Vaughan, Bradley, Joffe, Seifer, & Bargelow, 1987).

The following situations illustrate some of the factors that create diverse experiences of pregnancy. Because social work practitioners help many types of people, I have tried to bring as much diversity as possible to these and other examples.

Brenda, a 16-year-old student, is pregnant. Though not married, she plans to keep the baby. Her parents are concerned, as is her grandmother, who is a single parent herself. As time passes, Brenda observes her body changing. The tension surrounding her pregnancy builds up; there is an uneasy atmosphere in the family.

Mary and John have been married for 12 years. After trying to conceive for two years, they decide to get help. They visit several clinics and take various medications. At last Mary becomes pregnant with her first child. There is an air of excitement in the family, for they have waited a long time and

have plenty saved up to provide for this new member of the family.

Jim and Kim have been married for 14 years and have seven children. Kim is expecting their eighth child. This family is overburdened with financial problems. They live in a crowded three-bedroom apartment and cannot afford to move to a better dwelling. Kim suffers from high blood pressure. Another child will be an additional burden to the family.

In each of these situations, the family's reactions and attitudes to pregnancy depend on the problems it faces and on the uniqueness of the pregnant woman. An impending birth affects the entire family and is influenced by the family's income, health, age, religious background, and marital status.

Social and economic factors are also strong determinants of whether medical services will be used (Watkins & Johnson, 1979). Prenatal care and advice are closely linked to ethnic, cultural, and racial differences. Expectant mothers are more likely to follow professional advice on prenatal care if the health care providers' attitudes reflect an understanding and acceptance of the family's cultural patterns. For instance, the recommendation of a high-protein diet, such as steak and potatoes, may shock and confuse a new immigrant from Mexico who is used to spicy food or alienate a middle-class college graduate who is a strict vegetarian.

Another major factor in pregnancy, of course, is how a pregnant woman changes physiologically. Some women experience discomfort during pregnancy, because of weight gain and other complications; others do not. Further, women respond to discomfort differently. Thus, physiology and attitude, as well as the factors that contribute to them, may affect a mother's attitude toward her unborn child.

In short, no child is born in a vacuum. Almost from the moment of conception, the child becomes a part of the psychosocial as well as physical environment. Later in this chapter, we shall look at the effects of environmental influences on the fetus and newborn, after we have explored the biological and maturational aspects of the prenatal periods and childbirth.

## The Social Worker's Role

Before we move on, let us look briefly at the role of the social worker in the early stages of pregnancy. Please consider the following case:

> Tina is a young, pregnant teenager. She wants the baby despite the protests of her parents and her boyfriend. Though determined to have the child, she is frightened and angry because she does not receive any support from her family. She is also confused about herself and does not understand the sudden nausea and light headedness she experiences. She imagines she is losing her mind and her self-control. A social worker at a women's health center educates Tina through counseling and shares basic literature on what it means to be a pregnant woman.

Social workers might participate in either family planning or crisis intervention, including decisions about abortions. Practitioners should be knowledgeable enough to participate effectively in any such social action. Helpful social action promotes (1) concrete support services and (2) healthy attitudes toward pregnancy regardless of the status of the pregnant woman. For instance, a pregnant single teenager or a married woman with a serious mental conflict may experience a great deal of confusion, but support systems could help each develop a healthy attitude toward pregnancy.

## PRENATAL DEVELOPMENT

### Conception

When a new life is conceived, a process begins in the mother that leads to the development of a unique human being. One person grows tall, another is short. One is shy, another domineering. Human beings are the products of both heredity and experiences in the environment.

How does the creation of a human being begin? Once every 28 days on average, an ovum (egg) ripens in one of the two ovaries and is discharged into one of the fallopian tubes, which lead to the uterus. The ovum is one of the largest cells in the human body. The sperm, which comes from the man, is one of the smallest cells in the human body, only 0.05 millimeters in diameter. Egg and sperm cells are called *gametes*. The mature ovum survives for only two or three days. A man's sperm deposited in a woman's vagina during intercourse can survive as long as three days. Of the 300 million spermatozoa deposited in the vagina, it takes only one traveling from the uterus to the fallopian tube to fertilize the ovum at this critical period.

If the ovum does not become fertilized, it continues down to the uterus, where it disintegrates and is flushed from the body during menstruation. However, if the sperm penetrates and fertilizes the ovum while it is traveling to the uterus, a new life begins. The fertilized egg is called the *zygote*. The zygote represents a special combination of genetic potential, half from the father and half from the mother. Its gender is determined by the sperm; all ova carry an X chromosome, whereas a sperm cell has an equal probability of carrying either an X or a Y chromosome. When X and Y chromosome are paired, the child will be male. With an XX combination, the child is female.

Within 48 hours after fertilization, the new cell has duplicated its nucleus and divided into two identical cells. Then, in a geometric pattern the two cells become four, the four cells become eight, and so forth. This process of reproduction is called *mitosis*. The cluster of cells is nourished by the yolk of the ovum. The cells in the cluster continue to divide. Then, *differentiation* begins: The cells separate into groups according to their future roles. At this point, the cluster is called a *blastocyst,* a hollow ball of cells. Half of this ball consists of two distinct layers of cells; this half will eventually become a baby. The other half contains only a single layer of cells. This forms the housing and life-support systems for the fetus: the placenta, the umbilical cord, and the amniotic sac.

The blastocyst, which at first floats in the uterus, soon plants itself in the uterine wall. If the blastocyst does not implant itself properly at the right time and place, the cell mass will die before it can reach the embryonic stage. If everything goes well, the blastocyst will be firmly implanted about two weeks after conception.

Though fertilization seems to take place easily, many married couples face infertility. In the United States, approximately 10% to 15% of couples are infertile or otherwise unable to conceive (Denney & Quadagno, 1992; Papalia & Olds, 1992). This problem affects mostly older couples. Medical specialists can often help couples identify the causes of infertility and help them become parents through a variety of medical-surgical and educational techniques.

> Harry and Elaine, both in their mid-thirties, go to the Planned Parenthood clinic because they have tried to have a baby for a long time, and feel cheated by their failure. They receive counseling for their apparent lack of self-esteem, particularly Elaine's. Both seem to have fears, doubts, and anxieties about trying anything new, so their counselor encourages them to think about several options. Since the basic problem seems to be Harry's low sperm count, the counselor suggests artificial insemination as well as adoption of a hard-to-place child as possible alternatives. Together they discuss the risks and expenses involved. The couple thus receives emotional support and practical help in making their decision.

In spite of the help generally available, some couples do not successfully achieve parenthood. *Infertility* is defined as "the inability of a couple to achieve pregnancy, usually defined after a year or more of sexual intercourse without pregnancy" (Masters, Johnson, & Kolodny, 1988, p. 681). This condition has many causes. Men are responsible for 40% to 50% of all cases of infertility (Grunfeld, 1989); about 15% of couples share responsibility for their inability to conceive (Hudson, Pepperell, & Wood, 1987). Hyde (1990) cites four major causes of infertility in women: failure to ovulate, blockage of the fallopian tubes, abnormally thick mucus in the cervix, and hormonal abnormalities accompanied by emotional stress. Infertility in men is due to a low sperm count and decreased sperm motility (Hyde, 1990). Low sperm count can be caused by numerous factors including varicose veins in the scrotum and testes, drugs, congenital birth defects, and undescended testes (Masters et al., 1988).

The limited research literature on the emotional impact of infertility suggests that this is a major source of stress in the family. Infertility makes couples reassess the meaning and purpose of their marriage. It also raises questions of self-worth for both of them. Further, it often disrupts the couple's sexual satisfaction because of their need to share this personal problem with others (Sabatelli, Meth, & Gavazzi, 1988). These problems grow more acute when couples cannot identify any specific cause for infertility; this is seen in 20% of infertile couples (Crooks & Baur, 1990).

To make things worse, infertile couples often face harassing questions from relatives and friends. When people learn that a couple cannot get pregnant, they often ask, "What are you going to do about it?" or "Let me suggest to you this and this and this . . ." They usually do not realize that they have intruded and hurt a couple already in agony about their inability to conceive naturally. After four or five years of trying, many women begin to feel that they are less of a woman because their body is not doing what it is "supposed" to do. Similarly, an infertile man may feel like he is less of a man; in our paternalistic culture, he may even have to endure jokes about not being virile.

Fortunately there are ways to negate this situation. In 1990 an estimated 1 million new patients sought treatment for infertility (Elmer-Dewitt, 1991).

## Alternatives to Conventional Pregnancy

Revolutionary methods are now available to couples who have problems in conceiving or successfully completing a pregnancy: artificial insemination, in vitro fertilization, gamete intra fallopian transfer, vivo fertilization, and surrogate mothering.

*Artificial insemination* is the best-developed alternative to natural fertilization. In this technique, the woman goes to a clinic every month and has sperm injected into her vagina. Usually this sperm belongs to other men through donation and has been frozen. Ordinarily, sperm banks keep a record of the characteristics of the person who donated the sperm but keep all other information anonymous. This procedure allows the couple to select the sperm of a donor who closely resembles the husband. The Office of Technology Assessment reports that approximately 172,000 women in the United States undergo artificial insemination and about 65,000 babies are conceived in this fashion every year (Byrne, 1988).

*In vitro* ("in glass" or test tube) *fertilization* is also called *fertilization in an artificial environment.* On July 25, 1984, Louise Brown was born in England to delighted parents. Her mother could not conceive, because there was a blockage in her fallopian tubes that prevented fertilization. Her doctors transferred a ripened ovum from her body to a special culture and then fertilized it with sperm obtained from her husband (Lenard, 1981). When the fertilized ovum had grown into an embryo, the doctors transferred it to the uterus of the mother, where it attached itself and continued to grow.

A survey of 146 clinics that perform in vitro fertilization found the procedure successful in about 9% of the cases (Sperling, 1989). A current version of this procedure is called *sperm injection.* A single sperm is injected into an egg. Several eggs are fertilized in this manner and implanted into the mother's uterus. One Belgian physician reported that there were 100 births

associated with this new method (Associated Press, 1993).

In *gamete intra fallopian transfer* (GIFT), eggs and sperm are transferred from a test tube into a woman's fallopian tubes. Fertilization takes place normally and within the mother's reproductive system. The eggs and sperm could come from the husband, wife, and/or other donors. The fetus in the mother's womb could be related to the husband, the wife, both, or neither.

In *vivo fertilization* (fertilization in a living body), a wife and her husband involve another woman in conception. The other woman, a donor, has also demonstrated her fertility and the husband's sperm is artificially inseminated into the donor's body. Once the embryo is formed, doctors transfer it to the wife's uterus, which becomes the gestational environment. The wife is treated with additional hormones to maintain a normal pregnancy. In this case, the child is genetically related to the husband but not to the wife.

In *surrogate mothering,* sperm from an infertile woman's husband are injected into the body of a surrogate donor during her monthly ovulation period. The surrogate mother bears the child and returns it to the parents at birth. At the start of this process, the surrogate mother signs a legal document promising to give the child to the natural parents. According to Byrne (1988), 100 babies have been born to surrogate mothers. In one fascinating case, a woman agreed to be the surrogate mother for her own daughter who wanted a child but had been born without a uterus. At age 42 the donor gave birth to her own twin grandchildren (Elmer-Dewitt, 1991).

Though such donor techniques have created greater possibilities for couples with infertility problems, the legal, psychological, and ethical issues of such pregnancies are quite complex (Elmer-Dewitt, 1991; Elson, 1989). The man who gives the sperm should give consent to the procedure and assume responsibility for the legal guardianship of the offspring. The lack of official guidelines for screening donors raises many concerns. For instance, who is responsible for a child born with a severe genetic anomaly? Another serious concern is the sperm donor's rights to a relationship with the offspring. In 1983, a California man was granted weekly visitation rights to a child who had been conceived with his sperm.

In another case, widely discussed, Mary Beth Whitehead was paid about $10,000 to be a surrogate mother. After the birth of the child, Whitehead decided she wanted to keep the baby. In ensuing court battles, the New Jersey Supreme Court decided that the contract between the couple and Mrs. Whitehead was void and that it was illegal to pay a woman to bear a child for someone else. However, the court granted custody of the child to the donor parents, because they could provide the child with a stable environment. The court rejected the sperm donor's wife the rights to adopt the child and supported Whitehead's right to continued visitation.

This case creates a precedent that other states may follow. Another possibility is that surrogate parenting may be made illegal or may be so tightly regulated that it could become an underground practice. At this point, however, surrogate parenting is endorsed by the medical community (Lacayo, 1988, 1992; Silverman, 1989). As you can see, these sorts of procedures raise many ethical questions that need to be dealt with legally, socially, and morally.

## The Embryonic Period

After conception, the period of pregnancy lasts for typically 40 weeks. During the embryonic period, the embryo grows to a length of more than 1 inch. More bodily functions develop, and the embryo begins to look like a human being. Hetherington and Parke (1979) note that from the time of conception to the end of the embryonic period, the organism increases in size by 2 million percent. As the cells multiply, they differentiate into three distinct layers. The outer layer of cells is the *ectoderm.* The skin, nervous system, hair, and nails will eventually develop from this layer of cells. The middle layer of cells, the *mesoderm,* will eventually make up the muscles and bones of the body. The inner layer of cells, the *endoderm,* will develop into important components of the gastrointestinal system, the liver, lungs, several glands, and the adipose tissue.

In the embryonic period, which lasts approximately six weeks, the life-support systems—the placenta, the umbilical cord, and the amniotic sac—are refined. The part of the embryo attached to the uterine wall becomes the placenta. The *placenta* is a blood-filled, spongy mass that supplies the embryo with all its nutrients and carries its waste matter. The embryo is linked to the placenta through the *umbilical cord,* a tough, hoselike structure made up of two arteries and one vein surrounded by a gelatinous substance. The placenta continues to grow during pregnancy and has two sets of blood vessels connected to it. One set goes to the developing baby through the umbilical cord and the other goes to the mother's circulatory system. There is no direct link between these two blood systems. The semipermeable membrane in the vessels permits an exchange of nutrients and other elements small enough to pass through the blood vessel walls. Through this indirect passage the embryo receives oxygen, proteins, and other nutrients and eliminates waste products such as carbon dioxide. The embryo is basically a parasite on the mother's body (Brodzinsky, Gormly, & Ambron, 1986).

Agents that can produce malformations while the tissues and organs are forming are called *teratogens.* They take various forms such as viruses, alcohol, drugs, and environmental toxins.

By the third and fourth weeks, the embryo's cells differentiate rapidly, taking on the specialized structures of the body. Similar cells group together and emerge as body organs. The most important changes are the establishment of the body form as an elongated cylinder and the formation of precursors of the brain and the heart. The neural tube, the basis of the central nervous system, begins to take shape at the end of the third week. By the end of the fifth, the tube has differentiated into five bulging parts that will become the subdivisions of the brain. At this point, the embryo has increased 50 times in length and 40,000 times in weight since the moment of fertilization.

By the end of the second month, the embryo looks quite human. It weighs about 2.25 grams and is about 28 millimeters (1 inch) long. At this point, all the internal organs have formed as well as the face, limbs, fingers, and toes.

The embryonic period ends ten weeks after menstruation has stopped. By this time, the embryo looks like and represents a miniature human being. From this point on, the embryo is technically called a *fetus* until it is born.

It is estimated that 30% of all embryos are spontaneously aborted (Mussen, Conger, Kagan, & Gewitz, 1979). A spontaneous abortion or miscarriage is the expulsion of an embryo that cannot survive outside the womb. The following case shows the impact miscarriages can have.

> At age 29, Sonia looks emaciated. She has undergone three spontaneous abortions. Overwhelmed by the fear that she might again lose her unborn child she is afraid to get pregnant though she wants a child very much. A discussion of her lifestyle reveals that she works three different jobs and uses liquor to relax; she takes prescription pain killers as well. Her relationship with her husband is strained because he works seasonal jobs and has been unemployed for more than half a year. The couple decides they need marital counseling to improve their relationship before starting a family. They find that such improvement means cutting down the number of hours Sonia works and changing their lifestyle. Although these adjustments will not be easy, the social worker has pinned down the most visible problems.

Most miscarriages result from abnormal pregnancies. Chromosomal abnormalities could be present in half of all spontaneous abortions (Ash, Vennart, & Carter, 1977). Other possible causes include a defective ovum or sperm, unfavorable conditions for implantation, breakdown in supplies of oxygen or nourishment because of an abnormal umbilical cord, and physiological abnormalities of the mother (Papalia & Olds, 1986).

## The Fetal Period

As you know, from the end of the second month until birth, the developing organism is called a fetus. The rate of growth reaches its highest peak during the early fetal period and then slowly declines. During the fourth and fifth months, the mother starts to feel spontaneous fetal movements called *quickening*.

During the second trimester (three-month period), the fetus grows to 10 inches and almost 2 pounds. The fetus continues to grow at the rate of about an inch every 10 days from the fifth month until the end of pregnancy.

Qualitative changes also take place in this trimester. Kicking increases, and squirming decreases slowly. The presence or absence of reflexes helps caregivers evaluate the fetus's development, since there is a definite timetable for the development and cessation of most reflexes. At the end of the embryonic period and the beginning of the fetal period, the fetus responds to strong, direct stimulation of muscles. The response consists of a local contraction, called the *myogenic response*, which is a muscle response and does not involve the nervous system (Ambron & Brodzinsky, 1979).

At about 8 to 9 weeks, the fetus responds when a fine hair is drawn across its lips (Hofer, 1981). At 11 to 17 weeks, the fetus develops an increasing variety of responses in the limbs and in the trunk. This is the time when the facial muscles first respond to outside stimuli, and the body movements are flowing and graceful. At 16 weeks, the fetus reveals spontaneous movements that include squirming, jerks, and thrusts. All these movements are felt by the mother, beginning when the fetus is 7 inches long (Hofer, 1981). Other behaviors such as wriggling, reaching, kicking, grimacing, and pouting occur during this period.

When the fetus is about 17 to 18 weeks old, an extraordinary change takes place. The movements of the fetus slow down and finally become stilled. Those movements that can be elicited are sluggish, and spontaneous activity is limited to levels reached a month before. That is, the fetus regresses to an earlier level of functioning. This phase is called *the period of inhibition* and *the period of discontinuities in behavior development*. It is also called the *period of quiescence* (Hofer, 1981). This inhibition does not appear simultaneously in all parts of the fetus but rather one at a time, and it lasts until the fetus is 24 weeks old. Researchers think that the fetus might be subjected to partial anoxia (oxygen deficiency) during this period. Responsiveness reappears at the end of the quiescent period, when the fetus begins to respond as it had originally, beginning with the head and neck and progressing to the arms and finally to the lower limbs.

A large number of the neurons that make up the cerebral cortex are produced by the end of the second trimester. The regions of the cortex continue to mature over the first four years of life (Aoki & Siekevitz, 1988; Greenough, Black, & Wallace, 1987).

After the end of the second trimester, the fetus can survive outside the mother's body if it is placed in an incubator and given special care. However, a full-term baby has many advantages over a 28-week-old fetus: (1) the ability to begin and maintain regular breathing; (2) well-coordinated swallowing movements, stronger peristalsis, and therefore more efficient digestion and excretion; (3) mature regulation of body temperature (Newman & Newman, 1995).

The full-term baby can take full advantage of the mother's diet and the minerals in her body. The teeth begin to get enamel as the placenta starts to degenerate in the last month of pregnancy. Antibodies against various diseases that have been formed in the mother's blood pass into the fetal bloodstream and provide the fetus immunity to many diseases during the first months of life.

In the ninth month, the fetus continues to grow and begins to take a head-down position in preparation for the trip through the birth canal. From one to two weeks before birth, the fetus "drops" as the uterus settles lower in the pelvis. At this time, the mother's muscles and uterus may move sporadically. The fetus does not gain weight easily any more, and all is ready for birth.

Conception to birth takes about 266 days. Having begun with two cells at conception, the child at birth has as many as 200 billion cells.

## THE BIRTH EXPERIENCE

A branch of medicine called *perinatology* considers childbirth as beginning with conception and extending through the prenatal period to delivery of the child and the first few years of life (Norr, Block, Charles, Meyering, & Meyers, 1977). This multifaceted approach involves obstetricians, biochemists, and pediatricians. Social workers contribute their special awareness of the impact of medical problems on the family and community. As such, they can recommend and implement social programs needed to help families in coping with any difficulties that arise, as the following case demonstrates.

> Chin Lee and Susie are a refugee couple who have come to the United States with great difficulty. While expecting her first child, Susie has neither eaten enough healthy foods nor received prenatal care; she has also faced considerable emotional stress. The baby is delivered small, so weak she can hardly cry. Chin Lee can hardly speak English, and being confronted with a life-and-death situation for his wife and child petrifies him. In his own culture, members of the extended family would have taken care of the new mother, but here, he is on his own. The social worker on the ward tries to interpret the complicated realities to Chin and at the same time reassure him that the situation is hopeful. Help can be provided by the hospital's medical staff, the dietitian, and the social worker herself. The social worker provides emotional support both verbally and nonverbally, holding Chin's hands to reassure him. Eventually, Susie and her new daughter recover.

As this case shows, one cannot overemphasize the role of the social worker, who provides information as well as help in coordinating services.

Many changes take place when a child is about to be born. When a family already faces anxiety from a poor marriage, inadequate social supports, or conflicts in its own personal identity, the coming event can cause even more problems and greater emotional stress (Fleming et al., 1988). By the time of labor, most expectant parents have learned something about childbirth. The attitudes of the family are affected by the mother's experiences with childbirth as well as their culture. Those who have taken courses in prepared childbirth do appear to have a definite set of expectations about the events and procedures that will occur. Other parents gain information or hear stories from other family members, friends, or books.

Having a "baby shower" is at least one culture's way of preparing a woman for motherhood. Presenting a pregnant woman with items for the newborn baby in some ways prepares the pregnant woman for the birth of the child. As we know, though, not all mothers benefit from this custom, such as single teenage mothers with little or no approval from their families or society.

The mother's emotional state during pregnancy affects her experience of childbirth. Women who were depressed during pregnancy are more likely to continue feeling so during and after childbirth than those who were not. Studies show depressed mothers have difficulty feeling attached to their babies and are more likely to feel out of control or incompetent in their parenting role. They also show less affection toward their infants (Fleming et al., 1988; Field et al., 1985).

A group of Guatemalan women were studied with references to maternal anxiety during labor and delivery (Sosa, Kennell, Klaus, Robertson, & Urrutria, 1980). The hospital did not allow visitors to remain with any expectant mother on the maternity ward. Each woman in the study group was assigned a companion who stayed with her until she delivered. During this time, the companion held the pregnant woman's hand, talked to her, and provided emotional support during labor. These mothers had fewer complications during labor than a control group of women who had no companion, and their babies showed fewer signs of fetal distress. Also, the mean length of time was more than 10 hours shorter for those women who had a companion than for those who were alone.

Trends in the United States have leaned dramatically toward greater involvement of the father in labor and delivery. Husbands and wives attend classes together, which can add to the mother's sense of security while giving birth. It was found that when fathers were present, women tended to have shorter labors, experience less pain, and feel more positive about themselves and their childbirth experience (Grossman et al., 1980). Fathers also describe childbirth as a "peak experience." However, research findings do not show that fathers who participate in the birth experience have a more intimate relationship with their children than fathers not present at the birth (Palkovitz, 1985; Palm & Palkovitz, 1988).

## The Process of Birth

One can divide childbirth into three stages. The first stage, *labor,* is the period during which the cervix of the uterus dilates, through the involuntary contractions of the uterine muscles, to allow the baby to pass through. The average time for the first labor is 14 hours; for later labor, 8 hours (Danziger, 1979). The uterine contractions serve two important functions: effacement and dilation. *Effacement* refers to the shortening of the cervical canal; *dilation* refers to the gradual enlargement of the cervix from an opening only a millimeter wide to a diameter of 10 centimeters. Once the cervix has been fully enlarged, the mother can assist in the birth of the infant by "pushing," or exerting pressure on the abdominal walls around the uterus.

Delivery is the second stage. Depending on the baby's position, the average time from pushing to birth is 80 minutes for first pregnancies and 30 minutes in later ones (Masters et al., 1988, p. 126). About 95% of babies are born with their head emerging first, or in a *vertex presentation.* This type of delivery is normal and spontaneous. About 3% of babies are born with their buttocks and feet emerging first, or in a *breech birth.* Such births require special attention and are generally more difficult. In most cases there is a satisfactory delivery. An inverse presentation occurs in about 1 in 200 births. In this situation, the baby lies crossways in the uterus. During birth, a hand or an arm usually emerges first in the vagina. Generally such positions need special attention and present only two options. Either the baby must be turned during labor so that a normal birth can be accomplished or a caesarean section must be performed.

Doctors may also recommend a caesarean section when the baby is disproportionately large or the mother's pelvic opening is small. A *caesarean,* or *C section,* is a surgical delivery whereby an incision is made in the abdominal wall and the uterus, through which the child is removed. The incision is then carefully sewn. About 25% of all births in the United States are C sections (Stafford, 1990). Today such births are safe, with only minimal risks for the mother and the child. The mother's recovery takes longer than for vaginal births because the incisions have to heal.

A *forceps* or *instrument delivery* becomes necessary when the uterine contractions weaken or stop so that the baby cannot be pushed through the birth canal. In such situations, obstetricians use forceps, which are curved, tonglike instruments shaped to fit each side of the baby's head. In an emergency, a high-forceps delivery can be made during the first stage of labor or early in the second stage, at some risk. A low-forceps delivery, which is made at the time of natural delivery, does not involve much risk.

In the last part of delivery, the baby emerges completely. Assistants remove mucus from his or her mouth by using a vacuum aspiration device. They also place drops of nitrate or antibiotic ointment in the infant's eyes to prevent blindness from bacterial infections such as gonorrhea (Kelley & Byrne, 1992).

The third stage of childbirth is called the *afterbirth:* The placenta, the umbilical cord, and related issues are expelled from the mother's body. This stage is more or less painless and generally occurs about 20 minutes after the child is born.

The mother helps in the process by bearing down. With the delivery of the placenta, the birth process is complete. After the expulsion, the placenta and the umbilical cord are checked for imperfections that might signal damage to the newborn.

## Delivery of the Baby

Two medications frequently used today to relieve childbirth pain are Demerol® and Valium®. These are also amnesics, which obliterate all sensations. Recently researchers have begun to look at the possible effects of these drugs on newborn infants, especially in the light of the extreme danger of some drugs taken in early pregnancy. No studies confirm any long-term effects, though the baby temporarily moves sluggishly. However, if the mother has taken too much medication just before the delivery, it affects the baby's visual attentiveness, weight gain, general brain activity, and sucking behaviors for a few weeks.

Findings such as these have prompted more and more mothers to experience childbirth in an atmosphere free from the necessary impositions of the hospital regimen. Advocates of natural childbirth methods emphasize that hospitals treat childbirth as an illness, whereas natural childbirth implies maternal preparation, limited medication, and active participation. Natural childbirth also helps women to work through their fears of the unknown. Further, natural childbirth emphasizes relaxation techniques. Mothers are taught how to relax when under stress through breathing and other techniques. More and more women prefer natural childbirth because it allows them to experience and enjoy the birth to the fullest extent. When done correctly, pain is minimized.

There are several types of natural childbirth. Fernand Lamaze (1970) developed techniques that involve both parents. In a course of six to eight sessions, the mother learns exercises in relaxation, breathing, and muscle strengthening, while the father learns to serve as an active coach.

The French obstetrician Frederick Leboyer (1976) developed a method of childbirth that is thought to minimize trauma for the child. His approach follows from the thinking of Otto Rank, who indicated that the dramatic expulsion of the neonate from the safe, comfortable environment of the uterus creates the first basic trauma in a child's life. Leboyer proposed a reorganization of hospital procedures so that an infant could be born in a quiet, dimly lit room, placed immediately on the mother's abdomen, and then bathed in warm water.

Hospital maternity wards have seen several changes since then. Many hospitals can now better accommodate parents' wishes. *Alternative birth centers* permit the inclusion of family members in the total birthing experience. Some hospitals encourage rooming-in, an arrangement whereby the mother keeps the baby with her rather than in the hospital nursery and feeds the baby on demand. Of course not all mothers prefer these options—some, for instance, want the nursery staff to care for the baby while they get extra rest. But such services are becoming increasingly available.

Apart from these options, parents may choose home delivery. In doing so, however, parents must develop an emergency plan in case hospitalization is required. Home deliveries are common in Sweden, Finland, and Japan, where highly trained nurses serve as midwives. Although until the early 20th century home deliveries were the norm in the United States, the rate of home births has remained at an insignificant number, about 1% since 1975. Though midwives could be a valuable addition to the medical establishments, they have not yet become part of mainstream medical care in the United States. The home birth of babies in poor rural U.S. families has been associated with high mortality rates and failure to discover early disorders in the infant.

## The Neonate

During the first month of development, a newborn is called a *neonate*. Having just left the closed, protective environment of the mother's womb to enter the outside world, the neonate enters a period of adjustment. In many ways, the first month is a time of recovery from the birth process as well as adjustment to the body's respiration, circulation, feeding, crying, sleeping, and body-heat regulation.

The weight of the neonate at birth typically falls between 5½ and 9½ pounds, and height ranges from 19 to 22 inches. The newborn commonly arrives with puffy eyelids, an absent gaze, and blood spots in the eyes. The nose may also suffer temporary distortion from being pressed down during birth, and the head has not yet assumed its normal shape. The neonate's appearance may come as a surprise to first-time parents, but it soon changes for the better.

The rate of infant mortality—that is, the proportion of babies that are born in a given year and die within the first year of life—is larger in the United States than in 21 other industrialized countries. Approximately 7% of babies born in the United States have low birth weights—about 1 of every 14 babies (U.S. Department of Health and Human Services, 1990). These babies average less than 5½ pounds; low birth weight causes many problems and plays an important part in infant deaths. Even so, premature infants with their less developed physiological systems are more likely to die than babies with low birth weights. Reasons for this vary demographically, that is, by the mother's age, race, and education; medical reasons such as the baby's abnormally low weight gain; and the mother's use of drugs and alcohol (Papalia & Olds, 1992).

*Assessment*    Professionals strive to catch any problems in infants as soon as they are born. Using a standard scoring system developed by Virginia Apgar in 1953, hospitals can evaluate an infant's condition quickly by observing pulse, breathing, muscle tone, general reflex response, and skin color (Apgar, 1953). An evaluation of all these signs usually occurs twice—at 1 minute and again at 5 minutes after birth. A maximum score of 10 is possible; when a baby scores between 7 and 10 he or she is considered to be normal and healthy. Scores below 4 indicate that the baby has problems that need immediate attention. Most states require a mass screening for phenylketonuria (PKU) since a prompt introduction of a special diet can prevent it from causing retardation.

Another scale, called the Brazelton Neonatal Behavioral Assessment Scale (1973), has also been developed. While the Apgar scale addresses the immediate basic or gross functioning of the newborn, the Brazelton assesses the functioning of the central nervous system and the behavioral responses of a newborn. The scale is used to measure finer distinctions of behavior such as an infant's rooting and also the ability of the infant to respond to various types of external stimuli. This scale is usually administered 2 to 3 days after birth and again about 9 to 10 days after birth. The scale is useful for detecting neurological problems (Als, Lester, & Brazelton, 1979).

One can classify the behavior of the average newborn baby into four broad categories: sleeping, crying, feeding, and eliminating. The neonate has many complex impulses that usually disappear by the age of 3 to 4 months. Crying in the newborn is an unlearned, involuntary response but is readily shaped; it is an infant's first adaptive technique for interacting with the environment. Other useful reflexes include the rooting reflex: When one cheek is touched, a baby "roots" or moves his or her mouth toward the stimulus, seeking a nipple. Though the newborn's vision is blurred and he or she cannot see beyond 7 to 20 inches, vision improves slowly as weeks pass.

Not all children are born healthy, of course, and some have inherited genetic defects. In the following section, we shall look at the mechanisms of inheritance, genetic defects, and genetic counseling. Then, we shall move on to examining environmental influences in pregnancy and for newborns.

## MECHANISMS OF INHERITANCE

As you know, half an individual's genetic material comes from the mother and half from the father when the sperm fertilizes the ovum, uniting to form a unique genetic potential. The fertilized egg, or *zygote*, holds the materials that bear the pattern of a new person who is different from his or her parents, yet somewhat like them. What are these materials? Inside the zygote there are 46 *chromosomes*, the rod-shaped structures containing the unique genetic pattern of a person, which are present in every cell. Genes contain the mechanisms for directing the actions of every cell. All normal human cells contain 46 chromosomes except the germ cells (sperm and ovum), which have 23 chromosomes. Each chromosome contains 20,000 *genes*, which are the basic units of heredity. There are about 1 million genes in each cell (Schiamberg, 1985).

Each gene is composed of a chemical called *deoxyribonucleic acid* or *DNA*. DNA is an extremely long macromolecule that is the main component of chromosomes and is the material that transfers genetic characteristics in all life forms. It is constructed of two nucleotide strands coiled around each other in a ladderlike arrangement with the side pieces composed of alternating phosphate and deoxyribose units and the rungs composed of the purine and pyrimidine bases adenine, guanine, cytosine, and thymine. The genetic information of DNA is encoded in the sequence of the bases and is transcribed as the strands unwind and replicate. DNA determines what is passed from one generation to the next.

Nearly all of an individual's tens of thousands of genes occur in pairs, one inherited from the mother and the other from the father. Alternate forms of genes are called *alleles*. Each person carries two alleles for the same trait, one from the father and one from the mother. Sometimes, both alleles offer the same instructions for the determination of the trait, in which case the individual is said to be *homozygous* for that trait. For example, if the trait in question is eye color, and both of an individual's eye-color alleles call for blue eyes, then the individual is homozygous for eye color. A person whose alleles both call for brown eyes is also homozygous. When one of the person's alleles calls for brown eyes and the other for blue, the individual is *heterozygous* for eye color. Such an individual will have brown eyes because the allele for brown eyes is dominant.

Another aspect of inheritance has to do with twins. Sometimes the dividing zygote cells become separated and develop into two individuals. These two individuals are called *identical* or *monozygotic twins. Fraternal twins* develop from two different zygotes—two eggs, each fertilized by a different sperm. Monozygotic twins are more closely related than fraternal twins throughout the prenatal period. They usually develop together in one amniotic sac, both bathed by the same amniotic fluid, whereas fraternal twins usually have separate sacs.

Genetic determinants of (1) the rate of development, (2) individual traits, and (3) defective traits are the three genetic sources of individuality. Most traits, such as weight, height, blood group, and skin color, are controlled by the combined action of several genes. Gene pairs may interact in various ways; for example, one gene pair may allow the expression of another gene pair or inhibit it. Of course, genetic individuality does not provide the final script—it merely supplies the earliest elements of human identity and behavior. For instance, when compared with identical twins reared together, identical twins reared apart show the greatest differences in such traits as weight and intelligence. This finding suggests that some variables are more susceptible to environmental influences than others.

## Genetic Abnormalities

There are many genetic abnormalities that can affect human development. These do not necessarily cause birth defects; they may have no effect at all. Here we shall discuss aberrations that can harm the developing fetus.

*Chromosomal abnormalities* A missing or extra chromosome or a gross chromosomal abnormality is usually dangerous to the fetus. Often the defective gene has been in the family for generations, passed from parent to child. Down's syndrome, or mongolism, is a well-known genetic disorder in which a person is born with a limited mental capacity because of an extra chromosome or part of one. Mothers who give birth to such children are usually either over 40 or extremely young (Papalia & Olds, 1989). Down's syndrome is found in one out of every 500 babies born in the United States (Ambron & Brodzinsky, 1979). Some research indicates a relationship between Down's syndrome and the father's age (Abroms & Bennett, 1981). As in the case of the mother, the risk rises slowly as the father ages until he turns 49. This risk abruptly increases for men 50–55 and older.

Another birth defect found in 1 out of 500 babies, *spina bifida,* is a condition in which the spinal column has not fused and closed, leaving the nerves exposed. At times, this defect can be corrected surgically in the first months of a baby's life.

For most parents, the birth of a child affected by genetic abnormalities is an unanticipated and traumatic event. The majority of parents have little or no knowledge of birth defects before their child is born. Not even childbirth preparation classes offer this information, presenting only the situation of having a normal baby. The following comments were made by the parent of a congenitally handicapped child (Darling, 1983):

> I never heard of Down's. . . . Mental retardation wasn't something you talked about in the house. . . . There wasn't much exposure.
> I heard mongoloid—something I had read in passing in a book or something. Just a freak of nature. I remember thinking, before I got married, it would be the worst thing that could ever happen to me.

Most parents enter the birth situation expecting events to proceed normally and to take home a normal infant. Giving birth to a genetically disabled child can create feelings of meaninglessness, powerlessness, and helplessness.

*Sex-linked defects*  A *sex-linked trait* is one that is carried on the chromosome that determines a person's gender. A dramatic example of a sex-linked genetic abnormality is hemophilia, or bleeder's disease. In hemophilia, an element of blood plasma needed for normal clotting is deficient. A hemophiliac could bleed to death from a small wound that would normally clot within a few minutes. Internal bleeding, if not noticed, can lead to death. Hemophilia is carried as a recessive gene only on the X chromosome. Because the Y (male) chromosome is much shorter than the X chromosome, it has no site for a corresponding gene to pair with and counteract the hemophilia genes. Thus, any male child who inherits this gene will express it, regardless of whether the gene is dominant or recessive. Women do not suffer from this disorder, because they have two matching X chromosomes.

Another sex-linked disease, Lesch-Nyan syndrome, involves a severe behavior disorder and is transmitted as an X-linked recessive gene. In this disease an enzyme deficiency alters the metabolic rate of children, which causes them to hurt themselves compulsively. At about the time their first baby teeth come in, they begin to bite their lips and fingers (Plomin, Defries, & McClearn, 1990; Rothwell, 1988; Thompson & Thompson, 1986). In addition, such children are mentally disabled and have physical disorders such as kidney disease.

*Other defects*  Other hereditary defects include sickle-cell anemia, cystic fibrosis, Tay-Sachs disease, and a predisposition to diabetes. Certain disorders occur almost exclusively among specific national, racial, or ethnic groups. Sickle-cell anemia is a hereditary disease characterized by malformed red blood cells. This disease is most common among Africans, African Americans, and some Mediterranean populations. In cystic fibrosis, the respiratory and digestive systems malfunction; a thick, sticky mucus obstructs the airways and increases vulnerability to infection. This recessive disease is found mostly among Caucasians. In Tay-Sachs disease, infants inherit

two alleles that keep them from producing an enzyme necessary for fat metabolism. For such children, the normal developmental process is severely disrupted. Although they may appear to be normal at birth, within a few months these children begin to lose their eyesight. They stop growing and lose whatever motor coordination they have developed. Most of these infants die before they reach 2 years of age (Plomin et al., 1990; Rothwell, 1988). This disease is primarily found among Eastern European Jews.

Discovering that they are carrying "bad" genes is a scary experience for most people. Should they marry? Should they have children? However, most people who harbor potentially lethal genes are not even aware of them. Many recessive and non-sex-linked genes will not be expressed. Still, when the need arises, people can find out about their genetic inheritance and that of their potential marital partners.

## Genetic Counseling

Genetic counseling is a way of protecting the next generation from genetic defects. In such counseling, individuals and couples concerned about transmitting a genetic disease to their children can have a blood test for genes that may result in a given inherited disorder. They may also decide to have their genealogy studied to learn whether they are likely to carry defective genes. For instance, a woman aware of congenital blindness in her family can find out the likelihood of her carrying the gene. Further, the woman can find out if her gene alone can transmit blindness to her children or whether the defect could occur only if her husband also carried the gene. This is determined by family history and blood tests. This sort of information helps couples decide whether or not to begin a pregnancy.

Social workers engaged in adoptions, family planning, and services to the physically or mentally disabled see many clients who might benefit from genetic counseling. A genetic counselor can prepare a family history of the prospective parents and determine the risks of abnormality in the offspring. This type of prenatal diagnosis, though, has not gained much acceptance and is used most often by middle-class people and those with more than an average education. Sometimes the counselor's family history and test findings are confirmed, such as when an abnormal chromosomal arrangement is found in a developing fetus. Certainly, the odds of having a defective child can be determined to a given degree of accuracy. Further, a couple with an abnormal child whose problem was not of genetic origin can be reassured that the risks of having another abnormal child are minimal. Social workers can be employed in such clinics to insure continuing support for such families.

*Genetic technology*  Genetic technology might affect the future of genetic counseling in that direct modification of a person's genetic structure might be possible. In January 1989, the National Institutes of Health (NIH) launched a project to map the human genome; that is, to identify and list in order the full set of human chromosomes, which carry all the inherited traits of a person— approximately 3 billion base pairs. This map would let us predict an individual's vulnerability to genetic diseases, treat genetically caused diseases, and possibly enhance a person's genetic potential through gene modifications (Jaroff, 1989; NIH/CEPH Collaborative Mapping Group, 1992). For instance, the defective gene that causes cystic fibrosis has been identified. The biochemical process associated with this defective gene has been analyzed and a wide variety of therapeutic techniques are being developed, including both drug and gene therapy (Collins, 1992).

In 1988, the United States Government scrutinized and approved the transplanting of foreign genes into humans. The first gene-transfer experiment, conducted in the National Institutes of Health, was limited to ten cancer patients who were not expected to live for more than 90 days. The transplanted gene served as a marker to help keep track of the progress of an experimental cancer treatment. This experiment was not considered to be gene therapy because the transplanted gene was not expected to produce therapeutic benefits (Roberts, 1989). By 1992, 11 active clinical procedures were carried out that involved gene marking or gene therapy and 9 others were approved for implementation (Anderson, 1992).

Genetic engineering, gene transfer, the patenting of new life forms, and the use of genetic fingerprinting to identify criminals have all raised new ethical concerns. Most people agree that using gene therapy to treat diseases such as cancer and cystic fibrosis is ethical. But there is not much agreement on whether we should alter a zygote's genetic code to enhance aspects of normal development in human beings. Through debate, discussions, and court cases, we are setting new precedents regarding not only specific issues but also the way we conceptualize life itself (Newman & Newman, 1995).

*Techniques for finding defects*  Professionals use several techniques to discover genetic defects in unborn babies, including ultrasound, amniocentesis, fetoscopes, and chorionic villi sampling. Using *ultrasound,* doctors scan the uterus with extremely high-level sound waves to get a picture of the skeleton of the fetus. The presence of twins can be detected in this manner. Pictures obtained by ultrasound mapping reveal the location of the placenta, position of the fetus, size of the fetal skull, and characteristics of the fetal heartbeat. An ultrasound could disclose anencephaly, a rare and fatal defect in which parts of the brain are missing or malformed (Ambron & Brodzinsky, 1979), as well as other gross defects.

If a pregnant woman fears that she may give birth to a child with a genetic defect, she can also undergo *amniocentesis,* which allows doctors to test the fetus's general makeup. In this procedure, doctors use a needle to remove a small amount of the amniotic fluid that surrounds the fetus. The procedure can be performed with minimal risk if ultrasound is used to guide the needle (Moore, 1989). Amniotic fluid contains loose cells and other materials discarded by the fetus. The cells are separated from the fluid, grown in a culture, and analyzed for evidence of any suspected defect. More than 70 genetically caused disorders can be identified through this procedure (Plomin et al., 1990). One serious limitation of this procedure is that there is not usually sufficient fluid before the 13 or 14th week to permit sample taking. By the time the cells are cultured, the pregnancy has progressed to the 15 or 16th week (Moore, 1989)). If there are no fetal defects, the mother is spared many months of unnecessary anxiety. If defects are found, the parents must decide whether to have an abortion or to go ahead with the pregnancy in the hope that the child will lead a fairly normal life in spite of the problem. In this way, parental planning and adjustment to the child's condition can begin before the child is born.

To find defects, doctors can also use a *fetoscope,* which is a long, hollow needle with a small lens and a light at its end. Inserted into the mother's uterus, it enables the doctor to observe the developing fetus and look for any abnormal conditions.

Another technique, *chorionic villi sampling (CVS),* serves as an alternative to amniocentesis. In this procedure a small amount of fetal cells are plucked directly from the chorionic villi, or part of the placenta. This is a "method for diagnosing defects in the developing fetus; done by inserting a catheter through the vagina and cervix to take a small piece of tissue from the edge of the chorion, the membrane surrounding the fetus" (Masters et al., 1988, p. 681). This procedure can be performed when a woman is eight months pregnant, and results are usually available within a few days. However, this procedure is more limited than amniocentesis in the number of disorders it can detect (Moore, 1989).

*Public issues*  Several public issues yet surround genetic counseling. For instance, social workers who deal with genetic counseling or screening must be aware of current public policies for the prevention of genetic defects. The least controversial programs involve low-cost, low-risk mass screening to prevent severe birth defects that might otherwise require costly institutionalization; for example, 11 states have compulsory screening for phenylketonuria. But controversy rages over the abortion of fetuses with symptoms of Down's syndrome and other genetic defects and over questions like whether people who are severely mentally disabled should be sterilized. The following case illustrates this last point:

> Sally, age 23, is severely retarded, and her mother is retarded as well. The family is preoccupied with its financial and day-to-day problems. Sally spends a lot of time with men and has mothered two severely retarded children who have been institutionalized. If Sally gets pregnant a third time, should the state have a say in whether or not she bears the child?

Some of the trickiest questions involve the rights of the newborn, the rights of the family, the financial costs to the community of lifetime care for the severely disabled, and the potential impact on future generations:

> Kathleen and Michael, both strict Roman Catholics, are extremely troubled because they have two children who are mentally retarded, one of whom is also congenitally blind, and Kathleen is pregnant again. Her pregnancy is an accident. They see a social worker for genetic counseling. After the family history and genetic screening are done, it is obvious that the next child's chances of being normal are pretty low. The social worker presents the facts and offers emotional support. Although he personally favors abortion in this situation, he is careful not to push the couple toward a particular decision, in tune with the great importance that social workers place on respecting the client's right to self-determination.

How does society deal with its "defective" members? Should those who are "unfit" be sterilized, or should they be offered a full range of social services in the belief that all people are entitled to quality care? Our current policies fall between these two extremes. Through research, lobbying, and social action, social workers should be able to make a significant contribution to the difficult task of establishing and monitoring these policies (Specht & Craig, 1982).

Today, increasing numbers of hospitals test pregnant women for genetic defects, but gene therapy—the manipulation of individual genes to correct certain defects—is still in its infancy. Besides techniques concerned with only heredity, many important sociophysiological factors influence the total development of an individual.

## ENVIRONMENTAL INFLUENCES IN THE PRENATAL STAGE

Though the fetal environment is simple compared with the outside world, there are variations in the former that can result in significant psychological and physical differences in infants. The ability to produce a child usually begins one and a half years after *menarche* (onset of menstruation) and ends at *climacteric* (menopause). Women between the ages of 18 and 35 tend to provide a better uterine environment and give birth to children with fewer complications than do women under 17 or over 35.

Annually 5% to 8% of the children born in North America have some type of birth defect. Some are due to hereditary, others to environmental causes. As you know, a teratogen is an agent that disturbs the development of the fetus. Correspondingly, the study of developmental abnormalities is called *teratology*. For many years, people believed that the infant in the uterus was completely insulated from all outside influences, but we now know this is not true. Environmental influences ranging from radioactivity to drugs, chemicals, and viruses in the mother's bloodstream can affect prenatal development. Even though the placenta acts as a filter and keeps the mother's blood and that of the fetus from mixing, many dangerous substances can pass through. Exaggerated emotional stress during pregnancy may also bring about chemical changes and cause muscular tensions that can affect the environment of the developing fetus

(Ambron & Brodzinsky, 1979). Finally, the effects of environmental influences vary according to the stage of prenatal development in which such influences are encountered.

> Sula comes from a conservative Muslim home that is extremely superstitious. Her parents married when they were barely out of high school, and Sula has done the same. She and her new husband live in a run-down neighborhood and have financial difficulties. An alcoholic, he has lost his job and is on welfare. Sula believes that the conception of a child has brought them bad luck, and she seems to have negative feelings for the unborn child. This belief is reinforced when her father gets mugged.
>
> At the Social Service Center, Sula tells the social worker that the unborn child could be defective because of the negative things that have happened in her life, including having been frightened by a black cat in the night. The worker tries to help Sula understand that frightening and negative incidents in her own and family members' lives will not affect the baby and that Sula's own attitude toward the child is important. The worker spends a few sessions educating Sula about her responsibility as a parent as well as relieving many of her fears about the child. Malnutrition also appears to be a problem with Sula. Besides administering multivitamins, the worker gives her both advice and educational materials about eating inexpensive nutritious food.

### Maternal Diet

Pregnant women should have adequate diets to maintain their own general good health as well as to deliver a healthy infant. Mothers who follow a well-balanced diet have fewer complications such as anemia and toxemia and suffer fewer miscarriages, stillbirths, and premature deliveries. Such mothers are also generally healthier after childbirth than those who have not followed a well-balanced diet. Further, mothers with nutritionally sound diets tend to have babies less likely to contract bronchitis, pneumonia, or colds during early infancy, and their babies' bones and teeth are well developed (Restak, 1979).

## Toxemia and Anoxia

A disorder of pregnancy, *toxemia* is character-ized by high blood pressure (hypertension); waterlogging of tissues (edema); and proteins in the urine (proteinuria). Toxemia creates a chemi-cal environment in the mother's body that inter-feres with the proper functioning of the placenta. A fetus's chance of surviving toxemia is 50% (Jones & Smith, 1973). If untreated, toxemia can be fatal to both mother and child; it is ranked as the second or third cause of maternal mortality. Doctors usually treat toxemia by administering magnesium sulfate to control convulsions, enforc-ing bed rest, and reducing the woman's blood pressure with appropriate medication.

Toxemia is one of several diseases that can cause *anoxia* (oxygen deficiency or starvation) in a fetus. Brain cells are particularly vulnerable to a lack of oxygen: Once they have been destroyed by an insufficient supply of oxygen, the body cannot replace them. By contrast, the skin can be renewed after a cut or laceration. Thus, anoxia is a potentially serious complication.

When labor is difficult, infants may suffer gross oxygen deprivation. Severe damage or even death can occur. Lesser degrees of oxygen starvation may lead to mental disability, cerebral palsy, learning disorders, and behavior disorders. At least 10% of U.S. children have learning disabili-ties related to anoxia (Vaughan et al., 1984). If the damage to the brain is not too severe, one can compensate for the disorder. For instance, epilep-sy can be controlled with drugs, and many victims of cerebral palsy can gain some control of their affected muscles through medication.

## The Rh Factor

One particular incompatibility between a mother and her baby is commonly called the *Rh factor*. When the unborn child's blood contains a certain protein substance but the mother's blood does not, antibodies in the mother's blood may attack the fetus, which can result in spontaneous abor-tion, stillbirth, heart defects, anemia, mental retar-dation, and even death. How does this happen?

All blood is either Rh positive or Rh negative. Each blood factor is transmitted genetically, with Rh positive usually dominant. Normally the maternal and fetal blood supplies are separated by the placenta, but some exchange can occur. When an Rh negative woman is carrying an Rh positive baby and some fetal blood escapes the placenta and enters the blood system, the moth-er's body will then produce Rh antibodies. Usually the production of these antibodies does not pose a threat to the first baby because of the low level of antibodies produced. As time passes, however, the mother's body produces more anti-bodies, which will be in full force for the next Rh-positive child unless the mother received an antibody vaccine shortly after her first delivery. This vaccine destroys the Rh antibodies in the mother's blood so that she will not pose a danger to her next Rh-positive child (Apgar & Beck, 1972; Moore, 1989).

## Drugs and Related Issues

The range of drugs used by pregnant women today is enormous: iron, diuretics, antibiotics, hormones, tranquilizers, appetite suppressants, and other drugs, prescribed or not. In addition to these, some women also take other drugs such as alcohol, nicotine, caffeine, marijuana, and cocaine (Chasnoff, 1988). Studies show that drugs taken by pregnant women are metabolized in the pla-centa and transmitted to the fetus. Their effects on the fetus can be dramatic.

Before we discuss the effects of drugs we need to remember that genetic disposition may make some developing fetuses more vulnerable than others to the negative effects of certain drugs or toxins. Such effects are also determined by dosage, duration of exposure, and timing of exposure.

*Nicotine* There are many studies that associate smoking with "lower birth weights, shortened pregnancies, higher rates of spontaneous abor-tion, more frequent complications of pregnancy and labor, and higher rates of perinatal mortality (death of the fetus or newborn near the time of the birth" (Masters et al., 1988, p. 122). Heavy smokers risk miscarriages and stillbirths (Streissguth, Barr, Sampson, Darby, & Martin, 1989). Also, smokers' babies who were examined at 9 and 30 days after birth had decreased levels of arousal and responsiveness, compared with non-smokers (Fried, Watkinson, Dillon, & Dalberg, 1987).

*Alcohol*   Prenatal exposure to alcohol can influence brain growth, interfering with cell development and modifying the production of neurotransmitters, which are critical to the maturation of the nervous system (West, 1986). The impact of alcohol on the development of the fetus is called *fetal alcohol syndrome* (Abel, 1984; Clarren & Smith, 1978; Jones, Smith, Ulleland, & Streissguth, 1973). This syndrome is associated with disorders of the central nervous system, low birth weight, and malformations of the face, eyes, ears, and mouth. Babies with this syndrome also have a poorly developed *philtrum,* or natural groove between the nose and the upper lip (Rosett & Weiner, 1984). Even moderate drinking during pregnancy can produce some of these symptoms, particularly when the mother is also malnourished. About 1 to 3 infants per 1000 live births are affected. Fetal alcohol syndrome is the greatest source of environmentally caused disruption to the prenatal central nervous system.

*Caffeine*   Caffeine easily crosses the placenta and reaches the fetus in the womb. Caffeine is consumed in sodas, coffee, tea, and the like. Heavy coffee consumption, described as three cups or more per day, is associated with risk of low birth weight with a moderate connection to prematurity. Women who reduced the amount of coffee they drank after the sixth week of pregnancy did not reveal any ill-effects associated with early coffee consumption (Fenster, Eskenazi, Windham, & Swan, 1991; McDonald, Armstrong, & Sloan, 1992).

*Narcotics*   The use of narcotics such as heroin, cocaine, and methadone (used to treat heroin addiction) has been linked to high and increased level of birth defects, low birth weight, and higher rates of infant mortality (Zuckerman, Frank, & Hingson, 1989). Infants exposed to some or all of these drugs prenatally are born with a pattern of extreme irritability, high-pitched crying, evidence of neurological disorganization, poor sleep patterns, fever, feeding problems, muscle spasms, and tremors (Hans, 1987). These babies are also at high risk of sudden infant death syndrome. Children who survive still face problems with motor coordination and difficulty focusing and sustaining their attention, which will likely affect their school performance later.

*Sudden infant death syndrome*   Also known as *crib death, sudden infant death syndrome (SIDS)* occurs when a child is two to four months old. Research reveals that crib deaths are due to a variety of reasons (1) overwhelming infection by an unknown virus, (2) an unknown system that leads to sporadic closure of the larynx or failure of the cardiac system, and (3) *apnea,* or cessation of breathing for a brief period while sleeping. More recently it has been found that sudden death syndrome becomes a high-risk probability when the child's mother took narcotics when pregnant.

*Drug addiction*   Due to the indiscriminate use of cocaine and crack, the number of crack babies increased—from 30,000 to 100,000 a year—during the late 1980s (Gittler & McPherson, 1991). Given the high incidence of drug abuse among pregnant women, 19 states have passed laws that allow criminal charges to be brought against women who have exposed their child to these harmful and illegal substances (Sachs, 1989). In one case, a woman in Florida who had a second cocaine-addicted baby was arrested for child abuse; her child was placed in foster care.

Should such mothers be charged with child abuse? One serious consideration is how prosecution would affect these mothers' finances. Also, should the newborn babies be taken away from such mothers and placed in foster care (Feinman, 1992; Willwerth, 1991)? These issues of human rights must be reviewed carefully by social policy makers. Meanwhile social workers can help in such situations by teaching the crack mothers basic parenting skills.

> Denise is a pregnant drug addict in prison. When her baby is born, Denise finds it practically impossible to take care of him. She sees her son at regular intervals, but the baby is highly irritable and cries all the time. This angers Denise, who starts abusing the child whenever she handles him. The social worker who offers counseling to this young mother advises her to place the child in foster care until Denise has served her prison sentence. Meanwhile special efforts are made to find the child a home where appropriate parenting can be offered to an infant affected by drugs.

*HIV and AIDS*   Intravenous drug use has led to the spread of the human immunodeficiency virus (HIV) and acquired immunodeficiency syndrome (AIDS) from pregnant women to their unborn children. Among habitual drug users, nearly 70% of the women have been infected with HIV through either their own drug use or that of a sex partner. The co-relation between cocaine use, prostitution, and sexually transmitted diseases, including AIDS, is posing dangerous problems to unborn children, particularly in poor urban areas (Darney, Myhra, Atkinson, & Meier, 1989; Judson, 1989). Children born to mothers with the HIV virus have a 50% chance of developing the disease; 95% of those infected will die within the first three years. Because the newborn babies' immune systems are deficient or inoperative, they cannot fight off the many infections that babies typically encounter (Seabrook, 1987).

### Radiation and Chemicals

Radiation in early pregnancy from repeated X rays and from radium treatment for cancer have produced marked effects on prenatal development. *Radiation* occurs when a radioactive source emits energy in the form of waves or particles that can penetrate the living tissue and alter the nature of cells. Radiation has many sources: cosmic rays, certain geologic formations, X rays

for medical diagnosis and treatment, leaks from nuclear power plants, and releases from nuclear weapons production and testing (Ecker & Bramesco, 1981).

Prenatal exposure to radiation has been linked with death of the fetus, elevated rates of cancer, and brain damage and other malformations. Alternatively, genetic changes in fetal cells may not come to light for generations (National Research Council, 1990).

*Methyl mercury* is another pollutant that affects infants. An epidemic of severe brain damage and mental retardation was found among children born in Minimata, Japan. Mercury, the chemical that caused it, was traced to fish contaminated with this substance. Women who consumed this tainted fish in sufficient quantity during pregnancy had babies who suffered from what is now called Minimata disease (Moore, 1989; Shepard, 1983). Similar results were seen in Iraqi babies born to mothers who consumed mercury-contaminated bread during pregnancy (Shepard, 1983).

Since different chemicals have many different effects on infants, in the absence of certainty, cautious parents will avoid any unnecessary exposure to strong chemicals or known sources of chemical waste.

### Maternal Stress and Age

Stress during pregnancy initiates the same set of internal responses as stress under ordinary circumstances: The heart rate and blood pressure increase, blood flow is diverted to internal organs and to the skeletal muscles, and various hormonal changes take place. The result is that the blood flow to the placenta is reduced and various hormones associated with stress are transmitted across the placenta to the fetus. These hormones act as a stimulant to the unborn child and increase its need for oxygen at the same time that its oxygen supply is lowered because of diminished maternal blood flow (Steuer, 1994). Research has also shown that the mother's listening to music affects the fetus; fast music leads to more fetal movement, and slow music to less.

This effect is apparently connected with the mother's heart activity, which accordingly affects the flow of blood in the umbilical cord (Hall, 1970).

How does the stress of war affect pregnant mothers and their infants? A study done by Sontag (1944) showed that infants born during war were dramatically more active prenatally, were smaller at birth, had more feeding difficulties, and were more irritable and active after birth. Many recent studies have reported similar findings (Levin & DeFrank, 1988; Sameroff & Chandler, 1975; Stechler & Halton, 1982). These and other studies clearly show that women should avoid unnecessary stress during pregnancy.

Stress in pregnancy goes hand in hand with stress after birth. Stress-induced irritability only creates more pressures for the parent and the child. As we shall explore later, "the child and his caretaking environment tend to mutually (affect or) alter each other" (Sameroff & Chandler, 1975, p. 237).

Besides stress, a woman's age can also affect her unborn child. Women over 40 show an increased risk of giving birth to children with problems such as Down's syndrome and other birth defects. Spontaneous abortions also take place more frequently in older women.

Teenagers run the elevated risk of poor pregnancy outcomes for different reasons, such as immaturity of the adolescent reproduction organs combined with lack of prenatal care and poor nutrition (Hughs, Johnson, Rosenbaum, & Liu, 1989; National Center for Children in Poverty [NCCP], 1989). One study, however, found relatively little risk in young mothers who are in good health and are under the care of a physician (Roosa, 1984).

Adolescents do not appear to be aware of the risks inherent in early childbirth. In 1989, about 518,000 babies were born to women under 20. Over 400,000 legal abortions were performed that year for women the same age, accounting for 26% of all induced abortions that took place (U.S. Bureau of the Census, 1992). Social workers play an important role regarding teenage pregnancies. They can help a pregnant teenager decide whether she should have the baby or an abortion, or whether she should keep or give up the baby for adoption. Other factors in the counseling process include the environmental support systems available to the single pregnant teenager.

## The Impact of Poverty

Poverty is the most powerful psychosocial factor affecting the birth of babies. Poor women often experience the cumulative effects of the many factors associated with infant mortality and developmental vulnerabilities (Swyer, 1987). Compared with most women, poor women are less likely to be vaccinated against the infectious diseases, such as rubella, that can harm the developing fetus. Poverty is also linked with malnutrition, higher instances of infection, and higher rates of cardiovascular diseases—all of which are linked to low birth weight and the baby's physical vulnerability (Cassady & Strange, 1987).

Many of the risks poor pregnant women face can be remedied by an accessible system of health care facilities combined with an effective educational program on pregnancy and nutritional support; these significantly improve the health and vigor of babies affected by poverty (Swyer, 1987). For instance, when researchers evaluated a program of coordinated maternity care for women on medicaid in North Carolina, they found that a comprehensive prenatal care program improves birth outcomes, even in a high-risk population (Buescher, Roth, Williams, & Goforth, 1991). One could say, then, that the chance and quality of survival of infants born to the poor reflect the value a given society places on social justice. If we overlook our poor, then malnourished and vulnerable babies will become a significant part of our population. Timely help is needed for such women.

## The Family Environment

The greatest miracle in life is not the explosion of knowledge or the transplanting of an organ from one human being to another but the creation, development, and birth of a new life. Each new life is born into a mosaic of physical, psychological, and cultural surroundings that determine how much of the new person's potentials become realized.

Various factors may influence a woman's decision to become pregnant: pressure from parents or peers, early gender-role identifications with her parents, delight in relating to young children, a desire to procreate, and so forth.

Pregnancy affects not only the physical appearance of the woman but also the relationship between husband and wife. Research (Specht & Craig, 1982) reveals that couples may experience stress as long as six months after the first baby is born. Stressful factors may include sleeplessness, anxiety about how well one is coping with child care, interruption in sexual intimacy, jealousy, preoccupation with the infant, and differences of opinion regarding how to care for the child. For many new parents, the birth of the first child creates a crisis environment, in the sense that couples have to adapt to new roles and relationships. Thus pregnancy could be viewed as a period of rehearsal for parenthood. The extent to which the situation appears to be a crisis depends on the state of the marriage, family organization, the couple's preparation for marriage, and certain social background factors and situational variables, such as the number of years married. After the first child, the number, gender, and ages of other children become important factors. Frequently, infants are born to single women, who often belong to a lower socioeconomic group and do not follow a traditional lifestyle. Further, the number of 30- to 40-year-old professional women who are becoming single mothers has increased. Because single mothers have fewer support systems, they tend to face more stresses in childbirth and after than do married women.

The decision to have a baby, the social experience of pregnancy, the particular style of help that is available for delivery of the baby, care given to the mother and baby after delivery, and the attitudes toward them are all components of family lifestyles and cultural patterns.

> Puri comes from a rich, Far-Eastern family. Her children have always been born at home with the help of a woman gynecologist. However, when she gets pregnant in the United States, she cannot find a woman doctor who will help her give birth in her home. In labor at the hospital, she is shocked when her pubic hair is shaved off. Worse still, her doctor cannot make it, and a male gynecologist is the only one who can help her deliver her new baby. Puri is scared and overwhelmed by this new experience of childbirth.

There is a growing awareness of multiculturalism in the United States. Each year brings new immigrants from over 60 countries. Therefore, social workers should try to understand the cultural norms of the pregnant woman and her family. They should also interpret the key elements of the birth culture in the United States for women who are not familiar with it, so that they can understand and possibly reinterpret those aspects that may appear disrespectful or threatening to them (Hahn & Muecke, 1987).

## SPECIAL CIRCUMSTANCES OF THE NEWBORN

All newborns face environments in some ways unique, in others universal. The family environment, bonding, temperament, and parent-infant relationships all affect how the newborn will develop. The following sections examine these influences in turn.

### Family Environment

For some couples, parenthood is so romanticized that there is little effective preparation for parental roles. As one mother put it, "Because you read in books and you talk with people and you think all of a sudden there is going to be this motherly surge of love, which is not true. . . .

I had this colicky baby that spit up and we had to stay home. It took me a long time . . ." (Dyer, 1963). In Dyer's study, many husbands and wives mentioned that things were not as they expected them to be after the child was born.

> At 17, Melissa decides to leave home and live with her boyfriend Tom because she is expecting his child. Both of them are excited at the prospect of becoming parents. Then reality hits them. Unprepared to see his girlfriend spending all of her time with the baby, Tom becomes resentful and angry with the baby for being demanding. Melissa fears that he may hurt the baby. With the help of a social worker, Melissa's mother and aunts intervene to help the two; Melissa and Tom adjust to their new roles as parents.

The family environment for the birth of the child also varies from culture to culture. Clark and Howland (1978) describe childbirth for Samoan women:

> The process of labor is viewed by Samoan women as a necessary part of their role and a part of the life experience. Since the baby she is producing is highly valued by her culture, the mother's delivery is also commendable and therefore ego-satisfying. Pain relief for labor may well present the patient with a conflict. She obviously experiences pain as demonstrated by the skeletal muscle response, tossing and turning, and placing her body in fixed positions, but her culture tells her that she does not need medication. It is the "spoiled" palagi (Caucasian) woman who needs pain-relieving drugs. Moreover, the culture clearly dictates that control is expected of a Samoan woman, and no overt expression of pain is permissible. (p. 166)

At the positive end of the scale, birth is seen as a proud achievement:

> Among the Ila of Northern Zimbabwe, women attending at birth were observed shouting praises of the woman who had a baby. They all thanked her, saying, "I give thanks to you today that you have given birth to a child." (Mead & Newton, 1967, p. 174)

Again, a similar sentiment is expressed in Karmel's (1983) description of the Lamaze method of childbirth:

> From the moment I began to push, the atmosphere of the delivery room underwent a radical transformation. Where previously, everyone had spoken in soft and moderate tones in deference to my state of concentration, now there was a wild encouraging cheering section, dedicated to spurring me on. I felt like a football star, headed for a touchdown. (pp. 93–94)

More and more, the U.S. view of childbirth emphasizes both safety for the mother and child and building a sense of competence in the mother and father as they approach the care of their newborn (Sameroff 1987). With two more or less caring parents, the child is born under special, comfortable circumstances. Eiduson (1980) studied a variety of family lifestyles that reflect the pluralistic development of the family in the United States today. These families included 50 single-mother households, 50 social-contract (rather than legal-contract) couples, and 50 communities or living groups (including religious and charismatic-leader groups; triads; and domestic, rural, and urban communities). His comparison group consisted of 50 traditional two-parent families. After an intensive study, he concluded that single mothers brought up their children differently than two-parent families, regardless of circumstances. Eiduson also found this to be true in general: Different lifestyles have different effects on the upbringing of children.

Viewing parenthood as a crisis situation or merely as a transitional event for parents is only a semantic difference. In either case, it is a true turning point in the family's lifestyle, structure, and relationships.

For most couples, the stress of giving birth to a normal child appears to be short-lived. Feelings of powerlessness and helplessness that at first overwhelmed the parents are reduced as the child interacts with his or her parents and responds to parental handling. Social support from significant others is also helpful. As the child becomes less dependent and more familiar with the routine, the parents' feelings of chronic exhaustion simply fade away.

> Anne gets up often each night to care for her restless newborn daughter. Because he has to leave for work

early in the morning, her husband cannot relieve her. Anne is constantly exhausted and angry. She wonders what happened to the bundle of joy that they both looked forward to. She finds breast feeding a bore and envies her husband's ability to leave home and go to work. However, her daughter soon begins to respond to her with smiles. This makes Anne happy. In time, mother and daughter become more attached to each other, and Anne looks forward to feeding and playing with her baby. Chronic exhaustion is replaced with new energy and an enthusiasm for working at family relationships.

## Bonding

Like other species, human beings must accommodate themselves to their natural settings. Besides the physical environment, though, people have to adapt themselves to cultural systems. As these cultural systems grow out of human action, they create their own restrictions, limiting and shaping the direction of change. For instance, the relationship between parent and child is influenced by the culture of the family.

The parent-child relationship is special. *Bonding* is the process of establishing strong emotional ties between a parent and a child. In an early important study, Klaus, Kennell, Plumb, and Zuehike (1970) reported that early mother-child skin-to-skin contact appeared to facilitate bonding. Klaus and Kennell (1976) first described bonding as a process, possibly biochemical, that ties the mother closely to the child in the first hours after birth. Then they suggested (1982) that bonding begins before the birth of the child. The amount of bonding that occurs seems to depend more on social-system reinforcement than on the behavior of the fetus itself. However, fetal behavior might also affect bonding. The fetus's kicks and its heartbeats, which can be heard through the stethoscope and later on by ear, reinforce the bond.

Bonding increases with the birth of the child, and this increase is consonant with the environmental reinforcements available to parents. At birth, reinforcements increase substantially; there is a recognizable visual stimulus—the baby is more than a swelling in the mother's abdomen or

a great kicker. For many women, the birth process is an exhilarating experience. After birth the child can be touched; touching appears to be a critical component in relating (Klaus & Kennell, 1976, 1982) and an important reinforcer. Touching is an essential part of early feeding, early comforting, and many other positive contacts. The child can now make eye contact, track voices, make noise, and calm down with comforting. Through birth the infant has increased its potential to reinforce his or her bond with parents. Flowers, visits from friends and relatives, and congratulatory cards and gifts are also reinforcers. In these ways and others, the social environment plays a part in intensifying the infant's contact with its new parents.

The arrangements made between newborns and their parents vary from culture to culture. In many cultures, the mother and child are placed together immediately after birth. In U.S. culture, however, infants are often separated from their chief caretakers, at least for the first few days of their lives. Thus culture and environment, the family background, and the birth experience shared by parent and child begin to shape each child toward a unique development. According to birth order, age, socioeconomic status, and in some cases religious background, transactions take place between parents and child that result in an upbringing appropriate to the needs, desires, and outlook of that particular family in a specific culture.

*Temperament*  Neonates develop at individual rates. Born with their own temperament, they manifest their uniqueness almost immediately. Some infants are born more irritable than others. Some protest while lying naked on their backs to be changed. Some may show little tolerance for stomach upsets and as a result cry more than others. In a short time, each infant begins to display his or her individual temperament in interaction with the environment. Family members in turn respond to the child's behavior in a variety of ways.

Interaction with the family is as important an influence on the child as inborn temperament.

Psychologists interested in understanding how personality is formed concentrate on the child's early environment. Thomas, Chess, and Birch (1970) found that children could be grouped by three clusters of characteristics: those who were "easy" and biologically regular and rhythmical; "difficult" babies who withdrew from new stimuli and adapted more slowly to change; and those who were "slow to warm up"—that is, children who withdrew from activities quietly and who showed interest in new situations only if allowed to do so gradually, without pressure. About 35% of the children studied did not follow these types. In the other 65%, some of the characteristics became less prominent as the children developed and adapted to different circumstances.

The investigators found that any demand that conflicted strongly with a child's temperament placed the child under tremendous stress. Parents who understand their child's temperament and recognize what he or she can and cannot do may be in a position to avoid many problems in development as well as behavior. Further, because personality differences exist between parent and infant, parents need time and patience to become acquainted with the child's unique personality and develop a relationship. How the parent-child relationship affects the neonate's development will be discussed in the following section.

## Parent-Infant Relationships

Social workers, psychologists, and psychiatrists have emphasized the profound influence of parents and extended families on shaping an infant's personality. Recently, social behavioral scientists have begun to recognize that in the socialization process children are not only influenced but in turn influence their caretakers, as the following case shows:

Pat is a quiet, timid teenage parent who expected to give birth to an infant that she could take care of like a doll. But her baby, Nina, has other ideas. She cries noisily and demands constant attention. The only technique that seems to calm Nina is to pick her up and rock her rhythmically. However, Pat hates doing this—after all, *her* child is supposed to

be quiet. She starts to neglect this one-month-old baby out of disgust, turning to her own mother for help. At this point, the worker assigned to Nina meets with them and discusses the differences in babies, underscoring the need for Pat to understand and accept the baby as she is and work at creating a mutually satisfying relationship.

The characteristics of an infant elicit various responses from adults. A cuddly baby, a crying baby, and a squirming baby each bring out different responses in adults.

Though we cannot minimize the importance of the infant's constitutional characteristics in creating the initial pattern of mother-infant interaction, clearly the mother and the baby are caught up in an interacting spiral, whereby the behavior of each influences the responses of the other. As such, it is difficult to determine the variables that belong to a person's makeup; they blend together as part of a continuous, expansive spiral of interaction.

We do know that children play a significant role in determining the form and direction of parental behavior. Even young children can influence and control their caretakers' actions. For example, suppose a mother and child are looking at each other. If the infant looks away and then turns back, the baby may find he or she has lost the mother's gaze. When this happens, the infant starts to fuss and whimper, stopping as soon as the mother's gaze is regained. Infants swiftly learn elaborate means of securing and maintaining a caretaker's attention. Thus, socialization is a two-way process: a reciprocal relationship that involves both parent and child.

Researchers also note that the child's gender and position in the family may play a part in influencing parental behavior. Brown et al. (1976) studied a group of urban African-American mothers and found that they rubbed, patted, kissed, rocked, and talked more to their male newborns than to their female newborns. Mothers of first-born children spent more time feeding their babies than did mothers of later-born children. Thus, quite early in the developing relationship, different styles of interaction between parent and child become established, and both parent and child contribute to its patterning. Parents also need to recognize that a child behaves in a certain way not out of willfulness, hostility, laziness, or stupidity, but because of inborn temperament. By knowing this, parents can respond with less guilt, anxiety, and hostility and with less impatient, inconsistent, or rigid behavior. Most of all, a recognition of children's basic temperament relieves parents of a feeling of omnipotence—that they, and they alone, are responsible for turning them out in a certain mold (Papalia & Olds, 1986).

As we have seen, the environment initially created varies from home to home. It includes physical surroundings, other people, and the myriad social and cultural forces that influence the family. Human babies depend on others for sustenance. If babies are not fed or protected, they will die. Through nourishment and nurturing, as well as observation and imitation, children acquire the language, customs, attitudes, and skills of their group. Each cultural group has its own social heritage, derived from the history of its people and from other cultures. A culture shapes the children brought up in it, and they in turn, develop their attitudes, concepts and modes of thinking on the basis of their physical, sociocultural environment.

## TWO SIGNIFICANT ISSUES

Here we shall look at two important issues that many social workers face when helping pregnant women or new parents: infant death and abortion.

### Infant Death

Although most parents tend to think of infants as being invincible and make long-term plans for their childhood, unfortunately the unthinkable can happen at any time in a child's life. SIDS, a premature infant, an unusual illness, or a defective organ formation can cause infants to die. How do parents deal with this?

U.S. culture is uncomfortable with death, particularly that of an infant. Today infant death is viewed as a failure of medical technology. The immediate reaction of the family is shock, disbelief, anger, pain, and the haunting question, "Why me?" They may direct their anger toward health care professionals, a spouse, or themselves for allowing the death to occur; toward God for taking the child; or even the infant for dying. While dealing with their guilt feelings, parents also have to face friends and relatives. For many, dealing with other people has always been the most difficult part of the grieving process. Most people do not know how to respond to parents experiencing a child's death; Helmirth and Sternitz (1978) refer to this as the "conspiracy of silence."

How long does this grief last? Responses to the loss of an infant appear to mirror the effects of other forms of grief. Although the death is never forgotten, the acute stage of grief subsides after several months. By the end of a year, most parents have reestablished normal behavior patterns. This analysis was validated by De Frain and Ernst (1978), who studied 50 parents at various times following their infants' deaths. This study also reflects parents' tremendous potential for coping with a crisis situation and eventually adapting to a loss. Dealing with the death and dying of young children is just one area in which social workers play an important role, especially in helping parents to move ahead with their lives rather than remain obsessed with blaming.

### Abortion

Another controversial issue that many social workers face is abortion. As you probably know, *abortion* is the termination of pregnancy before the fetus is able to live outside the uterus (Newman & Newman, 1995). Here, we shall focus on the voluntary termination of pregnancy in a obstetrical setting rather than on spontaneous abortion (miscarriage).

*How abortions are done*  Before 12 weeks, a pregnancy is aborted by a process whereby the cervix is dilated and the contents of the uterus are removed by suction or by scraping out the uterus. After 12 weeks, abortion can be brought about by the injection of a saline solution or prostaglandin, which stimulates labor. Another procedure involves removing the fetus surgically by a procedure similar to a caesarean section (Cunningham, MacDonald, & Gant, 1989).

Research in France brought out a drug called RU 486 that can interrupt pregnancy by interfering with the synthesis and circulation of progesterone (Baulieu, 1989). This drug is most effective when it is taken within the first seven to nine weeks of pregnancy. This results in the shedding of the lining of the uterus, so there is no need for vacuum aspiration or surgical intervention. Between January and September 1989, about 2000 French women per month used RU 486, with a success rate of 95% when it was used in the first seven weeks of pregnancy. Right now, this drug is being evaluated in the United States. Should it become available, it brings abortion directly under a woman's personal control.

Timing is quite important in abortion as Denney and Quadagno (1992, p. 250) indicate:

> Abortion-related health risks are greatly reduced if the pregnancy is terminated as early as possible, if the patient is healthy, if the clinician is skilled and uses sterile technique, and if the woman is confident in her decision to have an abortion (Hatcher, 1990). . . . The most common problems include infection, retained products of conception in the uterus, continuing pregnancy, cervical or uterine trauma, and bleeding.

In spite of controversy, abortion continues throughout the world. It has been practiced alongside of infanticide throughout history and across cultures (Krannich, 1980). The Aranda of Australia and the Hopi of Arizona, for instance, have been known to induce abortion by tying a belt very tightly around the mother's abdomen (Murdock, 1934). In modern China, one cannot have more than one child; therefore many pregnant women are forced to have abortions.

Though abortion has existed for centuries, only in modern times has it become legalized. In 1920 the USSR gave permission to a mother to abort at the mother's request. In 1973, the U.S. Supreme court made abortion legal in this country. Even so, controversy still affects new laws and interpretations, all of which affect social work practices.

*The legalities of abortion in the United States*
In the United States, a conflict has arisen between the rights of a woman and those of an unborn child. People who are "pro-choice" believe that a woman has a right to privacy and an absolute right to choose or reject motherhood. On the other hand, "pro-lifers" believe that they have to protect the rights of an unborn fetus because it cannot protect its own interests.

Many people fall in the middle, supporting the idea that abortion is acceptable under certain conditions. One such condition involves the mother's health, mental and physical. If the mother was a rape or an incest victim, should she be forced to carry the fetus to full term? Would this scar the mother's mental health for life and would the child become a victim of the mother's rejection, pain, shame, or anger? Should abortion be performed if carrying the fetus would kill the mother? Whose life is more important, the mother's or the child's? These questions and others just as controversial continue to rage.

In the 1973 case of *Roe* v. *Wade,* the U.S. Supreme Court proposed a developmental model to address the issue. The courts supported the division of pregnancy into three trimesters and claimed that women had the right to abort in the first trimester, in keeping with their Constitutional right to privacy. The Court specified that in the second trimester some restrictions could be placed on access to abortion because of its risk to the mother; the fetus's rights were not an issue. In the third trimester, when the fetus has a good chance of surviving outside the uterus, individual states could choose whether or not to permit abortion.

In 1989, however, the Supreme Court upheld a Missouri law that made it illegal for any public institution or public employee to perform an abortion. The Missouri law said that an individual's life begins at conception. In 1992, the Supreme Court reviewed a set of laws passed by the Pennsylvania legislature, which said that a woman must see a presentation by her doctor intended to persuade her to change her mind, then wait 24 hours before she can have an abortion. Further, the law suggests teenagers should have the consent of a parent or a judge before an abortion. If a teenager does not get such consent before an abortion, the law requires a physical to specify any medical emergency and expects the physician or clinic to make regular reports to the state.

These recent decisions reflect how political climates (the macro environment) can affect people's daily lives. Social workers need to follow these developments so they can serve their clients with current information.

*Emotional and psychological effects*   What is the impact of abortion on women's sense of self and feelings? In some instances abortion is associated with lingering negative feelings (Lemkau, 1988). Sometimes the woman has become attached to the fetus; this is most common in second- and third-trimester abortions. Often such women are consumed with guilt, anger, and regret, particularly when they cannot have another child (Miller, 1992). Newman and Newman (1995) indicate that postabortion adjustment depends on the woman's views about the acceptability of abortion. Women who believe that abortion is viable usually also have friends, family, and partners who accept it. These women are less likely than others to experience strong feelings of regret or emotional upset following an abortion.

Although the issue has often been overlooked, men have feelings about abortion as well. Some evidence exists that men initially deal with it in a calm, intellectual manner. But after time passes, their true feelings emerge (Shostak, McLouth, & Seng, 1984). They experience feelings similar to those of women—guilt, sadness, and anger.

Men's feelings toward abortion have not been studied aggressively, however. Perhaps a study of men whose wives have undergone abortion would throw more light on the subject.

Now we shall look at an overview of the implications that pregnancy and childbirth carry for social work practice, after a brief reminder of what social workers need in general.

## IMPLICATIONS FOR PRACTICE

Like anyone else, social workers also come from families with points of view based on life experiences of their own. To work with other families and individuals, social workers must be able to understand the behavior of other people. Because practitioners can do this only from their own frame of reference, their own experience, they need to have self-awareness and a capacity for self-development. Self-awareness includes self-perception—an awareness of one's own needs, values, attitudes, feelings, experiences, strengths, weaknesses, expectations, and expertise.

Besides self-awareness, the worker needs a knowledge of human development and behavior—in many contexts—to assess and help clients. For instance, an understanding of life-span development shows them what is considered a normal phase of development and what is not. With appropriate assessments, workers can more effectively and easily help bring about change in people's lives. Further, with an understanding of the different phases of development, workers can anticipate potential problems as well as alleviate or prevent future problems. For example, when a child has a learning disability, social workers can help parents understand the problems of such a child and offer the child special help to rejoin the same school setting or join special school settings, according to his or her developmental needs.

As we have seen in this chapter, social workers should know about the early phase of human life to deal with such concerns as the health of the pregnant woman, nutrition, parenting skills, infertility, unwanted pregnancy, birth defects, and painful situations such as child neglect and abuse in the background of family relationships. An awareness of family factors such as lifestyle, socioeconomic status, ethnicity, and race also helps practitioners understand a family's attitudes and child-rearing practices.

In dealing with pregnant women, a practitioner needs to be aware of their particular needs. Because many pregnant women have no support systems, they may need to belong to groups that provide information about the emotional and physical aspects of labor and childbirth. Such groups often teach special exercises for mothers-to-be and allow them to share with others the many problems that arise in pregnancy. Classes such as Lamaze also teach techniques for dealing with childbirth. Joining a group helps the expectant mother take on an active role, thus becoming a meaningful participant in her own labor and childbirth.

## Cultural Factors: An Illustration

Pregnancy, childbirth, and child rearing are viewed differently in various parts of the world. A look at the lifestyle prevalent in Samoa when Margaret Mead did her famous study in the early 1920s illustrates such cultural differences:

> The expectant mother goes home laden with food gifts and when she returns to her husband's family, her family provides her with the exact equivalent in mats and bark cloth as a gift to them. At the birth itself the father's mother or sister must be present to care for the new-born baby while the midwife and the relatives care for her. There is no privacy about a birth. Convention dictates that the mother should neither writhe nor cry, nor wail against the presence of twenty or thirty people in the house who sit up all night if need be, laughing, joking and playing games. The midwife cuts the cord with a fresh bamboo knife and then all wait eagerly for the cord to fall off, the signal for a feast. If the baby is a girl, the cord is buried under a paper mulberry tree (the tree from which the bark cloth is made) to ensure her growing up to be industrious at household tasks; for a boy it is thrown into the sea that he may

be a skilled fisherman, or planted under a taro plant to give him industry in farming. When the visitors go home, the mother rises and goes about her daily tasks, and the new baby ceases to be of much interest to anyone. The day, the month in which the baby was born is forgotten.

> The baby's first steps or first word are remarked without exuberant comment, without ceremony. It has lost all ceremonial importance and will not regain it until after puberty; in most Samoan villages a girl is ignored until she is married. Even the mother remembers only that Losa is older than Pupu and her sister's little boy, Fale, is younger than her brother's child, Vigo. Relative age is of great importance, for the elders may always command the younger—until the positions of adult life upset the arrangement—but the actual age will be forgotten. (Mead, 1973)

Although labor and childbirth are common events, they are as diverse and complex as the people involved. Different life and birth patterns, rituals, child-rearing practices, and family interactions—in short, different cultures—add different flavor, color, and texture to human behavior. The social worker needs to have sufficient awareness of such differences to deal comfortably with diversity. (Note that in recent times, Samoan lifestyle has changed a great deal and these customs are more outdated with the influence of Western civilization.)

## Other Topics of Concern

Here we shall discuss several concerns social workers face regarding conception, pregnancy, and childbirth: premature birth, infertility, unwanted pregnancy, birth defects, and family setting. Though this list is not exhaustive, it should give you an idea of how we as social workers can use the life-span perspective to help our clients.

*Premature birth*    In the following case, notice how Alice depends on outside help:

> A teenager, Alice gives birth to a premature baby. Though she is firm in her decision to keep the infant, she has great difficulty relating to the child,

who does not respond with smiles or tears. The young mother in turn attempts to reject the unresponsive child by purposeful neglect. Fortunately, help is available. A social worker gives the young mother information about prematurity and its effects on the response level of the infant and the necessity for proper care if the child is to develop into a caring adult. Alice is encouraged to discuss her needs and fears, as well as her anger toward the child for not being "normal." Three months of supportive intervention help the young mother in the difficult task of parenting the child. Alice's family is enlisted as a support system, her mother and sisters help to sustain Alice's ability to care for her child.

In Alice's case, the practitioner used the potential of the family as a support system, which enhanced Alice's ability to cope and adapt to her new role as a parent, alleviating some stress. She learned to care for her child: feeding, changing diapers, and so forth. Positive reinforcement of such actions led Alice to feel efficient and competent despite minimal reward from the premature infant; meaningful actions combined with family support led to a sense of accomplishment and greater self-esteem. The practitioner's timing in offering help and his knowledge of the developmental life cycle set the stage for positive results.

*Infertility* Social workers need to enable people to make their own decisions regarding the different options available to them when faced with infertility. Factors that workers must consider include socioeconomic status, family background, and religious values. Is the couple willing to experiment with artificial fertilization if it is physically feasible for the mother and do they have the financial resources for the same? They would need to know that artificial fertilization may not work for them, so they could decide how much money they would like to spend for this purpose. Another option the social worker could present to the couple is adoption.

All counseling and discussions should take place in the presence of both partners, if there are two. This gives them an opportunity to

understand each other's opinions and ideas and proceed accordingly. If they disagree, the worker should help them resolve their differences and reach conclusions feasible to both. In addition, the social worker should share his or her knowledge of the different resources and facilities available in the area.

*Unwanted pregnancy* While working with women who are dealing with unwanted pregnancies, the social worker can play the roles of enabler, educator, broker, and advocate (Zastrow & Kirst-Ashman, 1994). Social workers enable women to make decisions by discussing the pros and cons of each alternative. As educators, they give women accurate information about the abortion process, fetal development, and the birth process. As brokers, they help women look at different resources and services available to them. These include health counseling, adoption agencies, and abortion clinics. Finally, social workers can be advocates, particularly for poor women; in this role, workers might find financial support and abortion services for such women.

The final decision, though, always rests with the pregnant woman, as Chilman (1987) points out:

> The ultimate decision . . . should be made chiefly by the pregnant woman herself, preferably in consultation with the baby's father and family members. To make the decision that is best for the couple and their child, the pregnant woman—ideally, with the expectant father—needs to view each option in the context of the couple's present skills, resources, values, goals, emotions, important interpersonal relationships, and future plans. The counselor's role is to support and shape a realistic selection of the most feasible pregnancy resolution alternative. (pp. 33–34)

*Birth defects* In the case of birth defects, parents need a great deal of support and counseling. Usually such parents are shocked and in disbelief that such a thing could happen to their child. They also get into whose family background could be responsible for the defect. Before long, they are fighting, blaming, and miserable. Without help, the marriage may be permanently affected. A social worker in this situation should help them (1) learn constructive ways of handling a child with birth defects including literature and support groups; (2) learn specific parenting skills; (3) work on their marriage; and (4) seek genetic counseling before they decide to have another child.

*Family setting*  The social worker should be aware of the influence and effects of family relationships on new parents and find out about their support systems. New parents who come from abusive backgrounds themselves could be encouraged to take parenting skills classes, for often such adults tend to follow after their parents unless they consciously decide they do not wish to do so. This decision and others like it might begin to put an end to abusive intergenerational patterns prevalent in U.S. culture.

Abused children have a distorted image of themselves, and unless there is insight or professional help, they do not really understand the implications of abuse. As Pillari writes (1991), George, a young child, was abused from the time he was 4 years old.

> In his own private world, this child suffered from guilt and justification of guilt of psychological and interpersonal functionings. This perception that he somehow was the bad person affected the ways he judged and accepted himself and others. (p. 88)

George lived his adult life with the feeling that he did not measure up and had less power than others in all situations. At the beginning of therapy George believed and accepted this image of himself. In time he understood that the abuse had robbed him of his sense of self, and he began to work diligently on his own self-esteem and self-respect. To fall in love, to care for another human being, and to be a parent, he had to work at understanding and accepting himself as a decent human being who had survived and worked through his own pain, the effects of an abusive home.

## CHAPTER SUMMARY

- The human capacity for adjustment is almost infinite. Like any other developmental period of a person's life, pregnancy has both personal and social aspects.

- Prenatal development begins when a new life is conceived. Conception takes place when an ovum is fertilized by a sperm. When this fertilized ovum undergoes cell division it is called the zygote, which embeds itself in the uterine wall within a couple of weeks. Then the embryonic period begins, lasting until the end of the second month after conception.

- The fetal period follows and lasts until birth. Within the amniotic sac, the embryo develops and receives oxygen and nourishment through the placenta. By the time the fetus is ready for birth, all its organs are functional and it can respond to sound and touch.

- Infertile couples have many alternatives to conventional pregnancy, including artificial insemination, in vitro fertilization, gamete intra fallopian transfer, vivo fertilization, and surrogate mothering.

- Different cultures have their own ways of preparing a woman for motherhood; for example, in the United States expectant mothers can enjoy a baby shower.

- The process of childbirth is divided into three stages. First, *effacement* refers to the shortening of the cervical canal and the dilation or gradual enlargement of the cervix. Second, *delivery* occurs when babies are born usually with the head emerging first, or vertex presentation. Other types of birth include breech presentation, when babies are born with the buttocks and feet emerging first; inverse presentation, when the baby is born with a hand or an arm that emerges first in the vagina; caesarean birth, which is surgical delivery; and forceps delivery, where the baby's head is pulled out with a tonglike instrument shaped to fit each side of the baby's head. Third, in *afterbirth* the placenta and related materials are expelled from the mother's body.

- The many ways of delivering a baby include natural childbirth, the Lamaze method, and Leboyer's techniques.
- The newborn typically weighs between 5½ and 9½ pounds and is 19 to 22 inches long. Assessment is made to detect any problems in infants as soon as they are born. The Apgar scale and the Brazelton Neonatal Behavioral Assessment Scale are the main ways professionals do this.
- Not all babies are born healthy, however. Genetic defects include chromosomal abnormalities and sex-linked defects.
- Genetic counseling is a way of protecting the next generation from genetic defects. The techniques available for diagnosing possible genetic defects include ultrasound, amniocentesis, fetoscopes, and chorionic villi sampling (CVS), which is an alternative to amniocentesis.
- Environmental influences in the prenatal stage that affect the newborn include maternal diet, toxemia, anoxia, the Rh factor, drugs, nicotine, alcohol, caffeine, and narcotics.
- Sudden infant death syndrome (SIDS), human immunodeficiency virus (HIV) and acquired immunodeficiency syndrome (AIDS), radiation, methyl mercury, maternal stress, maternal age, poverty, and the family environment also affect the developing fetus and condition of the newborn.
- Environmental influences after birth, such as parental expectations and other aspects of family life, affect newborns.
- Bonding between the newborn and the parent involves establishing strong emotional ties. This can include early skin-to-skin contact between the mother and child.
- Parent-infant relationships are shaped by both temperament and reciprocal interactions between parent and child.

- Significant issues in pregnancy and in newborn infants include infant death and abortion, particularly the legalities involved in the latter.
- Knowledge of the early phase of development is especially valuable for social workers who deal with problems such as infertility, unwanted pregnancies, birth defects, and family relationships. Their client population may represent diverse socioeconomic, ethnic, racial, religious, and age groups.

## SUGGESTED READINGS

Andrews, A. B., & Patterson, E. G. (1995). Searching for solutions to alcohol and other drug abuse during pregnancy: Ethics, values, and constitutional principles. *Social Work, 40*(1), 55–64.

Danziger, S. K. (1995). Family life and teenage pregnancy in the inner-city: Experiences of African-American youth. *Children and Youth Services Review, 17*(1–2), 183–202.

Davies, L., & Rains, P. (1995). Single mothers by choice? *Families in Society, 76*(9), 543–550.

Marcenko, M. O., & Spence, M. (1995). Social and psychological correlates of substance abuse among pregnant women. *Social Work Research, 19*(2), 103–109.

Powell, M. (1995). Sudden infant death syndrome: The subsequent child. *British Journal of Social Work, 25*(2), 227-240.

Yoshino, S., Narayanana, C. H., Joseph, F., Saito, T., et al. (1994). Combined effects of caffeine and malnutrition during pregnancy on suckling behavior in newborn rats. *Physiology and Behavior, 56*(1), 31–37.

## SUGGESTED VIDEOTAPES

*Bloodborne pathogens in the workplace* (8 minutes). (1996). Available from Long Island Productions, 1432 Kearney St., El Cerrito, CA 94530; 510-232-5215

Concept Media (Producer). (1992). *Birth and the newborn* (27 minutes). Available from Concept Media, Inc., P.O. Box 19542, Irvine, CA 92623-9542; 800-233-7078; Email: info@conceptmedia.com; Website: www.conceptmedia.com

Concept Media (Producer). (1991). *Emotional/social development* (22 minutes). Available from Concept Media, Inc., P.O. Box 19542, Irvine, CA 92623-9542; 800-233-7078; Email: info@conceptmedia.com; Website: www.conceptmedia.com

Concept Media (Producer). (1995). *First responders to SIDS: You make the difference* (38 minutes). Available from Concept Media, Inc., P.O. Box 19542, Irvine, CA 92623-9542; 800-233-7078; Email: info@conceptmedia.com; Website: www.conceptmedia.com

Concept Media (Producer). (1991). *Physical growth and motor development: The first two-and-a-half years* (19 minutes). Available from Concept Media, Inc., P.O. Box 19542, Irvine, CA 92623-9542; 800-233-7078; Email: info@conceptmedia.com; Website: www.conceptmedia.com

Questar (Producer). (1993). *Childbirth: Journey into life* (29 minutes). Available from Concept Media, Inc., P.O. Box 19542, Irvine, CA 92623-9542; 800-233-7078; Email: info@conceptmedia.com; Website: www.conceptmedia.com

## REFERENCES

Abel, E. L. (1984). *Fetal alcohol syndrome and fetal alcohol effects*. New York: Plenum.

Abroms, K., & Bennett, J. (1981). *Paternal contributions to Down's syndrome dispel maternal myths*. ERIC.

Als, H. E., Lester, B. M., & Brazelton, T. B. (1979). Specific neonatal measures: The Brazelton Neonate Behavioral Assessment Scale. In J. D. Osofsky (Ed.), *Handbook of infant development*. New York: Wiley.

Ambron, S. R., & Brodzinsky, D. (1979). *Lifespan human development*. New York: Holt, Rinehart & Winston.

Anderson, W. F. (1992). Human gene therapy. *Science, 256,* 808–813.

Aoki, C. G., & Siekevitz, P. (1988). Plasticity in brain development. *Scientific American, 259,* 56–64.

Apgar, V. (1953). A proposal for a new method of evaluation of the newborn infant. *Anesthesia and Analgesia, 32,* 260–267.

Apgar, V., & Beck, J. (1972). *Is my baby all right? A guide to birth defects*. New York: Trident Press.

Ash, P., Vennart, J., & Carter, C. (1977, April). The incidence of hereditary disease in man. *Lancet,* pp. 849–851.

Associated Press. (1993, August 15). Baby on the way through new technique. *Columbus Dispatch,* p. 5A.

Baulieu, E. (1989). Contragestion and other clinical applications of RU 486, an antiprogesterone at the receptor. *Science, 245,* 1351–1357.

Brazelton, H. M. (1973). Neonatal Behavioral Assessment Scale. In *Clinics in developmental medicine* (No. 50). Philadelphia: Lippincott.

Brodzinsky, D. M., Gormly, A. V., Ambron, S. R. (1986). *Lifespan human development*. New York: Holt, Rinehart & Winston.

Brown, J. V., Bakerman, R., Snyder, P. A., Fredrickson, W. T., Morgan, S. T., Hepler, R. (1976). Interactions of black inner city mothers with their newborn infants. *Child Development, 46,* 677–686.

Buescher, P. A., Roth, M. S., Williams, D. C., & Goforth, C. M. (1991). An evaluation of the impact of maternity care coordination on medicaid birth outcomes in North Carolina. *American Journal of Public Health, 81,* 1625–1629.

Byrne, G. (1988). Artificial insemination report prompts call for regulation. *Science, 241,* 895.

Cassady, G. G., & Strange, M. (1987). The small-for-gestational-age (SGA) infant. In G. B. Avery (Ed.), *Neonatology: Pathophysiology and management of the newborn* (pp. 299–331). Philadelphia: Lippincott.

Chasnoff, I. I. (1988). *Drugs, alcohol, pregnancy, and parenting*. Hingham, MA: Kluwer.

Chilman, C. S. (1987). Reproductive norms and social control. In J. Figueroa-McDonough & R. Sarri (Eds.), *The trapped woman: Catch 22 in deviance and control* (pp. 34–53). Newbury Park, CA: Sage.

Clark, A. L. G., & Howland, R. T. (1978). The American Samoan. In A. L. Clark (Ed.), *Culture, childbearing, and the health professionals* (pp. 154–172). Philadelphia: Davis.

Clarren, S. K., & Smith, D. W. (1978). The fetal alcohol syndrome. *New England Journal of Medicine, 298,* 1063–1067.

Collins, F. S. (1992). Cystic fibrosis: Molecular biology and therapeutic implications. *Science, 256,* 774–779.

Crooks, R., & Baur, K. (1990). *Our sexuality* (4th ed.). Redwood City, CA: Benjamin/Cummings.

Cunningham, F. G., MacDonald, P. C., & Gant, N. F. (1989). *Williams' obstetrics* (18th ed.). Norwalk, CT: Appleton G. Lange.

Danziger, S. K. (1979). Treatment of women in childbirth: Implications for family beginnings. *American Journal of Public Health, 69,* 521–555.

Darling, R. B. (1983). The birth defective child and the crisis of parenthood: Redefining the situation. In E. J. Callahan & K. A. McClusky (Eds.), *Life-span developmental psychology*. New York: Academic Press.

Darney, P. D., Myhra, W., Atkinson, E. S., & Meier, I. (1989). Sero survey of human immunodeficiency virus infection in women at a family planning clinic: Absence of infection in an indigent population in San Francisco. *American Journal of Public Health, 79,* 883–885.

De Frain, J. D., & Ernst, L. (1978). The psychological effects of sudden infant death syndrome on surviving family members. *Journal of Family Practice, 6*(5), 985–989.

Denney, N. W., & Quadagno, M. (1995). *Human Sexuality* (2nd. ed.). Chicago: Mosby.

Doering, S. G., Entwistle, D. R., & Quinlan, D. (1982). *Modeling the quality of women's birth defects in society.* St. Louis: Mosby.

Dyer, E. D. (1963). Parenthood as crisis: A re-study. *Marriage and Family Living, 25,* 196–201.

Ecker, M. D., & Bramesoco, N. J. (1981). *Radiation: All you need to know to stop worrying . . . or start.* New York: Vintage Books.

Eiduson, B. T. (1980). Child development in emergent family styles. In M. Bloom (Ed.), *Life span development* (pp. 119–129). New York: Macmillan.

Elmer-Dewitt, P. (1991). Making babies. *Time, 13*(8), 56–63.

Elson, J. (1989, July 24). The rights of frozen embryos. *Time,* p. 63.

Feinman, C. F. (1992). *The criminalization of a woman's body.* Binghamton, NY: Haworth Press.

Fenster, L., Eskenazi, B., Windham, G. C., & Swan, S. H. (1991). Caffeine consumption during pregnancy and fetal growth. *American Journal of Public Health, 81,* 458–461.

Field, R., Sandberg, D., Garcia, R., Vega-Lahr, N., Goldstein, S., & Guy, G. L. (1985). Pregnancy problems, postpartum depression, and early mother-infant interactions. *Developmental Psychology, 21,* 1152–1156.

Fleming, A. S., Ruble, D. N., Flett, G. L., & Shaul, D. L. (1988). Postpartum adjustment in first time mothers: Relations between mood, maternal attitudes, and mother-infant interactions. *Developmental Psychology, 24,* 71–81.

Fried, P. A., Watkinson, B., Dillon, R. F., & Dulberg, C. S. (1987). Neonatal neurological status in a low-risk population after prenatal exposure to cigarettes, marijuana, and alcohol. *Journal of Developmental and Behavioral Pediatrics, 8,* 318–326.

Gittler, J., & McPherson, M. (1991). Drugs and drug abuse. In *Information Please Almanac, 1992* (45th ed.). Boston: Houghton Mifflin.

Greenough, W. T., Black, J. E., & Wallace, C. S. (1987). Experience and brain development. *Child Development, 58,* 539–559.

Grossman, F. K., Eichler, L. S., & Winickoff, S. A. (1980). *Pregnancy, birth, and parenthood.* San Francisco: Jossey-Bass.

Grunfeld, L. (1989). Workup for male infertility. *Journal of Reproductive Medicine, 43,* 143–149.

Hahn, R. A., & Muecke, M. A. (1987). The anthropology of birth in five U.S. ethnic populations: Implications for obstetrical practice. *Current Problems in Obstetrics, Gynecology, and Fertility, 10,* 133–171.

Hall, R. E. (Ed.). (1970). *Abortion in a changing world* (Vol. 1). New York: Columbia University Press.

Hans, S. L. (1987) Maternal drug addiction and your children. *Division of Child, Youth, and Family Services Newsletter, 10,* 5, 15.

Hatcher, R. A. (1990). *Contraceptive Technology* (15th ed.). New York: Irvington.

Helmirth, T. A., & Sternitz, E. M. (1978). Death in an infant: Parental grieving and the failure of social support. *Journal of Family Practice, 6,* 943–949.

Hetherington, E. M., & Parke, R. D. (1979). *Child psychology: A contemporary viewpoint.* New York: McGraw-Hill.

Hofer, M. A. (1981). *The roots of human behavior.* San Francisco: Freeman.

Hudson, B., Pepperell, R., & Wood, C. (1987). The problem of infertility. In R. Pepperell, B. Hudson, & C. Wood (Eds.), *The infertile couple.* Edinburgh, Scotland: Churchill Livingstone.

Hughs, D., Johnson, K., Rosenbaum, S., & Lui, J. (1989). *The health of America's children: Maternal and child health data book.* Washington, DC: Children's Defense Fund.

Hyde, J. S. (1990). *Understanding human sexuality* (4th ed.). New York: McGraw-Hill.

Jaroff, L. (1989, March 20). The gene hunt. *Time,* pp. 62–67.

Jones, K. L., & Smith, D. W. (1973). Recognition of fetal alcohol syndrome in early infancy. *Lancet, 2,* 999.

Jones, K. L., Smith, D. W., Ulleland, C. N., & Streissguth, A. P. (1973). Patterns of malformation in offspring of chronic alcoholic mothers. *Lancet, 1,* 1267–1271.

Judson, F. N. (1989). What do we really know about AIDS control? *American Journal of Public Health, 79,* 878–882.

Karmel, M. (1983) *Thank you, Dr. Lamaze.* Philadelphia: Lippincott.

Kelley, K., & Byrne, D. (1992). *Exploring human sexuality*. Englewood Cliffs, NJ: Prentice-Hall.

Klaus, M. H., & Kennell, J. H. (1976). *Maternal and infant bonding*. St. Louis, MO: Mosby.

Klaus, M. H., & Kennell, J. H. (1982). *Parent-infant bonding* (2nd ed.). St. Louis, MO: Mosby.

Klaus, M. H., & Kennell, J. H., Plumb, N., & Zuehike, S. (1970). Human maternal behavior at first contact with her young. *Pediatrics, 46,* 187–192.

Krannich, R. S. (1980). Abortion in the United States: Past, present, and future trends. *Family Relations, 29,* 365–374.

Lacayo, R. (1988, February 15). Baby M. meets Solomon's sword. *Time,* p. 97.

Lacayo, R. (1992, May 4). Abortion: The future is already here. *Time,* p. 97.

Lamaze, F. (1970). *Painless childbirth: The Lamaze method*. Chicago: Regnery.

Leboyer, F. (1976). *Birth without violence*. New York: Knopf.

Lemkau, J. R. (1988). Emotional sequelae of abortion: Implications for clinical practice. *Psychology of Women Quarterly, 12,* 461–472.

Lenard, I. (1981, August). High tech babies. *Science Digest,* pp. 86–89, 116.

Levin, J., & DeFrank, R. S. (1988). Maternal stress and pregnancy outcomes: A review of the psychosocial literature. *Journal of Psychosomatic Obstetrics and Gynecology, 9,* 3–16.

Masters, W. H., Johnson, V. E., & Kolodny, R. C. (1988). *Human sexuality* (4th ed.). Glenview, IL: Scott, Foresman.

McDonald, A. D., Armstrong, B. G., & Sloan, M. (1992). Cigarette, alcohol, and coffee consumption and pre-maturity. *American Journal of Public Health, 82,* 87–90.

Mead, M. (1973). *Coming of age in Samoa* (2nd ed.). New York: Morrow.

Mead, M., & Newton, N. (1967). Cultural patterning of perinatal behavior. In S. A. Richardson & A. F. Guttmacher (Eds.) *Childbearing—its social and psychological aspects*. Baltimore: Williams & Wilkins.

Miller, W. B. (1992). An empirical study of the psychological antecedents and consequences of induced abortion. *Journal of Social Issues, 48,* 67–93.

Moore, K. L. (1989). *Before we are born: Basic embryology and birth defects* (3rd ed.). Philadelphia: Saunders.

Murdock, G. P. (1934). *Our primitive contemporaries*. New York: Macmillan.

Mussen, P. H., Conger, J. J., Kagan, J., & Gewitz, J. L. (1979). *Psychological Development*. New York: Harper & Row.

National Center for Children in Poverty. (1989). *Five million children: A statistical profile of our poorest young citizens*. New York: Author.

National Research Council. (1990). *Health effects of exposure to low levels of ionizing radiation*. Washington DC: National Academy Press.

Newman, B. M., & Newman, P. R. (1995). *Development through life*. Pacific Grove, CA: Brooks/Cole.

NIH/CEPH Collaborative Mapping Group. (1992). A comprehensive genetic linkage map of the human genome. *Science, 258,* 67–86.

Norr, K. L., Block, C. R., Charles, A., Meyering, S., & Meyers, E. (1977). Explaining pain and enjoyment in childbirth. *Journal of Health and Social Behavior, 4,* 18.

Palkovitz, R. (1985). Fathers' attendance, early contact and extended care with their newborns: A critical review. *Child Development, 56,* 392–406.

Palm, C. F., & Palkovitz, R. (1988). The challenge of working with new fathers: Implications for support providers. In R. Palkovitz & M. B. Sussman (Eds.), *Transitions to parenthood* (pp. 357–376). New York: Haworth.

Papalia, D. E. & Olds, S. W. (1986). *Human development*. New York: McGraw-Hill.

Papalia, D. E. & Olds, S. K. (1989). *Human development*. (4th ed.). New York: McGraw-Hill.

Papalia, D. E. & Olds, S. K. (1992). *Human development*. (5th ed.). New York: McGraw-Hill.

Pillari, V. (1991). *Scapegoating in families: Intergenerational patterns of physical and emotional abuse*. New York: Brunner/Mazel.

Plomin, R., Defries, J. C., & McClearn, G. E. (1990). *Behavioral genetics: A primer* (2nd ed.). New York: Freeman.

Restak, R. M. (1979, January 21). Birth defects and behavior: A new study suggests a link. *New York Times,* p. C7.

Roberts, L. (1989). Human gene transfer approved. *Science, 243,* 473.

Roosa, M. W. (1984). Maternal age, social class, and the obstetric performance of teenagers. *Journal of Youth and Adolescence, 13,* 365–374.

Rosett, H. L., & Weiner, L. (1984). *Alcohol and the fetus: A clinical perspective*. New York: Oxford University Press.

Rothwell, N. V. (1988). *Understanding genetics* (4th ed.). New York: Oxford University Press.

Sabatelli, R. M., Meth, R. L., & Gavazzi, S. M. (1988). Factors mediating the adjustment to involuntary childlessness. *Family Relations, 37,* 338–343.

Sachs, A. (1989, May 22). Here come the pregnancy police. *Time,* pp. 104–105.

Sameroff, A. J. (1983). Developmental systems: Contexts and evolution. In W. Kessen (Ed.), *Handbook of child psychology: Vol. 1. History, theory, and methods* (4th ed.). New York: Wiley.

Sameroff, A. J. (1987). Reproductive risk and the continuum of caretaking casualty. In F. D. Horowitz, M. Hetherington, S. Scarr-Salapetek, & G. Siegel (Eds.), *Review of child development research* (Vol. 4, pp. 187–244). Chicago: University of Chicago Press.

Sameroff, A. J., & Chandler, M. J. (1975). Reproductive risk and the continuum of caretaking casualty. In F. D. Horowitz, M. Hetherington, S. Scarr-Salapetek, and G. Siegel (Eds.), *Review of child development research* (Vol. 4). Chicago: University of Chicago Press.

Schiamberg, L. B. (1985). *Human development* (2nd ed.). New York: Macmillan.

Seabrook, C. (1987, February 19), Children—"Third wave" of AIDS victims. *Atlanta Journal,* pp. IA, 12A.

Shepard, T. H. (1983). *Catalog of teratogenic agents* (4th ed.). Baltimore: Johns Hopkins University Press.

Shostak, A., McLouth, G., & Seng, L. (1984). *Men and abortions: Lessons, losses and love.* New York: Praeger.

Silverman, P. R. (1989). Deconstructing motherhood. *Readings: A Journal of Reviews and Commentary in Mental Health, 4,* 14–18.

Sontag, L. W. (1944). War and the fetal-maternal relationship. *Marriage and Family Living, 6,* 3–4, 16.

Sosa, R., Kennell, I., Klaus, M., Robertson, S., & Urrutia, J. (1980). The effect of a supportive companion on perinatal problems, length of labor, and mother-infant interaction. *New England Journal of Medicine, 303,* 597–600.

Specht, R., & Craig, G. J. (1982). *Human development.* Englewood Cliffs, NJ: Prentice-Hall.

Sperling, D. (1989, March 10). Success rate for in vitro is only 9%. *USA Today,* p. 1D.

Stafford, R. S. (1990). Alternative strategies for rising caesarean section rates. *Journal of American Medical Association, 263,* 683–687.

Stechler, G., & Halton, A. (1982). Prenatal influences on human development. In B. B. Wolman (Ed.), *Handbook of developmental psychology* (pp. 175–189). Englewood Cliffs, NJ: Prentice-Hall.

Steuer, F. B. (1994). *The psychological development of children.* Pacific Grove, CA: Brooks/Cole.

Streissguth, A. P., Barr. H. M., Sampson, P. D., Darby, B. L., & Martin, D. C. (1989). IQ at age 4 in relation to maternal alcohol use and smoking during pregnancy. *Developmental Psychology, 25,* 3–11.

Swyer, P. R. (1987). The organization of perinatal care with particular reference to the newborn. In G. B. Avery (Ed.), *Neonatology: Pathophysiology and management of the newborn* (pp. 13–44). Philadelphia: Lippincott.

Thomas, A., Chess, S., & Birch, H. (1970, August). The origin of personality, *Scientific American, 233,* 102–109.

Thompson, J. S., & Thompson, M. W. (1986). *Genetics in medicine* (4th ed.). Philadelphia: Saunders.

U.S. Bureau of the Census. (1992). *Statistical Abstract of the United States: 1992* (112th ed.). Washington, DC: U.S. Government Printing Office.

U.S. Department of Health and Human Services. (1990). *Health, United States 1989* (DHHS Pub. No. PHS 90-1232). Washington DC: U.S. Government Printing Office.

Vander Zanden, J. W. (1978). *Human development.* New York: Knopf.

Vaughan, B. E., Bradley, C. F., Joffe, L. S., Seifer, R., & Barglow, P. (1987). "Maternal characteristics measured prenatally are predictive of ratings of temperamental difficulty" on the Carey Infant Temperament Questionnaire. *Developmental Psychology, 23,* 152–161.

Vaughan, B. E., Kopp, C. B., & Krakow, J. B. (1984). The emergence and consolidation of self-control from eighteen to thirty months of age: Normative trends and individual differences. *Child Development, 55,* 990–1004.

Watkins, E. L., & Johnson, A. E. (Eds.). (1979). *Removing cultural and ethnic barriers to healthcare.* Chapel Hill: University of North Carolina Press.

West, J. R. (1986). *Alcohol and brain development.* London: Oxford University Press.

Willwerth, J. (1991, May 13). Should we take away their kids? *Time,* pp. 62–63.

Zastrow, C., & Kirst-Ashman, K. K. (1994). *Understanding human behavior and the social environment.* Chicago: Nelson-Hall.

Zuckerman, B., Frank, D. A., & Hingson, R. (1989). Effects of maternal marijuana and cocaine use on fetal growth. *New England Journal of Medicine, 320,* 762–768.

# 3

# *Infancy*

## INTRODUCTION

Lolitha has been abandoned in a garbage can on a dust-ridden, debris-laden street. Her panicked shrieks and cries find the compassion of two scared but surprised teenagers. They turn the child over to the police, who immediately place the child in a hospital.

Lolitha appears to be at least 3 months old but is emaciated and has ugly bruises on her body. What is Lolitha's history and who are her parents? Why was she abandoned? A police search leads to her mother. Lolitha is the product of a mother addicted to drugs and alcohol. How will this affect Lolitha when she grows up?

In this chapter, we shall examine the principles of infant development—physical, linguistic, and psychosocial. We shall then explore the theories of Erikson, White, and Piaget to learn various ways of viewing this stage in the life span. Taken together, these theorists provide a helpful and holistic view of infancy, defined in this book as about 1 month through 2½ years.

The second half of this chapter focuses on central issues for infants in their environment. We shall see how attachments, separation, and personality development form the basis of a child's future social interaction. Then, specific caretaking issues will be explored, followed by implications for social work practice.

## THE PRINCIPLES
## OF INFANT DEVELOPMENT

At 8 months of age, Anthony was a beautiful baby with a ready smile. Placid, he was happy playing with toys. He cried when his diaper needed changing but otherwise showed no symptoms of temper. Now, at 2 years of age, Anthony continues to be easygoing and gentle. He has little fear and is outgoing and friendly. He also has reliable eating habits.

Within a few days after birth, Sean revealed that he was a fussy baby. At 6 months, he was already throwing violent temper tantrums. He had distinct preferences for food, toys, and people. At 18 months Sean was independent and active. His sleep could be disturbed by small noises, so his parents had to be careful. He would get up in the middle of the night, howling and crying. Now, at age 2, Sean's expressions of joy, fear, and anger remain intense. His parents worry, for by nature they are calm, quiet people.

Maya is the daughter of a single teenage mother. Though born premature, Maya received more than enough love, nurturing, and care to survive. She was surrounded by a network of grandparents, uncles, and aunts who looked out for both Maya and her mother. At 2 years of age, Maya is an outgoing, bright-eyed, lovable child with good eating habits and a good disposition.

Infants are far more competent than we once thought. Much new literature documents their many perceptual, cognitive, and social capacities, which genetic and environmental information guides. Even within the first six months of a child's life, we can notice individual differences in temperament as well as intellectual ability (Mandler, 1990). We are becoming aware that infants actively select and organize information and contribute to their own care, crying when hungry or wet (Belsky & Tolan, 1987; Bower, 1989).

The crucial place of genetics in infant development has now been well documented and the methods of studying infant behavior are reaching new levels of sophistication (Plomin, 1990, 1994). Several environmental factors influence genetics; for example, child care, cultural and religious beliefs surrounding child-rearing practices, and socioeconomic status all partially determine a child's vulnerability or resilience (Plomin & McClearn, 1993).

New information based on birth cohorts indicates that children born in the same historical period experience certain common patterns of opportunities and challenges. For instance, the restrictions in gas consumption led to creation of smaller cars and a different lifestyle in the 1970s.

In the 1990s we are experiencing a "baby boom," and we are paying special attention to newborn babies (Newman & Newman, 1995). There is an interest in how to respond to newborn babies to bring out their best potentials. For instance, there are attempts to understand when newborns begin to respond intellectually to outside stimuli. When more children are born, there is a need for more day cares that are efficient and stimulating. A great deal of attention centers on children affected by complex medical technology. The lives of children merely 2 pounds at birth are being saved. There is a renewed interest in studying infant temperament and early signs of personality. A growing baby industry provides food, toys, books, clothes, music, and other paraphernalia. Also, new mothers and pregnant women are spending more time in understanding and appreciating the newborn, showing a desire "to do the best I can" or "get it right the first time."

During infancy, rapid growth and achievement take place in all areas of development. Like other life-span stages, infancy follows the general principles that govern each stage of human development: (1) a characteristic growth rate, (2) a particular direction that growth follows, (3) a certain pattern of differentiation, and (4) the integration of a characteristic developmental sequence (Vander Zanden, 1977). Further, four developmental tasks are usually achieved during infancy: (1) primary motor functions such as early eye-hand coordination, reaching, sitting, crawling, standing, and walking; (2) a sense of the permanence of objects; (3) a behavioral, though not conceptual, understanding of the relationship between means and ends; and (4) social attachment.

Now, we shall look at the three main modes of development: physical, linguistic, and psychosocial.

## Physical Development

How does a baby grow? In this section, we shall examine a detailed list of the infant's physical development—everything from various principles of growth to feeding schedules.

*The holistic principle* Biological characteristics and environmental factors must work together for optimal development to be enhanced. Any negative interference from the "inside" such as neurological problems or hormonal imbalance, or from the "outside" such as improper diet or lack of stimulation, can turn the positive growth cycle into a negative one.

> At 18 months of age, Tanya is afraid of people. As an infant she was abused by her parents and ill fed. Now, whenever Tanya puts out her hand to touch something, she experiences physical pain. When others touch her, she shrivels up like a snail.

Mothers do not respond to children who have delayed language and verbal abilities the same way that they do to normal children. Lugo and Hershey (1979) and others found that when compared with normal children, delayed preschoolers generally spent more time in solitary play, initiated fewer interactions, and responded less frequently to maternal interactions and questions. Their mothers gave more commands, initiated fewer positive interactions, and were less likely to respond positively to their children's interactions, play activities, and cooperative behaviors.

*From mass to specific activity* At first, infants typically exhibit mass activity. For example, a pinprick on the foot will cause an infant to move his or her whole body around—head, arms, fingers, legs, toes, and torso—not just the affected part. As the infant grows older, mass activity is replaced by specific activity, characterized by distinct, individualized, and coordinated responses.

*Differentiation and integration* Specific activity that replaces mass activity is called *differentiation*. When a certain degree of differentiation has been reached, the infant moves toward *integration:* Small units of behavior combine and become coordinated into larger, more functional units. For example, the child will learn to follow a sequential behavior in order to obtain nourishment. This could take the form of crying, searching for food, or reaching toward the bottle, the breast, or a pacifier (if within reach) and placing it in his or her mouth.

*The cephalocaudal and proximodistal principles*    Infant development follows the cephalocaudal and proximodistal principles. According to the *cephalocaudal principle,* growth proceeds from head to feet. Improvements in function and structure also follow the same order, occurring first in the head, then in the trunk, and finally in the leg region. At birth, the head is disproportionately large, making up ¼ of the body, whereas in adults it is only ⅒ to ½ of the body. In contrast, the legs and arms of the newborn are disproportionately short compared with those of an adult.

Motor development also proceeds from head to foot. Infants learn to contract the muscles first of the head and neck, then of the arms and abdomen, and finally of the legs. When they begin to crawl, infants use their upper body to propel themselves and drag their feet passively behind. As they grow older and stronger they begin to use their legs to help them crawl.

The *proximodistal principle* indicates that growth proceeds from the head and torso toward the extremities. In early infancy, babies learn to move their heads and trunks. As they grow older, they learn to use their legs and arms independently. Control over the movements travels down the arms as children become increasingly able to perform precise and sophisticated grasping and other manual operations. Accordingly, children learn large-muscle control before fine-muscle control. Thus an infant can walk, jump, climb, and run before developing the ability to draw or write. Thus movements proceed from mass to specific activity.

*Rates of physical growth*    Although individual rates of maturing may differ, broad similarities mark the sequences of human developmental change. A person's growth may be rapid, slow, or uneven during the first 20 years of life. In general, however, growth in the first three years is rapid and slows down between ages 3 and 5.

After age 5, the rate of growth is slow and steady until puberty, during which a rapid acceleration of growth occurs called the adolescent growth spurt, to be discussed in Chapter 6.

In the young infant, not all parts of the system grow at the same speed. The nervous system develops more rapidly than others. At birth, the brain is already 25% of its adult weight; at 6 months, nearly 50%; at 2½ years, 75%; at 5, 90%; and at age 10 it has reached nearly 95% of its adult weight. Unlike the brain, the reproductive system grows slowly until adolescence, when it undergoes a growth spurt.

*Feeding*    As children grow up, they need to follow a routine. There is a time for eating and a time for sleeping. A schedule creates a tempo, rhythm, and balance in the infant's life that eventually becomes a pattern.

Infants' feeding schedules are based on various schools of thought. Some parents adhere to a strict schedule, believing that an infant should be encouraged to drink a given amount at each feeding, calculated according to the height and weight of the baby. Others believe that babies should be fed on demand: Whenever the baby is hungry, parents let the baby have as much or as little as he or she wants. Such feeding schedules depend on an infant's stomach size, constitution, and temperament. An infant's feeding schedule is also affected by the lifestyle of the parents. Not all infants have the advantage of a feeding schedule, however.

> At 24, Maria is the mother of five children. Her welfare check does not meet all her needs. She feeds her children the best she can, but poverty always lurks nearby. She feeds her older children well, but overlooks her youngest child, whose constant crying eventually turns to whining. This child's father is an abusive alcoholic, and somehow the infant reminds Maria of him. However, Maria does give the youngest child a full meal every day, at different times, whenever it suits Maria.

As a child grows older, his or her stomach can hold larger amounts, accounting for longer intervals between feedings. One common problem many infants face at this point is a digestive disorder.

Colic is one such disorder. The abdomen becomes distended with gas, producing severe pain. This usually happens with firstborn children. Tension in the mother does not help the situation, but usually colic disappears by itself and does not require medical attention.

> Rosa has become a single parent at 31. Before the birth, she read many books and really wanted to be an excellent parent. To her it did not matter if the child had a father present or not. She had chosen the lifestyle that offered her the greatest fulfillment. She was in for a bad shock, however. Her baby cries incessantly, her friends were tired of her frantic phone calls asking them what to do. When Rosa finally calls the doctor, the child is found to have colic. Rosa's anxiety and stress is relieved only when the colic begins to subside and, to Rosa's relief, finally disappears.

*Sleeping patterns*   The amount of sleep a child requires varies with age. At birth, full-term babies sleep 50% to 60% of the time; premature babies sleep about 80% of the time (Kaluger & Kaluger, 1984). Young infants need more sleep than toddlers. As a child's abilities increase and experiences widen, the child resists going to bed, and slowing down for bedtime becomes more and more difficult.

The quality of sleep that a child needs also changes dramatically. During the early months, sleep is relatively shallow, and the infant awakens whenever hungry or wet. Often the infant gives out sharp cries when waking up. But as children grow older, they learn to sleep more peacefully.

*Sensorimotor skills*   Infancy is a period of tremendous motor growth. *Motor* refers to muscular movements. Very young infants do not have enough strength and coordination in their head, neck, arms, and legs to initiate smooth, purposeful actions. Development in the brain and the spinal cord leads to muscle strength and coordination, which in turn leads to extraordinary changes in motor behavior over the first two years

of life. Motor development in infants follows two basic directions. First, as you know, it is proximodistal. Second, motor behavior shifts from being largely reflexive to being purposeful and voluntary. Reflexes help infants survive and lead them on to develop more complicated voluntary behavior. For instance, the sucking reflex helps infants gain nourishment relatively easily before this behavior comes under voluntary control.

Motor skills also develop as the bones, muscles, and nervous system grow and mature. By 12 months, babies can usually hold their heads and roll over by themselves. Earlier on, they begin to reach for things and grasp them. They learn to sit, crawl, stand, and eventually walk. Each accomplishment requires practice, refinement, struggle, and finally proficiency. Though children develop with progressive regularity, it is important to remember that there are late learners.

*Walking*   When infants begin to walk they falter and fall, but soon they begin to walk more efficiently (Clark & Philips, 1993). In the beginning, children must learn how to coordinate the thigh and the shank as well as the movement of both legs. Within three months of walking, infants appear to develop such coordination and walk much like adults.

Culture affects walking movements. For example, researchers observed that in African and West Indian child-rearing practices, babies spent much more time in a vertical position than do U.S. infants. Mothers in these cultures propped their babies up with pillows, carried them upright in a sling, and gently massaged the babies' backs, arms, and legs, all of which helped to strengthen the head and neck control and also orient the babies to upright locomotion (Hopkins & Westra, 1988).

By the time children are 14 months old, they begin to investigate by gently stepping and swaying at the top of a slope before descending. They develop a special strategy for descending; they also often slide down the ramp. In this way they learn to evaluate and navigate a slope that requires fine-tuning and exploratory behavior (Adolph, Eppler, & Gibson, 1993).

*Reaching and grasping*  As you know, the motor system moves from relatively gross unco-ordinated movements to finely tuned purposeful actions. Both grasping and reaching originate in reflexive behaviors (Fentress & McLeod, 1986). When quite young, babies can support their own weight by grasping an object. This reflex disap-pears after 4 weeks and is replaced by voluntary reaching, accurate grasping, clutching, and letting go (Bower, 1987).

The transition from involuntary to voluntary is guided by genetic inheritance as well as the prac-tice of coordinated muscle movements. For instance, when one baby, Clyde, discovers he has hands, he looks at them for long stretches of time, wiggles the fingers, and rotates the wrists. He clasps his fingers and views them from a dis-tance, pushing them to arms' length.

By the time children are about 4½ months, they can make contact with objects by reaching across, in front, and to the side. They also shift from exploring their fingers to sucking and biting to find out more about an object (Rochat, 1989). By 12 months babies can use their index finger and thumb to pick up tiny things like clots of dust, threads, piece of dry cereal, and spaghetti strands. Children between 12 and 15 months explore by lifting little things and by manipulat-ing things—they lift latches, turn knobs, and place small things into bigger things and try to get them out. By doing this, they learn how objects work and how they relate to one another. Often the baby at this point experiences conflict with the caregiver, who fears that the child may swallow such items.

Infants advance socially, emotionally, and intellectually as they achieve sensory-perceptual and motor skills. Motor development plays a role in determining developmental sequences or "timetables" in areas such as touch and depth perception. Increased motor development leads to an increased sense of control and is usually associated with positive emotions. It also influ-ences cognitive development (Bushnell & Boudreau, 1993). Between 11 and 18 months the child becomes an accomplished social being,

calling out to parents by saying "Dada" and "Mama" and using expressions such as "Bye-bye." The infants performs imitative actions such as talking on the telephone, reading a magazine, and sweeping the floor.

As you can see, many factors influence a baby's physical development. Factors as diverse as weather, type of clothing worn (overdressed or underdressed babies are uncomfortable), type of living arrangements made for the child, and the child's ordinal position in the family can all affect the infant's growth.

## Language Development

As infants grow older, language becomes an important and intimate part of their development. There is a difference between language develop-ment and speech development. *Language devel-opment* refers to words, their pronunciation, and methods of combining them. Language develop-ment concerns the length and patterns of sen-tence structure. *Speech* refers to *vocalization,* or the development of units of speech sound (phonemes) and the move toward proper articu-lation of such sounds.

*Speech*  Infant speech is important to observers because it provides them with a way to access the child's mental processes and thus to under-stand them better. Baby talk serves the expres-sive function of permitting the child to communi-cate needs and interests through means other than tears, smiles, shouts, and gestures. Thus infant speech becomes a vehicle of self-expression and communication as well as mental development. From a transactional perspective, it helps strengthen the infant's bonds with people. By talking, the child becomes more than just a small presence—he or she can ask for attention in a new and powerful way.

Infants make sounds from the time they are born. When a baby is 2 months old, her or his parents can distinguish a variety of cries, smiles, and sounds of contentment. Then, the infant moves quickly from vocalizing to babbling and talking.

*Language and culture*    By 1 year of age, children already favor sounds peculiar to the language of their caretakers. This pattern of selective phonemic learning reveals the significance of culture-specific linguistic systems. At this age, the child's speech is *holophrastic,* consisting of one-word utterances having more than literal meanings. That is, the child's manner of expression enlarges the meaning of the word, conveying delight, dismay, or the thrill of a new discovery. Later, the child moves on to *telegraphic* speech, achieving effective communication using only key words or phrases such as "Where dada?"

A cross-cultural view of languages reveals differences as well as similarities or universals. Different cultures promote various cognitive capacities in individuals (Cole, 1985; Rogoff, 1990). Further, one of the essential ways cultural beliefs and practices are communicated to children is through language. Rogoff (1990) points out that "there are striking . . . differences" in the ways adults and children communicate in different cultures (p. 119).

Exchanges of speech between child and caretaker tend to fall into one of two culturally determined patterns (Ochs & Schieffelin, 1984). These patterns reflect a culture's overall tendency to either (1) adapt the available situations to a child or (2) adapt a child to the situations that already prevail in daily life.

Middle-class families in the United States tend to fall in the former category. Usually they create special settings and experiences for infants and children. These include cribs, nurseries, preschools, special toys, and even unique ways of talking and socializing. Ochs and Schieffelin (1984) believe that adults in such cultures tend to be responsive when children attempt to communicate, talk to children in simplified ways, and cooperate with children to determine the meaning of utterances.

In the second type of pattern, children are raised to fit in with the ongoing practices of society. This produces a different type of linguistic communication between adults and children. Ochs and Schieffelin (1984) suggest that adults in such cultures tend to talk to children about topics that the adults select, to direct children's attention to other people, and often to demonstrate nonsimplified utterances for the child to repeat to another person. A mother in such a culture, then, might face her son toward his sibling and say, "There is your sister. Ask your sister to bring you the pillow."

These examples reflect North American middle-class culture. Some studies, though, explore other cultures' language development as well. For example, in studying language acquisition in Kaluli children of Papua New Guinea, Schieffelin (1985) found that mothers do not engage preverbal infants in the turn-taking "conversations" that typify North American adult-infant interactions. When young children begin to talk, Kaluli mothers often tell them what to say to someone else; they say *elema* which means "say like that" (Schieffelin, 1985, p. 531). Furthermore, in a linguistic interaction, the mother uses words that would help the listener understand rather than be understood by the child.

Also, in some cultures in the United States, adults and children do not frequently engage one another in conversations in the way middle-class families do. Rather, children appear to learn much about language by talking to peers, listening to conversations of adults, and watching TV. In short, children develop linguistic abilities to suit the habits and values of their own cultural groups. Cole (1985) specifies that some scholars argue that a full understanding of linguistic and cognitive development requires the study of cultural practices in all their variety.

## Psychosocial Development

Human infants are born into a social environment. From birth they take their place in that environment. To be human is to be a social product.

*Emotions*  Infants interact with their environment and create the beginnings of a social world for themselves. The term *emotion* implies a system of feelings. Many psychologists agree that emotion is, first of all, *affective*—that is, it has an element of feeling or awareness. Second, the central nervous system and the autonomic system are involved, providing characteristic motor, glandular, and visceral activities. Third, emotion can be classified into various types of phenomena, such as fear, anger, joy, disgust, pity, and affection.

Emotions provide an organizing framework for communication between infants and their caretakers (Campos & Barrett, 1984). There is a definite relationship between emotional states and organismic needs, which are both simple when the child is young. Most caregivers rely on the facial, vocal, and behavioral cues related to these emotions in order to determine an infant's inner states and goals (Malatesta & Izard, 1984). An infant's emotions are simple, spontaneous, and transitory but more frequently expressed than those of adults. As soon as an infant's emotion passes, it is forgotten, and the infant is free from strain and stress until new conditions arise that evoke an emotional response.

The chief caretakers provide the emotional environment: When interaction with an infant go astray and an adult cannot understand what a baby needs, the adult tries to repair the communication (Tronick, 1989). Think of a 7-month-old baby who wants a toy that is out of reach. The baby waves her arms in the direction of the toy, makes fussy noises, and looks distressed. Her father tries to figure out what she needs and watches her expressions to discover whether he is on the right track. Parents attuned to this form of communication often successfully help babies achieve their goals, and thus the infants are likely to persist in attempts to communicate because they have succeeded in the past.

Infants can also recognize and discriminate the affective expressions of others. Very young infants can differentiate facial expressions such as anger,

fear, happiness, sadness, and surprise (Hornik, Risenhoover, & Gunnar, 1987; Ludemann & Nelson, 1988; Walker-Andrews, 1986). Warmth, caring, and bodily satisfaction are equivalent to love for both the baby and the parent.

One of the infant's chief emotions is excitement—at seeing the loving caretaker, anticipating being fed, or getting ready for play. Another emotion is distress, which can be observed by the end of the second month. Between 3 and 6 months of age, infants show anger, disgust, and fear. As maturation and learning take place, complex interactions come into play. The chief caretakers, of course, greatly affect the infant's emotional development. However, the domain of emotions works two ways; infants and their caregivers establish *intersubjectivity,* a state in which both partners have the same understanding and take the same meaning from a situation. Infants and their caregivers are involved in a reciprocal, rhythmic interaction in which they take in each other's emotion or state changes and modify their actions according to this information. Through a shared repertoire of emotions, babies and their caregivers can understand one another and also create shared meanings. Exchange of mutual emotional expression can become a building block of trust.

*Social interaction*  Like adults, children depend on their social environment for their existence. The social group and available networks not only supply the infant's needs but to a great extent also determine what kind of individual the infant will become. The first social group with which a normal child interacts is the immediate family, which could consist of two parents, a single parent, or an extended family including siblings. The family plays an important part in establishing the child's attitudes and habits. Of course, as the child grows toward adulthood, his or her social networks change and expand, and reliance on the family decreases.

Infants make their first social responses to adults by 4 weeks of age. They stare at faces that are close by and appear to enjoy following the movements of objects and people. They begin to coo and babble. By the end of the third month, infants interact with people by responding to voices, turning their head or eyes toward the sound. At 5 months, they can respond to a person's smile by smiling in return. This stage marks the beginning of mutuality and reciprocity.

As infants' perspective powers increase, they interact more with whatever is in the immediate environment. By 7 months, they learn to play peekaboo or hide-your-face.

By the time children are 1 year old, they enjoy social give-and-take. They slowly come to understand that other people besides the family can be friendly. Playthings no longer hold their attention completely, because they enjoy being chased while they try to creep away. At 18 months, infants are into everything. Most of them can walk, and most enjoy being on their feet. They enjoy exploring and develop a great interest in household things and activities. During this period children are responsive to adults and are aware of social approval, which has become an important aspect of their lives.

> At 18 months, Nicholas lives in a crowded city with his mother, his mother's intermittently resident boyfriend, a couple of aunts, his grandmother, and six older siblings. Home life is chaotic: There are no rules for behavior, and the older the child, the greater the freedom. Alcohol and drugs are common features of family life. Nicholas is constantly neglected by his mother, who attempts to maintain the family on her meager welfare check and the income from drug trafficking. The real nurturer and caretaker in the family is the grandmother. In his mother's presence, Nicholas's behavior is quiet and timid. But when his grandmother enters the house, Nicholas babbles loudly and smiles as she responds with affection. Thus nurturing and social approval stimulate Nicholas's social behavior.

Now we shall turn to three theorists—Erikson, White, and Piaget—whose thinking on infants give social workers many helpful concepts and ways of working with infants and their caretakers.

## MAJOR THEORISTS ON INFANCY

### Erikson: Acculturation and Developmental Stages

A pioneer of developmental theory, Erik Erikson has carefully noted and described how human potentials are adapted to culture. He highlights psychosocial rather than psychosexual development through the life cycle, which he divides into eight stages of life (see Chapter 1). Perhaps because of his experiences in different cultures, Erikson emphasizes the importance of the child's world in the process of development; as such, he has been called a psychosocial theorist. His work on the life cycle is impressive, a carefully woven tapestry of biological, psychological, personal, cultural, historical, and political factors in the human life span. His theory thus focuses on the development of the reality-oriented ego within the social world of the individual. The following sections present each stage in order.

*Trust versus mistrust* Though analogous to Freud's oral stage, Erikson's infancy stage does not focus on the gratification of oral needs; rather, Erikson highlights the infant's relationship with his caretakers. Basic trust involves a positive orientation toward oneself, the world, and others; mistrust is shown in negative feelings, insecurities, and fears.

Once outside the womb, the infant remains completely dependent on the care of nurturing adults. That infant who is well cared for in terms of nourishment, contact, and attention develops a sense of contentment. For the nonverbal child, trust proceeds from experiences. If his or her needs are met, the infant feels valued and develops confidence in his or her surroundings. Trust can be inferred from an infant's ability to delay gratification and from the warmth and happiness it reveals in interacting with adults.

When their needs are either not recognized or treated inconsistently, infants can develop feelings of mistrust. When a crying infant is treated harshly, even the tiniest infants may conclude that they are not important enough to get attention. Such infants simply view their world as unfriendly and begin to see themselves as worthless.

Basic mistrust is soon revealed in behavior. Infants whose physical needs, such as nourishment and touch, are not satisfied react with prolonged crying. Ainsworth (1973) found that the amount and frequency of infants' crying reflect the degree of responsiveness that the parents have shown the child. Poor parental response increases the infant's crying episodes. Such infants believe that no one will come to them (Ainsworth, 1979).

Once infants adopt the orientation of mistrust, the environment works to reinforce it. In time, the child's caretakers come to view the child as cranky and unreasonably demanding. They scold and pick up the infant only in desperate attempts to quiet the child. Basic mistrust leads to self-defeating behavior, with a reduced sense of self-esteem and an inability to deal positively with others. Once entrenched, this transactional pattern between adults and infants affects the emotional development of the infant and the emotional responses of the adults.

Every culture inculcates its general rules through its child-rearing practices. Caretakers are influenced by their own socialization, cultural norms, environmental influences, and vision of an ideal parent. By receiving the child learns how to become the giver; thus, mutuality and reciprocity are established. Erikson (1978) ties the capacity for trust to the basic human strength of hope. "Hope is the enduring belief in the attainability of primal wishes, in spite of the dark urges and rages which mark the beginnings of existence and leave a lasting residue of threatening estrangement" (p. 26).

A psychosocial crisis at the infancy stage indicates tension between the developmental needs of the infant and the social expectations of his or her culture. According to Erikson, if everything does not go well in one stage of development, an individual does possess the ability to compensate for the setback by reworking the conflict during that period or at a later point in life. There are extreme cases, though, in which parents grossly neglect their infant. They leave the child with anyone they like; they do not bathe or feed the child, treat the baby's wounds, or protect the baby from danger. They may even express hostility toward the infant or refuse to communicate at all (Lyons-Ruth et al., 1987). Under such circumstances, infants discover painfully that their parents are not available for them, physically or psychologically (Egeland & Stroufe, 1981). This makes later compensation difficult or impossible.

The child's sense of identity gradually evolves through his or her mutual relationships with caretakers:

> Jane is a sad child. Neglected and abused, she's placed in a foster home at 18 months of age. She habitually withdraws from all human contact and shrieks when touched. Her foster parent learns to approach Jane by cooing and babbling in a soft voice, which seems to puzzle but not provoke the child. Jane's behavior continues to reveal lack of trust, but as time passes and she is well fed and treated with affection, Jane begins to break through her fears in small degrees and respond to the new parent differently, without fear and pain.

Jane's case proves two points: first, that the damage was not permanent; the child was removed from her harmful environment at a crucial time in her life and began to compensate and grow positively. Second, the interplay of person and environment is of obvious importance.

*Infancy and ritualization*    Erikson discusses *ritualization* and its effects on the infant and the caretaker. A daily ritual takes place between the infant and his or her chief caretaker. From the moment of waking, the infant evokes in the chief caretaker a whole repertoire of verbal, emotional, and manipulative behaviors. The caretaker approaches the child with a smiling or worried look, is either happy or anxious, and voices his or her opinions accordingly while commencing the morning routine. Through feelings, sight, and smell, the caretaker determines whether the baby is comfortable or uncomfortable and offers such services as changing, feeding, rearranging the infant's position, or picking the baby up. The caretaker feels obliged, if not a little pleased, to repeat a performance that arouses a predictably positive response in the infant, which in turn encourages the caretaker's agreeable behavior. Thus daily events between the chief caretaker and the child become a highly individualized ritual.

Ritual also takes place when a child is given a name. Name-giving ceremonies are usually considered significant by parents and extended family, as well as the larger community. The child also learns special names for caretakers. This arrangement has a special meaning in human ritualization; it is based on the mutuality of the physical and emotional needs of infant and caretaker, which becomes the fundamental basis for assimilating culture (Erikson, 1977).

*Autonomy versus doubt and shame*   As identified by Erikson (1980), the second stage of development in the life cycle, young childhood, is characterized by the quest for autonomy. As his or her muscles mature, the child moves toward three new activities: walking, achieving bowel and bladder control, and talking. Muscle control allows the child to engage his or her will in "holding on" and "letting go"—the mechanics of retention and elimination. These activities empower the child with a sense of autonomy. During this period, children become aware of their separateness. Through many experiences they learn that their parents do not always know what children want and do not always understand their feelings. This insight leads to a feeling of delight in their sense of self.

Toilet training plays an important role in the development of autonomy. If a child's parents are restrictive, rigid, and punitive about toilet training, the child may rebel by refusing to exercise the necessary control over bladder and bowel movements. Unfortunately, children defeat

their own purposes through this tactic, for they thereby deny themselves the growing sense of autonomy that accompanies control. As Erikson (1980) puts it, children are faced with a "double rebellion and a double defeat." Such children cannot be sure of themselves.

Other experiences also figure in the child's struggle for autonomy. Early on, children use primitive devices to explore their independence. For instance, they learn to say no to everything offered to them, whether they like it or not. This behavior is typical of the period called the terrible twos. Later in the development of autonomy, the emphasis changes from a somewhat rigid, nay-saying, ritualized style to an independent, energetic, persistent style of action. The older child's behavior is characterized by the assertion "I can do it myself." If children are allowed to experiment with autonomy, they develop a strong foundation of self-confidence and a delight in behaving independently.

The establishment of a sense of autonomy during childhood requires not only tremendous effort by the child but also extreme patience and support from significant others. The parents have to learn to cajole, teach, absorb insults, wait, and praise. At times, parents allow children to try things the children are not yet able to do. Only with constant encouragement from their parents do children continue to engage in new tasks, gaining a sense of competence when they succeed. Some parents constantly discourage and criticize their children, whose feelings of self-confidence and self-worth are then replaced by constant self-doubt.

Developing an overwhelming sense of shame and self-doubt to cope with stress is the negative resolution of the psychosocial crises of childhood. Young children who arrive at this resolution lack confidence in their ability to perform, and they expect to fail at what they do. Shame is the result of such feelings. The experience of shame is extremely unpleasant, and in order to avoid it children may refrain from participating in new activities. Thus learning new skills becomes a difficult task.

Two-year-old Neal and his parents suffer many problems. His father is an alcoholic, and his mother spends a lot of time away from home working at odd jobs. Neal's older sister, scarcely 8 years old, takes care of his needs. All family members are unnecessarily strict and harsh with Neal. At his young age, Neal has learned how to get his family's attention—by wetting himself. Though it makes his sister and parents angry, it gets him their negative attention. The more they reveal their disapproval of him, the more wetting he does. Toilet training has become a game to him, in which failure brings rewards.

When children take on new tasks and fail in them, caregivers need to help them understand that failure is not disaster—that they can safely take a chance and try again. This lesson has to be learned in all areas of development and reaffirmed throughout adult life.

## White: The Competence Model

Robert White (1963) applies the competence model to the normal development of the child. In their early dealings with the environment, says White, children have to learn to cope and adapt to their new surroundings. Infants' lives are dominated by imperatives such as hunger and by acute discomforts such as wetness.

*Coping*    Coping behavior consists of active efforts to resolve stress and create new solutions to the challenges of each developmental stage. White (1976) identifies three components of the coping process: (1) the ability to gain and process new information, (2) the ability to learn and maintain control over one's emotional state, and (3) the ability to move freely within one's environment. Further, coping behavior allows the individual to develop and grow rather than maintain equilibrium or become disorganized in the face of threat.

White's theory explains how people develop new, original, and inventive behaviors. It also helps us predict such behaviors, or at least that they will in some form occur in people's active social lives.

For infants, coping behavior involves improving their ability to do what they do well—crying and sucking. These actions produce consequences. The arrival of the nipple and the more rapid intake of milk may be presumed to give the infant a feeling of efficacy. Having been swamped by hunger, the infant's feelings of efficacy are impossible to untangle from those of gratification; therefore, gains in competence, if they occur, must be attributed to the transaction as a whole. In this transaction, the infant deals with stress by coping and adapting in meaningful ways that offer him or her satisfaction and gratification (White, 1963).

*Competence*    During the oral period, development is seen in terms of feeding and its effects on the personality of the infant. White indicates that as infants get older, they find meals increasingly entertaining; they investigate the utensils and play with their food. These behaviors affect their personalities positively, and they develop competency.

Playtime is also an important factor in development. Gesell's (1940) typical day for an infant shows an hour of play before breakfast, two hours before lunch, two hours during the afternoon, and maybe an hour of play before bedtime. Thus, when infants are 1 year old they are spending as much as 6 hours a day in play, not to mention play during meals and bath.

What happens during playtime? At first, visual exploration is the most concentrated form of activity, although babbling and gross motor movements also take place. Halfway through the first year, the child learns to grasp and is eagerly intent on playing. In the realm of social competence, children participate in social play because they have the opportunity to do something interesting with their environment. Exploratory play follows White's competence model: Children's active interactions with their surroundings start as fun but contribute steadily to the attainment of adult competence.

What types of competence does the child achieve through interacting with the environment? Consider locomotion: Children start as awkward toddlers, but by the middle of the second year they have become restless and get into everything. They experiment with their prowess by such stunts as walking backward or pushing their own carriages. Children's first upright steps may have been applauded, but their locomotor accomplishments soon become cause for parental despair and continue without the benefit of social reward. By their third birthday, children may display their astonishing gains by playing quite happily by themselves for long stretches of time. They engage in constant activity, carrying objects about, filling and emptying containers, tearing things apart and fitting them together, lining up blocks and eventually building with them, and digging and building in sandboxes. Such play may look meaningless to an adult, but it brings about a tremendous increase in the child's ability to deal with the physical world.

Because of their practiced maturing of general coordination and verbal capacity, children at 2 years reach a critical juncture in their ability to interact with their social environment: They attempt to exploit possibilities to increase their sense of social competence. At first their attempts appear to be somewhat crude and uncompromising. In their inexperience, children challenge rather forcefully their parents' sense of competence. These challenges are trying for parents. The temptation to prevail at all costs is powerful, not only for parents who would like to exercise authority but also for apostles of permissiveness who are startled to find such tyranny emerging in their young. In provoking these crises, how much sense of social competence can the child preserve? The child's first efforts to measure his or her efficacy against that of other people may leave quite a lasting impression on his or her confidence.

White views toilet training as another model for developing competence. During the anal period, and in some cases toward the end of it, children develop stubbornness, parsimony, and orderliness, which are necessary to prevent their being pushed around. The qualities of stubborn-

ness and parsimony emerge when they do because they depend on certain developmental achievements, namely, a sense of the constancy of objects and a continuity of play interests from day to day. Thus, White's perspective on human development is positive and competence based.

## Piaget: Cognitive Learning

The work of Jean Piaget (Flavell, 1963) concentrates on the cognitive development of children. His initial work was based on observations of his own children, following a variant of the case-study method. Children achieve cognitive learning by coping with and adapting to words, language, and nonverbal communication.

*Cognition* means knowing. As young people grow older, *knowing* comes to mean something more definite, certain, and lasting than immediate sense perception. Sometimes *cognition* can refer to the sum of mental abilities. According to Kaluger and Kaluger (1979), cognition includes imagination, perception, thought, reasoning, reflection, problem solving, and all verbal behavior. In infancy, cognition comes to be well developed, and this development is practically inseparable from that of the senses.

Piaget suggests that the child's cognitive development can be described in four main periods: (1) sensorimotor—infancy, or from birth to 2 years; (2) preoperational—ages 2 to 7; (3) concrete operations—ages 7 to 11; and (4) formal operations—age 11 through adulthood.

Piaget views the child as both an active and an interactive organism, whose behavior can be understood only in terms of the way it adapts to the world around it. Piaget emphasizes that the infant uses both assimilation and accommodation in adapting (Flavell, 1963). The development of assimilation and accommodation during the sensorimotor period has been cast into six successive stages, presented in the following sections.

*Stage I: Beginning of the systematic use of natural reflexes*   Estimated to begin during the first month of life, Stage I involves the increasingly smooth and systematic use of natural reflexes. The infant engages in "reflex exercises" such as blinking the eyes. For example, during the first few days of life, the infant gains competence in the sucking reflex, finding the nipple more readily when it slips out of his or her mouth. This improvement is called *functional assimilation;* it leads to *generalized assimilation* (in this case, the infant would suck on all kinds of objects) and *recognitive assimilation* (the baby would recognize the nipple as being different from other objects).

*Stage II: Primary circular reaction*    During Stage II, 4-month-old infants develop the habit of voluntarily putting their thumb into their mouth and keeping it there. This behavior differs from the reflexive thumb sucking seen in neonates; infants at this point recognize thumb sucking as a nursing activity. Systematic thumb sucking is a primary circular reaction—"primary" because the actual content of behavior has a biological base, and "circular" because the response is repetitive and appears to produce reinforcement.

*Stage III: Secondary circular reaction*    The secondary circular reaction begins when the child is between 4 and 8 months old. The child learns to make combinations or derivatives of primary reactions developed separately at an earlier time. For instance, shaking a rattle to hear the noise is a secondary circular reaction. The child has previously practiced reaching, grasping, and listening. Now the child learns to amalgamate these separate activities into a new and more complex behavioral sequence.

*Stage IV: Threshold of intelligent behavior*    During Stage IV, infants are at the threshold of intelligent behavior. Piaget notes that between 8 and 12 months infants seem to acquire truly instrumental behavior. He experimented with his son Laurent when the boy was 7 months and 13 days old. Piaget placed a toy in a visible location in front of the child and then covered it with a red pillow. Piaget found that visibility was not

essential to the child's locating the toy; Laurent found it under the red pillow. After some time, Piaget arranged two pillows, one red and one blue, and hid a toy under the red pillow while Laurent watched. Later he removed the toy, showed it to the child, and placed it under the blue pillow while the child watched. Then he asked Laurent to find the toy. Although the child had seen his father place the toy under the blue pillow, he looked only under the red pillow. The response of looking under a pillow represented the beginning of intelligent behavior, whereas the incorrect choice revealed the child's inability to recognize continuous processes. His consequent repetition of specific acts that had been successful in the past suggests that certain cognitive processes had not yet developed. Only when children are 12 to 18 months old will they learn to look under the blue pillow.

*Stage V: Tertiary circular reaction*    Between 12 and 18 months of age, infants begin to search for new means to reach objects. For example, the child sees an object on the rug and pulls on a near corner of the rug, drawing the object within reach. The child discovers that the movement of the rug also produces movement in the desired object. The use of this possibility is the milestone of Stage V. The basic idea may be discovered quite by accident, but the child then begins to experiment with the situation again and again. Repetition is neither absolutely stereotyped nor simply arbitrary. Instead the child seems to try out, in a more or less systematic way, variations in the newly discovered act to observe their effects (Piaget, 1971).

One of the most important accomplishments that generally occurs within this period is the infant's gradual gaining of the perceptual and mental ability to understand object permanence—the realization that objects are the same from one occasion to another. At first, infants think that when objects are out of sight they do not exist, but this idea disappears as children grow older. This lack of the concept of object permanence explains the excitement and delight of young children playing peekaboo. When they cover their eyes, what they have been looking at no longer exists. Uncovering their eyes, they are thrilled and happy to see the object again. The attainment of the concept of object permanence frees young children from total reliance on what they can see. This ability to hold the image of an object in the mind is the first step toward the beginning of complex representational thinking. The concept of object permanence is the fundamental building block of logical thought (Piaget, 1971).

*Stage VI: Schemata*   Stage VI begins when children are about 18 months old and lasts until age 2. The stage is characterized by an ability to combine various sorts of possibilities mentally to reach new and different solutions. During this period, the young child has begun to develop what Piaget refers to as *schemata*—miniature frameworks that enable the child both to fit and to manipulate new pieces of information and hence assimilate and accommodate the environment. At this time, the child's performance may be seen as the integration and completion of sensorimotor coordination; that is, as the rudiments of intelligence. The appearance of insightful behavior in infants marks the conclusion of one sort of cognitive development and the beginning of another—mental representation. Now the road for conceptual thinking is opened (Flavell, 1963).

Piaget stresses the organizing capacity of the intellect and uses it as an organizing principle in his theory of the personality. His cognitive theory focuses on the central organizing principles in higher animals and recognizes the partial autonomy of these principles, in the sense that a person interacts with, rather than simply reacts to, his or her environment. Erikson and White view the ego as an organizer, controlling motility and the perception of both the outer world and the self. The ego serves as a protective barrier against excessive external and internal stimuli. All these different theorists provide a balanced way of viewing the interactions of the person and the environment.

# THE BASIS OF SOCIAL RELATIONSHIPS

Infancy is a time when the first social bonds develop, forming the basis of later relationships. In this section, we shall explore how babies as well as their parents form attachments. We shall also see how separation can disrupt this bonding and introduce children to fear and grief. Finally, we shall look at the beginnings of personality development before moving on to issues of caretaking.

## Attachment

Attachment takes place between an infant and his or her significant others when they create a reciprocal relationship. This relationship forms the basis of human social relatedness.

*Defining the concept*   It is clear from the literature that the term *attachment* eludes definition. Cohen (1974) and Weinraub, Brooks, and Lewis (1977) have persuasively challenged most of the frequently preferred components of attachment definitions, and it has aptly been said that defining attachment is like trying to reach a platonic ideal. To illustrate some of these problems, note that Ainsworth (1963) distinguishes attachment, dependency, and object relations. She stresses that the hallmark of attachment is behavior that promotes proximity to or contact with the specific figure or figures to whom a person is attached. Ainsworth's concept of attachment appears markedly similar to what others call *dependency* (see Maccoby & Masters, 1970). In fact, Maccoby and Masters believe that dependency has a technical meaning that includes the same kind of behaviors that other authors such as Bowlby (1969) would call attachment.

The definition of attachment used throughout the remainder of this book represents an integration of diverse conceptions of attachment to form a consensus. As such, our definition has five components. If we proceed from the top, each successive component has progressively less consensus in the literature. The following, taken together, indicate attachment (Bowlby, 1969):

1. A person behaves in a way that secures or maintains proximity or contact.
2. This behavior is shown to one specific person or a few.
3. It elicits reciprocal behaviors in, or secures the presence of, such other(s).
4. The absence of reciprocal behaviors produces an aversive state (shown through distress behavior) for the person showing the attachment behavior.
5. The aversive state may lead this person to seek alternative attachment opportunities among his or her broader social network.

When psychologists and social workers apply the term *attachment* to infants, they usually mean that the infant directs most of his or her behavior—touching, reaching to be picked up, holding on, and clinging—toward a particular person, the chief caretaker (in most instances, the mother). The parent-child attachment, like any other, is reciprocal: Parents and infants become attached to each other.

How do parents become attached to their babies? For beginners, they see babies as "cute": Chubby cheeks and rounded profiles appeal to adults (Alley, 1981). Another important signal, smiling, is initially a reflexive response to almost any stimulus that could be triggered by voices at 3 weeks of age and by faces at 5 to 6 weeks of age (Bowlby, 1969; Wolff, 1963). When children begin to coo and babble, their parents can enjoy back-and-forth "conversations" with them (Keller & Scholmerich, 1987; Stevenson, VerHoeve, Roach, & Leavitt, 1986).

Caregivers and infants develop synchronized routines, similar to Erikson's rituals, in which partners turn to and respond to each other's leads (Stern, 1977; Tronick, 1989). These smooth interactions are likely to develop if the caregiver limits the social interaction to periods when the infant is alert and receptive and not tired and overstimulated. As Tronick indicates, the over-tired infant will fuss instead of responding, as if to say, "Cool it—I need a break from all this stimulation" (1989, p. 112). Further, Tronick describes an instance of this synchronous dance, a mother playing peekaboo with her child:

> The infant abruptly turns away from his mother as the game reaches its "peak" of intensity and begins to suck on his thumb and stare into space with a dull facial expression. The mother stops play and sits back watching. . . . After a few seconds the infant turns back to her with an inviting expression. The mother moves closer, smiles, and says in a high-pitched, exaggerated voice, "Oh, now you're back!" He smiles in response and vocalizes. As they finish crowing together, the infant reinserts his thumb and looks away. The mother again waits. [Soon] the infant turns . . . to her and they greet each other with big smiles. (1989, p. 112)

In short, infants play an important role in persuading parents to love them. They are equipped with physical appeal and many reflexes that promote attachment. Infants respond to their caretakers and can synchronize their behavior to that of their "dance partners."

*Behavior and preferences*  One can distinguish between attachment and affiliative behaviors (Lamb, 1977). Affiliative behaviors occur at a distance; for example, smiling, looking, talking, showing, or pointing. Unlike attachment, they involve no physical contact. For infants, attachment and not affiliative behavior reduces stress, a difference that, to Lamb, proves that the distinction is real. Ainsworth (1973), however, claims that these two classes of behavior reflect different qualities of attachment rather than distinct kinds of social behavior.

Kotelchuck (1972) exposed various groups of infants, ranging in age from 6 to 21 months, to 13 different episodes involving their father, their mother, or a stranger, alone or in combination, in a modified "strange situation" procedure—that is, an unfamiliar situation. Kotelchuck focused on the effects of the departure of an adult on the infant's playing, crying, and touching. For all measures, the infants at 6 months and 9 months showed essentially no differences in behavior as a result of who left the room, implying that in this situation they had no attachment preferences for father, mother, or stranger. A clear pattern appeared with 12-month-old infants: They showed more distress when the mother left than when the father left, and relief when the stranger left. For example, play increased and crying decreased when the stranger left, but the opposite occurred when the mother or father left. Attachment peaked in all measures at either 15 or 18 months and declined in all thereafter (Kotelchuck, 1972).

Studies done by Cohen and Campos (1974) with 10-, 13-, and 16-month-old infants of white middle-class families attained results consistent with those of Kotelchuck. Studies by Dunn (1976) showed that 1-year-olds exhibited greater attachment to their mothers than to their fathers, but by 2½ years of age this difference disappeared.

From these studies, we can conclude that between 6 and 9 months, infants show no attachment preferences for parents or strangers; by 10 months, they prefer mothers to fathers and fathers to strangers. These strong preferences reach a maximum when the child is between 15 and 18 months of age. At 2 years of age, infants show essentially equal attachment behaviors toward both parents, still preferring them to strangers. These conclusions are based on group averages; in every experiment, some 10-month-old infants preferred their father to their mother. Being separated from their chief caretaker makes the children feel distressed, particularly in unfamiliar environments. When reunited with their mother, they usually calm down. Infants are unlikely to become scared when with their chief caretaker; they also can be more easily soothed. Finally, they are more likely to seek attachment when hungry, tired, bored, or afraid.

Is there a critical period for attachment and a specific time during infancy when the infant develops a strong, well-differentiated preference for one person? Soon after the infant's birth, the parents' attachment to the infant becomes specific: the parents would not be willing to replace their own child with any other child of similar age. Infants, on the other hand, require some time before they are developmentally ready to form a genuine attachment to another human being. They progress through the following phases as they develop ties with their own caregivers (Ainsworth, 1973; Bowlby, 1969):

1. *Undiscriminating social responsiveness* begins at birth and lasts up to 2 to 3 months. At this time young infants respond to voices, faces, and other social stimuli and to any human being who would interest them. They do not show a clear preference for one person over another.

2. *Discriminating social responsiveness* occurs between 2–3 months and 6–7 months. During this period infants begin to express preferences for familiar people. They direct their attention, their biggest grins, and most enthusiastic babbles toward those companions and are still quite friendly to strangers.

3. *Active proximity seeking/true attachment* falls between 6–7 months and about 3 years. At 6 or 7 months, infants form their first clear attachment, most often with their own mothers. The infant will crawl and follow his or her mother to stay close to her, protest when the mother leaves, and greet her warmly when she returns. The infant continues to form attachments to other significant others until age 3 or so.

4. *Goal-corrected partnership* takes place when a child is 3 years or older. Because children at this age have relatively advanced cognitive skills, they can take a parent's goals and plans into consideration and adjust their behaviors accordingly to keep close to the parent. Thus a 1-year-old will protest, cry, and try to follow when Dad leaves the house to talk to a neighbor. A 4-year-old, though, can understand that the father is going out to meet the neighbor; the child can control his or her attention until Dad returns. This final partnerlike phase of attachment lasts a lifetime.

Because much research has focused on maternal attachment, interest has increased in the attachment behavior of fathers. Greenberg, Morris, and Lind (1973) have used the term *engrossment* (absorption, preoccupation, and interest) to describe the powerful impact of a newborn on his or her father. They have identified several specific aspects of the father's developing bond to his newborn, ranging from his attraction to the infant and his perception of the newborn as perfect to extreme elation and an increased sense of self-esteem.

Parke (1974) observed parents in three different situations: the mother and father each alone with their 2- to 4-day-old infant and the father, mother, and infant together (triadic interaction) in the mother's hospital room. Strikingly, Parke's studies do not reveal any significant behavioral differences between fathers alone with their infants and mothers alone with their infants. In a triadic situation, the father tends to hold the infant nearly twice as much as the mother, vocalizes more, touches the infant slightly more, and smiles significantly less than the mother. When both parents are present, the father plays the more active role, in contrast to the cultural stereotype of the father as a passive participant (Parke, 1974).

*Cultural factors* Most of the research on attachment focuses on studies of middle-class Euro-American families. Their infants are typically raised in nuclear families and taken care of primarily by a single person, the mother. By focusing on two-parent families, such research overlooks other family lifestyles. In single-parent families, bonding takes place between one parent and the child. In extended families having more than one caretaker, children may become attached to a primary caretaker who is not their parent.

Clearly, cultural factors affect bonding. Klaus and Kennell (1976) studied infants' attachment behavior toward mothers and fathers in the Latino culture of Guatemala. Latinos belong to Spanish-speaking cultures of Indian-European stock. The families in this experiment lived in a small city and had a low socioeconomic status. The infants studied varied in age—9, 12, 18, and 24 months. Basically the infants' play behavior, crying, closeness, and searching were observed following the comings and goings of any adult.

Infants of all ages played more with either parent than with strangers. Crying increased when parents departed and decreased when strangers departed. Moreover, just as the data shows, infants at 24 months exhibited few differences in attachment to the three adults but marked differences at 18 months. Two major discrepancies between the Euro-American and Latino data stand out. First, unlike the former infants, 9-month-old Latino babies showed attachment. Further findings suggest that this could be true because Latino babies are much less frequently separated from their mothers than are Euro-American infants. Second, Latino infants were not as strongly attached to their fathers as were the latter. Findings note that Latino fathers spend much less time with their infants than do Euro-American fathers.

In a study of attachment behavior among the children of Israeli *kibbutzim,* or collective farms (Fox, Aslin, Shea, & Dumais, 1980), the infants were either 8–10, 12–15, or 21–24 months of age. Besides their mothers, there was a chief caretaker, the *metapelet.* All the infants had been cared for by metapelets for at least four months prior to testing. In the kibbutz, infants were brought to an "infant house" four days after birth, where they were placed in the care of the metapelet. Mothers spent as much time as possible there for the first 6 weeks and then gradually returned to work. As the mothers spent less time with their infants, the metapelet spent more. When the infants reached 3 or 4 months, they were placed with another metapelet, who cared for them until they reached age 3. During that period children had a daily 3-hour visit with both parents at their home. Job training and maternity leave caused a high rate of turnover amount the metapelets. Thus there was some variability in the amount of time the infants had been cared for by a particular metapelet.

This situation provided a good opportunity for studying the attachment behavior of infants toward adults. The researchers found few differences in behavior toward the three adults for infants 21 to 24 months old, marked differences for those 12 to 15 months old, and small differences for those 8 to 10 months old. During separation, infants displayed equivalent levels of attachment to mother and metapelet, both substantially greater than toward a stranger. During reunion, infants showed greater attachment to their mothers than toward the metapelet, and greater toward either than toward the stranger.

These studies suggest that infants reared in environments that are normal for a particular culture reveal attachment behavior toward their primary caretakers. The extent of the attachment depends on how enjoyable and extensive their interactions have been. Cuddling, hugging, and playing with the infant contribute to such enjoyment.

*Mutuality*  Though attachment develops at various times in a person's life, the first relationship, the infant-caretaker bond, appears to lay the ground for future development. Further, attachment behavior depends on infants' perceptual range and on their ability to understand the events in their world, which lead to changes in the way attachment takes place (Bowlby, 1969).

How does attachment behavior begin? The chief caregiver feeds the baby, changes his or her diapers, and satisfies his or her other physical needs. Infants appear to invite nurturant responses from the caregiver. Some researchers have suggested that during the first few days after birth, the caregiver and infant are highly receptive to cues from each other and that their early interactions determine the type of future relationship they will have.

This early mutual behavior may thus lay the foundation for long-term patterns of interaction. For instance, caregivers who respond promptly and consistently to infants in the first few months of life are likely to have infants who cry less than others by the end of the first year. Another result is the degree of confidence babies develop from the effectiveness of their communications. With inconsistent care, infants do not develop confidence; instead, they themselves become inconsistent and less responsive. When the caretaker creates a secure relationship, the infant develops a basis for establishing other competencies, such as active exploration, early mastery in play, and meaningful relationships with others in the immediate environment.

Touching, eye-to-eye contact, odor, body heat, body movements, and voice tones are all reciprocal behaviors that result in attachment. Bowlby (1969) explains a child's attachment to his or her mother in terms of a tendency he calls *monotropy:* the tendency of instinctual responses to be directed toward a particular person or group of individuals and not promiscuously toward many people.

How do adults become attached to their infants? For 12 months, Klaus and Kennell (1976) studied factors that led to parents' attachment to an infant and came up with seven crucial components of attachment:

1. The period just after a child is born is particularly crucial. Because attachment is a structured process, parents must have immediate close contact with their newborn to optimize later development.
2. The human mother and father (caretakers) appear to make a species-specific response to their infant when they first see him or her.
3. The process of attachment is so structured that parents will become optimally attached to one child at a time (the inverse of monotropy). If there are twins, there is attachment to one child, then the other.
4. For a mother to become attached to her infant, the infant must respond to the mother by some signal, such as body or eye movements. As Klaus and Kennell (1976) put it, "You cannot love a dishrag."
5. Individuals who witness the birth process become strongly attached to the infant.
6. Some people find it difficult to go through attachment and detachment simultaneously;

that is, to develop an attachment to one person while mourning the loss or threatened loss of another. Therefore the timing of birth in relation to other events may have long-lasting effects.

7. Anxiety about the well-being of a baby with a temporary disorder in the first day of life may result in enduring concerns that cast long shadows and adversely shape the development of the child.

No form of behavior is accompanied by stronger feelings than attachment behavior. The people toward whom it is directed are loved, and they are greeted with signs of happiness and joy. Loss of the attachment, or the threat of loss, creates anxiety; actual loss causes sorrow and often anger. The next section explores these responses in relation to separation.

## Separation

As soon as infants experience the pleasures of love, they also begin to discover the agonies of fear. One such fear is *separation anxiety*. When a child has developed a close relationship with a caretaker, separation from the caretaker causes a three-stage reaction in the child: protest, despair, and detachment (Bowlby, 1980a, 1980b). During the protest period, children may refuse to be separated from their caretaker. They reveal their tension by crying, kicking, and banging their heads. Second, children lose all hope and cry monotonously with despair but not anger. As children lose hope, they become very quiet. As time passes, separated children proceed to the third stage, when they accept attention from all people who are part of their environment. Interestingly, they show no special attraction to a former primary caretaker who visits them; instead, they may react to this person with disinterest or detachment. Bowlby views detachment as a form of the defense mechanism that is a regular part of mourning at any stage in the life cycle.

Separation anxiety usually appears at the time a baby is forming his or her first genuine attachment. It peaks at 14 to 18 months and then grad-

ually becomes less frequent and less intense throughout infancy and the preschool period (Kagan, 1976; Weinraub & Lewis, 1977).

The child's detachment from the mother correlates highly and significantly with the length of separation. A child who has been separated from his or her mother for a long period does not respond to her when the reunion takes place. Many mothers returning after separation are puzzled and wounded by this reaction; even when hurt, the child does not attempt to seek the mother's comfort.

We can conclude that long-term detachment of an infant from his or her chief caretaker has negative effects on the infant, which reverberate to the caretaker. Furthermore, the relationship between caretaker and infant is based on mutuality and reciprocity; each needs feedback from the other to maintain a meaningful relationship.

> Betty, a 24-year-old woman from the inner city, has many problems. Her only source of joy is her 18-month-old, Kristie. One day, everything goes wrong. Her boyfriend beats her up. When she goes home to her mother's, where she lives off and on, her stepfather, who has previously attempted to seduce her, beats her up on the pretext that she has been on the streets the whole day. Her only love is Kristie, but before she can make any attempt to see the child, her stepfather throws Betty out. In a short while, Betty is arrested for prostitution. Nobody bothers to bail her out. One month passes. She misses her baby, but nobody hears her pleas. She tells her story again and again, begging to see her child. Eventually, with the help of the jail's social worker, she gets a chance to vent her feelings. After a month and a half, she goes home, only to face the greatest disappointment of all—Kristie looks through her as if she does not exist.

As this case shows, separation is not always planned. Illness, unforeseen circumstances, or accidents can bring about separation. The infant's failure to understand can cause tremendous pain on both sides.

A second fearful response that often emerges at this age is *stranger anxiety;* that is, a fretful and uneasy reaction to the approach of an unfamiliar person. Most children react positively to strangers until they form their first attachment and then become wary of strangers. Anxious reactions to strangers are often mixed with signs of interest, which become common at 8 to 10 months of age and then gradually decline over the second year (Stroufe, 1977). Ainsworth (1973) and her colleagues emphasize that an attachment figure serves as a secure base for exploration. For example, at a neighbor's house, little Charles can check back occasionally to make sure his mother is still there, but he may stop exploring when she "disappears" briefly into the bathroom.

## Development of Personality

A concept of self begins to develop in infancy, when the child starts to differentiate himself or herself from the environment. By the age of 1, most infants indicate genuine interest in self-recognition. However difficult it is to determine when infants gain a sense of themselves as separate from the world, we get a first glimpse of this capacity in babies' first two or three months of life (Samuels, 1986; Stern, 1983). For example, 8- to 12-week-old babies whose arms and legs are connected by strings to mobiles and audiovisual equipment delight in producing interesting sounds and sights by pulling and kicking (Lewis, Alessandri, & Sullivan, 1990; Rovee-Collier, 1987). But when these strings are pulled and they no longer produce such effects, the infants pull and kick harder, becoming frustrated and angry (Lewis et al., 1990). This implies that they have a sense of self and recognize that they do exist apart from and can act on other people and objects.

Infants also take part in mirror play. As thought and self-awareness develop, children come to think of themselves as being tall, strong, talkative, healthy, slow, dull, awkward, and so on. Obviously children make these self-references because of their earlier learning experience.

Another way of understanding self-awareness in a child is to assess the child's use of personal pronouns: *I, my,* and so forth. Observing children ages 13 to 24 months, Kagan (1981) found a significant increase in 19- to 24-month-olds, in the use of both self-referent words and words to accompany action. For example, while climbing onto a tall chair, a little girl described her actions by saying, "Up." In a recent study of 2-year-old boys, Levine (1983) found that those who had a more advanced sense of self (measured by mirror and pronoun use) interacted more positively with other 2-year-olds than those who had a less mature view of themselves. Levine concluded that the possessiveness of a 2-year-old actually may reflect the child's attempt to interact socially with another child and thus develop greater self-awareness. The sense of self that develops in infancy increases in complexity with cognition and social maturity. As children grow older, they become more self-assertive.

Adults also influence children's personality development. Charles Cooley (1902) and George Herbert Mead (1934) were among the first to recognize the crucial role of social interactions. Cooley coined the term *looking-glass self* to emphasize that our understanding of self is a reflection of how other people respond to us, and our self-concepts are images cast by a social mirror. Through actions and words, parents and other caretakers communicate to infants that they are infants as well as boys or girls.

Social feedback helps children determine what they like and who can and cannot do well. Later, they forge new self-concepts through their social interactions. This development of self and social development combined with beginning cognitive development are closely intertwined in infancy.

By the end of infancy, children who have formed secure attachments with their parents recognize themselves in a mirror better and know more about their names and genders than do infants whose relationships are less secure (Pipp, Easterbrooks, & Harmon, 1992).

## CARETAKING ISSUES

Clearly, the social environment impacts how infants behave and how they see themselves and others. Now, we shall take a closer look at how caretaking affects development. Who watches over children, for how long, and in what circumstances all strongly affect who a child will become. Specifically, we shall explore how parental roles, day care, minimal caretaking, and abuse can influence infant development.

## Parental Roles

All parental actions play a part in shaping a child's personality. Infants cope, adapt, and develop in response to adults' actions toward them, whether the actions are purposeful or unintentional. The warmth or hostility of the parent-child relationship can be understood with reference to acceptance or rejection, the control or autonomy of the disciplinary approach (that is, restrictiveness or permissiveness), and the parents' disciplinary consistency.

*Mothers*   Society sees the newborn child as an extension of the mother, who has to live up to certain expectations of society. That is, mothers are usually judged by how their children follow the social norms of growth and behavior. The mother is expected—intuitively—to anticipate, elicit, and respond to phase-specific behavior of the child. During the child's first few months, the mother is expected to respond to his or her every need. The mother is the object of a symbiotic relationship: She is expected to shield the baby, mediate between the baby and excessive stimulation, and reciprocate the child's first efforts at playing and taking initiative. After the baby's sixth month, she is expected to accept both the assertiveness of the baby and the demands that she alone can meet.

The common assumption is that the mother's role comes naturally to all women. In reality, this is not true. Mothering is a trial-and-error process in which the mother learns to understand and take care of the baby. Some women find this role self-actualizing, but others do not.

Some studies of temperament have explored the relationship between maternal behavior and maternal ratings of a child's temperamental "difficultness." Kelly (1976) found that maternal ratings of difficult temperament were related to negative mother-infant interactions. However, a study by Bates (1977) found no significant relationship between maternal ratings of "difficultness" and maternal behavior. In a more recent study on the relationship between maternal perception and maternal behavior in a "normal" group of 9-month-old infants and their mothers, Never, Shore, Timberlake, and Greenspan (1984) found that the mothers tended to perceive their babies accurately and responded appropriately to their cues. Nevertheless, certain distortions did appear between the mothers' perceptions and their babies' behavior, as a consequence of which the others' behavior became less responsive and more interfering. This maternal response correlated with the anxiety level of the mothers; in addition, these distortions were associated with sleeping difficulties among the children. This study suggests that there is a range of normal interactions between mothers and infants. Further, some perceptual distortion, proceeding from feelings, is inherent in normal interpersonal interactions. Future research may help identify the point at which maternal misperceptions become pathological and the differences, if any, in the nature of distortions among pathological and normal groups.

A study was made of maternal stress and social support and their effects on maternal-infant relationships from the infant's birth to the age of 18 months. Social support is generally considered to encompass several dimensions, among them instrumental assistance, the provision of information, and empathy. In this study, Henderson, Byrne, and Duncan-Jones (1981) proposed that social support to reduce maternal stress operates on many ecological levels, including intimate relationships, friendships, and less formal neighborhood or community contacts. Having such a support framework theoretically indicates that the individual is cared for, loved, and valued, as well as belonging to a network of mutual obligation. Further, Cochran and Brassard

(1979) claim that social support networks outside the nuclear family influence parental attitudes and behavior and, in turn, have both direct and indirect effects on child development.

Crnic, Greenberg, Regazin, Robinson, and Basham (1983) studied an initial sample of 105 mother-infant pairs. Of the 105 infants, 52 were premature (born after less than 38 weeks of gestation and having a birth weight of less than 1800 grams) and 53 were full term (39 to 42 weeks of gestation and a birth weight greater than 2500 grams). None of the infants revealed gross neurological or physical impairment. Infants were matched with other infants for family ethnicity and mother's education; that is, there was no significant difference within the group in mother's marital status, type of delivery, or child's gender or birth order. Mothers' perceived levels of stress and social support were found to be significant predictors of maternal attitudes and of the quality of interaction with their infants when measured concurrently across an 18-month period. However, long-term predictions were poor; maternal stress and support factors were only moderately stable. The quality of the infants' interactional behavior was also affected by levels of maternal stress and support, but only during the early measurement periods of 1 to 4 months.

*Fathers* Most research on child development has focused on the relationship between mother and child, paying little attention to the relationship between father and child. Research evidence shows that children who have frequent and regular contact with their fathers do form early attachments to them. The stronger the attachment, the more influence the father has on the child. Father-child interaction begun in infancy usually lasts through later childhood; fathers who are accessible to their infants may find it easy to establish strong emotional ties later. In U.S. culture, the father is often viewed as the secondary caregiver, but he does play an important role in the complex family interaction. A study by Clarke-Stewart (1978) of three-way patterns in families shows that the mother's influence on the child is direct, whereas the father's influence is indirect, through the mother. The child influences both parents directly. Studies show that fathers tend to be physical and spontaneous with their infants, and play between fathers and children occurs in cycles of high excitement and attention followed by periods of minimal activity.

When fathers become primary caretakers in U.S. society, they tend to act more as mothers do. They smile more at their infants, imitate their facial expressions, and vocalize with them more than secondary fathers do.

> Tom is a 27-year-old single parent. A year ago, he won a custodial court battle with his estranged wife, a drug addict. He is a caring, loving father. When his child develops pneumonia at age 2, Tom panics. Overly anxious about the child, as well as fearful that his former wife will use the situation against him, he becomes unable to function as a "normal" parent. The social worker at the Family and Child Center reassures him through emotional support, emphasizing that if a child is sick all that a parent can do is to take care of the child. If problems arise with his former wife, he will need to deal with them as they appear and not spend time anticipating trouble.

## Infants, Work, and Alternative Caregiving

Every day millions of preschool children attend day care or nursery schools. This phenomenon has increased tremendously with the advance of double-income families and single-parent households in the United States in the 1990s. Many parents have regrets about leaving their children in the care of others. Should parents worry about leaving their children in child-care centers? It depends on the age of the child. Beginning day care after children have passed their first birthday could benefit them (Kail & Cavanaugh, 1996). Children who spend time in early childhood programs are more self-confident, outgoing, and self-sufficient than those who do not (Clarke-Stewart & Fein, 1983). Sometimes these young children are less agreeable and less compliant, but this could be traced to greater emotional maturity.

When babies are below 1 year of age, however, many parents fear that the secure attachment to a parent may be disrupted by extended separation. When parents work full-time outside the home, approximately 60% to 65% of their children under age 1 form secure attachments, compared with 70% of children who have a parent who stays home the first year of their life (Lamb, Sterberg, & Prodromidis, 1992).

Several factors increase the possibility of an insecure attachment for working parents (Jaeger and Weinraub, 1990; Lamb, Sternberg, & Prodromidis, 1992):

1. *Number of hours in alternative care:* Insecure attachments are more likely when infants spend more than 20 hours per week with an alternative caregiver.
2. *Gender:* The attachment relationships of boys are more affected by alternative caregiving than girls.
3. *Birth order:* A firstborn child is more affected by alternative caregiving than children born later. The younger children often have a sibling at day care, whereas the firstborn is lonely.
4. *Quality of parenting:* The stress related to work can affect a parent's interactions with an infant. When a parent worries, suffers fatigue, feels guilt, or undergoes marital conflict as a result of employment, his or her caregiving can become less responsive.

## Multiple Mothering

In the United States the usual environment for raising children is the nuclear family, which consists of two parents and their children. The concept that mothering should be provided by one individual has been underscored by most professionals as the key to mental health. But many have found this view to be a culture-bound perspective, for throughout the world children are cared for in situations of multiple mothering, an arrangement in which responsibility for a child's care is distributed among several people.

Children usually adapt well to multiple mothering. Take again the example of kibbutzim. From early infancy, children in Israeli kibbutzim are reared in a nursery with other children by two or three professional caretakers. The responsibility for disciplining and punishment falls on these caretakers (Devereux et al., 1974), but the children's need for affection is usually satisfied by their mothers.

*Shared parenting* is an egalitarian arrangement whereby each parent works part-time and takes care of the child part-time. The child has alternate but consistent care from adults who have a lot in common in terms of family living. The child learns to accept and become part of this two-parent rearing pattern.

Studies of socially adequate staffed institutions in Russia and China as well as Israel reveal that babies cared for by many responsive caregivers appear as normal and well adjusted later in childhood as are infants reared at home (Bronfenbrenner, 1970; Kessen, 1975; Oppenheim, Sagi, & Lamb, 1988). Also, Efe (Pygmy) infants in Zaire seem to thrive right from birth while being cared and even nursed by a variety of caregivers besides their mothers (Tronick, Morelli, & Ivey, 1992). Thus infants do not need to form a strong attachment to just one mother figure to be healthy.

## The Unattached Infant

Some infants have limited contacts with adults during the first and second years of their life and do not appear to become attached to anyone. For example, some children who grow up in institutions reveal the symptoms of unattachment. In an understaffed institution, children may see a caregiver only during meals or when changed or bathed. Quite often, babies are seen as a "job," and the institutional staff have no time to play or love them. In some of these institutions the staff are overworked and underpaid. The caregivers rarely interact with the infants except to prop a bottle against their pillow at feeding time. The babies lie in separate cribs with sheets hung over the railings, in effect isolated from the world around them. They have no crib toys and compared to a typical home they receive very little social or sensory stimulation.

Infants raised in institutions appear to be normal for their first 3 to 6 months. They cry for attention, smile and babble, and make the proper postural adjustments when picked up. By the second half of the year, though, their behavior changes. They rarely cry, coo, or babble, and they appear to be depressed and uninterested in social contact (Provence & Lipton, 1962; Spitz, 1945). An early classic study by Goldfarb (1943, 1947) compared children who left an understaffed orphanage during the first year with similar children who spent the first three years of their life in an orphanage before departing to foster homes. Goldfarb interviewed, observed, and tested these children at 3½, 6½, 8½, and 12 years and found that the youngsters who had spent three years in the institution lagged behind early foster children in virtually all aspects of development. They did not do well in IQ tests, were not mature socially, were dependent upon adults, had poor language skills, were prone to behavior problems such as aggression and hyperactivity, and were often loners who had a difficult time relating to peers or family members.

In two other studies, Tizard (1977) and Hodges and Tizard (1989) compared similar groups of long-institutionalized and early-adopted children and found that many of the developmental impairments described by Goldfarb also characterized the late adoptees. Though the institutions in which Tizard's children lived were adequately staffed, the staff turnover was so high that the children were taken care of by 80 different caregivers; therefore, the children rarely became attached to any one adult in their first few years.

By 8 years of age, the children were intellectually normal and socially outgoing; many of them had even formed close emotional ties to a housemother or an adoptive parent. In spite of these encouraging signs, children who had spent about four years in an institution were more restless, disobedient, and unpopular in elementary school and were also more emotionally troubled and antisocial at age 16 than those who were adopted early in life. Thus it appears that prolonged institutionalization can have adverse effects that could be difficult to overcome.

Luckily, socially deprived children can overcome many initial handicaps if they are placed in homes where they receive a great deal of attention and affection from responsive caregivers (Clarke & Clarke, 1976; Rutter, 1981). Even children who have experienced social and emotional deprivation over the first 2 years of life show a strong capacity for recovery when they are placed in a stimulating home environment and receive individualized attention. Also, severely disturbed children who are adopted after spending several years in understaffed institutions show dramatic improvements, compared with those who remain in a barren institutional setting (Dennis, 1973; Rutter, 1981).

Less often, unattached children are brought up in families where they are reared by abusive and neglectful parents. In many cases, even if negativity surrounds the child, he or she develops attachments based chiefly on fear.

## Child Abuse and Neglect

*Factors of abuse*   Child abuse can be described as a nonaccidental physical attack on or injury to children by a legally older individual. Called the *battered child syndrome,* a pattern of such mistreatment of a child, typically by a caretaker, can result in abrasions, burns, fractures, concussions, and bruises. Abuse takes many forms (Zuraivin, 1991), including not only physical abuse but also sexual abuse, which involves fondling, intercourse, or other sexual behaviors, and psychological abuse, which involves ridicule, rejection, humiliation, and neglect. *Neglect* can be described as the absence of adequate emotional, social, and/or physical care. Shockingly, more than 2000 children die annually from abuse and neglect, and about 150,000 are seriously injured

(U.S. Advisory Board on Child Abuse and Neglect, 1995). Steele and Pollack (1968) found that, with few exceptions, abusive parents were raised in an authoritarian atmosphere, which they recreate for their own children.

Besides being raised in authoritarian families, parents who abuse their children were sometimes maltreated themselves (Simons, Whitbeck, Conger, & Chyi-In, 1991). Such parents set up high expectations for their children and do little to help them achieve these goals (Trickett, Aber, Carlson, & Cicchetti, 1991). They also rely on physical punishment to control their children (Trickett & Kuczynski, 1986).

Abusive parents come from all segments of the population: all socioeconomic strata, all levels of education and intelligence, and all religious and ethnic groups. Abusers do not fall into a single psychiatric diagnostic category but represent an entire spectrum of emotional disorders that one can see in any clinical population. The typical abusive person is often an unhappy individual who has limited social skills and may find it difficult to interact appropriately with children who are vulnerable as well as their dependents.

Culture also affects child abuse. For example, abuse is more common in a country like the United States where the physical punishment of children is accepted, as opposed to countries like Sweden where it is not (Zigler & Hall, 1989).

Abuse occurs relatively often in families living in poverty, because the lack of money increases the stress of daily life (Straus & Kantor, 1987). It occurs more as well in families that are socially isolated from relatives and friends. This isolation deprives the children of adults who can protect them (Garbarino & Kostelny, 1992).

*Breaking the cycle*    The topic of child abuse and neglect is particularly depressing because the practice is self-perpetuating. Children learn how to love from their parents, but if they are unloved and abused, they often in turn become abusive or unloving parents. However, Kempe, Silverman, Steele, Droegenmueller, and Silver (1962) found that about 80% of abusive parents could be helped so that they no longer physically punish their children. Both short-term and long-term help are widely available. Many cities have hot lines for parents to call when they are losing control, and some areas offer 24-hour crisis nurseries to relieve parents in need of a few hours of peace. Long-term help, in the form of individual and family therapy, is also offered to caretakers who seek it or are mandated by the family courts to receive it. Finally, nationwide attention to child abuse has made people aware of the problem and in some ways has effectively curbed it.

> Teresa is a single parent from a lower socioeconomic group. She has little money, no steady job, and no place to call home. About a year ago, she left Puerto Rico with the hope of finding a job and making it big in New York. Instead, her boyfriend deserted her a few months after they arrived, leaving her pregnant with Juan. Now, she can't forgive the child for being born; he is definitely unwanted. Her stress, already high, increases every time she gets turned down for a job. By the time Juan is 6 months old, she can't stand him. Her impulse control is minimal, and so she begins to batter him. Feeling tremendously guilty after each episode, she attempts to make it up to the child, but she can't stop her abuse. Eventually Juan winds up in the hospital. The social worker sees Teresa as a lonely, lost young woman who has difficulty communicating in English. The worker attempts to help Teresa secure a job and gives her information about where to leave her child if she needs a few hours of rest and time away from him. Thus with the help of an extremely empathetic worker, Teresa learns to make use of the center for temporary day-care services.

As this case shows, help can make all the difference in stopping abuse. Social workers can also teach family members effective ways of coping with situations that might otherwise trigger abuse (Wicks-Nelson & Israel, 1991). Certainly, using social support systems helps. When parents are aware that they can turn to other adults for advice and reassurance, they can more readily manage the stresses of child rearing that might otherwise lead to abuse.

## IMPLICATIONS FOR PRACTICE

Infancy is a significant period in a child's life. To maximize their understanding of its developmental issues, social workers need to be aware of factors such as child-rearing practices in various North American cultures, as well as racial, ethnic, and demographic factors.

Parents' expectations regarding children's autonomy and self-discipline vary with their lifestyle and background. For instance, studies show that working-class families tend to do less talking and explaining to their children and to use more physical methods of discipline than do middle-class parents; they also expect a greater degree of compliance from their children (D. R. Miller & Swanson, 1966). Behind this type of discipline is the assumption that it teaches children the most effective behaviors for the bureaucratic and technological world they will be entering. On the other hand, middle-class parents usually pass on to children their verbal and negotiating skills, which they themselves value, believing that they will help their children as they grow older.

Disciplinary techniques also vary according to ethnic and racial background. Native-American Indian children are usually disciplined nonverbally by a stern look or verbally by occasional teasing (D. Miller, 1979). Some African-American children may learn in their families that it is dangerous to challenge white authority openly or ask certain questions. Researchers also note social-class differences in child rearing within minority groups (Boutlette, 1978; Scanzoni, 1971).

In assessing a family, the social worker should take into account the number of children and caregivers in the family, as well as the degree of flexibility or rigidity that characterizes the family, because they have a bearing on the type of counseling offered. Another important consideration is the parents' ability to set limits and make schedules without creating too much stress. Social work practitioners are frequently faced with parents who describe their child as "a living monster." Usually, effective parenting helps a child deal well with discipline. When a child is described as "impossible," especially by a family with emotional problems, the worker often discovers that the parents actually do not want the toddler to relinquish the aggressive behavior, because it satisfies the needs of some adults in the family. In such cases, the child may not give up the difficult behavior; social workers need to make the interaction in the family the target of therapeutic help.

In offering help with toilet training, social workers can call on a wide range of methods, depending on the family's own child-rearing practices. Social workers see a variety of adult attitudes toward children's explorations of their bodies as well as toward their need for autonomy. Some parents may be harsh and severe in toilet training, imposing strict rules about all behaviors that require self-mastery and independence, including feeding, dressing, and general exploration. Other parents tend to be tolerant, flexible, and responsive to the child's needs. Some parents view "accidents" as intolerable and dirty; some are severe when a child breaks a plate or cup; some regard children's games in mud and sand as unhygienic. Social workers should remember all these factors when they deal with parents so as to offer help appropriately.

Social workers should help parents respond meaningfully to behavioral cues from their infants. Accordingly, practitioners should have an understanding of the developmental changes that take place in infancy. They should also be aware of women's needs, as well as women's expectations of themselves as mothers. Some may need more help than others to play the role of mother, and some may need an understanding of the infant's growth and development. One way social workers can help, then, is to teach parenting skills to clients or refer them to classes.

Under any conditions, the practitioner needs to have a holistic understanding of the growth and development of an infant and the influence of racial, ethnic, and social-class factors on the parent-child relationship. Social workers should also be aware of the support systems available to parents and children.

To round out this discussion, here are two case studies that demonstrate a few ways knowledge of infant development can help social workers deal with certain issues and problems. In the first, a social worker learns that child abuse knows no boundaries.

Jason is born with a delicate stomach and cannot digest food easily. He cries for long hours because his immature digestive system causes him pain. His mother chose to have a baby so she would have someone to love her always, but she is not "rewarded" by this baby. His father was never anxious to have a baby in the first place, though he went along with it.

Jason's parents are well-educated members of the upper middle class. The mother has a degree in the social sciences; the father is about to take his final exam in engineering. With his exam a week off, the father becomes exasperated whenever Jason starts to cry. The mother is already nervous because she never envisioned parenting as being so demanding. While the baby cries and her husband screams, she feels unloved by both of them. Overcome by the mounting stress, both parents abuse the child.

Frightened and ashamed, they bring their 9-month-old to a crisis intervention center for child abuse. The child's body shows large bruises as well as bone fractures. The mother cries silently. After the child goes to the emergency room, the parents are referred to a staff social worker.

The worker refers the parents to a support group for counseling, where they will be helped to understand their own limitations as well as their misconceptions about the baby. They genuinely regret their behavior, and the social worker gives them an emergency number to call in case they again became overwhelmed by stress.

Notice in the following case how the social worker deals with limited resources.

Jim is a 1-year-old boy. His father has just been arrested for drug dealing, and his mother wonders how she will get by. Several times, neighbors have found Jim whining and crying because he hasn't eaten in a couple of days. At last the child is brought to the notice of the Social Services Bureau.

In time, Jim is placed in a foster home. The available foster home, though, can't offer Jim the sense of permanence that he requires, and the social worker is not sure that any other home can. Meanwhile, the mother is overburdened with emotional turmoil, visits from the police, and lack of income. She is offered supportive services to help her deal with the loss of her husband and the circumstances of his arrest. She claims that she loves her son but that the unusual circumstances of the preceding few months caused her to neglect him. The social worker tries to maintain as much contact as possible between Jim and his mother and continues to assess the mother's potential for offering Jim an environment in which he can grow up meaningfully without danger to his development.

## CHAPTER SUMMARY

- The principles of infant development reveal that perceptual, cognitive, and social capacities are guided by genetic and environmental factors.
- During infancy, rapid growth and achievement take place in all areas of development. The link between social and individual processes is important even during infancy.
- Development proceeds by the basic principles of movement from mass activity to specific activity, differentiation, and integration.
- The biological, psychological, and social environment of the child affects the development of sensorimotor skills, locomotion, manual skills, and language, as well as physical habits such as feeding and sleep. The child responds to positive and negative environmental cues and copes with and adapts to stresses according to his or her potential as well as available supports.
- Human infants show emotion and also recognize and discriminate others' affective expressions.
- Erikson, a pioneer of developmental theory, discusses the beginning stages of human development—*trust versus mistrust* and

*autonomy versus doubt and shame.* Crises at these stages may be reworked and satisfactorily resolved later in life.

- White emphasizes that all infants have an innate drive to be competent and efficacious. Eating, toilet training, and playing are explorations of competence and efficiency.

- Piaget's theory divides the child's cognitive development into four major periods, the first of which is the sensorimotor period (from birth to 2 yeas of age). This is subdivided into six stages: (1) the beginning of systematic use of natural reflexes, (2) primary circular reaction, (3) secondary circular reaction, (4) threshold of intelligent behavior, (5) tertiary circular reaction, and (6) schemata. During the sensorimotor period, infants acquire concepts connected with the use of familiar objects. They express their potentialities in play and in their growing use of language.

- The infancy stage lays the ground for social relationships. In a secure attachment, a child explores new things as well as new people. Loss of attachment leads to serious consequences for the infant's personality development. A child who is not given the opportunity to develop a pattern of consistent responses with a primary caretaker will be unable to develop an attachment relationship.

- Children can suffer from separation anxiety, a three-stage reaction that includes protest, despair, and detachment, when a parent is not available to the child on a regular basis.

- Infants first show anxiety about separation when they are about 12 months old. Separation is part of the normal development of children as they learn to distinguish between familiar caregivers and strangers.

- Personality development begins when children start to distinguish themselves as separate individuals. Exploration begins when the child starts to feel secure. Self-assertiveness lays the foundation for meaningful personality development.

- All parental actions shape a child's personality. In particular, the roles mothers and fathers play, which depend on many variables such as culture, can affect how a child develops.

- As the number of working mothers increases, the need for alternative care also increases. Research has found that fathers have begun to play a more significant role in an infant's life than in the past.

- An unattached infant, who has had limited contacts with adults during the first and second years of his or her life, does not appear to become attached to anyone. Institutionalized infants often suffer from parental deprivation and an insufficiently stimulating environment.

- Child abuse and neglect are problems that affect some infants and parents, and consequently concern social workers.

- Social work practitioners must be aware of such factors as child-rearing practices, race, and ethnicity as they affect infants, their families, and their support systems. A holistic understanding of infancy provides a context for dealing with developmental issues.

## *SUGGESTED READINGS*

Bonkowski, S. E., & Yanos, J. A. (1992). Infant mental health: An expanding field for social work. *Social Work, 37*(2), 144–148.

Brink,, J. H. (1994). The effect of infant rearing practices on the personalities of children in Egypt. *Pre and Peri Natal Psychology Journal, 8*(4), 237–248.

Dunn, M. A. (1993). The peek-a-boo game. *Psychoanalytic Review, 80*(3), 331–339.

Guerin, D. W., & Gottfried, A. W. (1994). Temperamental consequences of infant dificultness. *Infant Behavior and Development, 17*(4), 413–421.

Marriott, J. A. (1992). Panic attacks and abandonment. *Australian Journal of Clinical Hypnotherapy and Hypnosis, 13*(1), 1–8.

Soref, A. R. (1992). The self, in and out of relatedness. *Annual Journal of Psychoanalysis, 20,* 25–48.

## SUGGESTED VIDEOTAPES

CBC (Producer). (1974). *Out of the mouths of babes* (28 minutes). Available from Filmmakers Library, 124 E. 40th St., Suite 901, New York, NY 10016; 212-808-4980

Concept Media (Producer). (1994). *Compliance, self-control and prosocial behavior* (27 minutes). Available from Concept Media, Inc., P.O. Box 19542, Irvine, CA 92623-9542; 800-233-7078; Email: info@conceptmedia.com; Website: www.conceptmedia.com

Concept Media (Producer). (1991). *Physical growth and motor development: The first two-and-a-half years* (19 minutes). Available from Concept Media, Inc., P.O. Box 19542, Irvine, CA 92623-9542; 800-233-7078; Email: info@conceptmedia.com; Website: www.conceptmedia.com

Dartmouth (Producer). (1993). *Multiple sclerosis: Mystery disease* (29 minutes). Available from Aquarius Productions, 5 Powerhouse Ln., Sherborn, MA 01770; 508-651-2963

Telepool (Producer). (1981). *Developing the sense of family* (21 minutes). Available from FFH (Films for the Humanities and Sciences), 11 Perrine Rd., Monmouth Junction, NJ 08852; 800-257-5126

Uniview Worldwide (Producer). (n.d.) *Language development* (40 minutes). Available from FFH (Films for the Humanities and Sciences), 11 Perrine Rd., Monmouth Junction, NJ 08852; 800-257-5126

## REFERENCES

Adolph, K. E., Eppler, M. A., & Gibson, E. J. (1993). Crawling versus walking infants' perception of affordances for locomotion over sloping surfaces. *Child Development, 64,* 1158–1174.

Ainsworth, M. D. S. (1963). Patterns of attachment behavior shown by the infant in interaction. In B. M. Foss (Ed.), *Determinants of infant behavior.* New York: Wiley.

Ainsworth, M. D. S. (1973). The development of infant-mother attachment. In B. M. Caldwell & H. N. Ricciuti (Eds.), *Review of child development research* (Vol. 3). Chicago: University of Chicago Press.

Ainsworth, M. D. S. (1979). Attachment as related to mother-infant interaction. In J. S. Rosenblatt, R. A. Hinde, C. Beer, & M. Busnal (Eds.), *Advances in the study of behavior* (Vol. 9). Orlando, FL: Academic Press.

Alley, T. R .(1981). Head shape and the perception of cuteness. *Developmental Psychology, 17,* 650–654.

Bates, J. (1977). The concept of difficult temperament. *Merrill-Palmer Quarterly, 26,* 211–226.

Belsky, J., & Tolan, W. (1981). The infant as producer of his development: An ecological analysis. In R. Lerner & N. N. Bush-Rossnagel (Eds.), *The child as producer of its own development: A life-span perspective.* New York: Academic Press.

Boutlette, T. T. (1978). The Spanish surnamed poor. In *Child welfare strategy* (OHDS 78-30158). Washington, DC: U.S. Department of Health, Education and Welfare.

Bower, T. G. R. (1987) *Development in infancy* (2nd ed.). New York: Freeman.

Bower, T. G. R. (1989). *The rational infant: Learning in infancy.* New York: Freeman.

Bowlby, J. (1969). *Attachment and loss: Vol. 1. Attachment.* New York: Basic Books.

Bowlby, J. (1980a). *Attachment* (Vol. 1). New York: Basic Books.

Bowlby, J. (1980b). *Loss* (Vol. 3). New York: Basic Books.

Bronfenbrenner, U. (1970). *Two worlds of childhood: U.S. and U.S.S.R.* New York: Russell Sage Foundation.

Bushnell, E. W., & Boudreau, J. P. (1993). Motor development and the mind: The potential role of motor abilities as a determinant of aspects of perceptual development. *Child Development, 64,* 1005–1021.

Campos, J. J., & Barrett, K. C. (1984). Toward a new understanding of emotions and their development. In C. E. Izard, J. Kagen, & R. B. Zajonc (Eds.), *Emotions, cognition and behavior* (pp. 229–263). Cambridge, England: Cambridge University Press.

Clark, J. E., & Phillips, S. J. (1993). A longitudinal study of intralimb coordination in the first year of independent walking: A dynamical systems analysis. *Child Development, 64,* 1143–1157.

Clarke, A. M., & Clarke, A. D. B. (1976). *Early experience: Myth and evidence.* New York: Free Press.

Clarke-Stewart, K. A. (1978). And daddy makes three: The father's impact on mother and young child. *Child Development, 49,* 466–478.

Clarke-Stewart, K. A., & Fein, G. G. (1983). Early childhood programs. In P. H. Mussen (Ed.), *Handbook of child psychology* (Vol. 2). New York: Wiley.

Cochran, M., & Brassard, J. (1979). Child development and personal social networks. *Child Development, 50,* 601–616.

Cohen, L. J. (1974). The operational definition of human attachment. *Psychological Bulletin, 81,* 207–217.

Cohen, L. J., & Campos, J. J. (1974). Father, mother, and stranger as elicitors of attachment behaviors in infancy. *Developmental Psychology, 10,* 146–154.

Cooley, C. H. (1902). *Human nature and the social order.* New York: Scribner's.

Cole, P. M. (1985). Display rules and the socialization of affective displays. In G. Zivin (Ed.), *The development of expressive behavior: Biology-environment interactions.* Orlando, FL: Academic Press.

Crnic, K. A., Greenberg, M., Ragazin, A., Robinson, W., & Basham, R. (1983). Effects of stress and social support on mothers and premature and full-term infants. *Child Development, 54,* 209–217.

Dennis, W. (1973). *Children of the crèche.* East Norwalk, CT: Appleton-Century-Crofts.

Devereux, E. C., Shouval, S., Bronfenbrenner, U., Rodgers, R. R., Veneki, K. V., Keely, S., & Kenson, E. (1974). Socialization practices of parents, teachers and peers in Israel: The kibbutz versus the city. *Child Development, 45.*

Dunn, J. E. (1976) mother-infant relations. Continuities and discontinuities over the first 14 months. *Journal of Psychosomatic Research, 20,* 273–277.

Egeland, B., & Stroufe, L. A. (1981). Attachment and early maltreatment. *Child Development, 52,* 44–52.

Erikson, E. H. (1977). *Toys and reason.* New York: Norton.

Erikson, E. H. (1978). Reflections on Dr. Borg's life cycle. In E. H. Erikson (Ed.), *Adulthood* (pp. 1–31). New York: Norton.

Erikson, E. H. (1980). *Identity and the life cycle.* New York: Norton.

Fentress, J. C., & McLeod, P. J. (1986). Motor patterns in development. In E. M. Blass (Ed.), *Handbook of behavioral neurobiology: Vol. 8. Development of psychobiology and developmental neurobiology.* New York: Plenum.

Flavell, J. (1963). *The developmental psychology of Piaget.* New York: Van Nostrand Reinhold.

Flavell, J. (1977). *Cognitive development.* Englewood Cliffs, NJ: Prentice-Hall.

Fox, R., Aslin, R. N., Shea, S. L., & Dumais, S. T. (1980). Stereopsis in human infants. *Science, 207,* 323–324.

Garbarino, J., & Kostelny, K. (1992). Child maltreatment as a community problem. *Child Abuse and Neglect, 16,* 455–464.

Gesell, A. (1940). *The first five years of life: The preschool years.* New York: Harper & Row.

Goldfarb, W. (1943). The effects of early institutional care on adolescent personality. *Journal of Experimental Education, 12,* 107–129.

Goldfarb, W. (1947). Variations in adolescent adjustment in institutionally reared children. *Journal of Orthopsychiatry, 17,* 449–457.

Greenberg, M., Morris, I., & Lind, J. (1973). First mothers rooming-in with their newborns: Its impact on the mother. *American Journal of Orthopsychiatry, 43,* 783–788.

Henderson, S., Byrne, D., & Duncan-Tones, P. (1981). *Neuroses in the social environment.* New York: Academic Press.

Hodges, J., & Tizard, B. (1989). IQ and behavioral adjustment of ex-institutional adolescents. *Journal of Child Psychology and Psychiatry, 30,* 53–75.

Hopkins, B., & Westra, T. (1988). Maternal handling and motor development: An intracultural study. *Genetic, Social and General Psychology Monographs, 14,* 377–420.

Hornik, R., Risenhoover, N., & Gunnar, M. (1987). The effects of maternal positive, neutral, and negative affective communications on infant responses to new toys. *Child Development, 58,* 937–944.

Jaeger, E., & Weinraub, M. (1990). Early nonmaternal care and infant attachment: In search of process. In K. McCartney (Ed.), *Child care and maternal employment: A social ecology approach.* San Francisco: Jossey-Bass.

Jersild, A. T., Telford, C. W., & Sawrey, J. M. (1975). *Child psychology.* Englewood Cliffs, NJ: Prentice-Hall.

Kagan, J. (1976). Emergent themes in human development. *American Scientist, 64,* 186–196.

Kagan, J. (1981). The second year: The emergence of self-awareness. Cambridge, MA: Harvard University Press.

Kail, R. V., & Cavanaugh, J. C. (1996). *Human development.* Pacific Grove, CA: Brooks/Cole.

Kaluger, G., & Kaluger, M. F. (1979). *Human development.* St. Louis: Mosby.

Keller, H., & Scholmerich, A. (1987). Infant vocalizations and parental reactions during the first four months of life. *Developmental Psychology, 23,* 62–67.

Kelly, P. (1976). The relation of the infant's temperament and mother's psychopathology to interactions in early infancy. In K. Riegel & S. Meachem (Eds.),

*The developing individual in a changing world* (Vol. 2). Chicago: Aldine-Atherton.

Kempe, C. H., Silverman, F. N., Steele, B. F., Droegen-mueller, W., & Silver, H. K. (1962). The battered child syndrome. *Journal of the American Medical Association, 181,* 17–24.

Kessen, W. (1975). *Childhood in China.* New Haven, CT: Yale University Press.

Klaus, M. H., & Kennell, J. H. (1976). *Maternal-infant bonding.* St. Louis: C. V. Mosby.

Kotelchuck, M. (1972). *The nature of the child's tie to his father.* Paper presented at the annual meeting of the Society for Research in Child Development, Harvard University, Cambridge, MA.

Lamb, M. E. (1977). A re-examination of the infant social world. *Human Development, 20,* 65–85.

Lamb, M. E., Sternberg, K. J., & Prodromidis, M. (1992). Nonmaternal care and the security of infant-mother attachment: A reanalysis of the data. *Infant Behavior and Development, 15,* 71–83.

Levine, L. (1983). Self-definition in two-year-old-boys. *Developmental Psychology, 19,* 544–549.

Lewis, M., Alessandri, S. M., & Sullivan, M. W. (1990). Violation of expectancy, loss of control, and anger expressions in young infants. *Developmental Psychology, 26,* 745–751.

Ludemann, P. M., & Nelson, C. A. (1988). Categorical representation of facial expressions by 7-month-old infants. *Developmental Psychology 24,* 492–501.

Lugo, J. O., & Hershey, G. L. (1979). *Human development.* New York: Macmillan.

Lyons-Ruth, K., Connell, D. B., Zoll, D., & Stahl, J. (1987). Infants at social risk: Relations among infant maltreatment, maternal behavior and infant attachment behavior. *Developmental Psychology, 23,* 223–232.

Maccoby, E. E., & Masters, J. C. (1970). Attachment and dependency. In P. H. Mussen (Ed.), *Carmichael's manual of child psychology* (Vol. 2). New York: Wiley.

Malatesta, C. A., & Izard, C. E. (1984). The ontogenesis of human social signals: From biological imperative to symbol utilization. In N. A. Fox & R. J. Davidson (Eds.) *The psychobiology of affective development* (pp. 161–206). Hillsdale, NJ: Erlbaum.

Mandler, J. (1990). A new perspective on cognitive development in infancy. *American Scientist, 28,* 236–243.

Mead, G. H. (1934). *Mind, self and society.* Chicago: University of Chicago Press.

Miller, D. (1979). The Native American family: The urban way. In E. Corfman (Ed.), *Families today: A research sampler on families and children* (Vol. 1, pp. 79–815). Washington, DC: U.S. Department of Health, Education, and Welfare.

Miller, D. R., & Swanson, G. E. (1966). *Inner conflict and defense.* New York: Schocken.

Never, A., Shore, M. F., Timberlake, E. M., & Greenspan, S. I. (1984, April). Relationship of maternal perception and maternal behavior. *American Journal of Orthopsychiatry, 54,* 111–118.

Newman, B. M., & Newman, P. R. (1995). *Development through life.* Pacific Grove, CA: Brooks/Cole.

Oppenheim, D., Sagi, A., & Lamb, M. E. (1988). Infant-adult attachments in the kibbutz and their relation to socioemotional development four years later. *Developmental Psychology, 24,* 427–433.

Parke, R. (1974). Father-infant interaction. In M. H. Klaus, T. Leger, & M. A. Trause (Eds.), *Maternal attachment and mothering disorders: A round table.* Sausalito, CA: Johnston Systems.

Piaget, J. (1971). *Science of education and the psychology of the child.* New York: Viking Press.

Pipp, S., Easterbrooks, M. A., & Harmon, R. J. (1992). The relation between attachment and knowledge of self and mother in 1-year-old infants to 3-year-old infants. *Child Development, 63,* 738–750.

Plomin, R. (1990). *Nature and nurture: An introduction to human behavioral genetics.* Pacific Grove, CA: Brooks/Cole.

Plomin, R. (1994). *Genetics and experience.* Thousand Oaks, CA: Sage.

Plomin, R., & McClearn, G. E. (1993). *Nature, nurture and psychology.* Hyattsville, MD: American Psychological Association.

Provence, S., & Lipton, R. C. (1962). *Infants in institutions.* New York: International Universerts Press.

Rochat, P. (1989). Object manipulation and exploration in 2-to-5-month-old infants. *Developmental Psychology, 25,* 871–884.

Rogoff, B. (1990). *Apprenticeship in thinking: Cognitive development in social context.* New York: Oxford University Press.

Rovee-Collier, C. K. (1987). Learning and memory. In J. D. Osofsky (Ed.), *Handbook of infant development* (2nd ed.). New York: Wiley.

Rutter, M. (1981). *Maternal deprivation revisited* (2nd ed.). New York: Penguin Books.

Samuels, C. (1986). Bases for the infant's development of self-awareness. *Human Development, 29,* 36–48.

Scanzoni, J. H. (1971). *The black family in modern society*. Boston: Allyn and Bacon.

Simons, R. L., Whitbeck, L. B., Conger, R. D., & Chyi-In, W. (1991). Intergenerational transmission of harsh parenting. *Developmental Psychology, 27,* 159–171.

Spitz, R. A. (1945). Hospitalism: An inquiry into the genesis of psychiatric conditions in early childhood. In A. Freud (Ed.), *The psychoanalytic study of the child* (Vol. 1). New York: International Universities Press.

Steele, B. F., & Pollack, C. D. (1968). A psychological study of parents who abuse infants and small children. In R. C. Helfer & C. H. Kempe (Eds.), *The battered child*. Chicago: University of Chicago Press.

Stern, D. N. (1977). *The first relationship: Infant and mother*. Cambridge, MA: Harvard University Press.

Stern, D. N. (1983). The early development of schemes of self, other and "self with other." In J. D. Lichenberg & S. Kaplan (Eds.), *Reflections on self psychology*. Hillsdale NJ: Erlbaum.

Stevenson, M. B., VerHoeve, J. N., Roach, M. A., & Leavitt, L. A. (1986). The beginning of conversation: Early patterns of mother-infant vocal responsiveness. *Infant Behavior and Development, 9,* 423–440.

Straus, M. A., & Kantor, G. K. (1987). Stress and child abuse. In R. E. Helfer & R. S. Kempe (Eds.), *The battered child* (4th ed.). Chicago: University of Chicago Press.

Stroufe, L. A. (1977). Wariness of strangers and the study of infant development. *Child Development, 48,* 1184–1199.

Tizard, B. (1977). *Adoption: A second chance*. London: Open Books.

Trickett, P. K., Aber, J. L., Carlson, V., & Cicchetti, D. (1991). Relationship of socioeconomic status to the etiology and developmental sequelae of physical child abuse. *Developmental Psychology, 27,* 148–159.

Trickett, P. K., & Kuczynski, L. (1986). Children's misbehaviors and parental discipline strategies in abusive and nonabusive families. *Developmental Psychology, 22,* 115–123.

Tronick, E. Z. (1989). Emotions and emotional communication in infants. *American Psychologist, 44,* 112–119.

Tronick, E. Z., Morelli, G. A., & Ivey, P. K. (1992). The Efe forager infant and toddler's pattern of social relationships: Multiple and simultaneous. *Developmental Psychology, 28,* 568–577.

U.S. Advisory Board on Child Abuse and Neglect. (1995). *A nation's shame: Fatal child abuse and neglect in the United States*. Washington, DC: U.S. Department of Health and Human Services.

Vander Zanden, J. W. (1977). *Human development*. New York: Knopf.

Walker-Andrews, A. S. (1986). Intermodal perception of expressive behaviors: Relations of eye and voice? *Developmental Psychology, 22,* 373–377.

Weinraub, M., Brooks, J., & Lewis, M. (1977). The social network: A reconsideration of the concept of attachment. *Human Development, 20,* 31–47.

Weinraub, M., & Lewis M. (1977). The determinants of children's responses to separation. *Monographs of the Society for Research in Child Development, 4* (Serial No. 172.)

White, R. (1963). *The enterprise of living*. New York: Holt, Rinehart & Winston.

White, R. W. (1976). *The enterprise of living*. New York: Holt, Rinehart & Winston.

Wicks-Nelson, R., & Israel, A. C. (1991). *Behavior disorders of childhood* (2nd ed.). Englewood Cliffs, NJ: Prentice-Hall.

Wolff, P. H. (1963). Observations on the early development of smiling. In B. M. Foss (Ed.), *Determinants of infant behavior* (Vol. 2), London: Methuen.

Zigler, E., & Hall, N. W. (1989). Physical child abuse in America: Past, present and future. In D. Cicchetti & V. Carlson (Eds.), *Child maltreatment: Theory and research on the causes and consequences of child abuse and neglect*. New York: Cambridge University Press.

Zuraivin, S. J. (1991). Research definitions of child physical abuse and neglect: Current problems. In R. H. Starr, Jr., & D. A. Wolfe (Eds.), *The effects of child abuse and neglect*. New York: Guilford.

# 4

# The Preschool Years

## INTRODUCTION

At age 2, Frannie is becoming aware of herself as a person. She runs up and down and throws her toys around. She tells her mother that she wants to be taken out to the garden. Again and again she says, "Frannie good girl, Frannie go out." She makes up stories in which she is the most powerful person and says such things as "Frannie is nice." This is the beginning of assertiveness and the development of self.

By the time she turns 6, Frannie has changed. She can explain many of her feelings of loss and frustration and is developing into a more thoughtful person.

Toward the end of the infancy stage, we find two distinctive features of development: The range of individual differences becomes more apparent, and the range of activities gradually shifts from those dominated by biological forces to those influenced by the forces of cognitive, social, and affective domains.

## PRESCHOOL DEVELOPMENT: AN OVERVIEW

### Physical Growth

The various aspects of physical maturation in the preschool child follow a particular order. Becoming aware of the concrete world around them, preschool children need to make solid contact with the outside world of people and objects, and they do many things to accomplish this. Such tasks and others at this stage are a continuation of earlier developmental tasks.

These tasks emphasize the maturational processes, or the unfolding of the child's natural potential for increasing his or her skills. Kaluger and Kaluger (1979) have classified the preschooler's developmental tasks as follows:

1. Achieving integrated motor and perceptional control
2. Completing control of the elimination of bodily wastes
3. Achieving physiological stability
4. Improving the ability to communicate and to comprehend what others say
5. Achieving independence in self-care areas such as eating, dressing, and bathing
6. Learning gender differences
7. Forming simple concepts of social and physical reality and learning how to behave toward persons and things
8. Learning to relate emotionally to parents, siblings, and other people
9. Learning to distinguish between right and wrong and develop a conscience (make value judgments)

Two-year-olds work at becoming competent. They can walk, run, and manipulate objects, but their coordination is still slow to improve. The use of the word *toddler* to describe the life stage from 2 to 4 years shows the important role locomotion plays in the life of the child. By 3, the child's walk has changed from the precarious, determined, half-humorous waddle to a more graceful, continuous, effective stride (Clark & Phillips, 1993). Note that qualitative changes in locomotive behavior are not simply a result of the cerebral cortex's maturation (Kalverboer, Hopkins, & Geuze, 1993). Changes in body weight and muscle mass, combined with new capacities to coordinate feedback from limbs and to judge the amount of effort needed to achieve a motor goal, are components in a regular progression of motor behavior (Getchell & Robertson, 1989).

By the time the child is 3, he or she has already learned to extend only one hand to receive one item and has begun to show a preference for the right or the left hand. Four-year-olds can vary the rhythm of their running, and many can skip rather awkwardly and execute a running jump. They can also probably use a crayon to draw lines and circles, as well as simple faces.

## Developmental Tasks

While preschoolers' bodies and brains develop, many notable changes in cognitive and social development also take place. One developmental task that children learn at this age is *self-control,* which refers to their ability to control their own impulses. Another is *overt control,* or their sense that they can control events around them. Preschool children's responses are often vigorous and uncontrolled. They want their needs met right now. Often, temper tantrums express their extreme rage at the lack of gratification of some impulse. Although considerable attention has been paid to anger, there are other emotions equally difficult for the child to control, among them love, sadness, and fear. Preschoolers seem to find it particularly difficult to modify or interrupt an emotional response once it has begun. Although adults might succeed in distracting children and turning their attention to something else, toddlers often cannot do this for themselves.

As children grow older, they learn to control their impulses. In the later preschool stage, children develop the ability to withstand delays in the gratification of impulses without experiencing the intense frustration characteristic of infancy. One factor enabling children to control frustration is an increased, though still rudimentary, sense of time, which involves some sense of the future. Such control develops slowly as children come to understand that what they want, although not available to them at the moment, will often be available after a brief delay. The knowledge that a need will eventually be met reduces the intensity of the emotional response.

The development of symbolic imagination allows children to create imaginary situations in which problems that disturb them can be expressed and resolved. In fantasy play, children can control situations that far exceed their real-world capacities. In a make-believe world they can punish, forgive, harm and heal, fear and conquer fear, all within the boundaries of the imagination. They begin to take charge of their emotional needs.

Children also have high expectations of themselves. Many times, children's enthusiasm and confidence outstrip their real potential. They see a parent easily performing a task and would like to be able to do a similar task. Told by a parent that they may not try to do something, they become frustrated because they are certain that they will do a good job. They do not expect an unsuccessful outcome, and denial of the opportunity discourages them. The best way to help a child is to offer assistance only as needed. As children engage in tasks beyond their capacity, they learn to assess their strengths and skills more realistically. By the end of their preschool years, children will be able to evaluate the requirements of a wide variety of tasks and judge whether they can accomplish them or not.

## Physical Setting and Development

Physical surroundings affect a child's development. Some settings are more conducive than others to positive growth. Two premises underlie the work of researchers investigating the immediate significance of environments in human activities and experiences. One holds that activities and experiences ordinarily take place in environmental configurations such as settings, places, landscapes, and the like, while the other indicates that humans apprehend, interpret, appraise, evaluate, and adapt to environments within which they enact their activities and undergo their experiences. Premises like these indicate that environments make up an external source of information that is necessary for people to act in the world and undergo experiences. But they also suggest that people necessarily transact and interact with this information, and in the process, look for meaning in it. They further imply that such information is likely to be influenced by how it appears and how people process it. Therefore, it makes sense to take the person-environment-behavior episode as the rational unit for visualizing both affective appraisals and their resulting emotions (Amato, 1993).

> At midnight, 2-year-old Chris is rudely awakened by the sound of thunder and heavy, howling winds. He cries desperately until his mother enters his room and picks him up. Three days later, when there is a heavy windy storm with lightning, Chris cries and clings to his mother. The previous experience of the midnight darkness, being alone, and then hearing the thunder and howling winds has created a negative impact (perhaps temporarily) on Chris about darkness, storms, and loneliness.

People may process information with reference to their environments deliberately or respond to it impulsively. In any case, a definite connection exists between people and their environment, which in turn affects human development. The following cases demonstrate this connection.

> Shirley lives in the inner city. A single parent, she finds it hard to get by on her limited finances. A decent existence is all she wants. But she never received encouragement to complete high school, and her mother was a drug addict. Fortunately, Shirley's grandmother constantly reminded Shirley about the bad effects of drugs. Shirley wanted to better herself, but all around her she saw only squalor, dirt, drugs, drunks, and rage. Often, she felt hopeless. The man she loved left her with two children.
>
> Frequently away from home to look for work, Shirley often leaves her toddler Leonard in the apartment with her older daughter, Clarissa, who is 14. Shirley keeps looking for a way out of the inner city and perhaps a good job. However, she cannot manage her children and her home. The apartment is always disorderly, with clothing and food strewn everywhere. It always smells bad.
>
> Clarissa attends school irregularly. She is more interested in getting her boyfriend to come home with her and having a good time with him than in taking care of her younger brother. When Leonard cries with hunger, Clarissa hurriedly gives him whatever is on hand just to shut him up. If he cries too much, she beats him up, so Leonard has learned not to disturb his sister. If he is hungry, he whimpers and cries softly, for he does not know how to fend for himself in this disorganized atmosphere. Eventually his sister gives him something to eat. He is used to being beaten, so whenever his sister puts out her hand he shrinks away in fear. He spends a lot of time watching TV and sucking his thumb. Seldom bathed, he has a strong body odor. He regards all people with suspicion. He whimpers and cries when he sees strangers and shrinks away if anyone tries to touch him, a result of the neglect and abuse in his environment. Influenced by her environment and her own needs, Clarissa treats Leonard in ways convenient to her.
>
> Brought up in a middle-class neighborhood, Tony belongs to a close-knit family. Although Tony hasn't spent too much time with his father, he is comfortable around men, for his uncles, cousins, and grandfather live nearby and visit each other often. Thus, he has grown up as a member of a large family network. Even at a young age, he felt secure and was friendly with everyone. His family environment and his immediate outside environment were conducive to his growth. Now he is verbal, sociable, and self-confident, having been nurtured by a large number of caring people.

## COGNITIVE DEVELOPMENT

The study of cognitive development—that is, long-term changes in children's mental skills and abilities—is one of the more diverse and exciting topics in developmental science. In this section we shall begin to explore the developing mind, focusing on Piaget, who charted what he and others believe to be a universal patten of intellectual growth that begins to unfold during infancy, childhood, and adolescence.

What happens internally when children learn? Something has to occur neurologically, because it is the only way any kind of cognitive consciousness can take place. The perceptual-motor processes must be adequately developed if children are to learn, read symbols, and understand abstract concepts. The more abstract, intricate, and complex the stimuli, the more efficient the perceptual processes must be for the learner to recognize differences and attach meanings to them.

Developmental specialists and neurologists such as Gesell, Piaget, and Inhelder leave little doubt concerning the importance of combined conceptual and motor experiences in developing a neurological (mental) structure, organization, or pattern that can be responded to, retained, and recalled. All these factors are a result of the brain structure.

## The Brain

Brain development occurs in a complex process that involves the production of neurons or individual nerve cells in localized areas; the migration of these cells from their place of origin to the place they will ultimately be located; and the formation of *synapses,* which are connections among neurons. Synapses permit information to be passed from one neuron to another, a process accomplished via chemicals stored in the neurons themselves. An individual neuron forms two types of structures: dendrites and axons. *Dendrites* are treelike branches growing out of the neuron that carry information (nerve impulses) toward the center of the cell from adjoining neurons. The neuron's *axon* is a long fiber that carries information away from the cell body and, eventually, to other cells. An axon is quite efficient if surrounded by a *myelin sheath*—a segmented, fatty covering that insulates the axon and increases the speed of impulse transmission. Myelin is produced by *glial cells.* Though these cells exist in profusion in the brain, they are not part of the information-carrying network but transmit nutrients to the neurons and make myelin. *Myelination* is necessary for the brain to function as it should.

Different parts of the brain have growth spurts at different times. In general, the lower parts— that is, the spinal cord and the structures lying just above it—develop ahead of other areas. The cerebral hemispheres, which form the topmost and largest part of the brain, are next to develop, with the cerebellum last. Important in controlling finer motor movements and maintaining coordination, balance, and muscle tone, the cerebellum has its growth spurt in cell formation during the first year after birth (Huttenlocher, Haight, Bryk, Seltzer, & Lyons, 1991; Malina, 1990; Tanner, 1990).

The outer layer of the cerebral hemispheres (the surface of the brain) is known as the *cerebral cortex.* In this part of the brain, people carry out the most uniquely human functions, which include thinking, understanding, and planning. The cerebral cortex forms the largest part of the brain in humans.

The cortex is divided into four different areas or *lobes.* The *frontal lobe* occupies the top, front area; the *parietal lobe* is also at the top of the brain, just behind the frontal lobe; the *temporal lobe* lies along the side of the brain; and the *occipital lobe* occupies the back of the cortex.

The cerebral cortex develops rapidly during the first two to three years. Normal brain growth and development occurs region by region, with each area maturing a bit, and then another. Much remains to be discovered about this apparently orderly and extraordinarily complex process. In the cerebral cortex, the first location to mature is the *primary motor area,* which lies at the very back of the frontal lobe. Maturation in this area allows infants to achieve their first motor skills such as grasping and reaching. Development in all these areas follows the cephalocaudal trend; that is, the upper body matures first and then the lower. The next area of development is the *primary sensory area,* in front of the parietal lobe, where sensations of touch are received throughout the body. The *primary visual area* and the *primary auditory area* receive information from the eyes and the ears, respectively.

Children as well as adults store information in their brain. As Greenough, Black, and Wallace (1987) indicate, two separate processes may be involved in the brain's reaction to experiences. What they call *experience expectant* processes involve the storage of environmental events experienced by almost all members of a given ᴗpecies. The brain is ready to receive all kinds of experiences that a species can be expected to have. *Experience dependent* processes, on the other hand, involve the storage of the unexpected, unique experiences of an individual. The authors suggest that the brain must create new synapses for this information to be stored. Such multiple storage mechanisms may explain why the same experience influences adults' and children's brains differently.

From a theoretical point of view, the basic neural system for learning consists of (1) a pattern of reflexes, including primitive motor, visual, auditory, vocal, and kinesthetic reflexes; (2) a motor response capability, including a postural weight-shift mechanism that provides symmetry and balance; (3) a memory endowment to retain and recall bits of information that have been learned; and (4) the ability to imitate certain behavior after a period of maturation (Kaluger & Kaluger, 1979).

Babies are bombarded with a lot of information from the world around them. To keep young children from overloading, nature makes it possible for them to receive and perceive only the grossest stimuli and shut out the rest. As they become more capable of handling finer, more precise stimuli, they become more aware of them. Handling these stimuli and selecting those that are most significant for them are part of the perceptual process. For example, preschoolers learn to become part of a family by recognizing family and friends as well as their unique behaviors.

## Piaget: The Preoperational Stage

Recall that during the sensorimotor period, infants show by their interactions with the environment that their dominant mental activity involves overt actions. Little internal intellectualization takes place until the close of this period. During the preoperational stage, though, the child begins to differentiate between verbal and nonverbal symbols, responds to them accordingly, and internalizes these perceptions into his or her personality. If a mother smiles at her 5-year-old son and tells him not to take the cookie from the plate, the child will take it anyway, because he is responding to her nonverbal communication, which says that it is all right to take the cookie. Further, the child becomes able to make internal responses that represent objects or events even if those objects and events are not present.

The preoperational stage of cognitive development begins at approximately 2 years of age. There are several characteristics of cognitive function noted during this period that Piaget views as obstacles to logical thinking:

1. *Egocentrism:* The child is unable to imagine or realize that another person may be viewing the same problem or situation from another perspective or angle. The child believes, "Whatever I can see, everybody can see."
2. *Centering:* The child is centered on one detail of an event and cannot take into account other features that are also important. Thus, the child cannot see variations. Focusing on a single part, however salient, leads to illogical reasoning.
3. *Irreversibility:* The child is unable to change the direction of his or her thinking to return to its point of origin. For instance, a preoperational child taking a walk would be unable to retrace the route accurately.

*Stages of preoperational thought* The two substages of development in the preoperational period are called the *preconceptual stage,* or period of symbolic thought, and the *period of intuitive thought.* During the preconceptual stage, children begin to associate certain objects with other objects they represent. Children begin to participate in symbolic play. (Play and its importance in childhood will be presented in another section of this chapter.)

When a 4-year-old child is asked if he has a brother, the child replies affirmatively and mentions that his brother's name is John. When asked, "Does John have a brother?" the child answers no. The child cannot grasp the notion that having a brother necessarily involves being a brother or sister to someone else.

The period of intuitive thought runs from about 4 to 7 years of age. During this period, children can think in a more complex fashion, and they can elaborate their concepts. Their egocentrism tends to be replaced by social behavior and social interaction.

*Concept formation*    Children do not learn to internalize verbal images until the age of 2, when their language development provides them with words that represent objects and events in the environment. At first, words do not have much meaning other than labels—answers to the question "What is it?" At a later stage, children ask questions such as "Where does it go?" and "What makes it go?" Slowly, they begin to use words as mediators for reasoning. Concepts learned by children before the age of 5 have only surface meaning, with no depth of insight or relationship to other concepts (Kaluger & Kaluger, 1979).

Preschool children cannot cope with definite perceptions of various situations; they can take into account only one idea or dimension at one time. Concepts such as time and numbers mean little to such children. However, concepts of space and size develop more readily. When a child is mentally 3 years of age, he or she can select the largest as well as the smallest objects from a group of objects of varying sizes.

*Classification, seriation, and conservation*
According to Piaget (Piaget & Inhelder, 1969), *classification* is the ability to sort things such as colors, shapes, or sizes into categories according to their characteristics. From 2 to about 4 years of age, children learn to make figural designs. As children continue to grow, they perform quasi classification, moving freely from one basis to another and mixing colors and shapes.

*Seriation* is the ability to arrange objects in sequence according to one or more relevant dimensions, such as increasing or decreasing size, weight, or volume. By age 4 or 5, children learn to pick up longer or smaller sticks. Seriation by weight is not usually attained until age 9; full seriation is not usually attained until age 12.

*Conservation* is the recognition that matter remains the same quantitatively—substance, weight, length, number, and volume or area—regardless of changes in shape or position as long as nothing has been added or taken away. For example, if we have a row of eight pennies and spread them farther apart, we still have eight pennies, but a 4- or 5-year-old may think that there are more. When a piece of clay is made into a ball then remolded into a log, the child may think that the log has more clay than the ball because it looks longer. According to Piaget, a child cannot conserve substance until age 6 or 7. Children learn the principle of conservation only when they can decenter perceptions, reverse operations, and comprehend *transformations,* or tell that one stage or appearance has changed to another (Piaget & Inhelder, 1969).

## Vygotsky: Sociocultural Contexts

Besides Piaget's cognitive development, another theorist's thinking has aroused a great deal of interest lately: the sociocultural viewpoint of Lev Vygotsky (1934/1962, 1930–1935/1978). This Russian developmentalist was an active scholar in the 1920s and 1930s when Piaget was formulating his theory. As ill luck would have it, Vygotsky died at age 38, before his work was completed. His thinking is important to social workers because he insisted that (1) cognitive development occurs in a sociocultural context that influences the form it takes and (2) many of a child's most noteworthy cognitive skills begin in social interaction with parents, teachers, and other competent associates.

According to Vygotsky, infants are born with a few elementary mental functions such as attention, sensation, perception, and memory that are eventually transformed by their culture into new and more sophisticated mental processes called *higher mental functions.* For example, a child's memory in early years is limited to biological constraints based on the images and impressions he or she can produce. However, each culture provides its children with *tools of intellectual adaptation* that help them use their basic mental functions adaptively. In sum, Vygotsky claims that human cognition, even when carried out in isolation (such as a family with children living in a remote area), is inherently sociocultural—affected by the values, beliefs, and intellectual tools passed to individuals by their culture. Though such values may vary dramatically among cultures, each culture transmits them from one generation to the next. Vygotsky believes that neither the course nor the content of intellectual growth is "universal," as Piaget indicates.

Vygotsky agrees with Piaget that young children are curious explorers, actively involved in learning and discovering new principles. But he also stresses that self-initiated discovery is deeply influenced by social contributions to cognitive growth. Vygotsky indicates that truly important discoveries children make occur in the context of cooperative or collaborative dialogues between an adult who can be a skilled helper and the child. The adult can model the activity and give the child verbal instructions. Eventually the child internalizes this information and uses it to regulate his or her own performance.

For example, when 3-year-old Tommy is given a tricycle, he is initially confused until his older brother sits on it and starts to ride it. Tommy is still very nervous so his father sits on the tricycle and encourages him, saying that it would be fun. Tommy rides it hesitantly but soon he understands the concept; his father steps back and lets him work more and more independently as he gets more skilled at it.

This type of social interaction fosters cognitive growth. Tommy and his father are operating on what Vygotsky calls the *zone of proximal development*—that is, the difference between what a learner can accomplish independently and what he or she can learn with the guidance and encouragement of a person with more skill. With his father's help, Tommy internalizes the use of a tricycle and becomes an accomplished tricycle rider.

Like Piaget, Vygotsky encourages active rather than passive learning. Their major difference lies in the instructor's role. Whereas students in Piaget's classroom would spend more time in independent, discovery-based activities, students in Vygotsky's classroom would find guided participation by teachers who structure the learning activity and provide useful hints or instructions carefully tailored to the children's current abilities and then monitor their progress, thus gradually turning over more of the mental activity to their pupils.

Such teachers might also arrange cooperative learning exercises, in which students are encouraged to assist each other. For example, Freund (1990) asked 3-to-5-year-olds to help a puppet decide which furnishings—such as beds, stoves, and bathtubs—should be placed in each of the six rooms of the puppet's dollhouse. First, the children were tested to determine what they already knew about proper furniture placement. Then each child worked at placing the furniture either alone (as in Piaget's discovery-based classroom) or with his or her mother (Vygotsky's guided learning). Finally, to assess what they had learned, Freund had the children perform a final furniture-sorting task. The results were clear. Children who had sorted furniture with their mothers' help showed dramatic improvements in sorting ability, whereas those who had practiced on their own showed little improvement at all, even though they had received some corrective feedback from the experimenter (Diaz, Neal, & Vachio, 1991; Rogoff, 1990). Similarly, advances in problem-solving skills have been reported when children collaborate with peers as opposed to working alone (Azmitia, 1992; Gauvain & Rogoff, 1989). Youngsters who gain the most from these collaborations are those who were initially much less competent than their partners (Azmitia, 1988; Tudge, 1992).

Children do not always learn well when they function as solitary explorers seeking discoveries by themselves. Often, conceptual growth takes place more easily through children's interactions with other people—particularly with competent people who provide just the right amount of guidance and encouragement that the child needs (Shaffer, 1996).

## LANGUAGE DEVELOPMENT

### Cognition and Language

Language development is one of the major accomplishments of childhood. According to Piaget, preschool children talk to themselves, and quite often two children carry on separate monologues rather than truly converse with each other. Piaget calls these self-directed utterances *egocentric speech*. He adds that speech progressively becomes more "social" and less egocentric toward the end of the preoperational stage, when the child begins to assume the perspective of others and thus adopts a speech that listeners can follow.

Vygotsky, however, says that a preschool child's self-directed monologue occurs in some contexts with reference to others. Vygotsky indicates that children talk to themselves as they attempt to solve problems and when they are encountered with obstacles—this is the reason for nonsocial speech, which he calls *speech for self* or *private speech*. This speech helps children plan strategies and regulate their behaviors in order to accomplish their goals. According to Vygotsky, private speech plays a critical role in cognitive development and makes children more organized and efficient problem solvers. He also mentions that private speech becomes more abbreviated with age and then disappears. It simply goes underground, becoming silent or inner speech and the covert verbal thought we use to organize and regulate everyday activities.

Recently, other theorists have confirmed Vygotsky's theory (Berk, 1992). This is because Vygotsky's sociocultural theory offers a new lens through which to view cognitive development, stressing the importance of specific social processes that Piaget and others overlook.

Clearly, from a social worker's perspective, language development is closely related to and affected by a person's sociocultural surroundings.

Vygotsky's theory has not been so intensely scrutinized as Piaget's theory. As Rogoff indicates, however, there are some criticisms of Vygotsky's theory. Guided participation that relies heavily on verbal instruction may not be useful in some cultures. For example, a young child learning to stalk prey in Australia's outback or to plant, tend, and harvest rice in Southeast Asia may profit more from observing the practice than from joining in and taking verbal instruction (Rogoff, Mistry, Goncu, & Mosier, 1993). Also other investigators have indicated that collaborative problem solving among peers may undermine task performance if the more competent collaborator is not confident about what he or she wants or fails to adapt instructions to his partner's level of understanding (Levin & Druyan, 1993; Tudge, 1992). Despite these criticisms, Vygotsky's theory has provided a valuable service by reminding us that cognitive and other kinds of human development are best understood in their cultural and social contexts (Shaffer, 1996).

### Language and Culture

Every culture determines what uses of speech are appropriate, just as it dictates pronunciation, syntax, and vocabulary. In many Asian cultures, politeness is important; therefore children learn polite forms of expression at an early age. Learning the correct use of a language involves thousands of details, such as knowing what form of address to use, what tone of voice to adopt, and what is considered rude or polite.

Appropriate language usage depends on the social relationship between speaker and listener. People show their awareness of another person's status by their tone of voice, grammar, and mode of address. A domineering father will usually convey his expectations of obedience and respect from his children by his tone of voice and the use of commands rather than requests. His children may respond by modulating their voices and using polite forms of address. Generally, children are quick to perceive degrees of status and adapt their speech to conform to the requirements of a wide variety of social settings.

Status and role awareness are important aspects of language communication. The structure and content of language also reflect one's social class and ethnic identification. Latino cultures, for example, focus on people rather than abstractions and on familial values rather than the competitiveness and individual learning styles. This focus is developed in part via language.

Though research has shown the relationships between socioeconomic status and language style, considerable difference of opinion exists about the nature and implications of these relationships. Middle-class parents consciously use language to initiate questioning of cause and effect, whereas working-class parents tend to give commands that control behavior and to spend less time explaining rules and reasons to their children.

One can make a distinction between a lower-class restricted language (one understood only by that group) and a middle-class elaborated language. The middle-class language is more complex and offers children a wider choice of syntax to express themselves and greater opportunities to develop flexible and creative speech patterns (Specht & Craig, 1987). Even so, Labov (1970) cites the richness and complexity of African-American English as evidence that nonstandard English is no less complicated in structure than middle-class English. Labov and other recent researchers view African-American English as an ordered and syntactically consistent dialect rather than a collection of careless errors, and Labov addresses this issue in his theory of language deficiency (1970).

All cultures define appropriate social uses of speech, just as they dictate pronunciation, syntax, and vocabulary. For instance, in India, people say, "Namaste" as a common form of greeting when introduced to a new person; it literally means "I respect the good in you."

## LANGUAGE DISORDERS

Social workers need to be aware of children's language disorders because they lead to complications in the social world. In some children, language problems are due to a disruption in the sensory system, as in deaf children, or in the conceptual system, as in a mentally disabled child. Language problems could also arise from factors that influence a child's affective and social development, such as schizophrenia or autism (Bloom, 1980).

Children disrupt the form, content, and use of language when they have a language disorder. In some behavioral disorders, children develop some ideas about the world (language content) and appropriate principles for interacting with other persons (language use) but cannot learn words and structures that provide the forms of language. Some children may learn repetitive and mechanical ways of interaction but may not be able to represent regularities in language content in a meaningful way. For example, "Denny go" could mean Denny wants to go home, to the bathroom, or to the playground. Some children may learn linguistic forms to represent certain categories of content but will not be able to interact with other people so as to learn the use of such forms. Some children may learn language in the same way normal children do, but not as rapidly, and their language development may be arrested at some early stage (Bloom & Lahey, 1978).

A 2-to-4-year-old who is learning a language slowly and with difficulty may also have trouble learning to read and write later in school. Thus, by the time the child is 7 to 8, he or she is seen as having a learning disability. Bloom mentions that it is not clear how this language disorder affects such individuals through the life span. However, he adds that a language disorder is itself a learning disability (Bloom, 1980).

## THE PSYCHOSOCIAL ENVIRONMENT

Developmental issues in the preschool period include continued dependency and the growing need for autonomy, mastery, and competence. Erikson (1963) points out that hope and competency promote the feelings of autonomy essential to the development of greater independence. Preschool children also develop a sense of self-esteem. Growth during the preschool years takes place through the process of identification, the learning of gender roles, and a sense of morality or conscience.

### Erikson: Initiative versus Guilt

Erikson indicates that preschool children experience a developmental crisis as their decreasing dependency creates conflict in their lives—conflict between what is possible and what permissible; what is acceptable and what is unacceptable. As children develop their intellectual capacities, they also become aware of their *powers,* or ability to make things happen. They become more and more aware that they can control their own bodies and consequently affect their physical environment.

Their increased ability to be complex and creative is combined with newfound self-confidence and a well-established faith that parents watching from the background will provide any needed psychosocial supports. The preschool child is readier than ever to explore the world with vigor, incessant curiosity, and verbal eagerness.

During this stage, children are eager to learn and work cooperatively with others to achieve their goals. At the same time, they begin to understand that other people have different motivations and perceptions. They learn from and are willing to accept the guidance of parents, teachers, and others. The child's energy is directed toward possible and meaningful goals, which permit the dreams of early childhood to be attached to the goals of a future active adult life.

The crisis of this stage is that children's newfound energies lead them to act in ways that will make them feel guilty. The child has a great sense of power, but it comes with an increasing awareness of required limitations on behavior. Violating those limitations produces guilt.

> Aaron is angry with his little sister and wants to push her out of her crib, but he knows that if he does, his mother will punish him. He is angry with the baby for all the extra attention she is getting in the family, but he also understands that he has to control his impulse to hurt her because acting on it will bring him punishment.

> Four-year-old Julie is tempted to put her fingers into the trembling, shiny cream pudding sitting on the dining table. But she holds back her impulse because she knows (based on previous experiences) that this would result in punishment.

Of course, ethical behavior consists of more than avoiding punishments by behaving properly. It means understanding the needs of others as well as one's own. We shall discuss morality further in a later section of this chapter.

Like Aaron and Julie, children face two important revelations in the preschool period: first, experiencing themselves as more powerful than ever, and second, beginning to realize that they must control their own behavior and that they will feel guilty if they fail to do so. As Erikson (1963) puts it, "The child indulges in fantasies of being a giant and a tiger but in his dreams he runs in terror for dear life."

If children handle the crisis of guilt well, they will function in ways that allow them to use their initiative constructively. They will find it pleasurable to use their own power and be able to cooperate with and accept help from others. Erikson (1963) says,

> There is in every child at every stage a new miracle of vigorous unfolding, which constitutes a new hope and a new responsibility for all. Such is the sense and the pervading quality of initiative. The criteria for all these senses and qualities are the same. A crisis is more or less beset with fumbling and fear, and is resolved, in that the child suddenly

seems to "grow together" both in his person and in his body. He appears "more himself," more loving, relaxed and brighter in his judgment, more activated and activating. He is in free possession of a surplus of energy which permits him to forget failures quickly and to approach what seems desirable (even if it also seems uncertain and even dangerous) with undiminished and more accurate direction. (p. 75)

Some children, however, do not find a balance between initiative and guilt. Their own desires for control and mastery may come into conflict with either the wish for the acceptance and support of others or the dictates of conscience. The conflict may lead them to overcontrol themselves, and they may become resentful of their sense of inner control. Children who do not resolve such a crisis may grow into adults who feel inadequate.

School social workers sometimes see children who lack self-confidence and are not assertive with their classmates. Children whose parents do not encourage them in new activities or who frighten them when they wish to venture into new activities may become anxious and learn to deny, minimize, or even disguise their need for autonomy. Based on cultural influences, this pattern occurs more often with young girls than young boys.

> In play with the vacuum cleaner, 5-year-old Pam accidentally turns it on. Frightened, she screams and cries. Her mother comes running to her rescue but also punishes Pam for touching the vacuum cleaner. Scared, Pam will not go near a vacuum cleaner again for a long time.

If parents constantly curb their child's initiatives at this period through discouragement as well as punishment, they may induce anxiety in the child and prevent or slow down the child's development of autonomy.

Children with physical and mental disabilities have fewer opportunities than others to test their skills in interacting with the environment. However, actively employed disabled people are more visible than ever before and should provide meaningful role models for such children in developing their own autonomy and initiative.

## White: Developing Competence

White (1976) considers Erikson's formulation of the dynamics characterizing the preschool years in terms of the competence model. He believes that the child is brought nearer to his or her crisis by developments in three spheres of competence: locomotion, language, and imagination. Walking and running reach the point of being serviceable tools rather than difficult stunts. Children can walk and run freely, cover a large territory, and use a tricycle to get around wherever they want. They like to race up and down the stairs or the gym. The development of these seemingly adult patterns makes it possible for children to compare themselves with grown-ups, yet they wonder about the differences in size. They also like to dress in adult clothes and imitate adult behavior.

As their language skills increase, children gain a wider understanding of people's behavior and social exchanges. Rhyme-making attests to and produces a growing mastery of speech, and children begin to understand such subtleties as the meanings of *could* and *might*.

Imagination is the third sphere of competence in which marked development occurs during the fourth and fifth years. At this time, children can first maintain the fantasy of an imaginary companion. Children can dramatize themselves, assuming various adult roles. They begin to have frightening dreams involving injury—for example, being carried away by wolves. As Erikson (1959) expresses it, "Both language and locomotion permit him to expand his imagination over so many things that he cannot avoid frightening himself with what he himself has dreamed and thought up."

In terms of social competence, these developments help children to understand their place in the family as well as in society. To some extent, children continue to experiment with crude social power, especially with their peers, whom they may hit, boss, or threaten in various ways. Further, children at this age learn the culture's definition of gender roles, and they experiment with a variety of adult roles (White, 1976).

White indicates that the growth of competence leads to intrinsic emotional and interpersonal crisis. Though preschool children apparently have no interest in sex, they develop competency in other areas (White, 1976). They still make locomotor, linguistic, and imaginative progress; show interest in being like adults; and make comparisons, such as size and height. Such children are competitive and subject to defeats and humiliations. Curious, they ask endless questions and encounter rebuffs, have bad dreams, and feel guilty over imagined or real aggressive actions. They learn about roles and understand relationships to other family members. All these factors arise inescapably from progress in the growth of competence and have important emotional consequences. All these situations give children a chance to maintain and strengthen their sense of initiative as well as impose a burden of guilt (Mussen, Conger, Kagan, & Geiwitz, 1979).

## MORAL DEVELOPMENT

One of the important human abilities that people acquire as they grow is the ability to tell right from wrong. *Moral development, conscience,* and *ethics* are all terms that we use to discuss our efforts to deal fairly with others. *Morality* implies that a person has (1) the ability to distinguish right from wrong, (2) a cognitive component that centers the way they conceptualize right from wrong and make decisions on how to behave, and (3) a behavioral component that reflects how they actually behave when, for example, they experience the temptation to cheat or are called on to help a needy person. Through training and experience, preschoolers gradually learn which actions other people consider acceptable and which not. Children learn that doing certain things could lead to punishment, as we discussed earlier. *Morality* is a set of cultural and social

rules that governs the appropriateness of social behavior and that the individual has internalized (Kohlberg, 1964). Moral development is the internalization and organization of these guiding principles over time. Further, such development works toward the organization of priorities and values in social situations.

A study by Mussen et al. (1979) indicates that from the time children are 3 years old, they know that other people have feelings and that those feelings vary by situation. The researchers note that children can better recognize others' happiness and fear than their sadness or anger. The study found no difference between boys and girls in recognition of these emotions, but older children did reveal more empathetic capability than younger ones. (As Piaget specifies, egocentricity declines gradually toward the end of the preschool years.)

A child's increasing social awareness accounts largely for the early manifestations of sympathy, conscience, and generosity during the preschool period. As children become more conscious of the needs and concerns of others, they begin to desire the satisfaction of meeting others' needs as well as their own. Preschool children's behavior shows a growing capacity for sharing and compassion. When Mussen et al. (1979) studied generosity in young children, they found that it was linked to moral characteristics such as cooperation, altruism, lack of interpersonal aggression, and sympathy. These aspects of moral development in turn are closely related to the child's perception of the same-gender parent as being warm, affectionate, and nurturing and a role model.

Children develop a sense of social justice by the end of the preschool years. Kohlberg (1976) suggests that young children understand that returning a stolen toy is more appropriate than merely apologizing for having stolen it. Not only can they distinguish between right and wrong, but they can also recognize that an apology may not correct a wrong.

Though many of Kohlberg's studies on moral development use Piaget's work as their starting point, they do challenge Piaget's view of the preschooler as an egocentric being who behaves properly only in response to adult authority, Kohlberg found that preschoolers were well on their way to understanding and internalizing basic moral considerations (Lerner & Hultsch, 1983).

Theorists define morality in different ways. Current theoretical views of moral development take one of three approaches, stressing the role of nature (Freud's view), interaction (interactional theories), or nurture (social learning theory).

## Psychoanalytic Theory

Freud views all stages of development as following an intrinsically determined, universal course. According to Freud, all people experience an oedipal conflict in their phallic stage. The successful resolution of this conflict will result in the formation of the structure of personality. Freud claims that the mature personality has three components: the selfish and irrational id, the rational ego, and the moralistic superego. The *superego,* or conscience, has the essential task of ensuring that any plans formed by the ego to gratify the id's urges are morally acceptable. Infants and toddlers, Freud indicates, lack a superego and are essentially "all id." They will act out their selfish motives unless their parents control them.

During the phallic stage—that is, between 3 to 6 years—children are presumed to experience an emotional conflict over their love for the other-gender parent. This conflict creates the superego. A boy resolves his Oedipus complex by identifying and patterning himself after his father, particularly if the father is a threatening figure who arouses fear. The young boy learns his masculine role through a process called *internalization.* In this process he also follows the father's moral standards. In a similar fashion, a young girl resolves her Electra complex by identifying with her mother and internalizes her mother's moral standards. Freud believed that girls do not experience the intense fear of castration that boys experience and therefore they develop weaker superegos than do boys.

Freud points out that emotion is an important aspect of moral development and that having a superego is like having a parent inside a child's head, someone to tell the child what is right or wrong and to arouse such emotions as shame and guilt if the child thinks of violating the rules, even with no authority figure around. The specifics of Freud's theory, however, are largely unsupported because cold, threatening and punitive parents do not raise morally mature youngsters; also, men do not appear to have stronger superegos than women, and moral development begins well before the phallic period. Furthermore, when children reach 5 or 6 years of age Freud claims they have achieved moral maturity by resolving their oedipal conflicts, but we know that such children have *not* completed their moral growth. We gain much by examining Freud's broad themes but we should lay the particulars of his theory to rest. The newer psychoanalytic theorists are discovering that moral emotions and standards begin in infancy when children form loving rather than fear-provoking attachments to their parents and when they begin to notice their parents' emotional reactions to their good and bad behavior (Emde, 1992; Kochanska, 1993).

## Interactional Theory

Cognitive developmentalists such as Piaget and Kohlberg study morality by examining moral reasoning; that is, the thinking process that occurs when we decide whether an act is right or wrong. Both these theorists believe that moral development depends on thinking. Moral reasoning is said to progress through an *invariable sequence,* or a fixed and universal order of stages, each of which represents a consistent process of thinking about moral issues that differs from the stage preceding or following it. Cognitive-developmental terms center on *how* we decide what to do, not *what* we decide or actually do. For example, a young girl and an adult woman may both decide not to steal a pen; however, the reasons they give for making such a decision might be entirely different.

*Piaget's view*   Piaget sees children as passing through two moral phases: heteronomous morality and autonomous morality. In *heteronomous morality* the child is objective in his or her moral judgment; an act is right or wrong in terms of its consequences. One who breaks a teacup would be judged by a child in this stage as morally culpable, whether or not breaking the cup was an accident. Moral realism in the child is based on the fact that the child views rules as being unchangeable, externally imposed requirements for behavior that demand unyielding acceptance. In autonomous morality, children become subjective and autonomous in their moral judgments. They take the intentions of the person into consideration while judging the moral rightness or wrongness of an act. One who breaks a teacup out of spite or anger would be judged morally wrong, but one who broke the cup out of clumsiness would not. Piaget believes the second type of judgment to be based on the child's moral reasoning. He considers rules as the outcomes of agreements between people in a relation not of social constraint but of cooperation and autonomy.

Piaget's theory differs from that of the morally relativistic, response-centered approaches of psychoanalysis. It has stimulated considerable interest among developmental researchers because it offers a provocative framework for assessing changes in morality beyond the level of early childhood.

*Kohlberg's view*   As you know from Chapter 1, Kohlberg's theory of moral development has its roots in Piaget's thinking. Kohlberg (1976) obtained evidence that Piaget's two-phase model does not sufficiently take into account all the types of change in moral reasoning through which people progress. Kohlberg thought it necessary to devise a theory involving several stages of moral reasoning in order to encompass all the qualitative changes he discerned.

Kohlberg's theory of moral reasoning, like Piaget's, is based on the idea that by focusing only on the response in a moral situation, one

risks ignoring important distinctions in the moral reasoning of people at different points in the life span—reasoning differences that in fact may give different meaning to the same response at various developmental levels. Responses alone do not signify the underlying reasoning. An individual's response must be examined in light of how the person perceives the moral situation, what the meaning of the situation is to the person, and how the person's choice relates to that meaning; in other words, in terms of the cognitive and emotional processes involved in making the moral judgments (Turiel, 1969).

Here is Kohlberg's view of the preschool child's moral development (see Chapter 1).

*Level 1: Preconventional Morality.* At this level, rules are really external to the self rather than internalized. The child conforms to rules imposed by authority figures so that he or she can achieve personal rewards or avoid punishment. At this point the perspective of the self dominates— whatever the child can get away with, he or she will, particularly if it is personally satisfying.

*Stage 1: Punishment and obedience orientation.* In this situation the goodness or badness of a behavior depends on its consequences. A child may obey an authority figure to avoid punishment but may not consider an act wrong if it will not be punished. The greater the harm done or the more severe the punishment, the more "bad" the act will be considered.

*Stage 2: Instrumental hedonism.* In this stage of moral development, the child conforms to rules in order to gain rewards or satisfy personal needs. Children may have some concern for the perspectives of others but they are ultimately motivated by hope of some benefit in return. "If I do this for you, will you do it for me, too?"

This is the beginning of moral reasoning, whereby individuals become more apt at considering the perspectives of others than their own. Moral reasoning progresses from a crude egocentric focus on personal welfare at the preconventional level to a concern that revolves around other people like siblings, parents, extended family, friends, and neighbors.

## Social Learning Theory

Social learning theorists such as Albert Bandura (1986, 1991) and Walter Mischel (1974) are interested in the behavioral aspect of morality; that is, *what do we really do* when faced with temptation? Like other behaviorists, these theorists believe that moral behavior is learned the same way other social behaviors are learned: through reinforcement and punishment and through observational learning. Moral behavior is also strongly influenced by the nature of specific situations in which people find themselves. Thus a person who may behave morally in one situation may transgress in another. For instance, a person may proclaim that nothing is more important than being honest but lie when he or she deems it necessary.

To compare social learning with the theories we have discussed, consider the following situation. Let us say that Starling is about to take an important math exam. Will he or will he not cheat in his exam? From Freud's perspective, a great deal depends on Starling's upbringing and his identification with his father. Presumably, Starling strongly identified with his father in early childhood. If so, he has developed a strong superego as part of his personality and will be less likely to cheat, lie, or steal than a child with a weak superego, unless Starling's father had a weak superego.

Kohlberg and Piaget would have more interest in Starling's cognitive development, specifically in which stage of reasoning he is at and how this helps him deal with moral dilemmas. Although Kohlberg insists that one level of moral reasoning does not predict which decision one will make, he would claim that Starling's reasoning would be consistent in many moral situations. Because Kohlberg believes that each higher stage permits a more adequate way of making moral decisions, he might expect the child whose moral reasoning is advanced to be less likely to cheat than the child who still functions and thinks at the preconventional level.

In Piaget's theory, children progress from a premoral period to a stage of heteronomous morality and then to a stage of autonomous reality at about 9 or 10 years of age. Therefore, young children are more likely than older ones to display such aspects of heteronomous morality as a belief that there is imminent justice; they are also more likely to show a tendency to emphasize consequences rather than intentions when judging how wrong an act could be (Jose, 1990; Surber, 1982). Further, a child's moral development depends on his or her level of cognitive development.

In both the psychoanalytical and the cognitive-developmental perspectives, morality is viewed as a type of personality trait—that is, a quality one possesses and that consistently influences one's judgments as well as one's actions.

What would social learning theorists say about Starling? They would like to understand the moral habits that he learned and the expectations he has formed about the probable consequences of his actions. If Starling's parents have consistently reinforced him when he behaved morally and punished him when he misbehaved, he would be more likely to behave in morally acceptable ways than a child who has not had adequate moral training. According to social learning theorists, Starling's behavior would be more positive if he was brought up with models of acceptable behavior rather than brought up in the company of liars, cheaters, and criminals.

Social learning theorists are skeptical of morality as a single highly consistent trait or mode of thinking that will show itself in all situations (Sigelman & Shaffer, 1995). Even if Starling's parents have taught him to be honest, the learning may not translate well to the math class if Starling has an opportunity to cheat, if his classmates have bribed him with a reward such as a forbidden ice-cream cone, or if he sees his classmates getting away with cheating. That is, the specific situation appears to have a stronger influence than his prior learning. In sum, the social learning perspective on moral development shows that morality is situation-specific behavior rather than a generalized trait such as a strong superego or a postconventional mode of moral reasoning.

Specific learning experiences—that is, either moral or immoral habits—express themselves in various situations, where it is possible to cheat, be kind, help a person in need, and so forth. Thus every specific moral situation we encounter has an effect on our behavior.

Now that we have seen preschoolers' moral development from three major theoretical perspectives, let us examine various social factors that influence general development at this stage.

## THE SOCIAL ENVIRONMENT

Two-year-old children are egocentric. They take what others give them, they are possessive, and they believe that they are the center of the universe because they are treated as such by people close to them.

By age 2½, children are usually comparing themselves with adults in the family, brothers and sisters, and a few children in the immediate neighborhood, which is their social world. Through these associates, children learn their limitations and develop into socialized persons. As they grow older, their increasing interest in playmates of their own age corresponds with a decreasing interest in adult associations. By age 3, they have become more mature in their play activity. Social play increases because they have gained in their ability to control their body movements, to handle objects, and to talk. At 4 years of age, children are sufficiently mature, mentally and physically, to participate in play activities with others and are ready to learn social patterns.

### Play

Attempts at playing with peers have their ups and downs during the preschool years. Limited attention span, fatigue, insecurity in a new situation, and need for parental attention are a few of the potential problems in an extended play situa-tion. On the positive side, this age shows the beginning of child-to-child relationships. Given the opportunity, 4-year-olds will spend about half their playtime playing with others.

When children encounter frustrating experiences with one another, they argue. On the whole, however, 4- and 5-year-olds are more outgoing and cooperative than otherwise. By the time they are 5, most children can compete vigorously with other children.

Imaginative play peaks when a child is 4 years old, but it is not unusual for a 5-year-old to have an imaginary friend. Probably all imaginative life in children satisfies an inner need for companionship. Their imaginative play activity is also practical. Five-year-olds, both boys and girls, enter into home-centered dramatic play, making this age group ideal for trying out play therapy.

*Uses of play*   Much of the preschooler's time is spent in one form of play or another. Several theories consider such play serious and significant. Just as young animals frolic to practice survival skills, the play of boys and girls develops maneuvers that prove useful in adapting to life. The dedicated "inside-out" theorist might maintain that children have play instincts that serve the biological purpose of honing children's beginning survival functionings. But an "outside-in" theorist would argue that play is one of the processes by which young children incorporate into themselves some of the opportunities and expectancies provided by society (for instance, playing games with schoolmates and family). Both ways see play as significant and acceptable because it has a functional value beyond itself. Kastenbaum (1978) calls this general perspective the "play-as-practice view." Play for the child means fun, but sooner or later, play experiences will contribute to the child's adaptive, sociable behavior. Play is practice for later life.

Much of the physical play of childhood is *mastery play,* which leads them to acquire new skills. Children do not waste any opportunity to develop and practice their physical skills. A simple walk to the grocery store can become episode after episode of mastery play: The child walks on top of a wall, then jumps over every crack in the sidewalk, then skips, walks backward, or races to the store. While playing, children find ice patches to slide across, wind to run against, or puddles to jump over (Berger, 1986).

Other theorists view play as a way of letting off excess energy—"letting off steam". Indeed, there are no other socially established pathways for the release of excess energy or excitement in early childhood, and young children certainly do run, leap, shout, and hurl themselves about when excited. According to this view, fun and pleasure are acceptable outcomes, but the essential purpose of play is to discharge excess energy. This theory has its limits, however. It does not explain why the child discharges tension in one way instead of another. Nor does it account for quiet play, which uses very little energy. Furthermore, the relationship it assumes between the child's play and his or her psychological world is rather mechanistic: Inner or outer stimulation excites the child, who then discharges it pleasurably through vigorous play.

The psychoanalytical approach and others view play as a means of both learning skills and discharging excitation. Play for children is a sort of language through which they express thoughts and feelings naturally and spontaneously. Through play, children reveal their needs, fears, and triumphs, just as an articulate adult will verbalize them. This approach has practical implications. Play is a way of relating oneself to the outside world; the importance of play is not *that* children do it but *how* they do it—that is, repetitively.

The study of play often can help social workers treat emotional problems in young children. An experienced practitioner "reads" the nature of the child's problem from play behavior and offers help accordingly. This technique is often used for research purposes as well, for it reveals aspects of children's thoughts, feelings, and social development apart from any particular emotional problem.

The psychoanalytic view indicates that play can also be work. Through *play-work,* a term coined by Kastenbaum (1978), children learn to cope with new, challenging, and alarming situations. Because a range of problems and experiences have been identified as common to children, observers have a base for understanding what takes place in play.

Four-year-old David felt displaced when his stepfather entered the family; now, that feeling has worsened with the birth of a baby sister. Formerly his mother's only child, David is overwhelmed and has developed temper tantrums. He screams and cries at night, wets his bed, and has turned into a finicky eater. Worried, his parents take him to a child guidance clinic. The mother insists that she prepared David for the new stepfather and that both parents prepared him for the birth of his sibling by explaining in simple, direct language the birth process and what it might mean to him. Every time the mother looks at David, she says, "I told you everything, didn't I?" and he nods his head obediently.

Through the use of play, the social worker reaches a better understanding of David's feelings. In playing house, David consistently beats the baby and calls the older child "poor baby boy." The new father appears as a peripheral person to whom David expresses subtle hostile feelings. He says that he and his mother have had dinner but the father comes home late for dinner. At another point he mentions that the father and the new baby go in a car and are killed.

Observing David at play helps the worker understand how intensely David feels about his stepfather, sister, and mother. This manifestation of the insecurity, anxiety, and stress that David feels in facing the competition surrounding him (and his mother) is a revelation. Play therapy also helps relieve the child's fears and anxieties. As time passes, the social worker, through use of play therapy and the help of David's parents, works toward helping David accept the new situation and reassures him that he is still a valued member of the household. As David's trust and self-confidence increase, his disruptive behavior begins to diminish.

*Play and thought*    Like other human activities, play reflects the level and type of thought of its participants. A 4-year-old child throwing a ball differs from an 18-year-old quarterback releasing a pass. Although both are playing ball, they differ not only in physical skills but also in their thoughts and strategies.

One can observe different styles and types of play as young children progress from the sensorimotor stage to the representational stage. As they grow older, children can appreciate and enjoy having an effect on the world and on other people. Their play becomes more varied and idiosyncratic as they gain the ability to represent and symbolize. The world of "make believe" and "let's pretend" becomes available. Such games at the preoperational stage include people and animals as well as objects: "You be the bad guy and I will be the good guy," "You be the baby sitter and I will be the mommy coming home from work."

*Parallel and cooperative play* At times, preschool children playing in the same place at the same time do not seem to be playing with each other. In this phenomenon, known as *parallel play,* children may occasionally interact, reaching out for the same toy or imitating one another, but typically each child engages in solitary play while in a group.

*Cooperative play,* with its ups and down, begins during the preschool years. Parents and other adults can either facilitate or impede cooperative play by their attitudes and the kind of instructions they provide. At times, children may quarrel about which toy each child should play with. All the children may prefer a particular toy. Adults can help in solving such quarrels by having the children take turns. Adults partial to one child's needs alone will hinder cooperative play. Using sound principles, such as everyone taking a turn, helps children understand the concept of sharing and how it applies to themselves. Cooperative play reflects children's growing capacity to accept and respond to ideas and actions not originally their own. Healthy self-esteem and normal maturation, particularly preschoolers' growing communicative and social

skills, make it easier for them to cooperate (Lourenco, 1993). Cooperative play also contributes to the development of *prosocial behavior,* or behavior that benefits another person. Often, cooperation works because individuals gain more than they would by not cooperating.

*Fantasy* Fantasy play is a pleasant activity engaged in by children and adults alike. Through fantasy, children privately explore their ever-expanding social world (Singer, 1977). As children grow older, they often drink pretend milk from toy cups or have long telephone conversations with imaginary partners. For instance, Harris and Kavanaugh (1993) examined how easily children use props for make-believe, such as pretending that a popsicle stick is a spoon or a toothbrush. They asked the young children to pretend to brush a toy bear's teeth with the popsicle stick or use it to stir the bear's tea. Most of the subjects who were 28 months old did so readily. Children who were 21 months old played with the bear or the stick but did not comply with the request to use the stick in make-believe play.

Fantasy involves a substitution of one object or situation for another. Further, fantasy is often a reaction to real events, not a withdrawal from them. For example, a little girl may alleviate her frustration at being unjustly punished by having her mommy doll apologize to her baby doll. Imaginary companions may assume any form—human or animal, male or female—and have any type of relationship with and meaning to the child. They begin to disappear when the child becomes more involved with real playmates.

Fantasy or make-believe play not only entertains children but also allows them to explore topics that frighten them. For instance, a boy who is afraid of the dark may reassure a teddy bear who is also afraid of the dark. When the child begins to explain to the bear why he need not be afraid, the child comes to understand and regulate his own fear of darkness. As you have seen, through make-believe children explore other emotions as well, including anger, joy, and affection (Gottman, 1986).

## Peer Relationships

The most significant advance that preschool children make in their relationships involves their peers: They establish one-to-one friendships. Three-year-olds may have various playmates, but at this early age their egocentricity prevents them from seeing much importance in the differences among them. Soon they develop preferences, seeing one playmate as passive, another as aggressive, and so forth. They pick out the child with whom they have the most fun as their special friend. The relationship may not yet be sustained or consistent, however, because young preschoolers respond strongly to feelings that change from moment to moment.

*Gender differences in play* Preschoolers choose friends whom they perceive to be similar to themselves. Such a preference increases gradually during the preschool years; by age 6, youngsters pick same-gender peers as playmates about two-thirds of the time (La Freniere, Strayer, & Gauthier, 1984).

Is the pairing of boy with boy and girl with girl unique to U.S. or Euro-American culture? No. Around the world, when children choose playmates, girls prefer playing with girls and boys with boys. This segregation takes place without parental encouragement. When parents push children to play with children of the opposite gender, most children resist (Maccoby, 1990). Why does this happen? Usually boys and girls differ in the manner in which they play. When girls interact with other girls, their actions and remarks tend to support one another; they resolve conflicts through discussion and compromise (McCloskey & Coleman, 1992). Boys play differently. Their games are physically more active and rougher—intimidation, threats, and exaggeration are common as one boy tries to dominate the others. When girls and boys are together, girls find that their supportive, compromising style does not affect boys, who are more likely to respond with assertive overtures (Smith & Inder, 1993). Thus children begin to establish personal friendships with children of the same gender, which marks an important step in children's awareness of other people as distinct. In time, children begin to explore a new world of relationships, although the relationship with parents remains by far the most important as long as children continue to need their parents' protection. Both parent and child face an ongoing challenge to reach out for opportunities that lead to assertion, competency, and independence.

## The Family Environment

Every individual grows up in a different family situation, which either enhances or inhibits that person's growth. Successful people as well as murderers grow up in families. The nucleus of society, the family will continue to serve as a miniature society.

*The family as a social system* Although a large number of parents have ideals regarding parenting, often they do not consciously decide how to raise their children on a day-to-day basis. Their own parents' child-rearing practices may determine how their children will behave and develop. Early family researchers focused entirely on the mother-child relationship, operating under the assumption that mothers were mostly the ones who molded children's conduct and character (Ambert, 1992). However, modern theorists have rejected this simple, unidirectional model of family socialization in favor of a more comprehensive "systems" approach. This approach recognizes that both parents influence their children and also stresses that (1) children influence the behavior and child-rearing strategies of parents and (2) families are complex social systems—that is, they are networks of reciprocal relationships and alliances that constantly evolve and are greatly affected by the larger social context. Let us look at families from this perspective.

*Families are complex entities* Belsky (1981) indicates that a family as a social system is much like a human body—a holistic structure consisting of interrelated parts, each of which affects and is affected by every other part and each of which contributes to the functioning of the whole.

For example, say a family consists of a father, a mother, and three teenage daughters. The middle daughter is highly depressed and is under medical treatment. Her condition affects her parents' relationship, the daughter-parent relationships, the sibling relationships—indeed, all relationships in and outside the home.

Another example would be a nuclear family consisting of a father, mother, and a first-born child. According to Belsky (1981), even this man-woman-infant system is quite complex. Recall the process of reciprocal influence, which is evident when the infant's smile is greeted by the mother's smile or the mother's concerned expression makes the child wary. When the father enters the picture there is immediate transformation from a mother-child dyad to a family system where husband-wife, mother-infant, father-infant, and mother-father-infant relationships come into play. One implication is that family members influence other members through an indirect, or third-party, effect.

Even toddlers exert direct and indirect effects on parents. For instance, an impulsive toddler who does not comply with the requests of his or her mother may drive this mother to punitive coercive methods of discipline, resulting in direct child-to-mother or mother-to-child effects (Kochanska, 1993). This, in turn might make the child more defiant than ever (Crockenberg & Litman, 1990). If no help comes from the husband, the exasperated mother may then criticize her husband for his nonintervention and thereby precipitate an unpleasant discussion about parental obligation and responsibilities. Thus, the child's impulsivity and behavior may have a direct effect on the husband-wife relationship.

Now let us look at the complexity of an extended family, a nearly universal practice in some cultures in which parents and children live with other kin—grandparents, aunts, uncles, nieces, and nephews. Living in extended families used to be fairly common among African Americans. This adaptive arrangement allows economically disadvantaged African-American mothers to work, supporting their children without a father, through the assistance from grandparents, siblings, uncles, aunts, and cousins who may live with them. Extended family members may serve as surrogate parents for young children (Pearson, Hunter, Ensminger, & Kellam, 1990; Wilson, 1989).

Until recently, family researchers have mostly ignored or viewed extended families as unhealthy contexts for child rearing. However, this view is changing because research reveals how support from members of the extended families, particularly grandmothers, can help single mothers cope with various stresses outside the home and show them how to become more sensitive caregivers at home (Burton, 1990; Wilson, 1989). In single-parent, African-American homes, schoolchildren who receive ample kinship support also tend to receive competent parenting at home, which, in turn, produces positive outcomes such as a strong sense of self-reliance, competent academic performance, and fewer behavioral problems (Taylor, Casten, & Flickinger, 1993; Wilson, 1986). In some African cultures such as Sudan, social life is governed by ideals of communal interdependence and intergenerational harmony. Children routinely display better patterns of psychological adjustment if they are raised in extended-family households than in nuclear families (Al-Awad & Sonuga-Barke, 1992).

From all these cases, we can infer that the healthiest family context for child development depends heavily on both the needs of individual families and the values that families within a particular culture and subculture attempt to promote. Families are complex in all cases.

*Patterns of parenting* Erikson (1963) and Maccoby and Martin (1983) claim that two factors in parenting profoundly influence children— parental warmth and parental control.

*Parental warmth* refers to the amount of responsiveness and affection parents display toward their children. Some parents express a great deal of affection, although they might criticize a child who misbehaves. By contrast, hostile parents are aloof, unresponsive, and quick to criticize, belittle, punish, or ignore a child; further, they rarely show their children that they are valued or loved. The amount of regulation or supervision that parents give their children is called *parental control.*

These two aspects of child rearing are reasonably independent. As such, we can find parents who are warm and controlling, warm and uncontrolling, aloof and controlling, and aloof and uncontrolling (Shaffer, 1996).

How important is it for children to be accepted by their parents? Parental warmth and affection contribute to healthy cognitive, social, and emotional development. Children who grow up with affection form secure attachments to their caregivers and tend to be competent students, relatively altruistic, generally obedient, and high in self-confidence, self-esteem, and role-taking skills. They are satisfied with their gender identifies and refer to their internalized norms rather than fear of punishment as the compelling reason for following moral rules (Brody & Shaffer, 1982). In one study, Czechoslovakian children whose parents tried repeatedly to gain permission to abort them (David, 1994) were compared with wanted children. The former children were anxious, emotionally frustrated, and irritable; had more physical problems, made poor grades, and were less popular with peers; and often required psychiatric attention for serious behavior disorders throughout childhood, adolescence, and adulthood. Other investigators have found that the main contributor to clinical depression and other psychosocial problems in later life are that both or one of the parents treated the child as unworthy of parental love and affection (Lefkowitz & Testing, 1984; MacDonald, 1992).

## Child-Rearing Practices

*Parenting styles*   Maccoby and Martin's (1983) two-dimensional classification—parental warmth and control—fits an important set of findings

reported by Diana Baumrind (Baumrind, 1967, 1971, 1972a, 1972b; Baumrind & Black, 1967). After extensive research, Baumrind identified three distinct parenting styles: authoritarian, permissive, and authoritative.

The *authoritarian parent* tries to shape, control, and evaluate the child's behavior and attitudes, typically in accordance with a set of absolute standards. Parents of this sort value obedience to their authority and favor forceful, punitive measures to curb "self-will"—that is, whenever the child's behavior or beliefs conflict with those of the parent. The demand for obedience, a traditional parental value, is combined with an orientation to respect work and to maintain order within the accepted social structure. The authoritarian parent expects to be listened to and does not encourage verbal give-and-take. The child is expected to accept the word of the parent without question (Baumrind, 1972b).

The *permissive parent* is undemanding, nonpunishing, accepting, and responsive to his or her children. This parent attempts to maintain a laissez-faire attitude or blanket acceptance of children's behaviors, desires, and impulses, while making few rule-based demands. Baumrind found that these children showed the least self-reliance and self-control.

The *authoritative parent* attempts to direct the child's activities with a rational, issue-oriented style. Through explanations and reasoning, the parent tries to induce the desired behavior in the child. An authoritative parent encourages verbal give-and-take in order to share with the child the reasoning behind any particular policy or rule. This type of parent does exercise a firm control over the child, but not to the extent that the child is overburdened with restrictions. The child's interests, specific needs, and behavioral capacities are taken into consideration. Such parents see the rights and duties of parents and children as complementary, but they do keep their own parental and adult rights in mind, thus combining power with inducement.

Despite this classification, the lines dividing the three parenting styles are often unclear as parents attempt to find ways to do the best thing for their children as well as themselves. Most parents hope for the same results—children who show friendliness, cooperation, orientation toward achievement, and interpersonal dominance. This cluster of behaviors describes a socially competent, responsible, and independent person. Baumrind mentions that extremely authoritarian or extremely permissive parenting has negative consequences for children. Each parenting style has its pros and cons; we shall not debate which style is "best." It will suffice for us to understand that there are different styles of parenting and that each style influences children in various ways.

> Seven-year-old Peter belonged to a single-parent household for three years. His mother, Ruth, consistently took a permissive approach to child rearing. Then Ruth decided to remarry. Her new husband, Jay, is familiar and comfortable with an authoritarian upbringing. In his family, children were punished if they questioned parents. When Ruth consults Peter on what he needs to do for the weekend or plans things with him, Jay becomes uncomfortable and angry. He cannot understand how she can confer with and talk to a little boy as if he were an adult. In time, Jay starts to discipline Peter in his own way, causing Peter and Ruth a lot of heartache. Peter begins to act out, insults his stepfather, and finally decides to run away from home. The second time he runs away, Ruth decides to see a social worker. After several sessions with Peter and his parents, the social worker concludes that Peter needs a firmer kind of discipline than before the marriage, but one that begins with listening to Peter's point of view and reasoning things out with the child when a disagreement arises. With help from the worker and through collaboration, Jay and Ruth work out an effective way of disciplining Peter agreeable to both. Therapy works in this family because Ruth and Jay are committed to each other and sincere in their efforts to be good parents.

*Social class and parenting*   Social class or socioeconomic status refers to one's social standing based on money, power, background, and other factors. In some countries, the status of a person is determined at birth, but in the United States we are fond of saying that anyone can rise above his or her origins and that if a person works hard enough to succeed, he or she will.

However, Hess (1970) indicates that realizing the American dream is a belief more easily endorsed by the members of the middle or upper middle class, or people who have the economic resources to maintain or improve their own status. People from the lower and working classes have their own problems, goals, and values. Reaching the American dream of having it all appears far-fetched to many such people.

How do parenting styles differ by social class? According to Maccoby (1980, 1990), the lower class stresses obedience and respect for authority and places less importance on fostering independence, curiosity, and creativity. They tend to be restrictive and authoritarian and frequently use power-assertive discipline. They also talk and reason less with children. Maccoby claims that these class-linked differences are observed in many cultures and across racial and ethnic groups in the United States. However, we should remember that these are group trends, not absolute contrasts. Some middle-class parents are highly restrictive, power-assertive, and aloof in their approach to child rearing, whereas many lower- and working-class parents act more like typical middle-class parents (Kelly, Power, & Wimbush, 1992; Laosa, 1981). Generally, lower- and working-class parents seem somewhat more critical, punitive, and intolerant of disobedience than parents from the middle and upper socioeconomic strata.

*The influence of siblings*   Although families are getting smaller in the United States, the majority of U.S. children grow up with at least one sibling. Many people speculate on the roles siblings play in each other's lives. For instance, many parents fear that fighting and bickering among their children will undermine their children's ability to get along with others later in life.

Such rivalrous conduct can start on the day a new baby arrives (Dunn, 1993). The mother typically spends more time with the newborn, and the older child or children may respond to the "neglect" by being difficult and demanding, crying a lot and clinging to their mother, and at times pinching or hitting the tiny brother or sister (Stewart, Mobley, Van Tuyl, & Salvador, 1987). The older children resent losing the mother's attention and may harbor animosities toward the baby and do whatever they can to make their feelings known to recapture the mother's love.

Sibling rivalry develops in a spirit of competition, jealousy, or resentment among siblings. Fathers play an important role in increasing the time they spend with older children as the mother decreases hers (Steward et al., 1987). Mothers could also help by talking to older children, appealing to their maturity, and encouraging them to help out or care for the baby (Dunn & Kendrick, 1982; Howe & Ross, 1990). As they grow older, children pay close attention to what goes on between parents and siblings. Acutely sensitive to any signs of favoritism, they often feel resentment if they think their mom or dad likes the other kid(s) best (Dunn, 1993).

In some ways, sibling relationships are truly paradoxical because they are both close and conflictual. Furman and Buhrmester (1992) reveal that grade school siblings who were similar in age reported more warmth and closeness than other sibling pairs—but at the same time, more friction and conflict. Also, children viewed their sibling relationship as conflict ridden and less satisfying than their relations with parents, grandparents, or friends. Yet when they were asked about the importance of different social relationships and the reliability of their various social alliances, siblings were viewed as more important and more reliable than friends.

> A little boy begins to hit 6-year-old Anzana because he claims that she was cheating. Immediately Anzana's 4-year-old sister jumps in to protect her sister and begins to chase the little boy saying, "You better keep away from *my* sister!"

In addition to serving as caregivers, supporters, and emotional confidants, older siblings frequently teach new skills to younger sisters and brothers. Quite often, older siblings serve as important role models and tutors to their younger siblings.

*Coping with feelings*    According to the manner in which they are reared and socialized, children deal with their feelings in different ways. The strategic patterns that children develop for coping with emotions last a lifetime.

> Carlos is a quiet, shy child of 6 who has come with his family from Puerto Rico. His cooperative and industrious behavior impresses his new teacher. He is always neatly dressed and never gets into fights or arguments. One day, he is playing by himself in a muddy place on the school grounds, apparently trying to draw something on the ground. Just then, the school cat majestically walks over his drawing and moves on toward a tree. Carlos becomes angry. He runs after the cat, picks it up, and dashes it with all his might against the tree.

Why does the cat's behavior provoke Carlos so? He appears to be a model child. Why can he not cope with his anger? Perhaps his parental training has been extremely rigid, or he has not been allowed to show his own feelings.

*Reciprocity*    As we have seen, a reciprocity exists in parent-child relationships. Changes in parenting depend in part on the changing nature of the child. For instance, as the child's cognitive skills develop, reasoning and delay of gratification become effective disciplinary strategies. Such efforts would be meaningless with a 3-month-old baby, but an older child becomes increasingly capable of controlling his or her own behavior. Parental control and development of a child's cognitive skills are methods of supporting the child's emerging competence.

In the developmental approach, changes that take place in the child are seen as systematic and organized. Also, from a scientific standpoint, this approach illustrates the child's effect on his or her caregivers and thus the reciprocal nature of the parent-child relationship. Children's potentialities influence parents' behavior, which in turn influences subsequent child development.

## Divorce

About 60% of all children born in the 1980s and 1990s will spend more time—that is, about five years on average—in a single-parent home, usually headed by a mother (Teegartin, 1994). What effects does divorce have on children? It is helpful to view divorce from a systems perspective, where it is not an isolated event but rather a stressful experience for the entire family. Divorce begins with marital conflict before the actual separation and includes a multitude of life changes afterward. As Hetherington and Camara (1984) indicate, families must often cope with the diminution of family resources, changes in residence, assumption of new roles and responsibilities, and establishment of new patterns and relationships in the existing family.

Most families affected by divorce go through a crisis period of a year or more, during which the lives of all the family members are seriously disrupted (Booth & Amato, 1990; Kitson & Morgan, 1990). Usually, both spouses face emotional as well as practical difficulties. The wife obtains custody of the children about 85% of the time and may feel angry, depressed, or lonely. The husband may also feel distressed, particularly if he did not seek the divorce, and may feel shut off from his children. Often, both parents are isolated from former friends and other bases of social support. Also, divorced women with children usually face having to get by on about half the previous family income (Smock, 1993). Overwhelmed by responsibilities and by their emotional reactions to divorce, custodial mothers often become edgy, impatient, and insensitive to their children's needs. Divorced parents can become more restrictive and coercive in their child-rearing methods, seemingly transformed into more hostile and less caring parents (Fauber, Forehand, Thomas, & Wierson, 1990). Noncustodial fathers, on the other hand, usually become somewhat overpermissive and indulgent when they visit their children. Like their parents, children of divorce are often angry, fearful, and depressed about recent events. They may feel guilty as well, particularly preschoolers, who are likely to think they are responsible for their parents' separation. The parent-child relationship during this crisis phase is best described as a vicious circle in which the child's emotional dis-

tress and problematic behaviors and the adult's ineffective parenting style feed on each other, making everyone's life unpleasant (Baldwin & Skinner, 1989). This circle can also cause problems at school, including strained relationships with peers, academic difficulties, and conduct disorders (Fauber et al., 1990).

Alison & Furstenberg (1989) indicate that the impact of marital strife and divorce is more powerful and enduring for boys than for girls. Further, boys show more behavioral disruptions (Block, Block, & Gjerde, 1986, 1988). Other studies reveal that boys may appear to have problem behaviors in divorce situations because many researchers have limited their studies to the most common custodial arrangement—that is, mother-headed households. Boys whose fathers assume custody fare much better than boys who live with their mothers. It was found that children and adolescents of both genders seem more well adjusted and are less likely to drop out of high school when they live with the same-gender parent (Zaslow, 1989; Zimiles & Lee, 1991).

Thus divorce can strike a hard blow to children of both genders. From three to five years after a divorce, about 75% of the single-parent families go through another major change when the parent remarries (Hetherington, 1989). New marriage improves the financial and other life circumstances, and most newly married couples are satisfied with their second marriages. But new marriages also constitute more challenges to the children in terms of adjusting to a stepparent as well as new siblings.

Divorce itself does not necessarily disrupt children's functioning; children of maritally troubled homes often engage in aggressive and antisocial behavior. Hetherington (1989) and Hetherington, Cox, & Cox (1979) have documented that rather than divorce per se, the quality of the marital and postdivorce relations between parents is what directly influences child development. When divorced parents maintain reasonably friendly relations, mothers who have custody of their preschoolers tend to be more involved with and supportive of their children than mothers engaged in continuing strife with their ex-husbands.

Social workers need to understand the role that support systems such as informal networks and day-care facilities play in enhancing parental functioning. The discussion of divorce has shown that the support a marriage provides or fails to provide can make a sizable difference in the way children develop in the family.

## The Impact of Television

Television viewing has become a major force in the socialization of children in U.S. society. An amazing 98% of households own one or more television sets (Comstock, 1991).

Television watching is influenced by socioeconomic, intellectual, dispositional, and developmental variables. Children between the ages of 3 and 11 watch an average of 2 to 4 hours of television every day (Huston et al., 1992). By age 18, an average child born today will spend more time watching television than any other single activity except sleeping (Liebert & Sprafkin, 1988). Boys watch more television than girls and ethnic minority children living in poverty are especially likely to be heavy viewers (Signorielli, 1991).

Television can affect children negatively. U.S. television is incredibly violent. Almost 80% of all prime-time programs contain at least one incident of physical violence; the average child of 16 has already watched more than 13,000 killings on television (Gerbner et al., 1986; Signorielli, 1991). The Saturday morning cartoons for children average more than 20 violent acts per hour (Signorielli, 1991).

According to Gerbner, Gross, Signorielli, and Morgan (1986), children's cartoons number among the most violent shows on television. In addition, most westerns are violent, and some children watch violent adult programs. Some theorists argue that watching violent acts on television has a "purifying effect" on the audience: Television stimulates violent fantasies but acts as a substitute for excessive aggression. Those children who are adversely affected by TV are those who have limited real-life models and who spend considerable time in front of the TV set. Often these children have emotional problems.

> Robert spends a lot of time watching TV. His mother is a single parent who has to work, so 5-year-old Robert serves as a part-time babysitter to his 3-month-old brother. One day while Robert is watching a fascinating show, his baby brother starts to cry. Robert becomes angry, rushes to the kitchen, picks up a knife, and stabs his brother "just like the Mighty Mouse in the TV shows." Appropriate placement is arranged for him with the aid of a social worker and the cooperation of the mother, who needs help in dealing with him, particularly after her younger son dies.

How would you have dealt with this child? Could we call him a juvenile delinquent? No, but his life experiences are limited, and he does have some emotional problems and lack of caring by his mother, who has too much to do. Clearly, some intervention is called for.

Another negative impact of television on children is that, in spite of efforts to counter them, stereotypes abound on television, particularly regarding gender and minorities. Further, Latinos and many other ethnic groups remain underrepresented. And when non-African-American minorities do appear, they are usually portrayed in an unfavorable light, often cast as villains or victims (Associated Press, 1994).

Yet another negative factor is that the average child in the United States is exposed to 20,000 commercials every year, many of which extol the virtues of toys, clothes, fast foods, and candy. When children ask for products that they have seen on television and parents refuse, tears, sulkiness, and refusal to cooperate with parents take over (Kunkel & Roberts, 1991). Started by concerned parents, the organization Action for Children's Television monitors and tries to change television's impact on children. This group considers the potential harm of TV commercials as an even greater problem than TV violence! Policy makers are responding to the outcries, as evidenced by a recent law limiting the number of commercials on children's programs and requiring programmers to offer more educational programming or risk losing their licenses (Zigler & Finn-Stevenson, 1993).

Television is not, of course, all bad. As research has shown, it does have the potential to teach children many forms of positive social behavior, adherence to social rules, and attitudes of generosity, helpfulness, cooperation, and friendliness.

Carefully planned TV shows portray themes such as cooperation, sympathetic attitude toward others, affection, and control of impulses. The most effective television models resemble parents and teachers and thus can demand certain behaviors. Many programs broadcast on public television, such as *Sesame Street* and *Mister Rogers' Neighborhood,* are designed in part to illustrate prosocial activities such as cooperation, sharing, and comforting distressed friends. One major review of the literature found that young children who often watch prosocial programming do indeed become more prosocially inclined (Hearold, 1986).

In conclusion, TV is a potent socializer that can influence children's behavior in either positive or negative ways. In light of the case study included, one can say that a child who spends too much time in front of the TV set will grow up to be passive and imitative in comparison with children who spend time playing with their peers.

## IMPLICATIONS FOR PRACTICE

### Holistic Approach

Individual differences in children's growth are compounded by family background, socioeconomic background, and ethnic and racial issues. When Johnny does well in kindergarten but Jim, who sits next to him, daydreams all the time, it may not mean that Jim is a failure or is stupid. Jim could be suffering from any of several impediments, such as learning disabilities or emotional problems, chronically or situationally. Social workers must treat each child as unique and give help accordingly. Understanding and

evaluating the important factors that influence children is clearly a necessary aspect of the worker's assessment.

> Five-year-old Tasha has a hard time in school. She throws violent temper tantrums, gets into trouble easily, and is always aggressive. Concerned, the teacher refers the child to the school social worker. To the worker's surprise, Tasha's younger brother, nearly 3 years old and in the pre-kindergarten class, is cooperative, friendly, and obedient. The social worker does not understand how this can be. When her efforts to change Tasha's behavior by counseling Tasha alone fail, she calls Tasha's parents for a therapy session. Tasha's mother, Diana, comes for therapy, revealing familial factors in Tasha's behavior. Tasha's younger brother is her stepbrother, and her mother as well as her stepfather treat the two differently. It appears as though the mother wants her daughter to misbehave; to Diana, this daughter resembles her former boyfriend, Tasha's father, an alcoholic. Once the feelings stemming from associating her daughter and former boyfriend are explored and dealt with, Diana can work with Tasha on their problems and relationship. Efforts include concrete help, such as structuring bedtime and playtime, as well as counseling from the social worker.
>
> Through their ups and downs, counseling helps; Tasha's self-esteem improves, in the classroom as well as at home. Taking into consideration the environmental and individual interactions of her clients has allowed the social worker to counsel Tasha and her family effectively.

### Developmental Issues

Social workers need to be aware of preschoolers' developmental tasks. For example, some children may grow very quickly and look bigger than their age and may face problems for this very reason. Workers should also keep the cognitive differences in children's development in mind. If one child appears to be smarter or more outgoing than another, the practitioner should consider the family background of these children. Each child is unique, living in his or her own family culture and developing cognitive skills accordingly. If children use inappropriate language, the social worker should confer with caregiver(s) to understand the source of the problem; status and social roles greatly affect linguistic communication.

To help young children labeled as learning disabled or physically or mentally challenged, social workers must access all available educational and counseling resources. They should also be able to direct parents to appropriate support systems.

When a new child is born to a family, preschool siblings may face some adjustment problems. For example, they may throw temper tantrums at day care or school. In such cases, social workers need to make special efforts to talk to parents. With parental support, the worker can reassure the child that his or her place will not disappear because of the new child. The child could be helped to become a "tiny helper" in taking care of simple needs of the newborn. Often, such involvement changes feelings of anger and rivalry into love and caring.

Play is important for preschoolers' development. One can often recognize children's behavior problems when they are playing with their peers. Children who are sociable, withdrawn, bossy, foul mouthed, or overly aggressive reveal their behaviors accordingly. If negative behaviors persist during playtime, workers can then look for underlying causes. As mentioned earlier, the experienced social worker uses play situations to study and treat emotional problems. Play therapy also reveals children's thoughts, feelings, and social development apart from any particular emotional problems.

It is extremely important that social workers do not judge children who seem to be difficult to manage or communicate. Often, it is best to remember that behind every child stands a family with adult(s) in it. Often children merely reflect their own home life.

## Two Cases: Family Environments

Let us look at two children who have faced contrasting experiences in the development of their sexuality.

Garland enters kindergarten as a very unhappy youngster who wants the total attention of all children and adults. He kicks, screams, and teases other children. He disobeys every rule the teacher sets forth, and he yells and demands that they grant his every wish. Of course many children avoid him and do not enjoy playing with him. He attempts to bribe them with candy and toys but has only limited success. A streetwise boy, he uses slang and four-letter words. Punishment, scolding, and even attempting to talk to him do not stop these disruptive activities. Garland says to one little girl, "Pull up your blouse and show me your bra and boobs!" He pulls down other boys' pants and runs around the room, laughing.

Garland is highly verbal and says a lot about his home environment to the school personnel and the social worker. His mother is a single parent. He is not sure if his father is alive or dead. His mother has several boyfriends and he talks about the sexual activities that his mother and the men engage in. Other sources report that she uses cocaine. When she comes to pick up Garland, she is often intoxicated. Through the school, mother and son are referred for intensive counseling. Garland takes a liking to the school social worker and starts working on his positive social skills. He begins to gain more acceptance among his peers. However, the lack of helpful guidance from his mother and the unstable life still affect him quite negatively.

The second case offers a marked contrast to the first.

Five-year-old Tendra looks at her aunt and asks, "Aunt Mindy, isn't it time to go home and see my mommy and baby Alice? I want to hold the baby. I want to ask Mommy how she was born. . . ."

For months, Tendra has talked about her mother's pregnancy and the thrills of having a younger sister. Her teachers and peers all like her. Tendra is a well-adjusted child with sufficient knowledge to understand how her baby sister will arrive.

Tendra and her parents have discussed and made plans for the coming of their new baby. Tendra helped to choose the colors and the equipment for the nursery. Once she went with her mother to the doctor's office and the doctor let Tendra hear her own heart beat and that of the baby developing inside her mother's womb.

When the new baby is born, Tendra's mother hugs and kisses Tendra and later tells her to sit beside her so that she can see and hold her new sister.

The substantial contrast between Garland and Tendra involves their experience, their family, and the attitude of others toward them. Garland's developing sexuality is full of unhappiness and anger. He suffers from a continuing uncertainty as to how he will be treated in each situation he faces. He lacks self-confidence and support from others. Tendra, on the other hand, believes that the world is a pleasant place and that everyone is her friend.

Children learn by what they see and experience, as well as what others tell them. Tendra is fortunate to come from a caring family where she is made to feel valuable and where information about fathers, mothers, and babies is presented appropriately. On the other hand, Garland experiences inappropriate sexual exposure. His mother does not have time for him and he has to look out for himself.

Unless physical, children's problems stem to some degree from their family setting. As such, social workers should not be quick to label children without at least one family counseling session.

## CHAPTER SUMMARY

- The motor activities of preschoolers lay the foundation for future cognitive, social, and emotional development. Besides growing physically—in speed, coordination, and perception—children grow in their ability to learn.
- Physical growth follows a particular order. The process of learning a new activity involves readiness, motivation, and opportunity to focus on the activity, as well as feedback from the activity.
- The bodies and brains of young children reflect notable changes that affect their cognitive and social development.

- Preschool children are at the cognitive stage that Piaget calls *preoperational.* Piaget lists three obstacles to logical thinking: egocentrism, centering, and irreversibility.
- Language development is an important aspect of the preschool child's life. As children learn to speak, they also begin to learn about concept formation, which includes classification, seriation and conservation. These children develop the capability for symbolic representation and can use words as well as images to represent both thoughts and experiences.
- According to Vygotsky, cognitive development occurs in a sociocultural contest that influences the form it takes. Many of the child's cognitive skills begin in social interaction with parents, teachers, and other competent associates. Every culture provides its children with tools of intellectual adaptation that help them use their basic mental functions adaptively.
- Language development depends on the social relationships between the child and typical conversants.
- Language disorders can cause children many problems, including complications for them in the social world.
- In Erikson's thinking, preschoolers are in the stage of balancing initiative versus guilt. This is the period when their newfound energy helps them understand themselves as powerful beings. Secondarily they begin to realize that they should control their behavior. Crisis in this period appears as guilt, which arises when the child cannot control his or her impulses.
- In White's competence model, preschool children develop competence in three spheres: locomotion, language, and imagination. This is also the period when children experiment with several adult roles.
- Moral development begins when a person develops a "conscience." The child learns that doing certain things could lead to punishment. An increasing social awareness

appears in the early manifestations of sympathy, conscience, and generosity.

- Freud, interactional theorists, and social learning theorists each present unique views of moral development.
- An important aspect of children's lives is play, through which they learn to understand themselves and others. Different types of play include fantasy, imaginative, parallel, and cooperative. Play teaches the child to function as a member of society.
- The family is an important social system that enhances or inhibits the growth of an individual.
- Baumrind identifies three types of parenting: authoritarian, permissive, and authoritative. Child-rearing practices teach children patterns of behavior through the use of rewards and punishments.
- An important factor that affects the upbringing of many children is divorce. The manner in which a divorce is handled can make a significant difference in the way children develop in a family.
- Television plays an important role in socialization. Television watching is influenced by factors such as socioeconomic status and intelligence. Considerable debate concerns programming that portrays violence. Some children may not have adequate models to counteract the influence of television, and some children may suffer by spending an excessive amount of time watching it.
- The implications of the preschool stage for practice indicate that the social worker should never judge children for their problems. They must keep in mind that problems often stem from the child's family system.

## SUGGESTED READINGS

Guralnick, M. J., Connor, R. T., Hammond, M. A., Gottman, J. M., et al. (1996). The peer relations of preschool children with communicated disorders. *Child Development, 67*(2), 471–489.

Halliday, S. K., Urberg, K. A., & Kaplan, E. M. (1995). Learning to pretend: Preschoolers' use of metacommunication in social dramatic play. *International Journal of Behavioral Development, 18*(3), 451–461.

Holcombe, A., Wolery, M., & Katzenmeyer, J. (1995). Teaching preschoolers to avoid abduction by strangers: Evaluation of maintenance strategies. *Journal of Child and Family Studies, 4*(2), 177–191.

Kaiser, A. P., & Hester, P. P. (1994). Generalized effects of enhanced milieu teaching. *Journal of Speech and Hearing Research, 37*(6), 1320–1340.

Leaderbeater, B. J., Bishop, S. J., & Raver, C. C. (1996). Quality of mother-toddler interactions, maternal depressive symptoms, and behavior problems in preschoolers of adolescent mothers. *Developmental Psychology, 32*(2), 280–288.

Nabors, L., & Kayes, L. (1995). Preschoolers' reasons for accepting peers with and without disabilities. *Journal of Developmental and Physical Disabilities, 7*(4), 335–355.

## SUGGESTED VIDEOTAPES

Associate Productions (Producer). (1994). *A child's grief* (40 minutes). Available from Aquarius Productions, 5 Powerhouse Ln., Sherborn, MA 01770; 508-651-2963

CBC (Producer). (1996). *Autism: The child who couldn't play* (47 minutes). Available from FFH (Films for the Humanities and Sciences), 11 Perrine Rd., Monmouth Junction, NJ 08852; 800-257-5126

*Child development* (59 minutes). (1993). Available from FFH (Films for the Humanities and Sciences), 11 Perrine Rd., Monmouth Junction, NJ 08852; 800-257-5126

Meridian Education Corp. (Producer). (1996). *Communicating with preschoolers* (20 minutes). Available from Meridian Education Corporation, 236 E. Front St., Bloomington, IL 61701; 800-727-5507

Video Sales in Training (Producer). (1989). *Teaching beginning readers and writers* (28 minutes). Available from FFH (Films for the Humanities and Sciences), 11 Perrine Rd., Monmouth Junction, NJ 08852; 800-257-5126

WSMV (Nashville) (Producer). (1994). *Fatherless in America* (26 minutes). Available from FFH (Films for the Humanities and Sciences), 11 Perrine Rd., Monmouth Junction, NJ 08852; 800-257-5126

## REFERENCES

Al-Awad, A. M., & Sonuga-Barke, E. J. (1992). Childhood problems in a Sudanese city: A comparison of extended and nuclear families. *Child Development, 63,* 906–914.

Allison, P. D., & Furstenberg, F., Jr. (1989). How marital dissolution affects children: Variations by age and sex. *Developmental Psychology, 25,* 540–549.

Amato, P. R. (1993). Children's adjustment to divorce: Theories, hypotheses, and empirical support. *Journal of Marriage and the Family, 33,* 23–28.

Ambert, A. (1992). *The effect of children on parents.* New York: Haworth.

Anderson, S. (1979, March). *Register variation in young children's role playing speech.* Paper presented at the Communicative Competence Language Use and Role-Playing Symposium, Society for Research and Child Development.

Associated Press. (1994, May 14). Which practices work best in today's schools? *Atlanta Constitution,* pp. A1, A14.

Azmitia, M. (1988). Peer interaction and problem-solving: When are two heads better than one? *Child Development, 59,* 87–96.

Azmitia, M. (1992). Expertise, private speech, and the development of self-regulation. In R. M. Diaz & L. E. Berk (Eds.), *Private speech: from social interaction to self-regulation.* Hillsdale, NJ. Erlbaum.

Baldwin, D. V., & Skinner, M. L. (1989). Structural model of antisocial behavior: Generalization to single-mother families. *Developmental Psychology, 25,* 45–50.

Bandura, A. (1977). *Social learning theory.* Englewood Cliffs, NJ: Prentice-Hall.

Bandura, A. (1986). *Social foundations of thought and action: A social cognitive theory.* Engelwood Cliffs, NJ: Prentice-Hall.

Bandura, A. (1991). Social cognitive theory of moral thought and action. In W. M. Kurtines & J. L. Gewirtz (Eds.), *Handbook of moral behavior and development: Vol. 1. Theory.* Hillsdale, NJ: Erlbaum.

Bandura, A., & Waiters, R. H. (1963). *Social learning and personality development.* New York: Holt, Rinehart & Winston.

Baumrind, D. (1967). Child care practices anteceding three patterns of preschool behavior. *Genetic Psychology Monographs, 75,* 43–88.

Baumrind, D. (1971). Current patterns of parental authority. *Developmental Psychology Monograph, 4*(1 Pt. 2), 1–103.

Baumrind, D. (1972a). Socialization and instrumental competence in young children. In W. W. Hartup (Ed.), *The young child: Review of literature* (Vol. 2, pp. 202–224). Washington, DC: National Association of Young Children.

Baumrind, D. (1972b). Some thoughts about child rearing. In U. Bronfenbrenner (Ed.), *Influences on human development.* Hinsdale, IL: Dryden.

Baumrind, D., & Black, A. E. (1967). Socialization practices associated with competence in preschool boys and girls. *Child Development, 38,* 291–327.

Beck, A. T. (1976). *Cognitive therapy and emotional disorders.* New York: International Universities Press.

Belsky, J. (1981). Early human experience: A family perspective. *Developmental Psychology, 3*(23), 17.

Berger, K. S. (1986). *The developing person through childhood and adolescence* (2nd ed.). New York: Worth.

Berk, L. E. (1992). Children's private speech: An overview of theory and status of research. In R. M. Diaz & L. E. Berk (Eds.), *Private speech: From social interaction to self-regulation.* Hillsdale, NJ. Erlbaum.

Block, J. H., Block, J., & Gjerde, P. F. (1986). The personality of children prior to divorce: A prospective study. *Child Development, 57,* 827–840.

Block, J. H., Block, J., & Gjerde, P. F. (1988). Parental functioning and the home environment of families and divorce: Prospective and current analysis. *Journal of the American Academy of Child and Adolescent Psychiatry, 27,* 207–213.

Bloom, L. (1980). Language development and language disorders in children. In M. Bloom (Ed.), *Lifespan development* (pp. 99–104). New York: Macmillan.

Bloom, L., & Lahey, M. (1978). *Development and language disorders.* New York: Wiley.

Booth, A., & Amato, P. (1991). Divorce and psychological stress. *Journal of Health and Social Behavior, 32,* 396–407.

Brody, G. H., & Shaffer, D. R. (1982). Contributions of parents and peers to children's moral socialization. *Developmental Review, 2,* 31–75.

Bronfenbrenner, U. (1960). Freudian theories of identification and other derivations. *Child Development, 31,* 15–40.

Clark, J. E, & Phillips, S. J. (1993). A longitudinal study of intralimb coordination in the first year of independent walking: A dynamical systems analysis. *Child Development, 64,* 1143–1157.

Comstock, G. (with Paik, H.). (1991). *Television and the American child*. New York: Academic Press.

Crockenberg, S., & Litman, C. (1990). Autonomy as competence in 2-year-olds: Maternal correlates of child defiance, compliance and self-assertion. *Developmental Psychology, 26,* 961–971.

David, H. P. (1994). Reproductive rights and reproductive behavior: Clash or convergence of private values and public policies. *American Psychologist, 49,* 343–349.

Diaz, R. M., Neal, C. J., & Vachio, A. (1991). Maternal teaching in the zone of proximal development: A comparison of low- and high-risk dyads. *Merrill-Palmer Quarterly, 37,* 83–108.

Dunn, J. (1993). *Young children's close relationships: Beyond attachment*. Newbury Park, CA: Sage.

Dunn, J., & Kendrick, C., (1982). *Siblings: Love, envy and understanding*. Cambridge, MA: Harvard University Press.

Emde, R. N. (1992). Individual meaning and increasing complexity: Contributions of Sigmund Freud and Rene Spitz to developmental psychology. *Developmental Psychology, 28,* 347–359.

Erikson, E. H. (1959). Identity and the life cycle. *Psychological Issues, 1,* 1–71.

Erikson, E. H. (1963). *Childhood and society*. New York: Norton.

Fauber, R., Forehand, R., Thomas, A. M., & Wierson, M. (1990). A mediational model of the impact of marital conflict on adolescent adjustment in intact and divorced families: The role of disrupted parenting. *Child Development, 61,* 1112–1123.

Freud, S. (1950). Some psychological consequences of the anatomical distinction between the sexes. In *Collected papers* (Vol. 5). London: Hogarth.

Freund, L. S. (1990). Material regulation of children's problem-solving behavior and its impact on children's performance. *Child Development, 61,* 113–126.

Furman, W., & Buhrmester, D. (1985a). Children's perceptions of the personal relationship in their social networks. *Developmental Psychology, 21,* 1016–1024.

Furman, W., & Buhrmester, D. (1985b). Children's perceptions of the qualities of sibling relationships. *Child Development, 56,* 448–461.

Furman, W., & Buhrmester, D. (1992). Age and sex differences in perceptions of networks of personal relationships. *Child Development, 63,* 103–115.

Gauvain, M. S., & Rogoff, B. (1989). Collaborative problem and children's planning skills. *Developmental Psychology, 25,* 139–151.

Gerbner, G. (1972). Violence in television drama: Trends and symbolic functions. In G. A. Comstock & E. A. Rubenstein (Eds.), *Television and social behavior* (Vol. 1). Washington, DC: U.S. Government Printing Office.

Gerbner, G., Gross, L., Signorielli, N., & Morgan, M. (1986). *Television's mean world: violence profile* no: 14–15. Philadelphia: University of Pennsylvania, Annenberg School of Communications.

Getchell, N., & Robertson, M. A. (1989). Whole body stiffness as a function of developmental level of children's hopping. *Developmental Psychology, 25,* 920–928.

Gottman, J. M. (1986). The world of coordinated play: Same and cross-sex friendships in children. In J. M. Gottman and J. M. Parker (Eds.), *Conversations of friends*. New York: Cambridge University Press.

Greenough, W. T., Black, J. E., & Wallace, C. S. (1987). Experience and brain development. *Child Development, 58,* 539–559.

Harris, P. L., & Kavanaugh, R. D. (1993). Young children's understanding of pretense. *Monographs of the Society of Research in Child Development, 58*(Serial No. 231).

Hearold, S. (1986). A synthesis of 1043 effects of television on social behavior. In G. Comstock (Ed.), *Public communication and behavior* (Vol. 1). New York: Academic Press.

Hess, R. D. (1970). Social class and ethnic influences on socialization. In P. H. Mussen (Ed.) *Carmichael's Manual of Child Psychology* (Vol. 2). New York: Wiley.

Hetherington, E. M. (1989). Coping with the family transition: Winners, losers and survivors. *Child Development, 60,* 1–14.

Hetherington, E. M., & Camara, K. A. (1984). Families in transition: The processes of dissolution and reconstitution. In R. D. Parke (Ed.), *Review of Child Development Research: Vol. 7. The family*. Chicago: University of Chicago Press.

Hetherington, E. M., Cox, M., and Cox, R. (1979). Stress and coping in divorce: A focus on women. In J. E. Gullahorn (Ed.), *Psychology and women in transition*. Washington, DC: Winston.

Howe, N., & Ross, H. S., (1990). Socialization, prospective taking and the siblings relationship. *Developmental Psychology, 26,* 160–165.

Huston, A. C., Donnerstein, E., Fairchild, H., Fishbach, N. D., Katz, P. A., Murray, J. P., Rubinstein, E. A., Wilcox, E. A., & Zuckerman, D. (1992). *Big screen, small world*. Lincoln: University of Nebraska Press.

Huttenlocher, J., Haight, W., Bryk, A., Seltzer, M., & Lyons, T. (1991). Early vocabulary growth: Relation to language input and gender. *Developmental Psychology, 27,* 236–248.

Jose, P. M. (1990). Just world reasoning in children's immanent justice judgments. *Child Development, 61,* 1024–1033.

Kaluger, G., & Kaluger, M. F. (1979). *Human development* (2nd ed.). St. Louis, MO: Mosby.

Kalverboer, A. F., Hopkins, B., & Geuze, R. (1993). *Motor development in early and later childhood: Longitudinal approaches.* New York: Cambridge University Press.

Kastenbaum, R. (1978). *Humans developing.* Boston: Allyn and Bacon.

Kelly, M. L., Power, T. G., & Wimbush, D. D. (1992). Determinants of disciplinary practices in low-income black mothers. *Child Development, 63,* 573–582.

Kitson, G. C., & Morgan, L. A. (1990). The multiple consequences of divorce: A decade review. *Journal of Marriage and the Family, 52,* 913–924.

Kochanska, A. (1993). Toward a synthesis of parental socialization and child temperament in early development of conscience. *Child Development, 64,* 325–347.

Kohlberg, L. (1964). Development of moral character and moral ideology. In M. Hoffman and L. W. Hoffman (Eds.), *Review of child development research* (Vol. 1). New York: Russell Sage.

Kohlberg, L. (1976). Moral stages and moralization: The cognitive developmental approach. In T. Luckona (Ed.), *Moral development and behavior.* New York: Holt, Rinehart & Winston.

Kunkel, D., & Roberts, D. (1991). Young minds and marketing value: Issues in children's advertising. *Journal of Social Issues, 47*(1), 57–72.

La Freniere, P., Strayer, F. F., & Gauthier, R. (1984). The emergence of same-sex affiliative preferences among preschool peers: A developmental ethological perspective. *Child Development, 55,* 1958–1965.

Labov, W. (1970). The logic of nonstandard English. In F. Williams (Ed.), *Language and poverty.* Chicago: Markham.

Laosa, L. M. (1981). Maternal behavior: Sociocultural diversity in modes of family interaction. In R. W. Henderson (Ed.), *Parent-child interaction: Theory, research and prospects.* Orlando, FL: Academic Press.

Lefkowitz, M. M., & Tesing, E. P. (1984). Rejection and depression: Prospective and contemporaneous analyses. *Developmental Psychology, 20 ,* 776–785.

Levin, I., & Druyan, S. (1993). When sociocognitive transaction among peers fails: The case of misconceptions in science. *Child Development, 64,* 1571–1591.

Liebert, R. M., & Sprafkin, J. (1988). *The early window: Effects of television on children and youth.* (3rd ed.). New York: Pergamon Press.

Lourenco, O. M. (1993). Toward a Piagetian explanation of the development of prosocial behavior in children: The force of negative thinking, *British Journal of Developmental Psychology, 11,* 91–106.

Maccoby, E. E. (1980). *Social development.* San Diego, CA: Harcourt Brace Jovanovich.

Maccoby, E. E. (1990). Gender and relationships: A developmental account. *American Psychologist, 45,* 513–520.

Maccoby, E. E., & Martin, J. A. (1983). Socialization in the context of the family: Parent-child interaction. In E. M. Herrington (Ed.), *Handbook of child psychology: Vol. 4. Socialization, personality and social development* (pp. 1–101). New York: Wiley.

MacDonald, K. (1992). Warmth as a developmental construct: An evolutionary analysis. *Child Development, 63,* 753–773.

Malina, R. M. (1990). Physical growth and performance during transitional years (9–16). In R. Montemayer, G. R. Adams, & T. P. Gullotta (Eds.), *From childhood to adolescence: A transitional period?* Newbury, CA: Sage.

McCloskey, L. A., & Coleman, L. M. (1992). Differences without dominance: Children's talk in mixed and same sex dyads. *Sex Roles, 27,* 241–257.

Mischel, W. (1974). Processes in the delay of gratification. In L. Berkowitz (Ed.), *Advances in experimental social psychology* (Vol. 7), New York: Academic Press.

Moller, L. C., Hymel, S., & Rubin, K. H. (1992). Sex typing in play and popularity in middle childhood. *Sex Roles, 26,* 331–353.

Mussen, P. H., Conger, J. J., Kagan, J., & Geiwitz, J. (1979). *Psychological development: A lifespan approach.* New York: Harper & Row.

Pearson, J. L., Hunter, a. G., Ensminger, M. E., & Kellam, S. G. (1990). Black grandmothers in multigenerational households: Diversity in family structure and parenting involvement in the Woodlawn community. *Child Development, 61,* 434–442.

Piaget, J., & Inhelder, B. (1969). *The psychology of the child.* New York: Basic Books.

Rogoff, B. (1990). *Apprenticeship in thinking: Cognitive development in social context.* New York: Oxford University Press.

Rogoff, B., Mistry, J., Goncu, A., & Mosier, C. (1993). Guided participation in cultural activity by toddlers and caregivers. *Monographs of the Society for Research in Child Development, 58*(8, Serial No. 236).

Shaffer, D. R. (1996). *Developmental Psychology*. Pacific Grove, CA: Brooks/Cole.

Sigelman, C. K., & Shaffer, D. R. (1995). *Life-span human development* (2nd ed.). Pacific Grove, CA: Brooks/Cole.

Signorielli, N. (1991). *A source book on children and television*. Westport, CT: Greenwood Press.

Singer, J. L. (1977). Imagination and make-believe play in early childhood: Some educational implications. *Journal of Mental Imagery, 1*(27), 127–144.

Smith, A. B., & Inder, P. M. (1993). Social interaction in same and cross-gender pre-school peer groups: A participant observation study. *Educational Psychology, 13,* 29–42.

Smock, P. J. (1993). The economic costs of marital disruption of young women over the past two decades *Demography, 30,* 353–371.

Sprecht, R., & Craig, G. J. (1987). *Human development* (2nd ed.). Engelwood Cliffs, NJ: Prentice-Hall.

Stewart, R. B., Mobley, L. A., Van Tuyl, S. S., & Salvador, M. A. (1987). The firstborn's adjustment to the birth of a sibling: A longitudinal assessment. *Child Development, 58,* 341–355.

Surber, C. F. (1982). Separable effects of motives, consequences and presentation order on children's moral judgments. *Developmental Psychology, 18,* 257–266.

Tanner, J. M. (1990). *Fetus into man: Physical growth from conception to maturity*. Cambridge, MA: Harvard University Press.

Taylor, R. D., Casten, R., & Flickinger, S. M. (1993). Influence of kinship social support on the parenting experiences and psychosocial adjustment of African-American adolescents. *Developmental Psychology, 29,* 381–388.

Teegartin, C. (1994, July 25). Never married soar among single parents. *Atlanta Constitution,* pp. A1, A7.

Tudge, J. R. H. (1992). Processes and consequences of peer collaboration: A Vygotskian analysis. *Child Development, 61,*1364–1379.

Turiel, E. (1969). Developmental approaches in the child's moral thinking. In P. H. Mussen, J. Langer, & M. Covington (Eds.), *Trends and issues in developmental psychology*. New York: Holt, Rinehart & Winston.

Vygotsky, L. S. (1962). *Thought and language*. Cambridge, MA: MIT Press. (Original work published 1934)

Vygotsky, L. S. (1978). *Mind in society: The development of higher mental processes*. In M. Cole, V. John-Steiner, S. Scribner, & E. Souberman (Eds.). Cambridge, MA: Harvard University Press (Original work published 1930, 1933, 1935)

White, R. W. (1976). *The enterprise of living* (2nd ed.). New York: Holt, Rinehart & Winston.

Wilson, M. N. (1986). The black extended family: An analytical consideration. *Developmental Psychology, 22,* 246–258.

Wilson, M. N. (1989). Child development in the context of the black extended family. *American Psychologist, 44,* 380–385.

Zaslow, M. J. (1989). Sex differences in children's response to parental divorce: Two samples of variables, ages and sources. *American Journal of Orthopsychiatry, 59,* 118–141.

Zigler, E. F., & Finn-Stevenson, M. F. (1993). *Children in a changing world: Developmental and social issues*. Pacific Grove, CA: Brooks/Cole.

Zimiles, H., & Lee, V. E. (1991). Adolescent family structure and educational progress. *Developmental Psychology, 27,* 314–320.

# 5

# *Middle Childhood*

## INTRODUCTION

Eleven-year-old Peggy gets into the Internet as soon as she returns home from school. She is excited to get back to the safe world of the "chat room" where she carries on a long conversation with a person she has never met. She does not miss her real schoolmates as the chat room is less demanding and provides an easy escape to an unreal world. Peggy enjoys the chat room because it takes her away from the responsibilities of school and home.

Her parents are both professionals. The parental agreement with Peggy is that when she gets home from school, she is allowed an hour of TV before her homework has to be completed. But Peggy, who grew up without much real supervision, feels addicted to the Internet. Each day she enjoys the Internet conversations until she hears her mother's car in the driveway. Feeling guilty, she shuts down the computer and rushes to her room to begin her homework.

Middle childhood is a time of growth: cognitive, moral, and academic. Many issues arise as children learn the skills they need to cope with life at home and in school. In this chapter, we shall explore Piaget's concrete operations, several moral theories, Erikson's crisis of industry versus inferiority, and White's competency model. We shall also see how social settings affect children at this age; for example, culture, socio-economic status, divorce, and teacher expectations can all influence a child's development. First, let us look at the physical growth of children ages 6 through 12 and how it affects their development.

## PHYSICAL DEVELOPMENT

### Stable Growth

Middle childhood is a period of stable physical growth lasting more or less from age 6 to age 12. The child's rate of growth is slower at this stage than it was during infancy and early childhood. The child continues to change physically in a process called *stable growth*. During this period, many of the basic physiological functions are completing their transition to adult levels. A careful analysis of the child's anatomy will show that there is a shift from infant/young-child status to adult status. Many children begin to look grown up. The head-to-body ratio closely resembles that of adults: Whereas in infancy the head of the child was quite large compared with the rest of the body, now the arms, legs, and long muscles are catching up. The circumference of the head increases to about 90% of its final adult size. Physical coordination continues to improve, with the child performing movements too sophisticated for preschoolers. The child at this stage shows a more secure sense of balance in activities such as jumping rope and climbing. Attempts to overreach present abilities bring fatigue and distraction, and the child is susceptible to falls.

By the time children are 6 years old, their permanent teeth have begun to erupt, affecting the contours of their faces. By the time the child is 13, most of the permanent teeth have appeared, except for the wisdom teeth.

The basic developmental pattern is the same for both genders during early childhood. In middle childhood, individual differences are more important than gender; however, boys and girls differ in the use of their bodies. Boys tend to be taller and heavier and throw their entire bodies into actions, whereas girls tend to be more advanced in bone development, more flexible in the use of their muscles, and perhaps more adept at rhythmic movements (Kastenbaum, 1979).

*Size and shape*    Children grow more slowly during middle childhood than they did earlier in life. They gain about 5 pounds and about 2½ inches per year. During these years, the children become proportionately thinner as they grow taller. Muscles become stronger, thus enabling the average 10-year-old to throw a ball twice as far as the average 6-year-old. The lungs grow stronger and their capacity increases, so that each passing year children can run faster and exercise longer than before (Berger, 1986). The changes that these young people undergo are affected by experience and maturation.

Healthy children vary in height and weight; some children are small, some large. Nutrition, genes, and environment all affect growth. Further, the rate of maturation varies from child to child. Some 5-year-olds have better muscle maturity and coordination than some 7-year-olds. At the other extreme, some children undergo changes of puberty earlier than their peers, surpassing them not only in height but in strength and endurance as well. Thus various rates of development in this age group are normal.

## Motor Development

Children's ability to adjust to changes proceeds from their observation of their own bodies, which produces their body image. For example, children take advantage of the greater strength and longer arms they have, which contribute to a new sense of identity.

*Spatial orientation*    As young children mature, they gradually learn to orient themselves to their environments. Children learn to distinguish left from right when they are about 6. However, they continue to have difficulty regarding their orientation in space, particularly with reference to other people and objects. When children are walking straight toward you, they may regard your right side as your left because it aligns with their left.

When the ability to perceive spatial orientation develops normally, it accompanies the ability to represent a situation verbally. The right-left concept thus appears to develop as an integral part of children's total comprehension of their other relationships to the world, not as a single or isolated phenomenon.

Children under age 6 find it difficult to observe other people's actions and perceive that others literally see things differently. Piaget and Inhelder (1966) tested spatial egocentrism by asking young children to look at a miniature landscape of trees and mountains and report what a doll would see from various points around the scene. Most of those who were 6 years

old or younger believed that the doll's perception would be the same as theirs, no matter where the doll was standing. To a child at this age, the body is a secure home base, but they cannot yet recognize others' bases or frames of references. But as they grow older, they begin to notice others' points of view.

From age 6, children improve in their resistance to fatigue as well as their muscular dexterity and strength. Thus they can do increasingly fine work by using their small muscles over longer periods of time, resulting in rapid improvement in their ability to control their bodies and manipulate objects. This ability in turn improves their agility and accuracy as well as endurance. During this period children can jump and climb, throw and catch with ease. By age 9, the child's eye-hand coordination is quite good. The child is ready to experiment with crafts and shop work (Newman & Newman, 1995).

As their coordination becomes more sophisticated, children begin to observe and learn from watching and understanding others. Children's conceptions of human life show up in figure drawings and other forms of creative play. The child has different moods and purposes, and drawings represent them accordingly, as the following case shows.

> Seven-year-old Joshua is angry with his father, who lives away from home for long periods of time. Without him, Joshua cannot play some of the outdoor games he loves. When asked to make a drawing about his family, Joshua shows his anger with his father by representing a tree with a nest, and a mother bird in the nest with the small ones. The father bird is flying away, bleeding, with a broken wing. As Joshua explains it, the father bird lives away from home most of the time and is therefore a "bad bird," so he has been shot.

*Body image*    What types of body image do children develop? The physique most sought after is the muscular type, particularly by boys. Children who have the most popular type of physique and those who do not show important differences in the ways they view their bodies and how their total self-concept develops. In their heightened sense of selfhood, schoolchildren are commonly interested in comparing their developmental status with that of other children as well as with adults.

> Ron, age 7, is undergoing treatment for defective growth glands. Very short and slight of build, he looks like a 4-year-old. As the shortest boy in the second grade, he is self-conscious about his height. He constantly measures himself against his parents—particularly his mother, who is the shorter parent—and says, "I am up to here with you." Then he adds, "Next year, I will be up to there."

This child appreciates that physical growth continues—that there is more to come. In this significant sense, all children observe as well as participate in the developmental process. Further, children after age 6 develop a sense of their own role in maintaining health. When asked about their health, elementary school children seem to understand that good health is something they must work toward continuously rather than take for granted. Children recognize that nutrition and physical fitness are important for maintaining their health. As children grow older, they usually define health in more abstract and global terms (O'Conner-Francoeur, 1983). Some children, however, suffer poor health from factors beyond their control.

## Effect of Malnutrition on Physical and Mental Growth

Families with low incomes often survive on a substandard diet. *Subnutrition* is an impairment of the functional efficiency of bodies, which can be remedied by eating appropriate foods. Subnutrition or malnutrition can produce populations of children who are stunted, disproportionate in their growth, and afflicted with a variety of anatomical, physiological, and behavioral problems. In North America, despite its high level of industrialization, poverty continues to exist. Chronic subnutrition is often accompanied by dramatic manifestations of severe and even lethal affects.

Women malnourished as children experience more problems in childbearing and may suffer intrauterine problems, as well as prenatal risk to their children. This earlier malnourishment would also affect the functional adaptive capacity of the newborns. Animal studies have been constructed to test the implications in this chain of associations (Chow et al., 1968). The findings show that second- and later-generation animals derived from mothers who were nutritionally disadvantaged when young are themselves less well grown and behaviorally less competent than animals of the same strain derived from normal mothers.

Assuming that the primary criteria for normal intellectual development and formal learning are the abilities to process sensory information and to integrate such information across sense systems, evidence shows that both severe acute malnutrition in infancy and chronic subnutrition from birth into the school years result in a defective intake of information. Malnutrition may interfere with the orderly development of experience and contribute to depressed intellectual functioning (Birch, 1972).

Severe malnutrition usually occurs in conjunction with low income, familial disorganization, poor housing, and a climate of apathy, despair, and ignorance.

> Pat, a Child Protective Services social worker, visits a family in which the mother, a single parent, has been accused of neglecting her children. The family lives in a run-down neighborhood. To Pat's repeated knocks, the door is finally opened by a tiny boy, all skin and bones. It's dark inside, and as the social worker's eyes grow accustomed to the darkness, she sees filth and piles and piles of dirty clothes— even roaches and rats. The four children in the house are all severely malnourished, and all are kept away from school. Pat is sickened and shocked to see a child of about 1 catch a cockroach and eat it. Pat later finds out that this child is actually 3 years old. This is a case of complete neglect. Malnutrition has made the children quiet, dull, and totally submissive. The mother is a prostitute who stays away from home for long hours and does not care at all about her children.

# COGNITIVE DEVELOPMENT

In middle childhood, children learn more about themselves and their environments. Piaget called middle childhood the period of *concrete operations*. Bound by immediate physical reality, children cannot transcend the here-and-now. Therefore they have difficulty dealing with the remote future and with hypothetical matters.

In the period of concrete operations, one test of cognitive development uses a set of sticks of varying lengths. Children mentally survey the sticks and then quickly place them in order, without any actual measurement. In the preoperational period, children arrange sticks by size in their proper sequence by physically comparing each pair in succession. Children in the preoperational period are dominated by actual perceptions, and the task takes them several minutes to complete. However, children in the period of concrete operations finish the project in a matter of seconds because internal mental or cognitive processes direct their actions (Piaget, 1952).

It makes sense that many societies begin the formal education of their children when they have reached the concrete operations stage (age 6 to 7). Piaget (1971, 1976) indicates that this is precisely the time when children are moving from perceptual illusions and acquiring the cognitive operations that will enable them to understand mathematics, begin to understand words and language and the power of both, and learn about different animals, people, objects, and events. This is the time many children look forward to their own birthdays.

## Conservation Tasks

As concrete operational thought evolves, a liberation takes place in children's thought processes. For example, the principle of conservation involves recognizing that the quantity of any substance or liquid remains the same despite changes in shape or position. Children in elementary schools come to recognize that pouring liquid from a short, wide container into a long, narrow container does not change the quantity of the liquid. They understand that the amount of liquid is conserved. This realization implies that they are capable of *compensation:* making mental adjustments to account for various external changes in objects. A 7-year-old can compensate by focusing simultaneously on both the width and height of the containers with which he or she is working. A 7-year-old also displays *reversibility*—that is, the ability to mentally undo the pouring process and imagine the liquid in its original container. Children armed with these cognitive operations know that the two different containers each have the same amount of liquid, and they use *logic*—not misleading appearances—to reach their conclusions.

Children acquire some conservation skills earlier and some later. For example, they learn conservation of discrete quantities (numbers) somewhat earlier than conservation of substance. Conservation of weight (heaviness of an object) comes after conservation of quantity (length and area) and is followed by conservation of volume (the space occupied by an object). Piaget calls this type of learning *sequential development;* that is, the acquisition of each skill depends on the assimilation of earlier skills. According to Piaget, children usually achieve the notion of the invariance of quantity a year or so before that of the invariance of weight. Further, he uses the term *horizontal decalage* to indicate that repetition of behavior takes place within a single period of development, such as the period of concrete operations. Repetition of behavior leads to efficiency and a sense of competence.

*Challenging the notion of sequence* Piaget (1950) shows that all children pass through the same stages of intellectual functioning between birth and adulthood, and to him everyone's intellectual development appears to move in the same sequence. Other psychologists, however, have demonstrated that each of us has our own fairly consistent pattern of intellectual behavior, based on our exposure to various environments. This pattern can be described as a person's personal style, which is the stable preference that people exhibit in organizing and categorizing their perceptions.

Tomlinson-Keasey, Eisert, Kahle, Hardy-Brown, and Keasy (1979) conducted a study on the growth of logical reasoning between ages 6 and 9. They found that various concrete-operational abilities developed gradually but roughly in the same sequence for all children they studied. For instance, seriation occurred before conservation of number and weight, which seemed necessary for the development of class-inclusion skills and the conservation of volume. But other studies (Case, 1985; Kuhn, 1992) found less coherence, or consistency of development, during the concrete-operational period. It appears that some children breeze through the class-inclusion problems before they can seriate or conserve weight, whereas others acquire these skills in the opposite order. Therefore, the sequencing of different concrete-operational skills is highly variable. This finding challenges Piaget's notion that the operational proficiencies acquired early are simpler schemes that serve as prerequisites for those developing later (Shaffer, 1996).

Differences in people's cognitive styles also appear in their approaches to problem solving. Some individuals respond to a problem rapidly, without worrying about accuracy (impulsive behavior), whereas others who possess equal intelligence take considerably more time (reflective behavior) (Kagan 1966).

> Cindy and Karen, ages 10 and 11, are given assignments by their mother before she goes to work one Saturday morning. The apartment certainly looks chaotic. Dirty dishes sit in the sink and on the kitchen table to be cleaned. Opening the windows to let the sunshine in, the girls also allow some uninvited houseflies into the apartment. The temptation to go out and play in the street, with the sun warm on their backs, is too much to resist, so Cindy and Karen leave their household chores undone and go out to play. In their hurry, they drop their nighties right in the family-cum-living-cum-bedroom and leave their beds unmade.

Their 17-year-old brother Steve, who works in a fast-food place, comes home for an afternoon nap, having worked all night. Irritated by the mess, he calls out to his sisters, saying that he'll tell mom. His boisterous voice quickly brings the girls in. Cindy bursts out crying and starts to curse because she feels that her brother has treated them badly by yelling at them. Karen looks quietly at the mess in the rooms and starts to clean, whispering that they promised to clean up. Cindy's behavior is impulsive, whereas Karen's is reflective.

## Perception of People

The elementary school years are a period of rapid growth in knowledge of the social world and of the requirements for social interaction. When we enter a social setting, we attempt to place people in a broad network of possible social relationships and assess such aspects of people's status as age, gender, and roles.

*Global assessment*   Children under 8 years of age describe people largely in terms of external, readily observable attributes. They categorize people in simple, holistic, moralistic ways and employ vague, global terms such as *good, bad,* and *horrible.*

> At school, Paul gives Tommy candy but later changes his mind and takes it back. Later, 6-year-old Tommy complains to his mother that his classmate Paul is the "baddest" boy in his class.

An 8-year-old child's vocabulary increases rapidly. Phrases become more specific and precise, and the child steadily gains the ability to recognize certain regularities or unchanging qualities in the inner dispositions or overt behaviors of other individuals. Younger children characterize a person entirely by the quality the person is displaying at the moment, so the same person may sometimes be "bad," sometimes "good," and sometimes "nice." As they grow older, children become capable of integrating various qualities into the idea of a whole person. A 14-year-old girl says of her friend, "Sometimes she gets angry, but that doesn't last long and soon she's her normal self" (Livesley & Bromley, 1973).

*Culture* Sociocultural factors also influence one's perception of people. In some cultures, children are treated as adults when they reach 5 or 6 and are given adult roles to play. In the Koya tribe of India, girls become adults when they are 6 or so. They cook food, bring home firewood, and take care of their younger siblings. Koya girls learn at a very young age to cater to the needs of adult men as well as young boys, who are the hunters and go away from home for long periods of time in search of food.

> Zena is a 10-year-old girl who belongs to a conservative, lower-class Muslim family. At a young age, she learned to cook, take care of the house, and obey the commands of her brothers and her father because she was a girl. The family carefully follows the rules of their religion, which teaches that women are subordinate to men and must therefore cater to them.

What we see in this case differs dramatically from childhood culture in the United States. When working with diverse cultures, social workers need to be sensitive and ask questions if they do not understand a different culture, in order to be effective helpers.

## Self-Evaluation

During the middle years, children begin to receive feedback on their skill building, and this is accompanied by self-evaluation. Children begin to match their achievements to internalized goals as well as external standards. In school, children may be designated as the "red group" readers or receive stars in their notebooks and on the bulletin board. School plays an important role in self-evaluation. The children who perform well may be well liked by the teacher or be asked to sit on one side of the classroom, while children who do not do so well have to sit on another side or be sent off for tutoring. These external standards of social evaluation help children incorporate their own self-evaluations.

During the middle school years, the process of self-evaluation is complicated because the peer group joins the adult world as a source of social comparison, criticism, and approval. At this age children begin to imitate their peers out of curiosity or to learn new strategies while approaching a new task (Newman & Newman, 1995). At this point in their lives, children start to pay attention to the work of others in order to assess their own abilities (Butler & Ruzany, 1993). No longer do parents and teachers alone respond to the child's athletic skills, intellectual abilities, and artistic talents; peers also begin to identify with others' skills and to generate profiles of one another, such as "Randy is very good in math, but he is not good in sports." "Megan is fat, but she writes and tells nice stories." "I like Ardice because she is good at everything."

Harter (1985, 1993) studied children ages 8 to 13 and devised a method of assessing children's perceptions of competence in five specific domains: scholastic competence, likability by peers, physical appearance, behavioral conduct, and general or global self-esteem. Her research was guided by the idea that by the time children are 8 years old, they not only differentiate specific areas of competence but also view certain areas as more important than others. Being competent in relatively unimportant domains is not strongly related to overall self-esteem.

A study by Kupersmidt and Paterson (1991) compared childhood peer rejection, aggression, withdrawal, and perceived competence as predictors of self-reported behavior problems. Peer evaluation, teacher ratings of behavior problems, and self-perceived competence ratings were obtained for 613 second- and third-graders. Two years later a modified version of the Youth Self-Report and Profile were given to the children. Rejected and neglected girls appeared to have a greater self-reported nonspecific negative outcome (negative attitude) than other children. Such girls were also at a greater risk for depression. A varied set of predictors obtained from different informants emerged for each gender for each self-reported outcome of depression, unpopularity, delinquency, aggression, and self-destructive/identity problems. The quality of peer relationships affects self-esteem and seems to be important in screening children for subsequent maladjustment.

Another interesting study of self-esteem in preadolescents examined 320 African-American children in grades 5 through 8 who maintained their self-esteem in spite of some dissonant signals from the environment. The Coopersmith Self-Esteem Inventory was administered to the subjects in their regular classrooms. The application of the self-efficacy paradigm to the subjects' affective profile helped to explain the strength of their self-esteem. The study was sufficiently sophisticated to show the relationship between each of the following pairs of factors: (1) their zest for fun and the need to be mature, (2) parental closeness and discipline, (3) academic satisfaction and teacher stimulation, and (4) self-worth and emotional stress/distress. In a thorough interpretation of the factor analyses the true meaning of these distinctions was captured (Wentzel, Weinberger, Ford, & Feldman, 1990). Thus different factors, particularly the role of the family, has a tremendous influence on the growth and sense of self of children.

## MORAL DEVELOPMENT

People learn to live with their society's designations of right and wrong. All human enterprise requires rules. People also assume that the rules will be followed. Each person's own welfare, as well as the existence of justice and equality, depends on people's acceptance of certain moral standards.

As you know from the previous chapter, moral development is the process by which children adopt principles given to them, learn to evaluate behavior as right or wrong, and govern their actions by those principles. Psychologists have depicted moral development in many ways: as conformity to group norms, as an increasing capacity for guilt, as the internal regulation of behavior in the absence of external sanctions, as behavior that is socially positive or helpful, and as the ability to reason about justice (Carroll & Rest, 1982).

In this chapter, we shall continue and enlarge the discussion of moral development begun in Chapter 4. Carroll and Rest (1982) identify the major psychological components involved in behaving morally. They propose that a fully developed morality exhibits the following features:

1. *Recognition and sensitivity:* An awareness that goes beyond the perception of ambiguity; the ability to recognize the presence of a moral problem in a given social situation and the capacity to be sensitive and recognize that someone's welfare is at stake
2. *Moral judgment:* Determining what ideally ought to be done in a particular situation; also, being aware of what moral norms and moral ideals apply in a given situation
3. *Values and influences:* Application of values and influences to take into account the good that a situation may activate for a person as well as the influence of external pressures
4. *Execution and implementation of moral action:* Behaving in accordance with one's goals in spite of distractions, impediments, and incidental adjustments; organizing and sustaining behavior to realize one's goals

According to Carroll and Rest (1982), people can fail morally because of defects in any of the four processes:

1. Being insensitive to the needs of others, and therefore not noticing that there is a moral problem; being confused about a social situation and unable to interpret what is happening
2. Having simplistic and inadequate concepts of fairness and moral ideals
3. Having moral ideals that are adequate but are compromised by the pressures of the situation (for example, threats from others, controversial opinions, or physical danger)
4. Having insufficient energy to carry out the plan or becoming sidetracked by some diversion

The following case demonstrates the third point:

> Eleven-year-old George is picked up in the classroom for drinking. Both his parents and his teacher are shocked because George normally keeps within the range of acceptable behavior in school. He meets with the school authorities, who advise his parents to take him to see the school counselor. When George recovers from his alcoholic trance, he is ready to talk. He says that he never took a drink before, having been taught at home that it's wrong to drink or take drugs. However, at school, some older boys got hold of him and forced him to drink alcohol. When he refused, they threatened to hurt him physically. George knew that he could not attend class drunk or misbehave in a classroom, but despite the moral values of his upbringing he did what was asked of him because of the pressures of the situation and the fear of physical danger.

At this point, you may want to recall the major contemporary theories of moral development as discussed in Chapter 4 with reference to the preschool years. Freudian theory views moral development in terms of the innate structure of the personality. Social learning theory represents it as a function of conditioning and model experiences. Interactional theories formulated by Piaget and Kohlberg place moral development within a cognitive context. Now we shall look at each in relation to middle childhood.

## Psychoanalytic Theory

As specified in Chapter 4, children internalize parental prohibitions. How does such internalization take place? To avoid guilt, self-punishment, and anxiety, children "become" their own parents through the mechanism of the superego. External punishment is transformed into self-punishment; external control into self-control. By incorporating the parental evaluation of their own behavior, children incorporate into themselves the moral standards of the wider society. Thus, according to Freud (1930), guilt feelings are turned toward oneself. Freud also argues that excessive guilt is the foundation of many mental disorders. Though most behavioral and social sci-

entists do not accept orthodox psychoanalytical theory, the assumption that children identify with their parents remains a major tenet of much contemporary research and therapy.

Kochanska (1992) used a longitudinal study to evaluate children's development of conscience when they were 8 to 10 years old. Children were told stories and asked to answer questions about the characters in the stories and the moral dilemmas these characters faced.

From the study Kochanska ended up with a rich array of early maternal child-rearing techniques, children's temperaments, and levels of conscience development in children. Those children whose mothers de-emphasized power in controlling their toddlers showed the most advancement in conscience development when they reached middle childhood.

## Interactional Theory

*Piaget*   According to cognitive theory, morality, like intellect, develops in progressive age-related stages. Piaget's book *The Moral Judgment of the Child* (1932/1965b) discusses the development of children's moral judgments.

On the basis of his interactional view, Piaget believes that moral development occurs as children act on and modify the world they live in. In Piaget's two-stage theory of moral development, heteronomous morality (subject to external forces) arises on account of the unequal interaction between children and adults. Immersed in an authoritarian environment, young children occupy an inferior position and develop a conception of moral rules that is absolute, unchanging, and rigid. As children approach and enter adolescence, heteronomous morality gives way to autonomous morality, which arises out of interaction among peers. The relationship of equals, coupled with general intellectual growth and a weakening in the constraints of adult authority, creates a morality characterized by rationality, flexibility, and social consciousness. Through peer associations, young people develop a sense of justice, a concern for the rights of others, and a desire for reciprocity and equality in human relations. Piaget (1965a) describes autonomous morality as egalitarian and democratic—a morality based on mutual respect and cooperation.

Piaget presents four dimensions that characterize the heteronomous stage:

1. *Moral absolutism:* Young children assume that rules are universal and accept rules as given and unquestionable.

Tim, age 5, is not allowed to eat candy except after dinner. When he sees his friend Brad eating candy before dinner, he becomes upset and promises to tell on Brad. After all, if Tim is not allowed candy freely at home, Brad's family must have the same rules and regulations.

2. *Belief in immutability:* Children usually believe that rules are rigid and unalterable, as we saw in the case of Tim.
3. *Belief in imminent justice by God acting in the world:* Children think that misfortune is inflicted on wrongdoers by nature or God.

Eight-year-old Kathie skips breakfast and is thoroughly hungry before noon. When she sees some candy in her friend Susie's bag while Susie is away, she takes the candy and eats it. Then she is filled with remorse and guilt. While walking to the cafeteria, she falls down and bruises her knee, and she tells herself, "This happened to me because I stole the candy."

4. *Evaluation of moral responsibility in terms of its consequences:* Children appraise an act by its results rather than by the intent of the actor.

Seven-year-old Dean wants to go to the bathroom, but he's afraid to ask his teacher. Eventually he wets his pants and feels guilty and remorseful. He feels that he's bad, because he should have waited until the class was over. He also feels that he should have asked for permission to leave the classroom even if he was afraid of his teacher.

Piaget's stages represent the *growth* of a sense of morality rather than the *existence* of moral behavior. According to Piaget (1965a), children's

moral sense develops from the interaction between developing thought structures and widening social experiences. Eventually children reach the stage of moral relativism; they realize that rules are created and agreed on by individuals and that the rules can be changed as the need arises.

Over the course of middle childhood, obedience to authority declines in favor of *autonomy,* which is based on mutual respect. These moral feelings parallel the cognitive ability to understand conservation. In this period the child moves from a focus on *authority* to a focus on *interactions in concrete situations.* For instance, a preschooler may share toys with other children in the presence of his or her mother, who is the authority figure, because he or she is supposed to share. In the next period of moral development, the child may note that children who do not share their toys are not liked by other children.

The child begins to "conserve" or generalize sharing behaviors to many situations. This simply means the child is capable of *reversible operations.* In the toy-sharing example, the child who stops sharing and incurs the anger of his or her playmates returns to the beginning of the play sequence where sharing resulted in positive interaction. The ability to reverse thinking and return to the starting point helps the child develop and extend the principle of reciprocity and sharing. Piaget has suggested that such "reciprocal morality" is *autonomous;* that is, it is no longer "dependent" on the relationship of the child to an authority figure, as was true in the previous stage. The sense of morality in this stage depends on mental relationships between peers on an equal, give-and-take basis in a concrete situation (Lee, 1976). Further, this emphasis on the concrete distinguishes the moral behaviors of the beginning school-age child from those of adolescents and adults.

In his study of game playing, Piaget observed that boys become increasingly fascinated with the legal elaboration of rules and the development of fair procedures for dealing with conflicts, a fascination that he notes is not found among girls (Piaget, 1968). Piaget observed that girls have a more "pragmatic" attitude toward rules, "regarding a rule as good as long as the game repaid it" (Piaget, 1968). Girls appear more willing to make exceptions to rules and more easily reconciled to innovations. A legal sense, which to Piaget is essential in moral development, "is far less developed in little girls than in boys." Clearly, Piaget's thinking is biased in that he equates male development with child development (Gilligan, 1982).

*Kohlberg*  Kohlberg has extended Piaget's stages of moral realism and moral reasoning into five phases—the developmental types of value orientation—as described in Chapter 1. Further, Kohlberg and his associates have elaborated the major points of Piaget's general approach (Colby, Gibbs, & Kohlberg, 1983; Kohlberg, 1969, 1971, 1976). Kohlberg's theory and research include a collection of theories and methods, which share these basic points (Carroll & Rest, 1982):

1. They focus on the underlying interpretive frameworks (global, unified systems of thinking) of a subject in perceiving social-moral situations and organizing judgments about what ought to be done.
2. They assume that these basic cognitive structures are not rules but schemas of social understanding developed by the person in interaction with others. They are not developed by direct tuition, modeling, or reinforcement.
3. They hold that concepts of justice are key to developing moral understanding. People learn to understand progressively more complicated and encompassing systems of reciprocal cooperation.
4. They propose that development takes place through the successive transformations of basic organizing principles; hence five stages instead of Piaget's two (see Chapter 1).

Baumrind (1978) criticizes Kohlberg's theory because it ignores important differences in how cultures determine what is moral. In Baumrind's view, moral development may depend less on cognitive processes than on values instilled during the process of socialization. Power and Reimer (1978) cite other weaknesses in Kohlberg's theory. They claim there is a difference between thinking about moral behavior and acting morally. Moral decisions are made at times of crisis, when people's behavior may not reflect their beliefs. When Kohlberg reviewed his work (1978), he acknowledged these distinctions. In his modified thinking, Kohlberg specifies that behavior should be studied partially in terms of the moral norms of the group to which people belong and partially in terms of people's internalized attitudes. Kohlberg also grants that the last level of moral development, principle orientation, may not apply to people of all cultures.

In some cultures, stealing and even killing is not a crime. The gang tradition has been particularly strong and persistent in California and the southwestern United States in recent years. Among gangs, stealing and killing is acceptable. Some gangs in Los Angeles date back 60 or more years—at least in name and tradition. Donovan reports that "today a Hispanic in Los Angeles may be a fourth generation gang member" (1988, p. 7). Gang members do not necessarily devalue school and do not criticize others for doing well (Horowitz, 1983), but they tend to believe that formal public education has little to offer them. "In an environment where education is meaningless, the gang barrio fulfills the young man's needs. . . . The neighborhood gang is the stuff of living as the gang member knows it." (Pineda, 1974, p. 15).

The following excerpt from a *Chicago Sun-Times* editorial offers a graphic description of the nature of gang violence. In "One Weekend under Fire," this newspaper reported all 61 (gang) shootings between dusk Friday, August 19, and dawn August 21 in the city and surrounding suburbs:

Of the 61 victims here, 40 were African American, 13 were Hispanic, and eight were white. Twenty-six were teenagers, the youngest was 13. All the seven victims were men. All the suspected shooters were men. Forty percent of the shootings took place between 10 P.M. and 2 A.M. (1994, p. 21)

Youth join gangs for many reasons: status, security, money, power, excitement, and the desire for new experiences—particularly under conditions of social deprivation and community instability. The idea of a gang as a family pervades discussions of the function of gang life (Spergel, 1994). The sense of morality and responsibility thus differs from the larger society for gang members.

Kohlberg's theory has generated many research projects, which have confirmed some aspects of moral thinking but have neglected others. In a 20-year longitudinal study of 58 U.S. male youth who were 10, 13, and 16 years old at first testing, Kohlberg and his associates found that the boys progressed through the stages of moral development in sequence and none skipped a stage. Moreover, moral judgments correlated positively with the boys' age, education, IQ, and socioeconomic status (Colby, Kohlberg, Gibbs, & Lieberman, 1983). To some degree, cross-cultural studies confirm this sequencing of development.

The appropriateness of Kohlberg's definition of morality for women in U.S. society has also been questioned (Gilligan, 1982). We shall discuss this issue in later chapters.

In spite of its drawbacks, Kohlberg's theory has enriched our thinking about the way moral development occurs, has furthered an understanding of the relationship between cognitive maturity and moral maturity, and has stimulated research and the elaboration of moral theory.

## Social Learning Theory

According to Albert Bandura, Walter Mischel, and other psychologists, children learn socialization behavior through imitative play. They acquire moral standards in much the same way. These psychologists insist that social behavior depends on situational contexts, not on one single aspect of the superego. Thus social-learning theorists

believe that behavior is the result of modeling that employs an appropriate system of rewards and punishments (Mischel & Mischel, 1976).

Some studies by social-learning theorists center on the effect of models on observers' resistance to temptations (Bandura, Ross, & Ross, 1961). In an experiment conducted by Walters, Leat, and Meizei (1963), children saw a person who either yielded or did not yield to temptation. One group of boys watched a movie in which a child was punished by his mother for playing with some forbidden toys. A second group saw another version of the movie, in which the child was rewarded for the same behavior. A control group saw no movie. The experimenter took each boy to another room and asked him not to play with the toys there. The study showed that the boys' responses depended on the model they had seen earlier. The boys who had observed the movie in which the boy had been punished showed the greatest reluctance to play with the toys. The boys who saw the movie in which the mother rewarded the boy for disobeying proceeded to disobey the experimenter themselves and played with the toys more often than did the boys in the other two groups. In short, observing the behavior of another person did seem to have a modeling effect on children's obedience or disobedience to social regulations (Rosenkoetter, 1973; Ross, 1971).

## THE PSYCHOSOCIAL ENVIRONMENT

### Erikson: Industry versus Inferiority

According to Erikson, middle childhood is the period when children exhibit the belief, "I am what I learn." Children watch things and try to do them. Erikson's psychosocial theory suggests that a person's attitude toward work is established during the school years. As children develop their skills and acquire personal standards of evaluation, they evolve an initial assessment of whether or not they can contribute to the social community.

*Industry*  This period is characterized by the conflict of industry versus inferiority. *Industry* implies a willingness to perform meaningful work. In an attempt to develop a measure of industry, Kowaz & Marcia (1991) described it as having three components:

1. *Cognitive:* The acquisition of the basic skills, knowledge, and values of a culture
2. *Behavioral:* The ability to apply such skills and knowledge effectively through characteristics such as concentration, perseverance, work habits, and goals
3. *Affective:* A positive emotional orientation toward the acquisition and application of skills and knowledge, such as the curiosity to know and understand, desire to know, pride in one's efforts, and ability to handle the pain of failure as well as the joy of success

During middle childhood, many aspects of work are intrinsically motivating. Learning new skills brings children closer to the capacities of adults. Having skills also gives the child feelings of independence and responsibility, which increase self-worth. Children all over the world receive some type of systematic instruction during this period. In preliterate societies without schooling, for example, children learn by what adults and others demonstrate in their ways of behavior (acclamation) rather than by formal tutoring. They learn the basic skills of the culture, such as handling utensils, tools, and weapons.

In U.S. culture, the aim is to attain a sense of proficiency. In addition to the self-motivating factors associated with competence, external sources of reinforcement promote the development of skills. Parents as well as teachers encourage children to become better at what they do, offering material rewards and additional privileges. Peers also encourage each other to develop certain skills. Some social organizations, such as scouting, add to the acquisition of skills.

In middle childhood, the child is encouraged to gain independence. If not guided or prodded too often by the parent, the child develops a sense of initiative. If children remain tied to the parents for directives, however, their chances of becoming industrious diminish. Rather than initiative, such children feel shame.

Don is a bright 8-year-old, an only child overprotected by his mother. He loves to play ball and is quite good at it. One day his friends call him to play ball, and he goes without his mother's permission. In the course of the game, he falls and hurts himself. At this point, although enjoying the freedom of playing ball and the initiative that goes with it, he's filled with remorse and guilt because his mother has warned him that he should not play games without her permission. He feels that he should stay close to his mother and do only what she wants him to do.

*Inferiority*  The quality Erikson pairs with industry in this stage's characteristic conflict is *inferiority*. When do children generate a sense of inferiority? Feelings of inadequacy and lack of worth come from two sources: the self and the social environment. Reward structures are so attuned to competence that children who do not develop it have heightened feelings of inferiority. Individual differences in children necessarily result in differences in aptitude, preferences, and capacity for learning specific skills. Children usually experience some inadequacy regarding a specific skill. Success in one area can compensate for failure in another, minimizing the effect of individual areas of inadequacy on the resolution of the psychosocial conflict.

The environment provides different types of reinforcement for different types of success. In a 6-year-old, U.S. culture values reading a book more highly than playing with mechanical toys. Participating in team sports and winning is valued more highly than watching a TV show and enjoying it with the family. Thus the social environment does play a part in providing social comparisons. At school as well as at home, children are confronted with the message "You are not as good as so-and-so." Children are often judged by how their efforts compare with those of others. The intrinsic motive of engaging in a task for the pleasure of the challenge comes into conflict with messages that engender feelings of self-consciousness, competitiveness, and doubt.

The social environment stimulates feelings of inferiority by placing a negative value on failure. Thus failure is viewed as one form of embarrassment. Further, doubt and guilt intimately accompany feelings of inferiority. A few failures can generate strong negative feelings, so that a child avoids engaging in new tasks in order to avoid failure: "I can play tennis, but I am not as good as Joe, so I don't think I will try to play at all." As the child grows older, however, he or she can learn that work, effort, and perseverance will bring competence and approval.

> Zack, age 11, lives in the ghetto. His family does not value schooling. His mother, a single parent, cannot support her family of ten. Zack takes off from school often, and his mother does not question him. He steals food and picks pockets to bring home things that the family urgently needs. His stealing is overlooked—rather, subtly encouraged—for it satisfies the needs of the family. In school, Zack is below average and has difficulty spelling simple words; however, the family's approval of his competency in stealing helps him persevere. Although a child who does not do well in school normally develops negative feelings, Zack earns approval by engaging in new tasks that help his family, regardless of the fact that most people consider them antisocial.

According to Erikson, it is in middle childhood that children learn to deal with industry versus inferiority; demonstration of competence becomes critical for the child's developing self-esteem. However, Erikson is talking only about the male child, for which many have criticized him. For the female child, Erikson admits that the sequence is a bit different (1968). This difference will be discussed further in the section on gender-role development.

## White: Competence

According to the competency model (White, 1960), children reach a point of no longer being satisfied with just play and make-believe. In line with their interest in becoming adults, children need to feel useful and be able to make and deal with things significant to adults. Erikson discusses this need in terms of the humanly significant objective world; Sullivan (1953) relates it to the social world.

However, according to White, the growth of social competence follows a definite pattern. From ages 6 to 9, children find out how to get along with others in the sense of competing, compromising, protecting themselves from hurt, and learning the rules of the game. They do this partly because they have been thrown in with others at school and partly because children afford each other opportunities to do something interesting in the environment. During this period, however, children's needs for dependency, security, and affection still find their satisfaction almost entirely within the family circle. Only a few assertive youth would find a sense of security without it. As time passes, problems begin to emerge in the family, including a desire for a favored position in the family, jealousy among siblings or between a parent and child, guilt, and demands for affection from parents and others. All or some of these factors will characterize the child's emotional life at home.

> Joseph is the youngest of six children. The only son in the family, he is overprotected by his parents and shown favoritism. Joe nearly always gets what he wants. He has a special bed and extra toys and clothes, and his mother caters to him all the time. His sisters are treated differently merely because they're girls. His immediate older sisters envy him. At 7, Joe wants to get along better with them, but his need for love and attention as the favorite child in the family dominates other needs. In spite of the guilt he feels when his sisters accuse him of being the center of attention, Joe finds his sense of security in the family and isn't entirely secure in his relation to friends and the outside world.

When a child is about 9 years old, social competence and understanding advance to the point that the world of contemporaries begins to compete with the family circle. Membership in peer groups starts to have emotional appeal; what is known as the "we feeling" and friendships begin to supply some of the affective responses hitherto obtainable only within one's own family. Children begin to form alliances outside the home, which serve as an alternative to the family world and thus open the way for a new growth of independence.

White points out the considerable potential for crisis along this route, where one's sense of competence is challenged in many ways. The pursuit of proficiency in school work and other adult tasks can build firm self-esteem and social approval but can also produce a deep sense of frustration and inferiority. Outcomes of competition on the playground yield either tremendous self-confidence or painful feelings of inadequacy. Attempts to participate in group, gang, and team activities can confer rewards of membership or the punishment of rejection and ridicule. Young people seek friendships, which can open avenues for warm, cherishing feelings or can lead to rebuffs and withdrawal into self.

Do these crises have lasting importance for the development of personality? Freud has not attached much importance to crises that occur at age 9, during the period of relative sexual calmness between the turbulent preschool years and the storminess of adolescence. However, Sullivan (1953) identifies the juvenile period as the first developmental stage in which the limitations and peculiarities of the home as a socializing influence begin to open for remedy. Even more influential, in his opinion, are preadolescent friendships, which under fortunate circumstances might rescue young people otherwise destined for emotional trouble or even mental breakdown.

White agrees with Sullivan that developments in middle childhood can change the effects of the first five years of life substantially. In fact, a badly troubled first five years can lead to a relatively healthy outcome if later years encourage a rich growth of the sense of competence in many directions.

Many events in middle childhood confer self-confidence. A boy who becomes prominent in school life is likely to enjoy some fortunate friendships, as well as self-assured relationships with girls. As White humorously puts it, a youth could have one or more love relationships spoiled by "oedipal residues," but the young person will not be without alternative resources. In creating social relationships, young people have to deal with jealousy and other negative feelings. Again White's interpretation of development portrays the experience of boys as universal. He says that young men acquire several characteristics in latency that are available to them in middle childhood and offer them a wide range of confidence-building activities (White, 1960). (It is not surprising that White and other theorists have used the male model as the universal model for understanding behavior, both male and female, for this practice has been acceptable in our society until recent times.)

## SOCIAL ISSUES IN MIDDLE CHILDHOOD

### Diversity in Family Life and Parenting

*Diversity in family life*    Although the concept of a family life cycle is useful, it does not capture the diversity of adult lifestyles and family experiences (Rowland, 1991). A large number of today's families do not progress in a neat and orderly fashion through the stages of the traditional family life cycle—that is, marrying, having children, watching them leave home, and so forth. Instead, a small number of parents never marry and a relatively large number move in and out of wedded life by marrying, divorcing, and remarrying.

Many teenagers who have conceived children "accidentally" decide to keep their babies but remain single. Their lack of experience and limited finances do not help them much in their parenting. Quite often, such young mothers need the help of extended families and other social support networks.

Another group—older, single, educated, upper-class women with good careers—fear their biological clock time will run out and therefore choose to have babies out of wedlock. Such mothers are better prepared for parenting than the young inexperienced teenage mothers.

Some young singles today live with a romantic partner without being married. Such cohabitation is more common than it used to be, and about 10% of single adults in their 20s and early 30s cohabitate (Sweet & Bumpass, 1987). Living together typically does not substitute for marriage; instead, it is usually a temporary arrangement, sometimes seen as a test of compatibility that leads either to marriage or to a breakup (Tanfer, 1987). Unfortunately, when matters get rough, the couple can split, and any children they have had experience the pains of losing a parent, as in divorce. Children of unmarried couples who do stay together, though, experience a fairly stable home life provided there are no horrendous family problems such as alcoholism, drug abuse, or spousal battering.

We saw in Chapter 4 that married couples who divorce and remarry often form "reconstituted" families. As you know, most such families have experienced divorce as a genuine crisis of a year or more (Booth & Amato, 1991; Hetherington, 1989; Kitson & Morgan, 1990). After a period of emotional and often financial struggles, most single parents remarry, which puts the entire family through a major change (Hetherington, 1989).

Remarriage shortly after divorce can add to the pile of stressors that the family faces (Fine & Schwebel, 1991). If couples are not satisfied with their second marriages, they may seek another divorce. Second marriages are somewhat more likely to end in divorce than first ones (Booth & Edwards, 1992). Imagine children having to face a recurring cycle of marriage, marital conflicts, divorce, and remarriage (Brody, Neubaum, & Forehand, 1988). How do children fare when their custodial parent remarries? At first, they reflect

conflict and disruption as new family roles and relationships are ironed out (Hetherington, 1989; Hetherington & Clingempel, 1992).

This quick examination of the diverse family lifestyles has shown us the difficulty of generalizing about families in the United States. Although we do gain insights by tracking the progression of developing human beings through the different stages of the traditional family life cycle, we must recognize that an increasing number of individuals depart from this pattern (Rowland, 1991), and this affects child-rearing as well.

*Child-rearing*  Parental behavior affects children's behavior in many ways. First, parents serve as models. Most parents have specific expectations of what they want from their children and how they want their children to behave. Parents also control the rewards and punishments that children receive. Child-rearing practices thus affect socialization and the development of personality.

Depending on the child-rearing practices at home, children enter their middle years with different capacities to make friends. Family experiences and interactions in early life contribute to a child's sociability and social competence. Children who have secure attachments at home tend to be popular in preschool and engage in a large number of social interactions.

The way caretakers discipline a child at home, how they speak to the child, and what parenting values they hold all affect a child's social competence. Children whose chief caretaker interacts positively with them express their own feelings in positive friendships. These patterns become more established when a child moves from preschool to the middle years (Youngblade & Belsky, 1992). Children of parents who use power-assertive discipline techniques and who believe that aggression is an acceptable way of resolving conflicts follow suit; such children expect to get their way by asserting their power in social relationships (Dishion, Patterson, Stoolmiller, & Skinner, 1991; Haskett & Kistner, 1991). While observing the behaviors of children ages 8 to 12 years who had been physically abused, researchers found that the abused children had lower ratings of social status among their peers. Further, their peers described them as being aggressive and uncooperative, and their teachers described them as showing behavior problems (Salzinger, Feldman, Hammer, & Rosario, 1993).

> Richardo is abused by both his parents. His father is an alcoholic and a peripheral parent, and his mother is an uninvolved parent. However, when the father comes home drunk and angry, he beats his son; the mother, in fear of being caught in the crossfire, won't stand up for the son. Abuse has been part of Richardo's life as far back as he can remember. When he goes to school, all his pent anger and fears make him lash out at classmates. His teachers complain about his behavior repeatedly to the mother, but she never responds, because she is too afraid to deal with Richardo's issues or discuss them with her husband. Thus Richardo continues to act out his anger and family pain in the school system.

Child-rearing styles influence a child's social competence in at least three ways (Newman & Newman, 1995). (1) Children usually imitate their parents' behavior, whether positive or aggressive. If the parents are open and invite the child to ask them questions and respond to them sensitively, children begin to feel positive about conversations as well. Children from such homes tend to show interest in the ideas and opinions of others. (2) The way a parent disciplines a child also influences what a child will expect in a social interaction. For instance, children exposed to aggressive parental techniques believe that these same strategies will work with peers. When children become heavy handed and aggressive with peers, peers avoid them. This, in turn, leads to a sense of social rejection. (3) Parents who are highly restrictive and who are constantly trying to have complete control over their children's behavior tend to keep their young children from having many peer social interactions. Such children are less prepared for peer relationships, because they have less experience in peer play (Hart, Ladd, & Burleson, 1990; Pettit, Dodge, & Brown, 1988; Putallaz, 1987).

As we have seen, parents and children affect each other's behavior reciprocally. The defiant child is likely to elicit from his or her caregivers increasingly severe punishment strategies. In this pattern, the authoritarian parent may see the child's behavior as justifying this style.

Also, cultural trends in raising children, as well as pressures from families and friends, may change a parent's expectations. As parents become more mature and their values continue to develop, the resulting behavior may influence children as much as or more than the methods used in early childhood.

While parental patterns evolve, the child is also changing rapidly, as a result of his or her own cognitive development and peer relationships. As such, the child's and adults' attitudes and behaviors are not always well matched. Such complexities make it understandable that people turn away from socialization research in despair.

*Incest* In some families, parental power becomes deviant because of longstanding problems that one or both parents have and could affect a child brutally. One such continuing problem that has come to light in recent years is incest.

> Eight-year-old Martha is constantly preoccupied and timid in class. She has turned from a lively, high-achieving child into a quiet and frightened person. She will no longer talk to her classmates and has failed all her recent exams. The teacher knows that Martha's mother has recently remarried and that Martha must make many adjustments to having a new father in the family. Concerned about Martha's grades, the teacher speaks with Martha about her schoolwork, pointing out how her performance has changed. Martha bursts out crying but will not divulge any information.

The teacher sends Martha to see the school social worker. In this setting, Martha slowly but steadily reveals her painful story. Her new stepfather takes her with him everywhere because he "loves his little new daughter," and in the process an incestuous relationship has developed between them. Martha is scared to tell because her stepfather told her that it would break her mother's heart and Martha would be responsible for causing her mother unnecessary pain; moreover, he said her mother would never believe it. With much time and energy, the social worker intervenes and places Martha in a different setting until the stepfather moves out of the family home.

An incestuous situation throws all child-rearing practices into disarray. The practitioner must work with a child who has to play not only a child's role but also that of a lover to a distorted adult. The practitioner has to hold on to whatever is positive in the family's child-rearing practices and use them to work with the child.

## Gender-Role Development

Young children rapidly acquire (1) a gender identity in the knowledge that they are either boys or girls, (2) gender stereotypes or ideas about what boys/men and girls/women are supposedly like, and (3) gender-typed behavior patterns or tendencies toward "gender-appropriate" activities and behaviors over those typically associated with the other gender.

*Preferences*    Children rapidly come to behave in gender-appropriate ways and show preferences for gender-appropriate toys even in infancy. Babies clearly show preferences for "boy toys" or "girl toys" even before they have established clear identities as boys or girls or can correctly label toys as such (Blakemore, LaRue, & Olejnick, 1979; Fagot, Leinbach, & Hagan, 1986). Also, children quickly come to favor same-gender playmates. In a study by Jacklin and Maccoby (1978), pairs of 33-month-old toddlers (two boys, two girls, or a boy and a girl) were placed in a laboratory playroom and observed to see how often they engaged in solitary activities versus social play. Both girls and boys were more sociable with peers of the same gender than those who differed.

During the elementary school years, boys and girls develop even stronger preferences for peers of the same gender and show increased gender segregation, thus separating themselves into boys' and girls' peer groups and interacting and spending more time with their own kind far more often than the other (Thorne, 1993). Gender segregation occurs in a variety of cultures (Whiting & Edwards, 1988), and Maccoby (1988, 1990) suggests that this could be due to incompatibilities between girls' and boys' play styles. As we have seen, boys like to roughhouse, domineer, and be rowdy while girls tend to use polite negotiations rather than physical force to settle disputes (Bukowski, Gauze, Hoza, & Newcombe, 1993).

Because boys face stronger pressures to adhere to gender-role expectations than girls do, boys develop strong gender-type preferences at earlier ages (Bussey & Bandura, 1992; Lobel & Menashri, 1993). In a study of preferences for toys (Richardson & Simpson, 1982), researchers studied the type preferences of 750 children between 5 and 9 years of age as expressed to Santa Claus. Both boys and girls revealed gender-typed preferences, but more girls than boys asked for "opposite-sex items." This is still true in the 1990s (Etaugh & Liss, 1992). Girls can sometimes opt to be "tomboys" whereas boys who act like girls are called "sissies" or other disparaging names. In many ways the masculine role is well defined in U.S. society, and boys who do not conform are ridiculed and rejected (Martin, 1990). Girls can engage in cross-gender activities since they have begun to discover that the masculine role has greater status in society and many male activities are fun.

Gender-role development takes place rapidly. By the time they are in school, children have long become aware of their basic gender identities and how the sexes differ and have already come to prefer gender-appropriate activities and same-gender playmates. During middle childhood, their knowledge continues to grow, and they become more adamant in their thoughts about gender roles. Particularly among boys, behavior becomes more gender typed, with children segregating themselves more from "the opposite sex." How does this happen?

*Expectations*    Once a baby is born, biologically male or female, social factors immediately enter the picture. Parents and others begin to label and react to the child on the basis of the appearance of his or her genitals. If the child's genitals are abnormal, then she or he can be mislabeled as a member of the other gender. This incorrect label will affect the child's future development. For example, if a boy is consistently labeled and treated as a girl until 3 years of age, he will have acquired the gender identity of a girl (Sigelman & Shaffer, 1995). Biological factors enter the scene again at puberty when large quantities of hormones are released, stimulating the growth of the reproductive system, the appearance of the secondary sexual characteristics, and the development of sexual urges. These life changes accompanied by one's earlier self-concept as male or female provide the basis for adult gender identity and role behavior.

Gender stereotypes tend to be self-perpetuating; boys and girls tend to conform to cultural stereotypes. A youngster shown pictures of a boy playing with dolls and a girl sawing wood will probably remember the pictures as showing the girl playing with dolls and a boy sawing wood (Levy, 1989).

Gender roles are not etched in stone. Today more women work outside the home than ever before, accepting ever more rigorous challenges. What is the future of gender roles? The Family Lifestyles Project (Weisner & Wilson-Mitchell, 1990) examined families in which the adults had belonged to the counterculture of the 1960s and 1970s. Some of the families were deeply committed to living their own lives and to rearing children without traditional gender stereotypes. In these families, men and women shared the household financial and child-care tasks.

*Gay and lesbian parents*  How do the children of gay and lesbian parents fare? More than a million youngsters in the United States have a gay or lesbian parent; most of these children were born in a heterosexual marriage that ended in divorce when one parent revealed his or her homosexuality. Though still rare, children born to single lesbians or lesbian parents are becoming more common. What of the gender identity of these children? Because the number of studies conducted is small, our answers should be viewed as tentative. Preschool boys and girls born to lesbian mothers identify with their own gender and acquire the usual gender-based preferences, interests, activities, and friends (Patterson, 1992). In dimensions such as self-concept, social skills, moral reasoning, and intelligence, the development of such children resembles that of other children. For example, in one study of 15 lesbian couples and 15 heterosexual couples, the children were comparably intelligent and comparably well adjusted psychologically (Flaks, Filcher, Masterpasqua, & Joseph, 1995). If substantiated with further research, these conclusions would have important implications for social work practitioners who work with children of lesbian or gay parents.

## Socialization and the School Setting

*The school experience*  Children ages 6 to 12 enter school and spend a significant amount of time interacting with this new and complex social institution. School systems vary in standards of achievement as well as in norms of behavior. Many schools in the United States hire social workers to look into the problems that children encounter within the school system or bring from home.

When they enter school, children have to meet many expectations. Separated from their parents or chief caregivers for a significant period of time, they learn to take care of themselves in small ways, such as making sure that they are neatly dressed before they start their long day.

> Ten-year-old Justin is an only child with two working parents. In the mornings, he is responsible for preparing himself for school. He bathes, brushes his teeth, and dresses. He eats the cereal that is left for him on the dining-room table, leaves the dirty dishes in the dishwasher, makes sure he has his lunch money, then sets off for school.

In school children learn to cooperate with others and develop an understanding of school rules and regulations, which vary according to cultural values and educational philosophy. In the school setting most typical of suburbia, the teacher reviews and enforces certain codes of behavior: Children should listen before they speak, line up for recesses, and get permission to go to the bathroom. People generally accept that a teacher must spend a great deal of time and energy in keeping order as opposed to teaching the subject matter.

Eight-year-old Bill is a student at a private school that encourages "open classroom" behavior. Children can sit wherever they feel comfortable, select their own work for the whole day, and interact informally with the teacher and the other children in the classroom. By the unspoken rules of the classroom, each child works independently and can ask questions but should avoid disturbing others.

When his family moves to another town, Bill finds himself in a public school with standards that do not reflect the sort of creativity he experienced earlier. Discipline is strict, and Bill feels stifled by too many overt rules of behavior and the necessity of asking permission for "everything." He describes his teacher as a "law-and-order" person who concentrates not on teaching the kids but on punishing disobedience and rewarding obedience of the rules.

*Social values*   One of the major functions of a school is to teach the dominant values of society to its students. This traditional approach of instilling morals has been termed *character education* or *conduct development.*

In conduct development, students learn about and accept some of the responsibilities that they will have to face as adults. Because schools uphold middle-class values, some students from lower-class homes face conflict in learning the schools' values (Kay, 1975). Most upper- and middle-class children who attend public schools do not appear to have such conflicts.

Alice is a 7-year-old in a lower-class family. Her parents work for an upper-middle-class industrialist, employed in their home as a husband-and-wife team, and live in the servants' quarters. Thus Alice

has to attend a middle-class public school where neither the teacher nor her classmates understand her. Alice is a victim of neglect at home. Her parents spend all their energy fighting each other. Physical abuse in the family is excessive. Alice frequently goes to school hungry and sloppily dressed. Other children find her "rude" and unfriendly and look down on her, an attitude encouraged by the teacher, who is impatient with Alice's lack of self-discipline. The total lack of structure in Alice's family is reflected by Alice's classroom behavior: When she gets tired, she tries to sleep, and when she gets angry she curses and screams at the other children. In turn, the other children ridicule her, thus perpetuating a negative cycle that affects Alice's already low self-esteem. The chances of Alice attending a public school with lower-income children are nil. Regardless of the school system, Alice has personal problems that need attention. The school social worker spends time counseling Alice and her parents—helping Alice accept and adjust to her school.

Schooling also affects the sense of morality that children develop. Kay (1975) found that when a teacher was authoritarian, children withdrew into submission, and in a laissez-faire atmosphere they became indifferent and irresponsible. Democratic situations had positive effects on the children; they developed responsibility and, with the dispersion of social power, adopted adult values.

In the typical school setting, children interact for most of the day with many classmates in their own age group whom they had not known before. During loosely supervised recess and lunch periods, children learn to interact more closely with peers and build a value system that helps them function meaningfully in the school setting.

Martin, the firstborn of four sons, is concerned that he's not well liked in his new school. One day, he brings in his pet frog and shows his unusual pet to his classmates during free time. Having something to show creates an opportunity to initiate relationships with other boys. He tells the boys he has other pets, which he'll bring to school shortly. In this way, Martin begins to gain acceptance in his new school.

*Problems of individuality*   Like adults, children tend to be individualistic. A child's reactions to the school setting are affected by the complex interplay of intellectual, perceptual, physical, social, moral, and emotional factors.

Many kinds of problems may arise in a classroom. Sometimes a bright child is overlooked by a teacher because the child is restless or has poor motor coordination or poor writing ability. The child cannot participate in a reading group because of emotional immaturity and disruptive behavior. Unless the problem is addressed, the child will be viewed simplistically as disruptive and may not get appropriate help.

To understand a related problem, consider the child who does not speak English but must enter a school in a small suburban town where children are exposed only to the English language and U.S. culture.

> Feda is a Lebanese child who has been uprooted from her hometown and brought to New York City. With no facilities for bilingual education, Feda fails in school and is miserable. Her family is loving but cannot help her in her struggle to be bilingual. The school social worker puts Feda and her family in touch with community resources that can help Feda make the transition to a new language and culture.

Regardless of the type of school setting, children often face a tremendous gap between what is acceptable at home and what a new school demands (Holt 1964; Kozol, 1970; Read, 1971). Thus children internalize a whole range of new procedures. Children's ability to succeed in school depends on how they deal with the transition from home to school. Successful adaptation depends on factors such as how well they can cope with dependency, autonomy, relationship to authority, and the need to control themselves.

*Socialization*   School settings affect the social and emotional development of children. Concern for this effect is justified, for school is a fact of life for every child in the United States. As you know, schools play an important role in socializing children. Besides home, school serves as the main setting for the development of self-esteem,

self-image, identity, ego, and what one could operationally call a *sense of self.*

Because of changes brought about in the traditional U.S. lifestyle by such forces as feminism and the employment of women outside the home, the nature of child care in the preschool years is changing. Consequently, many children who are entering the public school system at 5 or 6 years of age have already been exposed to some previous school experience, such as nursery school or day care, or early interventions, such as Head Start. Early exposure to school helps children learn to socialize with children of similar backgrounds and in general makes the transition to a public school smoother.

*The influence of peers*   In school, peers play an important role in each other's lives. While parents may provide a sense of emotional security that enables young people to explore their environments and to appreciate that other people can make interesting companions (Hartup, 1989; Higley et al., 1992), contact with peers could be especially critical to the learning of social skills and normal patterns of social behavior (Hartup, 1992).

The influence of peers extends far beyond the realm of social development; that is, peers also contribute to emotional, physical, and cognitive development (Hartup, 1992). Peers, particularly close friends, contribute to emotional development by presenting opportunities for emotionally intimate relationships and by offering emotional support and comfort. Peers help each other feel better about themselves and weather difficult events such as divorce. They feel more confident in facing new challenges such as the first day of school, with its new grade and new teacher (Hartup, 1992; Ladd, 1990). By offering children opportunities to learn and practice new motor skills, peers also contribute to physical development. Social interactions also stimulate new cognitive growth. Children acquire new knowledge and problem-solving skills from peers and exercise their cognitive and linguistic skills daily in play (Gauvain & Rogoff, 1989; Tudge, 1992). For a child to grow normally, the child requires both close attachments to adults and close relationships with peers.

*School's effectiveness*    Schools expose children to an informal curriculum that teaches them how to fit into the culture of the school. Children learn to obey rules, respect authority, and become good citizens. Schools also instill basic democratic and social values. Increasingly, society expects schools to help combat social problems such as racism, drug abuse, teenage pregnancy, and AIDS (Corner, 1991; Linney & Seidman, 1989). As we have seen, schools are socializing agents that potentially affect children's social and emotional development and provide them with knowledge and skills to lead productive lives.

In his review of research on education, Rutter (1983) defines effective schools as those that promote academic achievement, social skills, polite and attentive behaviors, and positive attitudes toward learning, mandatory attendance, and the acquisition of skills that will enable students to find jobs. Clearly, some schools are more able than others to accomplish these goals, regardless of racial, ethnic, or socioeconomic backgrounds.

What makes for a good education? Many factors that people assume are relevant actually have little bearing on how effective a school is (Fraser, Walberg, Welch, & Hattie, 1987; Linney & Seidman, 1989; Reynolds, 1992). Factors that usually do not affect a school's performance include funding (unless it is totally inadequate) and class size. Reducing class sizes to 36 or to 24 is unlikely to increase student achievement; the optimum range is 20 to 40. Even a reduction from 30 students to 15 may have little effect by itself on student achievement (Odden, 1990). Further, it was found that tutoring students in kindergarten through third grade, even disadvantaged or low-ability students one-on-one or in groups no larger than three, does not make a big difference in the learning of reading and math (Odden, 1990; Slavin, 1989).

The pros and cons of ability tracking have been debated for years. In ability tracking, students are grouped according to ability and then taught to work with others who have a similar academic or intellectual standing. Particularly when it involves separate classes for students of different ability, ability tracking offers no clear advantage over mixed-ability grouping for most students (Kulik & Kulik, 1992). On the other hand, low-ability students are unlikely to benefit and may suffer if they are denied access to the most effective teachers and are stigmatized as dummies (Rutter, 1983). These are examples of some of the characteristics that do not seem to contribute a great deal to effective education.

*Multicultural concerns and teacher expectations*    Public schools have traditionally been middle-class white institutions staffed by middle-class white professors who have Euro-American values. Yet when we look at a state such as California, it is clear that a majority of the school children belong to various minority groups (Garcia, 1993).

Many low-income African-American, Hispanic, and Native-American students earn poorer grades and achievement scores than their Anglo-American classmates whereas Asian Americans— that is, Japanese and Chinese—tend to outperform Anglo students (Slaughter-Defoe, Nakagawa, Takaniski, & Johnson, 1990; Sue & Okazaki, 1990). These racial and ethnic differences persist even after ethnic group differences in family income and other indicators of socioeconomic status are accounted for (Sue & Okazaki, 1990).

The factors that seem to influence school performance and achievement are parental influences, peer influences, and teacher expectations. Even when parents value education and highlight its effects, if peers in school devalue education, students must choose between academic success and peer acceptance (Ogbu, 1990). Regarding teacher expectations, the underachievement of some minority students is rooted in stereotyping and discrimination on the part of the teachers.

In a classic study, Rosenthal and Jacobson (1968) demonstrated that a teacher's expectations about a student can influence a student's ultimate achievement in what is called the *Pygmalion effect*. Students actually perform better when expected to do well than when expected to do poorly; teacher expectancies become self-fulfilling prophecies. How does this Pygmalion effect work? It appears that some teachers who expect great things of a student are warmer, expose the student to more and difficult materials, interact with students more often, and give him or her many opportunities to respond (Harris & Rosenthal, 1986). On the other hand, a Mexican-American or an African-American student from a poor neighborhood might be tagged by a teacher as a low-ability student and treated in ways that do not facilitate learning. Thus, he or she might end up fulfilling the teacher's low expectations as a result (Sorenson & Hallinan, 1986).

To evaluate academic achievement in terms of motivational, affective, and self-regulatory processes among preadolescents, a group of 163 sixth-graders were studied. Measures included GPA (grade point average) and adjustment inventory. The study showed that low distress and high motivation were positively related to classroom achievement by way of their association with self-restraint. In contrast, the teachers' evaluations of the students' high distress and low restraint were negatively related to poor achievement through association with low motivation. These results suggest that motivational, affective, and self-regulatory factors play an important role in the achievement of academic competence both as intrapersonal processes as well as behavioral manifestation of students' efforts to achieve (Wentzel et al., 1990).

Thus more than any other factor, a stress-free environment leads to better performance in the school system. This includes stress in the family, with peers, and in other environmental situations.

*Computers and schoolchildren*   No discussion of educational performance is complete without considering the effect of computers on children. Adults who grew up without computers are sometimes not sure of what to make of them but buy them for their children anyway. Schools are increasingly making computers part of the educational process. Researchers have started to question whether students learn more from computer-assisted instruction or from traditional instruction. Some forms of computer-assisted instruction are simple drills, such as math problems. Other computer programs are more elaborate, allowing students to learn academic materials by playing highly motivational and thought-provoking games.

After evaluating the research literature, Leppe and Gurtner (1989) have concluded that computer-assisted instruction is indeed more effective than traditional instruction, especially among disadvantaged and low-ability children. Highly involved "tutorials" that encourage thinking seem to be more beneficial than simple "drills." Teaching students the computer language Logo and allowing them to use it to figure out how to design graphics on the computer screen can actually improve their ability to think about their own thinking, deal with problems logically, and solve problems creatively (Clements, 1990, 1991).

Do computers isolate children from their peers? Apparently not. Because children use the computer like any other toy, it does not interfere with their playtime with friends. Research suggests that children who are learning to use the computer engage more in collaborative conversations than children who work in the traditional style (Crook, 1992; Kee, 1986; Weinstein, 1991). Eventually the computer, like television, will probably turn out to be either a positive or negative force in development, depending on how it is used. If children end up playing on their computers in their rooms, zapping mutant aliens from space for hours on end, perhaps the effects will be bad. But if computers are used as tools to help them play with each other and learn in more creative and effective ways, the future will be quite positive (Sigelman & Shaffer, 1995).

## Same-Gender Peer Groups

While children grow up as part of the home and school settings, they also venture out as social beings. They look to their peers for support and care. As mentioned earlier, middle childhood is also called the period of same-gender peer groups.

Young boys and girls play together on school playgrounds during recess. By the third grade, however, schoolchildren have divided themselves into two camps: girls are friendly with girls and boys are friendly with boys. This separation into same-gender groups tends to peak at about the fifth grade, and much of the interaction between boys and girls at the fifth-grade level takes the form of bantering, teasing, name calling, and even displays of open hostility. This "us against them" view of the opposite sex serves to emphasize differences between the genders. Thus, this period functions as a protective phase in life during which children can fashion a coherent gender identity (Kerckhoff, 1972).

*Social acceptance and rejection*  Many peer relationships take on enduring and stable characteristics. In this regard they resemble a *group,* or an assemblage of two or more people who share a feeling of unity and are bound together in relatively stable patterns of social interaction. Group members normally have a sense of oneness, an assumption that their own inner experiences and emotional reactions are shared by other members. This like-mindedness lets each member feel not merely in the group but *of* the group.

> Bill, Arthur, and James are good friends. Although they have a larger group of friends in the neighborhood, they are especially close. All three of them are 8, and all like to play soccer and watch the same shows on TV. They are also members of a club they created. They share their secrets, ideas, and dreams. They are loyal to each other and follow certain patterns of behavior. When Bill forgot to bring his lunch to school one day, Arthur and James shared theirs with him. They visit each other in their homes and have good feelings for each other. Being together makes the three friends feel comfortable and well liked.

A group's awareness is experienced through shared values, or the criteria people use to decide the relative merit and desirability of such things as other people, objects, events, ideas, acts, and feelings. Elementary school peer groups are no exception. The children arrange themselves in ranked hierarchies with respect to a variety of qualities. Even first-graders have notions of one another's relative popularity or status. Children differ in the extent to which their peers desire to be associated with them.

●

## SPECIAL CONCERNS

### Obstacles to Learning

Some children in later childhood do face critical learning problems at home or in the school setting. Such problems vary from learning disabilities and attention-deficit hyperactivity to mental retardation.

*Learning disabilities*  For some children with normal intelligence, learning is a struggle. These youngsters suffer from a *learning disability,* which means they (1) find it hard to gain proficiency in one or more academic subjects, (2) have normal intelligence, and (3) do not suffer from other conditions that could explain poor performance, such as sensory impairment or inadequate instruction (Hammill, 1990). There are a great number of learning disabilities, each type with its own cause and treatment. For example, a reading disability may be connected to problems in phonological processing and understanding and using sounds in written and oral language. All vowels would sound alike. Children with this disability would benefit from explicit and extensive instruction on the connection between letters and sounds (Lovett et al., 1994). Another child might suffer from an arithmetic disability. Here the instructor would explain the goals of arithmetic problems, select the correct arithmetic operations, and help the child use the operations accurately (Goldman, 1989).

Social workers need to learn about the different types of learning disabilities so they can pinpoint the specific cognitive and academic deficits that hamper a child's performance in school. With a precise account of these deficits, workers and teachers could plan instructions to improve a child's skills (Moats & Lyon, 1993). It is not easy to diagnose a specific disability. A child may suffer from both reading and arithmetic disabilities as well as such learning disabilities as attention-deficit hyperactivity. In the United States, about 5% of school-age children are classified as learning disabled, or about 2 million youngsters (Moats & Lyon, 1993). Researchers still constantly debate the degree of overlap among the learning disabilities. However, one common classification distinguishes disability in language, listening, speaking, and writing as well as reading and arithmetic (Dockrell & McShane, 1993): attention-deficit hyperactivity disorder (ADHD).

*ADHD*    What is ADHD? Let's look at a case.

A 5-year-old boy, Willie, gets up at 5 in the morning and goes to the refrigerator. He takes out some milk to drink but the eggs catch his attention, so he pulls out a whole tray of them and breaks them on the floor. He's upset and wants to clean up the mess, so he goes to the laundry room to look for a mop. But as soon as he reaches the basement he forgets about the mess in the kitchen and instead pours the detergent in the washer, throws in some of his clothes, as well as his toy train, and turns on the machine. When his mother wakes up 2 hours later, it looks like a hurricane has passed through her house. She feels ready to cry out of anger and frustration.

According to the DSM-IV, ADHD has three symptoms:

1. *Inattention:* For example, if the child does not seem to listen and is easily distracted and does not finish his or her activities or complete his or her tasks.
2. *Impulsivity:* Behavior that comes out before the child thinks about it. He or she is action-oriented and cannot inhibit an urge to blurt something out in class or wait for his or her turn in a group activity.
3. *Hyperactivity:* Perpetual fidgeting, tapping, chattering, and restlessness.

Approximately 3% of all children are diagnosed as ADHD, with about three ADHD boys to every such girl. Many children with this learning disability are also diagnosed with aggressive, antisocial behaviors as well as conduct disorders

(Silver, 1992). ADHD children have difficulty performing well in school. They irritate adults and can become locked in coercive power struggles with their parents, teachers, and others, which only aggravates their own problems (Barkley, Fischer, Edelbrock, & Smallfish, 1991; Buhrmester, Camparo, Christensen, Gonzales, & Hirshaw, 1992). Because their behavior is so disruptive, their peers tend to reject them (Whalen et al., 1989). ADHD thus affects the cognitive, social, and emotional development of children in many ways.

How do parents, teachers, and others deal with ADHD? The key is remembering that the disorder has its roots in biological, psychological, and social factors. Some children inherit a predisposition to the disease. Stress at home, including sociocultural factors, also affects how children regulate their attention. Children could be medicated with stimulants such as Ritalin, which in reality calms the child. Besides medication, such children should be reminded to regulate their attention and behavior more effectively. For instance, children can be encouraged to remind themselves to read the instructions before they start their assignments.

Parents can also learn techniques for encouraging attention and goal-oriented behaviors. Anastopoulos, Guevremont, Shelton, & DuPaul (1993) took parents of ADHD children and gave them nine training sessions. The parents learned how to use positive reinforcement to foster their children's attention and compliance. These parents reported fewer symptoms of ADHD when they put their training to use. They also felt a greater sense of competence in their own parenting skills. Such techniques, combined with medication and instructions, can greatly help ADHD children.

*Mental retardation*    Mental retardation is a form of mental deficiency in which children have an IQ of 70 or below. According to the American Association on Mental Retardation, it is a "significantly subaverage general intellectual functioning existing concurrently with deficits in adaptive behaviors" (Grossman, 1983, p. 1). IQ is measured using intelligence tests such as the Stanford-Binet. Adaptive behavior is usually evaluated from interviews with parents or other caregivers. The competency of the mentally retarded is affected in four areas:

1. *Motor skills:* How well they use their arms and legs for movement and their hands and fingers to manipulate objects
2. *Communication skills:* How well they can speak and understand what others say
3. *Socialization skills:* How they respond to others showing responsibility and sensitivity
4. *Daily skills:* How well they can care for themselves, perform household chores, and use money (Sparrow, Balla, & Cicchetti, 1984)

The most severely retarded people have very few skills and must be supervised constantly. Most of them live in institutions where they are supervised and taught self-help skills such as dressing and feeding (Reid, Wilson, & Faux, 1991). Moderately retarded people may develop the intellectual skills of a nonretarded person of 7 or 8 years of age and can perform simple tasks under supervision. They can also work in a sheltered workshop. The remaining 90% of retarded people are mildly retarded and can learn many academic skills. Such individuals can often lead independent lives. Comprehensive training programs focus on vocational and social skills that can help individuals with mild mental retardation become productive citizens and satisfied human beings (Ellis & Rusch, 1991).

> Twelve-year-old Nathan can only play with younger children because children his own age call him a "dummy." In his neighborhood he's known as the "slow kid." Nothing his mother says will stop this name calling. Protective, Nathan's mother sends him out to play with younger children in her own backyard. Because he does not do well in regular schools, the mother sends him to a special school for retarded children.

While working with any kind of disability, social workers have to be sensitive to the child and the problems the parents of such children face. At times, some of the problems faced by young children can be misunderstood by adults.

Mentally retarded youngsters represent one extreme of human ability. At the other extreme we find gifted and creative children.

## Gifted and Creative Children

*Gifted children* have an IQ of 130 or greater. Modern definitions of *gifted* include not exclusively scholarship but also special affinities for art, music, creative writing, and dance (Ramos-Ford & Gardner, 1991). Gifted children tend to be more mature than their peers and have fewer emotional problems (Luther, Zigler, & Goldstein, 1992). Their thinking seems to develop in the same sequence as other children's thinking; however, it grows more rapidly. In a nutshell, gifted children think like older nongifted children (Jackson & Butterfield, 1986).

Creativity has to be cultivated in such children. For instance, they benefit from environments that value nonconformity and encourage children to be curious. Creativity can also be enhanced by experiences that help children to be flexible in their thinking and to explore alternatives (Starko, 1988).

> Seven-year-old Marty is a gifted child. His father, a single parent, has just changed jobs, so they live in a new neighborhood. Marty is curious about his neighbors and the community. In his new school, he quickly finishes his classwork and starts looking at the telephone directory that he's taken to school with him, to look up activities for his father and him. The teacher is initially irritated at his distraction, but when she finds that he has correctly completed the work she handed out a few minutes ago, which the rest of the class will take at least another forty minutes to complete, she begins work on placing him in an accelerated school program.

## Depression

Children who cannot deal with their problems and do not have any way to verbalize or vent them develop depression. Children display what is called *masked depression* or a depression in the guise of symptoms other than those associated directly with depression (Quay, Rueth, & Shapiro, 1987). A depressed child may not talk about being sad but might express this feeling indirectly by behaving aggressively or being anxious. Schoolchildren often express their depression by getting into fights (Weiss et al., 1992). Later in school, depressed children express more cognitive symptoms such as low self-esteem, hopelessness, and self-blame (Weiss, Dodge, Bates, & Pettit, 1992). As one 10-year-old said when he attempted suicide, "The devil is in me"; another depressed suicidal child exclaimed, "I am a burden on the family" (Kosky, 1983, p. 459). Suicide attempts by such children are rare, but when they claim they wish to die they should be taken seriously. The rate of suicides by young children is beginning to climb and many apparent accidents may actually be suicidal attempts (Joffe & Offord, 1990). Depressed children, like their adult counterparts, tend to have recurring bouts of depression; however, the children's are milder. Clinically depressed children have recurring episodes of serious depression during childhood, adolescence, and even adulthood (Pataki & Carlson, 1990). Such depression affects their overall performance—that is, their intellectual and school achievements and social adjustment (Kovacs & Goldston, 1991).

Fortunately, most depressed children respond well to psychotherapy (Petersen et al., 1993; Weisz & Weiss, 1993). Often, children's depression has a global effect on his or her parents and siblings, making work with the whole family necessary to bring about changes.

Depression could result from a combination of biological and environmental factors. The next issue, however, deals with a purely environmental problem created by people, usually family members in the young person's life. When parenting breaks down, the result can be abuse.

## Child Abuse

The family is by definition the most supportive and understanding place to get nurturing and love. At times, though, these very families can become the greatest source of anguish and pain. Every day in different parts of the country, children are beaten, starved, suffocated, sexually molested, or otherwise mistreated by their caretakers. Child abuse knows no bounds. Children in different racial, ethnic, and socioeconomic groups have been abused to the point of death, with some children murdered outright. Many such incidents are reported, but many are not.

How does a child who has no place but the family live in such a horrifying situation? As Pillari (1991) writes, the abused child has to endure a great deal.

> Learning to live with a person you do not love or respect and learning to live with a person you know does not love or respect you is like learning not to live at all. It requires learning to talk in frightened whispers; how to deny what you feel; how to hate without showing it; how to weep without tears; and how to hide that the shame you are living is your family reality. (p. xvi)

Abused children also suffer from psychological abuse such as rejection, ridicule, or even being terrorized by their own parents. Still others are neglected and deprived of the basic care and stimulation they need for normal development. There is growing evidence that psychological abuse and neglect may prove to be even more harmful to children in the long run than other types of abuse (Emery, 1989; Grusec & Walters, 1991).

In 1985, there were over 1.9 million reports of child maltreatment filed in the United States (U.S. Bureau of the Census, 1989). In a more recent national sample of families in the United States, almost 11% of the children had reportedly been bitten, kicked, punched, hit with an object, or threatened with a knife or a gun by parents in the past year (Wolfner & Gelles, 1993). A national survey conducted in 1991 found that more than 400,000 U.S. children were coerced into oral and/or genital intercourse (Finkelhor & Dziuba-Leatherman, 1994), usually by a father, a stepfather, an older sibling, or another male relative or family friend (Trickett & Putnam, 1993). In the face of this depressing and frightening picture, social workers can respond by working directly with such clients as well as lobbying for better legislation and making people in all parts of the United States aware of these issues.

*Causes*    Looking at child abuse from a systems perspective, we can say that (1) some adults may be more inclined than others to abuse children, (2) some children may be more likely to be abused than other children, and (3) abuse could happen more often in some contexts than others, such as certain communities or cultures.

Child abuse can also be an intergenerational pattern, in which abusive behavior takes on a transactional pattern. The destructive aspects of abusive behaviors begin when a child's ability to be destructive appears to be in direct proportion and relation to the degree to which adults critically undermine his or her trust.

New research shows that most often an abusive parent tends to be a young poverty-stricken mother who is unemployed and has no spouse to share her burdens (Gelles, 1992; Wolfner & Gelles, 1993). As mentioned before, however, child abusers come from all races, ethnic groups, and social classes, and a large number of them may appear to be loving parents except in their tendency to become extremely irritated with children and to do things that they later regret.

Here is a particularly chilling case of abuse:

> A police officer is called by a neighbor because she has heard the loud moaning of a child next door. When the police try to enter the apartment, they have to break the door down. They are amazed at what they see: A totally drunk woman with a lighted cigarette in her hand is systematically burning holes in her 6-month-old son's body. The child is no longer crying. Apparently he has been beaten on his face repeatedly. The police officers charge the woman with abuse and take the child away. In a short time, however, the mother goes to court and gets her child back. The police officers have to go to her house a second time to rescue the child.

The police officer who reported this case talked about his frustration and anger at the mother getting the child back. Why do such mothers retain their rights to their children? One of the most important tasks we face in this country is reviewing the rights of natural mothers who have presented themselves as unfit. Of course, the mother needs help too, but at whose expense? The child's? Society's? Do we want to risk another generation of abused children who will probably grow up to be abusers? Can the mother be given help and the child placed elsewhere permanently?

Physically abused and otherwise neglected children tend to display certain problems, including intellectual deficits, academic difficulties, and disturbed social relationships with peers and teachers (Malinosky-Rummell & Hansen, 1993; Salzinger et al., 1993). Abused children are also found more often in high-risk neighborhoods. Garbarino (1992) and Garbarino and Sherman (1980) indicate that in deteriorating neighborhoods parents struggle, with little in the way of community services such as parks, recreation centers, preschool programs, churches, and other support systems such as contact with friends and relatives. Isolated parents who have nowhere to go for assistance or advice take their stress out on their children. Garbarino (1992) is just one of several theorists who believe that a large number of U.S. children are likely to be molested because of political or economic decisions that have undermined the health and stability of low-risk, family-oriented neighborhoods.

*Role of social workers*    Social workers play an important role in recognizing and preventing child maltreatment. One way of doing this is to target high-risk families for training programs that teach effective methods of preventing miscommunication between children and caregivers. For example, how would you deal with a baby who is always irritable or one who is unresponsive to the caregiver? Often unresponsive babies can make inexperienced mothers uncomfortable because they expect a reaction to their nurturing, something in return, or they may feel like failures or martyrs.

Schinke, Schilling, Barth, Gilchrist, and Maxwell (1986) worked with a group of high-risk mothers—that is, single teenagers under a great deal of stress. The main goal was to teach them a wide range of stress-management skills such as relaxation techniques, problem-solving strategies, and communication skills that enable mothers to request help and refuse unreasonable demands. These mothers also learned how to build stronger social support networks. After three months, those who had received the training outperformed those in the control group on several measures. They had better problem-solving skills, had established stronger support networks, enjoyed higher self-esteem, and were more confident about their parenting skills. It appears likely that by learning effective techniques for coping with stress, high-risk parents can improve their ability to deal with the sometimes overwhelming challenges they face. Such parents also benefit from programs that teach them effective child-management skills (Wolfe, Edwards, Marrion & Koverola, 1988).

Other issues that social workers will need to be aware of include the random abuser—often a male relative of the child—and intergenerational patterns of abuse.

## IMPLICATIONS FOR PRACTICE

Social workers need to be aware that, during middle childhood, home and school play an important part in the child's life. The child is developing a gender identity, cultivating peer relationships, and learning the norms of family as well as society. During this period, the child attempts to gain competency in verbal and manual skills. Achievement of skills makes the child feel competent, whereas ridicule and a lack of caring from chief caregivers make the child feel inferior and unwanted. Problems could arise in any of these developmental areas, depending on the child and his or her environment.

### Problems at School

School becomes the child's second social world. Problems in the home can appear at school, as the following case demonstrates.

Erin, a child of an alcoholic mother, comes to school poorly dressed and hungry. Her attention span is limited. At 10 years of age, she flies off the handle when things do not go her way. Her peers resent and avoid her. Their avoidance makes her less willing to participate in sports activities. Her concentration on schoolwork is also limited. Though she seems aloof, this is only a facade, her way of dealing with rejection. She begins to dress more sloppily and does not do her homework. Finally, her teacher refers her to the school social worker.

After two interviews, the worker decides to make a home visit because none of her phone calls has been returned. Erin jumps up with anxiety. She does not want the social worker to go to her home; she is afraid and ashamed of what the worker may discover. When Erin realizes that the worker will visit her mother anyway, she begins to tell the "real story" about her mother's alcoholism. Erin changes from an aggressive, sulky, and angry person to a little child afraid of the consequences of what she reveals to the social worker. The social worker reassures her about confidentiality, and Erin realizes that her classmates will not know about the visit. She cries like a child (which she is) because at last she has found someone who will listen to her and help her.

Besides being worried about her mother's state and the appearance of her house, Erin expressed concern about what her peers would find out and how they would react. While working with sensitive issues, the worker must keep in mind the child and his or her needs. Regardless of their home situation, most children wish to be accepted by their peers.

Some schoolchildren face unique problems of weight and height. Overweight children get insensitively teased, as do children who are very short for their age. Social workers should deal with such issues by keeping in mind the child, the family, and the school as systems.

Being competent in school, either in studies, sports, peer relationships, or all of the above, matters a great deal to children. If unaccepted by peers, children can become overwhelmed by feelings of inferiority. The social worker should be aware of this issue in school children and help them make adjustments accordingly.

When children grow up enough to function fairly well away from their families, they must reconcile their self-images with any new and often unpleasant stereotypes they may encounter. Children who are the subjects of stereotypes become overwhelmed and anxious. In our multicultural society, creating ethnic awareness and pride in self is important.

## Family Background

Social workers need to be aware of the multifaceted aspects of the child's life and his or her place at home. Some children have special needs—those who come from deprived homes and those who suffer from mental or physical problems and need special attention. The type of family children come from and the child-rearing practices they have faced are critical factors for a social worker to look for while attempting to help children with their problems.

The child continues to be a part of a family; help in this life stage therefore may best be offered either individually or in conjunction with the family. The social worker should also take into account the pressure on parents to conform to society's expectations and to produce an average child who looks, apparently feels, and certainly behaves in accordance with norms. Many parents experience a severe shock when their child does not meet their preconceived expectations—that is, when their child's physical and intellectual growth does not follow a relatively predictable pattern. Social work practitioners need to discern such expectations so they can help parents deal with their children's existing reality supportively. They should also refer parents to parenting classes and to social-network groups whenever necessary. This is particularly helpful to parents who have children with learning disabilities, ADHD, or mental retardation.

Other family-based problems include abuse—physical, sexual, verbal, and emotional. Social workers need to watch for the signs of sexual abuse. Physical abuse of a child by a significant person in the family can be traumatic for a child. Even if a child does not talk about them, constant bruises on a child's body in unlikely places should reveal to the teacher and the social workers that the child is being abused. A family session should be conducted to find out the issues for effective helping.

When young children use sexual words far beyond their years, talk explicitly about sex or suffer from unfounded fears, workers should suspect sexual abuse. Sexual abuse of a child by a parent or a parent's lover, live-in boyfriends, uncles, and in some cases aunts and siblings needs to be looked at expeditiously.

Mrs. Johnson has noticed that Tabitha has been trying to talk to her privately. Mrs. Johnson has always been very fond of Tabitha and vice versa. One day in the playground, Tabitha starts by saying that she wants to tell Mrs. Johnson something that her daddy has told her not to tell anyone. The teacher quickly responds by saying if her dad does not want her to tell anyone, she should not tell the teacher. Tabitha replies, "He isn't my real daddy," and leaves. The next day after class, she starts to talk again: "I want to tell you the secret daddy and I have. It's a secret game—I touch daddy's big 'pee-wee' and he touches me down there. I want to tell you because you are my teacher—but don't tell anyone else our secret."

Although this was shared in innocence, the teacher saw it as a cry for help. Because the teacher had to report suspected molestation, she informed the school social worker, who then took the necessary action. In this case, Tabitha volunteered the information. Often, sexual abuse has to be detected through subtler signs, for victims of abuse are ashamed and scared, and they have no place to go except home. Social workers have to make the child comfortable and relaxed for therapy. They can introduce anatomically correct dolls and begin a discussion about families in general aimed at talking about the child's own family. As always, when working with children the social worker should make special efforts to involve family members as necessary or feasible.

## CHAPTER SUMMARY

- During middle childhood, ages 6–12, the child's horizon expands to include the school world. Physical development appears to be fairly balanced between stability and continued growth.

- The ages of 6 to 12 present a period of new self-awareness and responsibility. Children settle down, develop new skills, and are increasingly motivated to gain approval from family and from friends and other peers.

- Children at this stage improve their dexterity.

- Malnutrition during this period has an effect on physical and mental growth.

- Piaget called middle childhood the period of concrete operations. As concrete operational thought evolves, a liberation takes place in children's thought processes: (1) children take on conservation tasks, and (2) children's perception of other people moves from global, vague terms, such as *good, bad,* and *horrible,* to more specific descriptions that reflect a person's immediate behavior as well as how the person normally behaves.

- When moral development takes place, children adopt principles and evaluate behavior as right and wrong. They conform to group norms and develop an increasing capacity for guilt.

- In psychoanalytic thinking, the aggressive sexual instincts—the id—must be dealt with through parental discipline to help children internalize socially acceptable behavior. At some point this internalization becomes the superego.

- Piaget and Kohlberg indicate that moral development occurs when children act on and modify the world they live in. They move from moral absolutism to moral relativism.

- Social-learning theorists hypothesize that behavior is the result of modeling and an appropriate system of rewards and punishments.

- Erik Erikson calls middle childhood the period of industry versus inferiority. Children learn skills that bring them closer to their capacities as adults; when they do not learn such skills, they feel inferior.

- In keeping with his competency model, White comments that besides requiring play and make-believe, children need to feel useful. Competency develops both at home and at school as children learn the rules of society—how to get along with others and how to compete, compromise, and protect themselves from hurt.

- Parents affect children in many ways. There are single parents, teenage parents, unmarried couples, married couples, and divorced and remarried couples with children.

- Parents follow diverse parenting styles, which contribute to social competence or its lack.

- Gender-role development starts the day a child is born. Gender roles are attained through socialization by imitating parents and other adults as well as peers of the same gender.

- Gender-role development also takes place in the classroom. The structure of most schools reflects the gender differentiations of the larger society.

- Schools affect the child's socialization. In the school setting the child develops a sense of self-esteem and ego identity.

- The traditional way to instill values is through character education and conduct development. These teachings become a part of children's moral development.

- Special problems may arise in school settings because of physical factors, such as poor health and poverty, or emotional causes and problems of diversity.

- Peers influence each other's personality. Peer groups develop their own cultures and often their own customs, rules, games, values, and beliefs.

- Peer groups perform an important function by giving children experience in relationships in which everyone has an equal footing.
- A child's sense of social acceptance or rejection is played out in the school setting and depends greatly on the acceptance or rejection received there.
- Same-gender peer groups become very popular at this age.
- Special concerns that social workers face in helping children include learning disabilities, attention-deficit disorder (ADHD), mental retardation, giftedness, depression, and child abuse.
- Social workers need to keep in mind the special needs of school-age children.
- While dealing with children's issues and problems, workers must also look at the family system.

## SUGGESTED READINGS

Johnson, G. M. (1994). Family characteristics and parental social involvement. *Family Therapy, 21*(1), 25–33.

Khamia, V. (1990). *Victims of the infada: The psychosocial adjustment of the injured.* Washington, DC: Naim Foundation and the Georgetown University Conference of Culture, Conflict and Trauma.

Maehr, M. L., & Anderman, E. M. (1993). *Reinventing schools for early adolescents: Emphasizing task goals.* Ann Arbor: University of Michigan (Combined Program in Education and Psychology).

Midgley, C., Anderson, E., & Hicks, L. (1995). Differences between elementary and middle school teachers and students: A goal theory approach. *Journal of Early Adolescence, 15*(1), 90–113.

Nakamura, S. Y., Taira, N., & Kawamoto, H. (1994). Cross-cultural experiences by students of Korean middle schools in Japan. *Japanese Journal of Educational Psychology, 42*(3), 291–297.

Nash, R., & Harker, R. K. (1992). Working with class: The educational expectations and practices of class-resourced families. *New Zealand Journal of Educational Studies, 27*(1), 3–20.

## SUGGESTED VIDEOTAPES

CBC (Producer). (1979). *David: Portrait of a retarded youth* (28 minutes). Available from Filmakers Library, 124 E. 40th St., Suite 901, New York, NY 10016; 212-808-4980

Meridian Education Corp. (Producer). (1996). *Understanding learning disabilities* (17 minutes). Available from Meridian Education Corporation, 236 E. Front St., Bloomington, IL 61701; 800-727-5507

Social Media (Producer). (1995). *Listen to children: A moral journey with Robert Coles* (89 minutes). Available at PBS, 6360 LaPas Trail, Indianapolis, IN 46268; 800-424-7963

TS Media (Producer). (1995). *Attention? ADD in school: Identification* (26 minutes). Available from TS Media, 18 Halley Ct., Fairfield, CT 06430; 800-876-6334

TS Media (Producer). (1995). *Attention? ADD in school: Intervention* (19 minutes). Available from TS Media, 18 Halley Ct., Fairfield, CT 06430; 800-876-6334

TS Media (Producer). (1995). *Attention? ADD in school: Strategies* (24 minutes). Available from TS Media, 18 Halley Ct., Fairfield, CT 06430; 800-876-6334

## REFERENCES

Anastopoulos, A. D., Guevremont, D. C., Shelton, T. L., & DuPaul, G. J. (1992) Parenting stress among families of children with attention-deficit hyperactivity disorder. *Journal of Abnormal Child Psychology, 20,* 503–520.

Bandura, A., Ross, D., & Ross, S. (1961). Transmission of aggression through imitation of aggressive models. *Journal of Abnormal Psychology, 63,* 575–582.

Barkley, R. A., Fischer, M., Edelbrock, C., & Smallfish, L. (1991). The adolescent outcome of hyperactive children diagnosed by research criteria: Mother-child interactions, family conflicts and maternal psychotherapy. *Journal of Child Psychology and Psychiatry and Allied Disciplines, 32,* 233–255.

Baumrind, D. (1978). A dialectical materialist perspective on knowing reality. *New Directions for Child Development, 2.*

Berger, K. S. (1986). *The developing person through the lifespan*. New York: Worth.

Birch, H. G. (1972). Malnutrition, learning and intelligence. *American Journal of Public Health, 62,* 773–784.

Blakemore, J. E. O., LaRue, A. A., & Olejnick, A. B. (1979). Sex-appropriate toy preference and the ability to conceptualize toys as sex-role related. *Developmental Psychology, 15,* 339–340.

Booth, A., & Amato, P. (1991). Divorce and psychological stress. *Journal of Health and Social Behavior, 32,* 396–407.

Booth, A., & Edwards, J. N. (1992). Starting over: Why remarriages are unstable. *Journal of Family Issues, 13,* 179–194.

Brody, G. H., Neubaum, E., & Forehand, R. (1988). Serial marriage: A heuristic analysis of an emerging family form. *Psychological Bulletin, 103,* 211–222.

Buhrmester, D., Camparo, L., Christensen, A., Gonzales, L. S., & Hirshaw, S. P. (1992). Mothers and fathers interacting in dyads and triads with normal and hyperactive sons. *Developmental Psychology, 28,* 500–509.

Bukowski, W. M., Gauze, C., Hoza, B., & Newcombe, A. F. (1993). Differences and consistency between same-sex and other-sex peer relationships during early adolescence. *Developmental Psychology, 29,* 255–263.

Bussey, K., & Bandura, A., (1992). Self-regulatory mechanisms governing gender development. *Child Development, 63,* 1236–1250.

Butler, R., Ruzany, N. (1993). Age and socialization effects on the development of social comparison motives and normative ability assessment in kibutz and urban children. *Child Development, 64,* 532–543.

Cantwell, D. P., & Baker, L. (1992). Attention-deficit disorder with and without hyperactivity: A review and comparison of matched groups. *Journal of the American Academy of Child and Adolescent Psychiatry, 31,* 432–438.

Carroll, J. L., & Rest, J. R. (1982). Moral development. In B. B. Wolman, G. Stricker, et al., *Handbook of developmental psychology*. Englewood Cliffs, NJ: Prentice-Hall.

Case, R. (1985). *Intellectual development: Birth to adulthood*. Orlando, FL: Academic Press.

Clements, D. H. (1990). Metacomponental development in a Logo programming environment. *Journal of Educational Psychology, 82,* 141–149.

Clements, D. H. (1991). Enhancement of creativity in computer environments. *America Educational Research Journal, 28,* 173–187.

Colby, A., Gibbs, J., & Kohlberg, L. (1983). *Standard form for scoring manual*. Cambridge, MA: Center for Moral Education.

Colby, A., Kohlberg, L., Gibbs, J., & Lieberman, M. A. (1983). *Longitudinal study of moral development*. Presentation at the Center for Advanced Study in the Behavioral Sciences Institute on Morality and Moral Development, 1979.

Corner, J. P. (1991). The black child in school. In M. Lewis (Ed.), *Child and adolescent psychiatry: A comprehensive textbook*. Baltimore: Williams & Wilkins.

Crook, C. (1992). Cultural artifacts in social development: The case of computers. In H. McGurk (Ed.), *Childhood social development: Contemporary perspectives*. Hove, England: Erlbaum.

Dishion, T. J., Patterson, G. R., Stoolmiller, M., & Skinner, M. L. (1991). Family, school and behavioral antecedents to early adolescent involvement with antisocial peers. *Developmental Psychology, 27,* 172–180.

Dockrell, J., & McShane, J. (1993). *Children's learning difficulties: A cognitive approach*. Cambridge, England: Blackwell.

Donovan, J. (1988). *An introduction to street gangs*. Paper prepared for Senator John Garamendi, Sacramento, CA.

Ellis, W. K., & Rusch, F. R. (1991). Supported employment: Current practices and future directions. In J. L. Maytson & J. A. Mulick (Eds.), *Handbook of mental retardation* (2nd ed.). New York: Pergamon.

Emery, R. E. (1989). Family violence. *American Psychologist, 44,* 321–328.

Erikson, E. H. (1968). *Identity, youth and crisis*. New York: Norton.

Etaugh, C., & Liss, M. B. (1922). Home, school and playroom: Training grounds for adult gender roles. *Sex Roles, 26,* 129–147.

Fagot, B. I., Leinbach, M. D., & Hagan, R. (1986). Gender labeling, gender stereotyping and parenting behaviors. *Developmental Psychology, 22,* 440–443.

Fine, M. A., & Schwebel, A. (1991). Step-parent stress: A cognitive perspective. *Journal of Divorce and Remarriage, 17,* 1–15.

Finkelhor, D., & Dziuba-Leatherman, J. (1994). Victimization of children. *American Psychologist, 49,* 173–183.

Flaks, F., Filcher, I., Masterpasqua, E., & Joseph, G. (1995). Lesbians choosing motherhood: A comparative study of lesbian and heterosexual parents and their children. *Developmental Psychology, 31,* 105–114.

Fraser, B. J., Walberg, H. J., Welch, W. W., & Hattie, J. A. (1987). Synthesis of educational productivity research. *International Journal of Educational Research, 11,* 145–252.

Freud, S. (1930). *Civilization and its discontents.* London: Hogarth.

Garbarino, J. (1992). Children and families in the social environment (2nd ed.). New York: Aldine de Gruyter.

Garbarino, J., & Sherman, D. (1980). High-risk neighborhoods and high-risk families: The human ecology of child maltreatment. *Child Development, 51,* 188–198.

Garcia, E. E. (1993). Language, culture and education. *Review of Educational Research, 19,* 51–98.

Gauvain, M., & Rogoff, B. (1989). Collaborative problem solving and children's planning skills. *Developmental Psychology, 25,* 139–151.

Gelles, R. J. (1992). Poverty and violence toward children. *American Behavioral Scientist, 35,* 258–274.

Gilligan, C. (1982). *In a different voice.* Cambridge, MA: Harvard University Press.

Goldman, S. R. (1989). Strategy instruction in mathematics. *Learning Disability Quarterly, 12,* 43–55.

Grossman, H. J. (Ed.). (1983). *Classification of mental retardation.* Washington, DC: American Association of Mental Deficiency.

Grusec, J. E., & Walters, G. C. (1991). Psychological abuse and childrearing belief systems. In R. H. Starr, Jr., & D. A. Wolfe (Eds.), *The effects of child abuse and neglect.* New York: Guilford.

Hammill, D. N. (1990). On defining learning disabilities: An emerging consensus. *Journal of Learning Disabilities, 23,* 74–84.

Harris, M. J., & Rosenthal, R. (1986). Four factors in the mediation of teacher expectancy efforts. In R. S. Feldman (Ed.), *The social psychology of education: Current research and theory.* Cambridge, England: Cambridge University Press.

Hart, C. H., Ladd, G. W., & Burleson, B. R. (1990). Children's expectations of the outcomes of social strategies: Relations with sociometric status and maternal disciplinary styles. *Child Development, 61,* 127–137.

Harter, S. (1985). *The self-perception profile for children* [Manual]. Denver, CO: University of Denver.

Harter, S. (1993). Visions of self: Beyond the me in the mirror. In J. E. Jacobs (Ed.), *Nebraska Symposium on Motivation: Vol. 40* (pp. 99–144). Lincoln: University of Nebraska Press.

Hartup, W. W. (1989). Social relationships and their developmental significance. *American Psychologist, 44,* 120–126.

Hartup, W. W. (1992). Friendships and their developmental significance. In H. McGurk (Ed.), *Childhood social development: Contemporary perspectives.* Hove, England, Erlbaum.

Haskett, M. E., & Kistner, J. A. (1991). Social interaction and peer perceptions of young physically abused children. *Child Development, 62,* 979–990.

Hetherington, E. M. (1989). Coping with family transitions: Winners, losers and survivors. *Child Development, 60,* 1–14.

Hetherington, E. M., & Clingempel, W. G. (1992). Coping with marital transitions. *Monographs of the Society for Research in Child Development, 60,* 1–14.

Higley, J. D., Hopkins, W. D., Thompson, W. W., Byrne, E. A., Hirsch, R. M., & Suomi, S. J. (1992). Peers as primary attachment sources in yearling rhesus monkeys. *Developmental Psychology, 28,* 1163–1171.

Holt, J. (1964). *How children fail.* New York: Dell.

Horowitz, R. (1983). *Honor and the American dream.* New Brunswick, NJ: Rutgers University Press.

Inhelder, B. (1966). Cognitive development and its contribution to the diagnosis of some phenomena of mental deficiency. *Merrill-Palmer Quarterly, 12,* 299–319.

Jacklin, C. N., & Maccoby, E. E. (1978). Social behavior at 33 months in same-sex and mixed-sex dyads. *Child Development, 49,* 557–569.

Jackson, N. E., & Butterfield, E. E. (1986). A conception of giftedness designed to promote research. In R. J. Stennberg & J. E. Davidson (Eds.), *Conception of giftedness.* Cambridge, England: Cambridge University Press.

Joffe, R. T., & Offord, D. R. (1990). Epidemiology. In G. MacLean (Ed.), *Suicide in children and adolescents.* Toronto: Hogrefe & Huber.

Kagan, J. (1966). Reflection–impulsivity: The generality and dynamics of conceptual tempo. *Journal of Abnormal Psychology, 71,* 17–24.

Kastenbaum, R. (1979). *Humans developing.* Boston: Allyn and Bacon.

Kay, W. (1975). *Moral education: A sociological study of the influence of society, home and school.* Hamden, CT: Linnet Books.

Kee, D. W. (1986). Computer play. In A. W. Gottfried & C. C. Brown (Eds.), *Play interactions: The contributions of play materials and parental involvement to children's development.* Lexington, MA: Lexington Books.

Kerckhoff, A. C. (1972). *Socialization and social class.* Englewood Cliffs, NJ: Prentice-Hall.

Kitson, G. C., & Morgan, L. A. (1990). The multiple consequences of divorce: A decade of review. *Journal of Marriage and the Family, 52,* 913–924.

Kochanska, G. (1992). Children's interpersonal influence with mothers and peers. *Developmental Psychology, 28,* 491–499.

Kohlberg, L. (1969). Stage and sequence: The developmental approach to socialization. In D. A. Goslin (Ed.), *Handbook of socialization theory and research.* Chicago: Rand McNally.

Kohlberg, L. (1971). From is to ought: How to commit the naturalistic fallacy and get away with it in the study of moral development. In T. Mischel (Ed.), *Cognitive development and epistemology.* New York: Academic Press.

Kohlberg, L. (1976). Moral stages and moralization. In T. Luckona (Ed.), *Moral development and behavior.* New York: Holt, Rinehart & Winston.

Kohlberg, L. (1978). Revisions in theory and practice of moral development. *Dimensions for Child Development, 2,* 83–88.

Kosky, R. (1983). Childhood suicidal behavior. *Journal of Child Psychology and Psychiatry, 24,* 457–468.

Kovacs, M., & Goldston, D. (1991). Cognitive and social cognitive development of depressed children and adolescents. *Journal of the American Academy of Child and Adolescent Psychiatry, 30,* 388–392.

Kowaz, A. M., & Marcia, J. E. (1991). Development and validation of a measure of Eriksonian industry. *Journal of Personality and Social Psychology, 60,* 390–397.

Kozol, J. (1970). *Death at an early age.* New York: Bantam Books.

Kuhn, D. (1992). Cognitive development. In M. H. Bornstein & M. E. Lamb (Eds.), *Developmental psychology: An advanced textbook* (3rd ed.). Hillsdale, NJ: Erlbaum.

Kulik, J. A., & Kulik, C. C. (1992). Metanalysis findings on grouping programs. *Gifted Children Quarterly, 36,* 73–77.

Kupersmidt, J. B., & Paterson, C. J. (1991). Childhood, peer rejection, aggression, withdrawal and perceived competence as predictors of self-reported behavior problems in preadolescence. *Journal of Abnormal Child Psychology, 19*(4), 427–449.

Ladd, G. W. (1990). Having friends, keeping friends, making friends and being liked by peers in the classroom: Predictors of children's early school adjustment. *Child Development, 61,* 1081–1100.

Lee, L. C. (1976). *Personality development in childhood.* Monterey, CA: Brooks/Cole.

Leppe, M. R., & Gurtner, J. (1989). Children and computers: Approaching the twenty-first century. *American Psychologist, 44,* 170–178.

Levy, G. D. (1989). Developmental and individual differences in preschoolers' recognition memories: The influences of gender schematization and verbal labeling of information. *Sex Roles, 21,* 305–324.

Linney, J. A., & Seidman, E. (1989). The future of schooling. *American Psychologist, 44,* 336–340.

Livesley, W. J., & Bromley, D. B. (1973). *Person perception in childhood and adolescence.* New York: Wiley.

Lobel, T. E., & Menashri, J. (1993). Relations of conceptions of gender-role transgressions and gender constancy to gender-typed preference. *Developmental Psychology, 29,* 150–155.

Lovett, M. W., Borden, S. L., Deluca, T., Lacerenza, L., Benson, M. J., & Brackstone, D. (1994). Treating the core deficits of developmental dyslexia: Evidence of transfer of learning after phonologically and strategy-based reading programs. *Developmental Psychology, 30,* 805–822.

Luthar, S. S., Zigler, E., & Goldstein, D. (1992). Psychosocial adjustment among intellectually gifted adolescents: The role of cognitive-developmental and experimental factors. *Journal of Child Psychology and Psychiatry and Allied Disciplines, 33,* 361–373.

Maccoby, E. E. (1988). *Social development.* New York: Harcourt Brace Jovanovich.

Maccoby, E. E. (1990). Gender and relationships: A developmental account. *American Psychologist, 45,* 513–520.

Malinosky-Rummell, R., & Hansen, D. J. (1993). Long-term consequences of childhood physical abuse. *Psychological Bulletin, 114,* 68–79.

Martin, C. L. (1990). Attitudes and expectations about children with nontraditional gender role. *Sex Roles, 22,* 151–165.

Mischel, W, & Mischel, H. N. (1976). A cognitive social-learning approach to morality and self-regulation. In T. Luckona (Ed.), *Moral development and behavior: Theory, research and social issues.* New York: Holt, Rinehart & Winston.

Moats, L. C., & Lyon, G. R. (1993). Learning disabilities in the United States: Advocacy, science and the future of the field. *Journal of Learning Disabilities, 26,* 282–294.

Newman, B. M., & Newman, P. R. (1995). *Development through life* (6th ed.). Pacific Grove, CA: Brooks/Cole.

O'Conner-Francoeur, P. (1983, April). *Children's concepts of health and their health behavior.* Paper presented at the meeting of the Society of Research in Child Development, Detroit, MI.

Odden, A. (1990). Class size and student achievement: Research based policy alternatives. *Educational Evaluation and Policy Analysis, 12,* 213–227.

Ogbu, J. U. (1990). Cultural model, identity, and literacy. In J. W. Stigler, R. A. Shweder, & G. Herdt (Eds.), *Cultural psychology: Essays on comparative human development.* Cambridge, England: Cambridge University Press.

One weekend under fire fingers gangs. (1994, August 30). *Chicago Sun-Times,* p. 21.

Pataki, C. S., & Carlson, G. A. (1990). Major depression in childhood. In M. Hersen & C. G. Last (Eds.), *Handbook of child and adult psychopathology: A longitudinal perspective.* New York: Pergamon Books.

Patterson, C. J. (1992). Children of lesbian and gay parents. *Child Development, 63,* 1025–1041.

Petersen, A. C., Compas, B. E., Brooks-Gunn, J., Stemmler, M., Ey, S., & Grant, K. E. (1993). Depression in adolescence. *American Psychologist, 48,* 155–168.

Pettit, G. S., Dodge, K. A., & Brown, M. M. (1988). Early family experience, social problem-solving patterns and children's social competence. *Child Development, 59,* 107–120.

Piaget, J. (1950). *The psychology of intelligence.* New York: Harcourt Brace.

Piaget, J. (1952). *The child's conception of numbers.* New York: Humanities Press.

Piaget, J. (1965a). *The child's conception of numbers.* New York: Norton.

Piaget, J. (1965b). *The moral judgment of the child.* New York: Free Press. (Original work published 1932.)

Piaget, J. (1968). *Six psychological studies.* New York: Viking Press.

Piaget, J. (1971). *Science, education and the psychology of the child.* New York: Viking Press.

Piaget, J. (1976). *To understand is to invent: The future of education.* New York: Penguin.

Pillari, V. (1991) *Scapegoating in families: Intergenerational patterns of physical and emotional abuse.* New York: Brunner/Mazel.

Pineda, C., Jr. (1974). *Chicano gang—Barrios in East Los Angeles—Maravilla.* Sacramento, CA: Youth Authority.

Power, C., & Reimer, J. (1978). Moral atmosphere: An educational bridge between judgment and action. *New Directions for Child Development, 2.*

Putallaz, M. (1987). Maternal behavior and children's sociometric status. *Child Development, 58,* 324–340.

Quay, H. C., Rueth, D. K. & Shapiro, S. K. (1987). Psychopathology of childhood: From description to validation. *Annual Review of Psychology, 38,* 491–532.

Ramos-Ford, V., & Gardner, H. (1991). Giftedness from a multiple intelligence perspective. In N. Clongelo & G. A. Davis (Eds.), *Handbook of gifted education.* Boston: Allyn and Bacon.

Read, K. H. (1971). *The nursery school: A human relationships laboratory* (5th ed.). Philadelphia: Saunders.

Reid, D. H., Wilson, P. G., & Faux, D. (1991). Teaching self-help skills. In J. L. Matson & J. A. Mulick (Eds.), *Handbook of mental retardation* (2nd ed.). New York: Pergamon.

Reynolds, D. (1992). School effectiveness and school improvement: An updated review of the British literature. In D. Reynolds & P. Cuttance (Eds.), *School effectiveness: Research, policy and practice.* London: Cassell.

Richardson, J. G., & Simpson, C. H. (1982). Children, gender and social structure: An analysis of the contents of letters to Santa Claus. *Child Development, 53,* 429–436.

Rosenkoetter, L. I. (1973). Resistance to temptation: Inhibitory and disinhibitory effects of models. *Developmental Psychology, 8,* 80–84.

Rosenthal, F., & Jacobson, L. (1968). *Pygmalion in the classroom: Teacher expectation and pupil's intellectual development.* New York: Harper & Row.

Ross, S. A. (1971). A test of generality of the effects of deviant preschool models. *Developmental Psychology, 4,* 262–267.

Rowland, D. T. (1991). Family diversity and the life cycle. *Journal of Comparative Family Studies, 22,* 1–14.

Rutter, M. (1983). School effects on pupil progress: Research findings and policy implications. *Child Development, 54,* 1–29.

Salzinger, S., Feldman, R. S., Hammer, M., & Rosario, M. (1993). The effects of physical abuse on children's social relationships. *Child Development, 64,* 169–187.

Schinke, S. P., Schilling, R. F., Barth, R. P., Gilchrist, L. D., & Maxwell, J. S. (1986). Stress-management intervention to prevent family violence. *Journal of Family Violence, 1,* 13–26.

Shaffer, D. (1996). *Developmental psychology.* Pacific Grove, CA: Brooks/Cole.

Sigelman, C. K., & Shaffer, D. R. (1995). *Life-span human development* (2nd ed.). Pacific Grove, CA: Brooks/Cole.

Silver, L. B. (1992). *Attention-deficit hyperactivity disorder: A clinical guide to diagnosis and treatment.* Washington DC: American Psychiatric Press.

Slaughter-Defoe, D. T., Nakagawa, K., Takaniski, R, & Johnson, D. J. (1990). Toward cultural/ecological perspectives on schooling and achievement in African- and Asian-American children. *Child Development, 61,* 363–383.

Slavin, R. E. (1989). Class size and student achievement: Small effects of small classes. *Educational Psychologist, 24,* 99–110.

Sorenson, A. B., & Hallinan, M. T. (1986). Effects of ability grouping on growth in academic achievement. *American Educational Research Journal, 23,* 519–542.

Sparrow, S., Balla, D., & Cicchetti, D. (1984). *Vinland Adaptive Behavior Scales.* Circle Pines, NM: American Guidance Services.

Spergel, I. A. (1994). *The youth gang problem.* New York: Oxford University Press.

Starko, A. J. (1988). Effects of the revolving door identification model on creative productivity and self-efficacy. *Gifted Child Quarterly, 32,* 291–297.

Sue, S., & Okazaki, S. (1990). Asian-American educational achievements: A phenomenon in search of explanation. *American Psychologist, 45,* 913–920.

Sullivan. H. S. (1953). *The interpersonal theory of psychiatry.* New York: Norton.

Sweet, J. A., & Bumpass, L. L. (1987). *American families and households.* New York: Russell Sage Foundation.

Tanfer, K. (1987). Patterns of premarital cohabitation among the never-married women in the United States. *Journal of Marriage and the Family, 49,* 483–497.

Thorne, B. (1993). *Gender play: Girls and boys in school.* New Brunswick, NJ: Rutgers University.

Tomlinson-Keasey, C., Eisert, D. C., Kahle, L. R., Hardy-Brown, K., & Keasy, B. (1979). The structure of concrete-operational thought. *Child Development, 50,* 1153–1163.

Trickett, P. K., & Putnam, F. W. (1993). Impact of child sexual abuse on females: Toward a developmental psychological integration. *Psychological Science, 4,* 81–87.

Tudge, J. R. H. (1992). Processes and consequences of peer collaboration: A Vygotskian analysis. *Child Development, 63,* 1364–1379.

U.S. Bureau of the Census. (1989). Statistical abstract of the United States 1989. Washington, DC: U.S. Government Printing Office.

Walters, R. H., Leat, M., & Meizei, L. (1963). Inhibition and disinhibition of responses through empathetic learning. *Canadian Journal of Psychology, 17,* 235–243.

Weinstein, C. S. (1991). The classroom as a social context for learning. *Annual Review of Psychology, 42,* 493–525.

Weintzel, K. R., Weinberger, D. A., Ford, M. E,. & Feldman, S. S. (1990). The academic achievement in preadolescence: The role of motivational affective and self-regulatory processes. *Journal of Applied Developmental Psychology, 11*(2), 179–193.

Weisner, T. S., & Wilson-Mitchell, J. E. (1990). Nonconventional family lifestyles and sex typing in six-year-olds. *Child Development, 61,* 1915–1933.

Weiss, B., Dodge, K. A., Bates, J. E., & Pettit, G. S. (1992). Some consequences of early harsh discipline: Child aggression and a maladaptive social information processing style. *Child Development, 63,* 1321–1335.

Weiss, B., Weisz, J. R., Politano, M., Carey, M., Nelson, W., & Finch, A. J. (1992). Relations among self-reported depressive symptoms in clinic referred children versus adolescents. *Journal of Abnormal Psychology, 101,* 391–397.

Weisz, J. R., & Weiss, B. (1993). *Effects of psychotherapy with children and adolescents* (Vol. 27 of Developmental Clinical Psychology and Psychiatry). Newbury Park, CA: Sage.

Wentzel, K. R., Weinberger, D. A., Ford, M. E., & Feldman, S. S. (1990). Academic achievement in preadolescence: The role of motivational, affective and self-regulatory process. *Applied Developmental Psychology, 11*(2), 179–193.

Whalen, C. K., Henker, B., Buhrmester, D., Hinshaw, S. P., Huber, A., & Laski, K. (1989). Does stimulant medication improve peer status of hyperactive children? *Journal of Consulting and Clinical Psychology, 57,* 545–549.

White, R. W. (1960). Competence in the psychological stages of development. In M. R. Jones (Ed.), *Nebraska Symposium on Motivation.* Lincoln: University of Nebraska Press.

Whiting, B. B., & Edwards, C. P. (1988). *Children of different worlds: The formation of social behavior.* Cambridge, MA: Harvard University Press.

Wolfe, D. A., Edwards, B., Marrion, I., & Koverola, C. (1988). Early intervention for parents at risk of child abuse and neglect: A preliminary investigation. *Journal of Consulting Clinical Psychology, 56,* 40–47.

Wolfner, G. D., & Gelles, R. J. (1993). A profile of violence toward children: A national study. *Child abuse and neglect, 17,* 197–212.

Youngblade, L. M., & Belsky, J. (1992). Parent-child antecedents of 5-year-olds' close friendships: A longitudinal analysis. *Developmental Psychology, 28,* 700–713.

# 6

# *Adolescence*

## INTRODUCTION

Several changes mark adolescence, the period of transition from childhood to adulthood. Some of the most important changes are physical, but significant changes also take place in cognition and emotions. An adolescent is not just a person who has reached reproductive maturity or moved beyond the dependent role of a child; adolescence involves many changes—biological, social, psychological, cultural, and historical. Some aspects of young people may be adultlike, such as cognition, while others are childish, such as emotions. To define adolescence, one must therefore look at its most frequently occurring characteristics. When the emotional, sexual, intellectual, and physical processes of a person fall within the range typical of a child, that person is labeled a child; if the processes fall within the range typical of an adult, then the person is called an adult. Lerner and Hultsch (1983) define *adolescence* as a period within a person's life span when most of the person's processes are in a state of transition from what is considered typically childish to what is considered typically adultlike.

In this chapter we shall follow the physical and cognitive growth of the adolescent from ages 12 to 19 as well as deal with the adolescent's increasingly turbulent emotional life.

> Maria slams the door of her room. Her mother doesn't understand her; she still thinks Maria is a child. Maria says to herself, "Can't she see what everyone else does? I'm old enough to handle responsibilities. After all, I'm 15 years old." She adds, "Mother's never been outside the house, so what does she know?" Moodily, she lies on her bed. Her fingers wander to her body and face, where she notices a pimple on her forehead. On close examination, she finds a couple more. She is devastated. How can she go back to school for the party? Everyone will notice how ugly she is. Her day will be ruined. She looks desperately for any medicine that will quickly get rid of those ugly pimples, but finds nothing that will help. Finally she gets up and runs to her mother, with whom she has just had an argument about how grown-up she is. She begs her mother to help her get rid of her pimples so the school party won't be ruined for her.

The typical adolescent is a combination of child and adult, with physical growing pains as well as the need to be his or her own person.

Adolescence can be classified into three stages. *Early adolescence* is characterized by the bodily changes of pubescence and some cognitive changes. *Middle adolescence* occurs when the person is seeking an independent identity and beginning to date. *Late adolescence* or youth (Keniston, 1975) is a period in which decisions are made about further schooling, careers, and future paths.

At puberty, the young person develops the ability to procreate physically. He or she, however, has not yet achieved the psychosocial development necessary to function appropriately in an adult sexual relationship.

> Twelve-year-old Pam is an early bloomer. She menstruated at age 10. Her mother, who never married, is busy trying to survive financially, with four mouths to feed. Living in a ghetto isn't easy. If you're pretty, you're exploited. That's how Pam became pregnant. She never thought it could happen to her. After all, as she puts it, she "did it just once, and can you get pregnant the first time?" Thus Pam, who has years of physical and mental growth ahead of her, has been caught in the lifestyle of poverty and exploitation: She is still in the pubescent period and not ready for pregnancy, physically or emotionally.

## PHYSICAL CHANGES

An adolescent undergoes development at a rate equivalent to or similar to that of the first two years of life. Growth in adolescence brings about rapid development of the reproductive organs, as well as the appearance of secondary sexual characteristics. These modifications are made possible through the precipitation of hormones, which are the chemical products of the endocrine glands.

However, different parts of the body develop at different rates. Often, adolescents look "funny," with long hands and legs disproportionate to the rest of the body. There is a sequence to development—the extremities (hands, feet, and head) reach adult size before the torso.

Following the period of rapid growth comes an accumulation of fat, especially in girls, which sometimes causes embarrassment. Most of the changes that occur are gender-specific. In this period, when the production of hormones increases (Tanner, 1971), target tissues in the body respond selectively to the hormones circulating in the bloodstream, such as the sex hormones estrogen and progesterone (Garrison, 1973).

The delicate balance of the endocrine gland secretions leads to normal growth and functioning. The pituitary gland, located at the base of the brain, produces various types of hormones, including the critical growth hormone somatotrophin (Garrison, 1973). The pituitary gland also produces the secondary hormones that stimulate and regulate the functioning of several other glands, including the sex glands. The testes and the ovaries, inactive until this period, perform two functions: they produce gametes (that is, sperm and eggs) and they secrete hormones vital to the development of the reproductive organs (Specht & Craig, 1987).

## Puberty

Like a clock that never stops ticking, biological processes push us through life with relentless determination. Adolescence begins with puberty and extends to adulthood. In many cultures, puberty signals the beginning of adulthood—adolescence does not exist: With puberty, people believe that they are capable of sexual reproduction, and they assume the status and roles of adults. Even in Europe and the United States in the early 19th century the interlude between childhood and adulthood was either quite brief or nonexistent.

At age 13, Fatima belongs to a Muslim, rural, relatively poor family in India. She wears a *purdah*, which covers her body and head completely except her face. At her first menstrual cycle, which began when she was 11, she begins to do all the household work and relieves her mother of a large number of intricate household duties. Although only 13, she covers her head when the men of the family come into the house. She looks forward to her own marriage. She is like a miniature adult who knows what is expected of her and follows the family rules and traditions.

Today, Western culture delays adult status and considers many years of training and experience necessary for the transition to adulthood. The length of this training is not clearly defined. It may end when a person can vote, drive a car, or consume alcohol; or when he or she finds financial independence or completes formal education.

In contrast, the beginning of adolescence is quite clear. Purely biological, it starts with a growth spurt and the development of primary and secondary sexual characteristics. In some cultures, the start of the journey to full adulthood is celebrated with ceremonies marked by caution and celebration.

*Sexual development*    Sexual development is an important milestone of this age. The primary sexual characteristics—that is, the ovaries, vagina, uterus, and clitoris in the woman and the penis, testes, and scrotum in men—develop rapidly. When puberty begins, girls are about 11 years old and boys are 13; primary sexual organs make performing the reproductive function possible.

As they develop, boys experience spurts in height and growth in size of the penis, concurrent with development of the seminal vesicles and the prostate gland. Between the times of testicular growth and penile development, pubic hair starts to appear. An increase in the number of both oil-producing glands (sebaceous glands) and sweat glands causes body odor and acne (Tanner, 1971).

In girls, the breasts and clitoris start to enlarge, and the uterus and the vagina begin to grow. Menstruation, which occurs after the period of rapid growth, is the most dramatic and symbolic indication of a girl's changing status. Traditional psychoanalytic thought focuses on the potential of menstruation for causing emotional distress but pays little attention to girls who readily accept this event as a symbolic entrance into the female sexual role (Melges & Hamburg, 1976). Nontraumatic acceptance will be discussed further in the context of other cultures.

In our discussion of conception and pregnancy (Chapter 2), we saw the role of chromosomes as determinants of sexual identity. Sexual-response biases are built into the prenatal nervous system, and predispositions are created by the hormonal system (Diamond, 1976). The major part of gender identity occurs after birth as other factors intervene from earliest childhood through adolescence and into adulthood (Kagan, 1976).

When puberty begins, it takes about two years for the sex hormones, produced by ovaries in women and testes in men, to bring about a series of physical changes. Some of these changes eventually lead to ovulation and menstruation in women, and the production of sperm in men.

The first menstrual period, called *menarche*, usually occurs at age 11 to 13, although it may take another year for ovulation to begin. Young girls as well as young boys tend to reach puberty earlier than did previous generations. Improved nutrition is probably the reason for this change. Boys become capable of ejaculation at about age 14, but they may be 15 before they produce a normal amount of sperm (Chilman, 1983; Tanner, 1978, 1990).

Experimenting and being preoccupied with one's own body is an important aspect of this growth period. The flow of hormones also produces secondary sexual characteristics. For adolescent girls, breasts develop, hips broaden, and pubic hair appears. For adolescent boys, shoulders broaden, the voice deepens, and pubic and facial hair appears. Activation of sexual desire accompanies the development of primary and secondary sex characteristics in both male and female adolescents, fairly well controlled by the value system in which the young person grows up.

Fourteen-year-old Karla has fallen in love with one of her classmates. Although her older sister blows it off as an adolescent crush, Karla truly thinks she's in love. Her raging hormones make her want to "do things" with her boyfriend, but a strict and loving upbringing with strong values about what should and should not be done stands in the way of her giving in to raging emotions.

*Physical growth*    At the beginning of puberty, adolescents begin to grow more rapidly than before. Although growth takes place in all dimensions, the most obvious is height, especially when a girl reaches 12 and a boy 14 years of age. A young adolescent grows at a rate not experienced since he or she was 2 years old (Tanner, 1990). At the peak of such growth, a boy may grow 4 or 5 inches and a girl 3 or 4, besides other gains in the two or three years before and after this peak. With height, boys also gain weight, but very little fat, unlike girls. However, in the beginning stages of adolescence, they may be more obviously awkward than girls in terms of their body's proportion.

Before puberty, girls and boys of a particular body size are similar in strength. Because girls reach puberty sooner than boys, there is a period from about 12 to 13½ years when girls are stronger than boys of the same age. However, boys usually catch up and surpass girls in terms of lung and heart size and other such characteristics (Tanner, 1990).

The hormones that produce the growth spurt and the secondary sex changes also affect cognitive abilities by influencing neural processing or controlling brain functioning. Social factors also play a significant role in sexual differences and appear to overshadow biological differences (Kolb & Wishaw, 1990).

*Storm and stress*    All these factors label adolescence as the time of storm and stress. For a girl the first menstrual cycle could be seen as a positive sign of maturity of becoming woman or negative sign of lost childhood (Loehlin, 1992). For adolescent boys, uncontrolled erection and first ejaculation may cause a great deal of surprise and worry (Mussen, Conger, Kagan, & Huston, 1990).

Puberty does not begin at the same age for all young people. Early-maturing girls may feel self-conscious and also unhappy with their own body-image. They are overly conscious of their bodies, but by late adolescence they are more popular and more self-directed cognitively, socially, and emotionally than their late-maturing male peers. Girls who mature late do not seem to experience the same stress, although they may be concerned about the delay. Early maturing is a blessing for boys. Early maturing boys are usually stronger and bigger than their peers, with an advantage in athletics. Also they receive adult privileges at a younger age. Many studies have shown that personality differences between early and late maturers persist long into adulthood.

All adolescents have to adjust their body image. Adolescents watch themselves with pain and pleasure as they undergo change. They attempt to revise their self-image by comparing themselves with others. With their unique status—neither adults nor children—they show an increased need for conformity and an intolerance of deviations in body types, such as obesity (Specht & Craig, 1987). Representations of teenagers as slim, beautiful people without any pimples, braces, or unattractive awkwardness place a lot of pressure on young people: Acne and uneven growth are part of growing up. Many adolescents are uncomfortable with their bodies. Whether they mature early or late, boys and girls encounter stressful problems connected with physical changes; such problems are normal for this period (Ganter & Yeakel, 1980).

Many adolescents worry about their sexual competency—that is, whether they can perform a sexual act satisfying to them and their partners. There may be conflict between their own intuitive interest in masturbation and the urge to share sexual experiences with others. Further, their family or religious teaching may say that either behavior is wrong and even harmful to their bodies. In reality, masturbation is one form of meaningful experimentation with their bodies. In some extreme cases, adolescents are totally deprived of their right to experiment and, as adults, some such people often reject all human sexuality as wrong and associate tremendous guilt with sexuality. Other adolescents overemphasize sexual feelings and actions and measure their worth solely by them.

> At 19, Andy has been dating heavily. When confronted by his mother, who is concerned because he's been neglecting his schoolwork, Andy can only answer that he's "sowing his wild oats, *wildly.*" After all, he wants to become a man like his father, to "prove his manliness." Often, he has heard his father emphasize that a man has to prove himself sexually.

## Cultural Attitudes

Different cultures view adolescence differently. U.S. culture assumes that adolescence will bring with it dramatic changes. As the changes occur, children begin to define themselves in new ways, seeing themselves as men and women. Failure to change at the expected time could be a source of embarrassment and despair. With the physical changes come emotional changes that affect the way adolescents feel about themselves.

All changes take place within the social context of a culture, with its particular expectations and values. In the following case, we can see how U.S. cultural expectations affect one girl who does not conform.

> Fourteen-year-old Bernadette appears to be lagging behind her classmates in her physical growth. She is tiny and timid. The taller and more developed girls in her class are interested in boys, and their conversation revolves around dating. Bernadette becomes more and more introverted because she has not yet reached that stage in her life. Being told that she's just a late bloomer doesn't remove the sting from the jokes she hears about herself. She often hears "Aren't you ever going to grow up?" This affects her personality as well as her performance in class. At home Bernadette has grown increasingly moody because her parents do not understand her problems.

*Samoa* According to the traditional view put forth by Freud and others (Freud, 1946), growing up at any stage is difficult, but it becomes more complicated when the adolescent has to come to grips with increasing demands made by the world—that is, pivotal decisions about work, lifestyle, friends, religion, and politics. No person passes through this phase without being affected deeply by it.

Evidence from other cultures, however, has challenged this view. One of the first Westerners who viewed adolescence differently was Margaret Mead (1928), who, as a young anthropologist in the 1920s, visited the island of Samoa and made a study of the people in the South Seas. Mead wished to know whether the physical changes of puberty necessarily yield the Western portrait of adolescence.

Although the culture of Samoans has changed a great deal and some have criticized Mead's writings, her study of early Samoan life, as understood by her, is quite interesting. In the 1920s the people of Samoa lived in an idyllic, unsophisticated culture, surrounded by coconut palms and mango trees. There was clear gender-role differentiation. Women spent their time looking after their young and planting and gathering food. Men fished and hunted, constructed buildings, and farmed. Samoan girls stayed close to their mothers and siblings when they were young but participated in the communal dances and activities. By the time they were 7 or so, girls and boys had formed voluntary groups with members of their own gender, revealing strong antagonistic feelings toward members of the opposite sex. This segregation is similar to the behavior of preadolescents in U.S. culture, who form same-gender peer groups.

With the onset of puberty, Samoan young people entered the fabric of society. During this period boys and girls received formal names and roles through religious rituals. After puberty, girls and boys were involved in sexual relationships. Girls continued to participate in the group with their elders by playing the ceremonial roles, and later they assumed more of the daily tasks of sewing, gathering, and planting. Gradually girls and boys learned the roles that would soon dominate their social lives—those of wife or husband and parent.

As Mead (1928) described it, the adolescent period in Samoa possessed a gradualness, a smoothness and naturalness that distinguished it sharply from the adolescent years in Western society. Young girls, apparently aware of the roles they would play, assisted in adult activities and took responsibility for child care. Sex and love relationships were easily accepted, and there were no feelings of shame, privacy, or guilt about sex or any other matters.

According to Mead (1928), growing up in Samoa was less complicated than it is in Western culture. On the basis of her study, she commented that Samoan children had it much easier; they were less stressed and less conflict ridden than their peers in the United States. Mead concluded that the Samoan culture was characterized by an integrated set of activities and that U.S. culture was increasingly characterized by specialization, diversity, and fragmentation. Of course, in the Samoan culture children also experienced problems, but they were not as complicated or diverse as those seen in Western cultures.

## COGNITIVE DEVELOPMENT

During the preschool and middle school years, children learn to solve problems involving length, quantity, and number, and they learn crafts and sports. But as they reach adolescence, they develop mental powers of a qualitatively different kind. They learn to combine and recombine symbols, draw inferences, and develop their own belief systems in science, religion, politics, and the arts. Their ability to perceive and feel, as well as communicate both verbally and nonverbally, improves.

Adolescent thinking represents a new level of reasoning, an ability to deal with situations that is far more complex than before. The adolescent can state a group of principles about any set of objects, explain what forces act on them and how their behavior is altered by them, and explore the relationships among those principles (Gardner, 1978).

### Piaget: Formal Operations

In early adolescence, young people begin to think of the world in new terms. From adolescence to adulthood, the quality of thought changes in some significant ways, becoming more and more abstract. Young people can think about several dimensions at once rather than focus on just one domain or issue at a time. Their thinking also becomes more reflective: Adolescents are increasingly more aware of their own thoughts as well as the accuracy or inaccuracy of their knowledge. Further, adolescents can generate hypotheses about events they have never perceived (Keating, 1990). Recall that Piaget describes these complex cognitive abilities as *formal operations* (Chapman, 1988; Inhelder & Piaget, 1958; Piaget, 1970, 1972). Most adolescents and many adults approach problem solving in a practical, concrete way in everyday life. Under certain conditions, however, more abstract, systematic and self-reflective qualities of thought can be observed, reflecting formal operations in the way adolescents approach the analysis of information and the ability to acquire knowledge (Eckstein & Shemesh, 1992; Fischer, Bullock, Rotenberg, & Raya, 1993).

Recall that concrete operations are mental actions related to tangible things and events. For example, a young person mentally classifies animals into categories. *Formal operations* are mental actions on ideas. Thus a person who acquires formal operations can mentally juggle ideas that cannot be seen, heard, tasted, smelled, or touched. That is, formal operational thought is more hypothetical and abstract than concrete operational thought. For example, the school-age child might define the justice system in terms of policy and judges, whereas the adolescent may define it as a branch of the government concerned with balancing the rights of different interests in society.

*New skills*    These cognitive abilities lead adolescents to develop new skills. These skills have implications for how adolescents approach interpersonal relationships, form personal plans and goals, and analyze scientific and mathematical information. For example, adolescents can manipulate mentally more than two categories of variables at the same time, such as considering the relationship of speed, distance, and time in planning a trip (Acredolo, Adams, & Schmid, 1984). Six new conceptual skills emerge during the stage of formal operations (Demetriou & Elfdides, 1985; Neimark, 1982).

1. Adolescents can draw on many variables to explain their own behavior and that of others.
2. They can think about things that will change the future. For instance, adolescents realize that their relationships with their parents will be quite different in ten years' time.
3. Adolescents can hypothesize a logical sequence of possible events. For example, they can predict which colleges and occupations will likely work for them, given their academic performance in high school.
4. They can anticipate the consequences of their actions. For example, they understand that if they drop out of school, they will probably end up in a less lucrative job than if they stay.
5. Adolescents can detect consistency or inconsistency in a set of statements. They can test the truth of a statement by finding evidence that either supports or does not support it. In their own idealism, a large number of them are perturbed by statements such as "All men are created equal," when racial and sexual discrimination continues to be part of society.
6. They think in a relativistic way about themselves, other individuals, and their world. They know that they are expected to act in a particular fashion because of the norms of the community and culture. As they begin to learn about other cultures and communities, they come to understand that different norms can govern behaviors. Ideally they have an intense desire to make a more conscious commitment to their culture.

With the emergence of a restrictive government, Salma, a young Muslim girl, has fled with her parents to the United States from the Middle East. In the orthodox culture in which she was brought up, girls did not date boys; rather, marriages were arranged for them. Any form of relationship with young men was frowned on and, according to the rules in her small, traditional Middle Eastern hometown, a girl could be stoned to death if she developed a relationship without marriage.

Salma starts school in the United States. One young man in her class asks her for a date. Terrified, she runs home and cries, not at all sure if she should even return to school. It takes the school social worker tremendous effort and energy to understand the cultural background of this new student. She helps Salma understand U.S. culture, as well as the compliment that the young man has paid her by asking her out. At the same time, the young man is informed of the cultural differences between them and what they mean. This exchange eventually leads Salma and her admirer to respect each other's cultures and their respective lifestyles.

Adolescents can more easily accept members of other cultures once they have realized that all people are products of their cultures, with different rules and norms (O'Mahoney, 1989). Piaget claims that the stage of formal operations is the highest level of thought that one can attain. Conceptual development in early adolescence usually results in a flexible, critical, and abstract view of the world. Adolescents develop greater awareness of themselves and others as well as greater powers of imagination and judgment. Young people begin to think in terms of career goals, educational attainment, and beginning a family; they also have concerns about unemployment, environmental cleanliness, and the global economy.

## Egocentrism

Because these thought processes are accompanied by changes, adolescents frequently assume that others are fascinated by them and their behaviors. They anticipate the reactions of others and assume that their own self-assessment is matched by others' approval or criticism. Elkind (1975) proposes that formal operational thought leads to *adolescent egocentrism*—that is, a difficulty in differentiating one's own thoughts and

feelings from those of other people. This leads to an *imaginary audience* before whom adolescents try out their own feelings and behavior. This period of egocentrism recedes by the time adolescents are 14 or 15 years old, when they replace their imaginary audiences with real ones. At this time, adolescents begin to see themselves from others' points of view and to incorporate some outside judgments as part of their own self-concept.

The second form of adolescent egocentrism is the *personal fable*—that is, a tendency to think that you and your thoughts are unique and special (Elkind, 1975). If the imaginary audience is a product of failure to differentiate between the self and others, the concept of a fable is a product of differentiating too much. Thus an adolescent who is in love for the first time imagines that no one in the history of the human race has ever felt such heights of emotion. And when a love situation does not work out, they feel no one can understand the depth of their agony. The personal fable also makes them feel that rules that apply to others do not apply to them. For instance, they feel that speeding on a highway and not wearing a seat belt will be safe, or having sex without contraception will not lead to pregnancy *for them.*

Elkind hypothesizes that the imaginary audience and the personal fable phenomena intensify when a young person begins adolescence and then decrease as he or she gets older and begins to assume adult roles. Indeed, research shows that imaginary audience and personal fable are most evident in early adolescence and decline with age (Elkind & Bowen, 1979; Lechner & Rosenthal, 1984).

## Criticism of Piaget's Theory

Piaget's theory is the definitive thought on adolescent cognitive development. However, not every psychologist agrees with Piaget's formulation of this final cognitive stage. Some point out that not all adolescents or even adults can think in formal operational terms. A certain degree of intelligence seems to be necessary; cultural and socioeconomic factors, particularly at the educational level, also play a part in this development (Neimark, 1975). As Neimark (1982) found, problem-solving abilities progress from 11 to 15 years of age. As you know, children's ability to solve problems progresses from simple to complex. When very young, children believe that there are no rules of behavior. But as parents begin to place restrictions on what can and cannot be done, children become aware of a limited number of rules. As they become adolescents, they realize that there are collections of rules. A study of 13-year-olds in which formal operational thinking was considered as a crucial factor showed a significant correlation between performance across six different measures (Overton & Meehan, 1982). However, the researchers concluded that children at this age do not apply a formal operational reasoning approach to problems across various specific content areas. For instance, at 13 years of age they did not understand the abstract ideas and terms such as truth and justice.

Another criticism indicates that formal reasoning as a construct is not broad enough to encompass the many dimensions of cognitive maturation. There are at least two domains in which growth takes place: (1) the information-processing system and (2) the hypercognitive system, which increases the speed, efficiency, and capacity of information storage documented during this period (Thatcher, Walker, & Giudice, 1987). Improvements in logical thinking result, in part, from being able to handle greater quantities of information more quickly and efficiently, which is due to both schooling and increased competence in specific areas. This combination of information processing and broader knowledge base improves hypercognitive processing. Adolescents can approach a problem from several different angles, assessing which one offers the most promising avenue to solution (Keating, 1990).

Further, adults can regress to a lower level of thinking in certain situations. When adults face unfamiliar problems, they tend to fall back on concrete reasoning. Some psychologists have therefore suggested that formal operational thought be considered as an extension of concrete operations rather than a stage in its own right. Though Piaget recognizes that this may be the case, he emphasizes that elements of this last cognitive stage are essential for the study of advanced science and mathematics.

Another limitation of Piaget's formulation of higher-level cognitive skills is that it explains how adolescents can speculate, analyze their own thoughts, and form self-concepts, but it does not account for creative ability. Some creative adolescents exhibit capacities for unusual ways of thinking that differ from the cognitive modes commonly used by adolescents with high IQ scores. However, educational institutions and society typically reward the conventional model of functioning rather than the highly creative and divergent person. This oversight results in an unfortunate loss of a great deal of creative potential.

Why is it that most adults do not perform well on Piagetian tasks? It appears that a person has to obtain at least an average score on standardized intelligence tests in order to reason at the formal level. Most college students in our culture meet this criterion; however, cultures in which people had not received formal schooling totally failed in solving Piaget's problems. So it can be concluded that thinking in a formal operational manner requires *expertise* in a domain of knowledge. What appears to be more than basic intelligence is formal education (Neimark, 1982.)

Piaget himself suggests that adolescents and adults are likely to use formal operations in an area they find familiar and comfortable but return to concrete operations in less familiar areas. For instance, hunters in preliterate cultures who fail the Piagetian scientific-reasoning task will often reason at a formal level when they are tracking prey, because this is an important and well-learned activity in their lives (Tulkin & Konner, 1973).

Finally, does cognitive development really stop after formal operations? There are several intriguing ideas about what may lie beyond formal operations—that is, postformal modes of thought (see Commons, Richards, & Armon, 1984; Labouvie-Vief, 1992).

> Alor, an adolescent, has attained formal operations and is carried away with his new powers of logical thinking. He performs extremely well on a Piagetian problem in which everything is given in the problem and the only thing Alor has to do is generate logically possible solutions and identify the correct one. Impressed with his own thinking, Alor insists there is a logically correct answer for every question. He adds that if a person simply applies logic he or she can arrive at absolute truths.

Perhaps people like Alor are not equipped for the *real* world (as yet), for there are many ways to look at an issue, and often there is no one single right answer.

## MORAL DEVELOPMENT

As adolescents begin to think and mature, they pay increasing attention to the selection of ideals and moral values. The development of moral values is part of the process the child begins by learning not to tell lies or steal. As you know, external morality is created by identification, modeling, and rewards and punishments. In growing up, the child internalizes this morality. When children become mature adults, they eventually reassess it and often build their own coherent set of values.

### Generational Consistency in Adolescent Values

One can measure adolescent values in many different ways. I shall present three studies to demonstrate. In the first, adolescents were asked to rank-order a list of values according to their importance to themselves. A study done by R. P. Beech and Schoeppe (1974) used groups of children in grades 5, 7, 9, and 11; the Rokeach Value Survey (Rokeach, 1968) was used to assess the instrumental and terminal values of the subjects.

*Instrumental* (or means) values can be classified as cheerful, helpful, and obedient. *Terminal* (or end-state) values can be a world of beauty, true friendship, loving relationships, and so forth. By testing the given ranges of subjects, the authors could examine the extent to which values held by adolescents tend to remain stable or change over the adolescent years.

There was a great deal of similarity in spite of such factors as age and gender. For example, world peace, freedom, honesty, and loving received consistently high priority from both boys and girls in all grades, whereas values like salvation, logic, and imagination tended to have lower rankings. The concept of family security was given higher priority by younger children than by older children, and equality and social recognition were seen as important values by older adolescents. Instrumental values, such as cheerfulness, helpfulness, and obedience, tended to decline in importance by the 11th grade.

In the second study, a German translation of the Rokeach measure was used with 400 German high school students (Gunther, 1975). No age or gender differences were reported, but there were differences across religious affiliations and political persuasions. Significant differences among Catholic, Protestant, and agnostic adolescents occurred regarding five terminal and three instrumental values. Catholics gave a higher ranking than Protestants, and higher still than agnostics, to such values as world peace and salvation. Agnostics gave a higher ranking to values such as an exciting life and pleasure. Both the Catholic and the agnostic group gave higher ranking to social recognition than did the Protestants. Three instrumental values also distinguished the groups. Helpfulness was rated as highest by Catholics, whereas Protestants ranked it lower and agnostics ranked it still lower. Being logical and being independent were valued highest by agnostics, followed by Protestants and then Catholics.

Third, Friesen (1968) studied the value orientations of 1000 adolescents in two large Canadian cities. Both genders were adequately represented in the study, which included three levels of socioeconomic status. Within each of the status groups, three different ethnocultural backgrounds were represented. Friesen's major findings were consistent with what Offer and Offer (1975) and others have said: Most of the value indicators were directly related to the ethnocultural background of the students involved in the study.

The current popular line of reasoning that youth culture is separate and distinct from the parent culture receives very little support from these data. Another popular suggestion, that communication between generations is breaking down and that the generation gap is all-pervasive, also is not supported by these findings. The fact that youth's aspirations, activities, and attitudes are related both to socioeconomic background and, independently, to ethnocultural background suggests that forces in society other than the youth culture continue to shape the value structures of modern youth significantly (Friesen, 1968). A continuity of values between parent and adolescent appears to be a general finding for different ethnic, racial, and socioeconomic groups.

As a child, Ruby was battered by her parents—usually by her stepfather—for any mistake she made. At 9, if she spilled her milk, her stepfather belted her for being careless. Her mother supported her husband in his policy of strict discipline with Ruby. As she grew older, the physical abuse continued. Ruby grew up both careful and rigid in her idea of what was acceptable and what was not.

Now, at age 16, Ruby has found herself a part-time job as the baby-sitter of a 12-month-old boy. One day when she gives him milk to drink, he pours it on the ground, more in play than in mischief. Ruby loses her temper and beats him severely. The more he cries, the angrier she gets. According to her, he's supposed to stop crying, but he does not. After she's through, the child has a swollen eye, a split lip, and marks all over his body. When this case is investigated, Ruby's value system is exposed. Though not positive by comparison with those of the general society, it is the set of standards she experienced in her family, which

helped her set up her own standards of behavior for the young child.

## Schools and Value Development

Value development does not begin and end with the family. The school transmits its values to young people daily.

Damon (1988), a proponent of prevention of problems for teenagers, proposes the development of an effective moral education program that includes the following practices:

1. By advocating certain basic values, the moral education program should actively allow and encourage children/adolescents to reason independently about values.
2. Children and adults should be encouraged to participate in a give-and-take discussion in which the young person's right to make a moral decision is respected.
3. The moral development program should take place across the school curriculum and in extracurricular activities, not just in moral discussions.
4. Because young people are idealistic, community leaders actively involved in showing moral responsibility—through running a homeless shelter, providing funds for physically or mentally challenged people or other social services—should be invited to talk to students and act as moral mentors. Young people should receive opportunities to engage in such community activities themselves.

Teaching moral values in a school setting would increase the work of teachers. Even so, adding moral education to the school system could be an effective start at preventing delinquency, adolescent pregnancies, and truancy.

## Kolhberg's Theory

*Stages* Kohlberg believes that most children in U.S. culture outgrow the first stages of moral development by the time they reach adolescence, when they begin to conform to conventional roles. Although a large number of teenagers break the law now and then, adolescence is actually a period of considerable growth in moral reasoning and a time when many individuals become increasingly motivated to behave morally.

In a 20-year longitudinal study, researchers asked boys originally studied by Kohlberg to respond to moral dilemmas at ages 10, 13 and 16 (Colby, Kohlberg, Gibbs, & Lieberman, 1983). They found that preconventional reasoning dominates 10-year-olds but decreases considerably during the teen years. During adolescence, conventional reasoning becomes the dominant mode of moral thinking. So among 13- and 14-year-olds, most moral judgments reflect either an instrumental hedonism that says, "You scratch my back and I'll scratch yours," or a Stage 3 reasoning that says, "Good girls or good boys are concerned with being nice and earning approval." Over half of the judgments offered by 16- to 18-year-olds embody Stage 3 reasoning (mutual interpersonal expectations, interpersonal conformity, and relationships—see Chapter 1). But a fifth of them scored at Stage 4 (social systems and conscience), which highlights authority, social order , and maintaining morality. The older adolescents were beginning to develop a broad social perspective on justice and were concerned about acting in ways that would help maintain the social system.

*Shift to conventional reasoning*    When does postconventional reasoning (Level 3) take place? Kohlberg's work suggests that it does not appear until early adulthood. Basically the main developmental trend in moral reasoning during adolescence is a shift from preconventional thinking to more conventional reasoning. During adolescence most individuals seem to rise above a concern with external rewards and punishments. They express a genuine desire to live up to the moral standards that parents and other authorities have taught them and to ensure that laws are designed to create law and order in society.

Damon and Hart (1988) observed another important breakthrough in adolescent moral development. Adolescents begin to view morality as an important part of their own identity. More sensitive to the expectations of those around them, adolescents are motivated to portray and view themselves as honest and caring individuals. They begin to realize that they will lose self-respect if they ignore others' needs (Eisenberg, Miller, Shell, McNalley, & Shea, 1991). A few of them even become moral leaders who devote their lives to achieving social justice (Stage 4) (Colby & Damon, 1992).

In becoming aware that people hold different and relative values, adolescents emphasize procedures for reaching consensus among reasonable people. They view law as a changeable set of principles that should yield to consensus regarding the public good.

Adolescents also develop the universal-ethical-principle orientation: One chooses a course of action by drawing a conclusion from one's own ethical principles, which have been arrived at as a result of an appeal to comprehensiveness, universality, and consistency. As Kohlberg sees it, adolescents hold certain moral principles that do not allow for exceptions. Specifically, they uphold the universal principles of justice, reciprocity, and equality of human rights.

## Criticism of Kohlberg's Theory

Because Kohlberg's scheme of moral development has gained impressive research support, it has been used in many educational programs. It also has generated much controversy. Researchers who have studied Kohlberg have had the tools and knowledge necessary to apply the numerous measures and dimensions involved in assessing moral stages. However, work that has not received Kohlberg's sanction has an unclear status, and those who have worked to learn his complicated scoring system criticize the "cult" surrounding Kohlberg's group (Hogan, 1973; Kurtines & Greif, 1974; McGeorge, 1973).

*Bias*   Another line of criticism concerns Kohlberg's claims about the universality of the stages of moral development and their sequence. Is Kohlberg's theory biased? Some critics say that it reflects three biases: cultural, liberal, and sexist. The stage theory unfairly treats people from non-Western cultures, those with conservative values, and women in general as less moral.

Not all cultures follow Kohlberg's moral stages or postconventional reasoning as Kohlberg defines it. Critics claim that Kohlberg's highest stages reflect a Western ideal of justice, which is a bias against cultures that do not highly value individualism and individual rights (Gibbs & Schnell, 1985; Shweder, Mahapatra, & Miller, 1990). People from societies who emphasize social harmony and place the good of the group ahead of the good of the individual may be viewed as conventional moral thinkers in Kohlberg's system of development but in reality they may have very sophisticated concepts of justice (Snarey, 1985; Tietjen & Walker, 1985).

> Thirty-year-old Anand lives at home with his widowed mother and his unmarried sisters in a remote village in rural India. The rest of the family obeys him. As the chief wage earner, he looks for bridegrooms to marry his three younger sisters but does not intend to get married himself until his obligation to his younger sisters has been carried out. He has complete authority over the choice of husbands for all his sisters, which is not considered morally wrong in this traditionally rich culture.

The most serious criticism concerns Kohlberg's bias against women. Gilligan (1982, 1993) indicates that Kohlberg interviewed only boys. To fill in the gap, she hypothesizes that women develop a *feminine* orientation to moral issues. Gilligan continues that boys are traditionally raised to be independent, assertive, and achievement oriented—to see moral dilemmas as inevitable conflicts between the rights of two or more parties and to view laws and other social conventions as necessary for resolving these conflicts. Girls are brought up to be nurturant and empathetic, to define their sense of "goodness" in terms of their concern for other people.

*Judgment and behavior*   One major criticism of Kohlberg's work concerns the relation between moral judgment and moral behavior. Perhaps even more important is the question of how necessary it is to talk about moral dilemmas at all. In any case, Gilligan (1982) has shown that a person's reasoning only marginally predicts how a person behaves in a particular situation. How one acts matters more than how one construes or rationalizes actions. Thus, in the famous experiment by Milgram in which one individual was instructed to shock another, many observers consider as crucial not the reasoning involved but rather the decision either to apply or not to apply the shock. (The case is famous because so many subjects did shock other subjects.) In this experiment, simple reasoning should have been preferred over complex reasoning in favor of shocking; according to Milgram, "It will hurt" should have overridden "I am helping the experimenter in the pursuit of scientific truth." There was a dramatic divorce between reasoning and action. When asked how they thought they would behave in such a situation, subjects invariably predicted that they would give far fewer shocks than they actually did (Milgram, 1974). In response to these criticisms, Kohlberg (1973, 1981) changed his thinking and agreed that reasoning and action are separate enterprises, and there was good reason to disregard reason and to focus on actions and consequences.

Kohlberg insists that reasoning exists in all different stages, but critics view this assertion as a bit hollow. Often, people decide what they wish to do, and even if their motives are unworthy they still manage to concoct a reason that could justify their behavior. Besides reasoning, there are many other factors, such as motivation, habit, and emotional state, that contribute to human behavior, even in morally ambiguous situations.

*Evaluation*   How can we evaluate Kohlberg's theory? An impressive body of studies documents the basic developmental levels. There is a persuasive theoretical account of the sequences of stages and of the view that moral thought can be tied to other aspects of intellectual growth. The difficulties with Kohlberg's work arise from the manner in which scoring decisions are made and the problem of cross-cultural validity, sexual differences, and the relative importance of moral judgments and moral actions. In sum, we can conclude that Kohlberg's theory has been concerned mainly with moral reasoning rather than moral affect or behaviors. A person might decide either to uphold or to break the law at any stage of moral reasoning. What makes one stage different from another is the complexity or structure of a person's reasoning, not the specific decision he or she reaches. Also, many personal qualities besides level of moral reasoning would influence whether a person will behave morally or immorally in daily life (Kurtines, 1986; Thoma, Rest, & Davison, 1991).

## ERIKSON: IDENTITY

### What Is Identity Formation?

According to Erikson, adolescence is the stage of the identity crisis, which is considered to be the central crisis of all development. The term *identity* expresses a mutual relation in that it connotes both a persistent sameness within oneself (self-sameness) and a persistent sharing of some kind of essential character with others (Erikson, 1980). Adolescence is the period when autonomy dawns. Young people begin to choose their own friends and pastimes and to build meaningful emotional ties away from the family. They create their own value systems, often influenced by the family to which they belong, and plan for the future. These enterprises consume a great deal of adolescent time.

In U.S. culture, adolescents strive for heightened self-awareness, autonomy, sexuality, and a way to forge an adequate relationship with the wider society while realizing various personal goals. Thus, as Erikson asserts, an identity evolves that combines past identifications, future aspirations, and cultural influences.

As adolescents grow older, they become preoccupied with efforts to define themselves. They take into account the bonds that have been built between themselves and others in the past, as well as the direction that they hope to take in the future. Identity serves as an anchor that allows people the essential experience of continuity in their social relationships.

There is a cultural component to identity formation. Erikson believes that young people in this age level begin to pursue their personal goals actively. The goals of an adolescent, however, reflect to some degree the value orientation of the culture to which he or she belongs. In forming a personal identity, adolescents must learn and decide which cultural goals serve them and which do not. Resolving the identity crisis is the final step in the internalization of cultural values.

As young people pass through the stage of later adolescence, they find that family, teachers, neighbors, friends, and ethnic groups hold certain expectations for the behavior of a person at this age. Adolescents may be expected to marry, serve the country, attend church, vote, and, of course, work. Expectations of this kind differ from cultural values, but they too are accommodated in the formation of the individual's identity.

### Negative Self-Images

In the process of identity formation, a person may make certain decisions as a result of the persistent demands of significant others. *Identity foreclosure* occurs when a person slips into a role through premature decisions about his or her identity, often in response to the demands of others. For example, an adolescent may decide to become a doctor or a lawyer because the parents or grandparents expect it. The young person does not question the decision and firmly commits to carrying it out to please others, without even identifying his or her own goals (Newman & Newman, 1995).

Some young people develop a *negative self-image* (Erikson, 1980). Labels like "failure," "good for nothing," and "juvenile delinquent" can partly determine a person's identity. Adopting such labels encourages the person to behave in ways that will strengthen that identity.

The foreclosed identity and the negative identity both resolve the identity crisis—provide the person with a concrete identity—in ways that fall short of the goal of a positive personal identity. However, worse problems arise for young people whose identity resolution leads to *role diffusion:* They can neither commit to any single view of themselves nor integrate the various roles they have to play. Such individuals are often confronted with opposing value systems and lack confidence in their ability to make meaningful decisions. This condition of diffusion arouses anxiety, apathy, and hostility toward the existing roles because these people feel uncomfortable in all of them (Newman & Newman, 1995).

In evolving a personal identity, an individual may experience temporary periods of confusion and depression. Adolescents are likely to experience moments of self-preoccupation, isolation, and discouragement as the diverse pieces of their lives fall together meaningfully into a reordered total picture. Thus even a positive role identification involves some degree of role confusion. Some people, however, never formulate a satisfying identity that provides for the convergence of multiple identifications, aspirations, and roles. They have persistent fears of losing hold of themselves and their future.

Abandoned by his mentally ill mother when he was 2 years old, 17-year-old Gregory has lived in six different foster homes and has been labeled a "no-good troublemaker." Some families were good to him but did not love him enough to keep him with them for a long period; others viewed him as a problem. In one foster home he was sexually abused by his foster brother. In each of these homes, Gregory experienced different rules, regulations, and expectations of himself. Now, at 17 he belongs to a group home but receives little direction about what to do with his life. A confused young man, he has recently fallen into trouble with the law for stealing a car and shoplifting. Although he'll have to leave the group home after a year, he can't decide what he wants to do with his life. He is living up to his label of no-good troublemaker.

## Developing a Self-Image: Two Cases

How do individuals develop positive or negative self-images? We shall look at two people on the threshold of adolescence and attempt to follow their growth experiences in order to gain a better understanding of the identity crisis in adolescence.

When Jack was an infant he experienced the world as good, giving, supportive, and dependable. He was born in a lower-class African-American family whose stable, loving relationships strengthened his sense of the world's goodness, which he internalized. The outcome for him was a sense of basic trust in himself as well as the world. By 2 years of age, Jack enjoyed a sense of autonomy. He gained increasing control over mind and body through a nontraumatic achievement of bowel control and successful attempts in exploring the environment and making decisions on his own. He could love as well as cooperate and thus move easily to the next stage of development, in which he attained a sense of initiative. Jack was well loved and felt comfortable in exploring his own potentialities. When he entered the school system, he was challenged with the new demands of learning and peer competitiveness. Now, because he's prepared for a confident, meaningful life, Jack will enter high school with the feeling that he "can do it" and a sense of competence and industry.

Perry comes from a lower-class African-American family characterized by constant marital conflicts. As an infant, he cried but nobody catered to him; often he cried himself to sleep. A harsh hand hit him if he did not drink the milk that was slipped between his lips, whether he was ready for it or not. Constant experiences of frustration and deprivation led Perry to develop a feeling of mistrust. As he grew older he had difficulty meeting the standards of his parents. It took him a long time to gain bladder and bowel control. Exploring his environment proved to be stressful. Instead of security and self-confidence, Perry developed a foundation of doubt and shame. All these negative factors created a barrier to establishing an adequate love-identity relationship with his parents; rather, guilt became a dominant feature of his life. At a young age Perry was preoccupied with rejection and pain in his immediate environment. This preoccupation put him at a disadvantage when he entered the school system. Although school surroundings made new opportunities available, Perry felt a sense of inferiority. Now, as he thinks about high school, he tells himself, "I can't make it at school."

What is the possibility that Jack and Perry will experience adolescence in the same manner? Practically nil. They have different orientations toward the new challenges and opportunities available to them. Jack is entering the period of adolescence with positive experiences behind him, whereas Perry remains burdened with adaptive concerns that date back to difficulties in early childhood and infancy. However, the outside world will see them as two African-American teenagers. Stereotypes of teenagers will be applied to both of them, and they will both be expected to perform and conform. When problems arise, the period of adolescence itself might even be blamed. In our culture we are more apt to recognize problems at adolescence than at earlier points in the life span and to make assumptions that the problems are new and peculiar to this stage. What truly happens is that the earlier problems just take on new dimensions. Some of the negative attention that adolescents receive reflects the limited recognition of the problems children tend to bring with them into adolescence. A failure to have noticed these problems before says something about our own perceptions as well as our values.

Again, the distinctive feature of adolescence is the need to develop a sense of identity. In time, a person has to add new components to that identity and thus develop a clear and integrated self-image. The task of integrating identity is complex, taking into account past, present, and future selves. Moreover, the young person has to perform this task in the midst of many new developments, including physiological transformations. Every individual who enters this stage has to face the risky task of identity integration;

some will falter and leave adolescence with a sense of identity confusion. Contrary to stereotypes, adolescents who show strong signs of mental health and adaptive coping strategies often enjoy positive communication and trusting relationships with their parents or other close family members as well as strong feelings of trust and security among their friends (Levitt, Guacci-Franco & Levitt, 1993; Raja, McGee & Stanton, 1992).

## Criticism of Erikson's Theory

Erikson's scheme of development is basically male in orientation. In describing the adolescent period, Erikson uses the masculine gender to represent all people. The reason is obvious: Like Freud, Erikson does not pay much attention to female development. Erikson does, however, assert that a woman puts aside her identity as she prepares to define herself through the man she will marry. Though he maintains that identity should precede intimacy (discussed in Chapter 7), he specifies that women achieve both at the same time.

Freud described male and female differences with the statement "biology is destiny." Psychologists have added to this idea the notion that "socialization is destiny." There are indeed differences between the sexes in defining identity, and though there has been subtle but often sexist acknowledgment of these differences, it is only in recent years that the quest for female identity has been researched.

## GILLIGAN: FEMALE IDENTITY

### Intimacy and Identity

Carol Gilligan (1982) concludes that women define themselves less in terms of achievement and more in terms of relationships with other people, while preserving their separate identity. They tend to achieve identity through cooperation rather than competition (Papalia & Olds, 1986).

From her study of women, Marcia (1979) concludes that women develop stability in terms of identity as society pressures women to carry on social roles. Marcia argues, as Erikson's male-based pattern indicates, that women do not have to wait to develop intimacy; they develop both identity and intimacy at the same time. She concludes that differences in male and female patterns are also due to the different ways parents treat boys and girls. As several studies have shown, different child-rearing practices are associated with different identity statuses (Marcia, 1980). Further, much research indicates that intimate friendships are more important to girls than boys in grade school (Cooke, 1979).

Sherman (1971) asserts that adolescence is not a period of stress and storm for most girls, although it tends to be unhappier for girls than for boys. For girls, sources of unhappiness tend to lie in the vagaries of acceptance by the all-important peer group rather than biological factors, such as menarche. They struggle to manage conflicting feelings toward the mother, engendered largely by dependence-independence conflicts. The intense same-gender peer friendships of this stage may be a way of working through the mother relationship, and sisters as well as girlfriends may become more important than fathers at this point in providing substitute relationships that help to wean the girl from the mother. Thus, for girls, intimacy is a way of establishing identity, and proceeds along with it.

The discrepancy between womanhood and adulthood is very evident in a study by Broverman, Clarkson, and Rosenkrantz (1972). The findings of this study reveal what is deemed necessary for adulthood—the ability to think autonomously, make clear decisions, and take responsible action—and show that these traits are associated with masculinity. Thus the stereotypes suggest a splitting of love and work that relegates expressive capacities to women while placing instrumental abilities in the masculine domain. Yet, looked at from a different point of view, these stereotypes reflect a conception of adulthood that is itself out of balance, favoring the separateness of the individual self over connection to others and leaning more toward an autonomous life of work than toward the interdependence of love and care (Gilligan, 1982).

Some men discover in midlife what women have known from the beginning: the importance of intimacy, relationships, and care. However, because this knowledge in women has been considered intuitive or instinctive—that is, a function of anatomy coupled with destiny—psychologists have neglected to describe its development. Gilligan goes on to say that her research on women's moral development centers on the elaboration of that knowledge and thus delineates a critical gender difference in psychological development.

## Political Issues

In *Meeting at Crossroads*, L. M. Brown and Gilligan (1992) present the lives of adolescents. They explored the relationships between girls and their connectedness to others. This study of 100 girls has led to more discoveries about girls and women's relationships.

Girls at the edge of adolescence face a central relational crisis. They begin to see how their actions and new powers of reasoning and bonding could invoke great disapproval from a patriarchal society. Being true to such a culture often means denying their identity—particularly their bonds with girls and women—in favor of certain roles. This can produce great anxiety and other psychological problems, such as false relationships and confusion about what they feel and think.

A central paradox in women's psychology, however, is that girls give up relationships (such as false ones) for the "sake of relationships." Miller (1976) has powerfully articulated this paradox as it relates to psychological problems. For example, one can want to be in a relationship but at the same time not be comfortable with it if it is "fake." Gilligan and Brown (1992) have found in girls' strong voices a healthy resistance to false relationships. This speaks directly to the relational conflicts and problems that many women may suffer. From listening to girls at the edge of adolescence and observing their own development as girls, as well as other women's responses, researchers have seen the outlines of new pathways in women's development as well as new possibilities for women's involvement in the process of political change. When women and girls meet at the crossroads of adolescence, the intergenerational seam of a patriarchal culture opens. Thus, if women and girls together resist and give up (false) relationships for the sake of "relationships," this union holds the potential for societal and cultural change.

According to Gilligan, the subject matter of moral development not only provides the final illustration of gender differences in human development, but it also indicates more particularly why the nature and significance of women's development has been so shrouded in mystery.

All these observations about gender differences reinforce the conclusion reached by McClelland (McClelland & Power, 1975), who says that gender role turns out to be one of the most important determinants of differences in human behavior, right from the beginnings of empirical research. But it is difficult to say "different" without saying "better" or "worse," for there is a tendency to construct a single scale of measurement. This scale has been generally derived from and standardized on the basis of interpretations of research data drawn predominantly or exclusively from studies of men or boys. Psychologists "have tended to regard male behavior as the 'norm' and female behavior as some kind of deviation from that norm" (McClelland & Power, 1975, p. 81). If women do not conform to the standards of psychological expectation, the conclusion has generally been that something is wrong with women (Gilligan, 1982).

With new light being brought into the field by thought-provoking studies of women's development, I hope that we can resolve some of the issues of using man as an ideal model for all people and move toward using the male model as an ideal for men and the female model as an ideal for women. Then practitioners in therapeutic situations can offer help to clients according to their gender, using their knowledge of typical male and female roles.

## ETHNIC IDENTITY

Almost one third of adolescents and young adults who live in the United States belong to an ethnic group, such as African Americans, Asian Americans, Latinos, Italian Americans, Jewish Americans, and Native Americans. These people typically develop an ethnic identity—they feel part of their ethnic group and learn the unique elements of their group's culture and heritage (Phinney, 1990).

Acquiring ethnic identity seems to occur in three phases. In the first phase, ethnic identity is not an important personal issue. A teenage African-American girl once mentioned, "Why do I need to learn about who was the first Black woman to do this or that? I'm just not too interested" (Phinney, 1989, p. 44). In the second phase, young people begin to explore the personal impact of their ethnic heritage. As one Asian Indian said, "I like going to Indian festivals because I learn more about myself and my own culture." In the third phase, individuals achieve a distinct ethnic self-concept, which is a combination of their own ethnic group and U.S culture. As one Asian American student of mine said, "I was born in Korea, and I'm here in America, and people of different cultures are here, too. So I do not only consider myself Korean but also American."

## WHITE: COMPETENCE THEORY

White (1960) regards adolescence as the final stage of development, one in which biological changes and newly strengthened sexual impulses make sexual intercourse possible. White agrees with Anna Freud that because this period brings increased instinctual drives, it threatens established patterns of ego control. According to White, some kinds of behavior are well handled by a competence model but neglected by libido and interpersonal models. Because the adolescent is reaching adult size, strength, and mental development, his or her overall behavior lies in the realm of serious accomplishment—serious and important in terms of either the youth culture or the adult culture.

White equates competence with what Erikson calls a sense of industry in the latency period; however, White claims the quest for competency continues more seriously after puberty than Erikson's account implies. White adds that he works chiefly with late adolescents whose sexual problems and social relations have, for the most part, not overwhelmed them. They have plans for studies; they learn to become aware of their abilities and limitations; they struggle with materials and skills to be learned; they attempt to become aware of their occupational leanings and to make career plans; and they express concerns about modern society and its future. Adolescents search for competency in these many spheres of their lives.

Adolescents learn to do things: drive cars, set adult records for sports, play football or soccer, play in the band, and so forth. Some of them try their skills at writing, at scientific discoveries, or at music and drama. All such actions belong to the realm of work. At the same time, adolescents gain or lose ego strength. That is, White indicates that in theorizing about this subject we should not exclude the possibility that such developments significantly affect what happens in the erotic and interpersonal realms.

White argues that to view competence as a simple and sovereign concept is not sufficient. A person who has developed wholly in competence but has no dimensions of passion, love, or friendliness would never qualify as mature. Competence is not necessary for experiences such as enjoying food, immersing oneself in a sexual relationship, loving children, cherishing friends, and being impressed by great works of art, nor should it be used to repress problems that arise from aggression and anxiety. One should use the competence model in conjunction with other models that do full justice to such experiences as hunger, sexuality, and aggression. It may frustrate our desire for logical simplicity to suppose that several models are required to understand a problem. However, it can never be claimed that human nature was designed in the interests of logic (White, 1960).

## Social Competence

> Dan, age 17, has been brought up by parents who stress that to make it in life he must perform extremely well in school, spend his free time in studies, and devote all his time to intellectual pursuits. Dan has been trained to think that way from the time he was a few years old. Thus at 17 he takes great pleasure in matters that other teenagers consider lofty but boring. He'll spend hours in the library studying volumes on how to pursue a particular intellectual task that fascinates him. However, he completely neglects matters of etiquette and social and emotional relationships. He doesn't care how he dresses, so he looks sloppy most of the time, and yes, as often happens, he wears thick glasses. A loner who hasn't acquired the art of being friendly, Dan is viewed as "peculiar" by his classmates. He can't get a date. Although he's competent in his intellectual pursuits, to be well-rounded, Dan also needs to be able to make friends and deal with sexuality.

White points out that adolescents have to acquire social competence. Young people at this age attempt to become members of groups. Membership in a peer group is useful. This meaningful group behavior depends on group norms, an awareness of group expectations, and taking turns in handling group responsibilities. Particularly in informal games, played just for fun, the nature of norms and reciprocal roles becomes abundantly important.

Another important contribution of peer relationships to social competence is the provision of varied information about the human environment. Though not always noticeably tolerant, the youth culture offers adolescents an opportunity to compare notes on mothers, fathers, siblings, families, and family values that differ from their own. Adolescents also share their knowledge about teachers, whose personal qualities are subject to zestful psychological analysis on the way to and from school. In these ways young people shed light on their own society, as well as contribute to each other's education by exchanging information about both leading groups and rival groups. Successful handling of this portion of the social curriculum should help adolescents see the relativity of perspectives and gain a widening awareness of the vagaries of human behavior (White, 1976). In short, participation in groups can lead to a sense of interpersonal competence.

*Enslavement*   On the other hand, total commitment to peer groups and social competency can lead to *social enslavement*, which may betray itself in painful loneliness and anxiety when one is not in the company of one's friends. The most serious problem is compulsive conformity to group sanctions. The young person's preferences, tastes, and opinions are sanctioned by the group, and the person takes no chances in giving offense or incurring disapproval. Complete conformity takes a heavy toll on individuality and makes it difficult for a person to think of herself or himself as an autonomous agent. In this case, belonging to two groups with different value systems can produce severe conflict.

Social enslavement is a product of anxiety. What young adolescent would dare to wear a skirt that is 3 inches too long or too short, risking embarrassment and ridicule, even if a skirt of that length had been right two years ago and would be right again in another two years? This is conformity. From the peers' point of view, conformity appears to be a good adaptation to the group; however, it can be a form of enslavement.

*Alienation*   Some adolescents belong to no group. Such youth face *alienation* or social estrangement, which is an absence of social support or meaningful social connection (Mau, 1992). Alienated adolescents do not experience a sense of belonging to any group; rather, they are continuously uneasy around their peers. Parents might contribute to alienation if they press adolescents to restrict their association to a particular peer group, which in turn might not offer the adolescent membership. Alienation also occurs when an adolescent looks over the existing groups and does not find one that can really meet his or her needs. Slowly the adolescent will be shut out from existing groups. Some young people will attempt to follow adult values and norms and are left out from all social groups. When young people follow adult norms, the other adolescents view them as goodie-goodies or nerds and do not welcome them into the peer culture (Allen, Weissberg, & Hawkins, 1989). Still other adolescents have poor social skills—that is, either they are overly aggressive and domineering or overly withdrawn and socially inept. It is not unusual for adolescents to identify certain students in their high school as "loners" or "outcasts" (Brown, Mounts, Lamborn, & Steinberg, 1993).

Social isolation, which follows an adolescent's failure to gain acceptance by a peer group, may affect his or her social growth. When an adolescent's attempts to fraternize are met with indifference or rejection, it creates the most elementary frustration; anxiety and shame pile up and create feelings of inefficacy. This may lead to *withdrawal,* which stems from a combination of hurt feelings and moral indignation. Those whose social experiences are not pleasant may turn out to be shy, retiring, housebound, and limited in interests to things they can do by themselves. Unfortunately, such an individual does not develop skills in competition or compromise, does not experience the give-and-take of group membership, and remains a stranger to convivial peership (White, 1976).

## ADOLESCENT SEXUALITY

Today's teenagers have ideas about morality that differ dramatically from those of their parents and grandparents. Adolescents have become increasingly liberal in their thinking about sex, particularly during the 1960s and 1970s. More recently, with AIDS and other complex diseases, attitudes may be becoming more conservative (Carroll, 1988). Dreyer (1982) mentions three major changes in teenagers' sexual attitudes that describe the new morality and what it means to them (see Abler & Sedlacek, 1989). First, most adolescents today believe that "sex with affection" is acceptable. Further, a large majority reject the maxim that premarital intercourse is always acceptable. They believe that casual or exploitative sex is wrong, though a few of them might have had such experiences. However only a small number of adolescents—6% of boys and 11% of girls—mention love as the main reason for their first intercourse, and about 75% of girls and 80% of boys attribute their loss of virginity to strong social pressures, and list such pressures with curiosity and sexual desire as important reasons for becoming sexually active (Harris, 1986).

Another aspect of teenage attitudes is the decline of the double standard that sexual practices are more appropriate for men rather than women. This double standard has not disappeared entirely—some fathers still condone the sexual exploits of their sons (Brooks-Gunn & Furstenberg, 1989). Also, college students polled recently believed that when a woman has many sexual partners she is immoral (Robinson, Ziss, Ganza, Katz, & Robinson, 1991). Finally, diverse sexual attitudes and permissiveness create increased confusion about acceptable sexual norms. For instance, Dreyer's idea of sex with affection creates a great deal of ambiguity in young people. First and foremost, what is affection? When beginning to *like* each other, should a couple have sex? Second, how does affection relate to love?

Adolescents are constantly told to maintain their virginity, but how can they do this with all the pressure about being attractive and popular and having a close friend of the opposite sex? In our culture, more than 9000 glamourous sexual innuendos and behaviors, often among unmarried couples, are seen annually on television (American Academy of Pediatrics, 1986). Also, the behavior of older siblings adds to the confu-

sion as younger siblings begin to imitate a sexually active older sibling (Rodgers & Rowe, 1988).

In childhood young boys and girls go their separate ways but in adolescence they clearly come together in more intimate ways. As children reach adolescence they develop an intense intolerance for deviance from gender-role expectations. This is called *gender intensification*—that is, gender differences associated with increased pressure to conform to gender roles, particularly when adolescents reach puberty (Boldizar, 1991; Galambos, Almeida, & Petersen, 1990; Hill and Lynch, 1983). As they become more established as adolescents, teenagers become more comfortable with their own identities as men and women and also more flexible in their thinking (Urberg, 1979).

Adolescents begin to incorporate their own concepts of self and sexuality into their personalities. They express sexuality by (1) acting in relationships as young women or men and (2) developing an awareness of themselves as *sexual* men or women. As part of growing up, teenagers raise questions about their sexual attractiveness, sexual values, and goals in close relationships.

Some adolescents face particularly acute problems in exploring their sexuality, as the following case shows.

> Fifteen-year-old Aron is confused and scared. He has been sexually abused by his older stepbrother and stepfather. He is confused about his own sexuality. Is he a man, or—what is he? If he *is* a man, how did he get sexually abused? Is he homosexual, bisexual, or heterosexual? He feels victimized and afraid.

There is little sympathy for young men when they are sexually victimized. Of course, this does not mean that women have an easier time. But there is a particular aspect of this problem that only men face. Our culture provides no room for a man to be a victim; men are simply not supposed to be victimized. A "real" man is expected to protect himself in all situations. Also, men are supposed to be in control of their feelings all the time. But a sexually abused young man like Aron faces ongoing feelings of confusion, frustration, anger, and fear, which become further evidence of his "failure" as a man.

## Sexual Orientation

Part of developing a sexual identity involves learning one's preferences for sexual partners of the opposite or same gender. Many other cultures accept a continuum of sexual orientation; they do not categorize sexual preferences as Western culture does (Paul, 1993). We describe people as having primarily heterosexual, homosexual, or bisexual orientations. A large number of adolescents establish a heterosexual orientation without much soul searching. But young people attracted to members of their own sex face a long and torturous process. Usually they become aware of their initial desire in terms of sexual preference but they often do not accept being gay or lesbian or gather the courage to "come out" until their mid-twenties (Garnets & Kimmel, 1991).

A large number of adolescents (20–40%) may experiment with homosexual activity during adolescence (Masters, Johnson, & Kolodny, 1993), but eventually a small percentage (5–6% of adults) will establish a lasting homosexual or bisexual orientation (Smith, 1991). Unlike the popular belief that gay men are effeminate and lesbian women masculine, gays and lesbians, like the rest of the population, have many psychological and social attributes that heterosexual adults have.

What influences young people to develop alternative sexual preferences? There are two perspectives: the genetic and the environmental. Researchers hypothesized that identical twins are more alike in their sexual orientation than fraternal twins. However, this was proven to be wrong. The study showed that in half the given identical twin pairs, one twin was homosexual or bisexual whereas the other was heterosexual.

This suggests that the environment contributes as much as genes in the development of sexual orientation (Bailey & Pillard, 1991; Bailey, Pillard, Neale, & Agyei, 1993).

Other research (Bell, Weinberg, & Hammersmith, 1981; Green, 1987; Martin, 1990) says most gays and lesbians expressed strong cross-sexual interests when they were young despite being subjected to the usual pressures to adopt traditional gender roles. Green (1987) studied a group of boys who displayed more socially acceptable feminine behaviors than most boys but who did not engage in overt cross-sexual play or prefer female roles, toys, and friends. He also found that 75% of these boys, compared with 2% of a control group of gender-typical boys, tended to be exclusively homosexual or were bisexual 15 years later. Genetic research by others indicates that sexual orientation is every bit as heritable among gay men who are masculine and lesbian women who are feminine as among those who had early cross-sexual interests (Bailey & Pillard, 1991; Bailey, et al., 1993).

## Contraceptives

A large number of sexually active adolescents fail to use contraception because they are partly cognitively immature and fail to take seriously the possibility that their behavior could have unfortunate consequences. The Centers for Disease Control (1992) indicate that 60% of high school boys and about half of the girls have engaged in intercourse. Among college students, the rate is 70% to 80% (Baier, Rosenzweig, & Whipple, 1991; Reinisch, Sanders, Hill, & Ziemba-Davis, 1992). Because of social change, the percentages of intercourse have increased steadily in this century (Forrest & Singh, 1990; Sonenstein, Pleck, & Ku, 1991). Finally, the sexual behaviors of women have changed more dramatically than for men; as a result, gender differences in sexual activity have all but disappeared (Darling, Kallen, & VanDusen, 1984; Wielandt & Boldsen, 1989). There have been even more dramatic results. The number of teenage pregnancies has soared sky-high.

> Thirteen-year-old Alicia is pregnant. Overwhelmed, her whole family has come to therapy. With the support and help of her family, Alicia opts to have an abortion. Everyone sighs with relief. Alicia has

repeatedly stated that she "did it only once" and never thought that she would get pregnant. The parents had not prepared for contraceptive pills or had the "bird and the bee" talk because they thought she was too young for such talk! Well, they found out otherwise.

We shall see more on the problem of teenage pregnancy later in this chapter.

## SOCIAL RELATIONSHIPS

### Family

How do adolescents view their parents? What is a typical relationship between a teenager and his or her parents? Teenagers who are out all the time with their friends groan when their parents suggest they should spend a fun evening with the family. They resent the slightest attempt by parents to cramp their freedom. Also, teenagers think that their parents do not know anything and argue with them about virtually everything. Many parents wring their hands and wonder if they will ever survive their children's adolescent years. Many feel that this period of the family life cycle is particularly stressful. Often, parent-child relationships begin deteriorating into bitter tugs-of-war (Sigelman & Shaffer, 1995) while the adolescent struggles at becoming his or her own person.

How do adolescents feel about their relationship with their own parents? Although it is generally believed that adolescents lose respect for their parents and feel less close to them, these beliefs simply do not hold up (Galambos, 1992; Offer, Ostrov, & Howard, 1982). Most high school students, regardless of age and gender, respect their parents and describe their family relationships in positive ways. The majority of teenagers also view their parents as key sources of affection and support (Furman & Buhrmester, 1992; Lempers & Clark-Lempers, 1992). Thus it becomes clear that parent-child relationships do not change during adolescence; in fact, the degree of closeness determines the balance of power between parents and adolescents.

*Autonomy from parents* Over the last few decades the relationships of parents to their children have changed considerably. Families have become smaller, with fewer children and fewer friends. Most theorists agree that the critical developmental task of adolescence is to achieve *autonomy*—that is, the capacity to make decisions independently and to manage life tasks without too much dependence on others. If adolescents wish to grow up and move toward adulthood, they cannot rush home for reassuring hugs after every little setback or depend on parents to get them to work on time or manage their money or checkbooks. Most parents also want their adolescents to become autonomous, and adolescents need the freedom to experience their autonomy. As young adolescents grow up, conflicts between parents and children seem inevitable, particularly during puberty (Holmbeck & Hill, 1991; Paikoff & Brooks-Gunn, 1991; Steinberg, 1981). Usually the quarrels are about disobedience, homework, and so forth (Montemayor, 1982). As time passes, adolescents begin to assert themselves, so that the parent-child relationship changes from one in which parents dominate to one in which parents and their sons and daughters share a relatively equal footing (Youniss & Smollar, 1985).

Young people achieve autonomy not by cutting parental cords but rather by maintaining a loose attachment to their families even as they prepare to leave the home (Kobak, Cole, Ferenz-Gilles, Fleming, & Gamble, 1993; Lamborn & Steinberg, 1993). Parents, in turn, have to nurture autonomy and maintain a positive relationship with their teenagers. That is, autonomy, attachment, independence, and interdependence are the chief adolescent goals. Studies by Lamborn and Steinberg (1993) and Ryan and Lynch (1989) indicate that adolescents tend not to become confident and independent if they try to distance themselves from their parents. Adolescents are most likely to become autonomous, achievement oriented, and well adjusted if their parents continue to enforce rules and regulations about their behaviors but continue to be warm and supportive (B. B. Brown, Mounts, Lamborn, & Steinberg,

1993; Dishon, Patterson, Stoolmiller, & Skinner, 1991; Lamborn, Mounts, Steinberg, & Dornbusch, 1991). Parents need to find a balance between parental warmth and a style of control that is neither too permissive nor too restrictive.

> Dillon comes from a home where his mother, a single parent, greatly supports Dillon's after school jobs. She helps him plan and put away his money in savings; she has also helped him buy a car. Kind to his casual dates, she nonetheless states what time he should be back home, for he is still a high school student. Mother and son show each other mutual respect and love.

When the person-environment fit is not good and when the parents are rejecting, overly strict, or very lenient, adolescents tend to be psychologically distressed or get into trouble (Koestner, Zuroff, & Powers, 1991; Lamborn et al., 1991). Parents with adolescents who are rude, aggressive, or hostile may also react in hostile ways to them, adding to the young people's problems. Alternately, level-headed, responsible adolescents tend to have parents who are loving and reasonable in setting rules and regulations. Again, adolescent behavior reflects prior upbringing. As mentioned earlier, the best parent-adolescent relationship is a partnership in which both maintain positive feelings for one another while reworking and renegotiating their relationship so it eventually becomes equal.

## Peers

As we have seen, during adolescence, relationships with peers assume great importance. From peers, adolescents pick up attitudes, values, and behavior patterns that they can choose as their own. From peers, adolescents receive signs of belonging and being successful.

Friendship has various phases in friendships. Dunphy (1963) has studied the stages of group development during adolescence. First, as in Samoa, preadolescents in North America spend more time with members of the same gender. Second, as adolescence approaches, these groups are attracted to the opposite sex. Third, the two

groups, girls and boys, unite in interactions such as dating; usually the individuals with the highest status in each clique are the first to date. In later stages of peer relations, the cliques become more and more heterosexual. Thus small clusters of dating couples come to replace the larger groups of early adolescence in U.S. culture.

Although middle school children are highly involved with peers, in adolescence much more time is spent with peers and much less with parents (Buhrmester & Furman, 1990). Although the relationship with parents is still quite significant, peers surpass parents in importance as sources of intimacy and support (Furman & Buhrmester, 1992; Lempers & Clark-Lempers, 1992). Further, the *quality* of peer relationships begins to change.

Because adolescents grow tremendously in their ability to understand others, they develop deeper relationships with their friends. When asked to describe their friends, they provide sophisticated psychological profiles (O'Mahoney, 1989). They see people as unique, with specific personality traits.

Friendships change in adolescence. For children, friendships are based on loyalty and common interests, but as they grow older they become increasingly focused on intimacy and self-disclosure (Berndt & Perry, 1990). Teenagers continue to form friendships with peers who are similar to themselves and express feelings of loyalty toward their friends. They begin to choose friends who have similar psychological qualities, including interests, values, and personalities.

Intimate friendships among girls develop earlier than do those among boys (Berndt & Perry, 1990; Reis, Lin, Bennett, & Nezlek, 1993). Teenage boys get to know their friends well by doing things with them; their friendships are less emotionally intense and they talk less about their feelings than those of girls (Berndt, 1989). Although young adolescents have mostly same-gender friendships, they slowly begin to enter close cross-gender friendships.

As we have seen, same-gender friendships develop in late childhood. Boys and girls become members of the same-gender cliques and have little to do with the opposite sex. As they get older, boys of one clique begin to socialize with girls who belong to another clique. Thus the socialization process begins. Talking to a girl with your buddies is far less threatening than doing it on your own. This marks the third stage of adolescent friendships—the *heterosexual clique.*

As more adolescents join the heterosexual cliques they form a *crowd,* defined as a collection of four or more heterosexual cliques who come together to plan and carry out organized social activities for the weekend such as parties, outings, going to the mall, and so forth. In this manner, young people may get to know each other; as they interact with the opposite sex, they begin to date. Slowly, couples begin to form through double dating and spending time with other couples. The crowd has served its purpose of bringing boys and girls together.

Adolescents often begin to date when they are about 14 years old (Miller, McCoy, & Olson, 1986). Regardless of the many changes in gender roles, girls still tend to expect boys to take an active role in dating (Rose & Frieze, 1993).

As adolescents grow older, they continue to listen to their parents and their peers. Parents who are warm and neither too controlling nor too lax will find that adolescents have internalized their values. The warm, caring parenting style usually leads adolescents to foster academic and social competencies and gain entrance into crowds who value achievement and disapprove of drug use and other forms of delinquency (Brook, Brook, Gordon, Whiteman, & Cohen, 1990; B. B. Brown et al., 1993).

Finally, adolescent socialization is not a continual war between parents and peers. The two serve rather as essential sources of influence that combine to affect development. The parent-peer warfare is actually at a minimum because they each influence distinct aspects of behavior and decision making. Also, parents in helping children develop a value system have a hand in insuring that friends share their views on many important issues. Because of these factors, most adolescents develop healthy peer relationships and acquire social competencies that allow them to form and maintain good relationships as adults (Sigeleman & Shaffer, 1995).

## Gangs

When the family is not invested in a child or does not provide the nurturing or the values necessary for appropriate development, it leads to chaos in some young people's lives. Lost, lonely, and with an intense desire to belong, young people search for an identity. Adolescents join gangs because they receive the attention and the sense of belonging they lack at home. They join gangs for recognition, self-esteem, and status, particularly if they are doing poorly in school, are unemployed, or lack recreational choices. They also join gangs to feel successful.

Some youth join gangs to protect themselves. Often they are alienated from their own families, from the police, and from other authorities, so they rely on gang members to help protect them.

At times, adolescents join gangs because they are coerced by their friends or relatives to do so. A lack of effective responses to peer pressure can create the climate that favors gang membership.

The most important and illegal but gainful factor are the financial rewards of gang membership, such as shared profits from drug trafficking, extortion, or other illegal activities. To such teens, money often means social status, so if being a member offers that opportunity, some adolescents will take it.

*Prevention*  To prevent their children from joining a gang, parents should be actively involved in their upbringing. Young people should spend their free time in meaningful tasks. Parents and children should communicate well and spend time together. Setting limits is quite important, and parents should participate in the education of their children as well as community events. As the famous anonymous saying goes, "Kids can walk around trouble if there's some place to walk to and someone to walk with."

Social workers should be prepared to work with gang members to help them move away from antisocial activities.

Several programs have been developed to reduce gang activities. These include detached worker programs, in which workers join gangs and seek to transform their antisocial behaviors into prosocial behaviors, and formal supervision of ex-gang members to support and help them move toward becoming acceptable members of society. In addition, programs that strengthen and support families, particularly single-parent urban families, programs that prevent school dropout, and academic support also reduce gang activity.

## SPECIAL PROBLEMS OF ADOLESCENTS

### Teenage Pregnancy

Teenage pregnancy is a fast-growing problem that urgently requires attention. A teenager who becomes pregnant may receive assistance from her parents or a social welfare agency. Some churches or other denominational groups also offer help to teenagers. Many infants of teenagers are taken by adoption agencies, either because the teenage mother does not wish to bring up her child or because she has been persuaded by her parents or others to give up the child. If a teenager gets involved with a social service agency, the caseworker provides the help needed to make a decision.

*Getting help*  The worker provides teenagers with vocational and educational guidance as well as public financial assistance and birth-control information. If physical or emotional support are not available to the teenager through her home environment, and she does not wish to have an abortion, then the caseworker helps her find a temporary home until the baby is born.

> Trisha is a 14-year-old Roman Catholic girl who became pregnant the first time she had intercourse. Her parents are horrified. They don't wish to let her

have an abortion because of their religion, but at the same time they don't want the burden of explaining their daughter's absence from school, as well as her increased body size. After much contemplation, they decide to send her away to a temporary home where she can give birth without much outside attention. The home is maintained privately by a few responsible people, who help Trisha go through the pregnancy and accept the idea of giving the baby away. The young mother must part with her child, even if she learns to love the baby, for she must abide by the decision she has reached with her parents.

Rosen (1980), who made a study of 432 pregnant teenagers under 18 years of age, found that 50% involved their mothers in pregnancy-resolution decision making. Many young unwed mothers who have to give away their babies for adoption are traumatized. Without the help and understanding attitude of people in their home, they find it practically impossible to go through this period of separating, which involves agony as well as the guilt and responsibility associated with giving away a child.

For the pregnant teenage girl, most states offer educational facilities. Some schools, however, have policies that have not yet acknowledged local rulings in favor of such facilities, and some have yet to set times for termination of schooling during pregnancy. The Edgar Allan Poe School in Baltimore; agencies in Azusa, California; Emery University, Atlanta; and the Young Mothers Educational Development Program, Syracuse—all set up programs specifically to take care of young pregnant girls. These programs offer young parents several support groups, including medical and educational-vocational groups, and teach teenagers how to use contraceptives consistently if they are sexually active. Other programs offer teenagers counseling and help teenagers work on their self-esteem.

*Reasons for pregnancy*  A study by Donoghue (1992–1993) explores the reasons that young teenagers become pregnant. Donoghue compiled statistics from the U.S. Virgin Islands Department of Health on teenage pregnancy including birthrates, age of putative fathers, and age at first intercourse. It is suggested that the high rate of teenage pregnancy in the Virgin Islands is a symptom of a culture of poverty. Cultural elements such as matriarchy, a propensity for immediate gratification, punitive child-rearing practices, overcrowding, the absence of appropriate male role models, and a strong feeling of fatalism encourage the early sexuality of the island's adolescents. To reduce teenage pregnancy in this population, Donoghue indicates that we must reduce the level of deprivation.

What about the father? Because women get pregnant, we tend to think of pregnancy and its consequences for only women; however, men have feelings about it as well. Sexual relationships during adolescence have pitfalls as well as potential rewards for young men, even if there is no pregnancy. If a pregnancy does occur, the young man may have to pay for an abortion or enter a forced marriage; he may also abscond. At an emotional level, all such men would have to deal with the role they have created for themselves. Sometimes the young father may be emotionally involved with the young woman and may care about the baby but may not be ready to support them emotionally or financially.

A boy who has intercourse with a girl could become a candidate for a paternity suit—not an easy situation for him. Some young women are afraid to admit to getting pregnant through willing intercourse and may claim that they were raped (MacDonald, 1973). The accusation has its own consequences; even if not allowed in court, it may leave a scar on the accused young man.

Many issues and problems arise out of adolescent sexuality because adolescents are dealing with a changing world and a changing self, which places tremendous pressure on them. An adolescent must integrate all inner and outer changes in order to adapt to life.

## AIDS and STDs

Sexually active adolescents also have to deal with the probability of sexually transmitted diseases

(STDs), including the most difficult disease without a real cure—AIDS. Has the fear of AIDS affected adolescent sexuality? As we will see, most studies find some change has occurred but not enough. Nowadays teens are more likely to use condoms, at least some of the time, than they did a few years ago. However, only a very small percentage, about 1%, of college students are doing what is necessary to protect themselves from HIV infection by using a latex condom with a spermicide *every* time they have sex (Maticka-Tyndale, 1991). Many adolescents put themselves at risk by having sex with several sexual partners (Forrest & Singh, 1990; Maticka-Tyndale, 1991). As such, many educators are calling for stronger programs of sex education and the distribution of free condoms at school. The chances of reducing teenage pregnancy and their risk of AIDS are almost nil unless teens are willing to postpone sex or practice safe sex.

Other sexually transmitted diseases are variants of old ones and are quickly transmitted in today's sexually permissive culture. One example is herpes simplex 2, a virus closely related or akin to the type that causes cold sores in the mouth (Hamilton, 1990). Unlike diseases such as syphilis and gonorrhea, herpes has no cure so far. Once it has invaded the body, its symptoms are usually blisters and sores in the genital area, which can recur indefinitely in unpredictable episodes. Herpes is thought to have reached epidemic proportions, with about 20 million people suffering from it (Berger, 1986).

In a therapy session, Washington says that he isn't sure of his own sexuality, because his mother and sister call him weird names like "sissy" and because he doesn't have a girlfriend. His sister smirks when he brings home some of his male pals. Washington mentions that he likes girls but doesn't know how to approach them. However, while therapy is progressing, Washington's mother, a single parent with five adult children, suggests that Washington see a prostitute to "set himself straight," which he does. Soon he discovers he has herpes. At first he is shocked. Then, though unhappy about the disease, he looks at the social worker with all the confidence of an "indestructible" teenager and comments proudly that "he's a man" because he slept with a woman—an *older* woman. And the herpes? "It will go away."

Another example of a rapidly spreading STD is chlamydia, a bacterial disease that infects approximately one out of every ten college students (Meyer, 1987). Although chlamydia can be detected by a simple laboratory test and cured by antibiotics, it remains a serious problem. That it often does not produce noticeable symptoms increases the likelihood of its spread. Untreated, it can lead to sterility.

## Juvenile Delinquency

Young people (between 16 and 18 years of age) are labeled *delinquent* for various reasons. Some of them violate criminal law through rape, theft, assault, or even homicide. As state law requires, they are arrested and punishable if found guilty. Some juveniles are called *status offenders*. Status offenses are actions that are illegal only because of the offender's status—typically age and gender. Status offenses include truancy and promiscuity.

The question of whether an adolescent is a delinquent can usually be answered by looking at his or her arrest records. Arrest practices for teenagers vary considerably. Some communities "warn" adolescents, whereas others "book" (arrest) them.

> Donald, a young man of 16, is arrested for running away from home and also for breaking into a mailbox. The police officer who deals with him takes a special interest in him. After discussing the situation with a social worker, he places the boy in seclusion in a jail cell for a night just to help him understand the stark realities of prison life. This cell, with only a commode in the corner and barely large enough to hold a tall man, has an effect on Donald. Frightened of what he sees, he vows not to get involved in such crimes again, not even "for the fun of it."

Many adolescents have at some time been involved in illegal behaviors such as shoplifting, drinking, and drug use. Whether or not they have been labeled delinquent depends on whether they were apprehended, as well as on their race and socioeconomic status. Lower-class teenagers are caught more easily than those from the upper class. Also, upper-class teenagers have more support systems and finances to bail them out of trouble. Some delinquent acts are petty offenses; others are serious. Virtually all teenagers admit to some sort of illegal behavior (Henggeler, 1989). Boys are usually more involved than girls in delinquent behavior (Steffensmeier & Streifel, 1991). Low-income members of minorities are more likely to be arrested than other adolescents and judged to be delinquent by courts, although, based on a self-report survey, these youth may not commit a delinquent act again (Henggeler, 1989).

A large degree of delinquent acts are committed *with* peers and *for* peers. Ages 15 to 16 are the peak for delinquent behaviors. Peers wish to impress each other by stealing the red flasher from the police car or moving the teacher's car to another corner of the parking lot (Gold & Petronio, 1980). A large number of youth who commit delinquent acts do not go on and develop a criminal career. Often this is only a phase they pass through.

Those who commit serious crimes and commit them habitually often come from troubled homes. Their parents reject them, fail to monitor their activities, and use negative, power-assertive forms of discipline (Dishion et al., 1991; Sampson & Laub, 1993). Further, researchers have discovered a cause-effect relationship, whereby family attitudes toward education can contribute to juvenile crime. People who commit serious crimes tend to perform badly in school because the family usually gives little attention to education (Lynam, Moffitt, & Stouthamer-Loeber, 1993). So, one thing feeds another. The youths are not encouraged to study at home, so they fail at school. Their poor performance and minor delinquent acts cause their peers to reject them. This, in turn, causes them to commit more delinquent acts (Dishion et al., 1991).

Young serious criminals are likely to continue and become more involved in criminal and violent behaviors in adulthood (Eton, 1987). Rehabilitative programs are important because they target high-risk youth and help them get a good start in schools, they work at improving their home and community environments, and they build academic and social competence that can protect youth from getting involved in antisocial activities later in life (Mulvey, Arthur, & Reppucci, 1993; Zigler, Taussig, & Black, 1992).

*Prevention*    Many attempts have been made to change the life of the delinquent through study programs, family therapy, foster homes, youth homes, various kinds of psychological assistance, and educational programs. Phillips, Phillips, Fixen, and Wolf (1973) found that such efforts were successful in small group homes consisting of six to eight boys and two professional "parents" sharing their living quarters.

> It has taken 16-year-old Julio several months of therapy to understand that he cannot go back to his home and live with his mother. She constantly changes the men in her life and has also set Julio against his own younger brother because she has a hard time showing love for both her sons at the same time. With the help of his social worker, Julio has come to understand how his home situation frustrates and angers him and has led him to commit petty crimes such as stealing and committing minor assaults on children who live on his block. After he accepts the reasons for his relocation, he goes to live in a group home, where he enjoys independent living and at the same time learns to respect his staff and group members and deal meaningfully with responsibilities. The structure and the consistent discipline, caring, and therapy help Julio move away from delinquent ways and develop a more responsible attitude toward life.

## Substance Abuse

*Substance abuse* is the misuse of a drug or other chemicals, usually to alter the psychological or emotional state of the user. The two classifications of drug dependency are physical and psychological. Abused drugs are often grouped as narcotics, stimulants, depressants, inhalants, hallucinogens, and marijuana.

The magnitude of the drug-use problem among teenagers is staggering. Alcohol is the most frequently used drug by almost all adolescents. Alcohol use begins early. About 90% of high school seniors have tried alcohol, and about 39% reported that they have had at least one episode of "party drinking"—that is, over five drinks (Johnston, O'Malley, & Bachman, 1985). About half of the seniors have tried to use marijuana after drinking. Marijuana moves some adolescents to experiment with other illegal drugs (Yamaguchi & Kandel, 1984).

The use of all these substances has begun to decline from the 1980s (Kandel & Davies, 1991). Not all adolescents who experiment with drugs become drug abusers, but some do. The question is, why do they participate in habitual drug use? Some researchers assume that adolescent problems are learned ways of achieving important goals such as independence from parents and peer acceptance (Jessor, 1987; Jessor, Donovan, & Costa, 1991).

Some teenagers suffer from what is called problem drinking. These youth get drunk an average of 20 times a year and experience adjustment problems associated with drinking. Jessor et al. (1991) conducted a longitudinal study of problem drinkers of adolescents ages 13 to 15. The researchers tracked the teenagers until they reached the ages of 25 to 27. Three factors distinguished problems drinkers from others: personal qualities, social environment, and other behavioral problems.

With reference to personal qualities, such youth tend to be alienated from conventional values. They place little value on academic achievement, are not very religious, and generally are not attached to any important social institution. Second, in terms of social environment, their parents are unsupportive and have little impact on them whereas their peers model and reinforce drinking and other problem behaviors. Evidence shows that young people who do drugs hang out with others who abuse drugs as well and do not have close relationships with their parents (Brook et al., 1990; Ellickson & Hays, 1992). Third, regarding behavior, drinking problems occur within the context of the other adolescent behaviors. That is, problem drinkers are more likely than other adolescents to commit delinquent acts and become members of gangs and less likely to engage in conventional behaviors.

As researchers found, any particular adolescent problem is part of a larger syndrome of unconventional and norm-breaking behavior (Farrell, Danish, & Howard, 1992; Rowe, Rodgers, Meseck-Bushey, & St. John, 1989). Preventing and treating such problems may require changing the values of adolescents themselves and reworking their relationships with parents, peers, and schools and other social institutions.

As his single parent mother tries to work two jobs to make ends meet, Garland has gotten into bad company. When she has free time, she's busy trying to find herself a boyfriend and a social life. She has no time for her son, so he goes out with kids who soon help find a place for him in their gang. In the process, Garland learns to drink, smoke pot, become sexually involved, and commit petty theft. He is hardly at home. One day he's caught shoplifting. Seeing her son at 15 with a cop by his side, his mother has to consider the possibility of life without her son. Garland, who looks defiant, is really scared of what's happening to him. Thus mother and son start afresh and with love, care, a new school, and a new environment. Garland has a second chance at becoming a healthy and decent human being. Many others have not been this lucky or successful.

Other teenage drug problems include smoking and, less common because of its immediate dangers, huffing. Smoking is seen as a novel experience, a way of being "grown up." When smoking becomes a habit, a teenager can smoke one or two packs of cigarettes a day, which may lead to serious health problems. *Huffing* is inhaling from paints, aerosol sprays, or air-conditioner vents to get an immediate high that makes users temporarily happy. Huffing leads to serious effects such as brain damage, paranoia, and sometimes death.

## Depression and Suicide

The incidence of suicide in people ages 14 to 19 has quadrupled in the past two decades. Some authorities believe that preadolescents look to others for their love relationships and therefore are afraid to kill themselves, whereas older adolescents see the world as revolving around them. When things seem hopeless and they believe that there is no way out, some kill themselves. Statistics show that more boys than girls commit suicide. They do so mostly in high school or in the first semester of college (Garrison & Garrison, 1975). Depression appears to be an important reason (Angold & Rutter, 1992) along with changes in hormonal levels, which tend to increase negative moods in adolescence. Further, having one foot in childhood and another in adulthood can create an identity crisis that causes depression.

Social factors rather than biological changes explain most depressive symptoms (Angold & Rutter, 1992). Adolescents can suffer depression because of problems such as substance abuse, eating disorders, and antisocial behaviors.

More mature than children, adolescents display the same symptoms of depression that adults do, such as hopelessness, feelings of worthlessness, suicidal thinking, and dark negative thoughts (Garber, Weiss, & Shanley, 1993). As depression takes over, they become involved in suicidal thoughts and attempts. Suicide has been the third leading cause of death among white male adolescents (U.S. Bureau of the Census, 1993).

Teenagers do not succeed at suicide as well as adults do. For this reason, the adolescent attempt is characterized as a "cry for help," a desperate attempt to get others to notice and help resolve problems that have become unbearable (Berman & Jobes, 1991). Adolescent suicide attempts should never be taken lightly, for if they do not receive the help they require, those adolescents may succeed in killing themselves.

Young Winter is very unhappy with her home life. Her mother deserted the family when Winter was 7, and ever since, Winter has played mom to her younger brothers and sister. When she was 17, her father married a fairly young woman. Strife developed between Winter and her stepmother. Her father, who was often not home, readily took his new wife's side. Winter felt isolated, threatened, and unloved. She had been the center of attention as the "housework-responsible person." Suddenly things had changed dramatically; Winter felt that she was a "nobody." She could turn neither to her father, who would no longer listen to her, nor to her stepmother, who viewed Winter as her rival. To make matters worse, she failed in exams at school. The report card became a point of contention between Winter and her stepmother, who ridiculed her performance.

Winter spent so much time at home with her younger siblings that now she doesn't have any close friends at school. She gradually withdraws from interactions at home and becomes depressed. Nobody seems to care; in fact, the stepmother is relieved that Winter's out of the way. Winter schemes to run away, but reality strikes her too hard: There is nowhere to go. Eventually, in despair, she attempts suicide. She takes an overdose of sleeping pills but is discovered in time.

In family sessions, several issues that divided this family were reconstructed. With empathetic help from the social worker, the family was able to get back together again and work on the issues that troubled them. Through understanding and support, Winter obtained the kind of nurturing she herself needed as a person. The case ended happily with the establishment of meaningful relationships among Winter, her father, her new mother, and the rest of the family.

## Eating Disorders

Some adolescents gain weight as they enter their teens; this change leads to a lifelong struggle to maintain a healthy, attractive body. In many ways the effort reflects our society's stringent standards of female beauty, which exalt slenderness above everything else.

Eating disorders among adolescents are receiving increasing attention. Two types of eating problems have recently gained popular notice: anorexia nervosa and bulimia. They reflect two different way sufferers attempt to meet the standards of beauty through bizarre eating habits. Both disorders affect adolescent girls, women, and more recently, young men.

*Anorexia nervosa*  Someone suggests to an adolescent girl that she should lose weight—just a few pounds. The young woman loses the weight and continues to diet obsessively; she refuses to eat until she has lost at least 25% of her original body weight. Her behavior is characteristic of *anorexia nervosa*. If untreated, she may eventually die. This disease affects people ages 9 to 30 and older. The typical patient is a bright, well-behaved, appealing young woman in her teens or early 20s, well-educated and usually from a well-to-do family. Preoccupied with food, she enjoys talking about it, cooking it, and urging others to eat it. Although she is a walking skeleton, weighing about 60 or 70 pounds, she insists that she is well-nourished and can stand to lose a few more pounds (Hsu, 1990). She herself does not eat. Anorexic people have a distorted image of themselves and consider themselves beautiful when they are pathetically and gruesomely skeletal. Once they start to starve, other symptoms begin to appear. For women, menstruation stops; they grow thick, soft hair on their bodies, and their level of activity becomes intense.

What causes anorexia? Researchers suggest various theories. It may be a physical disorder, caused by a deficiency of a crucial brain chemical (Fisher & Brone, 1991). It could be a psychological disturbance related to depression or a fear of growing up; a sociological reaction to extreme societal pressures for slenderness; or the product of a seriously malfunctioning family. So far, no hypothesis has been conclusively supported, and research continues (Yager, 1982). According to the renowned family therapist Salvador Minuchin and his associates (Minuchin, Rosman, & Baker, 1978), eating disorders may emerge because of disturbed family relationships that trigger compulsive dieting. Why does this happen? Because parents of such children tend to be strict and overprotective and tolerate very little dissent or negative emotions. When young people cannot free themselves of their parents and desperately need some control over their own lives, they think they can achieve it through dieting (Smolak & Levine, 1993). Treatment for this disorder involves applying behavioral modification techniques and, in the worst cases, tube-feeding. Once such people have begun to eat, therapy with the family involves supporting and convincing anorexics that they can achieve control over themselves through autonomy and by developing good self-esteem.

*Bulimia*    A disorder closely related to anorexia is *bulimia,* which is becoming more common among teenagers and young women. A bulimic person indulges in binge eating—up to 5000 calories in one sitting. After binging, the bulimic vomits or uses laxatives to empty the body of food. Often depressed, bulimics commonly suffer from such physical complications as hair loss, excessive tooth decay, and gastric irritation (Papalia & Olds, 1986). Some bulimics are also anorexic, while others maintain a normal weight. Bulimics differ from anorexics because they are more extroverted and impulsive rather than quiet; they experience open conflicts at home and talk about the lack of affection in their family (Smolak & Levine, 1993). Bulimia is most common among college students, where as many as 5% of the women and less than 1% of the men regularly partake in this "binge/purge" syndrome (Hsu, 1990).

Treatment includes individual psychotherapy and antidepressant medication for those who show signs of depression. Helping bulimics understand that they have a serious problem is part of the process: It is estimated that most bulimics do not recognize that they have a potentially serious problem and, if left untreated, may continue to binge without seeking help.

## Dropping Out of School

Although the educational level of people in the United States continues to increase, only 85% complete high school. An equal proportion of boys and girls drop out of high school, mostly during the junior or senior year. All states have some form of compulsory attendance; the law requires school enrollment until the age of 16 or 17. Often after that, parents and the school cannot force or convince a young person to attend school; thus a restless student drops out.

In 1990, in the United States, about 75% of the adolescent and young adult populations had completed high school and another 18.7% had some college education. During 1993, the national dropout rate was 11.2%. There was a great deal of variation in different states, with Alaska having the smallest percentage of people who did not finish high school and Washington, D.C. having a relatively high percentage. Ironically, the latter also had the largest number of people with college degrees (U.S. Bureau of Census, 1993).

More than 800,000 adolescents dropped out during the 1991 school year. The ethnic distribution of this population consists of approximately 10% Anglo, 11.3% African American, and 29% Latino youth. Only about 55% of Spanish-speaking students finish high school. The completion rates for both boys and girls of this group do not differ significantly (U.S. Bureau of the Census, 1993).

Most dropouts do not return to get their degrees. Some, however, do graduate by taking the high school equivalency examination. Even so, less than 1% of those graduate by attending night school or day school part-time programs (U.S. Bureau of the Census, 1993).

Adolescents may drop out of school because intellectual stimulation is not valued at home or because they feel pressured by their family to provide economic support. A small percentage of parents may actually encourage their children to drop out because the parents do not see the value of education. Nonacademic reasons for dropping out of school include depression and low self-esteem. Also, adolescents who get little help from home may get into trouble with teachers and administrators, show poor school attendance, and behave in ways not tolerated in school.

The consequences of dropping out of school are difficult to assess. Evidence suggests that dropouts do not do as well economically, generally speaking, as those who complete high school. High school dropouts can expect a lifetime earnings of about $575,000 on the average. High school graduates earn substantially more, about $855,000. Those who earn a college degree may expect earnings of about $1,120,000, according to the U.S. Bureau of the Census (1977). Based on Livitan, Gallo, and Shapiro (1993), the changing social and economic environments have negatively affected the standard of living for the uneducated. Money is only one criterion, however. There is also more unemployment among dropouts. Those who are employed hold blue-collar jobs that require minimal skills. Thus one's educational level determines one's employment opportunities.

Although they cannot be directly connected with incomplete high school education, numerous other factors are related to a lower educational level. People with less education than most are often products of a lifestyle that includes poverty, early marriage, high rates of marital disruption, high mortality rates, and early death (Spanier & Glick, 1980).

> Following his arrest for hitting a man in a street brawl, 24-year-old David is sent to see a social worker. He mentions that he's normally easygoing but that the tension over money in his family has made him edgy—and that's the reason for his sudden outburst.
>
> David married when he was 17, has fathered four children, and is now unemployed. He loves his wife, he says, but regrets that he married so young. All he can do is minimal-skill blue-collar jobs, which do not pay enough for his family to make ends meet. David feels that if his parents had encouraged him, he would have stayed in school and studied. However, the importance of education was overlooked in his family, so David dropped out of school.
>
> David informs the caseworker that he wants to go back to school under any circumstances, for he realizes that education will help him progress in his skills, get a better job, and move ahead in life. With the social worker's help, David decides to enroll in a night school so that he can get his high school diploma.
>
> David was lucky because at 24 he recognized the value of the diploma. Some people are 40 or more before they realize their situation. In most of these cases, they feel it is too late to change the situation, because they have already created a place for themselves in their jobs, family, and friends.

## IMPLICATIONS FOR PRACTICE

Social workers need to understand not only the overall needs and development of adolescents but their particular problems as well. Here we shall look at practice issues rearding adolescent sexuality and identity, and various problems.

### Sexuality

For adolescents, the acceleration of physical growth marks the end of childhood. Such biological maturation prompts changes in their feelings about themselves, which are often uncomfortable. For example, they may experience a great deal of uncertainty about becoming sexually competent. Their intuitive interest in masturbation and in sharing sexual experiences with others conflicts with their awareness of the persistent normative expectations that these activities are wrong and even harmful to their bodies.

Social work practitioners need to be aware of the sexual conflicts of adolescents and offer them information about their own bodies. Guilt is dysfunctional and does not make young people feel at home with their own bodies. Adolescents who are deprived of the opportunity to experiment with their own bodies may reject all human sexuality as bad and wrong. Others may overemphasize sexual feelings and actions, measuring themselves by sexuality alone. Social work practitioners should be able to identify the sexual issues that adolescents present and counsel them accordingly.

Social workers can serve as a support system by offering advice on birth control, teenage pregnancy, and abortion. While offering help, the social worker should be careful about the sensitive nature of their relationship with the adolescent. Adolescents are attempting to develop their autonomy from their own family of origin and from other adults. Social workers, as adults, therefore need always to be aware of the adolescent's struggles with adults.

## Identity

A few adolescents struggle seriously with sexual identity, but a larger percent struggle with values, self-image, and their place in society. They are caught between their own identity formation and the expectations of others. Recall that identity foreclosure is a premature decision on an identity based on other's expectations. Such issues need to be dealt with carefully by social workers, who must keep in mind the family and its values as well as the adolescent with his or her own personal desires. Negative self-images, social isolation, and alienation from peers and others can be the beginning of trouble for adolescents.

As you know, adolescence is defined by an inner striving for identity and a desire to experiment with adult roles, let go of childhood dependency, and take more responsibility for oneself and for others. Some adolescents can attain a sense of self with relative ease, whereas others struggle with separation from their family of origin. Adolsecents show a great deal of vacillation between playing child and adult.

Almost all young people struggle through adolescence, but those with poor or no role models of the same gender have a much more difficult time in developing an identity of their own than those who do.

Chet is the fifth child born to a woman who has lived with several men. Chet's four sisters have babies and jobs. Chet is an only son. His mother ridicules him, saying that he looks like his father, a "no-good criminal." Chet's father has spent more time in prison than in the outside world. His mother's constant negative remainders of his father make Chet mad. There are few men he knows who would make a good model.

One day, sick of all the cursing he hears at home, he goes into a mall and steals clothes from a store. After he is arrested, his mother comes to see him and repeats the self-fulfilling prophecy, "Like father, like son."

With no proper role models and no support from home, how will Chet grow up? Everything depends on whom he meets and who impresses him as being a good role model. Social workers need to keep in mind that all teenagers need good role models. Some lower-income adolescents and those belonging to different ethnic groups lack opportunities to engage in the appropriate struggle for an identity of their own and to fulfill their potential. Social workers need to have an awareness of cultural, ethnic, and racial differences as well as a concern for the difficulties of the human struggle.

Although there is a tendency to lump all adolescents together as "teenagers," workers must understand that this group is not homogeneous, but shows differences among individuals and among groups. Opportunities differ, as does ability to learn. Further, there are no shortcuts to adulthood. No young person can move from beginning sexual behavior to adult sexual behavior without trial and error, and no person can move from play to the working world of adulthood in a short time. There are no guarantees that meaningful work roles will be accessible to all adolescents.

For many, adolescence may be the first time they face the real world, with its prejudices and problems. They quickly find out cognitively that *all men are not created equal*, that discrimination is well and alive. Standards used in offering employment vary depending on the job market, the kind of jobs available, and who is hiring. As one African-American teenager employed in an all-Anglo store mentioned, "I am a token African American to fulfill the affirmative action quota." Many non-Anglo teenagers wonder if they have obtained a job out of merit or to fulfill a quota. Developing good self-esteem and self-awareness may be the first step in being assertive and proudly aware of one's heritage. The requirements for a reasonably productive life may also include tasks such as completing high school, completing college, or learning some useful vocational skills.

Developing good interpersonal skills and becoming aware that people hold different values is important for adolescents.

> Andy complains, "Nobody likes me because I speak differently. I'd like to drop out of school." Andy, who immigrated to the United States from an old Irish village, hasn't been welcomed well by his peers. The school social worker helps him understand cultural differences and see that acceptance occurs through effort, diligence, and open-mindedness. Andy has to do his part by being willing to take risks with schoolmates he does not know very well.

## Specific Problems

Adolescents who thrive and develop good self-images are not the ones who come to the attention of the social worker. Rather, the adolescent who is confused about his or her roles and sexual identity; who has problems ranging from drugs or teenage pregnancy to suicide, AIDS, delinquency, belonging to gangs, participating in criminal activities; or who suffers from low self-esteem is the one who needs the attention and counseling of a social worker.

Of the different helping professionals, social workers are particularly well equipped with knowledge, values, and skills to develop interventive strategies for the wide range of problems adolescents face. Social workers can work one-on-one with delinquents and gang members as well as deal with relatively mundane problems such as petty antisocial behaviors and dropping out of school.

Social workers have also learned to work with families, useful when working with problems such as eating disorders.

> Sixteen-year-old Kasha wants to be thin like her older sisters, who are beautiful and slender, like models. A little plump, Kasha faces ridicule from her family.

> As soon as Kasha loses her pubescent fat, she takes the road to being slim. She diets to the point of starvation. At 5 feet, 6 inches, she weighs a mere 70 pounds but thinks she still needs to lose more weight. Referred by the school social worker, another social worker (in private practice) insists that Kasha's whole family come to the clinical sessions. The social worker finds out that the family has very high expectations of all the children and there is a great deal of strife from a lack of rules and regulations, to the point of chaos. Though they have high expectations, the parents tend to say things like "Let's go to see a movie right now; schoolwork can wait" and "Life is meant to be enjoyed." Kasha wants some control over her life and wants to be different from the rest of the family. While her sisters aspire to be models, she wants to be a schoolteacher. She doesn't mention her desires at home for fear of ridicule. Everyone in the family is busy but as Kasha sees it, the busyness only adds to their own chaos. In clinical sessions some of the intricacies of the family are unraveled, and Kasha receives help to get more control of her life not through dieting, but by managing her time and planning her life the way she wants it. After initial resistance, Kasha's parents accept that Kasha's condition is a family problem. They work to reduce the chaos, manage their own time, and help Kasha develop some control over her own life.

The social worker also works on behalf of the young person in the school system and workplace. Social work practitioners working with different adolescent problems can take on roles such as counselor, educator, enabler, and advocate. Following the values of the social work profession, the worker can help change a delinquent or a gang member from a destructive force in society to a constructive one. Helping young people with problems move toward self-understanding and self-determination is an important role of the social worker.

Adolescent suicide and depression are other problems that call for the help of social workers. With biological changes, or when life does not go well, the overly sensitive adolescent may contemplate suicide. Social workers should take seriously threats of or attempts at suicide and offer help accordingly.

## CHAPTER SUMMARY

- Adolescence is the stage of transition between childhood and adulthood. It involves an extended period of education and dependency.
- The biological changes of young people proceed at a rapid rate but on a variable timetable: Bodily growth and hormonal changes begin at an earlier age for some young people than for others.
- Sexual maturation has psychological as well as physiological effects, especially since adolescents place a high value and conformity in looks.
- Different cultures deal with puberty and adolescence in varied ways.
- Cognitive development reaches the stage of formal operational thought, which involves the capacity to analyze one's own thoughts as well as to see oneself from the point of view of others. Not all young people develop this ability at the same time, nor do they use it consistently, but attainment of this complex stage of cognitive ability is necessary for the construction of an independent and logical system of values.
- Adolescent values are strongly influenced by the previous generation's values.
- Moral development could be taught in schools to help reduce adolescent problems.
- Kohlberg states that when children become adults, they eventually reassess their principles and build their own coherent system of values. Kohlberg's theory has been criticized because it appears to generalize about people's moral development on the basis of an exclusively male perspective.
- Erikson describes adolescence as a period when several factors converge to form a consistent ego identity. The search for identity may bring about growth rather than stress, depending on several internal and external factors. Too many hurdles affect a person's growth and can lead to identity diffusion.
- Gilligan explores the female adolescents' search for identity. Women define themselves through their relationships with others. For a female adolescent, intimacy goes along with identity—that is, a girl comes to know herself through relationships with other people. This process is unlike men's development, in which identity precedes intimacy and generativity in the optimal cycle of human separation and attachment.
- Identity has a unique dimension for the one-third of adolescents and young adults who belong to different ethnic groups. Ethnic identity develops by adolescents' acceptance of their own group culture and the broader U.S. culture.
- White equates the concept of competence to what Erikson calls the sense of identity in the latency period. Both competence in work performance and competence in the social sphere become important.
- Adolescent sexuality involves developing a sexual identity, part of which is sexual orientation. While the majority of teenagers are heterosexual, about 5% to 6% become homosexual or bisexual (Smith, 1991).
- Autonomy from parents is gained with a struggle. The smaller size of families— fewer children and fewer extended relations—creates important implications for parents, as well as children. Usually strong parental identification is associated with good adjustment.
- Peer relationships become important at this period in life. Young people develop the attitudes, values, and behavior patterns of their friends, but there is less conflict with parents as teens grow older.
- Adolescents join gangs if they need recognition and self-esteem when home does not provide them.
- Teenage pregnancy has become a widespread problem. Not only do the teenage

mothers have problems but studies show that young unmarried men also have conflicting feelings about pregnancy.

- Sexually active adolescents can develop sexually transmitted diseases (STDs). The most serious disease without a cure is AIDS (also transmitted through blood transfusion and infected needles). Others STDs include herpes simplex 2.
- Juvenile delinquency is another problem with serious implications for adolescence. Crime rate is higher during middle and late adolescence than at any other period of life.
- Adolescents are brought to court for criminal offenses such as theft, rape, and assault. Truancy and promiscuity are also illegal because of the offender's minor status.
- There are many sociological as well as psychological theories about the causes of delinquency.
- Substance abuse accounts for many juvenile arrests because the use of alcohol and drugs is as widespread among youth as in adult society.
- Smoking has increased among teenagers. Huffing, a fairly new problem, involves sniffing chemicals.
- Depression and suicide in the 14-to-19 age group has quadrupled during the past 12 years. Isolation, vulnerability, and disturbed emotional backgrounds are often the causes.
- Eating disorders, such as anorexia nervosa and bulimia, appear to affect young women (and some men) from childhood through the 30s and beyond.
- Anorexia nervosa is characterized by one's refusing to eat food to the extent of starving oneself; bulimia is binge eating followed by vomiting or the taking of laxatives.
- The outward purpose of eating disorders is to maintain a low body weight, but the deeper-seated issue is to gain control of self.

- High school students may drop out because of little encouragement toward intellectual achievement at home. Some young people drop out because of poor self-esteem. Often, such people are depressed.
- Social work practitioners need to understand the overall holistic development of adolescents, as well as to have an awareness of their specific needs, issues, and problems.

## SUGGESTED READINGS

Arroyo, C. G. and Zigler, E. (1995). Racial identity, academic achievement, and the psychological well-being of economically disadvantaged adolescents. *Journal of Personality and Social Psychology, 69*(5), 903–914.

Blankston, C. L. & Zhou, M. (1995). Religious participation, ethnic identification, and adaptation of Vietnamese adolescents in an immigrant community. *Sociological Quarterly. 36*(3), 523–534.

Blash, R. R. & Unger, D. G. (1995). Self-concept of African-American male youth: Self-esteem and ethnic identity. *Journal of Child and Family Studies, 4*(3), 359–373.

Horenczyk, G. & Nisan, M. (1996). The actualization of balance of ethnic identity. *Journal of Personality and Social Psychology, 70*(4), 836–843.

Snell, C. L. (1991). Help-seeking behavior among young street males [Special Issue: Men & men's issues]. *Social Work Theory and Practice, 61*(3), 293–305.

Tizard, B. and Phoenix, A. (1995). The identity of mixed parentage adolescents. *Journal of Child Psychology and Psychiatry and Allied Disciplines. 36*(8), 1399–1410.

## SUGGESTED VIDEOTAPES

Arts Council Films (Producer). (1996). *Africa I remember: A musical synthesis of two cultures.* (29 minutes). Available from Filmmakers Library, 124 E. 40th St., Suite 901, New York, NY 10016; 212-808-4980

Attainment (Producer). (1995). *Survivor's pride: Insight.* (29 minutes). Available from Film Ideas,

Inc., 3710 Commerce Ave., Suite 13, Northbrook, IL 60062; 800-475-3456

Media Education (Producer). (1992). *Pack of lies: The advertising of tobacco.* (35 minutes). Available from Media Education Foundation, 26 Center St., Northampton, MA 01060; 413-586-4170

Meridian Education Corp. (Producer). (1988). *Eating disorders: You are not alone.* (29 minutes). Available from Meridian Education Corporation, 236 E. Front St., Bloomington, IL 61701; 800-727-5507

Miles, K. (Producer). (1994). *Silent hunger: Anorexia and bulimia.* (46 minutes). Available from FFH (Films for the Humanities and Sciences), 11 Perrine Rd., Monmouth Junction, NJ 08852; 800-257-5126

Public Policy Prod. (Producer). (1995). *Sex, teens, and public schooling.* (55 minutes). Available from Filmmakers Library, 124 E. 40th St., Suite 901, New York, NY 10016; 212-808-4980

Research Press (Producer). (1980). *Harry: Behavioral treatment of self-abuse* (38 minutes). Available from Research Press, 2612 H. Mattis Ave., Champaign, IL 61821; 217-352-3273

## REFERENCES

Abler, R. M., & Sedlacek, W. E. (1989). Freshman sexual attitudes and behaviors over a 15 year period. *Journal of College Student Development, 30,* 201–209.

Acredolo, C., Adams, A. & Schmid, J. (1984). On the understanding of the relationships between speed, duration, and distance. *Child Development, 55,* 2151–2159.

Allen, J. P., Weissberg, R. P., & Hawkins, J. A. (1989). The relation between values and social competence in the early adolescence. *Developmental Psychology, 25,* 458–464.

American Academy of Pediatrics. (1986). Sexuality, contraception, and the media. *Pediatrics, 71,* 535–536.

Angold, A., & Rutter, M. (1992). Effects of age and pubertal status on depression in a large clinical sample. *Development and Psychopathology, 4,* 5–28.

Baier, J. L., Rosenzweig, M. G., & Whipple, E. G. (1991). Patterns of sexual behavior, coercion, and victimization of university students. *Journal of College Student Development, 32,* 310–322.

Bailey, J. M., & Pillard, R. C. (1991). A genetic study of male sexual orientation. *Archives of General Psychiatry, 48,* 1089–1096.

Bailey, J. M., Pillard, R. C., Neale, M. C., & Agyei, Y. (1993). Heritable factors influence sexual orientation in women. *Archives of General Psychiatry, 50,* 217–223.

Beech, F. A. (1976). Introduction. In F. A. Beech (Ed.), *Human sexuality in four perspectives.* Baltimore: Johns Hopkins University Press.

Beech, R. P., & Schoeppe, A. (1974). Development of value systems in adolescents. *Developmental Psychology, 23*(10), 644–656.

Bell, A. P., Weinberg, M. S., & Hammersmith, S. K. (1981). *Sexual preference: Its development in men and women.* Bloomington: Indiana University Press.

Berman, A. L., & Jobes, D. A. (1991). *Adolescent suicide: Assessment and intervention.* Washinton, DC: American Psychological Association.

Berndt, T. J. (1989). Friendships in childhood and adolescence. In W. Damon (Ed.), *Child development today and tomorrow.* San Francisco, CA: Jossey-Bass.

Berndt, T. J., & Perry, T. B. (1990). Distinctive features of early adolescent friendships. In R. Montemayor, G. R. Adams, & T. P. Gulotta (Eds.), *From childhood to adolescence: A transitional period.* Newbury Park, CA: Sage.

Boldizar, J. P. (1991). Assessing sex-typing and androgyny in children: The children's sex-role inventory. *Developmental Psychology, 27,* 505–515.

Brook, J. S. Brook, D. W., Gordon, A. S., Whiteman, M., & Cohen, P. (1990). The psychosocial etiology of adolescent drug use: A family interactional approach. *Genetic, Social and General Psychology Monographs, 116,* 111–267.

Brooks-Gunn, J., & Furstenberg, F. F., Jr. (1989). Adolescent sexual behavior. *Psychologist, 44,* 249–257.

Broverman, D., Clarkson, F., & Rosenkrantz, P. (1972). Sex role stereotypes: A current appraisal. *Journal of Social Issues, 28,* 59–78.

Brown, B. B., Mounts, N., Lamborn, S. D., & Steinberg, L. (1993). Parenting practices and peer group affiliation in adolescence. *Child Development, 64,* 467–482.

Brown, L. M., & Gilligan, C. (1992). *Meeting at the crossroads.* New York: Ballantine Books.

Buhrmester, D., & Furman, W. (1990). Perceptions of sibling relationships during middle childhood and adolescence. *Child Development, 61,* 1387–1398.

Carroll, L. (1988). Concern with AIDS and the sexual behavior of college students. *Journal of Marriage and the Family, 50,* 405– 411.

Centers for Disease Control. (1992). Sexual behaviors among high school students—United States, 1990. *Morbidity and Mortality Weekly Reports, 40,* 885–888.

Chapman, M. (1988). *Constructive evolution: Origin and development of Piaget's thought.* New York: Cambridge University Press.

Chilman, C. S. (1983). *Adolescent sexuality in a changing American society* (2nd ed.). New York: Wiley.

Colby, A., & Damon, W. (1992). *Pathways to commitment: Moral leaders in our time.* New York: Free Press.

Colby, A., Kohlberg, L., Gibbs, J. C., & Lieberman, M. (1983). A longitudinal study of moral development. *Monographs of the Society for Research in Child Development, 48*(Whole No. 200).

Commons, M. L., Richards, F. A., Armon, C. (Eds.). (1984). *Beyond formal operations: Late adolescent and adult cognitive development.* New York: Praeger.

Cooke, S. (1979). *A comparison of identity formation in preadolescent girls and boys.* Unpublished master's thesis, Simon Eraser University, Canada.

Damon, W. (1988). *The moral child.* New York: Free Press

Damon, W., & Hart, D. (1988). *Self-understanding in childhood and adolescence.* New York: Cambridge University Press.

Darling, C. A., Kallen, D. J., & VanDusen, J. E. (1984). Sex in transition, 1900–1980. *Journal of Youth and Adolescence, 13,* 385–399.

Demetriou, A., & Elfdides, A. (1985). Structure and sequence of formal and postformal thought: General patterns and individual differences. *Child Development, 56,* 1062–1091.

Diamond, M. (1976). Human sexual development: Biological foundation of social development. In F. A. Beech (Ed.), *Human sexuality in four perspectives.* Baltimore: Johns Hopkins University Press.

Dishion, T. J., Patterson, G. R., Stoolmiller, M., & Skinner, M. L. (1991). Family, school, and behavioral antecedents to early adolescent involvement with antisocial peers. *Developmental Psychology, 21,* 172–180.

Donoghue, E. (1992–1993). Sociopsychological correlates of teenage pregnancy in the United States, Virgin Islands. *International Journal of Mental Health, 12*(4) 39–49.

Dreyer, P. H. (1982). Sexuality during adolescence. In B. B. Wolman (Ed.), *Handbook of developmental psychology.* New York: Wiley.

Dunphy, D. C. (1963). The social structure of urban adolescent groups. *Sociometry, 26,* 230–246.

Eckstein, S., & Shemesh, M. (1992). The rate of acquisition of formal operational schemata in adolescence: A secondary analysis. *Journal of Research in Science Teaching, 29,* 441–451.

Eisenberg, N., Miller, P. A., Shell, R., McNalley, S., & Shea, C. (1991). Prosocial development in adolescence: A longitudinal study. *Developmental Psychology, 27,* 849–857.

Elkind, D. (1975). Recent research on cognitive development in adolescence. In S. E. Dragastin & G. H. Elder, Sr. (Eds.), *Adolescence in the life cycle.* New York: Wiley.

Elkind, D., & Bowen, R. (1979). Imaginary audience behavior in children and adolescence. *Developmental Psychology, 15,* 38–44.

Ellickson, P. L., & Hays, R. D. (1992). On becoming involved with drugs: Modeling adolescent drug use over time. *Health Psychology, 11,* 377–385.

Erikson, E. (1980). *Identity and the life cycle.* New York: Norton.

Eton, L. D. (1987). The development of aggressive behavior from the perspective of a developing behaviorism. *American Psychologist, 42,* 435–442.

Farrell, A. D., Danish, S. J., & Howard, C. W. (1992). Relationship between drug use and other problem behaviors in urban adolescents. *Journal of Consulting and Clinical Psychology, 60,* 705–712.

Fischer, K. W. (1980). A theory of cognitive development: The control and construction of hierarchies of skills. *Psychological Review, 87,* 447–531.

Fischer K. W., Bullock, D., Rotenberg, E. J., & Raya, P. (1993). The dynamics of competence: How contest contributes directly to skill. In R. Wozniak & K. Fischer (Eds.), *Development in context: Acting and thinking in specific environments* (IFS Series on Knowledge and Development, Vol. 1, pp. 93–117). Hillsdale, NJ: Erlbaum.

Fisher, C. B., & Brone, R. J. (1991). Eating disorders in adolescence. In R. M. Lerner, A. C. Petersen, & J. Brooks-Gunn (Eds.), *Encyclopedia of adolescence* (Vol. 1). New York: Garland.

Forrest, J. D., & Singh, S. (1990). The sexual and reproductive behaviors of American women,

1982–1988. *Family Planning Perspective, 22,* 206–214.

Freud, A. (1946). *The ego and the mechanisms of defense.* New York: International University Press.

Friesen, D. (1968). Academic-athletic-popularity syndrome in the Canadian high school society. *Adolescence, 3,* 39–52.

Furman, W., & Buhrmester, D. (1992). Age and sex differences in perceptions of networks of personal relationships. *Child Development, 63,* 103–115.

Galambos, N. L. (1992). Parent-adolescent relations. *Current Directions in Psychological Science, 1,* 146–149.

Galambos, N. L., Almeida, D. M., & Petersen, A. C. (1990). Masculinity, femininity, and sex role attitudes in early adolescence: Experiencing gender intensification. *Child Development, 61,* 1905–1914.

Gandelman, R. (1992). *Psychobiology of behavioral development.* New York: Oxford University Press.

Ganter, G., & Yeakel, M. (1980). *Human behavior and the social environment.* New York: Columbia University Press.

Garber, J., Weiss, B., & Shanley, N. (1993). Cognition, depressive symptoms, and development in adolescents. *Journal of Abnormal Psychology, 192,* 47–57.

Gardner, H. (1978). *Developmental psychology.* Boston: Little, Brown.

Garnets, L., & Kimmel, D. (1991). Lesbian and gay male dimensions of the psychologic study of human diversity. In J. D. Goodchilds (Ed.), *Psychological perspectives on human diversity in America.* Washington, DC: American Psychological Association.

Garrison, K. C. (1973). Psychological development. In F. Adams (Ed.), *Understanding adolescence* (2nd ed.). Boston: Allyn and Bacon.

Garrison, K. C., & Garrison, K. C., Jr. (1975). *The psychology of adolescence.* Englewood Cliffs, NJ: Prentice-Hall.

Getzels, J. W., & Jackson, P. W. (1959). The highly intelligent and highly creative adolescent: A summary of some research findings. In C. W. Taylor (Ed.), *The third (1959) University of Utah Research conference on the identification of creative scientific talent.* Salt Lake City: University of Utah Press.

Gibbs, J. C., & Schnell, S. V. (1985). Moral development "versus" socialization: A critique. *American Psychologist, 40,* 1071–1080.

Gilligan, C. (1977). In a different voice: Women's conception of self and morality. *Harvard Educational Review, 47,* 481–517.

Gilligan, C. (1982). *In a different voice: Psychological theory and women's development.* Cambridge, MA: Harvard University Press.

Gilligan, C. (1993). Adolescent development reconsidered. In A. Garrod (Ed.), *Approaches to moral development: New research and emerging themes.* New York: Teacher's College Press.

Gold, M., & Petronio, R. J. (1980). Deliquent behavior in adolescence. In J. Adelson (Ed.), *Handbook of adolescent psychology.* New York: Wiley-InterScience.

Green, R. (1987). *The "sissy boy syndrome" and the development of homosexuality.* New Haven, CT: Yale University Press.

Gunther, H. (1975). Einversuch der Anwendung der Rokeach Value Scale in der Bestimmung von Verhaltungen deutscher Austauschschuler. *Psychologische Beitrage, 17,* 304–320.

Hamilton, S. F. (1990). *Apprenticeship for adulthood: Preparing youth for the future.* New York: Free Press.

Harris, L. [with others]. (1986). *American teens speak: Sex, myths, TV and birth control: The Planned Parenthood poll.* New York: Planned Parenthood Federation of America.

Henggeler, S. W. (1989). Delinquency in adolescence. In *Developmental clinical psychology and psychiatry* (Vol. 18). Newbury Park, CA: Sage.

Hill, J. P., & Lynch, M. E. (1983). The intensification of gender-related role expectations during early adolescence. In J. Brooks-Gunn & A. C. Petersen (Eds.), *Girls at puberty: Biological and psychosocial perspectives.* New York: Plenum.

Hogan, R. (1973). Moral conduct and moral character: A psychological perspective. *Psychological Bulletin, 79,* 217–232.

Holmbeck, G. N., & Hill, J. P (1991). Conflictive engagement, positive affect, and menarche in families with seventh-grade girls. *Child Development, 62,* 1030–1048.

Hsu, L. K. G. (1990). *Eating disorders.* New York: Gilford Press.

Inhelder, B., & Piaget, J. (1958). *The growth of logical thinking from childhood to adolescence.* New York: Basic Books.

Jessor, R. (1987). Problem-behavior theory, psychosocial development and adolescent problem drinking. *British Journal of Addiction, 82,* 331–342.

Jessor, R., Donovan, J. E., & Costa, F. M. (1991). *Beyond adolescence: Problem behavior and young adult development.* Cambridge, England: Cambridge University Press.

Johnston, L. D., O'Malley, P. M., & Bachman, J. G. (1985). *Use of licit and illicit drugs by America's high school students 1975–1984* (DHHS Publication No. ADM 85-1394). Rockville, MD: National Institute on Drug Abuse.

Kagan, J. (1976). The psychology of sex differences. In F. A. Beech (Ed.), *Human sexuality in four perspectives.* Baltimore: Johns Hopkins University Press.

Kandel, D. B., & Davies, M. (1991). Decline in use of illicit drugs by high school students in New York State: A comparison with national data. *American Journal of Public Health, 81,* 1064–1067.

Keating, D. P. (1990). Adolescent thinking. In Feldman & G. R. Elliot (Eds.), *At the threshold: The developing adolescent* (pp. 54–90). Cambridge, MA: Harvard University Press.

Keniston, K. (1975). Youth as a stage in life. In F. J. Havighurst & P. H. Dreyer (Eds.), *Youth: the 74th yearbook of the NESSE.* Chicago: University of Chicago Press.

Kobak, R. R., Cole, H. E., Ferenz-Gilles, R., Fleming, W. S., & Gamble, W. (1993). Attachment and emotional regulation during mother-teen problem solving: A control theory analysis. *Child Development, 64,* 231–245

Koestner, R., Zuroff, D. C., & Powers, T. A. (1991). Family origins of adolescent self-criticism and its continuity into adulthood. *Journal of Abnormal Psychology, 100,* 191–197.

Kohlberg, L. (1973). Continuities and discontinuities in childhood and adult moral development revisited. In *Collected Papers on moral development and moral education.* Cambridge, MA: Harvard University Moral Education Research Foundation.

Kohlberg, L. (1981). *The philosophy of moral development.* San Francisco: Harper & Row.

Kolb, B., & Wishaw, I. Q. (1990). *Fundamentals of human neuropsychology* (3rd ed.). New York: Freeman.

Kurtines, W. M. (1986). Moral behavior as role governed behavior: Person and situation effects on moral decision making. *Journal of Personality and Social Psychology, 50,* 784–791.

Kurtines, W., & Greif, E. B. (1974). The development of moral thought and a review of Kohlberg's approach. *Psychological Bulletin, 81,* 453–459.

Labouvie-Vief, G. (1992). A neo-Piagetian perspective on adult cognitive development. In R. J. Sternberg & C. A. Berg (Eds.), *Intellectual development.* New York: Cambridge University Press.

Lamborn, S. D., Mounts, N. S., Steinberg, L., & Dornbusch, S. M. (1991). Patterns of competence and adjustment among adolescents from authoritative, authoritarian, indulgent, and neglectful families. *Child Development, 62,* 1049–1065.

Lamborn, S. D., & Steinberg, L. (1993). Emotional autonomy redux: Revisiting Ryan and Lynch. *Child Development, 64,* 483–499.

Lapsley, D. K., Harwell, M. R., Olsen, L. M., Flannery, D., & Quintana, S. M. (1984). Moral judgment, personality, and attitude toward authority in early and late adolescence. *Journal of Youth and Adolescence, 13,* 527–542.

Lechner, C. R., & Rosenthal, D. A. (1984). Adolescence self-consciousness and the imaginary audience. *Genetic Psychology Monographs, 110,* 289–305.

Lempers, J. D., & Clark-Lempers, D. S. (1992). Young, middle and late adolescents' comparisons of the functional importance of five significant relationships. *Journal of Youth and Adolescence, 21,* 53–96.

Lerner, R. M., & Hultsch, D. F. (1983). *Human development.* New York: McGraw-Hill.

Levitan, S. A., Gallo, F., & Shapiro, I. (1993). *Working but poor* (rev. ed.). Baltimore: Johns Hopkins University Press.

Levitt, M. J., Guacci-Franco, N., & Levitt, J. L. (1993). Convoys of social support in childhood and early adolescence: Structure and function. *Developmental Psychology, 29,* 811–818.

Livsen, N., & Peskin, H. (1980). Perspectives on adolescence from longitudinal research. In J. Adelson (Ed.), *Handbook of adolescent psychology.* New York: Wiley.

Loehlin, J. C. (1992). *Individual differences and development series: Vol. 2. Genes and environment in personality development.* Newbury Park, CA: Sage.

Lynam, D., Moffitt, T., & Stouthamer-Loeber, M. (1993). Explaining the relation between IQ and delinquency: Class, race, test motivation, school failure, or self-control. *Journal of Abnormal Psychology, 102,* 187–196.

MacDonald, J. M. (1973). False accusations of rape. *Medical Aspects of Human Sexuality, 7,* 170–194.

Marcia, J. E. (1979, June). *Identity status in late adolescence: Description and some clinical implications.* Address given at a symposium on identity development at Rijksuniversitat Groningen, The Netherlands.

Marcia, J. E. (1980). Identity in adolescence. In T. Adelson (Ed.), *Handbook of adolescent psychology.* New York: Wiley.

Martin, C. L. (1990). Attitudes and expectations about children with non-traditional gender roles. *Sex Roles, 22,* 151–165.

Masters, W. H., Johnson, V. E., & Kolodny, R. C. (1993). *Masters and Johnson on sex and human loving.* Glenview, IL: Scott, Foresman.

Maticka-Tyndale, E. (1991). Modification of sexual activities in the era of AIDS: A trend analysis of adolescent sexual activities. *Youth and Society, 23,* 31–49.

Mau, R. Y. (1992). The validity and devolution of a concept: Student alienation. *Adolescence, 27,* 731–741.

McClelland, D. C., & Power, C. (1975). *The inner experience.* New York: Irvington.

McGeorge, C. (1973). *Situational variation on level of moral judgement.* Unpublished paper, University of Canterbury, New Zealand.

Mead, M. (1928). *Coming of age in Samoa.* New York: Morrow.

Melges, F. T., & Hamburg, D. A. (1976). Hormonal changes in women. In F. A. Beech (Ed.), *Human sexuality in four perspectives.* Baltimore: Johns Hopkins University Press.

Meyer, C. H. (1987). Direct practice in social work practice: An overview. In A. Minahan (Ed.), *Encyclopedia of Social Work* (18th ed., Vol. 1, pp. 409–422). Silver Spring, MD: NASW Press.

Milgram, B. (1974). *Obedience to authority.* New York: Harper & Row.

Minuchin, S., Rosman, B. L., & Baker, L. (1978). *Psychosomatic families: Anorexia nervosa in context.* Cambridge, MA: Harvard University Press.

Money, J. (1988). *Gay, straight, and in-between: The sexology of erotic orientation.* New York: Oxford University Press.

Montemayor, R. (1982). The relationship between parent-adolescent conflict and the amount of time adolescents spend alone and with parents and peers. *Child Development, 53,* 1512–1519.

Mulvey, E. P., Arthur, M. W., & Reppucci, N. D. (1993). The prevention and treatment of juvenile delinquency; A review of the research. *Clinical Psychology Review, 13,* 133–167.

Mussen, P. H., Conger, J. J., Kagan, J., & Huston, A. C. (1990). *Child development and personality* (7th ed.). New York: Harper & Row.

Neimark, E. D. (1975). Intellectual development during adolescence. In F. D. Horowitz (Ed.), *Review of child development* (Vol. 4). Chicago: University of Chicago.

Neimark, E. D. (1982). Adolescent thought: Transition to formal operations. In B. B. Wolman (Ed.), *Handbook of developmental psychology* (pp. 486–499). Englewood Cliffs, NJ: Prentice-Hall.

Neimark, E. D. (1982). Adolescent thought: Transition to formal operations. In B. B. Wolman & G. Stricker (Eds.), *Handbook of developmental psychology.* Englewood Cliffs, NJ: Prentice-Hall.

Newman, B. M., & Newman, P. R. (1995). *Development through life: A psychosocial approach* (6th ed.). Pacific Grove, CA: Brooks/Cole.

Offer, D., & Offer, J. B. (1975). *From teenage to young manhood: A psychological study.* New York: Basic Books.

Offer, D., Ostrov, E., & Howard, K. I. (1982). Family perceptions of adolescent self-image. *Journal of Youth and Adolescence, 11,* 281–291.

O'Mahoney, J. F. (1989). Development of thinking about things and people: Social and nonsocial cognition during adolescence. *Journal of Genetic Psychology, 150,* 217–224.

Overton, W. F., & Meehan, A. M. (1982). Individual differences in formal operational thought: Sex role and learned helplessness. *Child Development, 53,* 1536–1543.

Paikoff, R. L., & Brooks-Gunn, J. (1991). Do parent-child relationships change during puberty? *Psychological Bulletin, 110,* 47–66.

Papalia, D. E., & Olds, S. W. (1986). *Human development.* New York: McGraw-Hill.

Paul, J. P. (1993). Childhood cross-gender behavior and adult homosexuality: The resurgence of biological models of sexuality. *Journal of Homosexuality, 24,* 41–54.

Phillips, E. L., Phillips, E. A., Fixen, D. L., & Wolf, M. M. (1973). Achievement place: Behavior shaping works of delinquents. *Psychology Today, 7,* 73–79.

Phinney, J. S. (1989). Stages of ethnic identity development in minority group adolescents. *Journal of Early Adolescence, 9,* 34–49.

Phinney, J. S. (1990). Ethnic identity in adolescents and adults. *Psychological Bulletin, 108,* 499–514.

Piaget, J. (1970). Piaget theory. In P. H. Mussen (Ed.), *Carmichael's manual of child psychology* (3rd ed., Vol. 1). New York: Wiley.

Piaget, J. (1972). Intellectual evolution from adolescence to adulthood. *Human Development, 15,* 1–12.

Pulaski, M. A. S. (1971). *Understanding Piaget.* New York: Harper & Row.

Raja, S. N., McGee, R., & Stanton, W. R. (1992). Perceived attachment to parents and peers and psychological well-being in adolescence. *Journal of Youth and Adolescence, 21,* 471–486.

Reinisch, J. M., Sanders, S. A., Hill, C., & Ziemba-Davis, M. (1992). High-risk sexual behavior among heterosexual undergraduates in a mid-western university. *Family Planning Perspectives, 24,* 116.

Reis, H. T., Lin, Y., Bennett, M. E., & Nezlek, J. B. (1993). Change and consistency in social participation during early adulthood. *Developmental Psychology, 29,* 633–645.

Robinson, I., Ziss, K., Ganza, B., Katz, S., & Robinson, E. (1991). Twenty years of sexual revolution, 1965–1985: An update. *Journal of Marriage and the Family, 53,* 116–220.

Rodgers, J. L., & Rowe, D. C. (1988). Influence of siblings on adolescent sexual behavior. *Developmental Psychology, 24,* 722–728.

Rokeach, M. (1968). Rokeach Value Survey. In M. Rokeach, *Beliefs, attitudes and values.* San Francisco: Jossey-Bass.

Rose, S., & Frieze, I. H. (1993). Young singles' contemporary dating scripts. *Sex Roles, 28,* 499–509.

Rosen, R. H. (1980). Adolescent pregnancy and decision-making: Are parents important? *Adolescence, 15,* 57.

Rowe, D. C., Rodgers, J. L., Meseck-Bushey, S., & St. John, C. (1989). Sexual behavior and nonsexual deviance: A sibling study of their relationship. *Developmental Psychology, 25,* 61–69.

Ryan, R. M., & Lynch, J. H. (1989). Emotional autonomy versus detachment: Revisiting the vicissitudes of adolescence and young adulthood. *Child Development, 6,* 340–356.

Sampson, R. J., & Laub, J. H. (1993). *"Crime in the making" pathways and turning points through life.* Cambridge, MA: Harvard University Press.

Shweder, R. A., Mahapatra, M., & Miller, J. G. (1990). Culture and moral development. In J. W. Stigler, R. A. Shweder, & G. Herdt (Eds.), *Cultural psychology: Essays on comparative human development.* Cambridge, England: Cambridge University Press.

Sherman, J. A. (1971). Imitation and language development. In H. W. Reese (Ed.), *Advances in child development and behavior* (Vol. 6). New York: Academic Press

Sigelman, C. K., & Shaffer, D. R. (1995). *Life-span human development* (2nd ed.). Pacific Grove, CA: Brooks/Cole.

Smith, T. W. (1991). Adult sexual behavior in 1989: Number of partners, frequency of intercourse and risk of AIDS. *Family Planning Perspectives, 23,* 102–107.

Smolak, L., & Levine, M. P. (1993). Separation-individuation difficulties and the distinction between bulimia nervosa and anorexia nervosa in college women. *International Journal of Eating Disorders, 14,* 33–41.

Snarey, J. R. (1985). Cross-cultural universality of social-moral development: A critical few of Kohlbergian research. *Psychological Bulletin, 97,* 202–232.

Sonenstein, F. L., Pleck, J. H., & Ku, L. C. (1991). Levels of sexual activity among adolescent males in the United States. *Family Planning Perspectives, 23,* 162–167.

Spanier, G. B., & Glick, P. C. (1980). The life cycle of American families: An expanded analysis. *Journal of Family History, 5,* 97–111.

Specht, R., & Craig, G. J. (1987). *Human development* (2nd ed.). Englewood Cliffs, NJ: Prentice-Hall.

Steffensmeier, D., & Streifel, C. (1991). Age, gender, and crime across three historical periods: 1935, 1960, and 1985. *Social Factors, 69,* 869–894.

Steinberg, L. (1981). Transformations in family relations at puberty. *Developmental Psychology, 17,* 833–840.

Sweder, R. A., Mahapatra, M., & Miller, J. G. (1990). Culture and moral development. In J. W. Stigler, R. A. Shweder, & G. Herdt (Eds.), *Cultural psychology: Essays on comparative human development.* Cambridge, England: Cambridge University Press.

Tanner J. M. (1971). Sequence, tempo and individual variation in the growth and development of boys and girls aged twelve to sixteen. *Daedalus, 100,* 907–930.

Tanner, J. M. (1978). *Foetus into man.* London: Open Books.

Tanner, J. M. (1990). Sequence, tempo, and individual variation in growth and development of boys and girls aged twelve to sixteen. In R. E. Muss (Ed.), *Adolescent behavior and society* (4th ed.). New York: McGraw-Hill.

Thatcher, R. W., Walker, R. A., & Giudice, S. (1987). Human cerebral hemispheres develop at different rates and ages. *Science, 236,* 1110–1113.

Thoma, S. J., Rest, J. R., & Davison, M. L. (1991). Describing and testing a moderator of the moral judgment and action relationship. *Journal of Personality and Social Psychology, 61,* 659–669.

Tietjen, A. M., & Walker, L. J. (1985). Moral reasoning and leadership among men in a Papua New Guinea society. *Developmental Psychology, 21,* 982–992.

Tulkin, S. R., & Konner, M. J. (1973). Alternative conceptions of intellectual functioning. *Human Development, 16,* 33–52.

U.S. Bureau of the Census. (1977, December). *Educational attainment in the United States, March 1977 and 1976* (Current populations report, Series P-20, No. 314). Washington, DC: U.S. Government Printing Office.

U.S. Bureau of the Census. (1993). *Statistical abstract of the United States 1993.* Washington, DC: U.S. Government Printing Office.

Urberg, K. A. (1979). Sex-role conceptualization in adolescence and adults. *Developmental Psychology, 15,* 90–92.

White, R, W. (1960). Competence and the psychosexual stages. In *Nebraska Symposium on Motivation.* Lincoln: University of Nebraska Press.

White, R. W. (1976). *The enterprise of living.* New York: Holt, Rinehart & Winston.

Wielandt, H., & Boldsen, J. (1989). Age at first intercourse. *Journal of Biosocial Science, 21,* 169–177.

Yager, J. (1982). Family issues in the pathogenesis of anorexia nervosa. *Psychosomatic Medicine, 44*(1), 43–60.

Yamaguchi, K., & Kandel, D. B. (1984). Patterns of drug use from adolescence to young adulthood: II. Sequences of progression. *American Journal of Public Health, 74,* 668–672.

Youniss, J., & Smollar, J. (1985). *Adolescent relations with mothers, fathers and friends.* Chicago: University of Chicago Press.

Zigler, E., Taussig, C., & Black, K. (1992). Early childhood intervention: A promising preventative for juvenile delinquency. *American Psychologist, 47,* 997–1006.

# 7

# *Early Adulthood*

# INTRODUCTION

Amy and Ward, both in their early 20s, have just gotten married. Ward has graduated from college with a degree in psychology. After Amy completed high school, she worked while waiting to marry her high school sweetheart. Their marriage is a fulfillment of their dream. They move into a small apartment of their own. Though they don't have much furniture, they hope to get some, and they save all the money they can. Amy wants to get a college degree eventually but feels that she should wait until Ward is further along in his career. Meanwhile, she also looks forward to starting a family in the near future. Their life has a sense of purpose, a sense of futurity, as well as a feeling that everything will work out meaningfully.

Carol and her boyfriend Joseph got married when both were in their early 20s. They both come from a lower socioeconomic background and do not have much money. Since their marriage, they've lived with Carol's mother. In the crowded living space, there isn't much privacy. Joseph doesn't have a job but hopes to find one soon. In spite of all these limitations, Carol and Joseph are very happy. They see their living arrangements as temporary and plan to move out of the house shortly. Their love for each other, combined with their youth and sense of futurity, helps tide them over their everyday problems.

A sense of purpose, growth, and directionality characterize young adulthood. This constellation of thoughts propels young people as they enter the prime of their lives. Many live by the self-imposed rule, "I will make it." Defining adulthood is not easy. Ganter and Yeakel (1980) describe it as the period between adolescence and old age. There is no definite point of identity that defines the beginning of adulthood. The end of the teenage years is a rough marker; early adulthood usually begins in the early 20s and ends at approximately age 39. During this period, people place less emphasis than before on physical maturation and are less preoccupied with body image. Depending on their childhood and

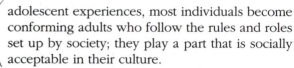

adolescent experiences, most individuals become conforming adults who follow the rules and roles set up by society; they play a part that is socially acceptable in their culture.

The type of adulthood a person experiences depends on family culture and the immediate environment. Some young adults experiment with different lifestyles, while others simply do what is expected of them and engage in routine work. Some may be denied freedom of choice by the nature of political, social, and economic forces over which they have no control.

A person could be perceived to have reached adulthood by physical changes alone, but adulthood is defined in social as well as physical terms. Some individuals continue to feel like children among adults well beyond their early 20s. In law, chronological age marks the points when people can drink, drive, and join the armed forces. Normative adult behavior is, however, associated with economic independence, productivity, and caretaking roles, all of which determine a kind of social timing within which it is presumed that people will fulfill their expectations (Ganter & Yeakel, 1980). Adulthood is the period when social development is transitional and intellectual development essentially comes to a state of completion (Kaluger & Kaluger, 1984).

# PSYCHOSOCIAL ENVIRONMENT

Young adults face many choices with respect to experiences and lifestyles. They learn to tolerate frustration and use logical reasoning and insight in making decisions. Up to the age of 30, men and women usually show underdevelopment in some areas of behavior and judgment but considerable maturity in others. New experiences and new expectations bring with them a more even development on a more mature basis.

The social and economic roles of early adulthood are so familiar and clearly defined that young adults have a clear picture of society's expectations. These expectations indicate developmental tasks, as this list shows:

1. Select a mate.
2. Learn to live with a marriage partner and/or choose a career.
3. Start a family.
4. Rear children.
5. Manage a home.
6. Get started in an occupation.
7. Take on civic responsibilities.
8. Find a congenial social group.

The successful achievement of these tasks leads to a more satisfying middle and late adulthood. Whether or not young people are aware of these options, the choices they make plant the seeds for the harvest in later years (Kaluger & Kaluger, 1984).

One of the most important aspects of young adulthood is learning how to fit into the different roles that become available at this stage of life. The most widely used criteria for deciding whether a person has reached adulthood are role transitions, which involve taking on new responsibilities and duties. The role transitions for a young adult involve completing their education, beginning full-time employment, establishing an independent household, getting married, and becoming a parent (Hogan & Astone, 1986). However, everyone faces adulthood in different ways. For instance, the average age for completing college has increased steadily in proportion to the number of people going to college. The numbers moved from a mere 10% in the early part of the 20th century to 50% in present times. The average age of first marriage and parenthood dropped steadily from 1950 to 1960 or so and rose sharply between the 1960s and the 1980s (Modell, 1989). Such complexities make using one event as the marker of adulthood difficult.

As Germain (1987) mentions, gender roles are being redefined. For instance, single parents are arranging to raise their own children by natural or surrogate means. Women have increasingly joined occupations and professions once considered exclusively male. Further, the two-provider family has always characterized human societies, whether hunting-gathering, agricultural, or industrialized. The current two-career family presents a higher social status and a new role for women. In at least some of these families, both parents take on new androgynous roles and tasks. Thus, men's roles are also changing. Men whose wives are partners and breadwinners are becoming homemakers by choice. There are also single-parent fathers. Finally, career choices have changed for men, who are now telephone operators, flight attendants, nurses, and in other positions that used to be exclusively female (Germain, 1987).

Let us look at role transitions in other cultures. In many non-Western cultures, marriage is the most important milestone for adult status (Schlegel & Barry, 1991). Adult status in many other cultures includes three criteria: one must provide, protect, and procreate. A young man has to have a job, be physically and mentally healthy, and have the qualities of someone who can protect and take care of another person, a woman. The requirements for girls are different. They are trained from a young age to clean, cook, and be obedient to their elders.

In some cultures, the onset of menstruation marks womanhood. The rite of passage for a young girl might be a coming-out party after her first menstruation, thus letting outsiders be aware that a daughter is available for marriage. In some male initiation rites, older men provide a role model and guide the young men through this transition (Keith, 1990). Because rituals change little through the years, they provide continuity for the young people. Through rituals, cultures all across the world maintain contact and social continuity with each other. In the United States, going to college is one of the most common rites of passage (National Center for Educational Statistics, 1993).

## COGNITIVE DEVELOPMENT

Two of the most important abilities young adults have are thinking and differentiating between knowledge and skills. Cognitive development includes both the differentiation and integration of component skills and an increasing knowledge of one's intellectual capacities.

> Dave has completed his bachelor's degree and is tempted to go to medical school. He has a girlfriend who wishes to make a more serious commitment. Dave struggles with his educational goals and his need for love and companionship. Eventually, after a lot of thought, he prioritizes his goals and decides that before he can make any serious commitment to his girlfriend, he needs to complete his education. Although full of pain, he discusses his plans with his girlfriend in a rational, cognitive fashion.

## Piaget and Beyond

According to Piaget, the highest stage of cognitive development occurs in adolescence under typical or favorable conditions. He sees the development of formal operational thought continuing in early adulthood.

Piaget (1972) characterizes the differentiation and integration of component skills in terms of (1) a new group of symbolic transformations—formal operations—operating on (2) abstract units as well as propositions, organized into (3) a simple, flexible structure having the properties of a mathematical system. The observable consequence of this restructuring of thought is the appearance of hypothetico-deductive reasoning; that is, starting from any initial assumption, one could imagine and explore its logical implications as a prelude to action. An additional characterization of formal operational thought invokes (4) different formal operational schemes; that is, general conceptual frameworks for dealing with such relations as proportion, correlations, equilibrium, and the coordination of different frames of reference.

Arlin (1980) differentiates the formal operational thought of adolescence from that of adulthood in terms of the consolidation and application of schemes. For the adolescent, learning schemes is an intellectual goal in itself; for adults, schemes become the means to further understanding. For example, the coordination of a frames-of-reference scheme underlies an appreciation of relativity. Relativity is an intricate concept; there are revolutionary advances in theories of physics and ethics that result from its incorporation. This is true of concepts derived from such other schemes as dynamic equilibrium and probabilistic (rather than strict) determinism, both of which influence theoretical advances in physical, biological, and social domains.

Arlin's description of the adult deals with the optimal capacity that one may attain. Much research and subsequent criticism of Piagetian theory has focused on mounting evidence (Neimark, 1982) that many individuals do not operate on this Hyperion plane. Partly as a result of such evidence, current research has turned toward identifying additional factors that moderate observed intellectual performance.

*Beyond formal operations*  How do we go beyond formal operations? Let us look at the following problem:

> Mike and Mindy have three children. Mike has a problem with alcohol. He tries to give up drinking because it affects his marriage and his relationship with his children. However his drinking has never kept him from bringing home a high salary. One day after an office party, he comes home drunk. Mindy warns him that if he ever drinks again she'll leave him, permanently.
>
> One week later, after another office party, Mike returns home. Totally drunk, he staggers at the doorstep. Mindy, in disgust, pulls him in. What should Mindy do? Leave him? Stay?

Adolescents and adults solve this problem differently. Adolescents will argue that Mindy gave Mike a clear ultimatum and because Mike ignored it Mindy should leave. Following a formal operational pattern, they reason deductively from the information given to them and come to a single solution based on their own experience. However, many adults would be reluctant to reach a conclusion based on such limited information. They would point out that there is much about Mike and Mindy that they do not know. How long have they been married? How long has he been drinking? Could Mindy support herself and the three children? From this perspective, the problem is ambiguous. Adults would eventually decide whether Mindy should stay or go, but only after they had considered the different aspects of the problem beyond the given information. Adults recognize that other people's problems and experiences may differ greatly from their own. Obviously the thought processes that these adults use differs from formal operations (Cavanaugh, Kramer, Sinnott, Camp, & Markley, 1985). Unlike formal-operational thinking, this approach involves considering situational constraints and circumstances—that is, understanding that reality constrains solutions. For example, one can consider the important role emotions play in all familial situations. As early as the 1960s, some researchers wondered if thinking differently might develop after adolescence. Though their work was grounded in Piaget's theory, they suspected that there might be a stage of thinking beyond formal thought. In a systematic study of cognitive development, Perry (1970) traced the development of thinking during the undergraduate years. He found that 18-year-old first-year students tended to rely heavily on the expertise of authority figures to determine which ways of thinking were right or wrong. For these students, thinking was tightly tied to logic and, as Piaget argued, the only legitimate answers were the ones that were logically derived. But by senior year, things changed. The students had gone through a phase in which they were much less sure of which answers were right or if there were any right answers at all. By the time they graduated, they were fairly adept at examining the different sides of an issue and had developed commitments to particular viewpoints. They realized that they were a source of authority and had to take a position on an issue and that other people may hold positions different from theirs but be equally committed.

Based on many longitudinal studies and numerous cross-sectional investigations since, researchers have concluded that this type of thinking represents a qualitative change beyond formal operations (Commons, Sinnott, Richards, & Armon, 1989; Kitchener & King, 1989; Kramer Angiuld, Crisafi, & Levine, 1991). As Commons et al. (1989) put it, postformal thought is character-

ized by a recognition that truth (the correct answer) could vary from situation to situation. To be reasonable, solutions need to be realistic. Ambiguity and contradiction are the rules rather than the exceptions. Finally, emotion and subjective factors usually play a role in decision making.

*Reflective judgments* The various research-based descriptions of adult thinking include *reflective judgment*; that is, the way adults reason through dilemmas involving current affairs, business, religion, science, personal and family relationships, and the like. Kitchener and King (1989) have refined descriptions and identified a systematic progression of reflective judgment in young adulthood. Though the stages presented are progressive, actual development is highly variable, making it difficult to tie specific ages to particular stages.

- *Stage 1:* Knowledge is assumed to exist absolutely and concretely and can be obtained by direct observation. There is a close correspondence between belief and truth and a correct answer to every question.
- *Stage 2:* Knowledge is absolutely certain but may not be immediately available. All knowledge can be obtained either by direct observation or from authorities. All beliefs that people have are justified by an authority.
- *Stage 3:* Knowledge is assumed to be certain or only temporarily uncertain. Any form of uncertainty can be remedied by intuition or bias until certainty is obtained. That is, when knowledge is certain, beliefs are justified by an authority, but when they are uncertain, they are justified intuitively.
- *Stage 4:* Often, knowledge is uncertain and idiosyncratic, because situational variables could dictate that we can never know anything with certainty. One justifies beliefs by appealing to evidence, but the choice of evidence is idiosyncratic. For example, one might pick only the evidence that already fits an established belief.

- *Stage 5:* All knowledge is affected by situations and is subjective. One makes his or her own interpretation of the world. One's beliefs are justified within a certain context or situation, but they are balanced against other beliefs, which may interfere with drawing conclusions.
- *Stage 6:* When one constructs knowledge, one evaluates the evidence, others' opinions, and so forth in different situations. Thus, one gets subjective and objective (as presented by others) personal constructions of issues. Usually, beliefs are justified by comparing evidence and opinions on different sides of an issue and by using one's own values.
- *Stage 7:* Based on practical factors, knowledge is constructed by reasonable inquiry into conjectures about the world, or reasonable solutions to problems at hand. Ordinarily, beliefs are justified either on the basis of evidence and argument or as the most complete understanding of an issue available.

From these seven stages, we can conclude that adults move from a firm belief in an absolute correspondence between personal perception and reality to the recognition that the search for truth is an ongoing, never-ending process (Kitchener & King, 1989).

Other researchers have found similar trends. Kramer (1989) and Kramer et al. (1991) claim that adult cognitive development involves three stages: absolutist, relativistic, and dialectical. With *absolutist thinking,* people firmly believe that there is only one correct solution to a problem and this solution can be reached through personal experience, which is the basis of all truth. This type of thinking is most common in late adolescence and the first few years of adulthood. *Relativistic thinking* involves realizing that there are many sides to an issue and that correct actions and solutions depend on circumstances. People in their early 20s through early middle age use this style. A potential danger arises from this type of thinking, which says "I'll do my thing

and you do yours." That is, because relativistic thinkers reason things out case by case, they are unlikely to commit to one position for a long time. Finally, *dialectical thinkers* see merits in different points of view and can synthesize them into a workable solution to which they can strongly commit. Clearly, in postformal thinking the progression is important; that is, individuals must learn one aspect of development to get to the next.

## Kohlberg

According to Kohlberg (1973), cognitive developmental tasks continue to take place in adults for the following reasons:

1. Adolescents who are slow in cognitive development because of biological and cultural factors and are still at the concrete operational level at age 15 may develop formal operational thought in early adulthood.
2. There is a continuous horizontal decalage of formal operational thought in early adulthood that could be applied to more spheres and activities. For instance, in middle childhood some forms of conservation are understood much sooner than others (like area or volume). Piaget was aware of this and many other developmental inconsistencies, and he coined the term *horizontal decalage* to describe them. Similarly, we can look at young adults, like college faculty members and graduate students, who are more proficient at both dialectical and systematic reasoning than undergraduate students. According to Piaget, one can argue that the viability of some formal operational undergraduates to resolve problems or to construct abstract "systems" and "supersystems" merely represents a type of horizontal decalage similar to that of a concrete operation, like a schoolchild who conserves liquids and mass but not volume (Shaffer, 1996).

3. Related to this decalage, a stabilization of formal thought can occur that could be equated with the increased subordination or rejection of lower forms of thought in favor of formal operational thought.

Given that these three types of cognitive development occur in adulthood, we might ask whether Kohlberg would support any new cognitive stage in adults. Since neurological maturation is apparently completed by adolescence, any such cognitive stage would be based on experience.

If there is some new adult stage, it is not likely to appear in logical-cognitive tasks as such. This conclusion has two bases: (1) Piagetian cognitive growth is correlated with both the hereditary and the age-maturational factors found in general intelligence and (2) logical stages by definition are normally experience-free. Experience appears to represent something of a hindrance to pure formal-logical thought, as evidenced by the fact that the greatest thinkers in mathematical and pure physical theory have commenced their work in late adolescence.

## ADULT EXPERIENCES IN MORAL DEVELOPMENT

As we saw in the previous section, one can argue that adult moral development has a cognitive structural component. However, moral changes clearly represent a greater focus in adult life than do cognitive changes. We do not need Erikson's studies of Luther and Gandhi to tell us that crises and turning points of adult identity are often moral in nature. Literature from Saint Paul to Tolstoy reveals that the classic biographies and dramas of maturity reflect transformations of moral ideologies. Further, most adults assume the responsibilities of parents, employers, or work supervisors; as such, their moral decisions affect not only their own lives but also those of the people around them.

## Kohlberg's Theory

Kohlberg's postcoventional moral reasoning begins to emerge in adulthood. In Kohlberg's (1973) study, most 30-year-olds still reasoned at the conventional level. About one-sixth to one-eighth of them had begun to use a postconventional level of reasoning—that is, to show a deeper understanding of the basis of laws and distinguish between just and unjust laws. Thus it is clear that there is moral growth in early adulthood (Walker, 1989).

As you know, Kohlberg also stresses the need for social experiences that require people to see things from others' perspectives in order to appreciate that they themselves are a part of a larger social order and that moral rules reflect a consensus of individuals. When people with different perspectives interact, this action creates cognitive disequilibrium. A conflict arises between cognitive structures and new ideas, which in turn stimulates new ways of thinking.

Living in a complex and diverse world can stimulate moral development as well. Just as we learn the give-and-take of mutual perspective by discussing issues with our friends, we can also learn that the opinions of many groups of people are diverse and that laws reflect the citizens' consensus rather than the arbitrary rulings of a dictator (or not, depending on where we live).

As you know, Kohlberg specifies three levels of morality and three different styles of relationships between self and society's rules and expectations (see Chapter 1). Like all stage theorists, Kohlberg believes that movement through his stages of development are progressive—always upward, gradual, and without significant regressions (Snarey & Kohlberg, 1985).

Of course, adults are faced with moral dilemmas. Take, for example, the case given by Kohlberg:

In Europe, a woman was near death from cancer. There was one drug that the doctors thought might save her. It was a form of radium that a druggist in the same town had recently discovered. The drug was expensive to make, but the druggist was charging ten times what the drug cost him to make. He paid $200.00 for the radium and charged $2,000 for a small dose of the drug. The sick woman's husband, Heinz, went to everyone he knew to borrow the money, but he could only get together $1,000 which is half of what it cost. He told the druggist that his wife was dying and asked him to sell it cheaper or let him pay later. But the druggist said, "No. I discovered the drug, and I am going to make money from it." So, Heinz got desperate and broke into the man's store to steal the drug for his wife. Should the husband have done that? Why? (Kohlberg, 1969, p. 379)

What do you think? Your *reasons* for the answer are more important then which position you take. A preconventional child might answer, "He shouldn't do it because he'll be punished" or "He should do it because if he lets his wife die he'll be in big trouble." Another young person, at the conventional level, might respond, "He shouldn't do it, because if people were allowed to take the law in their own hands, the social order would soon break down." An adult at the post-conventional level might say, "He shouldn't do it, because he would have to face his own self-condemnation in knowing that he had not lived up to his conscience and standards of honesty" or "He should do it because saving a life is a higher principle than disobeying the law." Kohlberg believes that "to act in a morally high way requires a high stage of moral reasoning. . . . One can, however, reason in terms of such principles and . . . live up to them" (Kohlberg, 1969, p. 38).

Kohlberg's theory does not apply to specific ages. To develop conventional morality, one must achieve Piaget's formal operations in adolescence. Again, just because a person is capable of formal operational thought does not guarantee that the level of postconventional morality will be reached. In fact, many people never reach this stage.

## Criticism of Kolhberg's Theory

Kolhberg's theory of moral development is subject to many criticisms, as follows:

First, Kolhberg based his early theorizing on interviews with white middle-class U.S. men. Although he later interviewed men and women of all ages in several cultures, many psychologists think there is insufficient evidence to support his belief in "an invariant developmental sequence" of the six developmental stages (Kurtines & Greif, 1974).

Second, the moral dilemmas that Kolhberg uses do not represent the types of moral dilemmas that children, adolescents, college students, and other individuals routinely face in their daily lives (Yussen, 1977).

Third, Kolhberg bases his theory on his own interpretations of subject's responses, and this may bias his conclusions (Flavell, 1985). Also, his levels may not adequately describe moral development within the many subcultures of the United States (Stack, 1986).

Fourth, Kolhberg's approach focuses on the rational and cognitive and therefore ignores emotional, empathetic responses, which could be related to moral growth (Vitz, 1990). For instance, Hoffman comments that moral values develop gradually from concrete experiences of empathy rather than in steps tied to cognitive stages as indicated by Kolhberg (L. Hoffman, 1981; M. L. Hoffman, 1984).

Finally, the strongest objection to Kolhberg's theory comes from psychologists who point out that his approach is "male biased." Kolhberg sees autonomy as the peak of moral development and objectivity as higher than subjectivity, just as Piaget does. However, Gilligan indicates that U.S. society socializes men to place a higher value on independence but teaches women to value interdependence, caring and sharing. If so, then women will always score somewhat lower on Kolhberg's tests than men will (Bloom, 1986; Gilligan, 1983, 1986). Gelman puts it this way, "What right has Kohlberg to say that "objectivity" is morally superior to "subjectivity?" (Gelman, 1985, p. 83). Therefore when we look at Kolhberg's theory should we see it as *descriptive,* not *prescriptive?* Kolhberg described what has happened in his particular sample, not necessarily what *should* occur, certainly not for all people. To move from description of observed changes to developments or improvements involves an *unproven assumption*—that moral decision making generally changes for the better as we get older.

## Gilligan: Stages of Moral Development

As we have seen, Gilligan (1982, 1985) sharply criticizes Kohlberg's theory with reference to women. She claims that care and responsibility in interpersonal relationships play a critical role in moral development, particularly for women:

> The moral imperative that emerges repeatedly in interviews with women is an injunction to care, a responsibility to discern and alleviate the "real and recognizable trouble" of this world. For men, the moral imperative appears rather as an injunction to respect the rights of others and thus to protect the rights to life and self-fulfillment from interference. (1982, p. 100)

Gilligan replaces Kohlberg's preconventional, conventional, and postconventional levels with a developmental progression in which people gain greater understanding of caring and responsibility. In the first stage, children are preoccupied with their own needs. By the second stage, people begin to care for others, particularly those who are less able to care for themselves, such as babies and older people. In the third stage, caring is combined with caring for others and oneself and an emphasis on caring for all human relationships.

Like Kohlberg, Gilligan specifies that moral reasoning becomes more sophisticated as individuals develop and progress through a specified number of distinct stages. However, Gilligan discusses care and helping people in need instead of justice and treating people fairly.

Let us turn now to Erikson's stage of young adulthood. In this discussion, we shall consider many views besides that of Erikson to provide a fuller view of human intimacy.

## INTIMACY VERSUS ISOLATION

### Erikson

According to Erikson, the major crisis of young adulthood is intimacy versus isolation. Erikson theorizes that one must achieve a sense of individual identity before becoming able to commit oneself to a *shared identity* with another person—that is, you must know yourself (adolescent task) before you can love someone else. The young adult who does not have a clear sense of identity may be threatened by the idea of entering a committed, long-term relationship and being "tied down"; alternately, he or she may become overly dependent on another as a source of identity (Sigelman & Shaffer, 1995). For Erikson, sexual intimacy is only part of true intimacy, which also includes psychological intimacy. Those who are unsure of their identity would shy away from interpersonal intimacy, but as they became more sure of themselves, they would seek intimacy in the form of friendship, combat, leadership, and love (Erikson, 1980).

The family is the appropriate context for sharing confidences and strong love, as well as revealing weaknesses and areas of dependency. However, the young adult faces a unique task: to establish an intimate relationship with someone who is *not* a member of his or her own family. Losing and gaining love represent the greatest challenges in adulthood.

*Intimacy* is the ability to experience an open, supportive, tender relationship with another person without losing one's own identity in the process of becoming closer. Stone (1973) describes intimacy as a relationship that supports the independent judgments of each member without stifling anyone. Intimacy implies mutual empathy as well as a mutual recognition of needs. One must give pleasure as well as receive pleasure.

According to Newman and Newman (1995), intimacy does not develop until a couple has been married for several years. Over that period of time, the couple's relationship may be influenced by the early period of mutual adjustment, the birth of the first child, and the social expectations of the members of the extended family.

> Don and Mary come for therapy after they have been married for 6 months. Don has turned from a loving and caring husband to a quiet robot who'll do everything his wife asks him to do but will not participate in any conversations. According to Mary, he has changed from a talkative and lively person to an unnaturally quiet person. Therapy reveals Mary to be a dependent person. She wants her husband to take her everywhere and help her with chores outside the home, calling herself "inexperienced." Although Don enjoyed Mary's dependency before marriage, it bothers him now. He feels that his wife is too dependent and has no identity of her own—she feels like a burden. Though their relationship seemed close at the start, it wasn't truly intimate, because both still needed to gain some adult perspective and, in the process, complete some developmental tasks, such as building a stronger sense of self or identity and a mature sense of intimacy.

## Male and Female Expectations

As you might have guessed, Erikson's formulation of the crisis in young adulthood is based on observations of men. Does it work the same way for women? Not really. As we have seen, the issues of identity and intimacy seem intertwined for women (Dyk & Adams, 1990; Hodgson & Fischer, 1979; Patterson, Sochting, & Marcia, 1992). Men are more likely to be psychologically ready for a serious relationship after they have either launched a career or settled on one after graduation. Career-minded women also tend to look at their identity before seeking intimacy (Dyk & Adams, 1990). Other women, however, resolve their intimacy issues before their identity issues. They might get married and begin to raise children before they stop and ask themselves who they are as individuals (Hodgson & Fischer, 1979; Schiedel & Marcia, 1985; Whitbourne & Tesch, 1985). Still other women forge identity and intimacy tasks simultaneously, forming a personal identity that centers on caring for other people or defining themselves in the context of a love relationship (Dyk & Adams, 1990). Perhaps one reason Erikson's theory fits men better than women is that women have had to find alternative ways of dealing with the issues of identity and intimacy. Gender differences regarding identity and intimacy may diminish as more and more women focus on careers and other options heretofore open only to men.

In today's world, men and women experience differences in socialization, which lead to differential expectations of intimacy and to different problems in the establishment of intimacy. Boys are taught during childhood to restrain from overtly expressing their feelings of dependence and to limit their emotionality. During late childhood and early adolescence, the emotional life of boys is guided by competitiveness and self-reliance. The male adolescent may withdraw from or resist expressing tenderness toward family members. His heterosexual relationships are often a way of expressing and demonstrating his virility to his friends. Although he may also express tenderness within those relationships, a young man will usually resist any commitment until he has established confidence in his own independence. The demand for intimacy may be difficult for him to meet, because he primarily resists intimate, interdependent relationships. However, the successful establishment of an interpersonal relationship offers him an opportunity to express emotion in a safe and supportive environment (Newman & Newman, 1975).

Today, women's upbringing differs from that of men. Usually well prepared for the emotional demands of intimacy, women not only define themselves in a context of relationships but also evaluate themselves on their ability to care (Gilligan, 1982). A woman's place in the man's life cycle has been that of a nurturer, caretaker, helpmate, and weaver of those networks of relationships on which she relies to help define her place in life (Gilligan, 1982). However, until recently, there have been no major studies on female development in adulthood that have age-related sequences comparable to the ones reported for men by Vaillant (1977) and Levinson (Levinson, Darrow, Klein, Levinson, & McGee, 1978). Female researchers, for their part, have not explored female psychology until recent times (Gilligan, 1982). *Seasons of a Woman's Life* (Levinson, 1996) does present the life stages of an adult woman.

Some essential points of difference between men and women lie in their paths to identity. Men traditionally individuate by separating from their families of origin, becoming autonomous, and pursuing individual interests. In contrast, as you know, women tend to develop their identities not by breaking away from relationships with other people but through those very attachments, as well as by accepting the responsibility that characterizes such ties (Baruch, Barnett, & Rivers, 1983; Chodorow, 1978; Gilligan, 1982).

A chief reason for these differences is that women tend to be the ones who take care of babies and small children; daughters observe their mothers performing child-rearing tasks and identify with them. Their personalities become defined early in life in relation to other people, more than men's personalities do (Chodorow, 1978).

Some researchers highlight the role of work in women's life, which differs significantly from that of men. Traditionally, women have defined themselves as mothers, wives, and daughters, not as professionals. Their work outside the home has been discontinuous because of child-rearing demands and societal expectations. In decades past, few women followed through on the career dreams of their early adulthood, and even fewer had mentors that could help. However, this pattern is changing, in keeping with society's new expectations for women (Papalia & Olds, 1986).

Today's woman faces a conflict between two sets of expectations. Although raised to think in terms of occupational fulfillment, women find out that society, including their partners, still expects them to take care of the tasks of homemaking and child rearing. Our present historical time is one of transition; today's men and women are writing psychological as well as sociological history.

Gilligan mentions that for those women who have been encouraged successfully to fulfill themselves only through work, an important element of personality is missing; that is, involvement with others. She further claims that current depictions of adulthood do not include an important line of development: progression in relationships toward a maturity of interdependence (Gilligan, 1982).

Because career and relationships are important in adult development, theorists must see not only the need to achieve in one's work but also the need to nurture and to care for oneself and others as a vital task of adulthood. For instance, Gilligan studied four 27-year-old women, all of whom were pursuing ambitious careers. When asked to describe themselves, none projected herself as a successful, achieving woman; all discussed themselves in terms of their relationships (mother, wife, past lover, adopted child), which highlighted the concept of the fusion of identity and intimacy.

Clearly, a well-rounded view of adult intimacy takes into account both Erikson's and Gilligan's views, as well as others. Now let us see what happens when this aspect of development goes awry.

## Isolation

The negative side of the crisis of intimacy, according to Erikson, is self-absorption and isolation. The possibility of closeness with others seriously threatens the self-identity of some young people. They imagine intimacy to be a blurring of boundaries—their own and others'—so they have great difficulty managing themselves in such relationships. People who experience isolation may erect barriers between themselves and others to keep their sense of self intact. Such a person has developed a fragile sense of self from a childhood that fostered either a rigid and brittle or a totally diffused sense of personal identity. People with this tenuous sense of self are so busy reminding themselves who they are—or so occupied in maintaining their identity or struggling to make sense out of diffusion—that they really cannot attain a sense of intimacy.

Gregory, as we saw in Chapter 6, lived in various foster homes as a child. He was taken care of reasonably well in some homes but was either overdisciplined or underdisciplined in others. To some extent he was also abused, both mentally and physically. At 17 he was living in a group home and enjoying the lifestyle it offered him, though he had various scrapes with the law. Later, he got a job in a gas station. Now he has met a pretty girl who has fallen in love with him. Gregory cares for her in return, but only superficially; his own needs are paramount. Nothing that she can do for him is sufficient. His ability to take is tremendous, but he cannot give in return. Always afraid of being overwhelmed by her, he distances himself when she tries to get emotionally close to him. The fear that he'll lose his identity in this relationship forces Gregory to push her away. Though offended and sad, his girlfriend doesn't really understand that his inability to give or to care for her isn't her fault. Gregory fears losing his identity because he has never really structured his own ego. Thus at 24 he appears to be floundering like an adolescent.

## ADULT IDENTITY

All people who reach adulthood face developmental tasks. They have to select and prepare for an initial occupation, achieve socially responsible behavior, and develop concepts for competency in the moral, ethical, social, economic, and political aspects of life. Adults have to cultivate desirable personality traits, social and communications skills, and healthy attitudes in preparation for marriage and family life. Last, they have to acquire a set of values by forming an identity and a concept of their place in society (Kaluger & Kaluger, 1984).

Kevin, 24 years old and very good-looking, still struggles with self-identity. He has dated several women and had intense sexual relationships with at least five of them at different points in his life. For Kevin, there has never been any kind of mutual, psychological intimacy, for he always drops a relationship as soon as his sexual partner wants more serious involvement. Laughingly, he comments that he likes sex but must know himself and his goals before he can make a serious commitment.

## Self-Image

How do young people develop a self-image? Earlier, in adolescence, self-image was not much of a problem: Adolescents either do what their parents want them to do or do the opposite. But most adults look for a stable, balanced self-image, a reliable view of themselves that will remain more or less steady throughout life. Such an image comes out of the values of the community, family, and groups of contemporaries.

However, in today's society it is becoming difficult for young adults to find their own self-image. Often they appear to stand alone in an unstructured moral climate. There are no absolute guidelines and standards to contemplate or patterns to follow in leading their lives. The emphasis is on "doing your own thing" without having a background of knowledge by which to judge what is desirable for you. Many young people have to proceed by trial and error and adopt those values with which they become comfortable.

## THE ROLE OF WORK FOR THE ADULT

In U.S. society there is no meaningful alternative to work. Most adults—the largest portion of the population—work. People define the characteristics of occupation, aside from pay, as enjoyment and the exercise of skills (Garfinkel, 1982):

1. Work defines our position in society. When we meet or introduce ourselves to new people, the first thing they inquire, after learning our name, is "What do you do?"
2. Work is the context in which we act out the main part of the human drama, in such areas as these:
   a. Competition (for example, in a sales job)—finding out who performs better than others, who gets a pay raise for better performance, and so on
   b. Territoriality—having one's name on the door, a corner room, a room with a view

c. Bonding (the mentor relationship)—
    associating with people in order to
    achieve
d. Nurturing (the mentor relationship)
3. Work is the opportunity for doing, creating,
    and achieving. What do a craftsperson and
    a corporate executive have in common? An
    interest in work. As Freud puts it, work
    and love provide opportunities for mean-
    ingful achievements in life.

The issue of work has been ignored by many developmental psychological theorists and human-factor engineers. Until recently, develop-mental psychology has emphasized only the early part of life. This focus on the early years assumed that human beings' "traits" and behaviors are formed and fixed by the time a person is 20 years old. Thus, unfortunately, researchers did not con-sider the topic of work in their studies.

Today, we have already learned that early decisions people make regarding work are relat-ed to their personalities. Holland (1973, 1985) makes explicit an intuitively appealing idea: that people usually choose occupations that will ide-ally optimize the fit between their individual traits—such as personality, intelligence skills, and abilities—and their occupational interests. However this is not always true. When jobs are scarce and layoffs common, people at some point take whatever job becomes available just to survive.

Reviewing Erikson's stages, we can see that in his conceptualization of the developmental tasks of adulthood, Erikson (1980) has completely omitted work as a developmental issue. This omission has been corrected by Vaillant (1977) and by Levinson et al. (1978) in their longitudinal studies of healthy adult men. Vaillant suggests adding a period he calls *career consolidation* to the developmental sequence. The concept of career consolidation is congruent with the chal-lenges and developmental tasks of adulthood, in which concerns about doing one's job skillfully, successfully, and appropriately are pervasive. One of Vaillant's subjects described his first 20 years of adulthood as the period of life in which he learned to get along with his wife and the next 10 as the time he learned to do his job. Vaillant modifies Erikson's scheme by suggesting that after adolescents make some progress with iden-tification, they begin to deal with intimacy and establish relationships with significant others. With the capacity for relationships established, the young adult attends to the task of work in the stage of career consolidation.

## Work and the Quality of Life

The orderliness of normative life events includes, but is not limited to, work activities, which strongly affect one's quality of life.

Phil is a 24-year-old construction worker who works in the inner city, where an old school build-ing is being renovated. Always tired at the end of the day, all he wants when he returns home is a good, hearty dinner, which he eats without a word. Then he plays with his little daughters before they go to bed. Later, Phil spends time talking to his wife before he dozes off to sleep by ten o'clock. Because his wife understands his need to go to sleep early, she doesn't feel offended when he dozes off while they're talking. He has to be up by five to leave for work in the morning. Phil's family is not wealthy by any standards—in fact, he makes barely enough money to meet all his financial obligations. But he enjoys his work. The family believes in making honest money, and that money comes by the sweat of Phil's brow.

Further, Hogan (1978) found that men who deviated from the normative order of completing school, getting a job, and then marrying were more likely to become separated or divorced than men who conformed to it. Of course, women face similar issues.

Marge works as a cook in a school cafeteria. She spends all her time cooking and cleaning. When she gets home, all she wants to do is go to sleep and get a good night's rest. Her job dictates her lifestyle.

Katie works as a teacher in an elementary school. She lives in a poor neighborhood and has to go home early so the wayside drunks won't cause her trouble. However, her job doesn't end in school.

She works with emotionally disturbed children and hopes to publish a book about them. So when she reaches home, her second job begins. She goes to work on her book about emotionally disturbed children and relives some of the earlier experiences of the day. Katie often works until midnight before going to bed, although her workday begins at eight in the morning. Her lifestyle is dictated by the kind of work she has chosen for herself.

If the developmental theorists are correct in that each life stage contains its own agenda of tasks and issues, then work must adapt over time to match the changing worker. The word *career* implies this dynamic quality of work. The structure of a career—its timing, sequence, and progress as well as its content—contributes to the evolution of an adult.

Though work is an important aspect of our lives, we seldom step back and think about it. For many of us, work is mostly a way of making a living. Clearly, though, money is not the only reward from a job. Even if it is the most important reward, the side benefits include friendships and a feeling of usefulness. We exchange the money we make for necessities and, perhaps, a few luxuries of life. Further, there are very few things that an individual can do without some connection to work. Often, time with friends and family depends on our work schedule. Parents choose daycare centers partly by proximity to their place of employment. Even mental flexibility, a component of intelligence, can be stimulated or stifled by work.

Sociology refers to *occupational socialization* as a process by which, over time, work experience fosters certain kinds of personal development. For some, work offers prestige and a sense of worth. For others, the excitement of creativity and the opportunity to give something of themselves make work meaningful. Such occupational priorities, or what people want from their employment, reflect the culture and the times in which people live (Kail & Cavanaugh, 1996). The personal development engendered by work in turn becomes a factor in promoting the direction, order, and stability of career progress. In this fashion, career and other facets of an individual's life, such as economics and family, influence each other.

As you know, Erikson postulated that the developmental process in each stage depends on the successful resolution of the preceding stage. Thus, in order to be able to establish intimate relations, one must have a sense of identity. A person who has not moved beyond the stage of intimacy and has never resolved the issues of work or career consolidation will be unable in later adulthood to deal with the developmental task of that period. Developmental psychologists indicate that such a person would stagnate and would be unprepared for the generativity stage of life.

## Contribution of Work to Adult Development

How does work affect an adult's adjustment and personal growth? Occupation is part of any person's central identity. It means a great deal for people to say that they are psychologists, social workers, teachers, nurses, electricians, and so forth. When a person gets fired or laid off, it often greatly affects a person's self-esteem and family relationships (Price, 1992). Being productive in the workplace can offer a person many personal rewards, including opportunities to face challenges, gain status, and form enjoyable relationships (Havighurst, 1982). On the other hand, the stress of work can spill over into family life and cause physical and mental disorders (Crouter & McHale, 1993).

Kohn and Schooler (1978, 1983) have explored the meaning and implications of the *substantive complexity* of a job—that is, the number of opportunities it provides for using one's mind and making independent judgments. For instance, a secretary with a substantively complex job would do more than perform merely what is required, such as typing assignments. She might also handle the department's budget, decide on office equipment, interact with the public, and assign work to clerical helpers. Thus she takes on the responsibility of making several important decisions every day.

Intellectually challenging work is associated with greater flexibility and the ability to handle intellectual problems adeptly, keeping an open mind on all issues. In contrast, people who engage in intellectually unchallenging work tend to be *relatively* ineffective thinkers. On the other hand, intelligent people can handle complex jobs. Further, Kohn and his colleagues demonstrate that the quality of one's job influences one's subsequent personal qualities (Clausen & Gilens, 1990).

So the manner in which we work as adults has important implications for intellectual and psychological well-being. Young adults who are intellectually challenged in school are likely to develop intellectual and personal qualities that will allow them to land substantively complex jobs, and their initial strengths will be further enhanced by their daily work activities.

### The Work Environment

The work environment can be conceptualized as a stimulus to which a person is exposed for a long time. Thus, the work environment can have a cumulative effect on adult development. Simply as a context, work exerts a multifaceted influence on us. We review and judge one another within a particular setting and, to a surprising extent, the context determines who we see and consequently who we become. For example, Shinar (1978) found that men and women are judged in different ways on such qualities as leadership and interpersonal adjustment, depending on the perceived gender appropriateness or inappropriateness of their occupation. For instance, a woman construction worker is seen as working in a man's field. Depending on how her supervisor feels about a woman in construction, she may be evaluated accordingly—that is, based on the positive or negative prejudices of her supervisor.

Evaluation of the worker is affected not only by the worker's performance but also by who does the judging. Feedback from other people is a vital source of information from which workers learn their value. Growth and learning can take place when such feedback takes the form of constructive advice. But when peers, supervisors, or subordinates respond to prejudged attributes instead of to the worker's actual performance, the result for the worker is confusion and anger. Responses that bear little relationship to the content and quality of one's work engender a feeling of helplessness and despair, which, if allowed to continue unabated, can ultimately contribute to depression. Thus the influence of work pervades one's self-concept even below the level of consciousness.

Work involves values and attitudes. One can describe an *occupation* as a complex social role as well as a set of behaviors and skills; incorporated in it are attitudes—what society expects of a person in that role. Lawyers, physicians, and insurance salespeople have different social roles. Young men and women as graduate students in professional schools of law, business, social welfare, or medicine are learning customary attitudes and habits from their professors as well as the specific knowledge and technology of their profession.

The social climate varies from one workplace to another. The faculty members of most colleges and universities have informal, easy, and democratic relations among deans, department chairs, and teachers. This structure differs from, say, a hospital, where the physician has an authoritarian role in relation to other staff.

### Occupational Development

For a large number of people, getting a job is not enough—they must also move up the ladder. Promotion is usually seen as a measure of how well one is doing in one's career. How quickly occupational advancement occurs or does not occur may lead to such labels as "fast-tracker" or "dead-ender" (Kanter, 1976). President Bill Clinton is a "fast-tracker"—that is, someone who wants to advance quickly—as was Kennedy. Such people learn how long to stay in one level and how to seize opportunities as they occur. Others, however, are too afraid to take a risk and must deal with the frustration of remaining in the same job with no chance of promotion.

As Kail and Cavanaugh (1996) indicate, how a person advances in his or her career depends on professional socialization, which includes such factors as expectations, support from co-workers, priorities, and job satisfaction. To understand this further, let us look at the general scheme of occupational development.

*Super's theory*    Over the past four decades Super (1957, 1980) has developed a theory of occupational development based on self-concept. In Super's framework, people's occupations begin to evolve in response to changes in their self-concept. This developmental process reflects and explains important life changes and follows what he describes as implementation, establishment, maintenance, deceleration, and retirement. All people in the labor force fit into a continuum of vocational maturity through their working years; the more congruent their occupational behaviors are with what is expected of them at different stages, the more vocationally mature they are.

In adolescence, young people begin to specify what they wish to do. In adulthood, their career takes on the distinctive characteristics described by Super.

1. The *implementation stage* begins in late adolescence or the early 20s when people take on temporary jobs and learn firsthand about work roles and try out possible career choices.
2. The *establishment stage* begins with selecting a specific occupation during early adulthood. It continues as the person advances in the same occupation.
3. The *maintenance stage* is a transition phase during middle age as workers begin to reduce the amount of time they spend fulfilling work roles.
4. The *deceleration stage* begins when workers begin to plan in earnest for their

upcoming retirement and separate themselves from their work.
5. The *retirement stage* begins when people stop working full-time.

For young adults, as Levinson and his colleagues (1978) describe, forming a dream with one career becomes one of their chief tasks. As people progress through adulthood, they continue to refine and update their occupational expectations. At times they may make dramatic changes because of the economic environment or other important factors such as age, race or gender. Lack of opportunity can lead to obsolete skills and changing interests.

A *mentor* is part teacher, part sponsor, part model, and part counselor. The mentor helps young adults work through a new job without creating waves and provides valuable information about day-to-day activities in the workplace. The mentor also helps make sure that his or her protégé is noticed and receives credit for good work (Levinson et al., 1978).

## Women and Work

To this point, the schemes for work and life cycles have been drawn primarily from men. Most people have viewed men as the major breadwinners in the family, and men have dominated the labor force. But now it is time for us to look at women, since their role has changed substantially in recent years. Most women work outside the home; the percentage of married women with children under 6 who do so has skyrocketed from 12% in 1950 to 57% in recent years (Chadwick & Heaton, 1992). Women are working for more years as well as out of preference rather than pure necessity (Herring & Wilson-Sadberry, 1993). Also, women are entering a wide range of fields formerly dominated by men or even totally closed to women, such as coal mining, truck driving, and engineering.

Some things about women's work have not changed at all. For example, about 4 million women are employed as secretaries, with about 99% of all secretaries women (Waldman, 1985).

Many women work in clerical and service occupations, which are traditionally dominated by women and are low paying (Unger & Crawford, 1992). The gap between men and women's pay has narrowed but not closed: A woman made 66 cents for every dollar a man made in 1989 (Sorensen, 1991).

Women still face barriers to career achievements because of gender discrimination and conflicts between family and work. Gender-based discrimination takes many forms, such as the argument that the woman's job is *only* a secondary income; therefore, a woman often hears, "Its a small job, so don't bring home your problems." In the workplace, too, women are pressured to remain in their traditional roles—that is, to be "feminine" rather than display "masculine" behaviors that often lead to career advancement (Gutek, 1985; Unger & Crawford, 1992). Also, one out of two women face some degree of sexual harassment during their academic career or work life (Fitzgerald & Shullman, 1993). This can create anxiety, depression, and stress, which could lead to physical ailments that could hurt work performance (Gutek & Koss, 1993). Finally, there are no "old-girl" networks, while old-boy networks still help young men to make the right connections and rise to the top quickly.

A certain degree of role conflict causes women to feel pulled in different directions. Role conflict occurs when, for example, a woman faces competing demands in family roles versus work roles. A large number of modern women feel that they have to be "jugglers" (Crosby, 1991).

Because many different cultures in our world view women as the primary caretakers of the family, many working wives have to subordinate their career goals to family responsibilities. When a woman tries to do her very best at home, in her marriage, and in an uninterrupted career, she can become susceptible to work overload.

Melanie is an untenured assistant professor in a small rural college. She is married and has three children. Her husband, who comes from a long line of farmers, has reverted to farming in spite of his engineering degree. He wants to "feel the earth" and work on the farm. Melanie feels overloaded but carries on her different roles as efficiently as she can. She cooks, cleans, and works outside the home. Her schoolwork, which includes grading papers and preparing for classes, does not give her time for any type of writing or leisure activities. Her hope that some day things will slow down makes her a determined mother, wife, and professor.

Clearly, both women and men face developmentally crucial challenges through their work. Many areas of adult work demand further research, as in the case of women. You can see how adult identity depends a great deal on the workplace and related issues. Other aspects of adult development center on the patterns of home life: whether one is married or single, how one defines gender roles, effects of sexual identity, and so forth. In the next section, we shall take a close look at issues in the first stage of adulthood that relate to patterns of intimacy. In later sections, we shall look at adult problems and at parenting issues.

## PATTERNS OF INTIMACY

A large percentage of the population will at some point get married, but others will choose to remain single or to enter cohabitation. Still others will choose gay or lesbian partners. Here we shall explore the varied aspects of life at home.

Erikson indicates that the principal task as well as the goal of a young adult is the establishment of intimacy, as opposed to living alone. According to Rogers (1979), young women have a much easier task in establishing intimacy than their male counterparts.

### Women's Role

Research by Gilligan (1982), Dinnerstein (1977), Eichenbaum and Orbach (1983), Miller (1976), and others has established that women have the ability to create relationships. Psychological development starts at birth and occurs within the context of the relationship that the infant has with his or her caregiver. Thus, in the formation of women's psychology, the mother-daughter relationship is critical. Mothers and daughters share a gender identity and a social role, as well as social expectations. A woman brings up a daughter to be like herself, whereas she helps her son become a man: Mothers inevitably relate to their daughters and their sons differently. To a large extent, this difference is deliberate and is prescribed by common stereotyping; for instance, a son's sexual adventures are to be encouraged, whereas a daughter's sexual behavior is to be overtly restricted.

All mothers have been daughters, and nearly all have been brought up by mothers. Thus in most mothers' experience, there is the memory, buried or active, of the struggles they had with their own mothers in the process of becoming a woman—of learning to curb their activities as required and to direct their interests in particular ways (Eichenbaum & Orbach, 1983). Women's development, unlike men's, builds on a context of attachment and affiliation with others. Many women perceive the threat of disruption of affiliation not just as a loss of relationship but as something closer to a total loss of self. This type of structuring leads to depression in women when they lose a significant person.

Women throughout their lives are taught to be vehicles of the basic necessity of human communication. Men go a long way without recognizing it as a necessity, whereas women are groomed from a young age for this role they have to play.

Women also learn at a young age that they should place their faith in other human beings, in the context of being a social being related to other human beings. Women learn early in life that they must depend primarily on this faith. They cannot base their own individual development solely on achievement or power. An awareness of the female perspective enables people to appreciate the importance of both genders and their connectedness with each other. That is, both men and women need each other. We cannot survive as a human race without each other. Thus, one of the most important

things that happens in young adulthood is healthy sexual intimacy.

## Sexual Issues

*Sexuality and intimacy*   All adults, whether single, married, or divorced, are to some extent involved in sexuality and sexual intimacy in reality or fantasy, and some have to work on their own unresolved issues. Adolescent sexuality differs from adult sexuality in the sense that the former is often confusing, embarrassing, and overwhelming. Also, adults move away from merely physical sex to a sexuality that is part of an enduring, satisfying emotional bond. Among some older adults, relationships may involve an emotional bond without much physical expression of sexuality.

> Allen is a young adult who was involved during his early 20s in a long-term relationship that ended because of personality clashes. Now, four years after that separation, he has met a beautiful woman, and there is a strong attraction between them. As they develop their relationship, Allen mentions that he used to close his heart to women because he had been hurt. After reflecting on his earlier relationship, though, he realizes what he misses most is the emotional companionship and togetherness rather than sex. Allen explains to his new girlfriend what he wants from the relationship. He describes a satisfying, meaningful, emotional relationship as a piece of cake and the sexual aspect of the relationship as the icing on the cake. The icing in a relationship is good to have, he says, but it isn't much without the cake—a good mutual understanding and a strong emotional bond that hold a couple together.

McCary (1978) and Rawlins (1992) present several components of intimacy, including mutuality and choice. Two people usually choose each other because of mutual attraction. They exchange confidences, develop a sense of trust, and accept each other's vulnerabilities as part of sharing their lives.

An enduring bond helps couples build up their relationship firmly and deal with problems as they arise. When people fail to present themselves to each other because they fear rejection, their intimacy is blocked; such people deny their feelings, such as anger, and cover up their emotional needs. Certain courtship and dating patterns actually discourage intimacy because they block the honest exchange of feelings (McCary, 1978). For instance, in many dating situations, couples "put their best foot forward" because they have a plan for marriage or just want to be accepted.

> Derek dislikes "aggressive" women. He and Janine—a beautiful, timid young woman—have been dating for two years. One day as they're sitting down to a spaghetti dinner she's just made, she says she wants to get married. When Derek says he's not ready, Janine tries to convince him otherwise but cannot. She loses her temper and throws the entire bowl of spaghetti at him. Derek is shocked. Never in the two years they've been together has she shown such a temper. Afraid of assertive/aggressive women, Derek runs out of her house. Later he comments that even if he had married her, they would have divorced sooner or later because of her temper.

> At 23, Gail wants to get married because all her friends from high school are already married. She has dated several men, but nothing ever came of them. Now, though, she has finally met a man who can provide well for her. In her version of a common dating ritual, she tells him what he wants to hear and agrees with all his dreams for the future, even though in reality she knows that she'll never agree to some of the things he's planning. She compromises her values and desires verbally so that she can end up in front of the altar with him. Secretly she hopes to change him to her way of thinking because, as she tells herself, after marriage he'll have no choice but to listen to her—she'll make him miserable otherwise. But what Gail has forgotten in the process is that the permanency of the marriage cannot be assured if they enter into it without any meaningful discussions of their joint dreams and hopes.

Here is another example of "games" that interfere with intimacy.

> Mason is 27 years old, good looking, and poor. He has a short police record from doing drugs and stealing from an apartment. Finally, he lands a small, stable job. At work he meets a woman who is attractive, well-educated, well-to-do, and caring. Excited, he plans to marry her, and begins to use all the games he knows to lure her to him. He's willing to say and do anything to make her a part of his life. What Mason ignores is the fact that the relationship might not last long after marriage because the woman knows nothing of his earlier lifestyle or his likes and dislikes.

People often enter into the marriage contract on the basis of such games or without too much thought, which can lead to early divorce.

*Cultural differences*   Sexual behavior depends a great deal on culture. For instance, where there are arranged marriages, as in Orthodox Jewish culture or in the Far East, a couple may not know each other when they marry, but they participate in sex immediately after marriage because a legal bond has been created between them. This sudden intimacy would appear strange to a person in mainstream U.S. culture, where two people are expected to know each other well before marriage. But people become acclimated to what is acceptable in their own cultures and tend to accept available lifestyles without question.

One can say that people from the Far East who have arranged marriages get married and then fall in love, whereas in the United States people fall in love and then get married.

Among the Samoans in the 1920s, sex was more straightforward—when two people liked each other they participated in sexual activities. At the other end of the spectrum, the farmers and fishers who live on the island of Inis Beag in the North Atlantic receive very little sex education (Specht & Craig, 1987). Nudity is not tolerated, and intercourse is performed very quickly without the removal of clothing. There is little or no premarital sexual experience, and neither marital partner expects to derive much pleasure from sexual activity. Historically, men in this culture marry only after inheriting property, usually in their late 30s or 40s.

People in different cultures learn different sexual roles and are taught behaviors considered appropriate to those roles. In many cultures, men and women are expected to acquire distinctly different behavior patterns. U.S. culture shows a relatively broad acceptance of various lifestyles as well as sexual behaviors.

*Dimensions of human sexuality* Masters, Johnson, Kaplan, and Money are some of the professionals who have discussed the various dimensions of sexuality. Among them, Gochros (1977) clearly identifies five dimensions of human sexuality: sensuality, intimacy, reproduction, interpersonal influence, and sexual identity.

*Sensuality* in U.S. culture means the mental enjoyment that an individual experiences with the release of sexual tension. Often, sexual satisfaction is associated with a love relationship. When a person says, "I love you" in the beginning of a relationship, the statement implies passion and sensual feelings.

*Intimacy* is the interdependence and closeness of two people. People in U.S. culture experience psychological closeness with only a few people, such as a spouse or other person with whom they have a sexual relationship.

At 25, Andrew, through inheritance, has become economically self-sufficient. He dates several women because he claims that he's a sensuous person. He quickly realizes that the women like him for what he has, not for who he is. As time passes, he becomes more and more selective when dating. Eventually he begins living with a woman with whom he develops both a sensuous and an intimate relationship.

*Reproduction* is another dimension of sexuality. Bearing children remains important to many couples. Procreation carries with it not only responsibilities, but also the pleasures of seeing one's own child grow up. Historically, the desire for children has often been the main reason for sexual intercourse.

*Interpersonal influence* is the use of sexual activities for nonsexual purposes, such as gaining power and control over a partner. As Haley (1984) indicates, the power struggle between husband and wife is ever present. When young men engage in sexual activities to prove their adequacy, this exemplifies the use of sex for interpersonal influence. At the extreme, rapists use sexual attacks to express aggression, power, and control.

Rita, a fairly assertive woman from a traditional middle-class home, works for Frank; they fall in love. Frank is painfully aware that he comes from a family in a much lower socioeconomic class than Rita's. Even so, the two get married. Frank soon creates rules and regulations about when she can see her parents and when she can invite them to their home. He threatens to beat her if she doesn't follow his rules. She doesn't believe that he'll do such a "horrible" thing. To her surprise, when she "disobeys" him, he beats her black and blue. At a family counseling center, the couple learn to deal with Frank's feeling of inferiority about his family's status, his low self-esteem, and his need to control his wife.

*Sexual identity* is complex because it involves a person's biological gender, self-image, and sexual preference, or choice of love objects. Some people face a physiological or psychological ambiguity about gender. For instance, transsexuals have the anatomical features of one gender but clearly perceive themselves as belonging to the opposite sex. Similarly, hermaphrodites have physical characteristics that are neither entirely male nor entirely female.

Social work practitioners may see clients who appear to be clear about their gender identity but are confused about their sexual identity because of their attraction to a particular love object. For example, they may see themselves as "straight" (heterosexual), but find themselves attracted to people of their own gender. Does this make them homosexual? Bisexual? Or are they merely curious? Clearly, social workers can help such people sort out these and other issues concerning sexual identity.

Pamela falls in love with an extremely good-looking man who appears to care for her. But as time passes she finds that he does not get closer to her

violence

physically. All he appears to be interested in is her earlier sexual relationships with men. When she tries to confront him with his lack of physical interest in her, he teases and taunts her about being a "loose woman." Confused and emotionally upset almost beyond repair, Pamela begins to see a social worker. She is amazed to find out that her boyfriend sexually prefers men and that he entered a relationship with her in order to test himself out and find out whether he is also attracted to women. In the process, Pamela has been terribly hurt, having been made to feel that she is not attractive and does not have much to offer him.

*Intimacy*  Intimacy or the need for affiliation becomes clearer as a person grows older. Young adults take on many roles as friend, lover, and spouse. Each role requires some personal sacrifices, in terms of giving of oneself to others. As Erikson explains, the young adult must

"face the fear of ego loss in situations which call for self-abandon: in the solidarity of close affiliations . . . sexual unions, in close friendship and in physical combat, in experiences of inspiration by teachers and of intuition from the recesses of self. The avoidance of such experiences . . . may lead to a deep sense of isolation and consequent self-absorption. (Erikson, 1980, p. 171).

For a large number of adults marriage is the favored path to intimacy. Contemporary U.S. sanctions a period of living independently from one's parents before marriage (Goldscheider & Goldscheider, 1987). After a period of living by themselves in dormitories, in apartments shared with friends, young adults slowly begin to test their wings and create their own nest. Many young people either live together or get married, but others continue to live alone, and still others struggle to understand their own sexuality.

## Single Adults

Between the ages of 20 and 25, 75% of men and 60% of women are single. Most young people enjoy this time of life, because they do not have to be responsible for another person and are free to pursue their own education and careers. For women, being single during this period also means they may attend college or find a satisfying job more easily than young married women of the same age (Burns, 1992).

A small number of young people decide to remain single between ages 25 and 30 (Phillis & Stein, 1983). Why? The various reasons include sexual standards, the increased financial independence of women, liberation movements, and changes in views about marriage (Stein, 1978). When some single people indefinitely postpone the decision about getting married, they may slowly slip into singlehood; that is, they never marry.

Because such people spend a lifetime without a spouse, they may develop alternative social patterns based on friendships. Never-married women tend to be more career minded and may become highly involved with relatives—that is, caring for an aged parent, living with a sibling, or actively helping nieces and nephews—and have strong social networks. Loneliness is not a problem among these women (Essex & Nam, 1987; Rubinstein, 1987). Although there is very little statistical information about never-married men, they tend to do the same—become involved with nieces and nephews, have an occasional date, and create strong friendships with men as well as with women who may be older than them or who treat them as a brother.

Also, never-married adults tend to have more androgynous gender identities than most and have high achievement needs; they also are more autonomous and wish to maintain close relationships with others (Phillis & Stein, 1983). Usually they have successful careers and do not wish to take the *risk* of getting married. The most difficult problem they face is other people's, including parents' and other relatives' desire for them to marry. This pressure to get married is stronger for women than men, but both endure the most frequently asked question, "Haven't you found anyone yet?" Many single people feel left out when their friends get married. Though attitudes are changing in the United States, much of our culture remains highly couple oriented. Even so, a large number of never-married people report that they are happy in their lifestyles, and the satisfaction derived from careers and friendships is sufficient (Alwin, Converse, & Martin, 1985).

*Cohabitation*   Some single people do not wish to get married but are in committed relationships and decide to live with another person (cohabitate) and participate in a shared daily life. At times cohabitation may lead to marriage (Bumpass, Sweet, & Cherlin, 1991). Women who cohabitate are much more eager to marry their partners than are men. Without a strong emotional commitment, women may feel exploited (Macklin, 1988). Cohabitation, however, does not make for better marriages (Booth & Johnson, 1988): Cohabitating couples tend to be less religious, be less conventional, and come from lower socioeconomic backgrounds, which may put them at a higher risk for divorce (DeMaris & Rao, 1992). Further, because the couple have already lived together, marriage does not cause much change in the relationship, and such a couple lack the newly wedded bliss seen in those who have not cohabitated (Thompson & Colella, 1992).

## Gay and Lesbian Couples

What does it mean to be in a gay or lesbian relationship? Certainly it means facing resistance in society, such as homophobia. However, less is known about the developmental course of gay and lesbian relationships than heterosexual relationships, largely because research has not focused on them (Kail & Cavanaugh, 1996). Even so, in comparison with heterosexual couples, two important aspects of gay and lesbian relationships have been examined: sexual expression and interpersonal relations.

Regarding sexual expression, on average, gay men have sex with each other early in the relationship more often than any other type of couple, but the frequency decreases as the relationship continues (Blumstein & Schwartz, 1983). Lesbian women, on the other hand, are more likely to have an intense, intimate monogamous relationship than gay men and tend to have sex less often than any other group (Blumstein & Schwartz, 1983). Lesbian women tend to stay together longer more often than do gay men.

There are a large number of similarities between gay/lesbian couples and heterosexual couples. Financial problems and decisions, household chores, and power are issues for all couples. In terms of parenting, gay and lesbian parents do not differ substantially from heterosexual parents in terms of style (Harris & Turner, 1986). Like other couples, gay/lesbian couples must define the roles of nurturer and provider and decide whether the relationship will be sexually open (Blumstein & Schwartz, 1983). However, gay and lesbian couples are more egalitarian than heterosexual couples, with lesbian couples the most egalitarian (Peplau, 1991).

Gays and lesbians are now trying to achieve the same rights and status as married couples. The following section presents a relatively traditional account of marriage; however, most of the issues also apply to less traditional relationships as well.

## Marriage

For most young people, dating eventually raises the possibility of marriage. Intimacy often leads to sexual activity and commitment. At its best, sexuality has the qualities of intimacy, trust, and devotion. Before a person's identity has been established, a sexual union is usually dominated by physical urges. Intimacy involves the possibility of being hurt or being rejected by one's partner. Some men who struggle with their own identity will not chance this. They may have multiple relationships without commitment. Men fall in love more easily than women, being more satisfied with their own qualities and believing in romantic love, and fall out of love more quickly as well (Hill, Rubin, & Peplan, 1979). Women as a rule take more time, are more practical, and exercise more caution in choosing a partner.

However, not all cultures follow this pattern. In traditional Korean culture, parents arrange marriages for young men and women. After marriage, the son continues to live with his parents, with the wife becoming a part of the husband's household. Even after they have a child, the couple remain under the control of older adults in the family.

Marriage serves two purposes. First, in a traditional North American setting, it is a means to achieve certain individual or social needs. Marriage is entered by legal contract and ritualized by ceremony; it provides opportunity for progeny and independence from parents, as well as security. In North American culture, marriage typically signals that full adulthood has been legitimized with sexual monopoly and gratification and the opportunity for the couple to procreate.

Second, marriage serves as a terminal event. It is considered a *terminal* event because once people marry, they give up their status of being single forever. Even if divorce takes place, the singleness differs from the singleness faced before they were ever married. Dreyer (1975) says that a large number of young people see it as a long-lasting event whereby they affirm their personal identity, attain psychological intimacy, experience mutual pleasure, promote personal growth opportunities, and achieve transcendence and permanency. However, this promise does not always hold; when young adults marry for egocentric reasons and life does not fall into place, they instead experience disagreements, misunderstandings, and, in most cases, divorce.

In U.S. society, about 90% of adults choose to get married, and most of them marry for love. In some cultures, marriages are not formed on the basis of love but are arranged by leaders of kin groups who are concerned with acquiring property and allies. As Nydegger (1986) says, "These matters are too important to be left to youngsters" (p. 111). Thus there are different ways of establishing a family.

Getting married is an important life transition; it involves taking on a new role as a husband or wife and adjusting to life as a couple. Usually weddings are witnessed as a celebration where the union of two people takes place; the new couple often appear supremely happy. Yet even in planning a marriage, each partner may struggle to achieve or maintain autonomy and yet make the compromises necessary to adapt to each other's personalities and preferences.

*After the honeymoon*    What happens after the marriage? Huston and his colleagues found that the honeymoon is short (Huston, McHale, & Crouter, 1986; Huston & Vangelisti, 1991). In a longitudinal study of 100 newly wedded couples, the researchers found that several aspects of the marriage deteriorated from 3 months to 15 months after the marriage ceremony. For instance, couples were less satisfied with their marriage and their sex lives, they said "I love you" less frequently, and they complimented and disclosed their feelings to each other less frequently. They spent more time getting tasks done and less time talking with each other or doing fun things. The couples whose relationships degenerated the most severely were those who had engaged in a great deal of criticism and other negative ways of communicating.

On the positive side, Huston and his colleagues found that more couples were far more satisfied than dissatisfied with their relationships after the "honeymoon" was over. Even blissfully happy marriage relationships evolved into still happy but more ambivalent ones. Whether the couples began to see "warts" that they had not noticed before marriage or they simply started to take each other for granted, marital relationships no sooner began than they changed in systematic ways (Sigelman & Shaffer, 1995).

Like any other relationship, marriage has peaks and valleys. All marital satisfaction tends to be highest at the beginning of the marriage and may decrease until the children begin leaving home, then rise again in later life (Berry & Williams, 1987). For most couples, marital satisfaction improves after the children begin to leave (Rhyne, 1981). This upward shift is especially apparent in wives. It stems from increased financial security after the children leave, relief from the day-to-day responsibilities of parenting, and the additional time that spouses can spend with each other.

Flexibility and adaptability are important factors in a marriage. Couples who have been married for a relatively long time show an ability to roll with punches and adapt to changing situations in the relationship.

*Dual-earner marriages*    In recent years one of the greatest changes affecting U.S. families has been the increase in the number of married women in the workplace. The percentage of employed women rose from 30% in the 1960s to 58% in 1991. The percentage of working women with young children below three years of age was 33% in 1975 but rose to 57% in 1991 (U.S. Bureau of the Census, 1992). Instead of dropping out of the labor force when their children are born, a majority of the women stay in the labor force throughout the early years of parenthood (Piotrkowski, Rapoport, & Rapoport, 1987).

Working couples need to redefine traditional parental roles and the division of labor. Sometimes this takes place amicably but other times it poses a threat. The partners may not really be aware of each other's expectations until they are married. Not until the laundry has not been washed for a couple of weeks does it become evident that the couple should decide who should do the task or how it should be shared.

In some families, both partners are high-powered professionals. Thomas, Albrecht, and White (1984) claim that these couples find high levels of marital satisfaction when the husband supports the wife's career, when they have a satisfying social life, when the husband is empathetic to his wife's stress and vice versa, and when they have a good sexual relationship. Also when such couples discuss work-related problems, there is role complementarity and role sharing, and with it comes shared activities and companionship.

## Ethnic Considerations

Whereas most research in the past has focused on middle-class white populations, there is a new branch of research to identify the various ways other populations meet needs for intimacy, companionship, and caring. The review of this new research by Staples and Mirande (1980) is summarized here.

Research on African Americans has changed positively, reflecting a tendency to move away from the perspective of defining African-American families as deviant and pathological toward seeing them as variant forms (for example, in terms of extended-family units and "fictive kin") that may be culturally equivalent to modal white forms. Some of the critical findings are that the majority of adult African Americans are unmarried; the African-American divorce rate has increased in the past decade; and there has been a sharp increase in marriages between African-American men and white women, which also show a high rate of dissolution.

Research on the Latino family has stressed machismo as either a negative or positive factor in family life. However, the role of machismo has changed recently. In Latino families, marital roles seem to be predominantly egalitarian across educational levels, urban/rural residency, and region. Latino families are characterized by high fertility, and most children under 18 live with both parents in intact families; about 60% of Latino families are headed by a married couple. Relatively more families are intact and fewer people are divorced or widowed than in other ethnic groups.

Native Americans show great diversity in customs and languages. Unfortunately, they have generally been studied by white anthropologists who see them as cultural deviants posing a problem to society. Native Americans have high fertility rates. They have many children born out of wedlock. There are many female head-of-household families, unemployment is high, and extended families form the basic family unit.

Asian Americans constitute a relatively small percentage of U.S. population. Their cohort differences are marked because many of the oldest were immigrants in a previous historical era. Younger groups again include recent immigrants.

Usually, compared with other North Americans, they have more conservative sexual values, lower fertility rates, fewer illegitimate births, and more obligatory kinship customs. Asian Americans have found it more difficult to maintain the traditional "honorable" kinship status of elders, which is reflected in intergenerational tensions.

## PROBLEMS IN RELATIONSHIPS

Many problems can arise when adults strive for intimacy. Four issues that many young adults face are violence in relationships, sexual difficulties, divorce, and remarriage.

### Violence

Relationships are mostly viewed as being healthy and relatively positive. But there is an ugly side to some relationships that social workers see more and more. In U.S. society, you can see astonishing violence just by switching channels on TV. Date rape is not uncommon anymore. When relationships become violent, one person becomes aggressive towards the partner and creates an abusive relationship. Such relationships have received increased attention in the past few decades. As the U.S. criminal justice system believes, the abusive relationship can be seen as an explanation for antisocial or criminal behaviors (L. E. A. Walker, 1984).

It is difficult to measure family violence. It occurs in the privacy of a home, and the victims are often reluctant to report incidents because they fear reprisal. Family violence involves rape, robbery, and assault among individuals such as spouses, ex-spouses, domestic partners, and friends. According to the *National Crime Victimization Survey Data,* women/girls are more likely than men/boys to be victims of family violence (Zawitz et al., 1993). Of all the kinds of violence, family violence holds the greatest potential for injury. Compared with victims of strangers, victims of family violence are twice as likely to be injured (Bachman, 1994).

*Battering* There are many battered people, particularly battered women, in U.S. society. Strong and DeVault (1983) describe *battering* as a catchall term that includes slapping, punching, knocking down, choking, kicking, hitting with objects, threatening with weapons, stabbing, and shooting. The battered wife often stays because of lack of self-confidence, adherence to traditional beliefs, guilt, economic dependence, fear of the abuser, fear of isolation, fear for her children, and love.

Based on a decade of research on abusive partners, O'Leary (1993) argues that there is a continuum of aggressive behaviors: verbally aggressive behaviors, physically aggressive behaviors, severe physically aggressive behaviors, and murder. This progression implies it is crucial for an abused partner to recognize the problem as abuse and not as a passing phase because it could get worse. Abusive people need help—the sooner abuse is recognized, the better it would be for everyone concerned.

The reasons for abuse include the following: patriarchal society, that the abuser was abused as a child, the abuser's bad temper, and intergenerational patterns. As Pillari (1991) writes,

> So what has happened in these families is that the threads of behavior patterns from their own original family cultures have been woven into their present lives. The quality of life in these families is born out of their own recreation of what they have taken from their original family cultures without being aware of it. Among these people I observed a helplessness about changing their own destiny, for they do not know how to change. (p. xvi)

Whatever the reasons, it is time for intervention by social workers. It is *never too soon* to look out for such people before partners are physically or emotionally harmed.

Many communities have established shelters for battered women and their children. There are also programs to treat abusive men, including more police intervention (see Chapter 3). However, the legal system in many areas is not set up to deal with domestic violence. Women in some locations cannot even use restraining orders to protect themselves from additional abuse. A great deal needs to be done to protect women and children from the fear and reality of dangerous abuse.

*Rape and sexual assault*    Date rape has progressively come to the attention of public authorities and the media as young, horrified, courageous women have come forward to tell the story of their rape. Women are beginning to reject the reasons for date rape, which vary: the woman had on a sexy dress or she "led on" the man.

There are many kinds of rape. Rape is an intimate violation of a person' privacy and dignity. It is a crime of violence, *not* a sexual crime. In rape, intense emotions such as anger, hatred, and fear are acted out sexually, although society views rape as an act of sexual passion. The rapist uses verbal and physical force to control and subordinate the victim. In its legal definition, rape is a sexual assault where penile penetration of the vagina occurs without mutual consent.

Although most rapes reported to law enforcement officials are perpetrated by strangers, victimization studies show that women face the greatest risk of rape during their adolescence and early 20s. They are also at the greatest risk of being raped by people they may know casually. Income is not related to the risk of rape. Rape destroys victims' sense of self and confidence and traumatizes victims for a long time. Many rape crisis centers are now affiliated with social service agencies or health care organizations (Byington, Martin, DiNitto, & Maxwell, 1991).

The need for specialized treatment of victims has been recognized because of the work of rape centers. Burgess and Holmstrom (1974) pioneered some of the first research that identified the common problems faced by victims of rape and sexual assault, which they called *rape trauma syndrome.*

This syndrome is now considered a specific aspect of posttraumatic stress disorder. It involves individualized reactions, including shock and disbelief as an immediate response to the sexual

assault or rape followed by a period of superficial adjustment (Forman, 1980).

From about two weeks to several months, victims experience physical and emotional turmoil from trauma, then increased insomnia, an easy startle response, fear of crowds, and unexpected fits of crying and terror around any of the circumstances surrounding the rape.

Social workers are involved in all phases of working with rape victims; some practitioners work with perpetrators. Social workers associated with hospitals stay with the victims while the rape examination takes place. Some practitioners work in the criminal justice system to act as liaisons and advocate for their clients. Finally, they may work in avoidance and prevention programs to help women and men understand the scope of the problems that lead to rape and to develop individual and community solutions.

## Sexual Problems and Treatment

Couples who have sexual problems with either their spouses or their lovers need help. Various resources are available. Masters and Johnson (1985) found that about 75% of people seeking help with sexual problems are treated by professionals other than doctors. Social work practitioners also treat sexual dysfunctions. Some professional organizations offer continuing education in human sexuality, so that social work practitioners can better understand and deal with sexual functioning (Specht & Craig, 1987).

Most problems brought to sexual counselors involve heterosexual adults—married couples and single individuals who are concerned about either their own or their partner's sexual adequacy.

Kim and her husband enter therapy because Kim is very unhappy in her sex life. She feels that her husband just gets what he wants and goes to sleep. He really does not care whether he satisfies her needs. She has never had an orgasm. The therapist attempts to deal with her clients' psychological blocks and also explains the importance of foreplay for women in sex.

One of the chief complaints brought to social workers is that women experience less physical gratification than men do (Hite, 1976; Hunt, 1974; McCary, 1978). Female dissatisfaction may be related to differences in the physiological and psychological patterns of men and women, with men climaxing before their partners have had sufficient stimulation to reach orgasm. Fortunately there is a growing awareness of the importance of clitoral rather than vaginal orgasm in women and correspondingly less emphasis on simultaneous male and female orgasm (Gordon & Shankweiler, 1971).

Psychologically, women need to express tender emotion along with sexual intimacy, whereas men have been taught not to express these emotions. Because of these substantial differences in male and female needs, couples who improve their communication can usually adapt more successfully to each other's needs than those who do not.

After the publication of Masters and Johnson's *Human Sexual Inadequacy* (1970), there was tremendous optimism about and interest in short-term behavior techniques that were claimed to be effective in achieving erection, delaying ejaculation, and facilitating orgasm (Fischer & Gochros, 1975). However, Masters and Johnson's research has been criticized for being too methodical and for being flawed in failing to provide a sound theoretical base for sex therapists or to show cures for sexual dysfunction (Zilbergeld & Evans, 1980). The therapists' criticism highlights the fact that Masters and Johnson do not set behavioral criteria for defining successful treatment outcomes; they simply speak of having only a 20% failure rate. The extent of change achieved by the 80% is not discussed, and what the researchers regard as failure is also not discussed.

Zilbergeld and Evans (1980) also question how to measure success in treating a man's premature ejaculation when the criterion for success is the partner's subjective sense of satisfaction. Sex is such an intimate matter that when a partner's dissatisfaction stems from other than physiological causes, such as interpersonal conflicts and struggles for power, objective evaluation is not possible. What is needed is an integration of behavioral management with insights into relationships provided by psychodynamic theories. Symptoms may thus be relieved by short-term methods when the client is supplied with proper information and counseling. However, in most cases, the social worker must deal with the client's total pattern of relationships in order to be helpful.

## Divorce

When people marry, they hope that the relationship will last for a long time. Unfortunately, fewer and fewer couples experience this permanence. Rather than growing together, couples grow apart. Further, the marital relationship is often evaluated differently by each partner. One cannot speak of a happy or an unhappy marriage but only of how happy or unhappy each partner is.

> Married for 15 years, Sam and Cynthia belong to a lower socioeconomic level. Cynthia has depended on her husband since she was 17. At first her husband viewed their relationship as "fun." It pleased him to have someone depend on him when he was 25. As time passed, he got tired of having a completely dependent wife, and when he demanded that she do things by herself, he would be met with a burst of tears. She interpreted Sam's unexpected demands as a sign that he no longer loved her. Eventually the situation got more complicated. Now Sam wants to get out of the marriage. With counseling and the help of the extended family network, the marriage is dissolved.
>
> From the point of view of a social worker, Cynthia and Sam clearly view their marriage differently, and in divorce they also experience different pain. Reluctant as first, Cynthia goes along with the divorce proceedings, but in the process she begins to find her own strengths.

The same principle applies to separation as well as divorce: A marital disruption is seldom symmetrical in its effect on the partners.

Drew and Tanya have been married for 11 years. In a relatively traditional marriage, Tanya at first stayed home and took care of the babies. But now that the children are older and less dependent physically, she has found herself a job. At first her husband is happy with the extra money, but as she starts to climb the career ladder he becomes envious and insecure. Their bickering starts in the morning and does not end even at bedtime. Eventually they get a divorce.

Drew cannot believe that Tanya has left him. He has been completely dependent on her for doing housework. With divorce has come the revelation that he must learn to do housework on his own. Though painful, this marks the beginning of his becoming a whole person.

Compared with that of other countries, divorce in the United States is common; couples have about a 50–50 chance of remaining married for life (Fisher, 1987). However, divorce rates in Canada, Great Britain, Australia, and Sweden are about one in three, and only one in ten in Japan, Italy, Israel, and Spain (U.S. Bureau of the Census, 1992). Other statistics throughout the world show that if marriages fail, they do so on average within 3 or 4 years (Fisher, 1987).

*Causes*   Divorce is not simple. Its social implications include disrupting the lives of the couple and any children they may have brought into the world. Those involved may temporarily feel anger and loss. Divorce may not necessarily reflect maladjustment in the marriage, however. Sometimes it is brought about by a crisis such as the injury or death of a child; in a state of depression the partners start to blame each other, and before long the marriage is dissolved (Wallerstein & Kelly, 1980).

Aaron is an only son. When he is 15, he goes fishing with his friends in spite of the family rule that he can't go to the river that time of the year. While out of town on business, Aaron's father receives a call saying that his son has drowned. The father cannot forgive his wife; he sees her as the cause of their son's death. He blames her because the son did not obey the family rule, and, in the father's

perspective, it was his wife's duty to make sure that the rules were followed. She, in turn, blames him for failing as a parental figure because he was never available to them. She also blames his constant absence from home. Their son's death has caused their marital problems to surface. Their anger and depression and the tremendous blame each levels against the other ends their long marriage in divorce.

In 1948, divorced women cited excessive drinking and nonsupport as the most common reasons for divorce (Goode, 1956). By 1985, the reasons had shifted to communication problems, unhappiness, and incompatibility (Cleek & Pearon, 1985). Infidelity and other sexual problems also often contribute to marital breakup.

*Effects*   Divorce might come as a welcome relief in a conflicted, intolerable marriage. However, many studies reveal that divorced people are the unhappiest in U.S. society. Though changes in attitudes toward divorce have eased the social trauma associated with it, divorce takes a high toll on a couple's psyches. A national study shows that divorce can impair an individual's well-being for at least five years after the event and produce a greater variety of lasting negative effects than even the death of a spouse (Nock, 1981). One longitudinal study of divorced people showed them as more depressed than when they were married (Menaghan & Lieberman, 1986). Also, a large number of people underestimated the pain the divorce would cause (Wallerstein & Kelly, 1980). In some cases, even ten years after a divorce, many people still reported feeling angry, lonely, disappointed, abandoned, and betrayed (Wallerstein & Blakeslee, 1989).

Divorce also affects parents' relationships with their children, especially when custody battles develop. Usually about 90% of the time, the mother receives custody of the child and the father becomes an occasional parent. For many mothers, the price of custody is very high in terms of the stress of caretaking. On average, divorced mothers face a 70% decline in their standard of living within the first year following divorce, while typically ex-husbands enjoy a 40% rise (Weitzman, 1985). Child care is expensive, and most divorced fathers contribute less than before the separation. However, divorced fathers pay a psychological price (Furstenberg & Nord, 1985). Though perhaps many would like to remain active in their children's lives, few actually do.

## Problems in Remarriage

A large majority of divorced people appear to believe in the one-man–one-woman relationship and tend to marry again within a few months or a few years (Glick & Norton, 1977). There is some evidence that remarried couples have their share of sexual problems and adjustments. The reemergence of marital problems in the second marriage is often due to each individual's belief that the problem is in the other partner and the consequent refusal to search themselves to find their part in it. In the absence of attempts at self-understanding, problems are apt to arise in new relationships as well. After a divorce, a person usually needs to remain single to understand his or her own issues and personality and to develop emotional distance from the earlier relationship.

> Brenda is a 30-year-old woman who married at 18 and divorced at 22. She has taken charge of her life, studied, and found an extremely well paying job. She has met some good men in social situations and workplaces, but she views them strictly as people with whom she can have pleasure. She doesn't want to get married. Though she's had two gratifying relationships, she has made a decision that she isn't ready for marriage at this point in her life.

Nearly 80% of divorced people remarry within the first three years (Glick & Lin, 1986). However, differences exist among various ethnic groups. Usually African Americans remarry a bit more slowly than European Americans, and Latinos remarry more slowly than either of these (Coleman & Ganong, 1990).

Eloise is a 30-year-old woman who has remarried after having been divorced for three years. She has three sons, and as a single parent she has been more lenient than before in raising her children. The oldest, Jonathan, who is 12, stays out late, but Eloise does not question his behavior. He also helps the most in household chores and feels responsible for his younger brothers as well as his mother.

Eloise's new husband, Terence, is the custodial parent of two sons, Justin and Philip, ages 12 and 10. He is a loving father but strict. The boys have rules to follow and cannot leave the house at will. For almost everything they do, the boys need permission.

Now, soon after the marriage, the children face many adjustment problems. Although both parents have 12-year-old sons, Eloise's son Jonathan is more adultlike and willing to take responsibilities but also wants more freedom, whereas Justin is more like a young child. This situation leads to conflicts between Eloise and Terence, as well as between the stepbrothers. Therefore each parent must reflect, compromise, and create new, joint rules and regulations for behavior.

Adapting to new relationships in remarriage differs for men and women (Hobart, 1988). For remarried men, the primary relationship is with their new wife while other relationships, such as those with children from the first marriage, take a back seat. But for remarried women, a new husband is relatively marginal, compared with the relationships with the children from the first marriage.

Remarried men and women both report that they experience the second marriage differently from their first. They claim that they enjoy much better communication, resolve disagreements with more understanding and goodwill, arrive at decisions more equitably, and divide chores more fairly (Furstenberg, 1982). In some cases, though, the remarriage does not work well at all. Second marriages have a 25% higher risk of dissolution than first marriages, and the divorce rate for remarriages involving stepchildren is about three times higher than the rate for first marriages (Glenn, 1991).

## PARENTHOOD

One element of parenting is that it is cyclical. First, an individual leaves her or his household—that is, her or his own family of origin (the family of orientation)—to establish an independent household. This step is usually followed by marriage, the second stage—a relationship with a new individual, developing a new family network. The third stage is the birth of the first child and the beginning of parenting (the family of procreation). There are many milestones in marriage, including the birth of the first child, the cost of raising a child, the departure of the last child from the family of origin, and the death of a spouse.

One can classify as *dysfunctional* those families who face constant conflict and problems. Those who have minimal problems are termed *functional* families. All families have structures, from an extended-family structure to a nuclear-family structure.

During the past 50 years, the family life cycle has varied. Not only do people live longer but the age level at which they first marry has risen drastically. There is also an increase in the number of women who wish to have their children after the age of 35 (Specht & Craig, 1987).

### The Tasks of Parenting

*Handling crisis*  All families experience what are called normal family crises. A *crisis* can be described as a turning point or point of no return, such as marriage or an adult child's leaving home. If handled meaningfully, a crisis can help people mature or develop. If not handled well, conflicts can cause problems in the family situation; this in turn could lead to more serious problems and weaker relationships or a state of weaker mental health among different family members (Okun & Rappaport, 1980).

Becoming a parent produces many normal crises. For instance, the initial adjustment to par-

enthood is sometimes difficult. Previous lifestyle and routines may be disrupted, and both parents may find their freedom curtailed. After the birth of a child, parents have to learn different ways of behavior that help them to adjust.

At 4 months old, Ashley sleeps most of the day, but at nightfall she is up and crying for attention. Her parents are usually very tired and do not wish to stay awake. If they attempt to ignore Ashley, she starts to cry and will not stop until they pick her up. So with great difficulty the parents reach a decision and a compromise. On workdays, when the father must leave early and return late, the mother gets up at night to take care of the child's needs. But during the weekends, the father attends to the child. Thus the parents' earlier behavior patterns have been changed to suit the child, and with that change their lifestyle of partying and going out at night has changed considerably.

*Four stages of parenthood*  Rossi (1968) has divided parenthood into four stages:

1. *The anticipatory period:* Pregnancy leads the expectant parents to new roles. Couples face both domestic and external social adjustments as they prepare to become a family. Getting the home ready for a new baby involves obtaining necessities such as furniture, clothes, baby food, and diapers. Socially, the couple are no longer just husband and wife; their roles expand to include those of father and mother.
2. *The honeymoon period:* Parent-child attachment is formed. Although when the baby is new the parents are constantly fatigued, they also derive pleasure from their new roles as parents.
3. *The plateau period:* Parents assume the roles of father and mother and learn to deal with family and community problems. Parenting includes socialization of the child and future family planning.
4. *Termination:* This final stage is usually reached when the last child leaves home to get a job, attend college, or get married.

Termination can happen prematurely when a child leaves because of a custody settlement.

Some parents cope with parenting very well. Others cannot deal with one particular aspect of parenting, such as taking care of the newborn, but are perfectly capable of taking care of preschool and school-age children. When parents have difficulty, they often find it helpful to include other people in the parenting of the child, with responsibilities shared among extended families, support systems, and nursery and play groups.

## Family Shapes

A common form of family in North America is the nuclear family, consisting of a husband, a wife, and their children. Depending on the structure of the family, the rules, regulations, and ways of behavior vary. Minuchin and Fishman (1981) classify families into groups by "shape," some of which are described as follows.

The *pas de deux family* has only two household members. They can be either a couple or a parent and a single child. In some cases this child is an adult. The two-person structure has the possibility of a lichenlike formation, in which the individuals become symbiotically dependent on each other. In such homes, individuals may be overly involved with each other.

*Three-generation families* are more typical of lower socioeconomic groups. In such multigenerational families, where there are grandparents, parents, and children, the question often arises: Who is parenting which child?

In so-called *accordion families*, one spouse leaves and enters the family as career dictates. For instance, in Navy families, one spouse takes on additional responsibilities as the nurturer, executive, and guide of children when the other spouse is not living at home.

In *fluctuating families*, the family moves from place to place; the ability of members to belong to a particular place or identify a place as home is diminished. Similarly, in such families, an adult may move from one relationship to another, viewing no one relationship as meaningful.

From a systems perspective, the concept of family shape has some usefulness in understanding the structure and the responsibilities families share.

## Single Parents

The number of single parents has increased dramatically during the past few years. The causes vary: high divorce rates, the decision to keep children born out of wedlock, teenage pregnancies, and the desire of many single adults to have or adopt children.

A large number of divorced couples report feelings of frustration, failure, guilt, and ambivalence about the parent-child relationship (Van Hoose & Worth, 1982). Frustration arises over the lack of companionship and the loss of friendship with other couples. It dawns on single parents that they each have to play father and mother to the children. Irrespective of gender, single parents face considerable obstacles. Financially they are usually much less well off than couples, except for the well-to-do career woman who wishes to have a baby without a partner. Integrating work and parenthood are difficult unless one has a great deal of money.

Partially because of a rising rate of out-of-wedlock births, researchers project that about half of all children born in the 1980s will spend some time in a single-parent family (Castro-Martin & Bumpass, 1989). In the 1960s only 9% of children lived with one parent, who was usually widowed; today, 24% live with a single parent, usually never-married or divorced once (Demo, 1992). Father-headed single homes have increased so that now fathers head 15% of all single-parent families (Meyer & Garasky, 1993). The problems that single mothers and fathers face differ. Financially, single mothers are hit the hardest.

*Mother-headed families* Another important factor for single-parent families is that half of those headed by a woman rely on welfare payments at least as a temporary source of income. Further, poverty affects single-parent families more often than two-parent families. The differences in the average income levels of single-parent, mother-headed families and two-parent families is devastating. About 34% of mother-headed families are in poverty compared with 8% for two-parent families (U.S. Bureau of the Census, 1992). The situation has continued to worsen for African Americans and Latinos. In 1991, about 67% of the African-American mother-headed families and 70% of Latino-headed families were living in poverty.

White mothers who live in poverty are most likely to have been married. Their single status is due to divorce, separation, or death of spouse. In the case of African-American women, about 64% of births were from unmarried mothers, versus 19% of all white births in 1989 (U.S. Bureau of Census, 1992, p. 69).

Women have traditionally taken care of children. Without additional help, poverty coupled with crime appears to be a way of life for certain families. Moreover, women's jobs usually provide little opportunity for advancement.

*Adjustments*    All families have in common the need to establish an income, maintain a household, develop social and economic relationships in the neighborhood and at work, and relate to children in a way that makes them productive members of society. The difference between an intact family and a single-parent family is seen in the types of relationships that are maintained in the family, both between parent and child and between spouses. Whatever caused the couple to break up has its own impact on the rest of the family. The length of separation, age of the child at the onset of separation, socioeconomic status, and birth order of children are also important factors (Hetherington, 1972).

Although intact families are similar in their performance of functions, the likelihood of diminished functioning in the single-parent family is increased by the added stress of modifying the family structure.

Debra is a single parent living in the inner city of New York. Debra came from Atlanta with her parents when she was 15 years old but was married by the time she was 17 and divorced by 20. She has one son, 8-year-old Lee. Her background is middle class. Single parenthood and economic responsibilities have reduced her status to a lower-income bracket, and she finds herself constantly overloaded with the task of being two parents to her child as well as holding on to her jobs as a cleaning woman, a part-time employee at a grocery store, and a part-time waiter. At times, when she comes home tired, she would love to slip into a hot tub, but her active 8-year-old boy makes it all but impossible. Debra finds that she must spend time with Lee. She realizes that her life revolves around her child, and she really does not have much of a support system. Her social life is practically nil. But she has decided that when Lee grows up, she'll have time for herself, so for the time being she can overlook some of her own needs.

For young adults, parenting poses many challenges, especially in these changing times. Now let us look at how social workers can help young parents as well as other adults cope with issues particular to this phase of the life span.

## IMPLICATIONS FOR PRACTICE

Most young people do what society expects of them, and their self-assessments frequently depend on how well they perform their assigned roles. The role expectations of young adulthood are primarily those of marriage, parenting, occupation, and social value. These roles give people both inner assuredness and recognition from others who count in their lives.

All these expectations are part of the developmental tasks that a young person faces. These may also include selecting a mate, getting married or living together, choosing a career that stabilizes them, and starting a family. Young adulthood dawns quickly. In this crucial period, people begin to see the paths they wish to take in life. Many clear-headed young people know where they wish to go in life, but others are lost, dissatisfied, and in need of help. Such people could use the services of a social worker. When social workers meet a young adult, they should be aware of the issues of this age group. Further, they need to remember that role transitions are more difficult for young adults than others.

U.S. society provides an idealized family model that emphasizes romance in marriage and fairly inflexible distinctions between caretaker and provider roles with regard to parenting and child rearing, all of which emphasize the marital partnership. For many young people, disenchantment and new identity conflicts arise when life goals are not shared. For some people, caring is associated with mutuality of regard and allowing for growth and change in the partnership arrangement (Ganter & Yeakel, 1980).

Young heterosexual couples may need the help of a social worker to resolve initial adjustment problems when they are newly married; they may need help in dealing with two sets of parents—natural parents as well as in-laws—and in acquiring skills for handling the home situation when a child is born. Living together brings its own set of problems for a new couple; the social worker needs to help members understand their family background and their own expectations of themselves and each other.

Homosexual couples, too, present themselves for therapy. Social workers need to understand this lifestyle from an emotional aspect as well as a sociological one, so they can offer the best kind of therapeutic help. Further, some homosexual couples, as well as single people, want to adopt children. The social worker needs to understand individuals' hopes and aspirations, as well as their capacities, in order to help them formulate realistic yet exciting goals for themselves.

Violence in relationships is an ugly reality that social workers should know how to handle. This includes making referrals and knowing all the hot lines available. Other strategies that social workers can use to help include offering support, reviewing alternatives, furnishing information, and advocating. A social worker also needs to keep in mind the special counseling needs of vic-tims, who experience powerlessness, limited behavioral and emotional options, anger, inadequate communication, and failure to nurture themselves.

Social services for rape and sexual assault victims may be short- or long-term. Short-term services include concrete services, supportive counseling, notifying family members, victim-assistance, and advocacy for victims. Long-term services may include individual or group psychotherapy to deal with lingering trauma, ongoing problems, and familial or spousal/romantic relationships affected by the rape. Social workers need to offer clients a great deal of reassurance that they did not precipitate the rape regardless of any errors in judgment they might have made (Byington, 1996).

Divorce brings a whole bag of problems for couples with children. Finances, visitation rights, and custody arrangements affect both adults and children. Social workers need to work with the concerned adults as well as pay special attention to children, who mourn the loss of the noncustodial parent, as well as the loss of family with two parents.

Remarriage involves two adults adjusting to each other and, as often happens, to each other's children. Creating new family rules, the husband and wife have to accommodate and compromise to "fit" all their children into the new stepfamily.

Single parents have the difficult double role of playing mother and father to their children. In addition, they may have financial problems and lack of time for themselves, work overload, and so forth. Services for children and for single parents should be made available by the social worker. The social worker also needs to remember that single parents have differing needs. Accordingly, the worker has to be sensitive, caring, and willing to look at their issues creatively.

Some people can accept their limitations as well as their strengths more easily than others. Counselors should help clients make the transition from an adolescent peer culture to the demands of work and an adult lifestyle. For a large number of young people, the issues of establishing autonomy and intimacy are not resolved during adolescence; they continue throughout the young-adult years. Social workers need to be aware of such unresolved conflicts.

Besides emotional situations, social workers are often presented with problems such as lack of a job or a poor economic situation. People who often have difficulties finding jobs include people of color, women, unskilled workers, and the disabled. Their situations have a psychological as well as an economic effect; such situations influence their aspirations and perceptions of what they can achieve.

## CHAPTER SUMMARY

- Human behavior and development take a new turn in adulthood. In adults, growth no longer stems from physical development and the rapid acquisition of cognitive skills. Adult growth is defined to a large extent by social and cultural milestones, as young individuals terminate their dependent relationships with parents and assume responsibility for themselves and others.

- Cognitively, adults continue to develop formal operational thought and beyond.

- Erikson's sixth psychosocial crisis is intimacy versus isolation. According to Erikson, to develop successfully, adults have to maintain their identities in order to develop close, intimate, heterosexual relationships that lead to procreation. The alternative and negative outcome for this period is self-absorption and isolation.

- Studies of adult women suggest that they develop identity uniquely. Traditionally, men have defined themselves in terms of separation and autonomy, whereas women seem to achieve identity through relationships and attachment.

- All people who reach adulthood face developmental tasks, which include selecting and preparing for an initial occupation and achieving socially responsible behavior.

- Work is an important part of an adult's life. It exerts a multifaceted influence on people, including effects on values and attitudes. Most adults feel that work is a major aspect of their identity.

- Some women view their careers in the same way men do, whereas others define themselves primarily in terms of familial roles. The proportion of women to men in the labor force has increased dramatically.

- Preparation for work includes both formal and informal training.

- Early socialization, as well as cognitive and emotional development through the early years, sets the stage for later career choices. Career choice is a serious decision for young adults, some of whom may need assistance in developing effective strategies for making choices.

- Being successful in work depends on one's socialization, one's ability to adapt to new challenges, and the relationship between one's skills and the demands of the labor market.

- Young people in the labor force have different needs. Some get caught in making a marginal livelihood. Others find work that gives them personal fulfillment.

- Super's theory of occupation shows how self-concept and adaptation to an occupational role contribute to a continuum of vocational maturity through the working years.

- About 57% of women work in the 1990s. Women still face barriers to career achievements because of gender discrimination and conflicts between family and work.

- Women's traditional role in the family has been based on creating and maintaining relationships.

- Sexuality and intimacy are important aspects of a young adult's life. Sexual behavior and roles in relationships vary in different cultures.

- Sensuality, intimacy, reproduction, interpersonal influence, and sexual identity are aspects of human sexuality.

- Couples who have sexual problems with their spouses or lovers can receive help from professionals.
- Some people choose to remain single all their lives.
- Cohabitation without marriage is in many ways a maturing experience, although there are problems associated with it.
- Gay and lesbian couples have problems similar to heterosexual couples, although they have more egalitarian relationships.
- For young people, dating often leads to marriage. During recent years, one of the greatest changes in the United States is the increase of dual-earner couples.
- Family violence holds the greatest potential for injury of all kinds of violence, and with family members twice as likely to be injured.
- Rape and sexual assault are receiving more attention; many social services are available for victims.
- The high rate of divorce in the United States could be, in part, the result of the increase in the number of women in the labor force and the increased acceptance of the view that unhappy marriages are to be terminated.
- Divorce entails a painful period of adjustment, even for the spouse who initiates it.
- Divorced people normally remarry after two to three years.
- Parenting confers a new social status on young adults. It also makes unexpected demands on them. One can divide parenthood into four stages: the anticipatory period, the honeymoon period, the plateau period, and termination.
- Besides the nuclear family, Minuchin and Fishman have developed structures for familial groups: pas de deux families, three-generation families, accordion families, and fluctuating families.
- The rise in single-parent households is due partly to increased rates of divorce, unmarried mothers who have unplanned children, and the desire of single women to have children.

- A large number of single parents have economic problems and so need economic as well as social supports.
- Social workers need to deal with the main issues of young adulthood: intimacy, marriage, career, and parenthood.

## SUGGESTED READING

Bullis, R. K. and Harrigan, M. P. (1992). Religious denominational policies on sexuality. *Families in Society, 73*(5), 304–312.

Lavee, Y. (1991). Western and non-Western human sexuality: Implications for clinical practice. *Journal of Sex and Marital Therapy, 17*(3), 203–213.

Lundberg, U. (1996). Influence of paid and unpaid work on psychophysiological stress responses of men and women. *Journal of Occupational Health Psychology, 1*(2), 117–130.

Lynn, S. A., Cao, L. T,. and Horn, B. C. (1996). The influence of career stage on the work attitudes of male and female accounting professionals. *Journal of Organizational Behavior, 17*(2), 135–149.

Shernoff, M. (1988). Integrating safer sex counseling into social work practice. *Social Casework, 69*(6), 334–339.

Todres, R. (1990). Effectiveness of counseling in the transmission of family planning and sexuality knowledge. *Journal of Sex Education and Therapy, 16*(4), 279–285.

## SUGGESTED VIDEOTAPES

Boulder County Rape Crisis Team (Producer). (1989). *From victim to survivor* (29 minutes). Available from Filmmakers Library, 124 E. 40th St., Suite 901, New York, NY 10016; 212-808-4980

Conn, D. (Producer). (1996). *After a suicide* (12 minutes). Available from Filmmakers Library, 124 E. 40th St., Suite 901, New York, NY 10016; 212-808-4980

Holland, J. (Producer). (1994). *Abused women: Survivor therapy approach with Dr. Lenore Walker* (59 minutes). Available from FFH (Films for the Humanities and Sciences), 11 Perrine Rd., Monmouth Junction, NJ 08852; 800-257-5126

Jeremiah Films (Producer). (1991). *AIDS: No second chance* (27 minutes). Available from EVN (Educational Video Network), 1401 19th St., Huntsville, TX 77340; 800-762-0060

JVD Productions (Producer). (1996). *Paving the way* (52 minutes; video about women in the workplace). Available from Filmmakers Library, 124 E. 40th St., Suite 901, New York, NY 10016; 212-808-4980

*Solving black inner-city poverty: William Julius Wilson* (29 minutes). (1994). Available from FFH (Films for the Humanities and Sciences), 11 Perrine Rd., Monmouth Junction, NJ 08852; 800-257-5126

Zanum, N. (Producer). (1995). *Beyond black and white* (28 minutes). Available from Film Ideas, Inc., 3710 Commerce Ave., Suite 13, Northbrook, IL 60062; 800-475-3456

## REFERENCES

Alwin, D. E., Converse, P. E., & Martin, S. S. (1985). Living arrangements and social integration. *Journal of Marriage and the Family, 47,* 319–334.

Arlin, P. K. (1980, June). *Adolescent and adult thought: A search for structures.* Paper presented at meeting of the Piaget Society, Philadelphia.

Bachman, R. (1994). *Violence against women* (NCJ 145325). Washington, DC: U.S. Government Printing Office.

Baruch, G., Barnett, R., & Rivers, C. (1983). *Lifeprints.* New York: McGraw-Hill.

Berry, R. E., & Williams, F. L. (1987). Assessing the relationship between quality of life and marital income satisfaction: A path analytical approach. *Journal of Marriage and the Family, 49,* 107–116.

Bloom, A. H. (1986). Psychological ingredients of high moral thinking: A critique of the Kolhberg-Gilligan paradigm. *Journal for the Theory of Social Behavior, 16*(1), 89–103.

Blumstein, P., & Schwartz, P. (1983). *American couples.* New York: Morrow.

Booth, A., & Johnson, E. (1988). Premarital cohabitation and marital success. *Journal of Family Issues, 9,* 387–394.

Brooks, L. (1991). Recent developments in theory-building. In D. Brown, L. Brooks, & Associates (Eds.), *Career choice and development: Applying contemporary theories to practice* (2nd ed.). San Francisco: Jossey-Bass.

Brown, B. B., Mounts, N., Lamborn, S. D., & Steinberg, L. (1993). Parenting practice and group affiliation in adolescence. *Child Development, 64,* 467–482.

Bumpass, L. L., Sweet, J. A., & Cherlin, A. (1991). The role of cohabitation in declining rates of marriage. *Journal of Marriage and the Family, 53,* 913–927.

Burgess, A. W., & Holmstrom, L. L. (1974). Rape trauma syndrome. *American Journal of Psychiatry, 113,* 981–986.

Burns, A. (1992). Mother-headed families: An international perspective and the case of Australia. *Society for Research in Child Development: Social Policy Report, 6,* 1–22.

Byington, D. B. (1996). Sexual assault. In *Encyclopedia of social work,* (19th ed., Vol. 3, pp. 2136–2141). Washington, DC: NASW Press.

Byington, D. B., Martin, P. Y., DiNitto, D. M., & Maxwell, M. S. (1991). Organizational affiliation and effectiveness: The case of rape crisis centers. *Administration in Social Work, 15*(3), 83–103.

Castro-Martin, T., & Bumpass, L. L. (1989). Recent trends in marital disruption. *Demography, 26,* 37–51.

Cattell, R. B. (1971). *Abilities: Their structure, growth and action.* Boston: Houghton Mifflin.

Cavanaugh, J. C., Kramer, D. A., Sinnott, J. D., Camp, C. J., & Markley, R. J. (1985). On missing links and such: Interfaces between cognitive research and everyday problem solving. *Human Development, 28,* 146–168.

Chadwick, B. A., & Heaton, T. B. (1992). *Statistical handbook on the American family.* Phoenix: Onyx Press.

Chodorow, N. (1978). *The reproduction of mothering.* Berkeley: University of California Press.

Clausen, J. A., & Gilens, M. (1990). Personality and labor force participation across the life course: A longitudinal study of women's careers. *Sociological Forum, 5,* 595–618.

Cleek, M. B., & Pearon, T. A. (1985). Perceived causes of divorce: An analysis of interrelationships. *Journal of Marriage and the Family, 47,* 179–191.

Coleman, M., & Ganong, L. H. (1990). Remarriage and stepfamily research in the 1980s: Increased interest in an old family form. *Journal of Marriage and the Family, 52,* 925–940.

Commons, M. L., Sinnott, J. D., Richards, F. A., & Armon, C. (Eds.). (1993). *Adult development: Vol. 1. Comparisons and applications of adolescent and adult developmental models.* New York: Praeger.

Crosby, F. J. (1991). *Juggling: The unexpected advantages of balancing career and home for women and their families.* New York: Free Press.

Crouter, A. C., & McHale, S. M. (1993). The long arm of the job: Influence of parental work on childrearing. In T. Luster & L. Okagaki (Eds.), *Parenting: An ecological perspective*. Hillsdale, NJ: Erlbaum.

Demaris, A., & Rao, K. V. (1992). Premarital cohabitation and subsequent marital stability in the United States: A reassessment. *Journal of Marriage and the Family, 54,* 178–190.

Demo, D. H. (1992). Parent-child relationships: Assessing recent changes. *Journal of Marriage and the Family, 54,* 104–117.

Dinnerstein, D. (1977). *The mermaid and the minotaur*. New York: Harper/Colophon.

Dishion, T. J., Patterson, G. R., Stoolmiller, M., & Skinner, M. L. (1991). Family, school, and behavioral antecedents to early adolescent involvement with antisocial peers. *Developmental Psychology, 27,* 172–180.

Dreyer, P. H. (1975). Sex, sex roles and marriage among youth in the 1970s. In F. J. Havighurst & P. H. Dreyer (Eds.), *Youth: The 74th Yearbook of the National Society for the Study of Education* (Part I). Chicago: University of Chicago Press.

Dyk, P. H., & Adams, G. R. (1990). Identity and intimacy: An initial investigation of three theoretical models using cross-lag panel correlations. *Journal of Youth and Adolescence, 19,* 91–110.

Eichenbaum, L., & Orbach, S. (1983). *Understanding women*. New York: Harper/Colophon.

Erikson, E.H. (1980). *Identity and the life cycle*. New York: Norton.

Erikson, E. H. (1982). *The life cycle completed: A review*. New York: Simon.

Essex, M. J., & Nam, S. (1987). Marital status and loneliness among older women. *Journal of Marriage and the Family, 49,* 93–106.

Fischer, J., & Gochros, H. (1975). *Handbook of behavior therapy with sexual problems*. New York: Pergamon Press.

Fisher, H. E. (1987). The four-year itch. *Natural History, 96*(10), 22–33.

Fitzgerald, L. F., & Shullman, S. L. (1993). Sexual harassment: A research analysis and agenda for the 1990's. *Journal of Vocational Behavior, 42,* 5–27.

Flavell, J. H. (1985). *Cognitive development* (2nd ed.). Englewood Cliffs, NJ: Prentice-Hall.

Forman, B. (1980). Psychotherapy with rape victims. *Psychotherapy: Theory, Research, and Practice, 17,* 304–311.

Fraser, M. W. (1995). Violence overview. In *Encyclopedia of Social Work* (19th ed., Vol. 3, pp. 2453–2460). Washington, DC: NASW Press.

Furstenberg, F. F., Jr. (1982). Conjugal succession: Reentering marriage after divorce. In P. B. Baltes & O. G. Brim, Jr. (Eds.), *Life-span development and behavior* (Vol. 5, pp. 108–146). New York: Academic Press.

Furstenberg, F. F., Jr., & Nord, C. W. (1985). Parenting part: Patterns of childbearing after marital disruption. *Journal of Marriage and the Family, 47,* 893–912.

Ganter, G., & Yeakel, M. (1980). *Human behavior and the social environment*. New York: Columbia University Press.

Garfinkel, R. (1982). By the sweat of your brow. In T. M. Field, A. Huston, H. C. Quay, L. Troll, & G. G. Finley (Eds.), *Review of human development*. New York: Wiley.

Gelman, B. P. (1985). Cognitive development of women. *New directions for student services, 29,* 29–44.

Germain, C. B. (1987, December). Human development in contemporary environments. *Social Service Review,* pp. 566–579.

Gilligan, C. (1982). *In a different voice*. Cambridge, MA: Harvard University Press.

Gilligan, C. (1983). *In a different voice: Psychological theory and women's development*. Cambridge, MA: Harvard University Press.

Gilligan, C. (1985, March). *Remapping development*. Paper presented at the biennial meeting of the Society for Research in Child Development, Toronto.

Gilligan, C. (1986). On "In a different voice": An interdisciplinary forum: Reply. *Signs, 11,* 324–333.

Gilmore, D. (1990). *Manhood in the making: Cultural components of masculinity*. New Haven, CT: Yale University Press.

Glenn, N. D. (1991). The recent trend in marital success in the United States. *Journal of Marriage and the Family, 53,* 261–270.

Glick, P. C., & Lin, S. (1986). Recent changes in divorce and remarriage. *Journal of Marriage and the Family, 48,* 737–747.

Glick, P. C., & Norton, A. (1977). Marrying, divorcing, living together in the U.S. today. *Population Bulletin, 32,* 5.

Gochros, H. L. (1977). Human sexuality. In *Encyclopedia of Social Work.* (15th ed., Vol. 2). Washington, DC: NASW Press.

Goldscheider, C., & Goldscheider, F. (1987). Moving out and marriage: What do young adults expect? *American Sociological Review, 52,* 278–285.

Goode, W. J. (1956). *After divorce.* Glencoe, IL: Free Press.

Gordon, M., & Shankweiler, P. J. (1971, August). Different equals less: Female sexuality in recent marriage manuals. *Journal of Marriage and the Family,* pp. 459–465.

Gutek, B. A. (1985). *Sex and the workplace.* San Francisco: Jossey-Bass.

Gutek, B. A., & Koss, M. P. (1993). Changed women and changed organizations: Consequence of coping with sexual harassment. *Journal of Vocational Behavior, 42,* 28–48.

Haley, J. (1984). *Problem solving therapy: New strategies for effective family therapy.* New York: Harper & Row.

Harris, M. B., & Turner, P. H. (1986). Gay and lesbian parents. *Journal of Homosexuality, 12,* 101–113.

Havighurst, R. J. (1982). The world of work. In B. B. Wolman (Ed.). *Handbook of developmental psychology.* Englewood Cliffs, NJ: Prentice-Hall.

Herring, C., & Wilson-Sadberry, K. R. (1993). Preference or necessity? Changing work roles of black and white women, 1973–1990. *Journal of Marriage and the Family, 55,* 314–325.

Hetherington, E. M. (1972). Effects of parental absence on personality development in adolescent daughters. *Developmental Psychology, 7,* 313–326

Hill, C. T., Rubin, Z., & Peplan, L. A. (1979). Breakup before marriage: The end of 103 affairs. In G. Levinger & O. Moles (Eds.), *Divorce and separation: Context, causes and consequences.* New York: Basic Books.

Hite, S. (1976). *The Hite report.* New York: Macmillan

Hobart, C. (1988). The family system in remarriage: An exploratory study. *Journal of Marriage and the Family, 50,* 649–661.

Hodgson, J. W., & Fischer, J. L. (1979). Sex differences in identity and intimacy development in college youth. *Journal of Youth and Adolescence, 8,* 37–50.

Hoffman, L. (1981). *Foundations of family therapy.* New York: Basic Books.

Hoffman, M. L. (1984). Empathy, its limitations, and its role in a comprehensive moral theory. In J. Gerwitz & W. Kurtines (Eds.), *Morality, moral development and moral behavior.* New York: Wiley.

Hogan, D. P. (1978). The variable order of events in the lifecourse. *American Sociological Review, 43,* 573–586.

Hogan, D. P., & Astone, N. M. (1986). The transition to adulthood. *Annual Review of Sociology, 12,* 109–130.

Holland, J. L. (1973). *Making vocational choice: A theory of careers.* Englewood Cliffs, NJ: Prentice-Hall.

Holland, J. L. (1985). *Making vocational choices: A theory of vocational personalities and work environments* (2nd ed.). Englewood Cliffs, NJ: Prentice-Hall.

Holmbeck, G. N., & Hill, J. P. (1991). Conflictive engagement, positive affect, and menarche in families with seventh-grade girls. *Child Development, 62,* 1030–1048.

Horn, J. L. (1982). The theory of fluid and crystallized intelligence in relation to concepts of cognitive psychology and aging in adulthood. In F. I. M. Craik & S. Trehub (Eds.), *Aging and cognitive processes.* New York: Plenum Press.

Hunt, M. M. (1974). *Sexual behavior in the 1970s.* Chicago: Playboy Press.

Huston, T. L., McHale, S. M., & Crouter, A. C. (1986). When the honeymoon's over: Changes in the marriage relationship over the first year. In R. Gilmour & S. Duck (Eds.), *The emerging field of personal relationships.* Hillsdale, NJ: Erlbaum.

Huston, T. L., & Vangelisti, A. L. (1991). Socioemotional behavior and satisfaction in marital relationships: A longitudinal study. *Journal of Personality and Social Psychology, 6,* 721–733.

Kail, R. V., & Cavanaugh, J. C. (1996). *Human development.* Pacific Grove, CA: Brooks/Cole.

Kaluger, G., & Kaluger, M. F. (1984). *Human development: The span of life* (3rd. ed.). St. Louis, MO: Times Mirror/Mosby.

Kanter, R. M. (1976, May). Why bosses turn bitchy. *Psychology Today,* pp. 55–59.

Kaplan, H. S. (1974). *The new sex therapy: Active treatment of sexual dysfunctions.* New York: Random House.

Keith, J. (1990). Age in social and cultural context: Anthropological perspectives. In R. H. Binstock & L. K. George (Eds.), *Handbook of aging and the social sciences* (3rd ed., pp. 91–111). San Diego, CA: Academic Press.

Kitchener, K. S., & King, P. M. (1989). The reflective judgment model: Ten years of research. In M. Commons, C. Armon, L. Kohlberg, F. A. Richards, T. A. Grotzer, & J. D. Sinnott (Eds.), *Adult development: Vol. 2. Models and methods in the study of adolescence and adult thought* (pp. 63–78). New York: Praeger.

Kobak, R. R., Cole, H. E., Ferenz-Gilles, R., Fleming, W. S., & Gamble, W. (1993). Attachment and emotional regulation during mother-teen problem solving: A control theory analysis. *Child Development, 64,* 231–245.

Koestner, R., Zuroff, D. C., & Powers, T. A. (1991). Family origins of adolescent self-criticism and its continuity into adulthood. *Journal of Abnormal Psychology, 100,* 191–197.

Kohlberg, L. (1969). Stage and sequence: The cognitive-developmental approach in socialization. In D. Goslin (Ed.). *Handbook of socialization theory and research* (pp. 347–480). Chicago: Rand McNally.

Kohlberg, L. (1973). Continuities in childhood and adult moral development revisited. In P. B. Baltes & K. W. Schaie (Eds.), *Lifespan developmental psychology.* New York: Academic Press.

Kohlberg, L. (1976). Moral stages and moralization: The cognitive-developmental approach. In T. Likona (Ed.), *Moral development and behavior: Theory, research, and social issues.* New York: Holt, Rinehart & Winston.

Kohn, J. L., & Schooler, C. (1978). The reciprocal effects of the substantive complexity of work and intellectual flexibility: A longitudinal assessment. *American Journal of Sociology, 82,* 111–130.

Kohn, M. L., & Schooler, C. (With J. Miller, K. A. Miller, C. Schoenbach, & R. Schoenberg). (1983). *Work and personality: An inquiry into the impact of social stratification,* Norwood, NJ: Ablex.

Kramer, D. A. (1989). A developmental framework for understanding conflict resolution processes. In J. D. Sinnott (Ed.), *Everyday problem solving: Theory and applications* (pp. 138–152). New York: Praeger.

Kramer, D. A., Angiuld, N., Crisafi, L., & Levine, C. (1991, August). *Cognitive processes in real-life conflict resolution.* Paper presented at the annual meeting of the American Psychological Association, San Francisco.

Kurtines, W., & Grief, E. B. (1974). The development of moral thought: Review and evaluation of Kolhberg's approach. *Psychological Bulletin, 81,* 453–470.

Lamborn, S. D., Mounts, N. S., Steinberg, L., & Dornbusch, S. M. (1991). Patterns of competence and adjustment among adolescents from authoritative, authoritarian, indulgent and neglectful families. *Child Development, 62,* 1049–1065.

Lamborn, S. D., & Steinberg, L. (1993). Emotional autonomy redux: Revisiting Ryan and Lynch. *Child Development, 64,* 483–499.

Lauver, P. J., & Jones, R. M. (1991). Factors associated with perceived career options in American Indian, White, and Hispanic rural high school students. *Journal of Counseling Psychology, 38,* 159–166.

Levinson, D. J. (1996). *The seasons of a woman's life.* New York: Alfred A. Knopf.

Levinson, D. J., Darrow, C. N., Klein, E., Levinson, M. H., & McGee, B. (1978). *The seasons of a man's life.* New York: Knopf.

Macklin, E. D. (1988). Heterosexual couples who cohabit nonmaritally: Some common problems and issues. In C. S. Chilman, E. W. Nunnally, & F. M. Cox (Eds.), *Variant family forms* (pp. 56–72). Newbury Park, CA: Sage.

Masters, W. H, & Johnson, V. E. (1970). *Human sexual inadequacy.* Boston: Little, Brown.

Masters, W. H, & Johnson, V. E. (1985). *Human sexual inadequacy.* Boston: Little, Brown.

Masters, W. H., Johnson, V. E., & Kolodny, R. C. (1988). *Human sexuality* (4th ed.). Glenview, IL: Scott, Foresman.

McCary, J. I. (1978). *Human sexuality* (3rd ed.). Princeton, NJ: Van Nostrand Reinhold.

Menaghan, E. G., & Lieberman, M. A. (1986). Changes in depression following divorce: A panel study. *Journal of Marriage and the Family, 48,* 319–328.

Meyer, D. R., & Garasky, S. (1993). Custodial fathers: Myths, realities, and child support policy. *Journal of Marriage and the Family, 48,* 371–386.

Miller, J. B. (1976). *Toward a new psychology of women.* Boston: Beacon Press.

Minuchin, S., & Fishman, H. C. (1981). *Family therapy techniques.* Cambridge, MA: Harvard University Press.

Modell, J. (1989). *Into one's own: From youth to adulthood in the United States, 1920–1975.* New York: Holt, Rinehart & Winston.

Money, J. (1988). *Gay, straight and in-between: The sexology of erotic orientation.* New York: Oxford University Press.

Montemayor, R. (1982). The relationship between parent-adolescent conflict and the amount of time adolescents spend alone and with parents and peers. *Child Development, 53,* 1512–1519.

National Center for Educational Statistics. (1993). *Preliminary data: Participation in adult education, 1993.* Washington, DC: U.S. Government Printing Office.

Neimark, E. D. (1982). Cognitive development in adulthood. In T. M. Field, A. Huston, H. C. Quay, L. Troll, & G. E. Finley (Eds.), *Review of human development*. New York: Wiley.

Newman, B. M., & Newman, P. R. (1995). *Development through life: A psychosocial approach* (6th ed.). Pacific Grove, CA: Brooks/Cole.

Nock, S. L. (1981). Family life transitions: Longitudinal effects on family members. *Journal of Marriage and the Family, 43,* 703–714.

Nydegger, C. N. (1986). Asymmetrical kin and the problematic son-in-law. In N. Datan, A. L. Greene, & H. W. Reese (Eds.). *Lifespan developmental psychology: Intergenerational relations*. Hillsdale, NJ: Erlbaum.

Okun, B., & Rappaport, L. J. (1980). *Working with families*. Scituate, MA: Duxbury.

O' Leary, K. D. (1993) Through a psychological lens: Personality traits, personality disorders, and levels of violence. In R. J. Gelles & D. R. Loseke (Eds.), *Current controversies on family violence* (pp. 7–30). Newbury Park, CA: Sage.

Paikoff, R. L., & Brooks-Gunn, J. (1991). Do parent-child relationships change during puberty? *Psychological Bulletin, 110,* 47–66.

Papalia, D. E., & Olds, S. W. (1986). *Human development*. New York: McGraw-Hill.

Patterson, S. J., Sochting, I., & Marcia, L. E. (1992). The inner space and beyond: Women and identity. In G. R. Adams, T. P. Gullotta, & R. Montemayor (Eds.), *Advances in adolescent development: Vol. 4. Adolescent identity formation*. Newbury Park, CA: Sage.

Peplau, L. A. (1991). Lesbian and gay relationships. In J. C. Gonsiorek & J. D. Weinrich (Eds.), *Homosexuality: Research implications for public policy* (pp. 177–196). Newbury Park, CA: Sage.

Perry, W. I. (1970). *Forms of intellectual and ethical development in the college years*. New York: Holt, Rinehart & Winston.

Phillis, D. E., & Stein, P. J. (1983). Sink or swing? The lifestyles of single adults. In E. R. Allgeier & N. B. McCormick (Eds.), *Changing boundaries: Gender roles and sexual behavior* (pp. 202–225). Palo Alto, CA: Mayfield.

Piaget, J. (1972). Intellectual evolution from adolescence to adulthood. *Human Development, 15,* 1–12.

Pillari, V. (1991). *Scapegoating in families: Intergenerational patterns of emotional and physical abuse*. New York: Brunner/Mazel.

Piotrkowski, C. S., Rapoport, R. N., & Rapoport, R. (1987). Families and work. In M. B. Sussman &
S. K. Steinmetz (Eds.), *Handbook of marriage and the family* (pp. 251–284). New York: Plenum.

Price, R. H. (1992). Psychosocial impact of job loss on individuals and families. *Current Directions in Psychological Science, 1,* 9–11.

Rawlins, W. K. (1992). *Friendship matters*. Hawthorne, NY: Aldine de Gruyter.

Rhyne, D. (1981). Basis of marital satisfaction among men and women. *Journal of Marriage and the Family, 43,* 941–955.

Rogers, D. (1979). *The adult years*. Englewood Cliffs, NJ: Prentice-Hall.

Rossi, A. S. (1968). Transition to parenthood. *Journal of Marriage and the Family, 30,* 26–39.

Rubinstein, R. L. (1987). Never-married elderly as a social type: Reevaluating some images. *Gerontologist, 27,* 108–113.

Russell, D. E. H. (1982). The prevalence and incidence of forcible rape and attempted rape of females. *Victimology: An International Journal, 7,* 81–93.

Ryan, R. M., & Lynch, J. H. (1989). Emotional autonomy versus detachment: Revisiting the vicissitudes of adolescence and young adulthood. *Child Development, 60,* 340–356.

Schaie, K. W., & Willis, S. L. (1986). Can decline in adult intellectual functioning be reversed? *Developmental Psychology, 22,* 223–232.

Schiedel, D. G., & Marcia, J. E. (1985). Ego identity, intimacy, sex role orientation, and gender. *Developmental Psychology, 21,* 149–160.

Schlegel, A., & Barry, H. (1991). *Adolescence: An anthropological inquiry*. New York: Free Press.

Shaffer, D. R. (1996). *Developmental psychology* (4th ed.). Pacific Grove, CA: Brooks/Cole.

Shinar, E. H. (1978). Person perception as a foundation of occupation and sex. *Sex Roles, 4,* 679–693.

Sigelman, C. K., & Shaffer, D. R. (1995). *Life-span human development* (2nd ed.). Pacific Grove, CA: Brooks/Cole.

Snarey, J. R., & Kohlberg, L. (1985). The kibbutz as a model for moral education.: A longitudinal cross-cultural study. *Journal of Applied Developmental Psychology, 6,* 151–172.

Sorensen, E. (1991). *Exploring the reasons behind the narrowing gender gap in earnings* (Urban Institute Report 1991–1992). Washington, DC: Urban Institute Press.

Specht, R., & Craig, G. J. (1987). *Human development. A social work perspective* (2nd ed.). Englewood Cliffs, NJ: Prentice-Hall.

Stack, C. B. (1986). The culture of gender: Women and men of color. *Signs, 11*(2), 321–324.

Staples, R., & Mirande, A. (1980). Racial and cultural variations among American families: A clinical review of literature on minority families. *Journal of Marriage and the Family, 42.*

Stein, P. J. (1978, September). *Being single: Bucking the cultural imperative.* Paper presented at the annual meeting of the American Sociological Association.

Steinberg, L. (1981). Transformations in family relations at puberty. *Developmental Psychology, 17,* 833–840.

Stone, W. F. (1973). Patterns of conformity in couples varying in intimacy. *Journal of Personality and Social Psychology, 27*(3), 413–419.

Strong, B., & DeVault, C. (1983). *The marriage and family experience* (2nd. ed.). New York: West.

Super, D. E. (1957). *The psychology of careers.* New York: Harper & Row.

Super, D. E. (1980). A life span, life space approach to career development. *Journal of Vocational Behavior, 16,* 282–298.

Thomas, S., Albrecht, K., & White, P. (1984). Determinants of marital quality in dual-career couples. *Family Relations, 33,* 513–521.

Thompson, E., & Colella, U. (1992). Cohabitation and marital stability: Quality or commitment? *Journal of Marriage and the Family, 54,* 259–267.

Unger, R., & Crawford, M. (1992). *Women and gender: A feminist psychology.* Philadelphia: Temple University Press.

U.S. Bureau of the Census. *Statistical abstracts of the United States, 1992.* Washington, DC: U.S. Government Printing Office, 1992.

Vaillant, G. E. (1977). *Adaptations to life.* Boston: Little, Brown.

Van Hoose, W. H., & Worth, M. R. (1982). *Adulthood in the life cycle.* Dubuque, IA: Brown.

Vitz, P. C. (1990). The use of stories in moral development: New psychological reasons for an old education method. *American Psychologist, 45*(6), 709–720.

Waldman, E. (1985). Today's girls in tomorrow's labor force: Projecting their participation and occupations. *Youth and Society, 16,* 375–392.

Walker, L. E. A. (1984). *The battered woman syndrome.* New York: Springer.

Walker, L. J. (1989). A longitudinal study of moral reasoning. *Child Development, 60,* 157–166.

Wallerstein, J. S., & Blakeslee, S. (1989). *Second chance: Men, women, and children a decade after divorce.* New York: Ticknor & Fields.

Wallerstein, J. S., & Kelly, J. B. (1980). *Surviving the breakup: How children and parents cope with divorce.* New York: Basic Books.

Weitzman, L. J. (1985). *The divorce revolution: The unexpected social and economic consequences for women and children in America.* New York: Free Press.

Whitbourne, S. K., & Tesch, S. A. (1985). A comparison of identity and intimacy statuses in college students and alumni. *Developmental Psychology, 21* 1039–1044.

Willis, S. L., & Schaie, K. W. (1986). Training the elderly on the ability factors of spatial orientation and inductive reasoning. *Psychology and Aging, 1,* 239–247.

Woodruff-Pak, D. S. (1988). *Psychology and aging.* Englewood Cliffs, NJ: Prentice-Hall.

Youniss, J., & Smollar, J. (1985). *Adolescent relations with mothers, fathers, and friends.* Chicago: University of Chicago Press.

Yussen, S. R. (1977). Characteristics of moral dilemmas written by adolescents. *Developmental Psychology, 13,* 162–163.

Zawitz, M. W., Klaus, P. A., Bachman, R., Bastian, L. D., DeBerry, M. M., Rand, M. R., & Taylor, B. M. (1993, October). *Highlights from 20 years of surveying crime victims: The national crime victimization survey 1973–92* (NCJ 144525). Washington, DC: U.S. Government Printing Office.

Zilbergeld, B., & Evans, M. (1980, August). The inadequacy of Masters and Johnson. *Psychology Today, 538.*

# 8

# *Middle Adulthood*

## INTRODUCTION

This chapter will focus on continuity and change between the ages of 40 and 65—the middle years. We shall consider the viewpoints of psychologists, sociologists, and economists.

Middle age is a stage in the lifespan in which biological changes accompany aging and changes in social role. The physical process of aging is viewed either as a period of development or as a process of undoing or reversal of development. Socially, however, aging is an upward spiral. Researchers tend to think they know what is happening in childhood and adolescence, but in some ways they find middle age a difficult period to study. This in-between period does not lend itself readily to the traditional ways of viewing human behavior and experience.

In this stage, people integrate their value systems; they continue to form priorities and fulfill ambitions. Middle-aged people place a great deal of importance on work and career: Often, they base life decisions on career demands and work values. Family, friendships, and taking care of themselves are also important, and affect their decisions. Within the family, adults continue to bring their values together to create blends of family values. Sometimes, though, they find deep and difficult conflicts that do not seem to go away (Newman & Newman, 1995).

Middle-aged people tend to strike a balance between their values and actions. They often strive for and find new meanings of life. Further, every middle-agd adult engages in such developmental tasks as managing a career, nurturing an important relationship, expanding caring relationships, and managing a household.

> Sheila is a middle-aged woman who has lived all her life in the inner city. She has been married twice and has lived with two men. In her early 50s, she is the mother of four grown children, all of whom live away from home. A cleaning woman, Sheila earns her livelihood through various routine and sporadic cleaning jobs. Although she has taken good care of her children, she is frustrated, for her children visit her only when they have to or when they need some extra money. If she tries to be helpful and give advice, they protest. As the young and upcoming generation, they ignore her in order to seek their own power. But she tries hard not to relinquish her power, and she uses her financial position (which is better than her children's) to exert some control over them. In her unique position in the family, she sees stress, frustration, and harassment as part of her life.

Middle adulthood is the period that represents the peak of a person's social integration. Although Sheila feels that her children take advantage of her in some ways, she knows that she has to face important family and occupational responsibilities. To put it in another way, the middle-aged person is usually fully occupied with career, obligations, expectations, and available opportunities.

## CHARACTER OF THE MIDDLE YEARS

Though the middle years tend to fall from about age 40 to age 65, this period can be longer or shorter for different people. For example, some people are biologically slower; they appear forever young. During the middle years, people realize that they are separate from young adults as well as from the elderly. Middle agers are often called the "sandwich generation," for they must develop new ways of responding both to grown children and to aging parents.

People over 50 years of age differ in many ways from younger people. They have to learn to accept limitations, such as dietary restrictions, come to terms with what must be, and go on from that point. At age 50, the average person realizes that some of his or her dreams will not come true. For example, a person who always wanted to be rich will see that he or she will most likely never become rich. People accept the lifestyle that they have adopted, can lead the kind of life that makes them happy, and can be satisfied with what they have done.

Juan is a 50-year-old man who came to Los Angeles at age 12 with dreams of making it big in this country. However, he did not have the kind of education that he needed to make it on his own. As a young person, he was labeled as incapable of doing mathematics; that assessment demoralized him so much that he made no special effort to study the subject. His parents were fairly illiterate and did not push him to follow academic pursuits. After Juan graduated from high school, he found odd jobs to do until he became a superintendent of a large housing unit in a prestigious area of New York City. He held onto that job, married, and had three children. Meanwhile his aged parents, who also lived in New York City, became his dependents to some extent.

Juan found that he did not have time for following any of his own pursuits; he had to provide for his family as well as for his parents. To manage both, Juan took a second job as a cab driver during what would have been his leisure time. But there was only enough money to allow him just to get by financially. Over a period of time, his dreams of being a wealthy man dissolved. Now he has accepted his role as a wage earner and the chief supporter of his family.

Here is an example of a middle-aged person who returns to school and changes occupations. At age 52, Randy isn't a typical student, but he stands out for more than his age. He is embarking on his third occupation. He previously worked in the Air Force for 24 years, first as a pilot and later as a staff officer. His military experiences include participation in the Vietnam War. On his return from Vietnam, he taught some members of Congress how to fly, working primarily in the Pentagon. But dealing with politicians concerning military appropriations and other matters became so frustrating that he retired. At age 44 he was selling insurance. He soon became tired of using all types of tactics to sell it even to people who did not need it. Now he has resigned this job and has gone back to school to become a recreational therapist.

Though Randy's experiences may not seem typical, many people make two or more career changes in their lifetime. Notice that Randy's training to be a recreational therapist differs greatly from his other experiences. Many middle-aged men and women get forced out of a job—

recall the late 1980s and early 1990s. People in this position may take any type of job to get a paycheck. However, Randy's experience shows that it is never too late in one's life to retool and change occupations.

In personal life, matters can be a little different. Middle-aged married couples have learned to accept their partners as they are, with the idea of changing the partner in their life given up long ago. They accept the person along with his or her limitations. Positive attributes are praised and highlighted, whereas negative qualities are overlooked.

After 40, people also face some problems relating to death and mortality. They will probably begin to lose parents and old friends at this stage.

A person of 50 has no need to keep up with the Joneses. In fact, who cares about the Joneses? Middle-aged people are more worried about their own lives. They do what pleases them, and that is where they find their satisfaction.

Middle-aged people have developed common sense and learned valuable lessons from experience that typically have enabled them to get a better job than before. Some now have their goals well within sight, others have reached their goals, and still others have attained what they had barely dreamed. Many, like Juan in the case study, have put early goals aside in favor of meeting the challenge immediately at hand.

By 40, people know that they are similar to each other. People realize that they do not know everything about life—nobody does—but when they need information they know where to get it. People at this age tend to become more reality oriented.

Middle adulthood usually involves upward and forward movement. This is the period when a person attempts to gain competence in the external world and seek material gain. For one in middle adulthood, the characteristic thought is, "If I can maintain what I have already made, I will be happy in my life."

Certain psychological and social changes mark the start of middle age. People realize that because of their basic decisions about career and family the future no longer holds limitless possibilities. Some people face this challenge confidently, whereas others feel a sense of crisis. Older women realize that their children are moving out of the family; others who have not had children realize that they may never have any children of their own. Women who have taken care of children and seen them grow up may ask what they should do with the rest of their lives. This is why many older people, particularly women, reenter the labor force or go back to school to get a degree after a long hiatus: They are attempting to develop a new sense of self.

> Pat, at 48, finds that she has a great deal of time on her hands. Her children have grown up, so she is by herself at home. There are no extra clothes to wash and no need to make cookies or bake cakes for her children. Though married, Pat feels alone. Her husband is involved in his job and intent on making it up the social and economic ladder. At last, she reaches a decision. She makes up her mind to take a part-time job. But she finds it limiting—in fact, boring—to be a cashier in a supermarket. Pat has always been a creative person. Eventually, with a lot of fears and self-doubts, she decides instead to go back to school and find a field that will make her feel self-fulfilled and also offer her opportunities to become an economically productive member of society.
>
> At last Pat gets an opportunity to carry out these plans. Going to school changes her outlook on life. She finds that there are interesting topics that she can share with her husband and that she can pursue her own interests on her own terms. She also starts to measure her success by her achievement in school.

Middle age is generally regarded as the period between completion of the traditional roles of child rearing and becoming established as a provider. It is the time when a couple starts to establish and maintain an adequate standard of living; when adults develop leisure activities, adjust to the physiological changes of middle age, and adapt to aging parents. The most important challenge of this stage is to develop a command of one's inner impulses as well as compe-

tence in dealing with the responsibilities of the outer world. As Specht and Craig (1987) put it, middle-aged parents assume the power of the older generation and insure the future of the younger generation. Ideally, middle age brings more personal freedom, reduced economic strain, greater availability of leisure time, and fewer demands for material growth.

The developmental tasks of middle adulthood are both interpersonal and intrapersonal in nature. For many people, this is the first time they give weight to the comforts of life. This is also the first time they face certain physical changes, as the following section discusses.

## PHYSICAL CHANGES

### Health

The body functions at its peak just before middle adulthood, when a slowing down occurs. Barring diseases, most people can withstand the physical rigors of the middle adult years. A few wrinkles appear in the face as the skin becomes dry and loses elasticity. People see a redistribution of fatty tissues and experience a limit to how much energy they can expend. For example, few middle-aged people can pursue career goals relentlessly and hope to fulfill all their social goals as well.

People at this age place a lot of emphasis on physical fitness. Men are endlessly jogging, running, and working out in the gym. Women also tend to take care of themselves, but they focus more on their mates than they did when they were younger.

The sense organs of middle-aged people change at an amazingly uniform rate. One of the most notable changes occurs in the eyes. Many people confront the shock of being middle aged when they find that they have to wear bifocal lenses. This change is the reason older people begin to hold their books or other reading material at arm's length. The condition usually develops when a person is 40 to 50 years old.

There are internal changes as well—some physical decline and slowing down. Sensitivity to taste, smell, and pain decreases during this period. Other biological functions, such as reaction time and sensorimotor skills, may begin to slow. Further, as a person grows older, the reserve capacity of many organ systems declines; that is, they cannot respond as well to demands that require extraordinary output, as in emergencies (Goldberg & Hagberg, 1990). For instance, old and young do not differ much in resting heart rates but older adults, unless they are completely disease-free, will have lower maximal heart rates (Lakatta, 1990). That is, older adults who do not feel old at all as they go about normal routines but may feel old if they try to run up the stairs too fast. When people adjust themselves to a slower pace in life, they preserve their energies for special occasions. By exercising regularly, people can conserve and maximize strength in middle age (Timiras, 1972).

## Physical Appearance and Structure

People in their 20s and 30s experience only minor changes in physical appearance. However, when people reach their 40s their skin begins to wrinkle, and their hair becomes thin and turns gray.

As people grow older they lose bone mass. By the time they reach 50, they begin to show a dramatic reduction in bone mass. In the disease *osteoporosis,* the bones become porous and are extremely easy to break. Osteoporosis can cause the spinal cord to become brittle or a vertebra to collapse and cause a person to stoop and become shorter (Meier, 1988). Although this disease is more common in women over 60, it can occur in women in their 50s. Osteoporosis is more common in women than in men for three reasons: Women have less bone mass in general, some girls and women do not consume enough calcium to build strong bones, and menopause causes a decrease in estrogen and an acceleration in bone loss (Heaney et al., 1982). To prevent osteoporosis, women should eat foods high in calcium, take calcium supplements, and exercise.

Hormone replacement therapy, which refers to taking estrogen and progesterone, can compensate for losses caused by menopause and can prevent or slow osteoporosis (Soules & Bremmer, 1982). Hormone replacement therapy may also relieve symptoms of menopause and protect against coronary heart diseases associated with loss of estrogen (Mathews, 1992).

## Climacteric

Sexual changes take place for both men and women during middle age. The term *climacteric* refers to the complex changes—both physical and emotional—that accompany hormonal changes in midlife.

*Menopause* In women, climacteric consists essentially of a gradual decline in ovarian functioning and the associated products (sex hormones and eggs) and the eventual cessation of menstruation (menopause). Women at this stage can also have shortened orgasms and decreased vaginal lubrication (Masters & Johnson, 1970). The most important change during climacteric is a drop in estrogen, which is the primary female hormone (Mayo Clinic, 1992).

Some in the medical profession believe that the symptoms accompanying climacteric can be reduced by *hormone replacement therapy,* in which women take low doses of estrogen and progesterone. This treatment also relieves hot flashes. When women under 40 begin climacteric hormone replacement therapy, they usually continue it for many years. Controversy about hormone replacement therapy centers on evidence that it leads to breast cancer and other forms of cancer (Mayo Clinic, 1992). Even without hormone replacement, most women indicate that the symptoms accompanying the climacteric are not severe (Mathews et al., 1990).

How women experience menopause depends on cultural differences as well. About 69% of Canadian women reported that they experienced at least one hot flash, compared with only 20% of Japanese women (Lock, 1986). Flint (1982) found that in traditional India, very few women experienced any symptoms at all. Women who had not reached menopause looked forward to it, and women who had reached it were pleased with themselves. Being freed from the taboos of menstruation brought social rewards. They continued to have meaningful work roles and were seen as wise by virtue of their years. In contrast, while Indian women gain status in their culture, older women in the United States lose status.

Wright (1982) comments that among Navajo women, reaching menopause is easily acceptable as women would be freed from menstrual taboos and have meaningful roles in society. They would also become eligible to take on ceremonial roles. However, Wright found that menopausal complaints were as common among Navajo women as among Anglo-American women. Navajo women living in the reservations had poor health and low income and had to do hard physical labor. Other research shows that women with lower socioeconomic status have more difficulty with menopause than more affluent women (Unger & Crawford, 1992). Clearly, in every cultural group women differ tremendously in this universal silent transition.

Menopause generally seems to do little against women and can even improve their lives (Neugarten, Kramer, & Loomis, 1963; Unger & Crawford, 1992). However, sexual activity begins to decline in the adult years (Greene, 1984). Again there are individual variations, with some women feeling more sexual and others not. However, in most cases menopause is accepted as a natural part of life.

*Babies in middle adulthood*    Recently, controversy has arisen about postmenopausal women having babies. That is, reproductive technology such as in vitro fertilization (see Chapter 2) and using donated eggs has made it possible for postmenopausal women to have children if they have access to the proper medical centers.

This notion of having babies after menopause throws out the biological clock. Some women have children because their daughters cannot conceive, while others do it because their desire for a child was never fulfilled while they were young.

Right now, this is a controversial issue. As technology advances, we shall be confronted with complex ethical questions, such as should children be born to older parents at all or under what circumstances, such as the purpose and goal of the parents.

*Reproductive changes in men*    Although there is no menopause in men as in women, for obvious reasons, men also go through a critical sexual phase in middle age. While women go through it in a short period of time men experience a gradual process. By the time women reach their late 50s, almost all are postmenopausal. Men, though, can often father children even when they are much older. However, the sperm produced by older men may not be as active as those produced by younger men. Testerone in men also decreases as they get older (Schiavi, Schreiner-Engel, White, & Mandeli, 1991). In short, changes associated with the climacteric in men are more gradual, more viable, and less complete than those in women (Soules & Bremmer, 1982). The psychological impact of this period on men is called the "midlife crisis." Frequency of sexual activity declines as men become more involved in other responsibilities.

For both men and women, changes in the reproductive system are part of adult development. Some men and women experience similar symptoms in climacteric (Ruebsaat & Hull, 1975). That is, they both report a loss of self-confidence or become irritable, fatigued, and depressed. Some symptoms are caused by hormonal imbalance, while others are caused by psychological stress, such as job pressure, boredom with a sexual partner, family responsibilities, ill health, or fear of ill health. Any or all of these changes can affect a person's sexual abilities.

## Disease

On the positive side, aging itself in the absence of disease has little effect on physical and psychological functioning. However, resesarchers have found men who had minor traces of impending diseases to be deficient in many measures. Symptoms that progressed to the point of disease also seriously affected daily performance. Therefore, disease rather than aging itself accounts for many of the declines in functioning in later life (Houx, Vreeling, & Jolles, 1991). Although disease is the cause of serious aging in older people, it is difficult to distinguish between the two. Though aging and disease are distinct, increased vulnerability to disease is an important part of the normal aging process.

Further, disuse of the body also contributes to steeper declines in physical functioning for some adults (Wagner, LaCroix, Buchner, & Larson, 1992). Masters and Johnson (1966) use the maxim "use it or lose it" to describe the fact that sexual functioning deteriorates when a person engages in little or no sexual activity. The signs of deterioration in adults resemble those in people who have been confined to bed for a long time (Goldberg & Hagberg, 1990). The brain also needs meaningful exercise to continue to function effectively (Black, Isaacs, & Greenough, 1991), and the body thrives on use. But too many people become inactive as they grow older (Wagner et al., 1992). Forms of abuse include drinking too much alcohol, gaining too much weight, and smoking. In addition, some prescribed medications interact with the aging body and impair functioning (Cherry & Morton, 1989; Lamy, 1986).

*Fitness*   Shepard (1978, 1990) indicates that regular fitness can delay physical dependence and increase survival by as many as eight years. In midlife, people can avoid known health risks and adapt habits that promote good health (Margolis, Sparrow, & Swenson, 1989; Walford, 1983). The following sensible food and exercise habits can keep a person healthy for a long period of time.

In a classic study of 3400 men ages 39 to 59, Rosenman (1974) examined and reexamined them at the end of two-and-a-half, then eight-and-a-half years to determine how behavior habits affected the incidence of heart disease. At one

extreme, researchers found a group they called Type A personality people, who were highly competitive, aggressive, impatient, and achievement oriented. Their muscles were tensed and they always functioned with a sense of urgency.

> Adrian, 47, is a busy executive in a large company. He always attends company parties, works 14 hours a day, and flies around the country to expand his already large business. He'll make a deal with anyone who can help his company get bigger and better than his competitors. He hardly has time for his family, and all his wife and children see of him are his quick arrivals and departures. One day while traveling on a plane, he has a sudden heart attack and dies. Death at 47 of heart attack is not unusual for the Type A personality.

At the opposite extreme were men of Type B personality—patient, easygoing, and relaxed. In Rosenman's study, 10% of the subjects were defined as Type A or B personalities, with the rest somewhere in between. Among the men who developed coronary disease, twice as many Type A men as Type B men developed it. The researchers found that the biochemistry of Type A personalities resembled that of people who had a history of heart disease. In Type A men there were higher serum cholesterol levels and faster blood coagulation than in Type B men. Such men also had more stress hormones in their blood during working hours. Type B men rarely developed coronary heart disease, regardless of how much fatty food they ate, the number of cigarettes they smoked, or how little they exercised (Rosenman, 1974).

Clearly, both men and women in middle age face many physical changes as well as consequences of personality and lifestyle. They also undergo changes in cognition.

## COGNITIVE PROCESSES

Every person has an optimal level of cognitive performance, which shows itself in areas in which they have been well trained (Fischer, 1980; Fischer, Kenny, & Pipp, 1990). Adults may think and strengthen formal modes of thinking only in their areas of expertise. As we saw in the early adulthood chapter, there may be a next stage after formal operations. Here we shall look at several intriguing ideas about "postformal" modes of thought (Commons, Sinnott, Richards, & Armon, 1984; Labouvie-Vief, 1992).

## Postformal Thinking Revisited

Recall that adolescents, who have discovered new ways of thinking, look at problems from a logical perspective and find possible solutions based on "absolute truth." For instance, carried away with his new powers of logical thinking, Butch insists that there is a logical answer to every question and that if you simply apply logic, you will arrive at the absolute truth. Formal operational adolescents like Butch do not seem fully equipped for a real world in which there are many ways to look at an issue and often not just one right answer.

As mentioned in the previous chapter, in relativistic thinking a person's sense of knowledge depends on his or her subjective perspective. Several researchers have suggested that unlike adolescents, adults see knowledge as relative rather than absolute (Labouvie-Vief, 1984; Sinnott, 1989). Absolute truth is the idea that, given the nature of reality, there is only one truth. A relativist assumes that one's own starting assumptions influence the "truth" that is discovered and there are multiple ways of viewing a problem.

Recall from Chapter 7 how differently preadolescents, adolescents, and adults solved the problem given by Labouvie-Vief, Adams, Hakin-Larson, and Hayden (1983). Most preadolescents and many adolescents answered quickly and confidently. They simply applied logic to the information they were given. On the other hand, adults tended to see that different starting assumptions were possible and the answer depended on which assumptions were chosen. As one woman said, "There were no right or wrong answers" (p. 12).

Adults also engage in advance thinking or thinking about abstract systems (Commons, Richards, & Kuhn, 1982; Fischer et al., 1990; Richards & Commons, 1990). If a concrete operational thinker operates on concrete objects, and the formal operational thinker performs mental actions on *ideas*, the postformal thinker manipulates whole *systems of ideas*. Thus when a student in a bachelor's program is asked to compare and contrast different theories, to uncover overall principles behind several theories, or to form a supertheory based on several theories, the student is being asked to reason about systems (Sigelman & Shaffer, 1995).

Middle-aged adults also achieve advances in *dialectical thinking* (Basseches, 1984; Kramer, 1989), which involves the ability to uncover and resolve contradictions between two opposing ideas. For instance, they would see the contradiction in one's insisting that welfare mothers be single to receive benefits for their children and at the same time criticizing welfare mothers for their single status. Thus relativistic thinking, systems thinking, and dialectical thinking might qualify as a new and higher stage of cognitive development that evolves out of formal operational thinking. Some of these skills may actually develop alongside formal operational thought but not replace it (Chandler & Boutilier, 1992).

Cognitive development involves learning to think in more efficient ways as one gains expertise. As adults become experts in their own areas of specialization, they develop shortcuts that enable them to bypass formal methods of thought (Scribner, 1984). This development depends less on age than on the given person and his or her life circumstances. The different demands placed on a person to think at work, at home, and in the community often tell us more about that person than does mere age.

## Intellectual Functions

Early theorists surmised that intelligence reaches its peak when a person is between 18 and 25 years old (Wechsler, 1958). However, this early descriptive work suffers from several method-ological problems. Most of it was based on mea-sures of intelligence that were developed within a strictly theoretical framework. Later, the ques-tion was reframed: Does intelligence really decline with age? Although research has been extensive since Wechsler's study, we have wit-nessed an increase, not a decrease, in controversy over the timing, extent, and sources of intellectu-al change during adulthood. On the one hand, Baltes and Schaie (1974) conclude that general intellectual decline in middle and old age is largely a myth. On the other hand, Botwinick (1977) concludes that decline in intellectual abili-ties is clearly a part of aging. Such disagreements reflect differing sets of assumptions, which in turn reflect varying degrees of theoretical versus methodological approaches to the phenomenon.

One solution is to discriminate types of intelli-gence and the ways in which they develop. Certainly, intelligence does change as people grow older. There are two types of intellectual ability commonly discerned. The first broad area of functioning, called *fluid intelligence*, appears mainly in the speed and effectiveness of neuro-logical and physiological factors. This area includes such abilities as motor speed, induction, and memory. Here, *fluid* refers to the fact that this type of intelligence can "flow" into various intellectual activities, including perception, recognition, and dealing cognitively with new information (Horn, 1970; Neugarten, 1977). However, by the end of middle age it has declined only to the level that it occupied during the middle of adolescence, which is still usually high (Specht & Craig, 1987).

*Crystallized intelligence* can be described as the ability to process and record the kind of infor-mation one can acquire through both formal and informal education. This includes verbal reason-ing, vocabulary, comprehension, and aspects of spatial perception. Unlike fluid intelligence, crys-tallized intelligence increases over the life span, including through the middle years (Neugarten, 1976).

An increase in crystallized intelligence helps people in their 40s and 50s compensate for any decline in fluid intelligence and thereby maintain their earlier overall level of intelligence. For instance, people in their late middle age or early old age can remember things from the past very well; they also have experience, and often wis-dom, which make up for the slowing down of their fluid intelligence. The exception is *skills* requiring various psychomotor processes, which do slow down in later years (Botwinick, 1977). (Declines in intellectual performance because of memory problems are more noticeable after mid-dle age and will be discussed in Chapter 9.)

Knox (1977) and others use the term *cognitive style* to refer to a person's characteristic pattern of processing information. For instance, some peo-ple are characteristically reflective and deliberate, whereas others are impulsive. Some see the world in a clear black-and-white pattern, where-as others look at shades of gray. Some tolerate ambiguity, whereas others do not.

Does a person's cognitive style change as she or he grows older? For example, does a 50-year-old man solve a problem the same way he did when he was 20 years old? Research indicates that most cognitive patterns are developed in childhood and continue to be individualized in adulthood. They seem primarily to reflect per-sonality type but are also associated with early training and cultural lifestyle. Some people appear to shift toward analytic thinking sometime between childhood and adolescence, with the shift becoming more stable in early adulthood. Many aspects of cognitive style become rigid between middle age and old age, however (Knox, 1977). The 50-year-old man does tend to solve problems the way he did 30 years earlier.

The issue of cognitive style is particularly important in casework services, training pro-grams, and formal and informal education for the middle aged. It is important to recognize that some middle-aged people may have difficulty in learning concepts, not because of a lack of intel-lectual ability but because of their inflexible cog-nitive styles. Being aware of this phenomenon may enable educators to help older students improve their intellectual performance (Knox, 1977). If educators understand a person's thought processes, they can better represent information in a way that will be understood easily. This understanding can also help social workers assess the cognitive styles of their clients.

> At 50, Miriam is returning to school after being out nearly 30 years. In school, she appears to perform very well in one class that makes use of life experiences, but she fails miserably when she must deal with new material that is statistically oriented. Her problem appears to be not the subject per se but the cognitive style she developed toward the subject while she was still in high school, where anything dealing with numbers was considered difficult. Her intellectual abilities in the area of mathematics have not been developed and, coupled with her attitude, create problems for her as she studies statistics.

## THE PSYCHOSOCIAL ENVIRONMENT

### Erikson: Generativity versus Stagnation

Middle adulthood brings a new capacity for directing the course of action of one's own life and the lives of others. The adult now attempts to fulfill his or her long-term goals. From Erikson's perspective (1980), a middle-aged person grows by resolving the conflict of generativity versus stagnation; this growth can be understood as a response to pressure to improve life conditions for future generations. "Generativity . . . encompasses procreativity, productivity, and creativity, and thus the generation of new beings, as well as the new products and new ideas, including a kind of self-generation concerned with further identity development" (Erikson, 1982, p. 67).

According to Erikson's observations (Erikson, Erikson, & Kivnick, 1986) generativity occurs when people maintain the growth of society and nurture themselves and others. A basic dictionary meaning of the word *generate* is "to bring into existence." Developmental factors in middle adulthood include furthering one's ability to make decisions, plan for the future, and anticipate the needs of others in order to make a meaningful impact on the future.

One can describe *generativity* as the capacity for contributing to the survival of one's society. At some point, adult members of a society begin to feel an obligation to give their resources, skills, and creativity to the cause of improving the quality of life of the young. To some extent they are motivated by recognition of the inevitability of mortality. People cannot live forever, nor can they direct the overall course of events. As such, people in this age group often make contributions to society, on both personal and public levels, that will stand after their deaths. These contributions usually take the form of some personal, unique, creative expression of values and often reflect the wish to share what they have learned.

At a more practical level, generativity is expressed in the contribution of money, time, and/or skills to charitable groups. The skills of middle adulthood, as they give new direction to the efforts of growing institutions, thus become valued by the entire community.

At the other extreme of generativity is stagnation, which reflects a failure to meet the demands of the earlier stages of life. Stagnation usually implies a lack of psychological movement or growth. Adults who devote their energy and skills to the sole purpose of self-aggrandizement and personal satisfaction are likely to have difficulty looking beyond their own needs or experiencing satisfaction in taking care of others. Adults who cannot manage a household, raise children, or manage a career are likely to feel a sense of stagnation at the end of middle age.

The experience of stagnation may differ for the narcissistic adult and the depressed adult. Narcissistic adults may expend their energy accumulating wealth and material possessions. They relate to others in terms of how others can serve them. This kind of person can exist quite happily until the physical and psychological consequences of aging begin to affect them. At that point, their self-satisfaction can be undermined by anxieties related to death. Newman and Newman (1995) indicate that individuals of this type often undergo some form of religious "conversion" after a serious illness or an emotional crisis that makes them acknowledge the limitations of a totally self-involved lifestyle.

Depressed people who do not make contributions to society may perceive themselves as being incapable of doing so on account of insufficient resources. These people usually have low self-esteem, are very doubtful about opportunities for improvement in the future, and are unwilling to invest energy in conceptualizing future progress. Both the narcissistic and the depressed types fail to move beyond their own relatedness to themselves and cannot contribute to the future of the larger society.

> Isaac is a 50-year-old man who lives in the inner city. Orphaned at a young age, he has lived in many of his relatives' homes. He is used to periodic changes in the rules and regulations of behavior. His self-esteem has always been low because he never really learned to become part of any particular family. In middle age, Isaac remains unmarried. Quite involved with his personal problems, he views life in terms of his own needs. He expects everyone to cater to him, and this attitude prevents him from making friends and developing a career. He earns a comfortable enough living, but he spends all his time hoarding money and living a meager life. Isaac appears to be more of a stagnated individual than a productive, useful citizen who can think in broad terms.

True to the pattern of resolution of other psychological crises, a person cannot expect to have a sense of generativity until the end of this phase. All the person's life experiences with home, family, and career management contribute to the needed sense of competence, which in turn helps the person pursue a course of action that will have a direct impact on others. People who are generative in their middle adulthood become aware of the ways society needs improvement, begin to generate creative ideas for resolving societal problems, then put into effect many of the solutions they have conceptualized.

## Tasks of Middle Age

Throughout their lives, people must accomplish certain developmental tasks in order to feel satisfied with their lives. One can describe the tasks of middle age in practical terms: One needs to discharge adult civic and social responsibility and to establish and maintain an adequate standard of living. As we just saw, the basic issue facing people at this time is generativity versus stagnation.

Peck (1968) has added some key concepts to Erikson's formulation and proposed several issues or conflicts that people face in middle age:

1. *Valuing wisdom versus physical powers:*
   This period brings a decrease in physical stamina and an increase in health problems that cause people to shift a good part of their energy to mental rather than physical activities.
2. *Socializing versus sexualizing in human relationships:* Many people have physical and social constraints imposed on them by divorce or widowhood that force them to redefine their relationships and emphasize companionship rather than sexual intimacy or competitiveness.
3. *Emotional and mental flexibility versus rigidity:* People make adjustments in middle age as families and friends move away and as new situations call for changed mental attitudes.

The rest of Peck's stages relate more to old age, but they begin in middle age:

1. *Ego differentiation versus work-role preoccupation:* Many people define themselves solely in terms of work roles, but tend to become disoriented when they begin to lose those roles through retirement, unemployment, or having children leave home.

2. *Body transcendence versus body preoccupation:* Body transcendence occurs when a person's self does not wholly depend on a sense of physical well-being. It is central to the individual's ability to avoid preoccupation with the increasing aches and pains that accompany aging.

3. *Ego transcendence versus ego preoccupation:* Ego transcendence means that people should not be mired in thoughts of death; rather, they learn to age successfully and transcend the prospect of their own extinction by becoming involved with the younger generation and accepting the fact that their legacy will outlive them (Specht & Craig, 1987).

Unlike Erikson's stages, each of which corresponds to a specific life phase, none of Peck's dimensions is completely confined to middle age or old age. The decisions made early in life act as building blocks to the solutions of middle age, which in turn help to resolve some of the issues of old age.

## Men's Development

Vaillant (1977) headed the Grant study, a developmental project that began in 1938. A group of 268 male Harvard University students, chosen because they were healthy and self-reliant, were tested, interviewed, and followed for many years. The researchers found that the lives of their subjects were shaped not by isolated traumatic events but by the quality of their sustained relationships with other people.

The researchers also looked at the adaptive functions of defense mechanisms. They found that repression and projection were meaningful adult coping styles. Coping capacities were classified as mature, immature, or neurotic. Vaillant found that both mature and neurotic mechanisms were used by healthy men. However, those who used mature adaptive mechanisms were the most well-adjusted men.

Though Vaillant's findings coincide with Erikson's adult life scheme, Vaillant names a different stage—*Career Consolidation*—which occurs between intimacy versus isolation and generativity versus stagnation (see Chapter 7). One subject of this research explains the typical pattern of these bright and achieving men: "At 20 to 30, I think I learned how to get along with my wife. From 30 to 40, I learned how to be a success at my job. And at 40 to 50, I worried less about myself and more about my children" (Vaillant, 1977, p. 206).

Vaillant found that at age 20 these men were very much under parental dominance. In their 20s and sometimes their 30s, these men spent time gaining autonomy and finding women to marry. At ages 25 to 35 years, these men worked hard at consolidating their careers and, by age 40, the career consolidation stage had ended. After this period, men may leave the compulsive, unreflective busy work and start to explore their inner selves (Vaillant, 1977).

In another study, Levinson, Darrow, Klein, Levinson, and McKee (1978) at Yale University conducted in-depth interviews of 40 men between the ages of 35 and 45. There were ten men in each of the following occupational groups: hourly workers in industry, academic biologists, business executives, and novelists. The purpose of the study was to show that the goal of an adult person is to build a *life structure*. This structure has both external and internal aspects to it. The external consists of participation in the sociocultural world of the individual, including his family, his occupation, and other major external events. The internal consists of the individual's values, dreams, and emotional life. The researchers divided men's lives into two kinds of periods: stable periods, which generally last six to eight years, and transitional periods, which last up to five years during which the men reappraise their lives and explore new possibilities.

Let us go back to trace male development from adolescence, so we can better understand the middle-aged man's experience. There are four transitional periods leading into stable middle adulthood; the first three are called novice stages. The first stage, *early adult transition*, usually occurs between the ages of 17 and 24 as a man moves from preadulthood to adulthood. During this time, he leaves his parents' home and becomes financially and emotionally independent. The young man may go to college or into the armed forces, thereby entering an institution while he is midway between childhood and full adult status.

Here is a typical (humorous) letter from a 19-year-old who has just entered college and needs financial help from his family. It was written on a torn cover of a book and mailed in an envelope made from a shopping bag to show how desperate he was:

Dear Mom, Dad, and Cathy:

This is a plea for help from your beloved son and beloved brother at Elon College. Due to unexpected expenses, I have run into some financial difficulty.

If you can find it within your heart to send me a few pennies it would be greatly appreciated.

I hope you rich people at home think of me when you sit down to a good meal. This letter is not meant to be a joke. I am running kind of low on cash.

I meant to ask you on Sunday but I forgot.

Just send me a little gift in the mail this week.

Your poor college student,

Steve.

The second stage is called *entering the adult world* (ages 22 to 28). The young man is now more in the adult world and less in his family of origin. Now is when he begins to build his first life structure. He may choose an occupation and become involved with women, which may lead to marriage. Two major features of this phase are the dream and the mentor. The young person may dream of becoming a well-known writer, which may motivate greater achievements. If this dream is not fulfilled, he may experience an emotional crisis later in his life. The second major feature of this period is the influence of a mentor, who may be 8 to 15 years older than the young man. The mentor offers guidance and inspiration both in career and personal matters.

The third stage is called the *age-30 transition* (28 to 30 years). The young man now reevaluates the commitments he made during the preceding decade and makes strong commitments for the first time. Some men slip into this stage with ease, whereas others experience developmental crises. Marriage problems may arise, resulting in divorce. Some men change jobs or settle down after a period of uncertainty. This is a phase of transition, a time to reassess earlier choices. This period could also bring the stress of radical changes in living location. In some ways this is a crucial period. If a man has made sound choices, he will have built a strong foundation for his life structure. However, if he has made poor life decisions, he may have difficulty during the next stage.

*Settling down* is the fourth stage of transition to middle adulthood (ages 30–45), and it is during this period that a man builds his second adult life structure. By this time, he has set specific goals for himself and has established roots in family, occupation, and community. Now he attempts to become his own boss. At times he may be at odds with his wife, children, boss, and co-workers, and he may even discard his mentor. As identified by Levinson, the five different patterns occurring in this period are classified as sequences. A man may do any of the following:

1. Advance within a stable life structure
2. Experience serious failure or decline within a stable life structure
3. Start a new sequence in his life by trying a new life structure
4. Produce a change in life structure
5. Remain in flux and experience an unstable life structure

For men, age 40 brings about another transition, which may be traumatic—the so-called midlife crisis. This is the time when unfulfilled dreams of young people need to be put into perspective. Men come to the realization that they are not the unqualified success they aspired to be and that their time is running out. They explore the neglected areas of their life and attempt to find new meaning in their lives.

By age 45, most men have settled down into the next period of calm. Once again, the man is pursuing new, more attainable goals with vigor.

Age 50 brings another transition, when men reevaluate their goals and lifestyle. Those men who did not experience a crisis at age 40 are more likely to do so at this time than those who did.

Then comes another period of calm, which is a culmination of middle adulthood. This can be a period of great fulfillment when men can reap the rewards of the more realistic goals they set for themselves in their earlier periods of transition.

The end of this decade brings another phase of transition. At age 60, men begin to reappraise their lives. They review their achievements with mixed feelings of joy, pride, and despair (Levinson et al., 1978).

## Women's Development

I deliberately present women's development as separate from men's. Although men and women complement each other and need each other, they are brought up to respond differently to situations and to life itself.

Horner (1972) found that the anxiety women feel and show in reaching achievements is unique. McClelland (1975) presents the human experience of success in terms of both "hope of success" and "fear of failure." On the basis of her studies of women, Horner identifies a third category, "fear of success." When women have a conflict between femininity and success, we must view their dilemma as different from that of men. Sassen (1980) proposes that women may face this conflict because they think their success will be bought at the price of someone else's failure. This perception suggests women's underlying sense that something is rotten in the state when success is defined as being better than anyone else. Sassen reveals that Horner found success anxiety to be present in most women only when competition was directly connected with being successful at the expense of another person's failure.

Virginia Woolf observed that women's values differ from those of men. Women's deference to others is rooted in their social subordination as well as in the substance of their moral concern (Woolf, 1929). Being sensitive to others and

assuming responsibility for taking care of them may lead women to voice opinions other than their own and to include in their judgments other points of view. Thus a woman's sense of morality is manifest in an apparent diffusion and confusion of judgment that is inseparable from her moral strength and her dominant concern with relationships as well as responsibilities (Gilligan, 1982).

When men describe themselves, their involvement with others is tied to a qualification of identity rather than to its realization. Whereas attachment is central to a woman's identity, for men individual achievement and great ideas or distinctive activity define the standard of self-assessment and success (Gilligan, 1982).

Erikson (1968), Levinson (1977), and Vaillant (1977) have put forth the most influential theories to date pertaining to adult development. As you know, these embody a male orientation in their theoretical concepts and research examples. However, in recent years other researchers have begun studying the female experience of middle age and found it to differ in many ways from previous models of development (Barnett & Baruch, 1978; Baruch, Barnett, & Rivers, 1983; Rubin, 1979; Sheppard & Seidman, 1982).

*Mentor, love, and dreams* Papalia and Olds (1992, pp. 403–404) review four unpublished dissertations describing studies using women subjects and Levinson's research designs. The four investigators interviewed a total of 39 women 28 to 53 years old. The women were primarily white, with 8 of them African American. Most of the women interviewed were employed; Some were married, some unmarried; some had children, some did not.

Though these studies tend to support Levinson's views that women and men undergo similar kinds of age-linked changes, the researchers identify three important differences, as follows:

1. *The mentor:* Women were less likely than men to have mentors. Many of the women identified having a role model when they were in their 20s but only four achieved a

true mentor relationship. If these patterns truly are typical, many women are hampered in their career pursuits for lack of a mentor.

2. *The love relationship:* Levinson found that men wanted a special woman who would help them pursue their dreams. In the studies of women, all 39 respondents similarly sought out a special man. However, these women saw themselves as supporting this man's dreams rather than wanting a man who would support them in achieving *their* goals.

3. *The dream:* Many respondents had dreams— that is, goals that they wished to achieve in life. But their dreams were more vague, more tentative, and more complex, as well as more temporary and less career oriented, than those of men. Most of the women's dreams were split between achievement and relationships. As other research studies show, women were more likely to define themselves in relation to others—that is, husbands, children, parents, and colleagues. Men, on the other hand, tended to "find themselves" by separating from their own family of origin and pursuing their own interests. Women also tended to develop their own identity through the responsibilities and attachments of relationships.

Men thought in terms of career goals while women dreamed about a mix of family and career interests. Also many of the women worked to help their "special man" achieve his goals, but other women by age 30 began to make more demands on their husbands to accommodate their interests and goals in regard to career, marriage, and raising children (Zastrow & Kirst-Ashman, 1994).

In the next two sections, we shall look at two different studies of women that have brought out varying and at times contradictory findings.

*Mastery and pleasure* Researchers Baruch, Barnett, and Rivers used questionnaires to study 298 women between the ages of 35 and 55 who had an average educational level of two years beyond high school and an annual income range that averaged between $4500 and $50,000 (Barnett & Baruch, 1987; Baruch, Barnett, & Rivers, 1983). The participants included (1) employed women who had never married, (2) employed married women with children, (3) employed married women without children, (4) divorced women with children, (5) married homemakers with children, and (6) married homemakers without children.

In all, 60 women (about ten in each of the six groups) were individually interviewed. The purpose of the study was to learn about the pleasures, problems, and conflicts that these people found in their lives. This questionnaire was also administered to a random sample of 238 other women in the six categories just mentioned.

This research discovered that the two basic elements that determine the level of mental health experienced by these women are the degree of control that a woman had over her life, which the researchers called *mastery,* and the amount of *pleasure* the woman experienced from it. These criteria were not related to age, for the older women felt as good about themselves as younger women did. There was very little evidence of a midlife crisis. There was no relationship between the well-being of a woman and her marital status, whether she had children, or whether she was pre- or postmenopausal. What emerged was evidence that the combination of a woman's *work* and her *intimate relationships* was of vital importance to her mental health.

Receiving pay for work proved to be the most reliable predictor of mastery, while experiencing *positive relationships* with husband (including a good sex life) and children was the best predictor of pleasure. A challenging job with good pay that gave a woman an opportunity to use her talents and skills and to make decisions added to the psychological well-being of a woman. The women who scored highest on both mastery and pleasure were employed married women with children, and the lowest scores were from unemployed childless married women. The researchers concluded that the well-being of a woman is enhanced by taking on multiple roles, in spite of the stress that goes along with active involvement in several important aspects of life simultaneously. It was more stressful to be underinvolved, not having enough to do, with few personal and occupational demands. This study presented a positive view of women in their midlife transitions.

*Homemakers and career women*  Levinson's (1996) new study of women, presented in *Seasons of a Woman's Life,* is similar to his study of men about two decades ago. Levinson studied 45 women who were seen as either homemakers or career women (business women and faculty members). Levinson indicates that the work of midlife individuation, an especially important task of this period, forms the inner matrix out of which the modified self and life evolve over the rest of the era. Contrary to Baruch et al. (1983), Levinson found that women have more serious midlife crises. The midlife crises of both groups of women were similar in some aspects. They all went through the midlife transition at the same ages—about 40 to 46.

Even so, Levinson found important differences between the homemakers and the career women. The homemakers had attempted in early adulthood to make family the central component of their life structures within the framework of a traditional marriage enterprise. In midlife, most of them recognized that their marriage enterprise was a partial or massive failure. Whatever its previous value, they wanted a different kind of a marriage, family, and life structure in the next season of their lives. The career woman, in contrast, had attempted in early adulthood to pursue an antitraditional dream. Many chose the dual role of wife/mother and successful career woman, balancing a full-time career and a marriage and family. However, more time went into the career than into the marriage or family. They did not want to be seen as employed housewives but as women with their own neotraditional marriage and careers. They wanted an equal marriage with a satisfying motherhood and a career

that gave her a valued nonsubordinate place in the occupational world and in society generally.

At midlife, each woman came to reappraise and modify her life. She came to understand more fully the sexism inherent in work organizations. In midlife transitions, career women asked, "What do I want in life?" The answer often was, "More passionate engagement and equality in love and work."

As Levinson (1996) saw it, for all career women occupation would have a different place in the ensuing life structure than in the previous ones. These women hoped that work would provide a stronger experience of creativity, satisfaction, and social contribution; that it would become more playful and loving rather than a matter of proving themselves in a competitive world. Their greatest fear was that they would find no satisfactory place for themselves as valued members of a valued world—and that perhaps they may be squeezed out altogether or get stuck in a position that offered little to themselves and required little from them. Levinson concludes that these were one of the first generation of women in U.S. history who chose a nontraditional way of living. These women found new paths that brought them into the corporate/business and academic worlds on career paths. These career women juggled work and personal life, dealing with work institutions that gave mainly lip service to career advancement for women beyond middle levels, with the hope of making it better in time. The personal growth and development of these women were great as they struggled with the essential question of who they were and what they wanted to pursue further in life.

The homemakers in Levinson's (1996) sample were pioneers in transforming the traditional marriage enterprise. These women had entered adulthood expecting to live as unemployed homemakers within a traditional marriage. In their early 40s, they entered the midlife transition and the shift from early to middle adulthood. Among the 15 homemakers, only one was in her first marriage and unemployed. About 50% of the homemakers were divorced or in a second marriage. At this point in their lives, motherhood was becoming a less central component of the life structure. The terms of the marriage enterprise were changing, and the mental relationship had to be modified. About 80% of the homemakers were working outside home. It was not clear what new marriage enterprises these women would create in the new era of middle adulthood as they struggled to create better lives for themselves (Levinson, 1996).

## FAMILY ISSUES AND PATTERNS

In middle age, people face various challenges related to family relationships and styles. This section explores the challenges of the "sandwich generation" in facing such issues as parental care, the "empty nest," divorce, and being single. Notice how the developmental tasks of middle age come up—how an awareness of broader social concerns stems from these life experiences.

### Taking Care of Older Parents

In U.S. culture, relatively few families consist of three generations living together, with an additional aunt or uncle. The nuclear family remains a constant, despite the rising divorce rate. This type of family—two parents and children—plays a significant role in society by providing models for children. However, many functions associated with the family are taken over at least in part by outside agencies. The functions of vocational guidance, recreation, religion, and social activities are carried on largely outside the family. In the present society, the major function of the family is to provide housing, food, and clothes; serve as an economic unit; inculcate values; and provide a reference point for various governmental agencies in their implementation of rules and regulations (Glick, 1975).

Partly because of the model of the nuclear family, there is widespread myth that older parents are mostly neglected by their middle-aged children. This myth is sustained by an additional belief that at some time in the past (the "good old days"), parents were treated better. The myth says that today's children do not care for their parents the way people used to (Lee, 1985). These beliefs are wrong. Proportionately fewer older adults live with their children than they did a century ago because older adults now are far more financially independent (Lee, 1985). A century ago there were neither social security nor private pension plans, so older adults had to live with other family members out of necessity. But today a large number of them live within a 30-minute drive of one of their children. Also, middle-aged children and their parents contact each other fairly frequently. According to Krout (1988), about 80% of the older parents have seen their children in the past two weeks, regardless of whether people live in rural or urban areas. There is a good relationship between the older parents and their middle-aged children. The children enjoy visiting their parents. They also use these visits to reevaluate the meaning of the relationship as their parents approach death (Helson, & Moane 1987).

When the health of an older parent is precarious, living with grown children may be a necessity. Such household arrangements may offer advantages, since some elderly grandparents have an excellent rapport with young children and on occasion may look after their grandchildren. Some older parents also contribute financially to their grown children.

Rachael is a 55-year-old woman who has been widowed for 20 years. Although she has had many opportunities to get married, she has avoided them and brought up her children single-handedly. Since her children have grown up, she lives by herself and enjoys the independence and quietness that life offers her. She is well-to-do and does not depend on her children for anything; in fact, she helps them out considerably. She also helps her elderly widowed mother.

Rachael is an active member of a recreational club and heads many social and charitable organizations. She often contributes money to charitable causes.

The way older parents live depends on their socioeconomic status. Older people with upper-class status usually retain their high status until their demise and frequently live alone, whereas older people without adequate financial resources have to depend on their children or on the state. The care of such parents usually falls into the hands of the daughter or daughter-in-law. Even when all demographic characteristics have been ruled out, daughters are clearly three times more likely than sons to provide care to their older parents (Dwyer & Coward, 1991). This gender difference appears in other cultures as well. For instance, in India the oldest son is responsible for parental care but it is actually his wife who does the day-to-day parenting.

For middle-aged people, the often considerable hostility that arises between them and the older generations seldom involves money. Stress in taking care of older adults comes mainly from two sources (Robinson & Thurnher, 1979): parental decline and sense of confinement. First, middle-aged children might have trouble coping with their parents' declines, especially those that involve cognitive disabilities. They may not know why their parents are declining. At times, these children may become ambivalent and antagonistic toward their parents. Second, when children see their caregiving situations as confining or as encroaching on their responsibilities as spouse, parent, employee, and so forth, they may feel angry and/or guilty.

Middle-aged people may start to help their older parents if either becomes chronically ill or one of them dies. At this point, the roles of parent and child reverse as middle-aged children assume all or part of the caretaking role from their parents. Adult children offer their parents economic assistance and transportation, share holidays and travel, do chores for them, and give them gifts. When parents have a disabling disease and cannot or will not live alone, then their children's intervention is imperative. Action on behalf of the parent could mean having a housekeeper in the parent's home, sending the parent away to a nursing home or to another relative's home, or bringing the parent into their own home. In caring for an ailing parent in one's own home, patience and fortitude are crucial. Research indicates that middle-aged children spend a great deal of time, money, and energy in helping their old parents (Brody, 1990). Nearly 90% of the elderly receive help from their children and other relatives (Morris & Sherwood, 1984).

> David and Toni are in their fifties. They have four grown children, two of whom are in college and require their parents' assistance in pursuing their educational goals. Suddenly, Toni's 70-year-old father dies of a heart attack, and her mother is left alone without much economic support and no one to take care of her. She suffers from arthritis, which makes it difficult for her to do anything useful in the household. So Toni, together with her husband, have to decide whether it will be constructive to bring her mother into their household. Though agreeable, David worries about having enough space for his children when they come home. He and his wife are both concerned about money and the need to make provisions for their children as well as provide special medical attention for Toni's mother. Eventually, after a long discussion, the couple decide to bring Toni's mother into their home. Although at times they see her as a burden, she contributes to the family in terms of emotional support both for her grandchildren and for her daughter and son-in-law.

When middle-aged adults bring their parents into a home where they have children of their own, the logistics of maintaining life as usual involve reestablishing rules of behavior to insure everyone is treated with respect. Setting up such rules demands great skill. If the relationship between the older parent and the middle-aged child was good in the early years, then the child's expectations and feelings about the necessary adjustment will be realistic, making this task less overwhelming. In time it can become a rewarding experience. Some families may need to have counseling by family service agencies to facilitate the transitional phase of relocation.

> In her 50s, Irene lives with her second husband and their seven children. A few of the children are

grown and live away from home, but the rest live at home, attending school and holding part-time jobs. Irene and her husband both have to work to meet all the household expenses. Irene's mother, who has been a single parent all her adult life, lives with them. It is a blessing to have her in the house; she takes care of major household responsibilities and prepares a hot meal when the family comes home for dinner. Moreover, the grandmother receives social security benefits, which she shares with the family. This type of living arrangement facilitates a meaningful livelihood for all members of the household.

## Parenting Roles in Middle Age

According to Jones, Garrison, and Morgan (1985), middle-aged parents have two tasks: (1) they have to relate successfully to their children and help to emancipate them into the adult world and (2) they have to adjust to the children's absence. The first of these tasks is difficult; parents have to let go of their children and allow them to become independent. Parents have to compromise, at least partially, on matters that involve their children's friends, styles of dress, vocational interests, and personal tastes. As children get older, the only way parents can assist them is through discussion and examples that serve to inculcate values. When adult children have marital problems, many parents cannot stay out of their arguments, and their interference can complicate the situation. Keeping out of grown children's problems is difficult, particularly when they are serious—for example, the partner's drug abuse, multiple infidelity, or physical abuse.

The roles of middle-aged parents change according to the needs of their grown children. Some mothers reestablish close bonds with their children through advice giving and taking a keen interest in the grandchildren. If there are problems between a daughter and her husband or a son and his wife, the mother may attempt to help ease the situation. At times, though, interference from her as the mother-in-law may create problems.

Gutmann (1964) believes men in middle age become more passive and women become more protective and aggressive. Rosenberg and Farrell (1976) state that the mother's role in nurture and aggression is important to the family's emotional life. In time, "she pushes her husband from the stage and seems to draw strength from his decline" (p. 163). Men are less authoritarian during this period and men of lower class often abdicate any decision making about their children, leaving the field to their wives, particularly when the children have overtaken the men in education. Many mothers of all classes are seen as confidantes to their daughters.

> Vivian is 27. The more involved she becomes in her own family life, the more she seems to need the help and support of her 53-year-old mother. Vivian has more in common with her mother than ever before and spends time talking to her mother about her own children, husband, and money problems. She visits her mother frequently, helping her in household chores and sharing neighborly gossip.

*Intergenerational adjustment* Middle-aged parents have to prepare themselves for the time when the children will leave home. Before that time, problems relating to the children's completing their education and embarking on careers frequently involve the parents to a high degree.

There are probably fewer differences now between young adults and their parents than there were in previous years, because communication has improved and the structure of power in the family has shifted from authoritarian to democratic. Several authorities say that the roles of parents as guides and of children as listeners have remained essentially the same, and these roles cannot be altered without affecting society.

Through their children, parents learn different ways of doing and thinking. As parents grow older, they often stay current with their children's outside knowledge and contacts.

> Fifty-two-year-old Linda is happy that her daughter has pursued higher education and become a nurse. Linda once yearned to work as a professional nurse, but because of family responsibilities she

never completed her education. However, her dreams have come true through her daughter, cementing the sense of belonging and mutuality that the mother and daughter already shared.

## Postparenthood

The postparenthood family is becoming more and more common in Euro-American cultures. This could be due to the trend toward smaller families with few children. Further, only recently have both parents lived long enough to see the marriage of their youngest child. On the average, men are about 54 and women about 51 when their children start to get married, and many middle-aged couples have completed their child-rearing roles before they reach age 60 years. However, another new trend may also postpone postparenthood: starting families later. At any age, parents must readjust to the departure of children.

Although grown children leave home, their parents do not abandon them. They continue to provide considerable financial help, such as paying college tuition when feasible. The help they give varies from the mundane, such as providing a washer and dryer, to the significant, such as paying the down payment of a house.

Once children have left home, parents take stock and question what kind of job they have done as parents. Ryff, Lee, Essex, and Schmutte (1994) specify that such assessment is an essential part of the parents' midlife evaluation of themselves. To test this idea, these researchers assessed a random sample of 114 middle-aged mothers and 101 middle-aged fathers from different middle-class families in the Midwest who had a child over 21 years old. The researchers asked the parents to rate the child's adjustment as well as their educational and occupational attainment, to compare the child to others of that age, and to rate their child's and their own psychological well-being.

The results showed that parents' view of their children's overall and social adjustment correlated closely with measures of their parents' own well-being. Further, parents' sense of self-acceptance and purpose in life and environmental adjustments were strongly related to how well

they thought their children were adjusted. Somewhat weaker relations were found between children's accomplishments and parental well-being. No difference was found between fathers and mothers. Parents whose children did better than themselves in terms of education and occupation were better pleased than parents whose children did worse.

Ryff and his colleagues (1994) also showed that midlife parents' self-evaluations are clearly correlated with their own perceptions of how their children turned out. They surmised that this was one way that parents can justify the time and energy they have devoted to their children.

*When grown children return* Although parents are sad when children leave home permanently, they also begin to readjust to a new life without them. But at times, at least one grown child returns back home to live with them. Interestingly, this living arrangement is most common if the parents are in good health and parents continue to do most of the housework (Ward, Logan, & Spitz, 1992). These grown children return home not to help out but because they have financial problems or need help with child care, particularly after a divorce where the young adult has become a single parent.

Although middle-aged parents love their children, they are often not thrilled to have their grown children return back home. Both tend to view the situation positively when the child is in his or her 20s and the arrangement is temporary (Clemons & Axelson, 1985). Also, four of every ten parents report the conflict and tensions that exist when arguments about lifestyle, friends, and personal habits arise. Of course, when times are hard, grown children may lack options and therefore need to live with their parents. All caring parents never stop being parents, and most willingly extend their hearts, their money, and their home for their children whenever they need it.

*Filling the void* When children leave home, parents face many changes. Critical changes in roles affect many areas of development. For example, the relationship between husband and wife changes as the parental role diminishes. Further, each parent often undergoes an introspective evaluation of his or her performance as a parent. When children leave home during their parents' middle years, some women experience the "empty nest" syndrome, causing them to seek jobs or other activities. Finally, parents have to recognize that the energy and resources they formerly put into child rearing are available for other purposes, and so they search for new outlets.

If a couple has had a meaningful relationship, their quality of life usually improves when children leave home. If not, the change may lead to deterioration in the relationship, which may result in either a divorce or a poor marriage maintained for economic and social purposes. Improvement in the quality of life comes about as people have more time for themselves and as family resources that had been committed to educating and caring for children are used for travel, redecorating, clothes, and entertainment.

Grandparenting fills a void for many. Though young teen mothers whose children also become parents during their teens may achieve grandparenthood before they reach age 30 (Miller & Cavanaugh, 1990), most people become grandparents in their middle age. Grandparents take on new roles and often provide pleasure and gratification to their grandchildren without being responsible for raising them.

When they take care of grandchildren, adults feel a sense of continuity with future generations and the emotional satisfaction of feeling young again. Their pleasure depends to some extent on their degree of involvement and freedom to come and go as they please (Neugarten & Weinstein, 1964).

On the basis of several studies, Stevens-Long (1979) concludes that there is a high degree of satisfaction among women who enter employment after their children are grown and who still have time for grandparenting. Their satisfaction and happiness with their employment depend on approval or disapproval from their spouses. However, many men are happy and willing to see their wives work because they become more financially secure.

## Marriage in the Middle Years

All through adulthood, marriage ideally represents happiness and companionship. The "launching" of grown children is seen as a celebration and is accompanied by marital satisfaction. Often, women report an improvement in their marriages (Rhyne, 1981; Swensen et al., 1981). There are three possible reasons for improvement. First, financial security improves. Disagreements over finances slowly die out as the couple begin to plan and pull together to make their own future secure. Employed men and women can devote more time for their work and thus increase their pay. Often, there are fewer expenses as children become at least partly self-supporting (Berry & Williams, 1987). Second, marriages improve because when children are successfully raised and launched, the parents are relieved of many anxieties and can share in feelings of achievement. Third, the couple begins to do things together, like fixing a house, taking a vacation, and just having more time for activities that lead to marital intimacy.

Of course, not all marriages improve. Some couples face financial strain and stress, unemployment, or illness of either spouse, which reduces time and money for doing things together. At times couples find out that they have been too far apart from each other and are in fact becoming "emotionally divorced" (Fitzpatrick, 1984). In this case, the couple needs to spend more time together.

A partner's physical appearance correlates with marital satisfaction and sexual interest, particularly for men (Margolin & White, 1987). In U.S. culture, age-related changes in appearance can be judged harshly, especially for women (Katchadourian, 1987). However, couples that had a genuine physical attraction when they were younger find that it continues, and they can greet the changes of middle age with empathy.

Some people think that for a marriage to be healthy and satisfactory, the couple should be equal partners. Rapaport and Rapaport (1975) believe this principle is overrated. They contend that a marriage should be equitable rather than equal. They feel that people will change and shift at various points in their life, so that the domestic load will be shared as needed in household chores, child care, and leadership in family affairs.

> Wendy is 54 years old and has traveled widely with her husband. In her career as a journalist, she enjoys writing, meeting people, and traveling around the world. She and her husband have four children. While her husband does most of the housework, Wendy cooks. She's a good cook, and her family truly appreciates her meals. In spite of her being a well-known journalist, what her children and husband look to her for is the comfort she offers them both as a caring person and as a good cook.

## Divorce and Its Aftermath

Alternatives to traditional marriage include swinging marriages and group marriages, which are not popular alternatives if we judge from the number of people involved in them. Apparently they are too fragile and hazardous to be considered by the traditional majority (Rogers, 1979). An increasing percentage of people stay single longer; also, more people who get divorced remain single. Greater permissiveness in sexual mores and the ability to establish emotional and financial independence allows many people freedom of lifestyle and freedom from responsibility for others. Most divorced men are between 35 and 44; a smaller number are in the 45-to-54 group. Most divorced women are between 45 and 50, followed by the 35-to-44 age group. Being divorced even at these late ages offers women and men many alternatives, although for the older woman between the ages of 45 and 54, finding another partner may be more difficult than for men at that age.

A couple does not reach the point of divorce overnight, say Levinger and Moles (1979). Their model of marriage has two features: On the one hand, external support and internal attractions tend to keep the marriage together; on the other hand, external attractions work against the mar-

riage. If the internal attractions are strong enough, then the marriage will be healthy. If the internal attractions are insufficient, then the marriage may stay together because of external supports, such as legal barriers, children, or career needs. When the external attraction to escape is stronger than the emotional tie, the marriage will be broken. If the impetus of these stimuli—the attraction of another man or woman, growth opportunities, and so on—continues, then divorce is inevitable.

No matter how desirable relief in the form of divorce may be, divorce rarely occurs without problems. The anticipated euphoria is outweighed by guilt, anguish, the legal matters as they affect others (especially children), and the necessity of making numerous adjustments. Many people, particularly women, when considering their future loneliness without their spouse, give up the idea of separating. Men may reflect on the fact that the wife has looked after their clothes, food, home life, and the like, and may give up the idea of divorce out of sheer fright.

Research suggests that today's couples, as others before them, give their marriage a chance to survive. Most divorcing couples experience a few years of marital distress and often try out separation before they make the final decision to divorce (Gottman & Levenson, 1992; Kitson, Babri, & Roach, 1985). Although the stated reasons vary, they are no longer restricted to severe problems such as nonsupport, alcoholism, or abuse (Gigy & Kelly, 1992). In fact, today's couples divorce for many other reasons such as lack of communication, of emotional fulfillment, or of compatibility. Wives also tend to have longer lists of complaints than do their husbands and often initiate the divorce (Gigy & Kelly, 1992; Gray & Silver, 1990).

Most divorced and widowed people remarry—three out of four, according to Glenn (1991)—with the hope that the new marriage will succeed. Remarriages of divorced women are more apt to end in divorce than those of men. Many couples do avoid making the same mistakes they made before and try to avoid possible mismatches. The opportunities for men to marry are typically greater than those for women because men tend to marry younger women and women tend to marry older men. The pool of potential marriage partners gets larger for men and decreases for women because at every period of life, more men than women die.

## Single Middle Adults

There are several stereotypes of the single lifestyle. Some people think that single people are lonely, but this is not true. As we have seen, single adults often live with their family members, a roommate, or significant partners. Women and men choose to be single for various reasons. The profile of a single lifestyle is rather different for men and women. Highly educated women who value their career achievement and have a strong sense of self-determination are likely to see distinct advantages in the single lifestyle. They view their singlehood as an identity-related commitment—why get into a relationship that may make them compromise their occupational goals? By the time they have reached middle adulthood, they are even more into their career goals; the concept of being married begins to fade away unless they pursue it. Women who remain single do experience rapid advancement in both educational and occupational attainment (Houseknecht, Vaughan, & Statham, 1987). However, men have never been subjected to social pressure to choose between career and marriage. Men who are single into their 30s are likely to be less educated, less successful in the world of work, and also less desirable as partners than their female counterparts (Newman & Newman, 1995).

People choose to remain single for many reasons. Some take on responsibilities in their family of origin and, when they have completed their obligations, find they have lived a lifestyle with which they are comfortable, so they do not change. Other factors that contribute to singleness are the changes in sex-role expectations, particularly for women; the decreased emphasis

on childbearing; and the presence of special facilities and services geared to singles, such as housing, newspapers and magazines, and entertainment spots.

Little research has been done on the psychosocial development of adults who remain single. According to Stein (1989) it makes sense to see decisions about remaining single as linked to the broader theme of identity development. There are two groups of people who are single: those who intend to get married but are not ready to marry at present because they feel ambivalent (*wishful/regretful singles*) and those who do not intend to marry (*resolved singles*).

> Shelly has dated a man for 17 years and has a good time with him but wants to marry him when she turns 45. He refuses, for he wanted to marry her when she was 23, when Shelly was not ready. Now they continue to date but without any serious commitment. Shelly is sorry that she didn't marry him when he asked her to. Thus in many ways she is a regretful single.

We can assume that resolved singles are quite satisfied about the quality of their lifestyle and are effective in forming the kinds of relationships that support their choice. In contrast, wishful and regretful singles are involuntarily single. They may have regrets and be more depressed about their situation. Generalizations about singles in terms of their adjustment or well-being often fail to take into consideration these kinds of distinctions (Shostak, 1987; Stein, 1981).

## CAREER ISSUES

Work is an important aspect of adult development, and every person who enters the workforce has an occupational career. Careers do not necessarily appear to be orderly or progressive; one can argue that as long as a person is involved in an effort to make use of his or her talents and skills we can find significant transactions between the world of work and the individual development of that person (Newman &

Newman, 1995). That is, work and home life are not as separate as one might think. As a doctor once remarked to his pregnant patient, he had spent part of the previous Sunday watching a TV show about pregnancy—his favorite topic! Because there is a reciprocity between work and individual growth, we expect people with certain kinds of experiences, abilities, and values to enter certain kinds of work roles (Holland, 1985).

However, when middle-aged people reassess their lifestyles, some of them may regret the careers they have chosen. Further, rapidly shifting technology has made some jobs redundant or obsolete. Stress is placed on the entire family system when the wage earner becomes involuntarily unemployed. Affected employees may receive retraining to update their skills or assistance in making career changes. This also causes the family a certain degree of stress, but the availability of employment mitigates it.

Values, careers, and attitudes interact. Normally people select jobs that suit their value system. For instance, a person who has a strong desire to help children would not choose a career in chemistry. Just as a person's value system affects choice of career, work molds the value system through social roles, environment, and atmosphere, as discussed in Chapter 7.

A large number of people change their jobs because they are not physically suited for a particular type of work after a certain age. For example, professional athletes, police officers, firefighters, or army officers do work that requires a level of physical skill and strength they cannot sustain later in life. Some of these people move into supervisory or executive positions, whereas others must find new careers.

Usually, though, the middle years are a period of career stability. At this time, most men and women reach their highest status and income in their careers if they have been employed all their lives. Those who have made successful choices and applied their energy well reap the benefits of a productive career. Given a degree of success in this period, the career task is not so much to reach and maintain a peak of prestige and income as to

achieve a flexible role—one that is interesting and productive as well as financially satisfying.

## Women and Careers

More women than before have taken jobs, particularly since the 1970s, for many reasons. For example, the present economy often demands two paychecks. Families tend to have fewer children. The consensus is that the average number of children that a woman has in the United States during the remainder of this century will be slightly less than two (Havighurst & Levine, 1979).

If I were to ask what would a young woman who had just graduated from college be doing occupationally ten years from now, how would you respond? Would she be strongly committed to her occupation or would she have abandoned it for other things? Betz (1984) wanted some answers, so she examined the occupational histories of 500 college women ten years after graduation. She found that two-thirds of the women were highly committed to their occupations and about 70% of these occupations were traditionally female ones. Most of the women had worked continuously after graduation. Only 1% were full-time homemakers during the entire ten-year period. About 79% reported that they had successfully combined occupations with homemaking skills. Also, women who followed traditional female occupations changed their jobs less often than those in nontraditional ones. If they did change, the move was likely to be a job with a lower rank and pay, as opposed to the changes made by women in nontraditional occupations.

Would highly educated women leave what appear to be well-paid occupations? Studies of women MBAs with children identify several family and workplace issues (Rosin & Korabik, 1990, 1991). Often, family obligations such as child care appear very important to a working mother. For women who can afford not to work but would like to, adequate child-care arrangements or having the flexibility to be at home when children return from school often makes a great deal of difference between accepting a job or remaining at home. In contrast, mothers who have made the decision to work full-time as a matter of necessity have somehow resolved the issues of child care. The pivotal workplace issues for these women center on gender. Insensitive or unsupportive work environments, organizational politics, and the lack of occupational development opportunities are important for women working full-time (Schwartz, 1992). Often, women in difficult workplaces focus on barriers to their occupational development and ways of getting around them.

> Anita, an Asian American, has a high paying job, but the demands placed on her are much more than others carry. Although she has achieved many awards in recognition of her work, she has been turned down for promotions because the others in the workplace, which includes other ethnic groups, envy her and call her a "foreigner" although she's lived in the United States longer than anywhere else. Highly productive and efficient, she begins to understand that she has to become politically proficient in the workplace to receive her overdue promotion.

Despite the dramatic change in the proportion of women in the labor force, the picture drawn by Mueller in 1954 still holds true. Mueller describes the following categories of women in the labor force:

1. *Stable homemaking career:* The woman marries shortly after leaving high school or college and devotes herself to homemaking.
2. *Conventional career pattern:* The woman is employed for a relatively short time after completing her education and then marries and makes homemaking her career.
3. *Stable working career:* The career becomes the woman's way of life following preparation in college or a professional school.
4. *Double-track career pattern:* The woman goes to work after completing her education, then marries and continues with a double career of working and homemaking.
5. *Interrupted career pattern:* The woman follows the sequence of working, homemak-

ing, working. (The latter stage may involve both.) The resumption of employment depends on the ages of the children and the interests and economic needs of the woman and her family.
6. *Uninterrupted career pattern:* The woman simultaneously works and does homemaking. The amount of employment she takes depends on the economic needs of the family, her health, and the health of the family. This pattern is more common among lower-class women than among other groups.

## Ethnicity and Occupational Development

Although North America is becoming more and more multi-cultural, different ethnic groups still face many problems. Not much research has been done from a developmental perspective. Most research has focused on the limited opportunities of people belonging to different ethnic groups and the structural barriers they face, such as discrimination. In terms of occupational selection, we shall examine three topics: nontraditional occupations, vocational identity, and occupational aspirations.

African-American women and Euro-American women do not differ in terms of plans to enter *nontraditional occupations* (Murrell, Frieze, & Frost, 1991). African-American women who choose nontraditional careers tend to plan for more formal education than necessary, making them at times actually overqualified for their jobs. For instance, women with a college degree may work at a job that does not require that kind of education. A woman construction worker in a nontraditional job may have a college degree, unlike her colleagues.

According to Steward & Krieshok (1991), *vocational identity* carries with it both ethnicity and gender. Compared with Euro-American women and Latino men, African-American and Euro-American men have a *higher vocational identity* (define themselves in terms of work) when they graduate from college. The term *lower vocational identity* means that people define themselves primarily in terms of things in life rather than work.

An individual's *occupational aspiration* is the type of occupation he or she would like to hold. An *occupational expectation* is the occupation that the person believes he or she will actually get. Latinos differ from Euro-Americans in this regard. They have high occupational aspirations but low expectations. They also show a difference in educational attainment as a function of national origin (for example, Cuban and Mexican), generational status, and social class (Arbona, 1990). However they are both similar in terms of occupational development and work values.

Research that has been conducted on occupational development among ethnic groups is clear on one point. When an organization responds to the needs of ethnic groups it makes a big difference to the employees. Managers of all backgrounds who perceive their organization as responsive and positive for ethnic employees are more satisfied with and committed to the organization (Burke, 1991a, 1991b). A study by Greenhaus, Parasuraman, and Wormley (1990) reveals that African-American managers report less choice of jobs, less acceptance, more career dissatisfaction, and more rapid attainment of plateaus in their careers than do other managers.

## Bias and Discrimination in the Workplace

Although the United States has been sensitized to the issues of race, ethnicity, and discrimination in terms of hiring, promotion, and termination procedures, these issues are not entirely resolved. It may take a long time before such a resolution happens.

Although a large number of women work outside the home, they are not usually found in high-status jobs (Morrison, White, Van Velsor, & the Center for Creative Leadership, 1992). The subtle or at times blatant discrimination against women is called *sex* or *gender discrimination*. For example, though qualified for a job, a woman may be denied a job just because she is a woman. Women refer to the "glass ceiling"—that is, the level to which they may rise in a company but beyond which they may not go. This happens by drastically restricting women's career opportunities by blocking access to internal labor markets and their benefits (Baron & Bielby, 1985). Besides discrimination in hiring and promotion, women face discrimination in pay. Although the pay gap began to widen in the early 1980s, it began to close in the early 1990s because men's salaries were declining (U.S. Department of Labor, 1995).

Age discrimination is also a serious problem. Age discrimination appears in several ways (Snyder & Barrett, 1988). For example, employers can make certain types of physical and mental performance a job requirement and argue that older workers cannot meet the standard, or they can get rid of older workers by giving them early retirement.

## Retirement and Second-Career Decisions

In their upper 50s or early 60s, people begin to think of retirement. Many find that a decline in their physical condition, because of accidents or the aging process, affects their job performance. A person who works on an assembly line may be hampered by failing eyesight. A person who has to lift heavy weights may become limited as the back muscles lose their elasticity. Some people simply desire to make a change, regardless of physical factors.

Today, flexible retirement offers various options. Some people want to change the nature of their jobs as they grow older. A change in the number of workers in particular jobs also influences retirement options. The most desirable kind of retirement is one that maximizes the employment options of people after 50 years of age. Though the usual retirement age has been 65 years of age, encouragement to take early or flexible retirement in some companies has opened many options for these people.

> Fifty-year-old Glenn has opted for early retirement from his job as a policeman. His dream is to be a photographer, so he takes a part-time job in a photo studio, where he does what he enjoys most. He uses his free time to take his own photos and develop them in his studio. He also begins to participate in photo competitions. Immensely happy with his work, he feels fulfilled as a person.

Retirement is a fairly recent phenomenon. In the past, people worked at their jobs until they were overcome by ill health or their strength failed them. Today, people retire for various reasons. Studies of successful retirees show that people can maintain some involvement in their primary interest; for instance, an academician might continue to flourish through writing, research, and study.

As the U.S. population ages, we face older people's growing need for jobs that are socially acceptable. Some jobs are not really appropriate for younger people, who need to have stable jobs, so older people might benefit from any part-time or temporary work an employer might provide.

There is also a growing need for recruitment in the staffing of senior centers and the provision of home-care services to help older people live independently in their own homes. Staff positions are usually full-time jobs, many of which could be second-career jobs for people past 50 years of age interested in this kind of service.

## Work and Environment

A middle-aged person has spent so many years on the job that it is difficult to assess the developmental implications of work, for work conditions have not remained constant over the decades. What is expected on the job today in terms of loyalty, hours spent on the job, decision making, exposure to hazards, and so forth differs among people even in the same age group. However, one of the simplest illustrations of how life situations affect continued development in middle age is the matter of how much of a person's time is absorbed by work. Kastenbaum (1979) notes that the average person in 1870 started to work at about age 14 and worked until death at about age 61. He or she spent about 3120 hours on the job every year and accumulated about 146,640 hours in 47 years of work (Miernyk, 1975). However, today the average person enters the workforce at age 20 and retires at 65. The number of hours each worker spends on the job each year has shrunk to about 2000, amounting to about 90,000 over the entire span. This total represents a reduction of nearly 40% in the number of hours a person spends at work. Thus the working adult of today has more time free from on-the-job obligations than workers did a century ago.

This gain in discretionary time means more opportunity to develop interests, skills, and a breadth of knowledge that was hard to come by for workers who were extensively bound to the work situation. Moreover, entering the work situation at a later age allows more time for education, both formal and informal, that can add to fuller personality development.

The different meanings work has for different people become more distinct as people grow older. Those who enjoy their work become interested in learning and developing themselves in their particular areas. Some people learn to get the most out of their job situations, enriching themselves and developing specific personality traits they need to perform well. Other people grow stale and cease development early. There is much to be learned about the relationship between work and individual development through the middle years (Kastenbaum, 1979).

As the following six case illustrations show, people's lifestyles vary with their jobs.

> Dominique, 49, works as a telephone operator at a motel. She spends eight hours a day in front of the switchboard with a headset and answers telephone calls. People rarely see her as a person with her own needs and wants; all they want from her is politeness. The job creates a restrictive atmosphere for her; she is occupied with the telephone even when she needs to get herself a drink of water.

Although Dominique calls herself a happy-go-lucky person, she has little opportunity to show it because people take notice of her only as a telephone operator and just nod their heads if they wish to greet her. Her boss calls her by her first name, whereas she has to call him "Mr. Jones." Her role is quite limited, allowing for no personal opinions, and she has no opportunities for personal growth. Her job is isolating; however, she realizes that it is a necessity for the motel that employs her.

David, 49, is the executive director of a ready-mix concrete company. His day starts at 7 A.M., when he starts his rounds through the five concrete factories he owns. Following his morning rounds, David usually has breakfast with a client, followed by office and board meetings. Late afternoons he spends in budgeting and planning, as he has decided to open another new factory. Constantly overwhelmed with all the stress he faces in the office, David sees his home as a place where he can feel peaceful, but he doesn't spend much time there, and he feels guilty for neglecting his family. Office pressures always seem to be present, and he accepts them as part of his lifestyle.

Barbara has been a cleaning woman from the time she was 20. At 50, she is a "regular" cleaning lady for several families. She enjoys her job, but she isn't comfortable with some of her customers. Some people treat her as if she does not exist; except for a "hello" and instructions about what needs to be done, they go about their business. Some of them expect to be addressed respectfully by their last names, though most call her by her first name. In other homes, though, she is invited to have a cup of coffee, and she appreciates being treated more like a person. She enjoys listening to the conversations of the families, although they never invite her to participate. In spite of her limited interaction with the homeowners, Barbara enjoys her job. She works hard and cleans each place as well as she can.

Anthony is a cab driver who immigrated with his family from Puerto Rico. His job affects his lifestyle as much as the traffic affects his job. Anthony has little time for recreation, always hustling his cab through the New York City traffic. Though the rush and the hassle get to him, he has to do his job and compete for fares. He also fears robbery, particularly

in unsafe areas, and the possibility of running afoul of regulations in some way that will cost him his job. In spite of the dust, the sweat, and the agony of driving in a crowded city, Anthony is grateful for his job. He notices two types of people who travel in his cab—the talkers and the nontalkers. He enjoys the stories that people tell him and can even give advice to them based on his experiences with different types of people. Comfortable with his job, he feels relatively secure in it. His wife is a good woman who cooks for him and their four children. His family understands that he needs to lie down and sleep, and there is not much question about what he should or should not be doing at home. In this comfortable home atmosphere, he can unwind and release some of the tensions he faces while working.

Sandy has worked all her life as a waiter. She likes her job and appreciates the tips that customers give her. She has been at it for 25 years, and it shows. Some customers tip her generously because they have known her for so many years. Many still address her with remarks such as "Come on, girl" and "Beautiful baby." But one day she overhears a young customer refer to her as "the old waitress." At first, Sandy feels insulted, and then she is scandalized because she has always thought of herself as being young and beautiful. In shock ,she looks at herself in the mirror and sees a slightly older woman who has some gray hair and appears to be in her 50s. Realizing that she is no longer as young as she was when she first became a waiter, Sandy becomes momentarily depressed, especially in view of the value attached to youth in her culture. But after her initial depression, as well as anger at growing old, Sandy accepts her situation as inevitable. She thinks of her family and feels grateful toward them. They've been her only emotional support system through all her trials and tribulations and make her feel contented, proud, and comfortable.

Jake resigns his job as a "delivery boy" at age 50 and takes a job as a security officer in an apartment building. Both his job and the manner in which he is addressed are new to him. Used to being treated as a young person, he now feels that the people in the apartment building view him as an older person. Young girls ask Jake to watch their purses and mothers ask him to mind their babies while they run some brief errand. At first this role puzzles him, but soon he comes to accept it. Eventually Jake realizes that people's attitudes toward him are influenced by his age—and by his appearance, for he looks 60. This change is not painful for Jake; he enjoys being treated differently, having resented the label "delivery boy" given to him even in his late 40s.

The jobs or careers of these six people have affected their personal lifestyle, growth, and development. In these cases, we can see an overall relationship between life situations and the possibility of continued development from midlife onward. Each of these adults has undergone significant changes in his or her own personal development since the onset of adulthood and may continue to do so.

## Joblessness

Some people become alienated from work. They have no satisfaction in their work and find little opportunity for meaningful labor. One study shows the unemployment rate at 7.0% for men and 6.3% for women (Hopper, 1990). When we divide the unemployment rates of middle-aged adults by race, sex, and age, we see that African Americans and Latinos face more unemployment than do whites. Many middle-aged adults face chronic unemployment; historically, vagrants tramps, and other homeless people have been linked to the inability of the labor market to absorb all able-bodied people who want to work (Hopper, 1990).

The great deal of restructuring in recent years has caused many of the middle-aged men with a history of steady employment, including increased responsibility and advancement, to be fired or forced into early retirement. Often, men define themselves in terms of their work, so taking it away has long-term effects on them. A group of jobless men who had held managerial or engineering positions were compared with employed men. Most of the jobless men were experiencing their first encounter with unemployment in 20 years. They felt unwanted,

insignificant, and bitter. They were also reevaluating their long-held goals and felt that their college education was wasted. Further, they said that their friends had shunned them after they lost their jobs. Because of the importance of their previous work, these men were left with deep feelings of worthlessness and low self-esteem that persisted even after they were reemployed (Braginsky & Braginsky, 1975).

This also occurs in the present era. Unemployed men face self-doubt, which introduces family stress and strain and new levels of conflict, which in turn affect their self-respect (Piotrkowski, Rapoport, & Rapoport, 1987). A study of 300 unemployed men has revealed that with strong social support from close relationships, the unemployed person starts looking for a new job; he or she feels hopeful and encouraged and therefore engages in active job-seeking efforts. The global sense of worth and caring that social support provides is especially important when job-seeking efforts do not pay off. A lack of support can lead to demoralization and self-destructive behaviors (Newman & Newman, 1995).

> Jacob is a well-liked business man who runs a small construction company that was handed down to him by his father. However, with competition from big companies, Jacob cannot survive the financial pressures and goes into bankruptcy. As soon as this happens, his friends and his colleagues keep away from him. If they happen to see him in a restaurant, they pretend not to see him. Angry that he cannot find a job, his family ridicules him. He feels more and more devalued as he finds he cannot find *any* job. Though he was willing to do anything for a living, very few people call him for an interview.
>
> Later, after one year of being jobless, he feels beaten down and defeated. He has lost all support from home as finances have become more and more of a problem. Often he leaves home, saying that he is looking for a job, but quickly finds his way into a bar at ten in the mornings and drinks himself to oblivion. He feels totally unworthy, unwanted, and a burden to his family.

Jacob could use some help. Social workers can provide assistance to middle-aged people in several ways, as the following section shows.

## IMPLICATIONS FOR PRACTICE

### Developmental Issues

Middle-aged people differ so widely in the resolution of their developmental issues that social workers are seldom able to make general recommendations, although they can often help a family keep its balance during transitions. Some people make great efforts to prevent a decline in their physical strength, while others will surrender easily to the notion of being athletically "over the hill." Some widows and widowers reenter the competition for a new partner, whereas others (particularly women) substitute friendships primarily with members of their own gender. Activities for middle-aged people have to encompass their various adaptive styles.

Middle-aged people, like others, can be classified as simple or complex. Simple people tend to protect themselves from the environment, avoid stressful situations, and maintain a lifestyle that reveals neither many psychological resources nor many deficits. Complex people have a high share of resources as well as deficits and problems, have more motivation for growth, and seek to expand their personality as well as range of functioning and life experience. Stress contributes to an adventurous, stimulating life.

Most people are at neither extreme. A person's position on the simplicity-complexity continuum indicates the person's developmental status. The simple middle-aged person tends to be happier than the complex individual, who tends to achieve more and adapt better instead in early adulthood. Some complex people who have entertained high hopes and great expectations find themselves at a dead end.

### Health and Work Issues

In therapy for middle-aged people, one of the most important issues is the crisis that a breakdown in the health of a middle-aged person can precipitate in the family. When a middle-aged person is hospitalized, the person's resources may have to be reassessed. The social worker may have to find resources to help the family survive the crisis.

Social workers may also have to assist factory workers who have temporary disabilities connected with their jobs. The employees must rely on benefits from private disability plans, which do not always cover the costs of extensive rehabilitative services. Whenever long-term permanent services are needed, most people turn to federally funded programs of financial assistance for the permanently disabled.

In many ways, early retirement in middle age by subtle persuasion is made so attractive by employers that it appears better for the employees to stay home than continue to work. However, their monthly income is significantly reduced and staying home often makes a person feel less useful. Few resources offer retraining of middle-aged workers who are no longer employed. Social workers retained by the government or private employers as members of interdisciplinary teams can participate in preventive education, diagnosis, referral for training, and counseling for the families of early retirees.

Occupational dissatisfaction is another problem many middle-aged people face. Self-fulfillment through work is not always realistic. Social work practitioners should have the knowledge to understand and deal with the stress levels of different lifestyles and offer help accordingly.

Women appear to suffer more than men in this respect. Lowenthal, Thurnher, and Chiriboga (1975) found that many middle-aged women experience a midlife developmental crisis. Many women become liberated from their energy-consuming parental roles. In middle age, they reevaluate themselves and look for ways to express their abilities. Some find themselves trapped; new or renewed life goals are difficult to find or achieve.

Lowenthal et al. (1975) found that women high in competence and positive self-concepts were the most likely to deal with occupational dissatisfaction meaningfully. However, the more complex and growth oriented a woman was, the greater the possibility for frustration. Complex and talented men were also stymied as they groped their way toward second careers and other forms of self-renewal.

As women get older, the job market starts to shrink for them faster than it does for men. Thus they are burdened with two serious issues, ageism and sexism. Younger workers replace older workers in receiving promotions and climbing the social ladder. Such preferences are subtle, with so-called valid reasons offered for overlooking the older person. Though talented older people move toward second careers/jobs, they are the last to be hired and the first to be fired, as most employers prefer to employ younger people, symptomatic of U.S. society's negative attitude toward aging.

When a middle-aged person comes for therapy, social workers need to know where the person stands. Whether the individual views his or her life as being successful or unsuccessful depends on what the person has defined as his or her own adult responsibilities and personal goals. Such issues could be explored with less stress if society behaved as if it expected grownups to keep on growing. That awareness—both among social workers and in the larger environment—would make society a better place for adult development and eventually create a safe and facilitating environment for child development as well.

## Relationships

Middle-aged people who wish to become parents for the first time face unique issues. Time, money, and energy needed for a baby should be explicitly discussed when such couples come for help.

Middle age is also the time when couples reevaluate their marriages and come up with solutions. A large number of them may rework their marriage or seek a divorce. Social workers should offer constructive help to such people.

Extramarital affairs are another problem in this age group. Though unhappy in the marriage, a partner may not wish to break up the marriage, because he or she likes the stability and security of a home and does not wish to lose contact with the children. An affair is often a symptom of a bad marriage. If the affair becomes known to the other partner it can lead to a great deal of hurt, shame, and anger and could lead to divorce. Whatever the result, social workers could help the couple. evaluate themselves, their life situations, and their expectations from life. If both partners wish to remain in the marriage, they have to work at their issues and rebuild a home, with more sensitivity to each other. If they wish to get a divorce, they should be helped to understand their own needs and be aware that their chances at remarriage are slim, more so for women than men. Problems and issues of modern dating should also be discussed.

Taking care of elderly parent/s should be a joint decision by a couple so that it does not create resentment. If one grown child takes care of elderly parents while other siblings do not contribute money or time, how would this affect the relationship between the caretaking child and the parent? These are serious issues that need to be thought through carefully before any decisions are made.

There are more stresses, complications, and questions in middle age than in any other period of life, mainly because of people's responsibilities to two different generations: their children and their parents. According to the values of social work, social workers should have good self-awareness in order to help people to deal with their problems.

## CHAPTER SUMMARY

- The middle years extend from 40 to 65 years of age.
- People vary in their responses to the biological, social, and psychological cues of midlife.

- The middle-aged person is caught between two generations and has responsibilities to both.
- Both sexes undergo physical and emotional changes that are related to hormonal shifts. These changes take place gradually in men; in women, menopause brings radical changes but does not necessarily cause great stress.
- Osteoporosis affects postmenopausal women more often than men of the same age. Symptoms accompanying climacteric can be reduced by hormone replacement therapy in women.
- Recent controversy centers on whether postmenopausal women should have babies using donated eggs.
- Aging without diseases has little effect on physical and psychological well-being. In one study, men with Type A personalities had higher serum cholesterol and more accelerated blood coagulations than men with Type B personalities.
- As people get older, they usually slow down in performing certain cognitive tasks. Recent research developments have provided a better understanding of how intelligence changes as people grow older.
- Cognitive styles in middle-aged adults include relativistic thinking.
- Intelligence can be classified into two types: fluid intelligence, which declines after adolescence, and crystallized intelligence, which continues to increase with age.
- Middle age is a period of reassessment. Erikson's seventh psychosocial crisis is that of generativity versus stagnation. The generative person is concerned with establishing and guiding the next generation, and one who fails to develop a sense of generativity suffers from stagnation, self-indulgence, and perhaps physical and psychological invalidism.
- Peck has expanded on Erikson's conceptualization and discusses the issues and conflicts that people face in middle age, such as valuing wisdom versus physical powers.
- Vaillant's study coincides with Erikson's adult life scheme but adds the Career Consolidation stage.
- Levinson, Darrow, Klein, Levinson, and McKee studied how men build life structures.
- Women's development differs from that of men in many ways. Attachment is central to women's identity, whereas for men individual achievement and great ideas or distinctive activities define the standard of self-assessment and success.
- Some of the stresses common to middle age arise from postparenthood, intergenerational adjustment, marriage in middle adulthood, and divorce.
- Taking care of older parents can bring up resentment and frustration as well as many rewards. Women usually provide most of this type of care.
- The roles of middle-aged parents change according to the needs of their grown children.
- There are many reasons a middle-aged couple may divorce, which does not happen suddenly. Either strong external supports or internal attraction can keep a marriage together; when these two factors do not suffice, external attractions can work against a marriage.
- Most divorced people remarry. However, the opportunities for men to remarry are greater than those for women.
- The lifestyles of single middle-aged people are differ distinctly from those of other people their age.
- Because of interaction among values, careers, and attitudes, middle-aged people have usually selected jobs that fit their lifestyle. Nevertheless, many people make career changes as they grow older, despite problems involving retraining. Some individuals learn new career roles and obtain new jobs, but the potential of others may

be overlooked because many employers prefer younger people as employees.

- There are a large number of women in the labor force. Their career patterns may be classified as the stable homemaking career, conventional career, stable working career, double-track career, interrupted career, and uncertain career. Women form 40% of the labor force.
- Bias and discrimination based on ethnicity exists in many workplaces.
- Retirement has taken many shapes. Flexible retirement helps middle-aged people find new jobs as well as lifestyles that enhance their potentials.
- People's lifestyles vary with their goals.
- Joblessness can arise from the restructuring of companies. Unemployment for a long period of time leads to demoralization and self-destructive behaviors.
- Social workers can help middle-aged people with many issues regarding development, health and work, and interpersonal relationships such as parental care and marital reassessment.

## SUGGESTED READINGS

Caspi, A., & Herbener, E. S. (1990). Continuity and change: Assortative marriage and the consistency of personality in adulthood. *Journal of Personality and Social Psychology. 58*(2), 250–258.

D'Amico, R., & Maxwell, N. L. (1995). The continuing significance of race in minority male joblessness. *Social Forces, 73*(3), 969–991.

Glick, P. C. (1994). Living alone during middle adulthood. *Sociological Perspectives, 37*(3), 445–457.

Johoda, M. (1992). Reflections on Marienthal and after [Special Issue: Marienthal and beyond: Twentieth century research on unemployment and health]. *Journal of Occupational and Organizational Psychology, 65*(4), 355–358.

Massey, D., & Shibuya, K. (1995). Unraveling the tangle of pathology: The effect of spatially concentrated joblessness on the well-being of African Americans. *Social Science Research, 24*(4), 352–366.

Mittag, W., & Schwarzer, R. (1993). Interaction of employment status and self-efficacy of alcohol con-

sumption: A two-wave study on stressful life transitions. *Psychology and Health, 8*(1), 77–87.

Thomas, S. P. (1995). Psychosocial correlates of women's health in middle adulthood. *Issues in Mental Health Nursing, 16*(4), 285–314.

## SUGGESTED VIDEOTAPES

American Media Inc. (Producer). (1996). *Just incredible! Customer service story* (25 minutes). Available from American Media Inc., 4900 University Ave., West Des Moines, IA 50266; 800-262-2557

Heartland (Producer). (1995). *Menopause: Passage to paradise* (24 minutes). Available from FFH (Films for the Humanities and Sciences), 11 Perrine Rd., Monmouth Junction, NJ 08852; 800-257-5126

Laughlin, Kathleen (Producer). (1997). *Woman on fire* (89 minutes). Available from Filmmakers Library, 124 E. 40th St., Suite 901, New York, NY 10016; 212-808-4980

Pintar, Barry (Producer). (1995). *Menopause: A woman's quest for anwers* (24 minutes). Available from University of California at Berkeley, Media Center, 2000 Center St., 4th Floor, Berkeley, CA 94704; 510-642-0460

Rasmussen, Lorna (Producer). (1988). *Family to me* (28 minutes). Available from New Day Films, 22D Hollywood Ave., Hohokus, NJ 07423; 201-652-6590

Xene Jenex, Inc. (Producer). (1993). *What every woman should know about menopause* (28 minutes). Available from Walter J. Klein Co., 3611 Carmel Rd., Box 472087, Charlotte, NC 28247-2087; 704-542-1403

## REFERENCES

Arbona, C. (1990). Career couseling research and Hispanics: A review of the literature. *Counseling Psychologist, 18,* 300–323.

Arlin, P. K. (1980, June). *Adolescent and adult thought: A search for structures.* Paper presented at meeting of the Piaget Society, Philadelphia.

Bachman, R. (1994). Violence against women (NCJ No. 145325). Washington, DC: U.S. Government Printing Office.

Baltes, P. B., & Schaie, K. W. (1974). Aging and the IQ: The myth of the twilight years. *Psychology Today, 7,* 35–40.

Barnett, R. C., & Baruch, G. K. (1978). Women in middle years: A critique of research and theory. *Psychology of Women Quarterly, 3*(2), 187–197.

Barnett, R. C. & Baruch, G. K. (1987). Determinants of father's participation in family work. *Journal of Marriage and the Family, 49,* 29–40.

Baron, J. N., & Bielby, W. T. (1985). Organizational barriers to gender equality: Sex segregation of jobs and opportunities. In A. S. Rossi (Ed.), *Gender and the life course* (pp. 233–251). New York: Aldine.

Baruch, G., Barnett, R., & Rivers, C. (1983). *Lifeprints.* New York: McGraw-Hill.

Basseches, M. (1984). *Dialectical thinking and adult development.* Norwood, NJ: Ablex.

Berry, R. E., & Williams, F. L. (1987). Assessing the relationship between quality of life and marital and income satisfaction: A path analytic approach. *Journal of Marriage and the Family, 49,* 107–116.

Betz, E. L. (1984). A study of career patterns of women college graduates. *Journal of Vocational Behavior, 24,* 249–263.

Black, J. E., Isaacs, K. R., & Greenough, W. T. (1991). Usual versus successful aging: Some notes on experiential factors. *Neurobiology of Aging, 12,* 325–328.

Bloom, A. H. (1986). Psychological ingredients of high moral thinking: A critique of Kolhberg-Gilligan paradigm. *Journal for the Theory of Social Behavior, 16*(1), 89–103.

Blumstein, P., & Schwartz, P. (1983). *American couples.* New York: Morrow.

Booth, A., & Amato, P. (1991). Divorce and psychological stress. *Journal of Health and Social Behavior, 32,* 396–407.

Booth, A., & Johnson, E. (1985). Premarital cohabitation and marital success. *Journal of Family Issues, 9,* 387–394.

Botwinick, J. (1977). Intellectual abilities. In J. Birren & K. W. Schaie (Eds.), *Handbook of psychology of aging.* New York: Van Nostrand Reinhold.

Braginsky, D. D., & Braginsky, B. M. (1975, August). Surplus people: Their lost faith in self and system. *Psychology Today, 9,* 68–72.

Brody, E. M. (1990). *Women in the middle: The parent-care years.* New York: Springer.

Brooks, L. (1991). Recent developments in theory-building. In D. Brown, L. Brooks, & Associates (Eds.). *Career choice and development: Applying contemporary theories to practice* (2nd ed.). San Francisco: Jossey-Bass.

Brown, B. B., Mounts, N., Lamborn, S. D., & Steinberg, L. (1993). Parenting practice and group affiliation in adolescence. *Child Development, 64,* 467–482.

Bumpass, L. L., Sweet, J. A., & Cherlin, A. (1991). The role of cohabitation in declining rates of marriage. *Journal of Marriage and the Family, 53,* 913–927.

Burgess, A. W., & Holmstrom L. L. (1974). Rape trauma syndrome. *American Journal of Psychiatry, 113,* 981–986.

Burke, R. J. (1991a). Organizational treatment of minority managers and professionals: Costs to the majority? *Psychological Reports, 68,* 439–449.

Burke, R. J. (1991b). Work experiences of minority managers and professionals: Individual and organizational cost of perceived bias. *Psychological Reports, 69,* 1011–1023.

Byington, D. B. Sexual assault. In *Encyclopedia of Social Work* (19th ed., Vol. 3, pp. 2136–2141). Washington, DC: NASW Press.

Byington, D. B., Martin, P. Y., DiNitto, D. M., & Maxwel, M. S. (1991). Organizational affiliation and effectiveness: The case of rape crisis centers. *Administration in Social Work, 15*(3), 83–103.

Castro-Martin. T., & Bumpass, L. L. (1989). Recent trends in marital disruption. *Demography, 26,* 37–51.

Cattell, R. B. (1971). *Abilities: Their structure, growth and action.* Boston: Houghton, Mifflin.

Cavanaugh, J. C., Kramer, D. A., Sinnott, J. D., Camp, C. J., & Markley, R. J. (1985). On missing links and such: Interfaces between cognitive research and everyday problem solving. *Human Development, 28,* 146–168.

Chadwick, B. A., & Heaton, T. B. (1992). *Statistical handbook on the American family.* Phoenix, AZ: Onyx Press.

Chandler, M. J., & Boutilier, R. G. (1992). The development of dynamic system reasoning. *Human Development, 35,* 121–137.

Cherry, K. E., & Morton, M. R. (1989). Drug sensitivity in older adults: The role of physiologic and pharmacokinetic factors. *International Journal of Aging and Human Development, 28,* 159–174.

Chodorow, N. (1978). *The reproduction of mothering.* Berkeley: University of California Press.

Cleek, M. B., & Pearon, T. A. (1985). Perceived causes of divorce: An analysis of interrelationships. *Journal of Marriage and the Family, 47,* 179–191.

Clemons, A. W., & Axelson, L. J. (1985). The not-so-empty nest: The return of the fledgling adult. *Family Relations, 34,* 259–264.

Coleman, M., & Ganong, L. H. (1990). Remarriage and stepfamily research in 1980s: Increased interest in an old family form. *Journal of Marriage and the Family, 52,* 925–940.

Commons, M. L., Richards, F. A., & Kuhn, D. (1982). Systematic and metasystematic reasoning: A case of levels of reasoning beyond Piaget's stage of formal operations. *Child Development, 53,* 1058–1069.

Commons, M. L., Sinnott, J. D., Richards, F. A., & Armon, C. (Eds.). (1984). *Adult development: Vol. 1. Comparisons and applications of adolescent and adult developmental models.* New York: Praeger.

Crosby, F. J. (1991). *Juggling: The unexpected advantages of balancing career and home for women and their families.* New York: Free Press.

Crouter, A. C., & McHale, S. M. (1993). The long arm of the job: Influence of parental work on childrearing. In T. Luster & L. Okagaki (Eds.), *Parenting: An ecological perspective.* Hillsdale NJ: Erlbaum.

Demaris, A., & Rao, K. V. (1992). Premarital cohabitiaiton and subsequent marital stability in the United States: A reassessment. *Journal of Marriage and the Family, 54,* 178–190.

Demo, D. H. (1992). Parent-child relationships: Assessing recent changes. *Journal of Marriage and the Family, 54,* 104–117.

Dishion, T. J., Patterson, G. R., Stoolmiller, M., & Skinner, M. L. (1991). Family, school, and behavioral antecedents to early adolescent involvement with antisocial peers. *Developmental Psychology, 27,* 172–180.

Dreyer, P. H. (1975). Sex, sex roles and marriage among youth in the 1970s. In F. J. Havighurst & P. H. Dreyer (Eds.). *Youth: the 74th Yearbook of the National Society for the Study of Education* (Part I). Chicago: University of Chicago Press.

Dwyer, J. W., & Coward, R. T. (1991). Multivariate comparison of the involvement of adult sons versus daughters in the care of impaired parents. *Journal of Gerontology: Social Sciences, 46,* 259–269.

Dyk, P. H., & Adams, G. R. (1990). Identity and intimacy: An initial investigation of three theoretical models using cross-lag panel correlations. *Journal of Youth and Adolescence, 19,* 91–110.

Eichenbaum, L., & Orbach, S. (1983). *Understanding women.* New York: Harper/Colophon.

Elkind, D., & Bowen, R. (1979). Imaginary audience behavior in children and adolescents. *Developmental Psychology, 15,* 38–44.

Enright, R., Lapsley, D., & Shukla, D. (1979). Adolescent egocentrism in early and late adolescence. *Adolescence, 14,* 687–695.

Erikson, E. H. (1968). *Identity: Youth and crisis.* New York: Norton.

Erikson, E. H. (1980). *Identity and the life cycle.* New York: Norton

Erikson, E. H. (1982). *The life cycle completed.* New York: Norton.

Erikson, E. H., Erikson, J. M., & Kivnick, H. Q. (1986). *Vital involvement in old age.* New York: Norton.

Essex, M. J., & Nam, S. (1987). Marital staus and loneliness among older women. *Journal of Marriage and the Family, 49,* 93–106.

Fischer, K. W. (1980). A theory of cognitive development: The control and construction of hierarchies of skills. *Psychological Review, 87,* 477–531.

Fischer, K. W., Kenny, S. L., & Pipp, S. L. (1990). How cognitive processes and environmental conditions organize discontinuities in the development of abstractions. In C. N. Alexander & E. J. Langer (Eds.), *Higher stages of human development: Perspectives on adult growth.* New York: Oxford University Press.

Fisher, H. E. (1987). The four-year itch. *Natural History, 96*(10), 22–33.

Fitzgerald, L. F. & Shullman, S. L. (1993). Sexual harassment: A research analysis and agenda for the 1990s. *Journal of Vocational Behavior, 42,* 5–27.

Fitzpatrick, M. (1984). Typological approach to marital interaction: Recent theory and research. In L. Berkowitz (Ed.), *Advances in experimental social psychology* (Vol. 18). New York: Academic Press.

Flint, M. (1982). Male and female menopause: A cultural put-on. In A. M. Voda, M. Dinnerstein, & S. R. O'Donnell (Eds.), *Changing perspectives on menopause.* Austin: University of Texas Press.

Gigy, L., & Kelly, J. B. (1992). Reasons for divorce: Perspectives of divorcing men and women. *Journal of Divorce and Remarriage, 18,* 169–187.

Gilligan, C. (1982). *In a different voice.* Cambridge, MA: Harvard University Press.

Glenn, N. D. (1991). The recent trend in marital success in the United States. *Journal of Marriage and the Family, 53,* 261–270.

Glick, P. C. (1975). A demographer looks at American families. *Journal of Marriage and the Family, 37,* 15–36.

Goldberg, A. P., & Hagberg, J. M. (1990). Physical exercise in the elderly. In E. L. Schneider & J. W. Rowe (Eds.), *Handbook of the biology of aging.* (3rd ed.). San Diego, CA: Academic Press.

Gottman, J., & Levenson, R. (1992). Marital processes predictive of later dissolution: Behavior, physiology and health. *Journal of Personality and Social Psychology, 63,* 221–233.

Gray, J. D., & Silver, R. C. (1990). Opposite sides of the same coin: Former spouses' divergent perspectives in coping with their divorce. *Journal of Personality and Social Psychology, 59,* 1180–1191.

Greene, J. G. (1984). *The social and psychological origins of the climacteric syndrome.* Brookfield, VT: Gower.

Greenhaus, J. H., Parasuraman, S., & Wormley, W. M. (1990). Effects of race on organizational experiences, job performance evaluations, and career outcomes. *Academy of Mangement Journal, 33,* 64–86.

Gutmann, D. L. (1964). An exploration of ego configuration in middle and later life. In B. L. Neugarten and Associates (Eds.), *Personality in middle and later life.* New York: Atherton.

Havighurst, R. J. (1972). *Developmental tasks and education* (3rd ed.). New York: McKay.

Havighurst, R. J., & Levine, D. U. (1979). *Society and education* (5th ed.). Boston: Allyn and Bacon.

Heaney, R. P., Gallagher, J. C., Johnston, C. C., Neer, R., Pafitt, A. M., & Whedon, G. D. (1982). Calcium nutrition and bone health in the elderly. *American Journal of Clinical Nutrition, 36,* 987–1013.

Helson, R., & Moane, G. (1987). Personality change in women from college to midlife. *Journal of Personality and Social Psychology, 52,* 1176–1186.

Hetherington, E. M. (1989). Coping with family transitions: Winners, losers and survivors. *Child Development, 60,* 1–14.

Hetherington, E. M., Cox, M., & Cox, R. (1982). Effects of divorce on parents and children. In M. E. Lamb (Ed.), *Nontraditional families.* Hillsdale, NJ: Erlbaum.

Holland, J. L. (1985). *Making vocational choices* (2nd ed.). Englewood Cliffs, NJ: Prentice-Hall.

Hopper, K. (1990). Public shelter as a hybrid institution: Homeless men in historical perspective. *Journal of Social Issues, 46,* 13–29.

Horn, J. L. (1970). Organization of data on lifespan development of human abilities. In L. R. Goulet & P. B. Baltes (Eds.), *Lifespan developmental psychology: Research and theory.* New York: Academic Press.

Horner, S. M. (1972). Toward an understanding of achievement-related conflicts in women. *Journal of Social Issues, 28,* 157–175.

Houseknecht, S. K., Vaughan, S., & Statham, A. (1987). Singlehood and the careers of professional women. *Journal of Marriage and the Family, 49,* 353–366.

Houx, P. J., Vreeling, F. W., & Jolles, J. (1991). Rigorous health screening reduces age effect on memory scanning task. *Brain and Cognition, 15,* 246–260.

Jones, R., Garrison, K. C., & Morgan, R. F. (1985). *The psychology of human development.* New York: Harper & Row.

Kastenbaum, R. (1979). *Human developing.* Boston: Allyn and Bacon.

Katchadourian, H. (1987). *Fifty: Midlife in perspective.* New York: Freeman.

Kitson, G. C., Babri, K. B., & Roach, M. J. (1985). Who divorces and why: A review. *Journal of Family Issues, 6,* 255–293.

Kitson, G. C., & Morgan, L. A. (1990). The multiple consequences of divorce: A decade review. *Journal of Marriage and the Family, 52,* 913–924.

Kivnick, H. Q. (1982). *The meaning of grandparenthood.* Ann Arbor, MI: UMI Research.

Knox, A. (1977). *Adult development and learning: A handbook on individual growth and competence in the adult years for education and the helping professions.* San Francisco: Jossey-Bass.

Kramer, D. A. (1989). Development of an awareness of contradiction across the life span and the question of post-formal operations. In M. L. Commons, J. D. Sinnott, F. A. Richards, & C. Armon (Eds.), *Adult development: Vol. 1. Comparisons and applications of developmental models.* New York: Praeger.

Krout, J. A. (1988). Rural versus urban differences in elderly parents' contacts with their children. *Gerontologist, 28,* 198–203.

Labouvie-Vief, G. (1984). Logic and self-regulation from youth to maturity: A model. In M. L. Commons, F. A. Richards, & C. Armon (Eds.), *Beyond formal operations. Late adolescent and adult cognitive development.* New York: Praeger.

Labouvie-Vief, G. (1992). A neo-Piagetian perspective on adult cognitive development. In R. J. Sternberg & C. A. Berg (Eds.), *Intellectual development.* New York: Cambridge University Press.

Labouvie-Vief, G., Adams, C., Hakin-Larson, J., & Hayden, M. (1983, April). *Contexts of logic: The growth of interpretation from preadolescence to mature adulthood.* Paper presented at the biennial meeting of the Society for Research in Child Development. Detroit, MI.

Lakatta, E. G. (1990). Heart and circulation. In E. L. Schneider & J. W. Rowe (Eds.). *Handbook of the biology of aging* (3rd ed.). San Diego, CA: Academic Press.

Lamy, P. P. (1986). The elderly and drug interactions. *Journal of the American Geriatrics Society, 34,* 586–592.

Lechner, C. R., & Rosenthal, D. A. (1984). Adolescent self-consciousness and the imaginary audience. *Genetic Psychology Monographs, 110,* 289–305.

Lee, G. R. (1985). Kinship and social support in the elderly: The case of the United States. *Aging and Society, 5,* 19–38.

Levinger, G., & Moles, O. C. (Eds.). (1979). *Divorce and separation: Context, causes and consequences.* New York: Basic Books.

Levinson, D. (1977). The mid-life transition: A period in adult psychosocial development. *Psychiatry, 40,* 99–112.

Levinson, D. J. (1996). *Seasons of a woman's life.* New York: Knopf.

Levinson, D., Darrow, C., Klein, E., Levinson, M., & McKee, B. (1978). *The seasons of a man's life.* New York: Ballantine.

Lock, M. (1986). Ambiguities of aging: Japanese experience and perceptions of menopause. *Culture, Medicine and Psychology, 10,* 23–46.

Lowenthal, M. F., Thurnher, M., & Chiriboga, D. (1975). *Four stages of life: A comparative study of women and men facing transitions.* San Francisco: Jossey-Bass.

Margolin, L., & White, L. (1987). The continuing role of physical attractiveness in marriage. *Journal of Marriage and the Family, 49,* 21–27.

Margolis, L. H., Sparrow, A. W., & Swenson, G. M. (1989). *Growing into healthy adults: Pediatric antecedents of adult disease* (Health Monograph Series No.3) Lansing: Michigan Department of Public Health.

Masters, W. H., & Johnson, V. E. (1966). *Human sexual response.* Boston: Little, Brown.

Masters, W. H., & Johnson, V. E. (1970). *Human sexual inadequacy.* Boston: Little, Brown.

Mathews, K. A. (1992). Myths and realities of the menopause. *Psychosomatic Medicine, 54,* 1–9.

Mathews, K., Wing, R., Kuller, L., Meilahn, E., Kelsey, S., Costello, E., & Caggiula, A. (1990). Influences of natural menopause on psychological characteristics and symptoms of middle-aged healthy women. *Journal of Consulting and Clinical Psychology, 58,* 345–351.

Mayo Clinic. (1992). *Mayo Clinic family health book* (Interactive ed.). Rochester, MN: Mayo Foundation for Medical Education and Research. (CD-ROM published by Interactive Ventures, Inc.)

McClelland, D. (1975). *Power: The inner experience.* New York: Irvington.

Meier, D. E. (1988). Skeletal aging. In B. Kent & R. Butler (Eds.), *Human aging research: Concepts and techniques* (pp.221–244). New York: Raven Press.

Miernyk, W. H. (1975). The changing life cycle of work. In N. Datan & L. Ginsberg (Eds.), *Lifespan developmental psychology in normative life crisis.* New York: Academic Press.

Miller, S. S., & Cavanaugh, J. C. (1990). The meaning of grandparenthood and its relationship to demographic, relationship and social participation variables. *Journals of Gerontology: Psychological Sciences, 45,* 244–246.

Morris, J. N., & Sherwood, S. (1984). Informal support resources for vulnerable elderly persons: Can they be counted, why do they work? *International Journal of Aging and Human Development, 18,* 1–17.

Morrison, A. M., White, R. P., Van Velsor, E., & the Center for Creative Leadership. (1992). *Breaking the glass ceiling: Can women reach the top of America's largest corporations?* (Rev. ed.). Reading, MA: Addison-Wesley.

Mueller, K. H. (1954). *Educating women for a changing world.* Minneapolis: University of Minnesota Press.

Murrell, A. J., Frieze, I. H., & Frost, J. L. (1991). Aspiring to careers in male- and female-oriented professions: A study of black and white college women. *Psychology of Women Quarterly, 15,* 103–126.

Neugarten, B. L. (1976). *The psychology of aging: An overview* [APA Master Lectures]. Washington, DC: American Psychological Association.

Neugarten, B. L. (1977). Personality and aging. In J. E. Birren & K. W. Schaie (Eds.), *Handbook of the psychology of aging.* New York: Van Nostrand Reinhold.

Neugarten, B. L., Kramer, R. J., & Loomis, B. (1963). Women's attitudes toward menopause. *Vita Humana, 6,* 140–151.

Neugarten, B. L., & Weinstein, K. (1964). The changing American grandparent. *Journal of Marriage and the Family, 26,* 199–205.

Newman, B. M., & Newman, P. R. (1995). *Development through life* (6th ed.). Pacific Grove, CA: Brooks/Cole.

Papalia, D. E., & Olds, S. W. (1992). *Human development* (5th ed). New York: McGraw-Hill.

Peck, R. C. (1968). Psychological development in the second half of life. In B. L. Neugarten (Ed.), *Middle age and aging*. Chicago: University of Chicago Press.

Pillari, V. (1991). *Scapegoating in families: Intergenerational patterns of physical and emotional abuse*. New York: Brunner/Mazel.

Piotrkowski, C. S., Rapoport, R. N., & Rapoport, R. (1987). Families and work. In B. Sussman & S. K. Steinmetz (Eds.), *Handbook of marriage and the family* (pp. 251–283). New York: Plenum.

Rapaport, R., & Rapoport, R. N. (1975). *Leisure and family life cycle*. London: Routledge & Kegan Paul.

Rhyne, D. (1981). Basis of marital satisfaction among men and women. *Journal of Marriage and the Family, 43*, 941–955.

Richards, F. A., & Commons, M. L. (1990). Postformal cognitive-developmental theory and research: A review of the current status. In C. N. Alexander & E. J. Langer (Eds.), *Higher stages of human development: Perspectives on adult growth*. New York: Oxford University Press.

Robertson, J. F. (1977). Grandmotherhood: A study of role concepts. *Journal of Marriage and the Family, 39*, 165–174.

Robinson, B., & Thurnher, M. (1979). Taking care of aged parents: A family cycle transition. *Gerontologist, 19*, 586–593.

Rogers, D. (1979). *The adult years*. Englewood Cliffs, NJ: Prentice-Hall.

Rosenberg, S. D., & Farrell, M. P. (1976). Identity and crisis in middle-aged men. *International Journal of Aging and Human Development, 2*, 153–170.

Rosenman, R. H. (1974). The role of behavioral patterns and neurogenic factors on the pathogenesis of coronary heart disease. In R. S. Eliot (Ed.), *Stress and the heart*. New York: Futura.

Rosin, H. M., & Korabik, K. (1990). Marital and family correlates of women managers: attrition from organizations. *Journal of Vocational Behavior, 37*, 104–120.

Rosin, H. M., & Korabik, K. (1991). Workplace variables, affective responses, and intention to leave among women managers. *Journal of Occupational Psychology, 64*, 317–330.

Rubin, L. B. (1979). *Women of a certain age*. New York: Harper-Colophon.

Ruebsaat, H. J., & Hull, R. (1975). *The male climacteric*. New York: Hawthorne Books.

Ryff, C. D., Lee, Y. H., Essex, M. J., & Schmutte, P. S. (1994). My children and me: Mid-life evaluations of grown children and of self. *Psychology and Aging, 9*, 195–205.

Sassen, G. (1980). Success anxiety in women: A constructivist interpretation of its sources and significance. *Harvard Educational Review, 50*, 13–35.

Schiavi, R., Schreiner-Engel, P., White, D., & Mandeli, J. (1991). The relationship between pituitary-gonadal function and sexual behavior in healthy aging men. *Psychosomatic Medicine, 5*, 363–374.

Schmidt, S. (1984). Studying working intelligence. In B. Rogoff & J. Lave (Eds.), *Everyday cognition: Its development in social context*. Cambridge, MA: Harvard University Press.

Schwartz, F. (with Zimmerman, J.). (1992). *Breaking with tradition: Women and work, the new facts of life*. New York: Warner Books.

Scribner, S. (1984). Studying working intelligence, In B. Rogoff & J. Lave (Eds.), *Everyday cognition: Its development in social context*. Cambridge, MA: Harvard University Press.

Shepard, R. J. (1978). *Physical activity and aging*. Chicago: Year Book Medical Publishers.

Shepard, R. J. (1990). The scientific basis of exercise prescribing for the very old. *Journal of the American Geriatrics Society, 38*, 62–70.

Sheppard, S., & Seidman, S. (1982, March). *Midlife women, the women's movement, and sexuality*. Paper presented at 15th annual National Meeting of Sex Educators, Counselors, and Therapists, New York.

Shostak, A. B. (1987). Singlehood. In M. B. Sussman and S. K. Steinmetz (Eds.), *Handbook of marriage and the family* (pp. 355–368). New York: Plenum.

Sigelman, C. K., & Shaffer, D. R. (1995). *Life-span development* (2nd ed.). Pacific Grove, CA: Brooks/Cole.

Sinnott, J. D. (1989). Life span relativistic post-formal thought: Methodology and data from everyday problem solving. In M. L. Commons. J. D. Sinnott, F. A. Richards, & C. Armon, (Eds.), *Adult development: Vol.1. Comparisons and applications of developmental models*. New York: Praeger.

Snyder, C. J., & Barrett, G. V. (1988). The Age Discrimination in Employment Act: A review of court decisions. *Experimental Aging Research, 14*, 3–47.

Soules, M. R., & Bremmer, W. J. (1982). The menopause and climacteric: Endocrinologic basis and associated symptomatology. *Journal of the American Geriatrics Society, 30*, 547–561.

Specht, R., & Craig, G. T. (1987). *Human development: A social work perspective*. Englewood Cliffs, NJ: Prentice-Hall.

Stein, P. J. (1981). Understanding single adulthood. In P. J. Stein (Ed.), *Single life: Unmarried adults in social context.* New York: St. Martin's Press.

Stein, P. J. (1989). The diverse world of the single adult. In J. M. Henslin (Ed.), *Marriage and family in a changing society* (3rd ed.). New York: Free Press.

Stevens-Long, J. (1979). *Adult life.* Palo Alto, CA: Mayfield.

Steward, R. J., & Krieshok, T. S. (1991). A cross-cultural study of vocational identity: Does a college education mean the same for all persisters? *Journal of College Student Development, 32,* 562–563.

Swenson, C., Eskew, R. W., & Kohlhepp, K. A. (1981). Stages of the family life cycle, ego development, and the marriage relationship. *Journal of Marriage and the Family, 43,* 841–853.

Timiras, P. S. (1972). *Developmental physiology and aging.* New York: Macmillan.

Unger, R., & Crawford, M. (1992). *Women and gender: A feminist psychology.* Philadelphia: Temple University Press.

U.S. Bureau of the Census. (1992). *Statistical abstract of the United States, 1992.* Washington DC: U.S. Government Printing Office.

U.S. Department of Labor. (1995). *Bureau of Labor Statistics Report.* Washington, DC: Author.

Vaillant, G. E. (1977). *Adaptation to life.* Boston: Little, Brown.

Vinokur, A., Caplan, R. D., & Williams, C. C. (1987). Effects of recent and past stress on mental health: Coping with unemployment among Vietnam veterans and non-veterans. *Journal of Applied Social Psychology, 17,* 708–728.

Wagner, E. H., LaCroix, A. Z., Buchner, D. M., & Larson, E. B. (1992). Effects of physical activity on health status in older adults: Observational studies. *Annual Review of Public Health, 13,* 451–468.

Walford, R. L. (1983). *Maximum life span.* New York: Norton.

Ward, R., Logan, J., & Spitz, G. (1992). The influence of parent and child needs on coresidence in middle and later life. *Journal of Marriage and the Family, 54,* 209–221.

Wechsler, D. (1958). *The measurement and appraisal of adult intelligence* (4th ed.). Baltimore: Williams & Wilkins.

Woolf, V. (1929). *A room of one's own.* New York: Harcourt Brace Jovanovich.

Wright, A. L. (1982). Variation in Navajo menopause: Toward an explanation. In A. M. Voda, M. Dinnerstein, & S. R. O'Donnell (Eds.), *Changing perspectives on menopause.* Austin: University of Texas Press.

Zastrow, C. & Kirst-Ashman, K. K. (1994). *Understanding human bahavior and the social environment* (3rd ed.). Chicago, IL: Nelson-Hall.

# 9

# *The Older Years*

# INTRODUCTION

Seventy-nine-year-old Laila is thin and tiny. She sits in her old, creaky rocking chair, slowly rocking herself back and forth. In front of her is her 7-year-old grandson, who carries on a long monologue to which Laila responds with grunts and nods. Once in a while the child shouts, "Grandma, are you listening?" and Laila replies, "Yes, yes, what is it now, Tommy?" Then in a few minutes she dozes off again.

Laila lives with her adult daughter and pitches in whenever and wherever she can. She enjoys her grandchildren, most of whom are adults. Laila used to enjoy good health, but after two serious operations and a slow recovery, her energy level has diminished tremendously. Laila is well read and can participate in lively discussions on topics varying from politics to religion and sex, but her grandchildren do not pay much attention to her opinions because their mother does not seem to value them.

Attitudes toward aging affect the adjustments that the elderly have to make. Schaie (1973) claims that negative attitudes could contribute to observed maladaptive behaviors among the aged and in some cases could lead to premature death. Negative views about aging, about life in general, and about oneself could result in an older person's unwillingness or inability to seek needed help. The negative attitudes of aging adults about themselves can also affect others who live in their environs, in turn causing those people to respond negatively to old people or ignore them completely. To complete the circle, such attitudes can affect the way older people feel about themselves. If an elderly person is treated like a worthless person and is restricted in his or her behavior, the chances of this person's becoming an invalid—dependent and helpless—are high. In the following extended case, we can see how this negative cycle affects the elderly.

Tina marries her high school sweetheart when she is 18 and gives birth to four children, of whom only two survive. Though not wealthy, she and her husband share a good life; they care about each other and do everything to make each other happy. Tina stays home, cooks, and cares for the children.

Her twin sister Diana, who lives some distance away, never marries; she is a happy-go-lucky person who has her own job and enjoys friendships and the freedom of being herself.

When Tina turns 65, tragedy strikes her family. Her husband dies suddenly after a mild heart attack, leaving Tina devastated. She has never managed money and does not know how to take care of herself or her property. Her only son lives in another state. Her daughter Loretta, who lives close by, volunteers to take care of her. Loretta sells her mother's property and takes her mother home. She sets up a room for Tina upstairs, "away from noise and children," and lets her live there. When the children want to talk to Grandma, Loretta tells them that they are tiring Grandma out.

Within a year and a half, Tina is no longer allowed to go downstairs, because it is considered too exhausting for her. If the grandchildren wish to speak to her, they are politely told not to because "Grandma does not have the energy to listen." Even though Tina truly longs to participate in the conversations and the family life that goes on downstairs, permission is never granted to come down and be a person.

Loretta fusses over Tina's developing a cold when she comes out of her room; she fusses about allowing Tina to participate in conversations. Because of Loretta's attitude, Tina has become a virtual prisoner in her daughter's house. All that she is allowed to do is lie still in bed and not even get up except to go to the bathroom and go back to her room. The idea constantly put into her head is that she is an old person and therefore ill.

Soon, Tina develops asthma and then has a heart attack. Her twin sister Diana, who lives in another state, comes to see her. Diana bounces up the steps two at a time to see her sister. She looks young. Recently she went back to college to get an art degree; she's proud of herself and her achievements. Well liked by her friends, she appears to be overflowing with energy. Tina, after her heart attack, is pale and fragile, looks older than her years, and has difficulty moving out of her bed.

How have these twins grown up to be so different? Diana never married, but she always worked and knew how to survive in the world. Tina was always taken care of, so when her husband died, her daughter viewed her as a burden. Loretta makes no bones about the time and energy she had to spend on her mother and called her an invalid even before she became one. The constant pressure for Tina to stay in her room and the family atmosphere that Loretta has created send the message that Grandma is weak and should not be bothered. This attitude actually creates Tina's ill health. Tina really has nothing to do but lie in bed, waiting to die. And why not? Life does not have anything to offer her. For her sister Diana, though, life is meaningful; the energy and happiness she radiates reflect her attitude.

Being old can mean various things, depending on culture. A culture that respects tradition treats growing old differently from one that discards old values and technologies in favor of anything considered "progressive." For example, an elderly person in traditional India would experience life differently from an older person in the United States. But the reverence and respect shown the elderly in rural India are disappearing in the cities, where Euro-American culture pervades. The role of cultural values in the family system affects the role and status of the elderly. Even if a person is elderly and unemployed he still enjoys a good status in some cultures.

> Gopal is an elderly man in his 80s who lives in a rural area, where he owns land. He lives with his three married sons, their wives, and his grandchildren. His wife has been dead for a long time. All the household duties as well as work on the farms is taken care of by the sons and daughters-in-law. Gopal gets up early in the morning, has a heavy breakfast, and goes for a long walk; he meets the other villagers and chats with them. At noon he comes home, has his lunch, and takes a nap. When family members have problems requiring solutions, Gopal is always sought out for his advice, and the rest of the family respects and heeds his word. Thus, he carries a relatively high position in the family hierarchy.

## PHYSICAL ASPECTS OF AGING

### Biological Theories of Aging

What causes aging and "natural" death? We have no definitive answers, but several complementary biological theories together provide some insights (Hayflick, 1994). In all there are four types of major biological theories: (1) wear-and-tear theories (2) cellular theories, (3) metabolic theories, and (4) programmed cell-death theories.

*Wear and tear theories* suggest that the body, like a machine, gradually deteriorates and finally wears out. Such theories explain some diseases very well. For example, in osteoarthritis years of use of the joints causes protective cartilage to deteriorate, which results in pain and stiffness. However, such theories do not explain other aspects of aging very well.

*Cellular theories* explain that processes occurring within individual cells lead to the buildup of harmful substances over a lifetime and cause aging. Most of these theories claim that certain substances have destructive effects on cellular functioning. Some theorists believe that free radicals—that is, chemicals produced randomly during cell metabolism—bond easily to other substances inside cells and cause cellular damage that impairs functioning; the cumulative effects of free radicals over the life span cause aging.

The "waste product" theory indicates that the accumulated waste products in the body play an important role in the process of senescence. Various chemical wastes do collect in some tissues, but there is no evidence that wastes interfere with cell functioning in any important way.

The "cross-link" theory is much more promising. This theory indicates that over time, molecules in the body develop links either among their parts or with other molecules. These cross-links, which are quite stable and accumulate over time, bring about chemical as well as physical changes that affect how the molecules function. Evidence for the cross-link theory comes from studies of collagen, a substance associated with connective tissue. Research shows that cross-links result in the loss of elasticity in various tissues, including blood vessels and skin. Specific enzymes have been isolated that can break down cross-links in collagen. Other chemicals have been found to inhibit the rate at which cross-links are formed. However, none of this research can yet be applied to humans (Schock, 1977).

*Metabolic theories* focus on aspects of the body's metabolism to explain why people age. These aspects include two important processes—calorie intake and stress. A limited amount of calories and a well-balanced diet are related to longer life expectancy and lower rates of disease (Monczunski, 1991). Further, how well one adapts to physical stress is important. Younger adults tolerate more physical exertion than do older adults. Such exertion can cause death when an older adult can no longer adjust to stress.

*Programmed cell-death theories* propose that aging is genetically programmed. There may not be a single aging cell, but evidence suggests that a genetic code could control cell life. The genetic components of age-related chronic diseases such as Alzheimer's disease, cardiovascular disease, and some forms of cancer also support these theories.

## Physical Aging and Disease

What changes sturdy young people into fragile elderly people is difficult to understand. Certainly, the physical effects attributed to aging do not develop at equal rates, even within one body. A person may be confined to a wheelchair or be totally blind, yet be more mentally alert than another individual who may look years younger.

*Physical decline* To see oneself growing older can be a shock, particularly if one wishes to avoid facing the fact of growing old. U.S. society encourages adults to look younger than they are and looks down on growing old. This attitude of avoidance shows in the use of hair dyes and face lifts.

No matter what, the elderly eventually find that their skin has become less elastic, drier, and more wrinkled. Poor posture may be accentuated by shrinking muscles and the decrease in elasticity that follows calcification of ligaments and loss of space between vertebral discs. These skeletal and ligament changes in old people cause loss of stature and slumping (Tonna, 1977). Warts may

appear on the face, trunk, and scalp, some blood vessels break, producing black-and-blue marks. As muscle weight decreases with age, the structure and composition of the muscle cells change, and they accumulate more fat. The heart, a highly specialized muscle, suffers the same problem as other muscles.

As people grow older, their hearing becomes less efficient Severe loss of hearing results in communication problems, which increase the social isolation of the elderly.

You might have observed as you walk briskly on the sidewalk that older adults often walk more slowly than young people. Some of them take short, shuffling steps and do not have much arm movement (Murray, Kory, & Clarkson, 1969). For one thing, the sensory organs do not function as well in old age as they did in earlier years (Ochs, Newberry, Lenhardt, & Harkins, 1985). Older adults actually perform many motor activities quite slowly compared with younger adults (Stelmach & Nahom, 1992).

Some older adults, though, move quickly. This could be because they either have no diseases or have quicker responses because they exercise (Spirduso & MacRae, 1990). As you know, aging itself without diseases and other disasters has very little effect on physical and psychological functioning.

Good nutrition plays an important part in the lives of the elderly; the poor health of old age may be related to poor diet. The diminished physical activity typical of old age causes a slowdown in metabolism, and so the elderly require less food than younger adults. The diet of the elderly may include insufficient quantities of nutritious food for various reasons, such as inadequate income, depression, loneliness, or problems getting to the grocery store.

Anna, 82, has recently lost her husband. It was the biggest loss of her life; she had lived with him for more than 60 years. Her eating habits have been influenced by their joint lifestyle: Anna and her husband would eat whenever they were hungry, not on any specific schedule. Since her husband's death, Anna has become depressed. She eats sporadically and infrequently. One day, while walking on the sidewalk of a busy street, she faints. The hospital to which she is admitted for long-term care finds that malnutrition was her biggest problem.

As most people grow older, they become aware of stiff joints, shortness of breath, and longer reaction time. As they focus on their limitations and decreasing agility, they become cautious about going down a staircase and feel vulnerable when crossing the street.

Aging can seem to occur suddenly. An illness or a serious fall can make a person feel that he or she has turned into an old person overnight. Recovery time in old age may be prolonged, and in fact the former energy level or muscle tone may not be regained. This sudden and drastic change could cause considerable confusion, stress, and frustration.

Many older people also suffer from chronic illness. As Hippocrates put it, old people have fewer diseases than younger people, but their diseases never seem to leave them. Chronic conditions account for many of the problems that the elderly face. The *Fact Book on Aging* (National Council on Aging, 1978) indicates that at least 85% of the problem conditions of the elderly are chronic, and most people over 65 years of age have at least one chronic condition. The most common conditions are vision and hearing impairments, arthritis and rheumatism, hypertension, and heart disease. Specht and Craig (1982) report that a smaller percentage of the chronically impaired are not limited in their activities. Other chronic conditions common among the elderly include obesity, abdominal-cavity hernias, cataracts, varicose veins, hemorrhoids, and prostate disease. The elderly are susceptible to neurodegenerative diseases, EEG slowing, chromosomal changes, and immune dysfunctions.

The health of the elderly is fragile—a balance so delicate that a minor illness can lead to major complications. For instance, taking aspirin for a headache can cause peptic ulcers to flare up. Physicians may advise caution in exercise, drug usage, and other matters if an elderly person is recovering from a serious illness.

## Mental Impairment

Some of the mental problems that the elderly face stem from *organic disorders,* which include temporary or permanent damage to the brain tissues, causing impaired memory, poor judgment, intellectual decline, and disorientation. The impairment could be slight or serious enough to require hospitalization. Individuals who have the best coping abilities before they become disabled will be the best equipped to deal with the developmental tasks of disability and will thus be the most successful in dealing with organic impairment (Havighurst, 1982).

Cardiovascular and cerebrovascular diseases also negatively affect cognition, but the extent of the effect differs widely and depends on the severity of the illness and the type of behavior examined. Studies that contrast patients having cardiovascular or cerebrovascular conditions with normal control groups almost invariably report poorer performance for the patients on both verbal and nonverbal measures. In contrast, comparison of hypertensive patients with age-matched normals produces a more complex pattern of outcomes. Hypertension impairs speeded psychomotor performance more than it affects untimed tests of verbal abilities. Sometimes mild hypertension appears to enhance performance and has been postulated to improve flow of blood to the brain. However, more severe hypertension ultimately lowers intellectual performance. Therefore, it is unclear whether chronic use of antihypertension medications influences cognitive abilities in a systematic way (La Rue & Jarvik, 1982).

A small percentage of people are affected by serious organic disorders. For example, psychosis affects a larger percentage of older people than those 35 and under. Sometimes, mental symptoms are caused by *chronic brain syndrome*—a gradual irreversible deterioration of the brain cells—or by cerebral arteriosclerosis, which impairs the flow of blood to the brain.

With advancing age and its attendant physiological decline, factors such as duration of disease and severity of symptoms, in combination with socioeconomic factors and patterns of intellectual as well as physical stimulation, appear to account for the variance in observed relationships between disease and cognition more than any single factor. One could say—in jest but with an element of truth—that for old age health + wealth = happiness, if happiness is viewed as the retention of those mental abilities that enable individuals to attain pleasure (La Rue & Jarvik, 1982).

## PERSONAL ADAPTATION TO AGING

Havighurst (1982) says that the developmental tasks of the elderly vary with their lifestyles and personal histories. Sociologists have advanced many theories to describe the changes that take place in the elderly.

### Disengagement and Activity Theories

*Disengagement theory*  In the 1960s, Cummings and Henry (1961) formulated the *disengagement theory,* which assumes that aging is a progressive process of physical, psychological, and social withdrawal from the wider society. At the physical level, people slow their activity level and conserve their energy. At the psychological level, they withdraw their concern from the wider world and begin to focus on those aspects of life that immediately touch them, shifting attention from the outer world to the inner world of their own feelings, thoughts, and actions. At the social level, a process of double withdrawal begins; the elderly withdraw from younger people, who in turn move away from the elderly. Cummings and Henry speak of the elderly as wanting to disengage, and, by doing so, reducing the number of roles they play and weakening or severing relationships.

In some sense, society encourages the disengagement of the elderly by transferring their functions to the young, both in work and in family responsibilities. Society thereby minimizes the problems that may be associated with increasing incompetence, illness, or death of the elderly.

According to disengagement theory, the withdrawal of the elderly person is natural and even beneficial because the aging person's diminished life then can match his or her decreased physical and psychic energy. The person may maintain a sense of satisfaction but curtail social involvements and activities because he or she has less desire for them.

The disengagement theory has been both thoroughly criticized and defended by large groups of people. Many articles have questioned its meaningfulness. Both sides have used cross-sectional studies, as well as generational and age differences. On the whole, the bulk of evidence seems to weigh against its main tenets (Maddox, 1969; Palmore, 1975). So, why consider it? Because, like most theories, there is perhaps some truth to it that can help social workers serve older people.

Some features of the disengagement theory do have merit. Some older adults may take a passive stance toward the world around them because they have become more introspective than they were earlier in life. This kind of psychological withdrawal could be seen as a kind of disengagement. Also, more older people today withdraw from certain roles and activities voluntarily. Further, older and younger members of society support the idea of retirement, suggesting that disengagement satisfies both the individual and society.

*Activity theory*  Several sociologists, including Havighurst and Neugarten (Vander Zanden, 1978), have developed *activity theory* as an alternative to disengagement theory. The theory says that people will be more satisfied if they are involved in life and actively resist the isolating effects of negative social attitudes. Older people will make better adjustments to retirement by finding productive substitutes for work and making new friends to fill the emotional gap.

Activity theorists indicate that the majority of older people maintain fairly stable levels of physical and social activity (Neugarten, 1973; Palmore, 1975; Shanas, 1972). The amount of engagement or disengagement that occurs depends on past life patterns and socioeconomic forces rather than on any inherent or inevitable process. Successful aging, then, is seen as requiring a substantial level of physical, mental, and social activity.

*Drawbacks to both activity and disengagement theories.* P. S. Fry (1992) indicates the relationship between the mere level of activity and life satisfaction or well-being is quite weak. Many individuals are quite inactive but nonetheless satisfied with their lives; others are very busy but nonetheless unhappy. This implies that the *quality* of one's activity is probably more important than its quantity.

Further, neither activity theory nor disengagement theory adequately allows for individual differences in personality traits and preferences. Some people will benefit from maintaining an active lifestyle, while others are happy when they disengage from society. Neither scenario is true for everyone. Most people would be satisfied in old age when they achieve a good fit between their lifestyle and their individual needs, preferences, and personality (P. S. Fry, 1992; Seleen, 1982). An older woman denied the opportunity of outside work and pay may be happy working at home rather than being inactive; a man who had a horrendous job outside the home would enjoy a retirement in which he spends time gardening and going out with his friends. Still another person may withdraw from small activities but be involved in more central roles that are few but satisfying (Rapkin & Fischer, 1992).

## Role-Exit Theory

Z. S. Blau (1973) has formulated the *role-exit theory*. According to Blau, retirement and widowhood terminate participation by the elderly in the principal institutional structures of society—the job and the family. This termination undermines opportunities for the elderly to remain socially useful. The loss of job and marital roles can devastate a person, for these are core roles—the main sources of adult identity.

Rosen (1974) and Keith (1990) take a similar position, saying that in the United States people are not effectively socialized into old age. The social norms as well as myths about the elderly describe them as old, weak, limited, and unworldly. The elderly therefore have very little motivation to move into this socially-ascribed role, which U.S. culture does not value. Rosen concludes that this role excludes people from equal opportunities for participation and rewards in society.

Critics of the role-exit theorists say they exaggerate the social losses felt by most elderly people. Many elderly people indicate that their loss of work and parental roles is offset by increased freedom, as well as by opportunities to do things they always wanted to do but had little time for when they were younger.

## Social-Exchange Theory

Dowd and other sociologists have applied the *social-exchange (interaction) theory* to the aging process. According to this theory, people enter into relationships because in doing so they derive rewards such as economic sustenance, recognition, a sense of security, love, or social approval. In seeking such rewards they incur costs, such as negative experiences, fatigue, or embarrassment. They may abandon their quest for a given reward if the costs are too high; they may also do it for the sake of pursuing a potentially more rewarding experience. Thus, in interaction theory, people are viewed as engaging in a sort of mental bookkeeping that involves a ledger of rewards, costs, and profits. In this view, a relationship tends to persist only as long as both parties profit from it (Homans, 1974).

Quite often, the elderly find themselves increasingly vulnerable because of their deteriorating bargaining position—emotional as well as economic. As they decline in power, the elderly retire with the hope that social security and medicare will provide for them.

Social-exchange theorists believe that the quality of the relationship between the elderly and society has been determined by the speed with which industrialization has taken place. Publications by Bengston, Cueller, and Ragan (1975), Cowgill (1974), and Cowgill and Holmes (1972) state that the position of the elderly in preindustrial societies was to accumulate knowledge and control through years of experience; the theorists believe that industrialization undermines the importance of traditional knowledge and control.

## Consolidation Theory

*Consolidation theory* posits a consolidation of commitments by the elderly, as well as a redistribution of their energies so that they can cope with lost roles, activities, and capacities. With the disappearance of some of their active roles, older people may find it easier to redistribute their energies among their remaining roles. Engagement in such roles may either match the preloss level or show a reduction in the energy expended. Some people may not have enough activities to perform, because their remaining roles cannot absorb the energy left by a specific role loss. Unless they find a substitute role, such people may be forced to waste themselves in losses. Consolidation theory will not hold true when a person faces a major loss; even if plentiful, the remaining activities cannot adequately serve as the basis of life.

> Ben and Charlotte, both in their 80s, are an extremely happy couple. Financially independent, they enjoy good health. Their children visit them frequently, they participate actively in their community's affairs, and they occupy a prominent and significant position in their social group. One morning Ben wakes up to find that Charlotte has quietly passed away in her sleep.
>
> This loss is devastating for Ben. Although there are still many activities in which he can participate,

the death of his wife makes him withdraw from his friends and family. Slowly and steadily, his pain is revealed in his disengagement from activities he had formerly embraced. The loss of Charlotte has not brought about any consolidation in his life.

Taken together, these developmental theories can offer insights into old age. The circumstances and personalities of clients should ultimately determine the sort of help social workers choose to give. Theories and observations concerning cognition can also help, as the following section shows.

# COGNITIVE FUNCTIONING

## Intelligence

There has been considerable controversy about the ability of older people to maintain their intellectual abilities. According to Horn and Donaldson (1976) and other psychologists, to declare that intellectual abilities diminish in old age or that the decline is inevitable or universal does a great disservice to the elderly. Their research reveals that there is a greater degree of elasticity in old age than we have traditionally accepted. However, they do not deny that mental abilities do decline with old age.

*Cross-section studies*    Older adults have difficulty with Piagetian tests of formal operational thinking (Blackburn & Papalia, 1992). Sometimes elderly adults perform more poorly than young and middle-aged adults even on concrete operational tasks that assess conservation and classification skills (Blackburn & Papalia, 1992; Denney, 1982). However, these studies have involved cross-sectional comparisons of the different age groups. Further, the poorer performance of older groups does not imply that cognitive abilities are lost as one ages. There could be cohort factors; for example, an older person may have less formal schooling than the average younger adult has had. In Piagetian tasks, level of education is a better predictor of success than is age (Blackburn & Papalia, 1992). Older adults who attended college did perform as well as the younger adults when tested on formal operations (Blackburn, 1984; Hooper, Hooper, and Colbert, 1985). Also, older adults who have been out of school for a long time can improve their performance by very brief training, which implies that necessary cognitive skills exist and merely need to be reactivated (Blackburn & Paplia, 1992).

Thus, the effects of aging on intelligence have been overestimated, partly because of the results of cross-sectional studies. Such studies employ the snapshot approach, usually testing individuals of different ages and then comparing their performance. Longitudinal studies, in contrast, retest the same individuals over a period of years (Kagan & Moss, 1962; Thomas & Chess, 1977).

Baltes and Schaie (1973) found that cross-sectional studies do not allow for generational differences in performance on intelligence tests. Increases in educational opportunities as well as social changes mean that larger numbers of U.S. citizens are performing at successively higher levels of functioning. Therefore, the measured intelligence of older adults keeps increasing. Individuals who were 50 in the 1960s had higher intellectual scores than those who were 50 in the 1950s.

*Optimizing intelligence*  People have become increasingly aware that optimal intellectual functioning in the later years is related to maintaining good health, physical activity, and intellectual interests throughout life. In many cases, reduced physical and mental activity is caused by emotional crisis and accompanying grief or depression; it is also brought about by pessimistic expectations of deterioration. Often, physical exercising or meditation and exercise can awaken lines of thought that have lain dormant because of neglect. Higher education may stimulate a desire to stay mentally alert and also impart skills that help the elderly adjust to old age. Many people enjoy reading, analyzing, criticizing, and discussing throughout their lifetimes.

One outstanding example of lifelong engagement is the great anthropologist Margaret Mead. In her late 70s she was still traveling, participating in discussions, teaching classes, and continuing to write. An extremely alert person, she let nothing escape her notice, and she continually pointed out to her students areas in anthropology they needed to explore and study.

Some older people are homebound. To help them, some libraries have outreach programs whereby they bring books and cassettes to the home. Neugarten (1976) found that the most influential factors in cognitive decline are not intrinsic to the aging process per se but to tangential problems that often are relievable, such as failing health, social isolation, and minimal formal education.

*Individuality*  Baltes and Labouvie (1973) made a review of the literature and reached some noteworthy conclusions. They found that individual differences among the elderly are tremendous and therefore could badly erode the predictive value of age alone. Even more complicating, individual differences have differential impacts for various ability dimensions. In general, age changes are surprisingly small in comparison to generational (cohort) differences or to the change described as "terminal drop" that comes just before death. Further, age changes can be altered even after onset in old age.

Though biological aging undoubtedly influences intellectual functioning, there has been a tendency to underestimate or ignore the impact of older people's environments, many of which are not conducive to intellectual acquisition and maintenance. Botwinick (1970) concludes that, in terms of overall ability, education is extremely important in explaining individual differences.

## Memory and New Learning

An increasing proportion of older people show some memory loss as their age advances. Memory is related to learning and intelligence. Remembering is part of the evidence of learning, and learning is part of the measurement of intelligence. Although we regard memory, learning, and intelligence as three separate processes, we have not learned to evaluate them independently of one another.

### Alzheimer's disease    Take the following case.

> Seventy-year-old Theodore notices that his memory is starting to falter. He begins to forget days and dates. Slowly, the most familiar surroundings become strange to him, and he frequently becomes lost. As time passes, he becomes more and more confused, and it appears he can no longer recognize his own wife.

Theodore has Alzheimer's disease, a form of senile dementia affecting more than 1 million and killing nearly 100,000 people per year in the United States (Raeburn, 1984). Alzheimer's victims are usually irritable, restless, and agitated and suffer from impaired judgment. The final stages of Alzheimer's disease bring progressive paralysis and breathing problems. Often, these breathing problems lead to pneumonia, frequently a cause of death in Alzheimer's patients.

The brains of these victims show a destructive tangle of protein filaments in the cortex—the part of the brain responsible for intelligent functioning. Research indicates that there are biochemical causes for the disease, and in about 15% of the cases, there is evidence of an inherited disposition—passing from one generation to the next (Raeburn, 1984).

What causes Alzheimer's disease is becoming an important question. In many cases, it usually begins in middle age. Because of its hereditary components, Alzheimer's disease repeatedly strikes in some families and affects half the family members (Heston & White, 1991). Analyzing the blood in such families, genetic researchers located a gene for the disease on the 21st pair of chromosomes and concluded that anyone who inherits just one of these apparently dominant genes will eventually develop the disease (St. George-Hyslop et al., 1987). Individuals with Down's syndrome may find that one of the caus-

es of mental retardation is that they have three rather than the normal two 21st chromosomes and consistently develop Alzheimer's disease in middle age (Heston & White, 1991). Genes on other chromosomes have been implicated as well and continue to help explain how genes may contribute to Alzheimer's disease (Heston & White, 1991).

The search for causes continues. A great deal of attention has been placed on a deficit in the neurotransmitter acetylcholine, which is essential for normal learning and memory (Heston & White, 1991). Another theory proposes that a slow-working virus is responsible for Alzheimer's disease. One study reveals that injecting blood from Alzheimer's patients and their relatives into hamsters can cause degeneration of the hamster's brains (Manuelidis, De Figueriredo, Kim, Fritch, & Manuelidis, 1988). Another theory indicates that the immune system malfunctions and launches an attack on normal brain tissues (Heston & White, 1991). It could be pointed out that Alzheimer's disease will prove to have early causes, some genetic and some environmental. It may even turn out to be a group of distinct diseases, each with a different causality (Heston & White, 1991). So far, no magic medicine has been discovered that can cure this disease.

### Types and stages of memory    Individuals show essentially four types of memory:

1. *Short-term memory:* Recall after very little delay, varying from 5 to 30 seconds
2. *Recent memory:* Recall of events after a brief period of time, from one hour to several days
3. *Old memory:* Recall of events that took place long in the past and have not been rehearsed or thought of since
4. *Remote memory:* Recall of events that took place long in the past but have been referred to frequently throughout the course of the lifetime

Regardless of type, there are three stages of memory:

1. *Registration:* The "recording" of learning or perceptions, analogous to the recording of sound on a tape recorder
2. *Retention:* The ability to sustain registration over time
3. *Recall:* The retrieval of material that has been registered and retained

A failure in any of these stages could result in having no measurable memory (no recollection of events).

*Memory loss and retrieval*  Bright people are less susceptible to memory loss with increasing age than their less intelligent counterparts. Again, some older people escape memory loss completely. As a person becomes older, the ability to retain auditory information is better than the ability to retain visual information. People who exercise their memory tend to maintain both remote and recent memory well into old age.

Memory loss among some older people could be due to some failure in registration or the acquisition of new knowledge; among others, it could be related to the retention of knowledge; and among still others, it could be related to recall or the retrieval of knowledge. Older people tend to organize themselves less well and less completely than they did when they were younger (Denney, 1974; Hultsch, 1969, 1971, 1974).

After evaluating many studies, Craik (1977) reports that memory loss is not a complete, all-or-nothing occurrence. Some of the elderly compensate for memory deficit better than others. Recall per se appears to be improved in the elderly if they are given more time for a task and supplied with careful instructions on how the material has to be organized in order for it to be learned. He found that performance improved with experience. Therefore it would be inappropriate to conclude that people over 65 cannot learn or make use of completely new material. Older people may not be as efficient as younger students in their speed of learning, but their past experiences and knowledge may well compensate for their lack of speed in learning.

Many colleges now cater to the needs of the elderly because there are more and more older college-educated people who wish to be retrained for other skills. Adult education does help the elderly to face the difficulties that confront retirees in our work-oriented society.

## ERIKSON: INTEGRITY VERSUS DESPAIR

Erikson (1980) characterizes the period of transition to old age as a crisis of integrity versus despair. As a person's commitment to integrity increases, the ego strength of wisdom emerges.

### Integrity

During this period an individual begins to think in terms of life's coming to a close. According to Erikson, the integrity aspect of life now provides a person with both the knowledge and wisdom to understand his or her own life; it produces a balance between the decrease in potency and performance and the opportunity to serve as an example to the upcoming generations.

In old age, a person becomes more intrapersonally than interpersonally oriented, reminiscing about past actions. *Integrity* refers to the ability to accept the facts of one's life and to face death without too many regrets or fear. Older adults who have achieved a sense of integrity view their past in an existential light. They appreciate their lives; that is, the accumulation of personal satisfactions and crisis their individuality has produced. Such people accept this record of events and do not try to deny some facts or overemphasize others. Integrity is not so much a quality of honesty and trustworthiness as it is the ability to integrate one's past history with one's present circumstances and to feel content with the outcome (Newman & Newman, 1995).

A sense of integrity is not based on physical achievements. There are people who are physically handicapped but have maintained a feeling of contentment throughout their lives and are sat-isfied with their lot in life. And there are individu-als who have been fairly conflict free but who still view life with great dissatisfaction and unhappiness. In short, developing an attitude of integrity and not despair depends on the self-acceptance that comes through introspection.

## Despair

People who have lived their lives carelessly may regret what they could have done but did not. This recognition of lost opportunity affects the way they feel. Erikson calls this the despair stage of life. Older adults need to incorporate in them-selves a lifelong record of conflicts, failures, and disappointments along with their accomplish-ments. This is a difficult process by itself. Moreover, older adults have to face some degree of devaluation, even hostility, from the social community. When they face negative attitudes from family members, colleagues, and younger people about their incompetence, their depen-dence, or their old-fashioned ways, many of them may feel discouraged about their own self-worth. Older adults also become aware that they cannot perform certain tasks and that their domains of independent functioning and mastery have diminished. Further, society does not view the death of an older adult as a loss, because we tend to see people's contribution to society as coming when they are younger. Therefore, older adults believe that society is already letting go of them even before they are ready to let go of life (Jecker & Schneiderman, 1994). The gradual deterioration of certain physical capacities, par-ticularly loss of hearing, impaired vision, and limited motor ability, also feeds frustration and discouragement.

All these factors could also lead to a sense of regret about life and about oneself. People wish in a nagging way that things could have been dif-ferent. This attitude of despair about life makes it difficult to develop an attitude of calm resigna-tion toward death. Either the individual seeks death as a way of ending a miserable existence or desperately fears death because there has been no compensation for past failures.

> Norman is 72 years old. He married once, when he was 18, but because he played around his wife eventually divorced him. He never again felt the necessity to get married. Norman continued as a happy-go-lucky person and took life as it came, but before he knew it he was an old man without too much to offer to others. He suffered a serious heart attack and then found that part of his body was paralyzed, leaving him disabled.
>
> Norman has no one at home to take care of him, so he has been admitted as an invalid to a home for the aged. When he meets the social worker, he cries in despair and laments that he did not spend his life more meaningfully when he was younger so that he could have someone to take care of him now. Norman comments sadly that if he had his life to live all over again, he would have remained faithful to his wife and not played around. He would have been a good parent to his children and shown better treatment to his sisters, who to him have always been "second-class citizens." While relating his life history, he cries constantly because he is miserable and unhappy.

Finally, in this stage, an individual may deny or fail to deal with the crisis at all.

Questions arise about the adequacy of integrity as an organizing principle for development in later adulthood. Clayton (1975) notes that rela-tively few individuals achieve a commitment to integrity and thus achieve wisdom in old age. Many individuals become fixated at an earlier point of development or a crisis point, particular-ly at a point of adolescent identity or other crisis, and do not move ahead.

Thus, having come to the end of Erikson's stages does not mean that we have come to the end of psychosocial crises, or that all people resolve the integrity crisis.

# SOCIAL ASPECTS OF AGING

## Status of the Elderly

Besides sexism and racism, U.S. culture is guilty of ageism—a bias that will likely affect most of us as we grow older. U.S. society continues to value youth and beauty over any other capacity or ability. How do other cultures view becoming old? A few aspects of aging are universal; all cultures seem to define some aspect of the lifespan as old age although they do disagree on when old age begins (Amoss & Harrell, 1981). Further, when a person becomes very old, many biological changes occur and diseases take over, which eventually lead to frailness and dependence—this is common in all cultures. Even so, the experience of being an elderly person varies dramatically from one society to the next.

As mentioned earlier, in some cultures to be old is to be honored and revered. In rural Taiwan and traditional Korea, birthday celebrations are held only when there is something worth celebrating, such as a person's 60th, 70th, and 80th birthdays. In Taiwan, the 88th rather than the 90th birthday is celebrated, because nines are considered unlucky numbers (Harrell, 1981). In Taiwan, the word *old* (*lau*) is also applied to middle-aged and young adults to signify that they are worthy of respect as they age (Harrell, 1981), whereas in the United States to be called old is not a compliment.

In many traditional societies, the elderly have a higher status compared to industrial societies (Finley, 1982; C. L. Fry, 1985; Keith, 1990). However, Sokolovsky (1990) indicates that there are many examples of hunter/gatherer cultures where the elderly have low status and modern industrialized societies in which they have high status.

How does a society determine the status of older people? Two factors come into play (Amoss & Harrell, 1981). First, old people will be valued to the extent their contributions to society are higher than their costs to society. There is a difference between the frail elderly and the healthy elderly, with always more respect for those who pull their own weight (Barker, 1990). Healthy elderly people can control their own resources. They own their property and can leave their inheritance to their children, or they hold leadership positions in the community and are well respected because of their high status. For exam-

ple, people respect the likes of Margaret Mead and former president George Bush.

Modernization itself is not an evil for the elderly. A great deal depends on whether social changes involve a loss or a gain in the elderly's ability to contribute to society and to control resources. At times, older people may lose their status in society as it modernizes but regain it back if industrialization brings with it a higher standard of living and better health (Finley, 1982; Keith, 1990). Finally, we must keep in mind that there is no one experience of old age. Comparing human development in different cultures and subcultures is the only way to determine which developmental processes and pathways are universal and which are peculiar to a society.

In the United States, many people experience a reduction in wealth, influence, prestige, and political power as they age. They also cannot fail to see that being older disqualifies them from esteemed positions such as administrator, vice president of a company, and so forth. In this country, the entry criteria for employment are health, age, gender, race, experience, and educational achievement. As long as old age is not viewed positively, elderly people will have more difficulty obtaining jobs than younger people.

## Empty Nest in Old Age

Most couples are middle-aged when their children leave home, but some are in their old age. With the trend toward delayed marriage, it is becoming more common for parents to start getting the children ready to leave home rather than waiting for them to leave on their own.

People have different attitudes about their children leaving home. Some women tend to look forward to launching their children, seeing it as an opportunity for greater freedom. Others are less eager, especially if motherhood has been the focal point of their lives and they have very few outside interests. The male viewpoint has not yet been researched.

Though many have discussed the empty-nest stage and how it affects parents negatively, researchers have falsely attributed results to the empty-nest stage that are in fact caused by other factors. For instance, the absence of children may unmask an empty marriage, but it is the quality of the marriage that causes divorce rather than the empty-nest stage. There is no evidence to show that solid marital relationships are harmed by the departure of children. The stage is only a transition, and researchers will have to look at men and women both before and after the last child has left home in order to assess the effects on the marriage. Lifestyles and personal traits also influence responses to children's departure.

> Eleanor is the mother of six children. Life with her alcoholic husband is difficult, but she devotes herself to taking care of her children and commits all her time to them. As long as her husband brings home part of his wages, she's satisfied.
>
> When the children grow and leave, Eleanor finds time on her hands and an empty house. Without her children, her life is miserable; after all, her marriage died when her husband's companion became the bottle. With the help of her sisters, who are close to her, Eleanor plans frequent trips to interesting places. She contemplates divorce but does not have the courage to get out of the marriage. Thus, although she is married, in reality she leads her own life. She looks forward to having her children visit her and to taking trips with them.

> Rosalind turns 60 just before her last child leaves home. Though initially sad, she is happy to have time to do the things she always wanted to do. Her husband and she begin to behave like lovebirds, spending more time in bed, listening to music, and visiting the theater. Both Rosalind and her husband view this as a very happy aspect of their lives, for they have finally found time for each other.

## Family and Friendships

Despite talk about the rejected older person, there is considerable contact between older people and their grown children, even though the older person may live alone. According to studies by Shanas (1972) and Antonucci and Akiyama (1991), about three-fifths of older people had seen a child of theirs on the same day they were interviewed or within the preceding week; there were few parents who had not seen their children in the previous year. It was found that adult children and their parents maintained meaningful kinship relationships. Small services were rendered reciprocally between parent and child; in some cases, parents offered more services than the grown children. Moreover, most parents were free of regular monetary dependence on their children. Further, reciprocity of help was seen in shopping, housework, babysitting, and home repairs. This form of kin assistance is an important characteristic of family role relations.

McKain (1967) reported and still holds true that the attitudes of grown children affect retirement marriages. He realized that some people were shocked to learn that their parents were planning to get married. In some cases, the problem was related to the inheritance of property. A negative attitude on the part of the grown children prevented a large number of retirement marriages.

Although the postparental period is viewed as potentially traumatic, most families do not find it so. In spite of the picture painted, there is no gloomy empty-nest syndrome. In a survey of an urban, upper-middle-class neighborhood in Kansas City, 22 out of 49 older couples evaluated the postparental period as "better" than the preceding years, 15 said that it was as good, 7 said that changes were not clear, and 2 said that it was "as bad" as the preceding phases (Shanas, 1972).

Although older people interact less frequently with acquaintances and friends than do younger adults, they interact frequently with spouses and siblings and feel closer emotionally to significant people in their lives than do younger adults (Carstensen, 1992). Although elderly adults have fewer friends and smaller social networks overall, particularly if they are men (Connidis & Davis, 1992; Field & Minkler, 1988; Fischer & Phillips, 1982), they have as many close relationships with relatives as do young and middle-aged adults (Levitt, 1991). It appears that the elderly intentionally restrict their relationships to people who count (Fredickson & Cartensen, 1990). But they are very satisfied with their relationships and just as able to count on social supports as are younger adults (Antonucci, 1985; Bosse, Aldwin, Levenson, Spiro, & Mroczek, 1993). In other words, one's social network does shrink in total size from early adulthood to very old age, and most older adults have emotionally rich and supportive relationships with a small circle of friends.

When U.S. adults over 65 years old were asked about their problems, only 13% cited loneliness as one of their "very serious problems" (Harris, Pedersen, McClearn, Plomin, & Nesselroade, 1992). Older people may spend more time alone than younger adults (Lason, Zuzanek, & Mannell, 1985), but it is the young adults who report feelings of loneliness (Parlee, 1979). Perhaps young adults are less secure in their relationships and feel anxious when they are not with people, whereas the elderly have learned to be alone and can enjoy time by themselves. However, we need to get rid of the myth that older adults suffer from a lack of close relationships (Sigelman & Shaffer, 1995).

## Lifestyles

When we observe people, we see not only their roles, relationships, group memberships, and environments but also how those elements are forged together by choices, by selective commitments of attention and energy, and by personal mannerisms to make up a whole lifestyle. The values served by a person's lifestyle are determined in part by cultural traditions and in part by personal experience.

Growing old has the potential to alter life in many ways, affecting physical capacities, economic status, group memberships, activities, and environments. At the same time, aging brings with it a certain freedom from social restraints that can result in changes in way of life. Nearly all studies of lifestyles in later life are cross-sectional ones, which do not allow us to assess the impact of age on changes in lifestyle. All we

can see from this type of study is which lifestyles predominate at various life stages.

In a study of people in their 70s, Maas and Kuypers (1974) found that just over 40% had lifestyles that centered on their families. Over 40% of the men led more solitary lifestyles than before, revolving around hobbies and more cursory social contacts. The remainder of these men's lives was dominated by sporadic ill health. Women in their 70s had a diverse lifestyle, owing largely to the fact that half of the women were no longer married and that a great percentage of the married women had a lifestyle that was job centered.

A study made of lifestyles of people over 65 years of age found that they followed one of six types of lifestyle, characterized as familism, couplehood, world of work, living fully, living alone, and maintaining involvement. *Familism* implies that an older couple have children and other relatives to whom they are totally devoted. *Couplehood* means an older couple with no children, who spend a lot of time with each other and other couples. Some elderly people were extremely work-oriented, others lived a full life working and having fun with and without friends. A small percentage lived alone and did not socialize much. Finally, some people lived by themselves but were involved with others. Here is the case of a couple living fully.

> Will is 77 and Candy, 74. A well-to-do couple, they have been married for 44 years. Their two children arre married and have families of their own. Candy and Will start their day at eight in the morning, after a leisurely breakfast. Then they drive to the shopping center or go to church activities. After a midafternoon nap, they both exercise on stationary bicycles. In the evening, they visit their family or friends or see a movie. What is most important about this lifestyle is that they enjoy each other's company and are very much in love with each other.

People perform many different types of activities, for various reasons: One activity may be a source of personal identity or a source of legitimate interactions with other people; another may yield a sense of personal involvement with life—

a way to get the vital juices flowing; yet another confers prestige or status. Activities may provide a source of new experience, service to others, a way to pass time, something to look forward to, a source of variety in life, an exercise of competence, peace and quiet or a means of escape, a sense of accomplishment, or just plain fun.

## Retirement

Retirement is an institutional separation of people from their occupational positions with a continuation of income based on prior years of service. Although health could be a big factor in retirement, age is of primary consideration. About 80% of men and about 90% of women over age 65 do not have a job. With ever-larger numbers of people in the United States living longer, retirement is becoming an important issue. Floyd et al. (1992) define *retirement* as the time when people begin to receive social security or other pension benefits and are not required to work. Retirement also refers to a developmental transition, a predictable normative change that involves preparation, redefinition of roles and role behaviors, and ongoing psychological adjustment as the structure and significance of being a wage earner or bread winner is replaced by other activities.

Of course, some people never retire. Some die before they reach retirement. Some continue to work on a reduced schedule. Those whose skills involve creativity often continue to blossom in their older years; they focus on painting, writing, acting, and music throughout late adulthood (Herzog, House, & Morgan, 1991). In some ways, retirement is an opportunity to be who you want to be. At the turn of the 20th century, 70% of the men over 65 years old were in the paid labor force, compared with 16% in 1991 (U.S. Bureau of the Census, 1992; U.S. Senate, Special Committee on Aging, 1986). Nowadays men spend about 20% of their lifetime in retirement. As improvements in health make later adulthood longer, the length of retirement and proportion of people in it will increase considerably.

*Phases*   People adjust to retirement in individual ways. About one-third of retired adults report significant difficulty during this process (Fletcher & Hansson, 1991). Retirement takes getting used to. Atchley (1976) has proposed that adults progress through several phases in the transition from employee to retiree:

1. Preretirement
2. Honeymoon
3. Disenchantment
4. Reorientation

Adjustment to retirement begins with a preretirement phase where workers begin to plan for the future (Evans, Ekerdt, & Bosse, 1985). As retirement draws closer, workers start to think in terms of time that is left until the big day when they can leave. They often begin to separate themselves psychologically from their jobs, even viewing work as a nuisance or a hassle that will soon end (Ekerdt & DeViney, 1993).

Immediately after retirement, they experience a honeymoon period when they enjoy their new-found freedom and head for the beach, golf course, bowling alley, and campgrounds. Later, they move to the disenchantment phase, when the novelty dies off and they feel aimless and sometimes unhappy. Last, they move on to a reorientation phase, when they begin to put together a realistic and satisfying lifestyle for themselves. Ekerdt, Bosse, and Levkoff (1985) found that men who had been retired for a few months were in the honeymoon period, highly satisfied with life and optimistic about the future, whereas men who had been retired for 13 to 18 months were disenchanted with life. Lastly, men who had been retired for a long time were relatively satisfied once again (Williamson, Rinehart, & Blank, 1992).

*Emotional concerns*   When people leave their occupations, many changes occur in their lives, regardless of whether they retired voluntarily or were forced to retire. Retirement spells fear and self-doubt for most U.S. citizens who are not well-to-do. As we have seen, work provides people with their self-concept and self-esteem, as well as personal satisfaction, meaningful peer relationships, opportunities for creativity, and, in sum, enduring life satisfactions. Losing these experiences through retirement can be demoralizing and a precursor of major problems in older age (Black, 1969; Cummings & Henry, 1961; Miller, 1965).

> Adam is 61 years old and the manager of a big company. He has held his job for more than 30 years and thinks of himself as indispensable to the company. He is therefore shocked when the company invites all senior staff to retire with a glamorous retirement plan. Forced to choose the plan, Adan feels resentful that the company does not want him anymore. He leaves the company feeling angry and unwanted, in spite of the fact that they acknowledge what he has done for the company and give him a big farewell party.
>
> At home with time on his hands, he is scared and restless. Finding his days to be aimless, he faces the immediate challenge of giving structure to the long, shapeless hours. From recurring nightmares he wakes up in a sweat, having seen himself drowning or being dropped into a bottomless well. The fear of coping with a new life so suddenly thrust on him is almost too much for him. Though educated and well prepared for this type of life, he has to work consciously at scheduling his time and to find meaningful involvement in doing what gives him the most pleasure.
>
> It takes Adam about six months to understand that he is no longer working for the company, that his time is his own, and that he can really do what he wants with his time and his energy. Adam learns to understand and accept that he is responsible only to himself, his wife, and his grown children. They show concern about his welfare, especially because of his uncharacteristic disorganization. Slowly and steadily, Adam starts to put time and effort into disciplining himself.

Traditionally, retirement has implied a period in which people worry that they are unwanted by society or no longer useful. In contrast, nowadays some people work outside their homes even after they have retired. For others, work has never been the central feature in their lives. Further, few workers today find their primary social interests or relationships in the workplace. Research shows that what people miss most in retirement is money and that when people are assured an adequate income, they will retire early (Atchley, 1977; Shanas, 1972).

One meaningful way of dealing with retirement is to give people options. Some people would like to retire early; others would like to work longer. Some may want to start a new career, whereas others may prefer to withdraw from work obligations and spend time with family or by themselves.

*Factors affecting adjustment*   Many factors affect the way of life for retirees, such as the type of friends and colleagues a person has (Cox & Bhak, 1979). If a person's associates view retirement positively, then the person may retire without too much feeling of loss and make a successful adjustment.

A person's lifelong attitude toward work also affects feelings about retirement. Many people spend a lot of their time at their workplaces, and their self-esteem and sense of self-worth are bound up in their working roles. Retirement downgrades their roles. Disengaging from work roles is particularly difficult for people who have not found satisfaction in hobbies and other activities.

Unfortunately, many widows and minority-group members after living on a limited income during their working years must spend their "golden years" in poverty (Arber & Ginn, 1991; Clark & Maddox, 1992), for their retirement money and social security barely cover their needs. You have no doubt heard horror stories of older women being caught stealing food from grocery stores or buying dog food for themselves because it was cheaper than human food. We need to deal with such issues compassionately. With the help of social workers, the state or federal government needs to plan preventive and protective interventions.

The personality type of the retiree also affects retirement. Lowenthal (1972) found four personality types in retirees: work-oriented, self-protective, autonomous, and receptive-nurturant. A person who is extremely work-oriented would be depressed in facing retirement and may also have a fear of not being useful. The self-protective person sees retirement as a time of detachment and lack of responsibility for others. An autonomous person has usually selected a job from which he or she can determine when to retire. When this type of person can exercise that option, he or she is usually happy, but if retirement becomes mandatory then the person may experience depression and require reorientation. The receptive-nurturant individual is usually a woman who has developed intimacy; her positive adjustment to retirement depends on how she perceives her marital role and relationship. As long as she is satisfied with her marital status, she will view retirement as something meaningful for her.

A study by Reichard, Livson, and Petersen (1962) identified five personality types in terms of their adjustment to retirement:

1. *Well-adjusted people:* Those who have no regrets about their past lives, accept their present circumstances realistically, and find genuine joy and pleasure in their retired lives

2. *"Rocking chair" people:* Those who welcome old age as a time they are free to sit back and do nothing and who find satisfaction in being passive rather than active

3. *"Armored" people:* Those who use activity as a way of fending off old age; who develop a highly satisfying lifestyle after retirement, a system that serves as a defense against anxieties about feeling old

4. *Poor adjusters:* Those who find little satisfaction in retirement and blame others for any failure that they face in their lives

5. *"Self-blamers":* Those who blame themselves for everything that has not gone right in their lives.

As you can see, whether a person responds favorably to retirement or not is the result of many factors, including health, economic status, need for fulfillment, personal history, and atti-

tude toward life. Retirement in its essence is not a breaking away from a lifestyle but merely a continuation of what has gone before. Whatever coping styles people have developed will stay with them when they grow old.

*Gender differences*   Almost all research on retirement is based on men. Few data concern women. Because of their various perspectives researchers have made contradictory conclusions about women workers. Some studies reveal that a married woman's decision to retire is related to her age and her husband's work status, not to the characteristics of her occupation (George, Fillenbaum, & Palmore, 1984). Other studies show that a woman's retirement is related not only to her husband's wages but also to her independent financial status (Campione, 1988). These different findings may be based on the past few years, when women have remained in the workforce long enough to base the decision to retire on their own wage history and financial security. More studies need to consider why women retire and how their partners influence them.

*Ethnic differences*   Few studies on retirement consider ethnicity. Gibson, (1986, 1987) and J. S. Jackson and Gibson (1985) found that the characteristics of retired African Americans differ from those of Euro-Americans. The ability to label themselves as retired is not based on subjective disability, work history, and source of income; rather, it is simply based on whether or not they are currently employed. Further, gender differences do not appear among African Americans; men and women base their self-labels on the same variables. The findings of the Euro-American populations therefore should not be extended to the African-American population or any other ethnic group. Separate theoretical models should be developed for these groups (Gibson, 1987).

## Reminiscing

Older people tend to reminisce about their past lives. Reminiscing can help them evaluate how they have spent their lifetimes and their legacies. Old age is when they finally confront the question of whether they have lived up to their expectations and have conformed to their earlier beliefs and values (Specht & Craig, 1987). As we have seen, a person who looks back on a meaningless life and realizes that there is insufficient time to make up for past mistakes may develop a fear of death. Some individuals may not deal at all with this crisis. However, reminiscence is viewed mostly as an activity that facilitates the feeling that life is complete.

Butler (1974) indicates that successful aging involves both a life-review process and a shift of focus from the future to the present. Butler suggests counseling to help older people make use of this review process in order to relieve old guilts and resolve old conflicts.

Often, the elderly person reflects on the relationship between his or her personal history and the social history of the times, a reflection of great interest to historians who recognize life-review as oral history and an important source of historical data (Davis, 1985).

This process can take the form of written autobiographies of the famous and the not so famous. The life review also takes the form of nostalgia, reminiscence, or story telling, all of which can be quite useful to the older person, although it may not always be easy to listen to.

Butler and Lewis (1973) indicate that one of the greatest difficulties for younger persons, including mental health personnel, is to listen thoughtfully to the reminiscences of older people. We have been taught that this nostalgia represents living in the past and a preoccupation with self, and that it is generally boring, meaningless, and time consuming. Yet as a natural healing process it represents one of the underlying human capacities on which all psychotherapy depends. The life review should be recognized as a necessary and healthy process in daily life as well as in the mental health care of older people (Butler & Lewis, 1973).

Eighty-year-old Kendra lives in a nursing home. She always talks about her brother, whom she hasn't seen for over 20 years. She was responsible for his disinheritance from the family property but did not do anything about it until her husband died. Her sons, in turn, took away all her property, saying that she had "mistreated" their uncle many years ago. She keeps mumbling, "I did wrong . . . I did wrong . . . I'm being punished now." Kendra repeats her story of guilt, regret, and pain to the social worker almost every time she sees her. Those attempts at resolution do not work well, though, for her only brother has refused to talk to her ever again.

## Grandparenthood

Grandparenting plays an important function in old age. During the 20th century, we have seen a lengthening of the life cycle (Neugarten & Moore, 1968). Marriage, the birth and departure of children, and grandparenthood tend to occur later in life for people now than they did at the turn of the 20th century.

The grandparent's role is not defined clearly in today's society (Clavan, 1978; Kahana & Kahana, 1971; Robertson, 1976). Grandparents play varying roles. Some grandparents become babysitters to their grandchildren; others, who are well off but do not have time to spend with their children, lavish gifts on their grandchildren; distant grandparents, even if not well off, may lavish gifts in order to be remembered and show love in absence. Some grandparents make sporadic visits to see the grandchildren and merely play the role they have been assigned—that is, to be kind and caring and spoil them. Still other grandparents are economically dependent on their children or even grandchildren. Such older people may live in the homes of their grown children, and the attitude that the grandchildren develop toward them may stem from the attitude encouraged by their own parents.

Some grandparents are happy in their roles. However, a significant number find it difficult to accept the roles ascribed to them. The style in which such roles are enacted depends on the lifestyle and philosophy of the grandparents. In a classic study by Neugarten and Weinstein (1964), grandparenthood was judged to have five dominant themes, not all of them noted by all subjects:

1. A source of biological renewal and/or continuity, helping them feel rejuvenated and creating extensions of youth and self into the future
2. A source of emotional self-fulfillment, the development of the relationship between grandparent and grandchild evoking feelings of companionship and satisfaction that were sometimes missing from the earlier parent-child relationships
3. A source of vicarious achievement
4. The opportunity to be a resource person, offering financial aid as well as help based on their own life experiences
5. A feeling of remoteness and not really being well liked

Neugarten and Weinstein (1964) also identified two styles of grandparental interaction with grandchildren:

1. Traditional, including the following:
   a. Formal, in which the grandparents performed the prescribed roles
   b. Surrogate (found only for grandmothers), in which the grandmother actually took care of and responsibility for the grandchild while the parent worked
   c. Reservoir of family wisdom, in which the grandparents were a source of special skills and resources
2. Informal, including the following:
   a. Fun seeker, characterized by informality and playfulness
   b. Distant figure, in which the grandparents relate to the grandchild only on special occasions, such as birthdays or holidays

Neugarten and Weinstein (1964) found that the traditional style prevailed most, with the relationship seen as fun for the grandchildren as well as the grandparents.

Grandparents placed three types of emphasis on their relationships with their grandchildren (Neugarten & Weinstein, 1964). Some empha-sized social orientation, more emphasized personal orientation, and still others emphasized both aspects. Grandparents were classified as having a social orientation if they answered "yes" to a question about whether their grandchildren should be honest and hardworking. Younger grandparents, who emphasized social orientation, were usually married and working. Older grandparents, who placed an emphasis on personal orientation, were usually widowed and unemployed. They paid more attention to their grandparenting role because they were needed companionship and fun. They also spent more time with their grandchildren. Some of the grandparents wanted their grandchildren to be both honest and hardworking and spend time with them for fun. It was also seen that women had the greatest amount of interaction with their grandchildren. In a study by Robertson (1976), more than 80% of the grandmothers interviewed mentioned that they were excited, happy, and proud to be grandparents.

How do grandchildren view grandparenting, and how do they react to their grandparents? To some extent the attitude of a child is colored by the attitude of the child's parents toward their own parents. Some grandchildren follow this attitude, but some take the opposite one. Grandchildren ages 4 to 11 years old tend to value their grandparents for egocentric reasons; that is, for what the grandparents give them in love, affection, food, and gifts. Robertson (1976) found that young adult grandchildren hold favorable attitudes toward grandparents; about 90% of this group of grandchildren mentioned that they did not find their grandparents boring or see them as old fashioned or out of touch with their grandchildren, and about 70% of the teenagers mentioned that they did not feel that their grandparents were a bore.

Older adult grandchildren saw grandparents only in the role of people from whom they received gifts. About 59% saw the grandparents as providing financial aid. The ideal grandparent, however, was seen as enjoying grandchildren as well as showing an interest in them. Children most admired those grandparents who were gentle, helpful, and understanding, as well as industrious, talkative, and smart; or those who served as a companion, mediator, and teacher. Low-ranking grandparents were characterized as lazy, childish, or both dependent and childish.

*Great-grandparents* Because more people, specifically women, are living longer, more of them are becoming great-grandparents. Also, when people marry at a relatively young age, they are more likely to become great-grandparents.

Little research has been done on great-grandparenthood. Their sources of satisfaction and meaning differ from those of grandparents (Doka & Mertz, 1988; Wentkowski, 1985). Compared with grandparents, great-grandparents as a group are much more similar in what they derive from their role largely because they are less involved with the children than are grandparents. As the study by Doka and Mertz (1988) reveals, three aspects of great-grandparenthood are important. (1) Being a great-grandparent offers a sense of personal and family renewal, which is important for achieving integrity. That a grandchild has produced new life renews one's own excitement for life and reaffirms the continuance of the lineage. A four-generation family symbolizes immortality. Great-grandparents take pride in knowing that their families will live many years beyond them. (2) Great-grandchildren provide new diversions and more people to listen to reminiscing. (3) Becoming a great-grandparent is a major milestone and a mark of longevity that most people never achieve. Watching the fourth generation grow is always perceived positively.

## Religion

Religious orientations influence older people's self-images and personalities. A higher proportion of elderly rather than younger adults say that the religious person is best prepared for old age.

Religion also influences attitudes toward death. A sense of serenity and decreased fear of death are found among people who follow a conservative religious approach and view death as a portal to immortality. One can find many cultural efforts to deny death. Fear is associated most with what is left behind at death—the problems of survivors and responsibilities that have not been faced. Often, the greatest fear for the dying person is to leave behind friends and relatives. Nonreligious people facing death are less likely to have a reference group that can give them support and security.

For older adults, religion offers consolation and solutions. When asked their most common ways of dealing with problems in life, about half of the older people surveyed in one study mentioned that their coping strategies were connected to religion (Koenig, George, & Siegler, 1988). Praying and gaining strength from God were the most frequently used ways of coping.

Among African Americans, the elderly stressed religion in times of need and were intensively involved in religious activities (Levin, Taylor, and Chatters, 1994). African-Americans churches offer a solid support system. They also serve as an instrument for advocacy of social justice (Roberts, 1980); for example, Martin Luther King, Jr. and other ministers have advocated for equal rights. The role of the church in African-American lives is central: A key predictor of life satisfaction among African Americans is regular church attendance (Coke, 1992).

Older people of Mexican-American origin adopt a different approach to religion. Villa and Jaime (1993) reveal that the Mexicans use *la fe de la gente* (the faith of the people) as a coping strategy. The word *fe* implies varying degrees of faith, spirituality, hope, cultural values, and beliefs. As such, it implies that the older Mexicans identify with a cultural value or ideology rather than a specific religious community.

For Native Americans, the elderly serve as spiritual leaders and wisdom keepers: repositories of the sacred ways and philosophies that extend back in time indefinitely (Wall & Arden, 1990). The wisdom keepers share dreams and visions, perform healing ceremonies, and may make apocalyptic prophecies. Wisdom keepers play a more central role in the tribe than religious leaders do in Western society.

Social workers who help the elderly need to be aware of the place of religion and church in the lives of such clients unless they specifically mention that religion is not important to them. Social workers should keep in mind the self-reported importance of religion in the lives of many older adults and design interventions accordingly. Older people are more willing to talk to their minister than to a social worker about their problems; if they seek out help, it is usually with someone connected with the church. As 80-year-old Emma mentioned, "I talked to my friend, Wendy, she is at my church and a good Christian." Thus, in interventions with the elderly, the use of religion, church facilities, and support networks from the church could be quite helpful.

## SPECIAL CONCERNS OF OLD AGE

The elderly face many problems, which we can classify into those due to age and biological status and those due to difficult social situations.

### Biological Problems

One problem that some of the elderly deal with is *dementia*. Nothing scares the elderly more than losing their minds. *Dementia* is the technical term for senility, or a progressive loss of cognitive capacities that leads to severe declines in tested intellectual ability, poor memory, poor judgment, and difficulty in thinking abstractly. Personality changes may also come about. Senility is not a normal aspect of the aging process. Serious cognitive impairments and senility affect only 5% of the 65-and-older population overall (Regier et al., 1988), although in some susceptible elderly it increases as they grow older (Regier et al., 1988).

People often mistake certain symptoms as dementia. A person may be unnecessarily labeled

as "senile" and then viewed as a lost cause. Many different conditions produce the symptoms we associate with senility; some of them are curable or reversible (Heston & White, 1991). Many people misplace keys or cannot remember a person's name just because they are absent minded or forgetful. Small losses of memory in later life do not affect daily functioning. If all it took to warrant a diagnosis of dementia is forgetfulness, then many young and middle-aged adults would qualify!

*Depression* is another ailment affecting the elderly. Often, they must face losses; without a support network to ventilate their pain, the elderly can slip into depression. One can base a diagnosis of depression on one of two clusters of symptoms. As with adolescents, the most common symptom of depression is feeling sad, or *dysphoria*. While younger people may report that they are feeling depressed, the elderly will say that they are "feeling helpless" and "feeling pessimistic" (P. S Fry, 1986). Older adults more often appear apathetic and expressionless, confine themselves to bed, neglect themselves, and make derogatory remarks about themselves. The second group of symptoms includes loss of appetite, insomnia, and trouble breathing (Fry, 1986). When a person is not suffering from other health problems and is not taking any medication, such symptoms indicate depression.

Depression has biological and social causes. Some researchers believe that imbalances in the neurotransmitter levels in old age could lead to depression, thus making it a biochemical problem (Thompson & Gallagher, 1986). In another theory, depression occurs when one loses one's internal belief systems; how a person interprets a loss, rather than the event itself, causes depression. This ailment is connected to losing a job, to poor health, to experiencing an unpredictable and uncontrollable event such as the death of a spouse, or to the belief that one is personally responsible for the negative things that happen to one.

When there is a neurotransmitter imbalance, depression can be treated with drugs such as antidepressants. When the cause is psychosocial, one can treat depression with medications and counseling.

## Dependence

One of the most dreaded roles that the elderly may have to play is the dependent. They may need to depend on others either physically or financially; most adults find either position difficult to accept. This is easy to understand. We have been taught that it is important to be independent and self-sufficient. Therefore, it is not surprising that older people are hostile to the idea of giving up their autonomy. Further, with dependency come changes in roles, especially for those who have to depend on their grown children. An elderly person resents such dependence, becoming frustrated and angry by his or her reversal of positions and feeling guilty for being a burden to children. The elderly may pay in other ways when they depend on family members, as the following case shows.

> At 70, Rebecca has spent her lifetime helping her husband with his business. They do not have any children. After 40 years of married life, her husband passes away. Rebecca has always been dependent on her husband, and after his death she becomes dependent on her younger sister Margaret, who is financially very well off. Margaret looks down on her older sister, though, and does not encourage her to do anything but vegetate. When Rebecca comments that she would like to remarry, Margaret responds that she'll never be able to do it because she doesn't have the looks for it. Rebecca does not have the self-confidence to resist this type of criticism or act on her own initiative. Having always done what her husband told her, she still depends on other people's opinions. Her dilemma seems to be, "I want to do something, but I don't know just what it is or how to go about doing it."

## Elder Abuse

Although research has long reported fairly close ties between adults and their aging parents, the phenomenon of adults' abuse of dependent elderly parents has only recently come to light. Just as child abuse and spousal abuse are major social problems, mistreatment of elderly people is becoming an increasingly important social concern (Pedrick-Cornell & Gelles, 1982).

It is difficult to define elder abuse. Researchers and policy makers advocate several categories of elder abuse (National Aging Resource Center on Elder Abuse, 1990). These include beating or withholding care, verbal assaults, and social isolation. Such abuse can take many forms, such as neglect—the withholding of food, shelter, clothing, or medical attention—or psychological abuse—tongue lashings or threats of violence and abandonment (National Aging Resource Center on Elder Abuse, 1990). At times, the elderly suffer physical violence: the beating, punching, or burning of old people who cannot take care of themselves. Other abuses include misuse of funds or financial exploitation, sexual abuse, and violation of personal rights.

Because of problems of definition and reporting (it is probably more underreported than child and spousal abuse), estimates of the rate of elder abuse vary from 1.5 to 2.5 million cases in the United States every year (Pedrick-Cornell & Gelles, 1982).

The typical abuse victim is infirm, very old, and a woman; the abuser is apt to be a middle-aged daughter who views the mother as the cause of overwhelming stress (Pedrick-Cornell & Gelles, 1982). There is no research evidence that such abuse correlates with a history of family violence, but researchers suspect that people who abuse their parents were beaten when they themselves were children (Papalia & Olds, 1986).

Like child and spousal abuse, elder abuse has to be approached from the perspectives of both victim and abuser (Hooyman, Rathbone-McCuan, & Klingbeil, 1982). To protect the aged, we need to develop procedures to identify and report abuse, to take victims out of the house, and, if necessary and possible, to reduce the degree of isolation they feel, through contacts in the community, supportive legal and social work, and other services.

## Housing

The immediate environment looms large in the lives of most older people in the United States. The living space of the elderly diminishes with age. Eventually, older people stop going to work or traveling. As energy and health decline and financial resources shrink, the neighborhood grocery store and the nearby church may be the farthest points in an older person's travels. The living of the enfeebled and ill may be reduced to a home or an apartment or, ultimately, to a bed within four restricting walls. Thus, the quality of housing is particularly significant for the aged.

Since the 1960s, a new housing vocabulary has come into being. It describes many types of housing available to an aged population, such as condominiums, town houses, cooperatives, mobile homes, retirement communities, public housing, nursing homes, and geriatric centers.

The housing needs of the elderly are like those of any other group of adults. Most older people wish to experience independent living. *Independent* implies that they want housing that will enable them to control their own households, to care for themselves, and to be free to entertain friends and perform their accustomed roles.

Another important aspect of life for the elderly is their proneness to accidents such as falls. Dwelling places should be carefully designed, constructed, and equipped to minimize injury. Climate also affects older people, who grow less tolerant of extreme changes in heating, cooling, and ventilation. Special attention should also be given to lighting and noise control.

Most people have a sense of place—a feeling that they belong to a particular location and environment. Regardless of where older people live, they have a fundamental need to identify with a place—a dwelling, a neighborhood, a village or city, and a landscape. People who are forced to move have to develop a new sense of spatial identity.

A sense of relatedness is an important aspect of older people's lives, and the extent to which older people relate to and interact with other human beings is also affected by the design, size, and location of their dwellings. Like any other group of people, older people need to feel a sense of control over their environments; this may come about through gardening, decorating and furnishing the dwelling unit, displaying accessories, or making other such changes.

> Sharon is in her 80s. Her only daughter has died of cancer, so there is no one to take care of Sharon's medical needs. Because she is well-to-do, she is placed in a nursing home. All Sharon asks is that she be permitted to take her own furniture with her; however, the nursing home does not allow it. Denial of this request makes Sharon feel alienated and gives her the feeling of being institutionalized.

It is increasingly understood that the elderly person, like any other individual, needs psychological stimulation and a variety of other stimuli. Ironically, as an older person's living space diminishes as a result of declining health, the loss of significant others, or a limited income, the person's major source of daily stimulation becomes the housing environment. With such sensory decline, older people need more stimulation so their world does not turn drab.

People need social stimulation as well. Marriage sometimes provides too much of one kind, however. It is easy for two older people to be overinvolved with one another, and each other's constant company can lead to quarrels and misunderstandings. As husbands and wives retire, it is common for them to be together all the time, but they usually need to spend time apart. This separation should involve both auditory and visual barriers. In a real sense, houses are indispensable regulators of human interaction, because they encourage both withdrawal and association. Doors, windows, walls, and closets do much more than enclose space and conceal; they serve the crucial function of allowing privacy.

Insight into the housing problems of the elderly shows us how important living spaces are to them. Type of housing as well as lifestyle affects the aging person. Society should take steps to commit finances and technology to upgrade the services offered to the elderly.

## Crime

Frail older adults do not go out after dark. The fears of the elderly are based on their recognition of their frailty and diminished ability to protect themselves from an attacker. The incidence of the most serious violent crimes—murder, rape, and assault—is quite low among the elderly; however, 25% of the elderly respondents to one survey identified the fear of crime as a serious problem among the elderly (National Institute on Aging, 1982, 1984). People who are 75 years or older are most likely to be victims of violent crimes at home, whereas those between 65 and 74 are most likely to be victimized on the street (Bachman, 1992). Further, the lower the elder person's income, the more likely he or she will be a victim of violent crime. However, it was found that low-income people were the least likely to experience thefts or household crimes. Elderly people who were divorced or separated were more likely to be victims of all types of crimes than those who were married or widowed or had never married.

Only in recent years has special attention been given to problems of crime for the aging population. People have become aware that they need to develop special programs for the elderly in this regard.

## Cross-Cultural Problems of Aging

A person's culture affects his or her experience of aging. In some cultures, aged people are admired for their wisdom; in others they are left on an ice floe to die; in still others, they are simply ignored. The cross-cultural variables include typical lifestyle, level of health, medical care, diet, and exercise. Within the United States alone, cross-cultural factors vary considerably.

The African-American elderly face "double jeopardy"—that is, discrimination based on both race and age. This description holds true today for other groups as well, including Native Americans, Mexican Americans, and Puerto Ricans.

The general problems that the elderly face are intensified for minorities. They tend to be poorer, experience more frequent illness, and be less likely to have their illnesses treated. They tend to be less well educated, have a history of unemployment, live in poorer housing, and have shorter life expectancies. Though they show greater needs for social and medical services, they live in areas where such services are less accessible than in other areas.

Another tragedy common among minority groups is the inability of workers to collect the social security and medicare benefits they have earned; they often die too young to qualify for them. Further, many minority-group workers hold jobs not covered by social security.

The experiences of aging are made more meaningful by the families to which they belong. The family structure creates a sense of mutual responsibility for the elderly person. For instance, among Latino families, the elderly are treated with respect. Grandparents play an important role in child rearing, as well as exert considerable influence over family decisions. In recent years, because of assimilation, this pattern is breaking down, and the relationships between generations are becoming more like those in the population in general. The extended-family pattern still prevails in this group, however, and the position of the elderly is still relatively high.

African-American families protect their own through an extensive kinship network by which the generations help each other with financial aid, child care, advice, and other supports. This network usually supplements formal assistance from community and governmental agencies by providing extra help for needy family members (Mindel, 1983). However, African Americans still need help; statistics have shown that in every state twice as many African-American aged need financial help as white aged. The former also tend to define themselves as old at a chronologically younger age than the latter (Lowy, 1979).

As Tidwell (1997) indicates, the demographics of the African-American population have changed markedly over the years. For instance, growth of the African-American population has increased the collective economic and political power of this group in the larger society. It has boosted the potential for self-development initiatives. But this potential of growth has also brought some negative consequences. particularly for the young and the elderly.

In terms of the elderly, there need to be more effective day-care programs and greater availability of good nursing homes. The problem with the elderly is not how to keep the older African American out of an institution but how to get him or her into a good one. All minorities constitute about 4% of the total nursing-home population, with the African-American aged constituting about 3% of that total. Jackson proposes the development of a multipurpose, multiservice geriatric center that will provide both institutional and noninstitutional services, to be located in minority neighborhoods.

Lowy (1979) indicates that the average life expectancy for Native Americans is 44 years. There is very little information about the aged Native American. The majority live on reservations, with very little income and very poor housing.

Many old people of various ethnic groups in the United States—especially people born in other countries—do not take advantage of many community and governmental services for which they are eligible. They see such services as a form of charity, which they are too proud to accept. They are also unwilling to travel outside their own homes because they are uncomfortable in dealing with other groups whose ways they do not understand. The suicide rate for aged Asian Americans is three times higher than the national average, indicating that this population could greatly benefit from programs offered (Lowy, 1979).

## Older Women

Another group particularly discriminated against is older women. As mentioned before, there are two prejudices operating against them, ageism and sexism. Stereotypes abound: the ever-ready mother-in-law stories, the unmarried aunts scorned as old maids, and the grandmother who outlives grandfather and becomes a family nuisance. Older women in this country have low visibility and are rarely viewed as viable, valuable human beings.

> Seventy-year-old Winsome, a Jamaican, lives in the United States. She has three sons, whom she struggled to educate while she worked as a maid. With great difficulty, her sons graduated from college, married, and worked in their jobs to reach their idea of American middle-class standards. Two of the married sons have moved away. The youngest, who still lives close by, hardly visits his mother, who had a stroke and is hard of hearing. She feels neglected by her son and often complains to him about her situation.
>
> As a stroke patient, she comes to the attention of the hospital social worker. Through interviews, the worker begins to understand Winsome's plight, gets her a hearing aid, and visits her regularly. The social worker meets Winsome's son while he is visiting his mother. The son apologetically tells the social worker that he cannot visit his mother on a day-to-day basis because of the demands in his life. He works hard to reach the standards his mother set for him. He also feels that his mother is too demanding. The social worker spends the rest of the interview trying to help the mother and son understand each other's perspectives and to improve communication between them. This eases the situation and greatly improves the mother-son relationship. The son promises to visit the mother more regularly, and Winsome promises to try to understand her son's situation and not complain if he cannot visit every day.

There are two areas in which older women wield some power to help themselves and their peers. Politically, older women have an advantage. With a voting strength of many millions, about 90% of them are registered voters and vote regularly. They have the political strength to elect into office candidates who are sympathetic to their causes. Economically, although many older women are poor, some do have tremendous amounts of money. These women could use their resources to provide backing to women's movements, particularly to those attempting to solve the problems of their own age group (Butler & Lewis, 1973).

## The Rural Elderly

Between the years 1735 and 1812, a woman named Martha Ballard kept a diary of her daily activities in a rural area, now called Augusta, Maine. Every day for 27 years Martha recorded details of her everyday life as a midwife, a mother of nine children, a grandmother of dozens, the wife of a surveyor, a gardener, a boarder, and a neighbor. Ulrich (1990) has ingeniously restored Martha Ballard to life for the 20th century, drawing threads from Martha's diaries to weave a rich tapestry of everyday life in the late 18th and early 19th centuries. Simply woven into her life are facts about changing medical practices, insufficient medical help, relationships between men and women, time, budget, and travel activities. A great deal of the writing discusses the lack of facilities and amenities. How much has rural America changed since those days? Well, medical facilities are still insufficient, finances still depend on crop turnout, and relationships between men and women are still based on division of labor. Though Martha lived 200 years ago, what she so faithfully recorded still appears to some extent to hold true of the rural United States.

Morris (1995) writes that millions of rural people—children, young adults, elderly people, men and women, African American, whites, Latinos, and Native Americans—are challenged every day to confront and cope with the problems of rural poverty. High rates of rural poverty persisted throughout the 1980s and into the 1990s. Experts have associated such poverty with varied patterns of economic restructuring in rural areas in the 1990s and the complexity of problems resulting from the diversity of rural people.

Most elderly people who live in rural areas are poor. About one-third of the men and even more of the women have an average annual income of less than $2000. Only one-quarter of the elderly work after age 65. In nonmetropolitan areas,

about 60% of the elderly occupy substandard housing. Because the rural elderly were usually self-sufficient in their youth, they are often ashamed to ask for or take advantage of services. There is a need to develop outreach programs for such people, such as providing them with transportation (Manney, 1975).

## DEATH, DYING, AND RELATED ISSUES

### Defintions of Death

The final stage of life is death. *Death* can be defined as a process of transition that starts with dying and ends with being dead (Kalish, 1976). There are various ways of describing death. Dying is the period when the organism loses its viability. The term *dying* refers to a dying trajectory, which encompasses the speed with which a person dies and the rate of decline in functioning. The word *death* can be defined as the point at which a person becomes physically dead. When we mention that a person has died at a certain time, we usually refer to the process by which a person has passed from being some*one* to becoming some*thing*.

There are many sociocultural definitions of death. In Eastern culture, when a driver is killed in a traffic accident, this death is seen as one part in an eternal cycle of births and rebirths (Kalish, 1987). Other cultures view death differently. As Counts and Counts (1985) indicate, the Melanesian word *mate* includes the very sick, the very old, and the dead, and the word *to* refers to old living people. In older South Pacific cultures, many believe that the life force may leave the body during sleep or illness; sleep, illness, and death are considered together. Thus, it can be said that people "die" several times before experiencing "final death" (Counts & Counts, 1985).

Besides sociocultural definitions, we have legal and medical definitions. To determine when death occurred has always been subjective.

Physical death can be described as a physical process at the end of which people are no longer feeling, thinking beings. Social death occurs when the dying person is no longer capable of hearing, seeing, and understanding what others are saying. Sometimes social death occurs before physical death.

The most frequent causes of death of the elderly are heart attack, strokes, cancer, influenza, and pneumonia. In contrast, the leading causes of death for people between 25 and 44 are accidents, heart disease, cancer, suicide, and cirrhosis of the liver.

For many years, people have accepted and applied the criteria now called *clinical death:* lack of heartbeat and respiration. The most widely accepted criteria are those that characterize *brain death:*

1. No spontaneous movement in response to any stimuli
2. No spontaneous respirations for at least one hour
3. Total lack of responsiveness to even the most painful stimuli
4. No eye movements, blinking, or pupil responses
5. No postural activity, swallowing, yawning, or vocalizing
6. No motor reflexes
7. Flat eclectroencephagram (EEG) for at least 10 minutes
8. No change in criteria 24 hours later

For a person to be declared brain dead, all eight criteria must be met. Some conditions mimic death; deep coma, hypothermia, and drug overdose must therefore be ruled out. Finally, most hospitals feel that the lack of brain activity must remain in both the brainstem, which involves vegetative functions such as heartbeat and respiration, and in the cortex, which involves higher processes such as thinking. A person's cortical functioning can cease while brainstem activity continues; this is a *persistent vegetative state,* from which a person cannot recover. This condition can occur following a severe head injury or a drug overdose. The person's relatives must make difficult ethical decisions. For example, because doctors can stimulate artificially both breathing and heartbeat, a legal tangle has arisen over determining when a person is physically dead.

Contemplating death appears to occupy a large portion of the elderly person's life, particularly when the person is sick or bedridden with permanent physical disabilities. Although the inevitability of death does cross their minds, few people can really grasp the meaning of their own death or the idea of their own extinction, especially by natural causes (Kubler-Ross, 1969).

People usually view their own deaths as the result of an act of an outside force. This view makes it impossible to visualize lying quietly in bed and allowing death to overtake one. How people react to death or the dying depends on the manner in which they have been helped to cope with such situations, as well as on their previous patterns of coping and adaptation. Older people who live past their expected number of years may feel that they are living on borrowed time. Dealing with the deaths of their friends can help socialize older people toward acceptance of their own death.

Fear of death is also associated with the lack of religious belief. Those people who are religious do not fear death as much as those who are irreligious; and atheists do show more fear of death than do the religious. Uncertain and sporadically religious people show the greatest fear of death.

To deny death is to believe that people continue to experience some form of life after their physical death. Physical death is undeniable, but mental death is deniable. Belief in an afterlife; belief in the existence of ghosts, spirits, angels, or demons; and belief in reincarnation are all ways of denying death and the ability to experience death. Denial can also mean outright incomprehension; that is, when physicians tell their patients that they are going to die, the physicians realize later their message was not really heard (Kalish, 1976).

## Dying

Dying can be quick or lingering. When a person is diagnosed as terminal, he or she is assigned the role of a dying person. Young people with terminal conditions are expected to fight death, to try to finish business, and to cram as much experience as possible into their remaining time. We expect younger people to be active and antagonistic about dying. All dying persons are apt to find that the role of the dying person means having less control over their own lives than before. At first, the younger person fights to maintain control over his or her life, but slowly the person realizes that he or she does not have much control. Though this realization is even stronger among older people, society allows them less room than the young for expressing anger and frustration about death.

*Kubler-Ross's stages*  For a long time there was no literature on death and dying, but today there are books, magazines, and professional journals on the subject. The first person who made a detailed study of death and dying was Elisabeth Kubler-Ross. She focused on the short-term situation that follows a person's first recognition that death is imminent. For instance, when a person is overtaken by a fatal illness, the person may realize that he or she is involved in a serious situation. Kubler-Ross identified five stages of death and dying: (1) denial, (2) anger, (3) bargaining, (4) depression, and, (5) acceptance.

Once the initial shock that death is inevitable wears off, people may try to deny the coming event. Later, they are overcome with anger because they do not have any control over the situation. Next, people start to bargain, thinking that somehow they can prolong life. Eventually, hopelessness and depression may take hold, in one of two forms: reactive depression or preparatory depression. *Reactive depression* is a response to losses incurred so far—physical deterioration, depletion of financial resources, and the crumbling of one's hopes and dreams. *Preparatory depression* is grieving for oneself, just as elderly people, like others, may suffer anticipatory grief at the prospect of a spouse's death. Dying people find it quite difficult to speak of their own grief. However, their expressions of sorrow may help move them toward the final stage—acceptance of death, not only by themselves but to some degree by the rest of their families. When dying people are kept in the dark about their own impending death, they are deprived of participation in it and denied the opportunity of bringing any final, meaningful conclusion to their lives.

*Surrounding circumstances*  Many people die in health-care institutions, but most people prefer to die at home. Though a death at home imposes a heavier burden on the family, most family members are glad when death at home is possible.

A consideration receiving increasing attention is when and how long a person should be allowed to live. An elderly patient may ask that no extraordinary measures be taken to prolong his or her life. Kalish (1976) reports that some patients make "living wills" spelling out their wishes. The dying person has an important right to participate in decisions about the where and when of his or her death.

It is important that dying persons not be abandoned, humiliated, or lonely at the end of their lives. Encouraging as well as maintaining their intimate personal relationships with others is a critical aspect of the social care of the elderly.

A person who undergoes a long dying trajectory may understand and resolve the issues of dying and allow the survivors to work through their grief reactions in advance. In some cases, the dying process is so slow that the final event brings more relief than grief (Kalish, 1976).

## Ethical Issues of Death and Dying

The "right to die" movement advocates the rights of terminally ill patients to decide when they want to die, despite the wishes of their doctors to prolong their lives. Proponents of this movement favor the use of euthanasia (mercy killing), withholding the use of life-sustaining procedures and equipment, and letting nature take its course. Voluntary euthanasia has become an increasingly controversial issue as science and technology develop more and more methods for sustaining life. The laws that govern the rights of terminally ill patients to terminate treatment are often unclear and vary from state to state (Shapiro, 1978).

Euthanasia can be carried out in two different ways: active and passive. *Active euthanasia* involves the deliberate ending of someone's life, which may be based on a clear statement of the person's wishes or a decision made by someone else who has the legal authority to do so. One widely reported example of active euthanasia involved Dr. Jack Kevorkian, a physician in Michigan who created a suicide machine. Dr. Kevorkian's machine allowed several people with terminal illness to give themselves lethal doses of medication or carbon monoxide.

*Passive euthanasia* happens when a person is allowed to die by the withholding or withdrawal of available treatment. For example, chemotherapy can be withheld for a cancer patient, a surgical procedure may not be completed, or food may be withdrawn.

Euthanasia raises complicated legal and ethical issues. In most jurisdictions, it is legal only when a person makes his or her wishes known regarding medical interventions in a living will. For instance, in 1990 the U.S. Supreme Court took up the case of Nancy Cruzan, whose family wanted to end her forced feeding. But the court ruled that unless clear and incontrovertible evidence was presented that an individual desires to have nourishment stopped, another party cannot decide to end it.

*Hospices*   Hospices provide an innovative means of organizing the efforts of health service providers and families around the goals of minimizing the pain associated with terminal illnesses and allowing terminally ill people to die with dignity. The multidisciplinary hospice staff seeks to care not only for the dying but for their families as well.

The first well-known hospice, St. Christopher's, was started in 1967 by Dr. Cicely Saunders in London, with the primary function of freeing the patient of pain and any memory or fear of pain. Besides freedom from pain, the staff at St. Christopher's provides comfort and companionship to their patients. Families, including children, are free to visit at any time except on Mondays, when no visiting is permitted. Families are not made to feel guilty if they do not visit; however, family members are encouraged to help with patient care, and patients often go back and forth between hospice and home. The median stay at the hospice is two to three weeks. Half of the patients return home to die with dignity. Interest in hospices has grown rapidly.

In the United States, hospice care can be offered at home, in an institution, or in a hospital. There are approximately 1100 hospice programs in the United States. These programs highlight family-oriented, warm, personal patient care. In this setting, the medical and helping professions work together to ease the pain and treat the symptoms of patients, keep them comfortable and alert, as well as show interest and concern to the patient's family and help them deal with their loved one's impending death.

Hospital and hospice care differ. The hospice team can spend more time with the patients and their families in helping them cope with their situation (Kane, Wales, Bernstein, Leibowitz, & Kaplan, 1984). In contrast to hospitals, the chief aim of the hospice is comforting care; hospitals use more aggressive treatment approaches. But when a person is admitted to a hospice, he or she has been given less than six months to live by two medical doctors. Usually, hospice clients are mobile, less anxious, and less depressed. Spouses visit hospice clients more often and participate more in their care; hospice staff members are perceived as more accessible. Also, clients who have been in hospitals before coming to a hospice strongly prefer the care of hospice (Walsh & Cavanaugh, 1984).

However, hospice care is not always an alternative to hospital care. Some disorders require treatments or equipment not available at inpatient hospices. Some people may find that a hospice does not meet their needs or fit with personal beliefs. At times, the needs of the hospice clients, their families, and staff do not coincide. The staff and family members may be interested in pain management, but the clients may want to talk about death or their religious beliefs (Walsh & Cavanaugh, 1984). Staff need to stay involved in what the clients need rather than making assumptions about the same.

## Bereavement

Bereavement is the process of recovery from the death of another individual. It can end quickly or take a long time. It was found that 48% of widows felt that they got over their husband's deaths very quickly, whereas about 20% felt that they had never gotten over it and did not expect to. Individual reactions took three forms: physical, emotional, and intellectual. Some common physical reactions to grief include shortness of breath, frequent sighing, tightness in the chest, feelings of emptiness in the abdomen, loss of energy, and stomach upset (Kalish, 1976). These reactions are particularly common in the period immediately following the death and generally diminish with time. The mortality rates of widowed people are higher than those of married people.

Emotional reactions to death include anger, guilt, depression, and anxiety, as well as preoccupation with thoughts of the deceased (Parkes, 1972). These responses diminish with time. A longitudinal study of widowed people found that those who react to bereavement by becoming depressed are more likely than others to report disproportionately poor health a year later (Bornstein, 1973). To document the extra stress people feel due to grief, Norris and Murrell (1987) collected data concerning grief reactions and compared them with 63 older adults in families who had not experienced a member's death. The researchers gathered extensive information on physical health (including functional abilities and specific ailments), psychological distress, and family stress. The instrument used to measure distress tapped symptoms of depression. The family stress measure assessed such things as the new serious illness of a family member, having a family member move, additional family responsibilities, new family conflict, or new marital conflict.

The intellectual aspect of bereavement consists of what Lopata (1973) calls the "purification" of the memory of the deceased. In this process, the negative aspects of the person are stripped away, leaving behind an idealized, positive memory. Even women who had hated their husbands mentioned that they felt their husbands had been good people.

Harlow, Goldberg, and Comstock (1991) and Stroebe and Stroebe (1993) indicate that men and women react somewhat differently to bereavement. In terms of reaction to loss, men feel that they have lost part of themselves, whereas women feel that they have been deserted and left to fend for themselves. Recently bereaved people are exempt from certain responsibilities. Family and friends help with cooking and caring for dependents. Older women find their children making their decisions for them. Such social supports for the bereaved person are temporary. Usually people are expected to reengage in the social world as quickly as possible.

## Widowhood

Widowhood is usually seen as something that happens to women, but it happens to men as well. In U.S. society, widowhood is primarily a long-term role for older women. Young widows play the role for only a short time, after which people consider them as single rather than widowed (Lopata, 1973). Society sees widowhood as something that would make younger people feel stigmatized. Older widows, even those only in their 60s, often experience a change in status; the prevalence of widowhood in later life combined with low rates of remarriage can produce for older women a lower social position.

The role of the older widow is vague. Ties with the husband's family are usually drastically reduced. This role also brings many societal expectations. For example, older widows are to keep the memories of their husbands alive; they are not supposed to be interested in men but are supposed to do things with their children or with other widows. Additionally, widowed people of both genders may feel awkward as the third party or may view themselves as a threat to their married friends (Field & Minkler, 1988).

Becoming an older widow also changes a woman's self-identity. For *traditionally-oriented women,* the role of wife is central to life. Widowhood may therefore mean not only the loss of the person whom they can support but a changed concept of themselves as persons. How other widows cope with their identity crisis depends on how they define their status as well. *Role-invested people* may take up jobs, or they may increase their investment in jobs they already have. People who are primarily *acquirers* may place their identity in things rather than in people. If widowhood brings a substantial change in acquisitional power, acquirers must adjust their self-concept. Unfortunately, many widows find that their quality of life changes markedly. Sometimes all three orientations may be present in the same person, and coping strategies may reflect all three changes in investment of energy.

Loneliness is an important aspect of the widow's life because of the absence of a significant relationship. Further, both Atchley (1975) and Morgan (1976) have pointed out that economic conditions are an important factor in loneliness. Finally, Kunkel (1979) found low levels of loneliness in a small-town sample of widows; only a quarter felt lonely. But in urban areas, a larger percentage of widows felt lonely. Aloneness should not be confused with loneliness. Many widows quickly become accustomed to living alone, and more than half continue to live alone.

The experience of losing a spouse differs for women and men. Although statistics may change as more and more women join the workforce, today women tend to outlive men. As Lopata (1975) indicates, for most women, widowhood spells disaster because they have been economically dependent on their husbands. The income of the African-American widow was found to be far less than that of the Euro-American widow, but the ratios of widowed and married women were similar for both groups—that is, both had lower incomes than married women.

Women's adjustment to widowhood also depends on the social background and the social roles that the women played before the deaths of their husbands. Those women who were highly involved in the role of wife—particularly educated, middle-class women—suffered the strongest disruption after the deaths of their husbands (Lopata, 1975). Other women, who lived in a more sex-segregated world, who held jobs, or were involved in their neighborhoods, did not find the deaths of their husbands as devastating.

Lopata (1975) classifies widows into five groups:

1. The traditional widow, who spends time with her children, her grandchildren, and her siblings
2. The liberated widow, who leads a multidimensional life with several interests and activities and may live with a new partner
3. The merry widow, who is socially active
4. The working widow, who focuses on her job
5. The "return-to-work" widow, who spends much time on her work but does not get much economic reward

This last classification of widow is also called the "widow's widow"; she remains in this role and is unwilling to relinquish it through remarriage or devotion to grandparenting.

There are some important gender differences in how men and women react to widowhood. Widowers suffer a higher risk than widows of dying soon after their spouse dies, either by suicide or natural causes (Osgood, 1992). Normally, both men and women find all aspects of their life affected: their psychosocial needs, their household roles, nutrition and health care, transportation, and education. Usually widowers are lonelier, have lower morale, and are more dissatisfied with life than widows. Often, they need help with household chores, they eat poorly, and they have strong negative images of themselves. Widowers are often more unwilling to talk about widowhood or death than are widows. Many do not want a confidante. However, widowers tend to remarry; they view the loss of a wife as devastating.

> Harry retires at 65. When his wife dies a few months later, Harry is totally lost; he has depended on her for everything from cooking and cleaning to emotional support. She was the first person to whom her children turned when they needed help or advice. Her death alters Harry's life completely; he is devastated. He lies in bed for hours, not knowing if it is day or night. In a short period of time he ages considerably, most of it as the result of mourning for his wife. His children visit him sporadically and decide to place him in an institution for the elderly because they do not know if he will survive by himself. They do not consider Harry's opinions because at this point they view him as a burden and feel he would be better off under institutional care. Harry protests mildly but soon decides to take his chances and become a resident in a nursing home.

## Remarriage after Widowhood

Many people remarry in their old age. Remarriage constitutes a workable alternative for older widows and widowers; the number of remarriages has doubled during the past 20 years. In a study on older people who remarried, Vinick (1978) interviewed more than 60 people to determine how they experienced remarriage. Most widows as well as widowers chose to live alone for a while after the death of the spouse, but men tended to remarry rather quickly, whereas women tended to wait. Men usually remarried within a year of their widowhood, but only three women remarried in the three years following

the deaths of their spouses. Most of the new couples had known each other for a long time; they had been the spouses of friends or were introduced by mutual friends after the deaths of their spouses.

The most significant reason for remarriage was the need for companionship. Men also mentioned that they had a desire to care, whereas women mentioned that they liked the personal qualities of their respective spouses. Vinick (1978) further notes that a large percentage of these couples were satisfied in their new marriages—80% of the women and 87% of the men. It was only when people married for external reasons that they found they were not happy; one woman admitted that she married her husband for financial security but found him to be autocratic and miserly.

Older married people were found to have a serenity in their marriages that was not present among young married people. In many ways, older marriages present less stress. They are free from the strains of early marriages—child rearing, ambition for higher status, and conflict with in-laws. Often, older people have learned that it does not pay to get into an argument, that one should contain one's feelings, and that it takes two to get into an argument. One of the chief difficulties of marriage for older women is that there are fewer available men. Because men have a shorter life than do women, the number of potential male partners is drastically reduced.

## IMPLICATIONS FOR PRACTICE

Social workers can see human aging is developmental. From this perspective, there are losses and gains to be made at every point in life. An elderly person continues to grow as long as the gains outweigh the losses.

Older people need support systems to function independently. They need support groups to continue their active participation in society. They also need freedom of choice with regard to their degree of disengagement from activity, they need to integrate their life experiences, and they need protection of their integrity as their lives come to an end (Canter & Yeakel, 1980). Social workers should be aware of the elderly's social support systems, such as family, friends, and neighbors, as well as professional, occupational, religious, and self-help networks.

The causes of intergenerational conflicts cannot be determined in general terms; such conflicts arise and are dealt with differently by different social groups. The expected patterns of behavior and cultural values of Asian Americans and Puerto Ricans, for example, engender respectful behavior toward elders.

> Eighty-year-old Srinath is a farmer. He lives in an extended family home in rural India. His sons, grandsons, and their wives live in the same home. Srinath is revered as the head of the family. When any important decisions have to be made, Srinath's opinion is considered quite valuable. His children obey and respect him.

Abuse of the elderly is becoming more obvious in U.S. culture. Services for the abusers can reduce their stress and give them different options, allowing them to be caregivers instead of "paingivers." These services could include financial assistance, education, and emotional support, as well as caregiving help, so that the overstressed caregiver can take a day or a weekend off to revive themselves.

The attitudes of families toward their elderly and the attitudes that the elderly have toward themselves greatly affect the mental health of the elderly. While working with older people, social workers need to make special efforts to understand the social circumstances under which the elderly live. Attitudes and way of life determine whether the elderly find integrity or despair in their lives.

When older people retire, they usually experience an institutional separation from occupation and find time on their hands. Older people who have hobbies should be encouraged to pursue them.

With retirement also comes reminiscing. Older people tend to reminisce about their past lives.

Reminiscing serves as an evaluation of how they spent their lives and what they are leaving behind. When social workers work with the elderly, they will find that they have to listen to a great deal of reminiscing. The social worker should acknowledge this as a part of the older person's way of recounting his or her successes and failures.

While working with older adults, social workers should make a special effort to involve family members whenever the older person specifies such a desire. Further, if the older person enjoys being a grandparent, the social worker can encourage this interest with the help of the rest of the family.

Elderly people living by themselves should be allowed to have pets, which offer an opportunity for them to nurture and care for a living being. The pleasures and satisfaction they receive by doing so add to mental well-being.

Often, diseases accompanied by depression can overtake the elderly. Making sure that they receive the right medications and making them comfortable and offering them support are important.

Death looms large for older people. If the elderly wish to talk about it, social workers should listen without judgment and encourage others to do the same. Further, if a client shows any desire not to be kept artificially alive through a breathing apparatus, the social worker should encourage her or him to put this in a living will.

In work with an aged person, social workers act as a bridge between the individual and the social reality. One task is to help redefine social stereotypes. By helping older adults organize their lives according to their own goals, as well as helping them make social contributions that complement new goals, social workers can work against unhelpful social expectations. The pressures on the aging to conform to the societal stereotypes of infirmity and uselessness, however, make the task of orienting them toward productivity quite difficult. Social workers must recognize and support the rights of the elderly to continue to grow, to integrate their own life experiences, and to liberate themselves from restraints so that they can be who they wish to be. Without this liberation, the aged can devalue themselves and fail to move toward new accomplishments.

## CHAPTER SUMMARY

- In U.S. society, the prevailing negative attitude toward the elderly colors old people's feelings toward themselves as well as society's manner of treating them.
- There are various models and theories of aging, such as wear-and-tear, cellular, cross-link, metabolic, and programmed cell-death theories.
- Aging itself without diseases and other disasters has very little effect on physical and psychological functioning.
- Chronic diseases of the elderly include abdominal-cavity hernias, cataracts, and prostate disease.
- Mental impairments include temporary or permanent damage to brain tissues, impaired memory, poor judgment, intellectual decline, and disorientation.
- Disengagement theory speaks of the aged's withdrawal from society.
- Activity theory says that participating in activities can lead to more successful aging.
- Role-exit theory states that as people get older, the number of roles they play diminishes.
- Social-exchange theory proposes that when people enter relationships they find rewards such as a sense of security, and costs, such as fatigue.
- Consolidation theory describes a consolidation of commitments as well as a redistribution of energies so that people can cope with lost roles and have more energy for other activities.
- Considerable controversy attends the issue of whether or not older people can maintain their intellectual abilities. Research

shows a great deal more elasticity in old age than traditionally accepted. This is related to maintaining good health, physical and mental activity, and intellectual interests throughout life. Further, a person's overall cognitive functioning is most closely related to his or her education and previous levels of performance. People vary in their abilities to compensate for cognitive deficits.

- The eighth and final stage of life in Erikson's theory is that of integrity versus despair. Aging people develop either an acceptance of their lives or a fear of impending death accompanying the realization that time is too short to correct past mistakes.
- The effects of aging on the elderly vary by culture. In some cultures, the aged receive respect, and therefore continue to be active as older adults; in others they do not receive respect, and older people tend to devalue themselves accordingly.
- Though the elderly may go through an "empty nest" stage, they often form close relationships with their children.
- One study shows six types of lifestyle in the elderly: familism, couplehood, world of work, living fully, living alone, and maintaining involvement.
- Some people look forward to retirement and, thereafter, a gradual further disengagement; others find continued involvement in some job or perhaps an unpaid occupation necessary. Whether a person reacts well or poorly to retirement depends on health, income, personal lifestyle, and whether the retirement is chosen or not.
- Successful aging involves both a life review and a coming to terms with one's life and the inevitability of death. Such reminiscing is closely connected to retirement and other earlier conditions.
- There is no one role for grandparents in the United States. Different styles of grandparenting have been identified.

- Religion plays a role in the lives of many elderly people; self-images and personalities are influenced by religious orientations.
- Biological problems include dementia and depression.
- Many older people fear dependence.
- Elder abuse is causing ever greater concern in the United States.
- The influence of living arrangements on the quality of life increases as a person's mobility decreases. The variety of alternative living arrangements for the elderly has grown in recent times.
- Many older people fear crime, though statistics show that their fear far exceeds their likelihood of being victimized by violent crime.
- All problems faced by old people in the United States are complicated by membership in minority groups.
- Older women are more discriminated against than any other group of people because of ageism and sexism.
- The rural elderly face problems that date back 200 years.
- The inevitability of death becomes apparent as people grow older. Kubler-Ross identifies five stages of dying: denial, anger, bargaining, hopelessness and depression, and acceptance.
- There is an increasing concern for the psychosocial needs of the elderly ill. Terminally ill patients may want more control over their treatment and a lessened emphasis on prolongation of life. One major advance in care for the dying is the hospice movement, which began in Great Britain.
- Bereavement is the process of recovery from the death of another individual. Loss of spouse is a major stress affecting the aged population greatly.
- Given the different life expectancies of the sexes and the tendency of men to marry younger women, more women than men tend to be widowed.
- Although widowhood affects people differently, those who adjust best continue to lead active and engaged lives.
- Remarriage, particularly for companionship, tends to be a positive experience for the elderly.
- Social workers need to accept that losses and gains will be made in every point in life, including old age.

## SUGGESTED READINGS

McGoldrick, A. E. (1994). The impact of retirement on the individual. *Reviews in Clinical Gerontology, 4*(2), 151–160.

Noggle, B. J. (1995). Identifying and meeting the needs of ethnic minority patients [Special issue: Hospice care and cultural diversity]. *Hospice Journal, 10*(2), 85–93.

Ogozalek, V. Z. (1991). The social impacts of computing: Computer technology and the graying of America. *Social Science Computer Review, 9*(4), 655–666.

Strom, R., Collinsworth, P., Strom, S., Griswold, D., et al. (1992). Grandparent education for black families. *Journal of Negro Education, 61*(4), 554–569.

Wilson, M. N., Tolson, T. F., Hinton, I. D., & Kiernan, M. (1990). Flexibility and sharing of childcare duties in black families [Special issue: Gender and ethnicity: Perspectives on duel status]. *Sex Roles, 22*(7–8), 409–425.

## SUGGESTED VIDEOTAPES

ABC News (Producer). (1996). *Forget me never* (15 minutes). Available from Filmmakers Library, 124 E. 40th St., Suite 901, New York, NY 10016; 212-808-4980

Alzheimer Association (Producer). (1995). *Alzheimer's disease: Inside looking out* (18 minutes). Available from Terra Nova Films, 9848 S. Winchester Ave., Chicago, IL 60643; 773-881-8591

CBC (Producer). (1990). *I never planned on this: An affirmative approach to the later years* (46 minutes). Available from Filmmakers Library, 124 E. 40th St., Suite 901, New York, NY 10016; 212-808-4980

Gravity Productions (Producer). (1995). *You're not alone: Coping with the death of a spouse* (40 minutes). Available from Aquarius Productions, 5 Power-house Ln., Sherborn, MA 01770; 508-651-2963

United Nations (Producer). (1994). *Portraits of age* (29 minutes). Available from First Run/Icarus Films, 153 Waverly Pl., 6th Floor, New York, NY 10014; 800-876-1710

University of Hawaii (Producer). (1993). *Growing old in a new age: The future of aging* (55 minutes). Available from Annenberg/CPB, P.O. Box 2345, S. Burlington, VT 05407-2345; 800-532-7637; http://www.learner.org

WGBH (Producer). (1993). *Conquering cancer* (59 minutes). Available from FFH (Films for the Humanities and Sciences), 11 Perrine Rd., Monmouth Junction, NJ 08852; 800-257-5126

WPBT (Producer). (1990). *NBR guide to retirement planning* (47 minutes). Available from American Program Service, 120 Boylston St., Boston, MA 02116; 617-338-4455

Yorkshire Television (Producer). *Cigarettes: Who profits, who dies* (49 minutes). Available from FFH (Films for the Humanities and Sciences), 11 Perrine Rd., Monmouth Junction, NJ 08852; 800-257-5126

## REFERENCES

Amoss, P. T., & Harrell, S. (1981). Introduction: An anthropological perspective. In P. T. Amoss & S. Harrell (Eds.), *Other ways of growing old: Anthropological perspectives.* Stanford, CA: Stanford University Press.

Antonucci, T. C. (1985). Personal characteristics, social support, and social behavior. In R. H. Binstock & E. Shanas (Eds.), *Handbook of aging and the social sciences* (2nd ed.). New York: Van Nostrand Reinhold.

Antonucci, T. C., & Akiyama, H. (1991). Social relationships and aging well. *Geriatrics 15,* 39–44.

Arber, S., & Ginn, J. (1991). *Gender and later life: A sociological analysis of resources and constraints.* London: Sage.

Atchley, R. C. (1975). Dimensions of widowhood in later life. *Gerontologist, 15.*

Atchley, R. C. (1976). *The sociology of retirement.* Cambridge, MA: Schenkman.

Atchley, R. C. (1977). *The social forces in later life* (2nd ed.). Belmont, CA: Wadsworth.

Bachman, R. (1992). *Elderly victims* [Bureau of Justice Statistics special report]. Washington, DC: U.S. Department of Justice.

Baltes, P. B., & Labouvie, G. V. (1973). Adult development of intellectual performance: Description,

explanation and modification. In C. Eisdorfer & M. P. Lawton (Eds.), *The psychology of adult development and aging.* Washington, DC: American Psychological Association.

Baltes, P. B., & Schaie, K. W. (1973). *Lifespan developmental psychology.* New York: Academic Press.

Barker, J. C. (1990). Between humans and ghosts: The decrepit elderly in a Polynesian society. In J. Sokolovsky (Ed.), *The cultural context of aging: Worldwide perspectives.* New York: Bergin & Garvey.

Bengston, V. L., Cueller, J. B., & Ragan, P. K. (1975). Stratum contrasts and similarities in attitudes toward death. *Jounal of Gerontology, 32,* 76–88.

Black, K. W. (1969). The ambiguity of retirement. In E. W. Busse & E. Pfeiffer (Eds.), *Behavior and adaptation in late life.* Boston: Little, Brown.

Blackburn, J. (1984). The influence of personality, curriculum, and memory correlates on formal reasoning in young adults and elderly persons. *Journal of Gerontology, 39,* 207–209.

Blackburn, J. A., & Papalia, D. E. (1992). The study of adult cognition from a Piagetian perspective. In R. J. Sternberg & C. A. Berg (Eds.), *Intellectual development.* New York: Cambridge University Press.

Blau, P. M. (1964). *Exchange of power in social life.* New York: Wiley.

Blau, Z. S. (1973). *Old age in a changing society.* New York: New Viewpoints.

Bornstein, P. E. (1973). The depression of widowhood after thirteen months. *British Journal of Psychiatry, 122,* 561–566.

Bosse, R., Aldwin, C. M., Levenson, M. R., Spiro, A., III, & Mroczek, D. K. (1993). Change in social support after retirement: Longitudinal findings from the Normative Aging Study. *Journal of Gerontology: Psychological Sciences, 48,* 210– 217.

Botwinick, J. C. (1970). Learning in children and in older adults. In L. R. Goulet & P. B. Baltes (Eds.), *Life-span developmental psychology: Research and theory.* New York: Academic Press.

Butler, R. N. (1974). Successful aging. *Mental Hygiene, 58.*

Butler, R., & Lewis, M. (1973). *Aging and mental health.* St. Louis, MO: Mosby.

Campione, W. A. (1988). Predicting participation in retirement preparation programs. *Journal of Gerontology, 43,* 91–95.

Carstensen, L. L. (1992). Social and emotional patterns in adulthood: Support for socioemotional selectivity theory. *Psychology and Aging, 7,* 331–338.

Clark, D. O., & Maddox, G. L. (1992). Racial and social correlates of age-related changes in functioning. *Journal of Gerontology: Social Sciences, 47,* 222–223.

Clausen, J. A., & Gilens, M. (1990). Personality and labor force participation across the life course: A longitudinal study of women's careers. *Sociological Forum, 5,* 595–618.

Clavan, S. (1978). The impact of social class and social trends on the role of the grandparents. *Family Coordinator, 27.*

Clayton, R. R. (1975). *The family, marriage and social change.* Lexington, MA: Heath.

Coke, M. M. (1992). Correlates of life satisfaction among elderly African Americans. *Journal of Gerontology: Psychological Sciences, 47,* 316–320.

Connidis, I. A., & Davis, L. (1992). Confidants and companions: Choices in later life. *Journal of Gerontology: Social Sciences, 47,* 115–122.

Counts, D., & Counts, D. (Eds.). (1985). *Aging and its transformations: Moving toward death in Pacific societies.* Lanham, MD: University Press of America.

Cowgill, D. O. (1974). Aging and modernization: A revision of theory. In J. F. Gubrium (Ed.), *Late life.* Springfield, IL: Thomas.

Cowgill, D. O., & Holmes, L. D. (Eds.). (1972). *Aging and modernization.* New York: Appleton-Century-Crofts.

Cox, H., & Bhak, A. (1979). Symbolic interaction and retirement: Adjustment—An empirical event. *International Journal of Aging and Human Development, 9,* 3.

Craik, F. (1977). Psychopathology and social pathology. In J. Birren & K. W. Schaie (Eds.), *Handbook of the psychology of aging.* New York: Van Nostrand Reinhold.

Cummings, E., & Henry, W. E. (1961). *Growing old: The process of disengagement.* New York: Basic Books.

Davis, B. W. (1985). *Visits to remember: A handbook for visitors of nursing home residents.* University Park: Pennsylvania State University Cooperative Extension Service.

Denney, N. W. (1974). Classification abilities in the elderly. *Journal of Gerontology, 29.*

Denney, N. W. (1982). Aging and cognitive changes. In B. B. Wolman (Ed.), *Handbook of developmental psychology.* Englewood Cliffs, NJ: Prentice-Hall.

Doka, K. J., & Mertz, M. E. (1988). The meaning and significance of great grandparenthood. *Gerontologist, 28,* 192–197.

Ekerdt, D. J., & DeViney, S. (1993). Evidence for a preretirement process among older male workers. *Journal of Gerontology: Social Sciences, 48,* 536–543.

Ekerdt, D., Bosse, R., & Levkoff, S. (1985). Empirical test for phases of retirement: Findings from the Normative Aging Study. *Journal of Gerontology, 40,* 95–101.

Erikson, E. (1980). *Identity and the life cycle.* New York: Norton.

Evans, L., Ekerdt, D. J., & Bosse, R. (1985). Proximity to retirement and anticipatory involvement: Findings for the Normative Aging Study. *Journal of Gerontology, 40,* 368–374.

Field, D., & Minkler, M. (1988). Continuity and change in social support between young-old and old-old or very old-old age. *Journal of Gerontology: Psychological Sciences, 43,* 100–106.

Finley, G. E. (1982). Modernization and aging. In T. M. Field, A. Huston, H. C. Quay, L. Troll, & G. E. Finley (Eds.), *Review of human development.* New York: Wiley-Interscience.

Fischer, C. S., & Phillips, S. L. (1982). Who is alone? Social characteristics of people with small networks. In L. A. Peplau & D. Periman (Eds.), *Loneliness: A sourcebook of current theory, research and therapy.* New York: Wiley-Interscience.

Fletcher, W. L., & Hansson, R. O. (1991). Assessing the social components of retirement anxiety. *Psychology and Aging, 6,* 76–85.

Floyd, F. J., Haynes, S. N., Doll, E. R., Winemiller, D., Lemsky, C., Burgy, T. M., Werle, M., & Heilman, N. (1992). Assessing retirement satisfaction and perceptions of retirement experience. *Psychology and Aging, 7,* 609–621.

Fredrickson, B. L., & Cartensen, L. L. (1990). Choosing social partners: How old age and anticipated endings make people more selective. *Psychology and Aging, 5,* 335–347.

Fry, C. L. (1985). Culture, behavior, and aging in the comparative perspective. In J. E. Birren & K. W. Schale (Eds.), *Handbook of the psychology of aging* (2nd ed.). New York: Van Nostrand Reinhold.

Fry, P. S. (1986). *Depression, stress, and adaptation in the elderly.* Rockville, MD: Aspen.

Fry, P. S. (1992). Major social theories of aging and their implications for counseling concepts and practice: A critical review. *Counseling Psychologist, 20,* 246–329.

Gaylord, S., & Zung, W. W. K. (1987). Affective disorders among the aging. In L. L. Carstensen & B. A.

Edelstein (Eds.), *Handbook of clinical gerontology* (pp. 76–95). New York: Pergamon.

George, L. K., Fillenbaum, G., & Palmore, E. (1984). Sex differences in the antecedents and consequences of retirement. *Journal of Gerontology, 39,* 364–371.

Gibson, R. C. (1986). *Blacks in an aging society.* New York: Carnegie Corporation.

Gibson, R. C. (1987). Reconceptualizing retirement for black Americans. *Gerontologist, 27,* 691–698.

Glick, I. O., Weiss, R. S., & Parks, C. M. (1974). *The first year of bereavement.* New York: Wiley.

Harlow, S. D., Goldberg, E. L., & Comstock, G. W. (1991). A longitudinal study of the prevalence of depressive symptomology in elderly widowed and married women. *Archives of General Psychiatry, 48,* 1065–1068.

Harrell, S. (1981). Growing old in Tawain. In P. T. Amoss & S. Harrell (Eds.), *Other ways of growing old: Anthropological perspectives.* Stanford, CA: Stanford University Press.

Harris, J. R., Pedersen, N. L., McClearn, G. E., Plomin, R., & Nesselroade, J. R. (1992). Age differences in genetic and environmental influences for health from the Swedish Adoption/Twin Study of Aging. *Journal of Gerontology, Psychological Sciences, 47,* 213–220.

Harris Poll and the National Council on Aging. (1975). *The myths and realities of aging in America.* Washington, DC: National Council on Aging.

Havighurst, R. J. (1982). The world of work. In B. B. Wolman (Ed.), *Handbook of developmental psychology* (pp. 771–787). Englewood Cliffs, NJ: Prentice-Hall.

Hayflick, L. (1994). *How and why we die.* New York: Ballantine.

Herzog, A. R., House, J. S., & Morgan, J. N. (1991). Relation of work and retirement to health in older age. *Psychology and Aging, 6,* 202–211.

Heston, L. L., & White, J. A. (1991). *The vanishing mind: A practical guide to Alzheimer's disease and other dementias.* New York: Freeman.

Homans, C. C. (1974). *Social behavior: Its elementary forms* (Rev. ed.). New York: Harcourt Brace Jovanovich.

Hooper, F. H., Hooper, J. O., & Colbert, K. K. (1985). Personality and memory correlates of intellectual functioning in adulthood: Piagetian and psychometric assessments. *Human Development, 28,* 101–107.

Hooyman, N. R., Rathbone-McCuan, E., & Klingbeil, K. (1982). Serving the vulnerable elderly. *The Urban and Social Change Review, 15*(2), 9–13.

Horn, J. L., & Donaldson, G. (1976). On the myth of intellectual decline in adulthood. *American Psychologist, 31,* 701–719.

Hultsch, D. F. (1969). Adult age differences in the organization of free recall. *Developmental Psychology, 1.*

Hultsch, D. F. (1971). Adult age differences in free classification and free recall. *Developmental Psychology, 4.*

Hultsch, D. F. (1974). Learning to learn in adulthood. *Journal of Gerontology, 29.*

Jackson, H. (1975, August). Crisis in our nursing homes. *Urban Health Journal.*

Jackson, J. S., & Gibson, R. C. (1985). Work and retirement among the black elderly. In Z. Blau (Ed.). *Current perspectives on aging and the life cycle* (pp. 193–222). Greenwich, CT: Jai.

Jecker, N. S., & Schneiderman, L. J. (1994). Is dying young worse than dying old? *Gerontologist, 34,* 66–72.

Kagan, J., & Moss, H. A. (1962). *Birth to maturity: A study in psychological development.* New York: Wiley.

Kahana, B., & Kahana, B. (1971). Theoretical and research perspectives on grandparenthood. *Aging and Human Development, 2.*

Kalish, R. A. (1976). Death and dying in a social context. In R. Binstock & E. Shanas (Eds.), *Handbook of aging and social sciences.* New York: Van Nostrand Reinhold.

Kalish, R. A. (1987). Death and dying. In P. Silverman (Ed.), *The elderly as modern pioneers* (pp. 320–334). Bloomington: Indiana University Press.

Kane, R. I., Wales, J., Bernstein, L., Leibowitz, A., & Kaplan, S. (1984, April 21). A randomized controlled trial of hospice care. *Lancet,* pp. 890–894.

Keith, J. (1990). Age in social and cultural context: Anthropological perspectives. In R. H. Binstock & L. K. George (Eds.), *Handbook of aging and the social sciences* (3rd ed.). San Diego, CA: Academic Press.

Koenig, H. G., George, L. K., & Siegler, I. C. (1988). The use of religion and other emotion-regulating coping strategies among older adults. *Gerontologist, 28,* 303–310.

Kubler-Ross, E. (1969). *On death and dying.* New York: Macmillan.

Kunkel, S. R. (1979). *Sex differences in adjustment to widowhood.* Unpublished master's thesis, University of Miami, Florida.

Larson, R., Zuzanek, J., & Mannell, R. (1985). Being alone versus being with people: Disengagement in the daily experience of older adults. *Journal of Gerontology, 40,* 375–381.

La Rue, A., Dessonville, C., & Jarvik, L. F. (1985). Aging and mental disorders. In J. E. Birren & K. W. Schaie (Eds.), *Handbook of the psychology of aging.* (2nd ed., pp. 664–702). New York: Van Nostrand Reinhold.

La Rue, A., & Jarvik, L. F. (1982). Old age and behavioral changes. In B. J. Wolman & G. Stricker (Eds.), *Handbook of developmental psychology.* Englewood Cliffs, NJ: Prentice-Hall.

Levin, J. S., Taylor, R. J., & Chatters, L. M. (1994). Race and gender differences in religiosity among older adults: Findings from four national surveys. *Journal of Gerontology: Social Sciences, 49,* 137–145.

Levitt, M. J. (1991). Attachment and close relationships: A life-span perspective. In J. L. Gewirtz & W. M. Kurtines (Eds.), *Intersections with attachment.* Hillsdale, NJ: Erlbaum.

Lopata, H. (1973). *Widowhood in an American city.* Cambridge, MA: Schenkman.

Lopata, H. Z. (1975). Widowhood: Societal factors in lifespan disruptions and alternatives. In N. Datan & L. H. Ginsberg (Eds.), *Lifespan developmental psychology: Normative life crisis.* New York: Academic Press.

Louis Harris and Associates (1981). *Aging in the eighties: America in transition.* Washington, DC: National Council on Aging.

Lowenthal, M. F. (1972). Some potentialities of a life–cycle approach to the study of retirement. In F. M. Carp (Ed.), *Retirement.* New York: Behavioral Publications.

Lowy, L. (1979). *Social work with the aging.* New York: Harper & Row.

Maas, H. S., & Kuypers, J. (1974). *From thirty to seventy.* San Francisco: Jossey-Bass.

Maddox, G. L. (1969). Disengagement theory: A critical evaluation. *The Gerontologist, 4,* 80–83.

Manney, J., Jr. (1975). *Aging in American society.* Detroit, MI: Wayne State University, Institute of Gerontology.

Manuelidis, E. E., De Figueriredo, J. M., Kim, J. H., Fritch, W. W., & Manuelidis, L. (1988). Transmission studies from blood of Alzheimer's disease patients and healthy relatives. *Proceedings of the National Academy of Sciences, 85,* 4898–4901.

McKain, W. C. (1967). Community roles and activities of older rural persons. In E. G. Youmans (Ed.), *Older rural Americans.* Lexington: University of Kentucky Press.

Miller, S. J. (1965). The social dilemma of the aging leisure participant. In A. M. Rose & W. A. Peterson (Eds.), *Older people and their social world.* Philadelphia: Davis.

Mindel, C. H. (1983). The elderly in minority families. In T. H. Brubaker (Ed.), *Family relationships in later life.* Beverly Hills, CA: Sage.

Monczunski, J. (1991). That incurable disease. *Notre Dame Magazine, 20*(1), 37.

Morgan, L. A. (1976). A re-examination of widowhood and morale. *Journal of Gerontology, 31,* 6.

Morris, L. C. (1995). Rural poverty. In *Encyclopedia of Social Work,* (19th ed., pp. 2068–2075). Washington, DC: NASW Press.

Murray, M. P., Kory, R. C., & Clarkson, B. H. (1969). Walking patterns in healthy old men. *Journal of Gerontology, 24,* 169–178.

National Aging Resource Center on Elder Abuse. (1990). *Elder abuse and neglect: A synthesis of research.* Washington, DC: Author.

National Council on Aging. (1978). *Fact book on aging: A profile of America's older population.* Washington, DC: Author.

National Institute on Aging. (1982). *Crime and the elderly.* Washington, DC: U.S. Government Printing Office.

National Institute on Aging. (1984). *Be sensible about salt.* Washington, DC: U.S. Government Printing Office.

Neugarten, B. L. (1973). Personality change in late life: A developmental perspective. In C. Eiserdorfer & M. P. Lawton (Eds.), *The psychology of adult development and aging.* Washington, DC: American Psychological Association.

Neugarten, B. L. (1976). *The psychology of aging: An overview.* Presentation from APA Master Lectures. Washington, DC: American Psychological Association.

Neugarten, B. L., & Moore, J. W. (1968). The changing age-status system. In B. L. Neugarten (Ed.), *Middle age and aging.* Chicago: University of Chicago Press.

Neugarten, B. L., & Weinstein, K. K. (1964). The changing American grandparent. *Journal of Marriage and the Family, 26.*

Newman, B. M., & Newman, P. R. (1995). *Development through life* (6th ed.). Pacific Grove, CA: Brooks/Cole.

Nolen-Hoeksema, S. (1988). Life-span views on depression. In P. B. Baltes & R. M. Lerner (Eds.), *Life-span development and behavior* (Vol. 9, pp. 203–241). Hillsdale, NJ: Erlbaum.

Norris, F. N., & Murrell, S. A. (1987). Older adult family stress and adaptation before and after bereavement. *Journal of Gerontology, 42,* 606–612.

Ochs, A. L., Newberry, J., Lenhardt, M. L., & Harkins, S. W. (1985). Neural and vestibular aging associated with falls. In J. E. Birren & K. W. Schaie (Eds.), *Handbook of the psychology of aging* (2nd ed., pp. 378–399). New York: Van Nostrand Reinhold.

Osgood, N. J. (1992). *Suicide in later life.* Lexington, MA: Lexington Books.

Palmore, E. (1975). *The honorable elders.* Durham, NC: Duke University.

Papalia, D. E., & Olds, S. W. (1986). *Human development.* New York: McGraw-Hill.

Parkes, C. M. (1972). *Bereavement: Studies of grief in adult life.* New York: International University Press.

Parlee, M. B. (1979, October). The friendship bond. *Psychology Today,* pp. 42–54, 113.

Pedrick-Cornell, C., & Gelles, R. J. (1982). Elder abuse: The status of current knowledge. *Family Relations, 31,* 457–465.

Raeburn, P. (1984, March 5). Alzheimer's disease of the aged. *Wisconsin State Journal,* p. 1.

Rapkin, R. D., & Fischer, K. (1992). Personal goals of older adults: Issues in assessment and prediction. *Psychology and Aging, 7,* 127–137.

Regier, D. A., Boyd, J. H., Burke, J. D., Rae, D. F., Myers, J. K., Kramer, M., Robins, L. N., George, L. K., Karno, M., & Locke, B. Z. (1988). One-month prevalence of mental disorders in the United States. *Archives of General Psychiatry, 45,* 977–986.

Reichard, S., Livson, F., & Petersen, P. G. (1962). *Aging and personality: A study of eighty-seven older men.* New York: Wiley.

Roberts, J. D. (1980). *Roots of a black future: Family and church.* Philadelphia: Westminister.

Robertson, J. F. (1976). Significance of grandparents: Perceptions of young adult grandchildren. *Gerontologist, 16,* 137–140.

Rosen, I. (1974). *Socialization to old age.* Berkeley: University of California Press.

St. George-Hyslop, P. H., Tanzi, R. E., Polinsky, R. J., Haines, J. L., Nee, L., & Watskins, P. C. (1987). The genetic defect causing familial Alzheimer's disease maps on chromosomes 21. *Science, 235,* 885–889.

Schaie, K. W. (1973). Reflections on papers by Looft, Peterson and Sparks: Intervention towards an ageless society. *Gerontologist, 13,* 31–36.

Schock, N. (1977). Biological theories of aging. In J. Birren & K. W. Schaie (Eds.), *Handbook of the psychology of aging.* New York: Van Nostrand Reinhold.

Seleen, D. R. (1982). The congruence between actual and desired use of time by older adults: A predictor of life satisfaction. *Gerontologist, 22,* 95–99.

Shanas, E. (1972). Adjustment to retirement: Substitution or accommodation? In F. Carp (Ed.), *Retirement.* New York: Behavioral Publications.

Shapiro, M. (1978). Legal rights of the terminally ill. *Aging, 5*(3), 23–27.

Sigelman, C. K., & Shaffer, D R. (1995). *Life-span development* (2nd ed.). Pacific Grove, CA: Brooks/Cole.

Sokolovsky, J. (1990). Introduction. In K. Sokolovsky (Ed.), *The cultural context of aging: Worldwide perspectives.* New York: Bergin and Garvey.

Specht, R., & Craig, G. J. (1982). *Human development.* Englewood Cliffs, NJ: Prentice-Hall.

Specht, R., & Craig, G. J. (1987). *Human development.* (2nd ed.). Englewood Cliffs, NJ: Prentice-Hall.

Spirduso, W. W., & MacRae, P. G. (1990). Motor performance and aging, In J. E. Birren & K. W. Schaie (Eds.), *Handbook of the psychology of aging* (3rd ed.). San Diego, CA: Academic Press.

Stelmach, G. E., & Nahom, A. (1992). Cognitive-motor abilities of the elderly driver. *Human Factors, 34,* 53–65.

Stroebe, W., & Stroebe, M. S. (1993). Determinants of adjustment to bereavement in younger widows and widowers. In M. S. Stroebe, W. Stroebe, & R. O. Hansson (Eds.). *Handbook of bereavement: Theory, research and intervention.* Cambridge, England: Cambridge University Press.

Thomas, A., & Chess, S. (1977). *Temperament and development.* New York: Brunner/Mazel.

Thompson, L. W., & Gallagher, D. (1986). Treatment of depression in elderly outpatients. In G. Maletta & F. J. Pirozzolo (Eds.), *Advances in neurogerontology: Vol. 4. Assessment and treatment of the elderly patient.* New York: Praeger.

Tidwell, B. J. (1997). *The black report.* Lanham, NY: Datadeeds, LLP, and University Press of America.

Tonna, E. A. (1977). Aging of skeletal and dental systems and supporting tissue. In L. E. Finch & L. Hayflick (Eds.), *Handbook of the biology of aging.* New York: Van Nostrand Reinhold.

Ulrich, L. T. (1990). *A midwife's tale: The life of Martha Ballard, based on her diary, 1785–1812.* New York: Knopf.

U.S. Bureau of the Census. (1992). *Statistical abstract of the United States.* Washington, DC: U.S. Government Printing Office.

U.S. Senate, Special Committee on Aging. (1986). *Aging America: Trends and projections.* Washington, DC: U.S. Government Printing Office.

Vandenbos, G. R., Deleon, P. H., & Pallack, M. S. (1982). An alternative to traditional medical care for the terminally ill. *American Psychologist, 37,* 1245–1248.

Vander Zanden, J. W. (1978). *Human development.* New York: Knopf.

Villa, R. F., & Jaime, A. (1993). La fe de la gente. In J. Sotomayor and A. Garcia (Eds.), *Elderly Latinos: Issues and solutions for the 21st century.* Washington, DC: National Hispanic Council on Aging.

Vinick, B. H. (1978). Remarriage in old age. *The Family Coordinator, 27.*

Wall, S., & Arden, H. (1990). *Wisdomkeepers: Meetings with Native American spiritual elders.* Hillsboro, OR: Beyond Words Publishing.

Walsh, E. K., & Cavanaugh, J. C. (1984, November). *Does hospice meet the needs of dying clients?* Paper presented at the meeting of the Gerontological Society of America, San Antonio, TX.

Wentkowski, G. (1985). Older women's perceptions of great-grandparenthood: A research note. *Gerontologist, 25,* 593–596.

Williamson, R. C., Rinehart, A. D., & Blank, T. O. (1992). *Early retirement: promises and pitfalls.* New York: Plenum.

# Index